Musical Theatre Beyond New York and London
Revised and Expanded Edition

The**Friendlysong**Company
Vancouver ⊙ London

Copyright ©2012, 2019 Mel Atkey

All Rights Reserved. No portion of this book, with the exception of brief extracts for the purpose of literary or scholarly review, may be reproduced in any form without the permission of the publisher.

Published by The Friendlysong Company, Inc.
4827 Georgia Street, Delta, British Columbia, Canada V4K 2T1

Cataloguing:

>Atkey, Mel (1958-)
>
>A Million Miles from Broadway – Musical Theatre Beyond New York and London (Revised and Expanded Edition)
>Includes bibliographic references and index
>ISBN 978-0-359-93061-6
>
>1 – Musicals – International – History and criticism.

Cover photo credits, clockwise from top left:
Athanaeum Theatre, Melbourne, photo by author
Royal Alexandra Theatre, Toronto, photo by author
Novello Theatre, London, 2007, photo by author
Dracula, Buenos Aires, 1991, photo courtesy of Angel Mahler
Anne of Green Gables, Theatre Under The Stars, Vancouver, 2003, photo courtesy of Roger Smith
Forbidden City, photo courtesy of Singapore Repertory Theatre

MEL ATKEY
DIED - DECEMBER 16/2022
AGE 64 - IN LONDON - ENGLD.

Other Books by Mel Atkey

When We Both Got to Heaven: James Atkey Among the Anishnabek at Colpoy's Bay

Broadway North: The Dream of a Canadian Musical Theatre

Running Away with the Circus (or, "Now is the Winter of our Missing Tent")

Breaking Into Song: Essays, Articles and Interviews on Musical Theatre

Something Magic: Mel Atkey and the Musical Theatre (Piano and Vocal Score)

Table of Contents

Dedication: "Normandy Lane"......3
Acknowledgements......5

Overture
Overture: A Search for Signs of Life......9

Act I: The Parents
European Musical Comedy (Oops, I Mean Operetta)......34
Musicals for the Masses: Emanuel Schikaneder and the Theater an der Wien......52
Give My Regards to Friedrichstrasse......66
Paris: Where Musicals Were Born, and Where they Go to Die......76
Cabaret: From "le Chat Noir" to the Algonquin Room......96
Declaration of Independence......121

Entr'acte: A New World Order
The New World(s)......136
Between the Wars......138
The Rock 'n' Roll Syndrome......146
Universality Part 1: "Do They Understand This Show in America? It's So Japanese......158
Universality Part 2: A Sense of Time and Place......185
"The Lore of It, the Craft of It, the Technique of It"......197

Act II: The Offspring
Europe after Hitler......217
"Who Will Buy?" Lionel Bart and the Post-war British Musical..263
Canada – "Still Deciding What it Will Be"......274
Larrikins and Sentimental Blokes: Musicals Down Under......319
Africa: "Freedom is Coming......367
"Down South American Way" – Musical Theatre in Latin America......406
"The Theatre Is Alive" – Musical Theatre in Asia......436
New Musicals: "You Have to Kiss a Lot of Frogs"......512

Finale
Are We Up For It?......536

Bibliography......548
List of interviewees......563
Author's biography......564

Dedication:
"Normandy Lane"

Norman and Elaine Campbell

A few years ago, Norman and Elaine Campbell, composer and co-lyricist of *Anne of Green Gables - The Musical*™, applied to the local authorities to change the name of the road leading to their farm house in Covehead, Prince Edward Island. They asked for it to be renamed "Normandy Lane". Eventually the word came back from a jubilant official, "Mr. Campbell, we've agreed to your request to rename it 'Normandy Road'". "No! You don't understand!"*

For those of us struggling to create new musical theatre, (especially those of us who do not live in New York) it seems we are always struggling against those in the majority who just don't "get it". Norman and Elaine were my mentors. Both professionally and personally, they were role models. As Canadian musical writers, we were all swimming against the current, but it was great comfort to know that at least we were swimming together. So this book is dedicated, not just to Norm and Elaine, but to all those in "Normandy Lane" – swimming uphill together.

Thanks to Cliff Jones for telling me this story.

---

* There is a fun postscript to this story, according to their son Robin Campbell in an email dated 10 October 2012: **"The sign that read Normandy Lane was knocked over by a snow plow years ago and replaced with a bilingual sign that reads 'Ch NORMANDY Ln'. It goes on..."**

Acknowledgements

The author would like to thank the following people who contributed to his Kickstarter campaign: Marilyn Atkey, Marion Atkey, Erin Beese, Jim Betts, Sharon Rooker Brade, Adam Brazier, Trixi Bücker, Vern Carter, Sue Culver, Amanda Drew, Gwen Eagleton, John Esche, Charles Finn, Willi Germann, Michael Koebel, Karl Lewkowicz, Sam Mancuso, Robert Moser, Stephen Robb, Andrew Sabiston, Airlie Scott, Joann Sickinger, Ciaran Sweeney, Percy Tucker and Patrick Young.

A book like this cannot be written without the invaluable assistance of others. I have consulted many experts in the field, including some specialists with experience and expertise far beyond my own.

For Argentina, I want to thank Elena Roger, who put me in touch with Pablo Gorlero, who has written the definitive history of Argentine musical comedy, and to Guillermo Masutti, who represents the team of Angel Mahler and Pepe Cibrian.

In Australia, I "dips me lid" to Ray Kolle, a musical book writer who introduced me to Tony Sheldon, Peter Pinne (who, in addition to his work in Australia, also shared his extensive knowledge of South American musicals as well) and Frank Van Straten, who have each given their own accounts of Australian musical theatre. Will Conyers and P. J. Buchanan had me as a guest on their show *Broadway at Bedtime*, and through Will I met Aaron Joyner of Magnormos and Dr. Peter Wyllie Johnston, whose doctoral thesis was on Australian musicals. Col Macdonald, the current owner of Collits' Inn, provided me with a copy of the original recording of his home's namesake musical, while Jonathan Harvey gave me a video of the more recent concert production of that work that he produced. From Kookaburra I want to thank Peter Cousens and Peter Ross. Thanks also to Jill Perryman, Jenny Benjamin, Neil Gooding (of Hayes Theatre Company), Rob Morrison and the late Peter Stannard.

In Canada, Bob Martin, Don McKellar and Lisa Lambert provided invaluable information on the development of *The Drowsy Chaperone*, and David Hein and Michael Rubinoff did the same for *Come from Away*, as did Ted Dykstra for *Evangeline*.

For China and Taiwan, I would like to thank Edwin W. Chen.

In Denmark, I would like to thank Helle Hansen and Søren Møller.

For Egypt, I would like to thank Sarah Enany.

For Greece, I would like to thank Dr. Lydia Papadimitriou.

For Israel, I would like to thank Dov Seltzer and Avivit Hochstadter.

For Italy I would like to thank Gabriele Bonsignori.

In Japan, very special thanks to Amon Miyamoto (and to his interpreter, Yuriri Naka). Dr. Leonie Rae Stickland in Perth, Western Australia supplied invaluable information on the Takarazuka Revue.

For Korea, I would like to thank Hong Sooyeon, Lee Jangwoo and Bae Sunghuck of the Daegu International Musical Festival, and Dr. Kim Shin Dong of Hallyum University. I would also like to thank Dr. Andrew Killick of the University of Sheffield.

For Malaysia, I would like to thank Teng Ky-gan.

For Mexico, I would like to thank Jaime Lozano, José Manuel Lopez Velarde and Fabián Polanco, author of a history of Mexican musicals.

For the Netherlands, I would like to thank René Driessen, Hugh Ross, Dr. Sanne Thierens, and Rosalie Mohr and Paul Eenens of Stage Entertainment.

For the Philippines, thanks to Ryan Cayabyab, Gimbey Dela Cruz, Girlie Rodis, and Joy Virata of Repertory Philippines.

For Portugal, I would like to thank Jorge Santos.

In Singapore, I would like to thank Dr. Kenneth Lyen, Stella Kon and Desmond Moey of Musical Theatre Live for their hospitality and information, and Veronica Goh of the Esplanade Theatres on the Bay. Dick Lee met up with me in London, and Ken Low corresponded by email. Aaron Hales in Perth, Western Australia also supplied helpful leads. Charlotte Nors of Singapore Repertory Theatre provided photographs.

For Spain, I would like to thank Iñigo Santamaria.

For South Africa, I would like to acknowledge Percy Tucker and Prof. Michael Simpson for their background information, and Esme Matshikiza, Irene Mennel, Pat Williams, Charl-Johan Lingenfelder and Daniel Galloway of the Fugard Theatre for material relating to their production of *King Kong*.

For Thailand, I would like to thank Napisi and Krisada Reyes of Mahidol University, Bangkok.

Thank-you to Grover Dale for sending me his memories of *Les Demoiselles de Rochefort*.

Julian Forsyth provided background information on the German cabaret composer Mischa Spoliansky.

Thanks to Stephen Cole for sharing his experiences in Qatar.

For help with *Irma la Douce*, thanks to Greg MacKellan of 42nd Street Moon, San Francisco, and very special thanks to Elizabeth Seal, Peter Brook and Nina Parry.

For help in locating Lehman Engel's manuscript for "Porgy in Ankara", thanks to Richard Boursy, archivist of Yale University's Gilmore Music Library.

From Broadway Asia International, thanks to Damon Brooks and Simone Genatt.

For help in locating Peter Stone's article "The Musical Comedy Book", I would like to thank Library and Archives Canada.

For information on the development process of new musicals, I want to thank Georgina Bexon; Chris Grady; Kerry Michael, (formerly of Theatre Royal Stratford East); Søren Møller of Fredericia Teater; Michael Rubinoff of the Canadain Music Theatre Project, Sheridan College; John Sparks of the Academy for New Musical Theatre; and Sarah Schlesinger of the NYU Tisch School of the Arts.

For their financial assistance in gaining my MA in Musical Theatre degree I would like to thank the Albert Baker Fund.

For their general support, I want to thank Mark Bentley; Leslie (Hoban) Blake; Gyles Brandreth; Vince Casey; Tony Castro; Ian Fenwick; Mark Fox, (archivist for LW Theatres); Kurt Gänzl (the author of many highly authoritative books on musical theatre, some of which are listed in my bibliography); Charles Gilbert of the Musical Theatre Educators Alliance International; Philip Godfrey; Dr. Michael Kunze; (the late) Joe Marchi; Tedde Moore; Ann Mortifee; Prof. David Overton; Michael Owen, (Archivist, Ira and Leonore Gershwin Trusts); Raymond Padua of White Rabbit Productions, Winnipeg; Virginia Reh of Brock University; Jeremy Sams; Victoria Saxton; Jason Saunders of Sheridan College; Stephen Schwartz; Athena Stanley-Yolgecen; Estée Stimler; Scott Ashton Swan of Applause Musicals Society, Vancouver; the late Martin Taylor; Richard Voyce; David Warrack; Ed Weissman; Lawrence Westlake; Phil Willmott; and the staff of the Victoria and Albert Museum's Theatre Collection (formerly the Theatre Museum). Thanks also to Barry Penhale and Jane Gibson of Natural Heritage Books.

Above all, I would like to thank my family – my parents, (the late) Ken and Marion Atkey, my sisters Marilyn Atkey and Beverley Atkey Beese and my brother-in-law Bill Beese for their continued support.

I have also found that what some people would call serendipity (I tend to think of it as a higher power) played a leading part. For example, when I was in Singapore, my hosts strongly urged me to talk to pop star and musical writer Dick Lee. How was I going to do that from the opposite end of the world? I found his website and sent him an email. Almost immediately I received a reply saying "I am in fact in London right now... and could meet up... I'm staying at The Soho Hotel..." He in turn insisted I talk to his Japanese collaborator, Amon Miyamoto. How on Earth was I going to do that? After a few weeks of playing email tag, I learned that he was directing the next show at the theatre where I worked. After that, I naturally concluded that God wanted this book to be written. In line with that epiphany is an email that the late Cheryl Hutcherson (1954-2012) sent to me at an early stage of this book's development:

> "My intuition tells me that you are going to be successful with your book and all will fall into place as it is needed. I am not a fortune teller or anything like that... it's just the gut feeling thing. I don't see you rolling in money at any point as you put this book together, but I see you getting what you need when you need it... and it will be there when the time is right, not just because you wish for it to be there right now. As a matter of fact, it will probably come in bits and pieces so you will never be able to say, 'Aha! Here it is. Here is the financial help I've been looking for all along!' No, it will come in small chunks... but you will notice that you are making the trip here, or the trip there, where months before you thought you couldn't do them because of lack of funds... just like your quick trip to Paris. It happened. It was productive... I'll leave you with a thought... it's something I strongly believe in, so do with it as you may. Thoughts may seem like fleeting moments, but in fact, they are energy coming from the energy within us... and as we know, energy is extremely powerful. So whatever thoughts you put out there, you are going to receive back tenfold. A thought *is* a reality, and once it is sent out, it can actually materialize. So, if you put out the thought(s) – 'Creating this book is my passion and it is going to happen. Everything I need to create this book, to compile my thoughts into book form and to get whatever I need to go to wherever I need to go to to finish this book, this is all going to happen, and happen in an order that will be useful to me'... So just make simple thoughts. 'Thank you for letting me complete this book and giving me the opportunities I need to finish it.' Anytime you feel a negative thought coming on, stop it and replace it with a grateful thought."[1]

Thank-you Cheryl, wherever you are, for it all happened as you said.

Within the text, I have indicated the dates of birth and death (where applicable) of the major players, in order to provide historical context. (If no birth or death is indicated, the information was unavailable at the time this went to press.) Where no direct citation is given, quotes from theatrical reviews are taken from promotional or other secondary materials.

Overture:
A Search for Signs of Life

For many decades, the world has accepted the notion that the musical theatre is basically an American art form and, therefore, that all of the great Broadway and Hollywood musicals were the result of uniquely American ingenuity. Like jazz, it is thought to be America's gift to the world, and requires good old American know-how to make it work.

Balderdash.

"*Musical Comedy* has often been called the only unique American contribution to the theatre", said Cecil Michener Smith (1906-56), former editor of *Musical America*. "This claim is not merely oversimplified; it is false... In its basic form, musical comedy is not specifically American even now."[1] He wrote this almost seventy years ago, during what some call Broadway's Golden Age. Nowadays, what he said is even more relevant.

British creative-life-coach Chris Grady maintains, "There is no country in the world that doesn't have music. It may be very different music from what you or I might hear in the West End, but there is a fundamental thing in the human condition which makes music. That tends to be the starting point for getting a piece of theatre."

Of course, the classic Broadway and Hollywood musicals are undeniably brilliant, and are enormously (and rightly) influential. They *may* even represent musical theatre at its pinnacle, and certainly set *an* example. However, it's one thing to say that the musical is an integral part of American culture; it's quite another to deny the rest of the world its birthright by claiming that America is an indissoluble part of the musical.

In fact, since World War II, Broadway has seen hit shows from Australia, Canada, France, Germany, Great

Britain and South Africa. There are Argentine musicals, Egyptian musicals, Greek musicals, Korean musicals... There is scarcely anywhere on Earth that does not claim to create musical theatre.

However, not everybody would see it that way. Peter Stone (1930-2003), a former president of the Dramatists Guild best known as the Tony winning book writer of *1776* and *Titanic*, once claimed that no musical theatre existed outside of New York City... and he wasn't joking. My guess is that there are others who still think that way.

Stone was not himself a native New Yorker. He was born in Los Angeles, the son of film writers – (his father John produced Shirley Temple's *Baby Take a Bow* in addition to several Charlie Chan and Mr. Moto films). He even spent thirteen years living in Paris – the musical's actual birthplace – as a journalist and newsreader for American broadcaster CBS.

He was a liberal-minded man, yet in 1989 Stone said, "Why doesn't a musical theatre exist anywhere but in New York? It doesn't, you know."[2] Bear in mind that, at that time, Broadway was dominated by *Cats*, *Phantom of the Opera* and *Les Misérables*, with barely an American-written musical to be seen (or heard). How could he have not have been aware of something that to me was so obvious? Cultural chauvinism alone doesn't fully explain everything. Even a decade later he still maintained, "I always thought the reason [*Waiting for*] *Godot* was a hit everywhere except in New York was because we were the only place in the world that had musicals."[3] Once one dismisses the rest of all possible worlds...

This puts me in an odd position. His assertion runs entirely contrary to the thesis I am about to put forward, yet I find myself partly defending him. It is important for us to understand the reasons why he believed what he did. To him, the art and the craft of the musical was something unique, something close at hand and something worth defending. Is it possible he was correct in his premise while at the same time being utterly erroneous in his conclusion?

This is the part of his argument that we have to reckon with: "It is in New York that it is passed along, the lore of it, the craft of it, the technique of it."[4] Now, not everybody these days cares about the lore, the craft, the technique, but I do. I care passionately, and people like me will therefore do whatever it takes to imbibe these things, regardless of where we live. And what I have discovered about the lore of musical theatre would, I aver, surprise even Mr. Stone.

He explains, "Musical comedy writing is something that is passed down and around from practitioner to practitioner, so it's not something you can do in a room in Cincinatti. New York is the place. You can see the shows that are working and synthesize what's to be gotten from them."[5]

It's true that historically the craft of musical theatre was handed down from one generation to another. Stone was himself mentored in this way by Frank Loesser (1910-69), the composer-lyricist of *Guys and Dolls*.

But what do you do if you live and breathe musicals, yet living in New York is not, for whatever reason, an option? Is there another way to learn the craft? You might take a tip from Jerome Kern, George and Ira Gershwin, Cole Porter and Charles Strouse.

Before New York had taken its place at the head of the queue, Jerome Kern studied privately for two years in Heidelberg, Germany, then moved on to London, where he lived and worked in the theatre for a further decade. Ira Gershwin also worked in London with people who had known and collaborated with his idols Gilbert and Sullivan, while his brother George returned from Paris – then considered to be the world's cultural capital – with suitcases filled with Debussy scores. Cole Porter was similarly drawn to Paris, where he studied at the Schola Cantorum, and a generation later Charles Strouse was tutored in the same city by Nadia Boulanger.

Consider also the many Broadway writers, including Victor Herbert, Frederick Loewe and Kurt Weill, who were born abroad and arrived in New York with their studies – and sometimes even their reputations – already a *fait accompli*.

Eventually, some people from New York turned their attention to training foreigners. Broadway conductor Lehman Engel (1910-82) declared, "Writers and composers in other countries have made serious attempts to rival the creative spirits of the American musical theatre. There seems to be no reason why they should not succeed."[6] In addition to his workshops in New York, Los Angeles and Nashville, he also taught in Toronto.

Nowadays, people from places like Korea come to study at the Tisch School in New York (or Goldsmiths in London), then they go back home to practice – and spread – what they have learned. Others just study the works themselves (the hits and the flops), see every show they can and read every biography they can get their hands on. They may also have a chance to see – and learn from – the more than eighty percent of musicals that fail.

In this sense, New York has, up until now, enjoyed an advantage, but does that mean it is really the only place where musicals can happen? I deeply admire Peter Stone's work, and there is a great deal to be learnt from him, but in denying the very existence of international musical theatre, he was clearly mistaken. Just as there are movies made outside of Hollywood, there are musicals written and performed away from Broadway. However, that still leaves the question: how do we master our craft?

At the time Stone was speaking of, many of the greats – including even George Abbott (1887-1995) – were still with us and plying their trade. Now, thirty years later, virtually all of those practitioners – including Mr. Stone himself – have left us. It is no longer possible to be directly mentored by them, no matter where you live, so we learn from the greats by whatever means are available to us.

Make no mistake – musical theatre certainly does exist outside of New York. I'm not talking about the many franchised versions of *Les Misérables* and *Hamilton* that have played everywhere from Tel-Aviv to Abu Dabi. I'm referring to indigenous musical theatre created in places other than New York by people other than New Yorkers and drawing on traditions other than just those of Broadway. We are now in the world of what Canadian academic Marshall McLuhan (1911-80) called the "global village".[7]

What we now call the American musical was the child of a European parent, to which some like to apply the one-size-fits-all label "operetta"[8]. (These archaeic labels relate to the musical in the same way as "Gramophone" relates to "mp3 player". In many cases, they eschewed operatic voice production and employed contemporary popular music forms.)

That same parent had other offspring as well, and therefore the Broadway musical has siblings, not just children. These siblings, some more closely related to the parent than others, have co-existed and borrowed from each other throughout their history (and continue to do so) to the enrichment of all.

Although some people argue that the American musical reached its zenith on Broadway in the 1940s and 50s, I have never believed that this was to be the musical's ultimate destination. "The history of the musical theatre", in the words of New Zealand-born historian Kurt Gänzl (1946-), "is no one-nation or one-center affair."[9] Alan Jay Lerner

(1918-86), the librettist behind *My Fair Lady* said, "Broadway cannot live without the musical theatre, but the musical theatre can live without Broadway. After all, its first home was Paris and then Vienna and then London and then New York. So changes of address are not uncommon."[10] American composer-lyricist Maury Yeston (1945-) adds, "Broadway is now a very long street running from the Kartnerstrasse in Vienna through Hamburg and Amsterdam, across to the West End, New York, Chicago, Minneapolis, L. A., to the Ginza[11] and beyond."[12]

Musical theatre is, in fact, universal, and if I may say so, I am living proof. Neither American nor English, I grew up in Vancouver, British Columbia, Canada, some three thousand miles away from Broadway, yet I write musicals[13]. The first professional musical I ever saw was a home-grown show, *Anne of Green Gables*, but whether professional, amateur, or just watching the movies, it seemed that in Vancouver, people everywhere were bursting into song. It was part of the whole Lotusland[14] atmosphere – beautiful scenery begets beautiful music. Could it be then that my home town was an artistically charged environment?

In the early 1970s, there emerged from this cocoon a remarkable group of people who were evidently drinking the same water as I was. Several of them eventually rose to international prominence, among them future Tony award winning actor Brent Carver, dancer Jeff Hyslop and singer-songwriter Ann Mortifee. They all emerged from the University of British Columbia Musical Theatre Society (MUSSOC) at around the same time, and after graduation, they continued to work together, known informally as the "Movers and Shakers"[15] club. For a time, they gave my home town a unique musical theatre scene.

I was too young to actually be a part of this group. I just watched from the sidelines, and got to know each of them personally. They were my first heroes, and, importantly for this book, they proved that local people *could be* my heroes.[16]

But, like most of the "Movers", I had to leave Vancouver, for I wanted to study the masters and to combine the discipline I would learn abroad with the uniqueness that I found at home. Sometimes it takes an entire lifetime to learn that the first idea you had was the right one. While I have since then worked in Toronto, New York and London, the influence of the "Movers and Shakers" is still with me.[17]

It wasn't until the mid 1990s – some twenty years after I wrote my first musical – that I actually saw my first show on Broadway.[18] Like *The Drowsy Chaperone*'s "Man in Chair" character, I was more familiar with the Broadway cast albums than I was with the shows themselves. I saw them from a remote distance, and so they were filtered through local perceptions. (You can be a Christian, but if you were born on Saturn, your perspective is going to be different.) New York may have been literally about 3,000 miles away, but it might as well have been a million.

Music is a universal language. I believe that it is hardwired into us. Some say that it stems from the beating of the heart, our natural metronome.

"Singing is as essential for humans as it is for our fellow musical creatures", says David Rothenberg, author of *Why Birds Sing: A Journey into the History of Bird Song*. "Birds, whales and humans all sing because we must, because it is of our very essence."[19]

Since prehistoric times, music and dance and storytelling have formed a part of religious rites of all kinds. A cave painting between 11,000 and 17,000 years old was discovered in Ariège, France that depicted a man manipulating a musical bow while dancing in the wake of a herd of reindeeer. The first Greek dramas were sung, although until recently[20], the music had long been thought lost. Why? What makes us sing?

The noted Indian classical musician Hazrat Inayat Khan says that "the human body was made in tone and rhythm."[21] Lyricist and psycho-therapist Pat Williams (1931-) adds, "It seems to me that a community surrounding children with music and movement and song so that they come 'instinctively' to dance and sing, works in exactly the same way as surrounding children with words, so that they may learn 'instinctively' to talk."[22] Sarah Schlesinger, chair of the Tisch School of the Arts Graduate Musical Theatre Writing Program explains, "To my mind, the merging of words and music is the most powerful mode of expression available to us. When this power is used in the service of storytelling, there is no limit to what is possible."[23]

Perhaps the question we should really be asking is what *stops* us from singing? Diana Deutsch (1938-), a psychologist at the University of California at San Diego has discovered an interesting phenomenon. When a recording of a short, spoken phrase is played back several times in succession, it begins to sound like music. "It brings to the fore a real mystery – why don't we hear speech as song all the time?" The answer, she believes, is that the human brain suppresses our recognition of pitch, and that the exact repetition of a sound we've already processed over-rides this. "It stops the inhibition of the pitch region of the brain so we hear song, which is really what we ought to have been hearing in the first place."[24] When I asked her how this worked with tonal languages such as Chinese and Thai, she said "Other researchers have found that it works in a variety of different languages also, including tone language. However the effect appears not to be so strong in tone language, such as Chinese - as would be expected from the use of tone to convey lexical meaning."[25]

Certain harmonies have an emotional effect on an audience – so much so that, at some points in our dark and distant past, authorities have actually tried to ban augmented fourths (or "tritones") on the pretext that they were "diabolus in musica" (the devil in music) due to their dissonance. Conductor Marin Alsop (1956-) describes it as "An interval that requires a resolution, and without resolution it just hangs there and makes you uncomfortable."[26] (Leonard Bernstein used tritones extensively in *West Side Story*.)

It also seems that music is an innate talent. Whether the product of nature or nurture, it defies scientific analysis. It's what I call the *je ne sais quoi* factor – you can have a PhD in composition, and not have the "talent" of some kid with a guitar who plays by ear. "Songwriters are a breed apart", said composer and conductor André Previn (1929-2019). "Application of musical sophistication has very little to do with basic melodic genius. It isn't an inflammatory opinion to say that Irving Berlin's songs are better than Leonard Bernstein's, nor is the fact that Bernstein had more musical knowledge in his eyelashes than Berlin had in his whole persona up for debate."[27]

Music also has regional characteristics. Edward Elgar (1857-1934) is thought to be quintessentially English, while Sergei Prokofiev (1891-1953) is believed to be unmistakably Russian and George Gershwin (1898-1937 is surely uniquely American, even though, in each case, the music may not actually be indigenous to that place. (American music, for example, is a fusion of European and African forms.) Nevertheless, musical styles can evoke a sense of place and time. They are also subject to sense memory: if the opening strands of Beethoven's Fifth Symphony are used in a *Bugs Bunny/Roadrunner* cartoon to underscore a dramatic "uh-oh" moment, this precedent is then set in our minds.

What gives it that unique imprint? Dr. Aniruddh Patel of the Neuroscience Institute in San Diego argues that even instrumental music is influenced by language in its rhythm and accent. "Composers, like every other person in their culture, learn the patterns of their language and it's latent in their minds, so when they compose, they have those patterns to draw on."[28] American composer and lyricist Stephen Sondheim (1930-) expands on this. "It seems to me that the music of any country is a reflection of its language, and that the rhythms of that particular country's language are what is appropriate." This can make translation very challenging. "As soon as you translate it, it's very very hard to make it sound as if it is really wedded to the music."[29]

When composer Howard Goodall (1958-) related a story in his book *Big Bangs* of how a particular piece of music came to him in a somewhat mystical way, somebody suggested to him that it was the most convincing proof he had yet heard of the existence of God. "There are no easy answers to account for being moved to tears by notes on a page, or of being stirred to anger and action, or being comforted in our loneliness", says Goodall. "It's a mystery how Rachmaninoff's flowing melodies and ripe harmonies make people feel romantic and amorous, or how Ravel's Boléro conjures up sexiness."[30]

As I have said before, we are in the beauty expressing business. Ralph Vaughan Williams (1872-1958) defines art as "the means by which one man communicates spiritually with another."[31] Peter Link (1944-), the Tony-nominated composer of *Salvation* and *King of Hearts* says that "the worst music that I write comes from me, and the best of it comes through me."[32] Now a composer of "inspirational" music, he believes that the best music has a spiritual origin, a purer language than words. I have found myself that when a character is singing on stage, they often come closer to the truth than when they are speaking.

If music and theatre are primal and have existed since the beginning of civilisation, it should follow that musical theatre is also universal. Chris Grady says, "Almost every country in the world *does* create musical theatre. It maybe not 'musical' with a capital 'M', 'theatre' with a capital 'T' care of Broadway, but it's pieces of drama, theatre, live performance which involve words and music blended together to create an experience for the audience."

That is the premise of this book: to explore the diversity of a multi-national musical theatre, and to learn its craft by examining the works that have gone before – in all parts of the world.

Each country that I discuss in the ensuing chapters is struggling to find its own unique voice. For some the struggle has been greater than for others: some have to deal with oppressive political regimes, some with domestic indifference, and many are shouting to be heard over louder and more prosperous voices. Some countries have been turning out artists of international stature for many years, while others are nascent. There are, I maintain, phases of development. Countries like Thailand or Singapore are new to the game, and the work they produce may not yet have developed to the level of sophistication of the more mature countries. This is to be expected. As they develop, they may find ways of combining what they have learned from Western musical theatre with their own traditions, and with the ways they have found to cater to their home audience. The musical's future may well lie in one of these nascent places.

My aim is to combine the craft that has been developed by the writers of classic Broadway and West End musicals with the indigenous elements that are associated with the other places where musicals either have been or will be developed. Can this craft be passed on? It can if people want it to be. I believe that it is possible to teach the craft without necessarily imposing the Broadway/West End style. It takes a combination of teachers who are sensitive to the needs of other cultures, writers and creatives who are willing to learn the skills, and audiences who will demand them. In a country with a very limited modern musical theatre heritage, it may take some research to find other ways of making the connection between music and drama. For example, in places like China or Thailand, notions of dramaturgy may be very different from those in the West. With their tonal languages, the mechanics of fitting words to music will certainly be different.

Before *Show Boat* and *Oklahoma!*, neither the creatives nor the audiences were demanding that musicals told viable stories. (And, in spite of *Show Boat*'s major success, it was some decade and a half before somebody successfully tried it again.)

On the other hand, during the so-called Golden Age, audiences expected to come out of the theatre humming the tunes. Only rarely does that happen now, unless it's a jukebox musical. Perhaps in the future, there will be another element that musicals will require that we are not now fulfilling.

We can examine shows from our past, determine why they worked, and under what circumstances, or similarly, why they didn't. That way, we learn from them in order to create better shows in the future. A show that is a hit in London can flop in New York and vice versa, and one that is a hit in both is by no means guaranteed to work in Melbourne, Tokyo or Buenos Aires.

We will re-examine the heritage of the musical in order to re-cast its development in a "universal" context and how it relates to the world; to show how London and New York developed their own forms to differentiate themselves from their predecessors, or in a few cases, where American or British musicals have been affected by their regional or ethnic sources. This is not in any sense anti-New York or anti-London. It's just that the lights of Broadway (and the West End) are so bright that it's often difficult to see anything else. Sometimes, just as a ship travelling at night must block out its own lights in order to maintain forward visibility, so we have to dim those bright lights of Broadway so that we can see (hear) ourselves think.

The fact is that the world is changing, and its

centre of gravity is shifting. "At the military and political level, we still live in a unipolar [i.e. US dominated] world," says Fareed Zakaria (1964-), author of *The Post-American World*. "But along every other dimension – industrial, financial, social, cultural – the distribution of power is shifting, moving away from American dominance. In terms of war and peace, economics and business, ideas and art, this will produce a landscape that is quite different from the one we have lived in until now – one defined and directed from many places and by many peoples."[33]

Until the Second World War, there were not two centres for musical theatre, but at least four. I believe that musical theatre is evolving back toward being this kind of an international form again.

Even within the United States, musical theatre is shifting away from Broadway. Maury Yeston (1945-) and Arthur Kopit (1937-)'s *Phantom!* is an example of a show that has been produced very profitably in the regions and received over a thousand productions in German, Japanese and Korean as well as English without ever playing in New York. "Of course, people dream of having their shows discovered and raised to the Tony Award or Olivier Award winning level in a commercial production in New York or London", says John Sparks, the artistic director of the Academy for New Musical Theatre in Los Angeles. "But this is no longer the primary focus. Writers, producers, non-profit theatres and others involved in the form are focusing on more local audiences."[34]

In this book's first "Act", I tell the story of the musical's origins in France, Britain, central Europe, and its migration to (and partial reinvention in) America. This is not just an academic exercise or a history lesson; it is to point out the foundations both of our existing musical theatre and of potential future developments. In order to understand where musical theatre is going, you need to know something about where it came from.

It all started in Paris – a city now regarded ironically by outsiders as the graveyard of musicals. I went there in search of its actual birthplace. Just around the corner from the Quatre Septembre Métro station, up the Rue Monsigny, lays the Théâtre des Bouffes-Parisiens. Originally dating from 1826, it was opened by Louis Comte (1783-1859), a ventriloquist and director of the École de Comédiens, a theatre for children. However, it was the man with whom, some three decades later, Comte's son Charles would go into business that would make this place special. His name was Jacques Offenbach. The year was 1858 and the show that would change the face of musical theatre forever (and have people dancing the can-can in the aisles) was called *Orphée aux Enfers* – "Orpheus in the Underworld".

Paris was, at the time, the cultural capital of the Western world, and as the Belle Epoque approached, things would only get better. The people who invented champagne also invented the cabarets where audiences could sip it. And of course, the Folies-Bergère and the Moulin Rouge. And "comédie-musicale". A revolution was in the air – and it spread from Paris to Vienna, Berlin, Budapest, London, New York and the world.

Yes, musical theatre is revolutionary. As I began my research for this book, one of my most startling discoveries was the extent to which the development of popular musical theatre coincided with the development of middle-class democracy. There had always been the low-brow type of folk music, and there had always been so-called "classical", or posh music. Now, the two were beginning to meet in between – the "middle brow", so to speak. Sometimes it was part of the democratic struggle, but more often it was a by-product of that evolution.

John Gay's *The Beggar's Opera* of 1728 was a political satire, but since it and its 1729 sequel *Polly* led – indirectly – to the Licensing Act of 1737 which introduced censorship, its relation to democracy was somewhat testy, to say the least. Although it was later appropriated by the elite, Mozart's *The Magic Flute* (which premiered only two years after the French Revolution), was written for the masses. Gilbert and Sullivan poked fun at the upper classes and those in authority. It is hardly surprising that the Americans embraced the form so enthusiastically – but they were not the only ones. Musical comedy and cabaret flourished in Weimar Berlin (but not under the Nazis, who were not noted for their sense of humour), and in late 19th century Paris.

Musicals – as opposed to most opera – are written and composed in the vernacular, and tend to be accessible to the masses. The emergence of an educated female population further enhanced the demographics for musicals. What Mozart (and after him, Kurt Weill, Leonard Bernstein and, more recently, Maury Yeston and Howard Goodall) sought to do was to educate those masses, and to bring sophisticated musical and dramatic forms to as wide an audience as possible.

So, if it's true that musical theatre developed alongside democracy, then why has it lost its leading role in Western culture? Starting in the 1950s, rock and roll usurped the musical as the "vernacular" form. It became the music of the streets, the voice of protest. (It was an uneasy coalition between the kids who bought the records and made the music, and the businessmen who saw a market niche and exploited it.)

On the other hand, the musical sought a rapprochement with opera. Some say that the musical failed to keep up with the times. "As a creative musical force, the contemporary West End musical is dead," says Neil Tennant (1954-) formerly of the 80s pop duo The Pet Shop Boys. "It contains the sort of music you only find in musicals; it has no relevance to contemporary music; it exists in a creative ghetto... The music and lyrics have one foot in the past and the other in parody."[35]

Others will argue that popular music has declined in craftsmanship. Rock and roll has seldom fulfilled Mozart's aim to elevate the tastes of the masses. A few shows have attempted to combine contemporary pop music with sophistication, but all too often the one defeated the other. (Tennant produced Liza Minelli's 1989 technopop disco version of Sondheim's "Losing My Mind", sandblasting away any trace of sophistication or subtlety, then goring it of whatever harmony or texture may have lain within.)

Still, musicals remain by far the most popular form of live theatre, and they've found support from some unlikely sources. "The musicals I've seen recently knocked spots off any modern drama", says British playwright and actor Steven Berkoff (1937-). "*Chicago* is unbelievably clever. Most new plays bore me to death."[36]

Music is a direct conduit to the human heart, and there is no more potent force and nothing bolder or more radical than splashing that across a stage. The American theatre critic Brooks Atkinson (1894-1984) said, "I have sometimes wondered whether it is not a more genuine and comprehensive form of theater than the spoken drama... It is the one element of poetry left in a form of entertainment that was all poetry originally".[37]

Musical theatre has a great tradition, yet it continues to break new ground. Like jazz, it has a devout following of highly literate enthusiasts. Of course, like any art form, there are camp and tacky elements, to be sure. Sometimes it descends into kitsch, but at its core, it is the most demanding of performing art forms.

Is the musical actually a form in and of itself? Is there a "Broadway" or "West End" sound? Does the musical demand a form that is distinct from all others? It depends to some extent on who you talk to. Personally, my own work falls roughly within the Broadway/West End paradigm. Yet there are musicals coming out of South

Africa that owe little to the tradition started by Offenbach. However, I also know that "it took Nixon to go to China".[38]

For full disclosure, I believe in the Hammerstein principle, in that the songs in a musical must support the drama. I also believe that the music should be memorable enough to stay with the audience when they leave. I believe that rhymes should be accurate. In some of this, I am at odds with many of my colleagues. Some would probably brand me "conservative", but I don't see it that way. Only those who build on a solid foundation will find it easy to move forward.

I'm often asked what my favourite musical is, or who is my favourite composer. I really don't have favourites, but I will say that if one is planning to write a through-sung show, the example to study is not *Jesus Christ Superstar* or *Les Misérables*, but Frank Loesser's *The Most Happy Fella*. When I heard Lucy Simon (1943-)'s score for *The Secret Garden* (1991) I thought it to be the finest Broadway score of its decade.

It is fashionable to say that since music is now there purely to support the drama, and that writers are no longer expected to provide song "hits", they have then been relieved of any requirement for songs to be "memorable".[39] Dramaturgical principles may vary from one culture to another, but the need for some level of craft remains constant.

Alan Jay Lerner said in 1971, "We've been living through a period when the gifted beginner has been so over-praised that it has deprived him of the incentive to grow and learn his craft, and the professional is so scorned that he has become fearful of picking up a pen. But far more dangerous than all that is, I think, the contantly continuing cry that we must attract the youth. Will the young people like it? Well, the theatre is not for the young. Nor is it for the old. It's not even for everybody. It's for the people who like the theatre, whatever their age. The people who go to be transported or amused or uplifted or enchanted on the highest possible level, the level that has made the theatre survive the ages."[40]

This brings me to declare that I love the musical for what it is capable of being, and not necessarily for what a lot of it in fact is. When great music is put together with the right lyrics, the result is that the music lifts the lyrics up to heaven.

As we move into this new global musical world, it is important to understand its heritage. However, as a lecturer I have encountered some resistance to this study. In fact, the course leader in the MA in Musical Theatre program of a major London conservatory[41] told me that the history of the craft could be of no more than "tangential" interest to his students, arguing that they are only interested in "practical" matters. (Sigh.) I talk to all too many young actors and actresses, straight out of stage school, who seem to think that musical theatre began with *Les Misérables* or even *Rent*. What are they going to do when they are asked to perform in *HMS Pinafore* or *Show Boat*?

The "history" (I actually prefer to call it "heritage") of how we got to where we are also helps us to find out where we might be going. As one of the readers of my previous book *Broadway North* told me:

> "I initially got an advanced diploma in Musical Theatre because my school did not offer a degree program and was one hundred percent practical. Now, fourteen years later they are offering a degree program and I was able to go back and complete my degree. What did this entail? The *History* of Musical Theatre, Dance and Acting. That is how I discovered your book… It was so valuable to me and I loved it so much! It was what was missing all those years ago. I think if I had understood the history sooner, not only would it have informed my work in a positive way, but it would have made me realize I was a part of something much bigger than the latest audition and given an importance and richness to

my work that was lacking. Not only should it be included in a MA of Musical Theatre program, it should be taught from first year!"[42]

If you are expecting a "scholarly" work, (i.e. one that never uses a two syllable word when a five syllable one is available), I must tell you that, while I aim to be thoughtful and accurate, as a show writer myself I cannot resist the urge to try to entertain an audience and, given this subject, I do not believe I would be able to write credibly about it if I did not try to do so. (Imagine reading an academic treatise on comedy written by somebody who evidently doesn't get the joke.)

When I was a participant in Toronto's Guild of Canadian Musical Theatre Writers workshops – based on the teachings of Lehman Engel – I was told to study the works that came before me. This, it was assumed, meant the great Broadway songwriters. What I learned was that, while Jerome Kern and George and Ira Gershwin had studied and been influenced by the great European operettas and musical comedies, they yearned to create something that was more identifiably American. It was, for them, part of the long process of overcoming a cultural inferiority complex. (Even today, many American artists, deep down, fear they may be "Rome" to Britain's "Greece".) As a Canadian, and a musical theatre writer, this was something I could relate to.

I also longed to hear my own culture represented. Inspired by the late composer Norman Campbell (1924-2004) (*Anne of Green Gables- The Musical*™) as well as by his colleague Mavor Moore (1919-2006), founder of the Charlottetown Festival, I began to study the history of musical theatre in my own country. The result was *Broadway North: the Dream of a Canadian Musical Theatre*, published by Natural Heritage Books/Dundurn Press in 2006.

It seemed to resonate with the Canadian musical

theatre community: John MacLachlan Gray (1946-), author of *Billy Bishop Goes to War* told me, "It's thanks to you there is such a concept as a 'Canadian musical'."[43] Composer and lyricist Ray Jessel (1927-2015), who with Marian Grudeff (1927-2006) wrote the score for Broadway's *Baker Street* said, "It will be *the* definitive book on the subject for a long time, I'm sure."[44] Composer and singer Ann Mortifee (1947-) wrote, "I have always so appreciated what you have done for musicals... It is a gift to us all."[45]

That book even seemed to strike a chord in other countries. I was featured on a Melbourne radio show called *Broadway at Bedtime*, and found that the situations for Canadians and Australians were uncannily similar. Australian actors longed to play in their own accents. Singaporeans wanted to see theatre that reflected their East-meets-West experience. South Africans sang for their freedom, and still burst into song at the drop of a hat.

I began to think about how the principle of (metaphorically) putting the audience "on stage" – might apply in a broader context. I could see that "universality" is an idea that has two parts – establishing an identity, then sharing it with the world. The Irish playwright John Coulter (1888-1980), who immigrated to Canada in 1936 said, "What virtue is there in becoming specifically Canadian? Why not aim at the idea of internationalism in the theatre at least? I should reply that in my belief the way to internationalism in the theatre as in all else lies through the prior achievement of the greatest degree of nationalism. It is an organic growth outward from a core which is the individual himself, in this case, the individual playwright."[46]

When I talk about "nationalism", I don't mean the narrow kind of parochialism that divides people; I mean a broader, more generous notion of sharing ourselves with the world, and of being comfortable in our own skin.

Howard Panter, creative director of London's

Ambassador Theatre Group has said, "A lot of the musicals that hit my desk are transatlantic. But I believe if you can be very local and very specific, you can actually have universal resonance."47

My original subtitle for this book was to have been *the Globalisation of Musical Theatre*. After all, "globalisation" does not have to mean "world conquest". On the contrary, it can mean that we engage with the world as equals. However, I conceded that in this context the word can be misleading. I now prefer to use the term "cosmopolitan", which British playwright Dan Rebellato defines as "a belief that all human beings, regardless of their differences, are members of a single community and all worthy of equal moral regard."48

If a show has universal appeal, it does not mean that one culture has spread its tentacles to its neighbours and subjugated them, but rather that the neighbours are able to feel some sense of ownership or involvement in a foreign work.

In Rebellato's view, when applied to musicals, "globalisation" implies something different: "When you buy the rights to put on *Phantom of the Opera*, you're not given a score and a script and told to get on with it; you buy the original production: sets, costumes, direction, lighting, the poster and all the merchandise. This means that all productions of *The Phantom of the Opera* are, to a very significant extent, identical... These are not new productions; they are franchises."49

I must tell you right now; this notion of "globalisation" is *not* what this book is about. Nor is it about making shows so bland that they lose all local resonance. I want to explore what that word "universal" does (and does not) mean. To me, it can suggest a single show such as *Fiddler on the Roof* that finds broad appeal in many different countries, knowing that it appeals to each of those cultures in a unique way. It can also imply a place where we are able to experience work from other cultures and thereby broaden our own horizons.

I believe that great cultures can take root anywhere, so long as they are nurtured. The seeds are there, they just need to be watered.

For the purposes of this book, I define a musical as a theatrical entertainment that is aimed at a popular audience (as opposed to a social, economic or intellectual elite), and in which music and drama (or at least theatricality) work together to create a whole that is greater than the sum of its parts. While many scholarly works are concerned with dividing the field into a more precise nomenclature such as revue, zarzuela or operetta, I am content to do the precise opposite, uniting all and sundry under the occasionally anachronistic title "musical theatre". This embraces musical comedy, operetta and revue, as well as certain operas (*Carmen*, *The Magic Flute*) and some of the more theatrical cabaret acts. This notion antedates *The Black Crook* and other American musicals. (In fact, antedating such terms is a commonly accepted practice. After all, Sir Isaac Newton predated the term "scientist"[50] by some two centuries.) It is this democratisation – the musical as a common man's opera – which leads me to the belief that it can be adapted to other cultures.

This book does not set out to be a comprehensive history of the musical, nor is it an in-depth dramaturgical analysis of individual shows. Rather, it is a manifesto with an agenda. Where I give the background of European and American musicals, it is to put them into a modern, international context. I'm concerned with how we can learn from our heritage and what roots we have to draw from. Because I am myself a creator of musicals, my view is toward the future. I'm interested in both the actual roots of the musical and the potential roots. I want this study to produce results.

Therefore, when I talk about the relationship

between musical theatre and cabaret, for instance, I am not just talking about its historic impact, but also its potential future influence. For example, if I were a French writer looking to write Parisian musicals, I would be studying everyone from Christiné to Monnot and Legrand as well as the songs of Brel, Aznavour and Trennet, and the cabaret and café-concert, as well as contemporary popular song. Since the 1930s, most French musical comedy has failed to keep pace with Broadway, yet I feel that there are ways they *could* have. Similarly, if I were writing musicals in Germany, I would want to learn about Weill, Holländer and Spoliansky, as well as the great director/impresario Max Reinhardt. When I talk about how the American musical found its own voice, it is to point the way for other cultures who also want to assert their own identities. We know that the American musical is a confluence of European operetta, jazz and vaudeville. When Lionel Bart wrote *Oliver!*, he created an equivalent cocktail of English music hall and folk traditions. (Even his so-called "Jewish" numbers – i.e., "Reviewing the Situation" – are London Jewish, not New York Jewish.) Therefore, when I look at musicals in other countries, I consider the allied forms – e.g. Irish drama with Celtic dance and music – that could potentially be combined, even if this has not yet happened.

In some cases, such as Canada and Australia, although they have arrived at their own variances, the musicals fall broadly within the confluence of European and American traditions. On the other hand, in South Africa, they have their own indigenous musical story telling tradition. Many of the cultures that I discuss in this book have yet to reach maturity in their theatrical development, and so I touch on avenues that might have future significance.

In recent years, Broadway has played host to *Sarafina!* (from Johannsburg), *The Drowsy Chaperone* and *Come from Away* (from Toronto) and *Priscilla – Queen of the Dessert* and *The Boy from Oz* (from Sydney). We now have something called World Music. Why not World Musical

Theatre? After all, nineteenth century New York – in what the British derisively still referred to as "the colonies" – was a pretty unlikely place for anything of cultural importance to prosper. What the musical theatre requires is people with talent and the need to express themselves in drama and in song, and an atmosphere in which that talent can be nurtured. It also requires skill – which can be learned. When you live and work away from the centres of New York and London, this means that you study both the great international works *and* the forms that come out of your own environment.

We should be aware of the works of the past, in order to create better works in the future. My objective with this book is practical. I want the musicals of the future to be well-crafted, and for their creators and performers to be well versed in their own heritage. If one writes musicals in Canada, you should be familiar not just with the works of Rodgers and Hammerstein, but also with *Spring Thaw* and *Anne of Green Gables*. If you're an Australian, you may want to know about *Collits' Inn* and *The Sentimental Bloke* as well as the *Phillips Street Revue*s. It is also helpful, for example, for First Nations people in Canada to understand how Australian aborigines are developing their own musical theatre forms. In Japan, how are the "Anime" and "Manga" traditions put to use in musicals? And the "Chanchada"s of Brazil? And what about Korean "Ch'angguk", South African "Mbaqanga", India's "Bollywood", Thailand's "Lakorn Rong" and the new work coming out of Singapore and Argentina? In the new "global village", the international musical theatre, you'll want to learn about all of them.

ACT I: The Parents

European Musical Comedy
(Oops, I Mean Operetta)

According to musicologist Wilfred Mellers (1914-2008), "Musical comedy – a Plain Man's popular art – had its origins in the impact of democracy on opera, which had been initially an aristocratic art"[1]. Perhaps it's not a coincidence that Mozart wrote *Die Zauberflöte* ("The Magic Flute") shortly after the French revolution, a time when the writing was on the wall for any autocrat with despotic tendencies. It's not so much that the early musicals were overtly political. It's more that demo*cratic* change begets demo*graphic* change. John and the Missus were now attending the theatre, and it was their lives and their values that would be represented on stage. (And, yes, I *am* calling *The Magic Flute* a musical.)

In later chapters, I will look at how Paris, Vienna and Berlin developed as centres for musical theatre, and at how London and New York first adapted the continental European forms and then ultimately created the English-speaking musical theatre that would, for a time, predominate. I will also discuss the unique contribution that cabaret – in its many forms – has made. Then, in "Act II", I will look at how other centres in other parts of the world are trying to follow their examples and create their own unique forms.

Many musical theatre historians will tell you that the musical is descended from "vaudeville", referring to the late-nineteenth and early twentieth century American form of music hall. In fact, its relationship with the French *vaux de ville* (street songs) or *vau de vire* (song of the Vire valley) goes back much further. The *comédie en vaudevilles* began toward the end of the seventeenth century combining satirical songs with acrobatic displays and pantomimes. This eventually led first to opéra-comique, then to opéra-bouffe, before finally emerging as comédie musicale, or musical comedy.

In the Viennese theatre of the late eighteenth century, there was no such thing as a "non-musical". This was especially true of the Volkskomödie, the popular theatre. A few decades earlier Emperor Charles VI had required the Kärntnertortheater[2] to combine German comedy with its repertoire of Italian opera in order to reach a wider audience. The result was a higher level of composition in their Singspiel – a popular form of opera that featured spoken dialogue. The aristocracy, who had developed a taste for French comedy, showed little or no interest in a German national theatre. While the theatre of the court had bizarre regulations – such as one prohibiting the intermingling of comedic and serious elements – the popular theatre had no such restrictions, and offered far greater scope for innovation. We know that Wolfgang Amadeus Mozart (1756-91) attended the Kärntnertortheater with his father Leopold (1719-87) in 1768, when the prodigy was twelve years old. Mozart the elder, a stage father of Mama Rose proportions, didn't approve. He wrote to a friend, "That the Viennese, generally speaking, do not care to see serious and sensible performances, have little or no idea of them, and only want to see foolish stuff, devils, ghosts, magic… witches and apparitions is well known, and their theatres prove it every day."[3] The son apparently disagreed. Twenty-three years later, in what was clearly an act of rebellion, he would write a show that would include all that and more.

Wolfgang Amadeus Mozart

The book – sorry, "libretto" – of *The Magic Flute* was furnished by Emanuel Schikaneder[4] (1751-1812), the actor-manager of Vienna's Freihaus-Theater auf der Wieden where it premiered on 30 September, 1791 with Schikaneder in the comic role of Papageno. In the Viennese popular theatre, the librettist was king, and the composer's name appeared in small print – if he was lucky. Since Schikaneder was the producer and director as well as the comic lead – and it was his name on the (sometimes rubber) cheques – he was effectively in control, and had some considerable influence over all aspects of the production, including the music.

All of this apparently didn't bother Mozart. He had anonymously contributed songs to previous Schikaneder productions, and for some time, he had been trying to reach beyond the stuffy confines of the state theatres and into "vaudeville". "He approved Schikaneder's aims and methods for developing a style of people's opera", says author and lecturer George Collerick. "Mozart saw such ventures as a means to raise standards of popular taste."[5] Eleven years earlier, his father had counselled him, "I recommend you in your work not to think only of the musicians in the audience, but also those who are not musicians. You should know that there are always 100 ignoramuses as against 10 true connoisseurs. Therefore, don't forget the so-called popular style which will tickle also the long ears." Mozart replied, "Don't worry about the so-called popular style, for in my opera there's music for all kinds of people – except for the long ears."[6]

According to Eva Badura-Skoda, professor of music at the University of Wisconsin-Madison, "Mozart broke the boundaries of the Viennese Singspiel and created a full-sized German opera... The high quality of popular music in Vienna in the time of Haydn and Mozart, and the affinity of these great composers to folk music... caused most probably the extraordinary world success of Viennese classical music, unbroken, valid, and alive even today."[7]

It wasn't just "classical" music that he was influencing. These were some of the first rumblings of what would later be called operetta, then finally emerge as musical comedy. Alas, *The Magic Flute* soon gained stature as a piece of grand opera, and in doing so its "vaudeville" origins were played down. (If I were being churlish, I might suggest that it had been hijacked by the very establishment that it was rebelling against.)

Although Vienna would eventually claim its place as *the* centre for operetta, the form first took root in Paris in the mid-nineteenth century. It was an actor-conductor-composer-organist (and, no doubt, usher and ticket seller) named Florimond Ronger (1825-92) who is credited with advancing the form known as opéra-bouffe. German critic Siegfred Kracauer describes him as "an impulsive and highly excentric person"[8]. Because of an unrepealed Napoleonic decree – an attempt to protect the hegemony of Paris' "legitimate" opera houses – he was only allowed to produce one-act shows with a maximum of two characters. This did not mean he was limited to two actors, merely two characters, so he was able to find ingenious ways of getting around the restrictions: for example, in one case he made the third person onstage into a corpse – albeit a corpse who could sing. Using the stage name Hervé, his hits included *Don Quixote et Sancho Pança* (1848).

But it was a German-Jewish immigrant from Cologne who was to create what many consider to be the first modern musical. Born in 1819 in Cologne-Deutz, Jakob Eberst was the son of Isaac Eberst, the cantor of Cologne's synagogue, who was known as "der Offenbacher" – the man from Offenbach-am-Main. Jakob began learning the violin at the age of six and by the time he was eight years old he was writing music.

Jacques Offenbach

In 1833, fourteen-year-old Jakob arrived in Paris to study at the Conservatoire. This was a time when France was in a political state of flux under the rule of Louis-Philippe. (The June Rebellion depicted by Victor Hugo in *Les Misérables* had occurred only a year before.) He changed his first name to the more

French sounding "Jacques", and used his father's byname "Offenbach".

Jacques Offenbach (1819-80) supported himself by playing cello in the orchestra of the Opéra-Comique, and quit the Conservatoire without ever receiving a diploma. In 1853, one year into the reign of Napoleon III, he began writing short comic operas, but was limited by law to only four actors and one act. Once this restriction was lifted, he was able to spread his wings, moving on from the burlesques and vaudevilles that were popular at the time. His somewhat subversive take on the Orpheus myth – in which the hero is forced to rescue his wife Euridyce from Hades – opened at his own Théâtre des Bouffes-Parisiens on 21 October 1858. The libretto was by Ludovic Halévy (1834-1908), the nephew of Offenbach's mentor and teacher Fromental Halévy (1799-1862), the composer of *La Juive*. (This libretto would later be revised by Hector-Jonathan Crémieux (1828-92).)

Orphée aux Enfers concluded with a finale called the "Galop Infernal" which included a chorus line of ladies dancing the infamous can-can, a dance that had originally begun in Paris' bordellos, but had been made popular, if not yet entirely respectable, by the younger members of fashionable society. "Revolutionary-minded romantics used the dance to express their derision and contempt for the sanctimonious social conventions of the new regime," says sociologist and cultural critic Siegfried Kracauer (1889-1966), "and for Louis-Philippe and his dynastic ambitions – the sorry result of their fighting at the barricades; while the young scions of the Legitimist aristocracy used it to show their disdain for the court balls and the bankers who attended them."[9]

Orphée aux Enfers was what, in modern terms, we would call a "sleeper". The review by Jules Janin (1804-74) in *Journal des Débats* decried the "profanation of holy and glorious antiquity"[10]. Offenbach issued a rebuttal, claiming that part of the show was actually based on Janin's own writings on Pluto. An open feud erupted in the media, the publicity from which ironically resulted in a respectable run of 228 performances. All of this was good news for Offenbach's many creditors.

Later, Halévy would team up with another librettist, Henri Meilhac (1830-97) on the libretto for *La belle Hélène, La Vie parisienne* and *La Grande-Duchesse de Gérolstein*. According to Offenbach's friend the German music critic Eduard Hanslick (1825-1904), "Offenbach would sit at the piano and sing to his librettist the music he had composed the day before. Now he would find that there were four lines too few, and Meilhac would write them; now he would want two lines deleted, but Meilhac would maintain they were absolutely essential. When one was unwilling to sacrifice his music and the other his lines, the discussions were apt to become very lively. But they always agreed in the end."[11] This suggests a true collaboration in the modern sense.

In creating this new form, Offenbach was, in fact, rebelling against what he believed to be the heavy handed and pompous tendency of Italian opera, then prevalent in Paris. Believing that opera's true French heritage was being discarded, the composer wrote "The idea of really gay, cheerful, witty music – in short, the idea of music with life in it, was gradually being forgotten"[12]. According to biographer Peter Gammond (1925-), he "assimilated every kind of traditional and popular song so that his music was always close to the tastes of the ordinary French citizen."[13] He explains, "Composers like Irving Berlin and Richard Rodgers would be disgruntled not to find people singing and whistling their works for they are written expressly for that purpose, and they, rather than the serious composers, who depend as greatly on official patronage to get their works produced as the early composers did on the nobility, are the real heirs to Mozart, Lully, Rossini, Donizetti and Offenbach."[14]

The opéra-bouffe was also, according to Kracauer,

reflective of its time. "The operetta would never have been born had the society of the time not itself been operetta-like; had it not been living in a dream world, obstinately refusing to wake up and face reality."[15] Although certain pieces by Offenbach have survived and continue to be performed, he fell out of favour in France at the end of the Second Empire, when the public were no longer interested in what was considered to be posh frivolity. The opéra-bouffe had, to Kracauer, "originated in an epoch in which social reality had been banished by the Emperor's orders, and for many years it had flourished in the gap that was left. Thoroughly ambiguous as it was, it had fulfilled a revolutionary function under the dictatorship, that of scourging corruption and authoritarianism, and holding up the principles of freedom" but "with the decay of the dictatorship and the growth of the Left opposition, social forces, whose place had been taken by Offenbach's operettas, once more came into play... Republicans had always wrongly regarded Offenbach as a representative of the Imperial regime."[16]

While he may have lost favour at home, *Orphée*'s fame beyond France grew slowly, as German language productions played in Vienna, Berlin and even New York. English playwright John Robinson Planché (1796-1880) admired Offenbach's music but loathed the libretto by Crémieux and Halévy, which included infidelity and suggestions of sadomasochism. On top of this, the then-risqué can-can was judged too racy for Victorian London, so Planché adapted their work into a pastiche called *Orpheus in the Haymarket*, which opened in 1865. One reviewer complained of the "washed-out and colourless result."[17] English author and broadcaster Leslie Baily (1906-76) says, "...in adapting these works for the English stage the Gallic naughtinesses were cut out and replaced by all the shoddy stock-in-hand of the English stage: puns, clumsy innuendoes, men dressed as women, women as men, feeble singing, slatternly acting. Any delicate Gallic spice which remained seemed to weather badly in its transportation into the strange foreign atmosphere of an

England where prudishness and vulgarity flourished side by side."[18] Not until twenty years later did it finally reach Broadway in English under the now famous title *Orpheus in the Underworld*, although his *La Grande-Duchesse de Gérolstein* had already been well received there.[19] Gammond concludes, "Offenbach was unquestionably the key figure and the most powerful catalyst in the establishment of our popular musical theatre... a task which he achieved by having one ear bent to operatic developments from Mozart to Donizetti and one to the earthier music of the cafés and music halls."[20]

While Offenbach certainly affected the work that followed, his real influence might be summed up in an expression used by modern political pundits – by reaching out to a new audience, he "changed the weather". "Offenbach possessed all the qualities essential to the successful composition of musicals;" wrote British light music composer and conductor Mark Lubbock (1898-1986) in 1957, "apparently inexhaustible fertility and musical invention, a predominantly personal idiom... together with range and variety."[21] "In the musical theatre", says Alan Jay Lerner, "he was indeed the father of us all."[22]

Even *Carmen*, one of the greatest and most popular of operas, is arguably really a musical – in structure, if not in vocal style. In fact, it is probably the only opera in the world whose arias are as familiar to the man in the street as are the songs from *Oklahoma!*. Written for Paris' Opéra-Comique, a more "middle-brow" establishment than the elitist Palais Garnier, it contained (in its original form) large tracts of spoken dialogue. The music was by Offenbach's friend Georges Bizet (1838-75), and the libretto was co-written by frequent Offenbach collaborators Halévy and Meilhac, based on a novel by Prosper Mérimée. Like Offenbach, Bizet was a student of Halévy's uncle Fromental Halévy, who was also his father-in-law.

Its premiere in 1875 received only mixed reviews. If he wanted his work to be accepted by the major opera houses of the world, then Bizet had to conform. Although he was contracted to write the necessary recitative for the Viennese premiere, he suffered a heart attack and died (at the age of only thirty-seven) before work was begun, and so the job was left to his American-born friend and protégé Ernest Guiraud (1837-92), who would also later complete Offenbach's *Tales of Hoffman*. Performing Arts critic and musicologist David Foil says:

> "As in a classic American musical comedy, the dialogue between musical numbers in an opéra-comique tends to underscore the characters' humanity, to reveal subtleties and interesting contradictions in their personalities. Instead of the alluring, vampish prima donna that reigns supreme in Guiraud's version, the Carmen of Bizet's opéra-comique is raunchy, sometimes wickedly funny, petty, tantalizingly remote, and unpredictable. Likewise, Bizet's Don José is not the bellowing overgrown boy he can sometimes seem in the Guiraud version, but a deeply conflicted young man full of repressed rage. He is teetering on the brink of insanity, an obsessive-compulsive who becomes a homicidal stalker. In the case of Don José, the opéra-comique version does not make the character lighter, but much, much darker."[23]

When Leonard Bernstein – one of the first modern conductors to champion the restoration of the original opéra-comique version – presented excerpts from *Carmen* on Japanese television in the early 1960s, he did the spoken dialogue alongside the recitative for comparison, using Broadway actors for the former and singers from the Metropolitan Opera for the latter.[24] His 1972 Metropolitan Opera production more or less permanently banished the Giraud version. Perhaps this structural similitude to the musical explains why Oscar Hammerstein II was so successful in adapting it as *Carmen Jones* in 1943, using less spoken dialogue than the original had.

Meilhac and Halévy would also between them provide the source material for two of the most popular operettas of all time – *Die Fledermaus* ("The Bat") (1874), with music by Johann Strauss Jr. (1825-99) and *Die Lustige Witwe* ("The Merry Widow", 1905) with music by Franz Lehár (1870-1948). While the former was based on Meilhac and Halévy's play *Le Réveillon* (which also formed the basis for Offenbach's *La Vie Parisienne*), they did not provide the libretto – Richard Genée (1823-95) did. Similarly, the libretto for *The Merry Widow* was by Viktor Léon (1858-1940) and Leo Stein (1861-1921), based on Meilhac's 1861 play *L'attaché d'ambassade*. According to American theatrical historian Marlis Schweitzer, "the new era in musical entertainment heralded by Lehár's operetta coincided with the rapid expansion of a transnational market in theatrical comodities, fuelled by the feminization of commercial theatre audiences and increased demands for exciting, moving or otherwise captivating entertainment."[25]

At this point, I feel that I should say something about this term "operetta". It has been used to describe everything from Offenbach and Strauss to Vincent Scotto. The *Oxford Concise Dictionary of Music* defines it as "Little opera. Strictly a play with [overture], songs, entr'actes and dances, but the term has become synonymous with 'light opera', e.g. Offenbach's *La Belle Hélène* and Strauss's *Die Fledermaus*, and 'musical comedy', e.g. Coward's *Bitter-Sweet*."[26] I tend to compare it to terms like "Victorolla" and "gramophone", which are simply archaic tradenames for what we would now call a media player. While "operetta" may imply the quasi-operatic world of Strauss, it is also applied to the works of Gilbert and Sullivan, who often employed singing actors, rather than opera singers. George Colerick describes operetta as "a variety of opera, just as demanding artistically, and with special features, such as the dependence on clearly enunciated speech and the combination of song with movement in set pieces which at the high moments bring audiences to a state of excitement relieved by synchronised clapping."[27] According to Stephen Sondheim, "'Opera' implies endless stentorian[28] singing; 'operetta' implies gleeful choirs of peasants dancing in the town square; 'opéra-bouffe' implies hilarious (in intent, at least) complications of mistaken identity;

'musical comedy' implies showbiz pizzazz and blindingly bright energy; 'musical play' implies musical comedy that isn't funny. For me, an opera is something that is performed in an opera house in front of an opera audience. The ambience, along with the audience's expectation, is what flavors the evening... Opera is defined by the eye and ear of the beholder."[29]

The world of the nineteenth century was not as clear-cut in separating "classical" versus "popular" as we are in the twenty-first century. Looking at it from a modern standpoint, works that are not performed in opera houses and that do not use operatic voice production would be classed as musicals (or, if they are not commercially popular, as "music theatre"). I will go further, and say that a show that aims for a popular audience is a musical, as is one in which the libretto is of equal importance to the music. Broadway conductor Lehman Engel writes that Offenbach, Strauss and Arthur Sullivan together "represented a synthesis, a fruition and a culmination. Though alike in intention, their respective works were totally dissimilar in style. In a narrow sense, despite their enormous popularity, these men produced no direct musical heirs of quality. Indirectly, however, the tradition they created was to be found most vitally developed in contemporary American musical theater."[30]

"What most impressed its admirers?" Professor Richard Kislan asks. "Two qualities. The serious artistic approach to the elements of the libretto (especially plot and characterization), and the music of composers of international stature. The European librettists introduced a frankness in dialogue and situation hitherto avoided in English-language musicals. The European composers set much of these lyrics to attractive and entertaining music that responded to valid dramatic considerations as well as the composer's need for a free musical imagination."[31]

Operetta finally took root on English soil with the fourth collaboration between playwright William Schwenk

Gilbert (1836-1911) and composer Arthur Seymour Sullivan (1842-1900), probably the first theatrical song writing team to receive equal credit for music and lyrics. At the time they came together, Gilbert and Sullivan were already fairly well established individually: Gilbert as a respected dramatist, and Sullivan as a composer and conductor. Both would work with other collaborators of renown, Gilbert with Carl Rosa (1842-89) and Sullivan with Alfred Tennyson (1809-92), among others. However, at this time virtually all light musical comedy was written to existing music. Leslie Baily says that Gilbert's "need was for a composer as original as himself."[32]

Their differences in temperament were legendary. Sullivan, who was born into genteel poverty in Lambeth, was a social butterfly and friend of royalty. Gilbert was, at least initially, somewhat to the political left of his partner and aimed his barbed wit at virtually anybody of higher social status than himself. He also closely controlled what went on stage, and as an accomplished illustrator, had much to do with the visual conception of the work. According to Leslie Baily, "By autocratic, hard-hitting methods he set about demolishing the turgid traditions of the Victorian stage, against the resistance of players who could not fathom why an author should have a say in their interpretation of what he had written."[33] Gilbert's lyrics were at least as important to the work as Sullivan's music – much sometimes to the latter's chagrin.

Their partnership began rather inauspiciously with *Thespis*, which ran for only sixty-three performances at the Gaiety Theatre in 1871. Gilbert himself described it as "a crude and ineffective work".[34] Only fragments of Sullivan's score survive from this early work. ("Climbing Over Rocky Mountain" was interpolated into *The Pirates of Penzance*.) It took one more modest success – *Trial By Jury* (1875) – and one more failure – *The Sorcerer* (1877) before that all-important breakthrough came when *H.M.S. Pinafore – or – The Lass that Loved a Sailor* opened at London's Opéra Comique on 25 May 1878. Gerald Bordman, author of

American Operetta says, "In the world of English-speaking theatre, it stands as the most important musical ever written... [it] determined the course and shape of the popular lyric stage in England and America for the final quarter of the nineteenth century."[35] Their greatest success, however, would come in 1885 with *The Mikado – or, the Town of Titipu* which although superficially Japanese (Sullivan actually borrowed from Japanese composer Yajiro Shinagawa (1843-1900) for part of the melody of "Mi-ya Sa-ma") was in fact a satire on English values. It remains one of the most performed pieces of musical theatre in history, and the one Gilbert and Sullivan piece that has crossed language barriers.[36]

This was not the beginning of musical comedy in Britain – that is usually dated to John Gay (1685-1732)'s *The Beggars' Opera* in 1728. However, Gilbert and Sullivan created the first successful English works with original music (*Beggars' Opera* borrowed established arias and folk tunes) to capture the imagination of the world. Many Americans – Alan Jay Lerner and Ira Gershwin among them – cite Gilbert as a master lyricist, which of course he was (although Stephen Sondheim has dismissed his work as "technically adroit but rarely as interesting in concept or surprising in progression"[37] as Cole Porter's). But his work was always quintessentially English. It is also of its time, yet much of it is relevant today to a modern, non-British audience.

"While Britain historically produced a fair number of musicals, these were the works of unique individuals (Noël Coward, Ivor Novello, Noel Gay, etc) rather than the product of a musical theatre culture,"[38] said the Theatre Committee of the Writers Guild of Great Britain, in a submission to the UK Parliament's Culture, Media and Sport Committee in November 2003. What is a musical theatre culture, if not a collection of such "unique individuals"? Unlike the Americans, they never coalesced into an identifiable "British school" because there was no imperative for them to do so. Britannia ruled the waves.

The very fact that they spoke English defined them. (Only by rebelling against this hegemony did the Americans put their own unique stamp on the form.)

And so they plodded along. Vivian Ellis (1903-96) (*Mr. Cinders, Bless the Bride*) wrote a number of pleasantly comfortable shows that were as English as warm beer and cold toast, and that had scarcely any impact beyond Britain's borders. Even Ivor Novello (1893-1951)'s success was, for the most part, confined to Britain – or at most, the British Empire. (In Hollywood, his chief claim to fame appears to be coming up with the line "Me Tarzan, you Jane".)[39] Only Noël Coward (1899-1973) seemed to catch the fancy of American audiences – and that was largely because this polymath not only wrote the book, music and lyrics, but also produced, directed and starred in such shows as *Bittersweet* (1929) and *Conversation Piece* (1934). Even so, he is better remembered for his many plays and his speciality songs ("Mad Dogs and Englishmen", "Mad About the Boy") than for his book musicals.

In the period after World War II, the English musicals began to look staid and quaint next to the brash American shows that began to dominate the West End – *Annie Get Your Gun*, *Oklahoma!* and even *My Fair Lady*. Only later did Lionel Bart, David Heneker and others begin to bring it back to life. (But that's another chapter.)

Other European countries developed their own musical theatre traditions, although these didn't travel as widely as the French, German and English ones. Spain (and the Spanish-speaking world) developed a form of its own. The term "zarzuela" literally means "bramble bush"[40], but refers to a form of (usually) light opera with spoken dialogue. The name actually refers to the royal palace near Madrid where these masque-like pieces were first performed. Although the form dates to the seventeenth century, it was revived in the 1850s with a government-subsidised aim of presenting opera with a Spanish accent. Francisco Asenjo Barbieri's (1823-94) works included *El barberillo de Lavapiés, Jugar con fuego, Pan y toros, Don Quijote, Los diamantes de la corona,* and *El Diablo en el poder.* It reached its apotheosis in the first half of the twentieth century with works by Jacinto Guerrero (1895-1951), José Serrano (1873-1941) and Amadeu Vives (1871-1932) whose *Doña Francisquita* (1923) is considered by some to be the pinnacle of the genre. Christopher Webber, author of *The Zarzuela Companion*[41] calls this "one of the few zarzuelas which has 'travelled' abroad. With its easy lyricism, fluent orchestration and colourful evocation of 19th Century Madrid – not to mention its memorable vocal and choral writing – it certainly encapsulates Vives' sweetly potent charm, and his love for the city where he worked and died".[42] In addition to its great popularity in the Spanish speaking world, it was also seen in French translation in 1934 in Monte Carlo, Vichy and Brussels, and more recently at the Washington National Opera in 1998.

Although their popularity never reached the English speaking world, the zarzuelas did spread to Latin America, especially Cuba and Mexico, as well as the Philippines (where it is called "sarswela"), and were performed in Catalan, Basque and Tagalog as well as Castilian Spanish. They have also indirectly influenced Greek musicals. The Spanish opera singer Plácido Domingo (1941-) was the son of zarzuela singers with their own Domingo-Embil Company in Mexico, and the song "El Cóndor Pasa", made popular by Simon and Garfunkel, is from a 1913 zarzuela of the same name by Peruvian composer Daniel Alomía Robles (1871-1942).

Even the Communist block produced musical comedies. Since 1929, the Leningrad State Musical Comedy Theatre had been the home of Russian operetta and musical comedy, and during the Second World War was the only theatre to remain open during the entire siege of Leningrad. From the land of Mussorgsky and Rimsky-Korsakov sprang Isaak Osipovich Dunayevsky (1900-55), who wrote some fourteen operettas, including *The Golden Valley* (1937) and *The Free Wind* (1947), and forty-two musical films, mostly for the director Grigori Aleksandrov (1903-83), a former collaborator of Sergei Eisenstein. He was one of the first Soviet artists to begin using jazz. Rimgaila Salys, Professor of Russian studies at the University of Colorado says, "Aleksandrov recognized that Russia was a singing country with a rich tradition of folk and urban melodies."[43] Their film musicals together included *Jolly Fellows* (1934), which might have languished unreleased as a "banned" film had it not been for the intervention of Josef Stalin. It produced a hit song "Yak mnogo devushek khoroshikh" ("Such a lot of nice girls") with lyrics by Pyotr Leshehenko. British novelist Graham Greene, writing for *Spectator* magazine in London, said that it was "the best thing to happen to the cinema since René Clair made *The Italian Straw Hat*. Alexandrov, who has been awarded a Soviet Order for his direction has produced, just as Clair did then, out of the smallest resources and apparently with poor-quality film, a picture of almost ecstatic happiness... I have no wish to criticize this film, but simply to rejoice in its wildness, its grotesqueness, its light, taking tunes, a sense of good living that owes nothing to champaign or women's clothes."[44]

This was followed by *Circus* (1936) from which "The Song of the Motherland" became the call-sign for Moscow Radio and for a while was the unofficial Soviet anthem.

During a visit to California in the mid 1930s, Alexandrov sang a popular folk song "Ponizovaya Volnitsa" while rowing with Charlie Chaplin in San Francisco Bay. This features the lines (translated into English):

> Volga, Volga, Mother Volga,
> Wide and deep beneath the sun,
> You have ne'er seen such a present
> From the Cossacks of the Don!

As a joke, Chaplin suggested the line as a movie title, but Alexandrov took him seriously. *Volga-Volga* (1938) was, according to legend, to become Stalin's favourite film, and, having seen it over a hundred times, one that he would re-enact by heart. With an inventive if sometimes frantic style, it told of a band of amateur performers sailing down the river of its title aboard a sternwheeler, bound for Moscow and the Musical Olympiad. This was one of the few Soviet musicals to be released in the West, albeit in a shortened version dubbed into English and featuring future star Trevor Howard as the voice of 'Uncle Kuzya' the water-carrier.

As one might expect from a two-time winner of the Stalin Prize, Dunayevsky's works often contained political messages, such as his cantata *Glory of the Railwaymen* and his *Rhapsody on Songs of the People of the Soviet Union*. Whereas I have argued that the musical grew up alongside democracy, in this case the genre came under the purview of the Peoples' Commissar of Enlightenment. Comedy films were given a mandate to "become a medium of Communist enlightenment and agitation, an instrument of the Party in educating and organizing the masses around the basic task of the period of socialist construction."[45] Needless to say, their work did not transfer to the West End and Broadway, although Dunayevsky's stage and film musicals remained popular within the Soviet Bloc.

In Dana Ranga's 1997 film *East Side Story*, which documents the phenomena of Soviet-bloc musical films, an East German audience member named Brigitte Ulbrich says, "When we were young and used to compare these films with films from the West or from America, [the latter] seemed rather removed from us. We saw them, we enjoyed them, we had fun. But our own films... they were our world."[46]

All of the pre-war musical theatre in continental Europe would soon grind to a crashing halt. The European musical theatre faced a challenge from the New World – and a holocaust in its own back yard. (For European musicals after World War II, please see the chapter "Europe

After Hitler".)

Musicals for the Masses:
Emanuel Schikaneder and the Theater an der Wien

Whereas New York is known as a centre for commerce and Paris for its fashion and art, Vienna is all about music – especially waltzes and operettas. More than any of the other historic capitals of musical theatre, Vienna is rooted in the classical world – of Mozart and Beethoven. "One of the oldest and richest traditions in world theatre"[1], says musical historian Kurt Gänzl. Yet, after the Second World War, it demolished most of its musical theatres, and largely turned its back on the form. In the modern era of megamusicals, its significance is in danger of being forgotten.

Since the fourteenth century, Vienna has been a centre for the study of music, existing at a cross-road of French, German, Dutch and Italian trains of thought. "Creativity is often the result of reconciling opposing ideas or influences"[2], says Michael Cherlin, professor of music theory at University of Minnesota. "Although every culture derives its own personality in part through being affected by the impact of other cultures, the musical life of Vienna is particularly remarkable in this regard... Ideals of clarity and grace, derived in large part from the French Enlightenment, intermingle with the conceptualization of music as drama derived in large part from the ascendancy of Italian opera." Like New York in the nineteenth and twentieth centuries, Vienna was a cultural melting pot. Yet, it is only since the late eighteenth century that important works began to be written in German – the language of the masses.

Vienna's time of musical prosperity roughly coincided with its period as the capital of the Austro-Hungarian Empire, and consequently it attracted the best musical talents – classical and popular – of not only Austria, but also Hungary and Bohemia (now the Czech Republic). Emperor Joseph's 1782 "Decrees of Tolerance" made it possible for Jews, Lutherans, Calvinists and others to enter areas of business previously denied them. "Vienna's many-sided musical culture, throughout the 19th century and beyond, had interesting racial implications, beyond the other important social ones", says George Colerick. "The Habsburg Empire offered for a long time an unusual kind of multi-racial stability. It stimulated an incomparable variety of musical achievements."[3] (The same was also then true of Berlin – how things would change in a few short years!) In fact, it has been a series of contradictions – a culturally conservative city that pioneered many social democratic policies, and a multi-cultural society that waffled between tolerance and bigotry.

In the late eighteenth century, political change was sweeping across Europe. The French revolution put Europe's ruling classes on notice, and the theatrical tastes of the general populace began to be felt in the development of singspiele, which would eventually become operetta and musical comedy.

Since the American musical theatre defined itself by imitating the Viennese, French and British operetta before moving on from it, it may be helpful to look at Viennese musical theatre within the context of the other places and works discussed.

As a musical writer, I've learned that when writing a musical biography, it is best to focus on a specific event or aspect of the subject's life. The cultural life of a city is no different. In the case of Vienna, I've narrowed in on one particular theatre, and the man who built it. In it you will find the story of the Viennese musical in a microcosm.

Although his name is seldom heard in the same sentence as those of Florenz Ziegfeld, Max Reinhardt, Harold Prince or Cameron Mackintosh, Emanuel Schikaneder (1751-1812) is, for me, one of the great (pardon the expression) unsung heroes of the musical. The friendship that he struck up with Leopold Mozart – and, more significantly with his son Wolfgang Amadeus –

would change musical and theatrical history, and add immeasurably to the development of popular musical theatre. His biographer Kurt Honolka says, "Schikaneder's universality and creative fantasy could be compared to Max Reinhardt's; to a certain extent he managed to achieve a thoroughly 'modern' form of theater presentation. His Singspiele and comic operas... anticipate the later Viennese operetta, while his extravagant spectaculars point toward the revue and the musical."[4] Most significantly, although he is credited with co-creating one of the grandest of all operas, his intended audience was largely working class.

Emanuel Schikaneder

Schikaneder was born in Straubing, Bavaria in 1751 to a poor family, and was educated by Jesuits in Regensburg, where he sang in the cathedral. He joined the acting company of Andreas Schopf at the age of 22, where he performed in opera, farce and singspiele. He began to write and act in his own musical pieces, creating both the libretti and scores. By the time he was twenty-seven, he had triumphed as *Hamlet*, and was running his own company. It was two years later, during an extended stay in Salzburg, that he met the Mozarts. The young composer became enthralled with the populist entertainments that Schikaneder produced, making anonymous musical contributions to a number of them. It was eleven years later that they created the work that would lay new foundations for both musical comedy and opera.

Honolka says, "Schikaneder was author, producer and director, controlling casting and the magnificence or sparseness of the scenery, all of which means his contribution to the success of the evening can hardly be overestimated."[5] I would go even further than that. *The Magic Flute* wouldn't have happened without both its composer and its librettist. It appears to have been

Schikaneder's idea in the first place; it was the librettist who hired Mozart, and not the reverse, as was often the case. In writing a show of this nature, Mozart was enthusiastically entering into Schikaneder's world of populist entertainment, and eschewing the snootiness of court-based Italian opera. It appears to have been a true collaboration: when Schikaneder suggested that Papageno should stammer when first meeting Papagena, Mozart obligingly rewrote the scene. Over the past two centuries, scholars and critics have debated the merits of Schikaneder's libretto. Only in the world of opera would it be suggested that a masterpiece could be created on the strength of the music alone, without first having a strong "book". Although Mozart himself dictated that the libretto must be the servant of the music, in a Broadway musical – at least in the post *Oklahoma!* period – the book writer is paramount.

The Magic Flute opened on 30 September 1791 at the Theater auf der Wieden and ran for an initial 223 performances there in repertory. Emboldened by its success, Schikaneder determined to eventually build his own theatre, and secured an imperial privilege from the then-Emperor Joseph, which was, fourteen years later, confirmed by Emperor Franz, his successor. With the backing of a wealthy merchant named Bartholomäus Zitterbarth, he opened the Theater an der Wien, designed in the Empire style by Franz Jäger, on 13 June 1801. A theatre-going journalist named Adolf Bäuerle wrote, "If Schikaneder and Zitterbarth had had the idea… to charge admission simply for looking at the glories of their Theater an der Wien, Schikaneder would certainly have been able to take in vast sums of money without giving one single performance."[6]

A year after opening his new theatre, he presented a revival of *The Magic Flute* with some revisions to the libretto, and a new scenic design that took full advantage of the expanded stage facilities. Unfortunately, by this time Mozart had been dead for a decade. Even though, as the capital of the Austrian Empire the city would soon emerge into its greatest era of political and cultural importance, the musical theatre revolution they had started together had stalled, and Schikaneder's greatest artistic achievements were behind him. Within two years, he and Zitterbarth had parted company, and they were forced to sell the theatre to Gesellschaft der Cavaliere ("Society of Cavaliers"), a consortium of court nobles, including Count Ferdinand Palffy von Erdöd, who acquired full ownership in 1813. Schikaneder's imperial privilege allowed him to retain some influence as Artistic Director, and he was able to appoint no less than Ludwig von Beethoven as his director of music, presenting the premiere of the latter's opera *Fidelio* in 1805. (Three years later, Beethoven's Fifth Symphony also received its world premiere here.) Schikaneder made his final appearance on the stage of the theatre he built on 23 December 1806, and he would die in poverty six years later. Honolka says that "his greatest contribution is found in his concept of popular theater of higher quality".[7]

In 2016, Broadway composer Stephen Schwartz opened a new musical at the Raimond Theatre (which is under the same management as Theater an der Wien) in Vienna called *Schikaneder* set during the period leading up to *The Magic Flute*'s opening. He told me it was "fun to know that someone else thinks of Schikaneder as one of the progenitors of contemporary musical theatre."[8]

Palffy attempted to court popularity with pantomime and variety, in addition to opera and ballet, but failed financially, and he was forced to sell the theatre in 1825. It would be some seven decades before the theatre Schikaneder built would make its next great mark on history. Under Carl Carl (Karl Andreas von Bernbrunn – 1787-1854) – who also ran the Carltheater in the Vienna suburb Leopoldstadt – it became Vienna's leading popular theatre, premiering many of Johann Nestroy's (1801-62) plays. (While Nestroy's comedies remain staples of the German-speaking theatre, few have ever been translated into English, although one became the basis for Thornton

Wilder's *The Matchmaker*, which later became the musical *Hello, Dolly!*)

In 1845, Franz Pokorny acquired the theatre after a benefactor paid its debts, and Carl was forced out. Pokorny updated the facilities, intending to produce operas, but in spite of several guest performances by the "Swedish nightingale" Jenny Lind, he quickly went bankrupt and in 1848 his son Alois took over.

In 1858, Offenbach's *Le Mariage aux lanternes* was presented for the first time in German in Vienna – the first of over sixty such presentations in his lifetime – and within a year, German-language writers began knocking off their own "opéra-bouffe"s. Franz von Suppé (1819-95), a pupil of Donizetti's, soon emerged as a leading light when his *Das Pensionat* ("The Girl's Finishing School") opened at the Theater an der Wien in 1860.

From 1862, under Friedrich Strampfer, the theatre continued on its new course, presenting the operettas of Offenbach. Marie Geistinger (1836-1903) and Maximilian Steiner (1839-80) took over in 1869, and five years later would present the show that would herald the so-called "Golden Age" of Viennese operetta.

It was a long time coming. For sixteen years, audiences had shown a decided preference for the French opéra-bouffe, despite the best efforts of Suppé and others. The city had been in an economic slump following a stock market crash that devastated the commercial theatres. Then from out of this gloom a French comedy, *Le Réveillon* ("The Midnight Supper") by frequent Offenbach collaborators Henri Meilhac and Ludovic Halévy (in turn based on *Das Gefängnis* ("The Prison") by Roderich Benedix) would give birth to what would become the touchstone of Viennese Operetta.

The original plan was simply to present the play but Steiner, unhappy with the translation he had commissioned, decided that it needed to be set to music. He approached the "waltz king" Johann Strauss Jr. to provide the score, and the libretto was by Richard Genée (1823-95), a composer in his own right.[9] The result would translate a Parisian comedy into something very Viennese. *Die Fledermaus*[10] ("The Bat") opened at the Theater and der Wien on 5 April 1874, starring the theatre's co-director Marie Geistinger as Rosalinde. It did not however immediately set the theatrical world alight, enjoying a very modest run in Vienna, but gaining greater acceptance in Berlin, and spreading throughout the Germanic world. Only much later would it become popular in English and other languages. In 1950, New York's Metropolitan Opera commissioned new English lyrics by Broadway and Hollywood legend Howard Dietz (1896-1983) for a production adapted and directed by Garson Kanin (1912-99).

By the end of the nineteenth century, the generation behind the "Golden Age" had almost all passed away, and the lights of Vienna appeared ready to dim. But then a new generation began to emerge, and with them, a lighter, breezier, less "classical" form. Although largely centred in Vienna, this new generation of writers would be drawn from throughout central Europe, especially from within the Austro-Hungarian Empire, where the talent pool was mobile.

After a 1900 renovation by theatre architects Ferdinand Fellner Jr. and Hermann Helmer, Wilhelm Karczag took over the management of the Theater an der Wien, as the operetta entered its so-called "Silver Age". (It may seem strange to us that the "Silver Age" produced even more enduring works than the "Golden Age" did, but Simon Broughton in the London *Independent* says, "Golden Age operetta was an escape from the present, Silver Age operetta was a retreat into the past."[11])

Die Lustige Witwe ("The Merry Widow", 1905) was originally offered to composer Richard Heuberger (1850-

1914), who had enjoyed some success in 1898 with *Opera Ball*, but he failed to provide a satisfactory score. The commission was then offered to a young Hungarian musical director, Franz Lehár (1870-1948), who had already enjoyed some success with *Wiener Frauen* and *Der Rastelbinder*, both in 1901. The book by Viktor Léon (1858-1940) and Leo Stein (1861-1921) was based on an 1862 play by Henri Meilhac, *L'Attaché d'ambassade* ("The Embassy Attaché"). (Another work by Meilhac had inspired *Die Fledermaus* a generation earlier. In fact, Léon and Stein were a bit of a holdover from that previous age: Léon had worked with Strauss on *Simplicius* in 1887.)

The setting for *The Merry Widow* was the Paris embassy of "Pontevedro", a thinly disguised Montenegro. For Lehár, this was an opportunity to add some Balkan musical colour, although some Montenegrin students were less than thrilled to have their homeland made the object of fun.

The Merry Widow's success was immediate. A London production opened in 1907, and it soon spread across Europe and North America. (Its influence on the later American musical is unmistakable: listen to the "Maxime's" sequence, then listen to the verse leading into "Shall We Dance?" from *The King and I* as well as to "Dance at the Gym" from *West Side Story*.)

With some of the money he was now earning, Lehár bought a baroque mansion in the suburb of Nussdorf that had once belonged to Emanuel Schikaneder. He was to be one of the few composers to stay behind – and prosper – under the Nazis, although to be fair, it was reportedly an uneasy truce. His wife Sofie had been a Jew until she converted to Catholicism, thus rendering her an "Ehrenarierin" (Honourary Aryan) in Nazi eyes. He is also reported to have fought unsuccessfully to save the life of his librettist Fritz Löhner-Beda (1883-1942).[12]

In 1901, writer and drama critic Felix Salten

presented a short-lived cabaret season – Austria's first – in the theatre's cellar. A more permanent cabaret known as Die Hölle ("Hell") was opened in the same theatre by Sigmund and Leopold Natzler in 1906 with art nouveau décor designed by Heinrich Lefler and Joseph Urban. With Fritz Grünbaum (1880-1941) as its Master of Ceremonies, it presented songs, comedies and even small operettas, including Franz Lehàr's *Frühling* ("Spring"), as well as works by future operetta composers Leo Fall, Edmund Eysler, Robert Stolz and Ralph Benatzky. In one incident in 1910, Grünbaum – who was to become one of Austria's greatest cabaret artists and actors – was injured in a duel after he slapped an Imperial officer for shouting out anti-Semitic remarks. Die Hölle closed in 1928 (although the space remains as one of the theatre's bars), and Grünbaum would eventually die in the Dachau concentration camp.

In the same year as Die Hölle opened, Grünbaum would also establish himself as a librettist in the main theatre upstairs. With co-author A. M. Willner (1859 - 1929) and composer Leo Fall (1873-1925), he wrote *Die Dollarprinzessin* ("The Dollar Princess"), based on a comedy by Gatti-Trotha with a contemporary American setting.

It travelled first to London, with a new book by Basil Hood (1864-1917) and lyrics by Adrian Ross (1859-1933) where it played successfully for over a year at Daly's Theatre in Leicester Square[13]. In New York it was given a new libretto by George Grossmith Jr. (1874-1935), (the son of a Gilbert and Sullivan veteran) and, as was common practice in those days, some additional music by Jerome Kern. The *New York Times* complained that it had been rather too anglicised. "If you care for the charm and grace of English musical comedy you are quite sure to enjoy *The Dollar Princess*. If you are looking for Austrian fire and dash you are quite likely to be disappointed."[14] Not for the last time, German-language musical theatre would indulge its fascination with the culture that would soon overtake it.

Like Fall, Oscar Straus (1870-1954) had also written

for the cabarets, including some presented by Max Reinhardt. Alan Jay Lerner says, "He was the only one of them all with an appreciation of comedy."[15] In 1908, Straus's *Der tapfere Soldat* ("The Courageous Soldier") opened with a libretto by Rudolf Bernauer (1880-1953) and Leopold Jacobson (1878-1943) based on George Bernard Shaw's *Arms and the Man*. While its success in Vienna was modest, an English translation by Stanislaus Stange (1862-1917), *The Chocolate Soldier* was loved by everybody – except Shaw, who forbade any further musical adaptations from his works.[16] (Lerner and Loewe would have to wait for him to die before they could turn *Pygmalion* into *My Fair Lady*.)

In 1909, another Hungarian composer with a cabaret background made his debut at the Theater an der Wien with a show that had premiered in Budapest the previous year. *Tatárjárás* ("Tatar Campaign"), with a score by Emmerich Kálmán (1882-1953) was translated into German as *Herbstmanöver*, and also played at the Knickerbocker Theatre in New York as *The Gay Hussars*, adapted by Maurice Browne Kirby with lyrics by Grant Stewart. This was the beginning of a long Viennese career.

Many of his best known works premiered at the theatre's rivals, including *Die Csárdásfürstin* ("The Csárdás Princess") which opened at the Johann-Strauss-Theater in 1915. Kálmán would make good use here of both his Hungarian and cabaret roots. The libretto by Leo Stein and Béla Jenbach (1871-1943) is set in Budapest's Orpheum cabaret, and concerns a star making her farewell appearance before embarking on a tour of the U.S. A hit throughout Europe, it missed out on English (*The Gipsy Princess*) and American (*The Riviera Girl*) success because of an apparent inability to come up with a decent adaptation, although in total it otherwise amassed some 12,000 performances. In New York, where it included a book by Guy Bolton and P.G. Wodehouse and additional songs by Jerome Kern, it played only 78 performances. Opening in 1917 while World War I was still in full swing, according to

Richard Traubner, it "indeed proved a dud, partly due to anti-Viennese feeling in the United States."[17] The war was over in 1921 when it opened in London with a new libretto by Arthur Miller and Arthur Stanley. It lasted 200 performances. Zoltán Imre of Eötvös Loránd University says, "The (relative) failure was partly due to the fact that the operetta dealt with the gipsy theme in a very conventional way... within the known and expected stereotypical representation of the Eastern Gipsy."[18]

Kálmán also spent some time in New York, contributing to the score of *Golden Dawn* with a libretto by Oscar Hammerstein II (1895-1960) and Otto Harbach (1873-1963). He was collaborating with Lorenz Hart on a show when the latter passed away in 1943. He died in Paris in 1953.

World War I adversely affected the operetta in two ways. During the war, nothing was exported to Britain or France. And after the war, the Habsburg Empire – and the glamour that went with it – was a distant memory. In a country that had thrown off its monarchy, people lost interest in stories about princes and counts. At the same time, New York was beginning to assert itself. Elegance and gentility were usurped by the rhythms of jazz. The centre of gravity was slowly shifting, but while it may have been the beginning of the end for European operetta, it wasn't quite done yet.

The stereotyped image we have of a Viennese operetta is an old-world vision of counts and baronesses sipping champaign as they waltz at a grand ball, an image derived from *Die Fledermaus* and *The Merry Widow*. In reality, the Viennese may not have kept pace with Broadway, but just as the Parisians moved on from Offenbach and Messager, so the Viennese moved on after Strauss and Lehár. The trouble was, English speaking audiences by and large were only interested in the stereotype, and so the jazzier "operettas" with contemporary – sometimes even American – settings tended to stay home. (I've discovered that this is a common theme – we tend to be interested in foreign musicals only if they're "exotic".)

Ralph Benatzky (1884-1957) secured an international reputation with *Im Weissen Rössl* in 1930 at Berlin's Grosse Schauspielhaus for director/choreographer Erik Charell (1894-1974), which travelled to London the following year as *The White Horse Inn*. Productions in Paris, Vienna, Budapest and eventually New York followed. In each case, the book was localised and songs by other composers interpolated, although Charell remained at the helm. It remains the most popular musical export from 1930s Berlin.

Karczag's son-in-law Hubert Marischka (1882-1959) took over the Theater an der Wien in 1923, continuing the policy of post-classical operetta that would come to an end with the rise of Hitler. Its swan song was Benatzky's 1936 jazzy Hollywood satire *Axel an der Himmelstür* ("Axel at the Gates of Heaven"). With a book by Paul Morgan (1886-1938) and Adolph Schütz and lyrics by Hans Weigel (1908-1991), it starred the Swedish actress-singer Zarah Leander (1907-81) as a Hollywood diva, and Danish actor Max Hansen (1897-1961) in the title role. One need only examine the fates of these collaborators to understand what happened to Viennese musical theatre. Benatzky escaped to the U.S., whereas Morgan died in a concentration camp. Leander, on the other hand, became a star of Nazi films.

During the Second World War the theatre was requisitioned by Kraft Durch Freude ("Strength Through Joy"), providing Nazi propaganda. From 1945, for ten years, it was home to the Vienna State Opera. In 1960, it was rescued from demolition by the municipality of Vienna, and became a venue for modern musicals, including *Cats*, which ran from 1983-88. In 1992, it hosted the massively successful German-language musical *Elisabeth*, with book and lyrics by Dr. Michael Kunze (1943-) and music by Sylvester Levay (1945-), which ran for six years. Although it has, since then, become a full-time opera house, I like to think that its builder would be proud of the fact that throughout most of its two hundred plus years' history it has catered to a wide audience with popular tastes.

Of course, the Theater an der Wien was not the only venue for operettas in Vienna. The Carltheater, home of many of Suppé's works, began its life as the Leopoldstädter Theater, and was comprehensively rebuilt in 1847. It closed in 1929, and having suffered bomb damage during the war, was demolished in 1951. The Raimund Theater, named for the playwright Ferdinand Raimund, opened in 1893 as a playhouse, and became a home for musicals and operettas from 1908. It survives as a commercial house and in recent years has hosted *A Chorus Line*, *Les Misérables*, *Kiss of the Spider Woman* and *Beauty and the Beast*, as well as German musicals *Dance of the Vampires* with music by Jim Steinman (1947 -) and lyrics by Michael Kunze, and *Rebecca* (with music by Levay and lyrics by Kunze). The Volksoper was built in 1898 as the Kaiser-Jubiläums-Stadttheater and has for most of its history housed plays, operas and musicals. In its early years it was Vienna's second opera house, behind the State Opera, but after 1929 focused on operettas. The Wiener Bürgertheater[19] was built in 1905 under the management of actor and writer Oskar Fronz, with Edmund Eysler (1874-1949) as house composer, also presenting hits by Lehár, Fall and Kálmán. It was demolished in 1960 as part of what seems to have been a "let's-destroy-our-cultural-heritage" campaign. The Johann-Strauss-Theater, built in 1908, and the Wiener Stadttheater of 1914 suffered a similar fortune – one which the Theater an der Wien only narrowly escaped. The fate of the "bricks and mortar" seems to echo that of the Viennese musical itself. What need would they have for theatres if the operetta is dead?

Of course, the traumatic events of the Nazi occupation are not the only reason for the decline of Viennese musicals. The writing was on the wall long before that. While revivals of the classic operettas sated the appetites of tourists, there was little interest in new work, which should be a warning to us all. For whatever reason, the generation of writers and composers who eventually followed after Kálmán, Lehár and Benatzky chose to largely ignore their examples and to follow instead the leads of American and British writers. Yet American composers such as Leonard Bernstein (1918-90) with *Candide* and Stephen Sondheim (1930 -) with *A Little Night Music* managed to create works that brought a late twentieth century sensibility to the Viennese operetta form.

Berlin:
Give My Regards to Friedrichstrasse

In a way, perhaps Adolph Hitler was right. It seems that in the musical theatre, there was a master race. Unfortunately for him, they were not the so-called Aryans, but the Jews – the very people he was persecuting. Evidently he didn't own a mirror, or else he might have noticed that he was not himself blonde haired and blue eyed.[1] Still, he dedicated himself to ridding Germany of many of the people that had brought it to the forefront of the arts and sciences, resulting in the greatest "own goal" in the history of humanity. He would discover, to his peril, that this included most of the top nuclear physicists who were now devoting their not inconsiderable intellects to making sure that no one atom in his body remained attached to any other. Equally humiliating to him was the fact that most of the greatest musical talents of the Third Reich (save for his beloved Wagner, who was already dead) were either being killed or driven into exile. Musical theatre in central Europe was brought to virtual extinction, and it was all his fault.

Not that Hitler was against the arts. Far from it – after all, he was a failed artist himself. It was just that he didn't like anybody to be better at anything than he was, and so he and his fellow Nazis did not suffer geniuses gladly. When the leading German conductor Wilhelm Furtwängler (1886-1954)[2] declared, in the *Deutschen Allgemeinen Zeitung* that the only dividing line in music was not between Aryan and Jewish but between "good and bad art"[3], the Nazi minister for "public enlightenment" Joseph Goebbels replied, "Only an art that draws from the full Ethnicity itself may in the end be good".[4]

It was not always thus. In the late nineteenth and the first quarter of the twentieth century – a period of remarkable racial tolerance – Germany, along with Hungary and Austria, not only had a strong indigenous musical theatre tradition, but it has had an inestimable influence on the rest of the world as well. The dual traditions of operetta and cabaret gave us Weill and Holländer among many, many others.

In fact, Kurt Weill is probably the first name to come to mind when you think of Berlin musical theatre, but he was by no means the first out of the starting gate. In fact, many people probably know the song "Glow-Worm" without realising that it came from a 1902 production of *Lysistrata*, with music by Paul Lincke (1866-1946). Richard Strauss (1864-1949) had suggested Lincke to Kaiser Wilhelm as a court composer, but the Kaiser – who was an admirer of Arthur Sullivan – thought him too vulgar. His early career had been spent writing opera parodies, and he honed his skills in Paris as musical director of the Folies-Bergère. His first great Berlin success was *Frau Luna*, a "burlesque-fantastic-spectacular" with a libretto by Heinrich Bolten-Bäckers (1871-1938), which began in 1899 as a simple one-act operetta. It struck a nerve with its hometown audience.

After World War I, the mood and temper of Berlin musical theatre changed. "German language operetta was at the crossroads, not just politically but artistically, as it attempted to reconcile the traditional and the new"[5], says Andrew Lamb. The "traditional" could be typified by the operettas of Strauss and others, while the "new" would include the cabaret-derived works of Brecht and Weill, Benatzky, Holländer and Spoliansky. "Berlin in the years after the First World War was in spirit the most American city in Europe", said Kurt Weill in a 1941 interview. "We read Jack London, Hemmingway, Dreiser, Dos Passos, we admired Hollywood pictures, and American jazz had a great influence on our music. America was a very romantic country for us."[6] Of course, German composers re-interpreted American jazz and Tin Pan Alley and "that re-interpretation created something highly individual and unique," according to Kevin Clarke, director of the Amsterdam-based Operetta Research Centre. "You can sense that in the newspapers of the period... Or you can sense it in [Emmerich] Kàlmàn recycling [Sigmund]

Romberg, after Romberg had recycled Kàlmàn (in *Desert Song*). I find this ping-pong game fascinating. At the time, audiences in Germany and Austria [were] obviously much more aware of what was going on on Broadway than now. And instead of just copying it... like now, they used it as a starting point for something new. "[7]

Viennese-born Max Reinhardt (1873-1943) was one of the leading directors of the twentieth century. His work straddled barriers between the traditional and new, populism and elitism, and intimacy and spectacle. In Berlin in 1919, he constructed the massive 3,500 seat Grosses Schauspielhaus ("Great Theatre"), a domed arena with a thrust stage and revolve where he staged epic classics such as Aeschylus' *Oresteia*. He became noted for his spectacular productions of *The Miracle* and *A Midsummer Nights' Dream*, both of which were eventually adapted for American audiences. But he also was a pioneer of intimate cabaret with his Sound and Smoke, where he nurtured the early careers of Friederich Holländer and Mischa Spoliansky.

Although he was a great lover of Offenbach, whom he regarded almost as a soul mate – he had staged productions of *La Belle Hélène*, *Tales of Hoffmann* and *Orpheus in the Underworld* – he had, according to his son Gottfried, "a deep aversion to the sham Vienna depicted by coy and sentimental operetta kitsch... He would not give a *Fuchzgerl*[8] for the operetta giants, Franz Lehár, Emmerich Kálmán, Robert Stolz, and the full weight of their carefully calculated schmaltz. He would not even give the negligible time it would have taken to sit through a performance of Oscar Straus's cloying *Waltz Dream* or *Chocolate Soldier*, although he esteemed the musicianship of Straus, a friend ever since they had collaborated on their mutual cabaret debut. And he would not let wild horses drag him into a theatre to sit through the saccharine *Merry Widow* or *Madame Pompadour*, even when their star was Germany's operetta queen Fritzi Massary, whose talent he found irresistible... Even Richard Strauss's *Der Rosenkavalier*, ("The Knight of the Rose") whose first performance he directed, made him uneasy. The elegant sophistication of its first act, the lyrical glamour of its second, followed by the broad buffoonery of its third, was a mixture too smooth for his comfort... While he considered Johann Strauss's music to be of Mozartian quality, the cute slapstick offended him."[9]

Still, he was persuaded to mount a revival of Strauss's *Die Fledermaus*, which opened in Berlin on 8 June 1928 at the Deutsches Theater with the composer's widow Adele in attendance. "As theatre, the Johann Strauss opus has hardly ever been taken seriously", Reinhardt Jr. continues, "With one exception... under Max Reinhardt's direction it took its place under what I would call his flawless productions." (Kurt Gänzl – who is not a Reinhardt fan – disagrees, dismissing it as "gaudy" and "typically big and typically botched"[10].) For this version, the book was revised by Ernst Marishka (1893-1963) and the music adapted by future Hollywood maestro Erich Wolfgang Korngold (1897-1957). The violinist Yehudi Menuhin saw this production, "which left me walking on air for three days afterward."[11] He then took his production to Paris, where it received a cool reception. In Vienna, it was pilloried for tampering with such a sacred cow, yet in Milan they loved it. In 1942, an English translation of this version opened on Broadway under the title *Rosalinda* with choreography by George Balanchine (1904-83). The English book was credited to John Meehan Jr. (1908-67) and Gottfried Reinhardt (1911-94) and the lyrics by Paul Kerby (1891-1971). *Time* magazine wrote that "Director Reinhardt has whipped *Fledermaus*' drama into a light fluff, flavored it with a medley of Strauss waltzes from other sources, given it a new prologue, a new name (*Rosalinda*) and a decorous, Victorian striptease... that leaves its leading lady more thoroughly clad than many of today's best-dressed bathing beauties."[12]

Reinhardt was not officially the director of this production: a former assistant of his, Felix Brentano, had teamed up with Korngold to remount the show using

Reinhardt's text and prompt book. When the great director got wind of this (it was Korngold who tipped him off), he stepped in to protect his legacy. It received excellent notices and ran for a total of 521 performances before going on tour.

"Musical quality alone was not sufficient incentive for him to come to terms with absurd stories and characters without character", says his son. "Operetta texts – *Die Fledermaus* not excepted – are synthetic fabrications. Their roles are stereotyped and their actions tend to bog down in structural impasses."[13] In other words, as Oscar Hammerstein demonstrated in *Oklahoma!*, the music must serve the book.

Reinhardt was a firm believer in popular theatre. "The so-called 'good' public is in reality the worst," he told his biographer Gusti Adler. "Dull sophisticates. Inattentive, blasé, used to being the centre of attention themselves... Only the gallery is worth anything."[14] German theatre critic Esther Slevogt says, "Reinhardt has never really been forgiven for pointing out that all democratic theatrical arts are dependent on the audience, in other words *the market*. The majority of German theatre makers continue to feel part of an elite with a diffuse task: that of enlightenment, or of truth itself. Max Reinhardt took another path and because of this he is still a provocation to subsidised culture."[15]

The Berlin of Max Reinhardt and of Kurt Weill (1900-50) is the child that was aborted. Reinhardt's Deutsches Theater, of which he had been artistic director since 1904 was, according to Brecht's translators John Willett and Ralph Manheim "at that time one of the world's three or four leading theatres"[16]. It was nationalised by Hitler in 1933 and eventually became the state theatre of the German Democratic Republic. Reinhardt and Weill, both Jews, became refugees of the Nazis. They had made two failed attempts to collaborate – they had intended to work together on *The Rise and Fall of the City of Mahagonny* and

The Silver Lake, but were unable to – before finally coming together on the ill-fated *The Eternal Road* — with a cast of 245 — in New York in 1937. Although their collaboration never really amounted to much, somehow we are left thinking that it *should* have. These were two of German theatre's brightest talents, but the rise of German nationalism had ironically strangled its sense of national identity. We are left to speculate what, in their hands, might have become of German musical theatre had they not been so rudely interrupted.

The "new" with which the operettas had to come to terms included the influence of the cabarets, which had existed in Germany since the early 1900s. Paul Lincke wrote few new works after 1918 because, according to George Colerick, "he did not have the feel for the new rhythms, especially those from the Americas."[17] It is only too ironic that it was American lyricist Johnny Mercer who adapted "Glow-Worm" into a popular song for the Mills Brothers in the very form that had eluded Lincke himself.

The new generation brought Friedrich Holländer, Mischa Spoliansky and, of course, Kurt Weill. The son of a cantor in Dessau, Weill came to Berlin in 1918 to study under Engelbert Humperdinck (1854-1921), composer of *Hansel and Gretel*, but he returned home, dissatisfied. He worked as music director at a theatre in Lüdenscheid. There he resolved that he would spend his life in the theatre, and returned to Berlin to study under Ferruccio Busoni (1866-1924). His timing was propitious: the end of the First World War had forced Germany to open its borders to foreign cultural influences, including American, French, English and Russian. For Weill and others, this meant exposure to jazz. One of the leading bandleaders touring Europe at that time was Paul Whiteman (1890-1967), a former classical violinist who championed "symphonic jazz" that largely eschewed improvisation. (It was Whiteman's orchestra that commissioned Gershwin to write *Rhapsody in Blue*.) Some might consider the jazz heard in Berlin to be watered down, even corrupted, but this was jazz filtered through German ears. Weill biographer Foster Hirsch writes, "Such jazz-based elements as syncopation, improvisation, a greater use of wind instruments, and a driving percussive beat mixed with native expressionist and atonal idioms... A fusion was born that was to prepare the way for Kurt Weill's music-theatre hybrids."[18]

It was his collaboration with Bertolt Brecht (1898-1956) that was to have the greatest impact on German musical theatre. They both shared a fascination with America – or rather, the America that they saw on the movie screen. To them it was the New World, not yet the world-dominating hegemony that it later became. Weimar Germany was freer than Wilhelmine Germany had been, but it was economically and politically precarious. Of course, Brecht was not one to tread lightly on eggshells. His outlook was radical, both politically and theatrically.

Their first project together was a setting of Brecht's *Mahagonny* poems, a songspiel describing a mythical American city that was later expanded into the three act opera *The Rise and Fall of the City of Mahagonny*. But the major stage work for which they are now remembered came about when a former actor named Ernst Josef Aufricht (1898-1971) bought the Theater am Schiffbauerdamm, and was determined to open it on his birthday with a new show. John Gay's 1728 *Beggar's Opera* had recently enjoyed a successful revival at the Lyric Theatre Hammersmith in London, and Brecht's assistant Elisabeth Hauptmann (1897-1973) was working on a German adaptation.

Aufricht apparently leapt at the idea, but was reluctant to take Brecht's suggestion that Weill write a new, original score. He had Weill prepare a few songs to "audition", and then gave the go-ahead. *Die Dreigroschenoper* ("Threepenny Opera") opened on 31 August 1928. The initial reception was not warm, but it gradually caught on, and played for more than 400 performances.

Soon dance bands all over Germany were playing music from the show, including its opening number, "Moritat von Mackie Messer" ("The Ballad of Mack the Knife"), a song written just before the opening to satisfy the ego of actor Harald Paulsen who played Macheath. (He was disappointed then to learn that while the song was about his character, he would not be singing it.)

With all the touring companies, *Threepenny Opera* amassed a staggering 4,200 performances in Germany in the 1928-29 season, and by 1933 had been seen over 10,000 times across Europe. A film was made by director G.W. Pabst (1885-1967) in both German and French (an English version was planned but never made). The German version cut half of the music, but included several members of the original cast, including Lotte Lenya (1898-1981) as Jenny. Although several attempts were made, it was not a success in the English speaking world until an off-Broadway production opened in 1954 with a translation by Marc Blitzstein (1905-64) and starring Weill's widow Lotte Lenya. "Mack the Knife" became a hit for Louis Armstrong and, later, Bobby Darin.

In stark contrast to conventional operetta – and to later "integrated" Broadway musicals, Brecht believed in keeping the elements separated, in order to "alienate" the audience, maintaining an emotional detachment. "Nothing is more revolting than when the actor pretends not to notice that he has left the level of plain speech and started to sing," he wrote. "The three levels – plain speech, heightened speech and singing, must always remain distinct, and in no way should heightened speech represent an intensification of plain speech, or singing of heightened speech… The actor must not only sing but show a man singing."[19] Richard Kislan, professor of speech, theatre and dance at Glassboro Stage College in New Jersey writes, "Since Brecht theorized much about devices in the theater for breaking illusion and keeping emotion in check through interrupting devices, it was natural for him to insist on wonderful, haunting, and idiosyncratic songs that interrupted the book."[20]

Brecht and Weill followed with *Happy End*, with a book by Elisabeth Hauptmann set in 1920s Chicago among gangsters and Salvation Army recruits. (Frank Loesser tackled a similar idea with much greater success a couple of decades later – *Guys and Dolls*.) While it contained some enduring songs, including "Surabaya Johnny", it was not a hit.

"The more the newer trends took hold," says historian Andrew Lamb, "the greater the nostalgia for the past, and there were various attempts to satisfy it by overhauling the operetta hits of the nineteenth century."[21] A 1922 revival of *Frau Luna* expanded it by interpolating songs from other Lincke shows, (including the aforementioned "Glow-Worm").

One composer working in Vienna and Berlin who managed to straddle the lines between cabaret, operetta and revue was Ralph Benatzky (1884-1957). Born in what is now the Czech Republic, he studied with Antonin Dvořák (1841-1904) before becoming the musical director of the Kleines Theater in Munich, and later the cabaret venue Bonbonnière. While working within the operetta tradition, he incorporated a jazzy, musical-comedy sound that revealed an American pop influence. In 1931, his greatest success, the "singspiel" *Im weissen Rössl*, for which he wrote the majority of the score, opened at Berlin's Grosses Schauspielhaus, Reinhardt's former home of spectacle. It travelled to London the following year as *The White Horse Inn*. It then opened in New York in 1936 under the same title, but with new lyrics by Irving Caesar. In fact, it was extensively adapted for each country in which it played, including France, Hungary and Australia. Although it was Benatzky's only world-wide hit, he enjoyed other successes in German-speaking countries, including his charming Hollywood satire *Axel an der Himmelstür* ("Axel at the Gates of Heaven") starring Zarah Leander (1907-81), staged in Vienna in 1936.

Alas, after 1933, musical theatre activity in Germany – and much of Europe – effectively ground to a screeching halt, never to regain its former glory. Sure, there were operettas and cabaret of a kind but, according to Bruce Zortman in his book *Hitler's Theatre*, "Artistic capability was disregarded, inspired talent was expelled and true quality was silenced."[22] Not only did Weill, Holländer and Spoliansky leave, but so did Max Reindhardt, deemed by many to be the greatest theatrical director of the century. The rest is a story of "woulda, shoulda, coulda". It did not die a natural death. It was murdered.

However, there is a coda to our story. A few years ago, when riding an S-Bahn train in Berlin and looking at the eclectic mixture of passengers, including some from Turkey and North Africa, I realised just how beautifully Hitler had failed.

Paris:
Where Musicals Were Born,
and Where They Go to Die

Alain Boublil, the co-creator of *Les Misérables* has said, "France is an empty space as far as musical theatre is concerned. Only old-fashioned operettas, but that's about it."[1] Far be it for me to argue with the most successful French musical theatre writer of the modern era, but he may as well claim that his country has no art, literature or architecture.

Yet, this notion has persisted. Cameron Mackintosh has said, "The French have hardly ever taken to modern musicals, and Paris has proved the early graveyard for most of the worldwide musical successes of the last fifty years; they prefer revivals of operettas, Euro-rock musicals of dubious origin and the occasional short, chic season of American touring musicals – performed in English."[2]

Irish music producer Gareth Murphy takes that logic even further, saying "The fact is, with the exception of classical music composers such as Ravel, Debussy or Fauré, France is not really a major player on the world's musical map."[3] What about their film composers – Maurice Jarre, Georges Delerue, Francis Lai, ? Michel Legrand, Alexandre Desplat? Murphy goes on to say that, "Caught in a split personality between the brooding of Northern Europe and the simplicity of Mediterranean culture, it's almost as if the French still don't know whether music is supposed to be stupid or serious, ironic or first degree... I suspect that theatre is the subliminal reference of what they think music should resemble. Sharing the same stage as thespians, impersonators, comedians and pantomime clowns, French musicians shift gears from mega-seriousness to social satire, even into slapstick muzak. In the French language, both drama and humour are represented by the one word: comédie." I would argue that what Murphy has described here is the essential ingredient of their cabaret tradition, and that is its strength, rather than a weakness.

Still, we love to brag about what we don't comprehend. Back in 1929, when Parisian musical comedy was still at its peak, a reviewer for *Time Magazine* remarked, "French musical comedy is seldom written home about. Tourists are either ashamed about it, or don't understand it, or spend their time in the Louvre".[4] A strange fate to befall the land of Offenbach and Bizet, to be sure.

The truth is that Paris' relationship with the musical theatre is rather complicated. In the past, it had its own quite vibrant musical theatre scene. The city was also the inspiration for many Broadway and Hollywood musicals. However, these two seldom if ever intersected. The odd Parisian number, such as "Mon Homme / My Man" would make it across the Atlantic, and stars such as Maurice Chevalier (1888-1972) and Yvonne Printemps (1894-1977) were known and admired by their English language contemporaries. But, for much of the twentieth century – so far as the English speaking world was concerned – a haze of obscurity hung over the musical theatres of Paris.

While the world embraced the music of Edith Piaf, Charles Trenet, Charles Aznavour and Jacques Brel, there was little musical theatre traffic – in either direction – between the stages of Paris and those of New York and London. In the past, few American musicals succeeded in France (with the odd exception, such as *Rose-Marie* or *No No Nanette*), and French musicals didn't travel well to the English speaking world. Why was this? Musical theatre historian Kurt Gänzl says, "If the American writers of musical comedy had studied these gents and their text writers rather more than they did, they might have produced rather better musical comedies. For me, these pieces are the acme of 20th century musical theatre writing."[5]

What is even stranger still is that now the French seem to retain more of an appetite for writing musicals than they do for going to see them – including, of course, Boublil and his partner Claude-Michel Schönberg. Boublil says, "Imagine two people in France creating something for which no tradition exists." Yet France has one of the richest traditions in all of the musical theatre, even if you have to dig a little bit to find it. Not only that, but Boublil and Schönberg are very much a part of it. Of course, *Miss Saigon* doesn't have the sauciness that has run through much of the Parisian musical comedy, from *Orpheus in the Underworld* to *Irma La Douce*. But still, Schönberg grew up listening to *Carmen* (Bizet) and *Tales of Hoffman* (Offenbach), while Boublil was steeped in Aznavour and Brel. And it shows. Their ballads have the highly wrought intensity of a Piaf chanson. "Empty Chairs at Empty Tables" could easily have come from the pen of Jacques Brel. (And Brel himself was a champion of musicals, having played in *Man of La Mancha* for 180 performances in 1968.)

History is written by the victors. Just as Thomas Edison – and not the Lumière Brothers – is credited with the invention of cinema, the Americans get all the credit for inventing musical comedy. Yet, even American musicals like *Gigi* and *Can-Can* seem to tacitly acknowledge that, from the Chat Noir to the Moulin Rouge and the Folies-Bergère, Paris has all of the ingredients.

Théâtre des Bouffes-Parisiens

In front of the Théâtre des Bouffes-Parisiens in Rue Monsigny in the second arrondissment there is a historical plaque indicating that the theatre, once run by Jacques Offenbach, was where the world premieres of *Orpheus in the Underworld*, *Veronique* and *Phi-Phi* took place. The first theatre on the site, the Théâtre Comte was opened in 1826 by Louis Comte (1783-1859) a ventriloquist who ran it as a children's theatre until his retirement in 1854. Two years later his son Charles sold a part interest in the theatre to Offenbach, who used it to present his own works until 1862.

However, Offenbach may have been a great showman, but he was a poor businessman. Management passed to a man named Alphonse Varney (1811-79) – who proved to be even worse, for he reduced the number of Offenbach shows presented, nearly bankrupting the theatre. All the same, he rebuilt it as an eleven hundred seat house, causing Offenbach to temporarily sever his ties with it in 1864 because the re-opening had been delayed. In spite of this, for over one hundred fifty years the theatre has been associated with the name Offenbach, and continues to be the premier venue for French musical comedy.

However, it was not the only musical house of importance in the French capital. Nearby in Boulevard Montmartre, the Théâtre des Variétés had been in business since 1807, and still exists today. It would house a number of Offenbach premieres, including *La belle Hélène*, *La Grande-Duchesse de Gérolstein*, *La Périchole* and *Les Brigandes*, and many years later, Reynaldo Hahn's *Ciboulette*. Also in the Opéra Quarter is the Théâtre Edouard VII, opened in 1916, which presented many of the Sacha Guitry shows, including *L'Amour Masque* with music by André Messager and *Mozart* with music by Reynaldo Hahn. (It also still exists.) The Théâtre Mogador, built in the manner of an English music hall, hosted Messager's *La Petite Functionnaire* in 1921 as well as two of the few Broadway musicals to take Paris by storm – *No No Nanette* in 1926 and *Rose-Marie* in 1927 – and continues as a commercial musical house to this day, housing *The Lion King* (in French) in 2007. The 200 seat Théâtre des Capicines built in 1889 which presented André Barde and Charles Cuvillier's *Son p'tit frère* in 1907 and Maurice Yvain's *Yes* in 1928 still exists, but not as a theatre. In 1993 it became a museum for the perfume maker Fragonard. The tiny Théâtre Marigny in the Champs-Elysées was originally established in 1835, but gained its greatest prominence as Offenbach's first Bouffes-Parisiens before his move to the Théâtre Comte. The present building, dating from 1880, received Messager's *Coups de Roulis* in 1928. The 450-seat art deco Théâtre Daunou, which housed one of Maurice Yvain's greatest hits, *Ta Bouche* was built in 1921. The Théâtre Nouveautés, the fourth of that name also built in 1921 in Boulevard Poissonnière – would present its follow-up, the equally successful *Pas sur la Bouche*. The Théâtre de la Michodière, where Messager's *Passionnément* opened in 1926, was built in the previous year for the impresario Gustave Quinson. Even the Folies-Bergère presented operettas in its early days, before gaining renown for more exotic popular entertainment.

Since Offenbach, there have been many composers who achieved great success within France – and sometimes in central Europe, but little if any of their work is known in English speaking countries. The reasons for this are complicated, and do not necessarily always reflect on the quality of their work. In some cases, the libretto lost too much in translation. In others, the frankness of the subject matter was deemed unsuitable for either British or American tastes.

Many French musical comedies were farces on the Feydeau model, a form that has seldom adapted well in English musicals. Lehman Engel writes, "The farces of Feydeau and Labiche cannot accommodate music because they are extremely complex without the additional and probably more confusing burden of another element. Also they are swift and the inclusion of songs would only slow them down. Without speed, they would fail to make their incessant – almost unrelenting – comic points."[6] *A Funny Thing Happened on the Way to the Forum* is a rare exception, because the songs offer a relief from this breakneck pace. "Farces are express trains, musicals are locals", explains Stephen Sondheim. "Savoring moments can be effective while a farce is gathering steam, but deadly once the train gets going. That's why the songs in *Forum* are bunched together in the first half of the first act, where there is more exposition than action, and then become scarcer and scarcer, until eventually in the last twenty minutes before the Finale there are no songs at all."7   It could be argued, however, that in the case of a show like *Pas sur la bouche* the music gives a pretence of elegance and sophistication to what is otherwise a vulgar form.

Opéra-Comique, Paris

André Messager (1853-1929), a pupil of the composer Camille Saint-Saëns (1835-1921), did double duty as a serious composer during the day while his nights were spent as a conductor at the Folies-Bergère. (Like many French composers of that period, he had one foot in so-called "serious" music, the other in popular culture.) His first break came when the composer Firmin Bernicat (1843-83) died prematurely while writing the score for *François-les-Bas-Bleus*, which Messager was commissioned to complete. He then combined light operettas with ballets and more substantial comic operas such as *La Basoche*, produced at the Opéra Comique in Paris in 1890. (An English version was produced in London in 1891 by Richard D'Oyly Carte.) His commercial breakthrough came seven years later when *Les P'tites Michu* was staged at the Bouffes-Parisiens, and was solidified the following year by *Véronique* with a libretto by Albert Vanloo (1846-1920) and Georges Duval (1847-1919). The plot concerned the pending arranged marriage between an aristocratic woman and a libertine. The two have never met, but when the young woman hears of the libertine's seduction of a shop worker, she sets out to teach him a lesson. Being an operetta, they fall in love.

Messager also enjoyed a career as a conductor at the Opéra-Comique (where he conducted the world premiere of Debussy's *Pelléas et Mélisande*) and at London's

Royal Opera House and the Paris Opéra. For a time, this took him away from composition, and by the time he returned, the fashions had changed, and he adapted. In 1919, he worked with the English librettist of *Maid in the Mountains* Freddie Lonsdale (1881-1954) on an adaptation of Booth Tarkington's *Monsieur Beaucaire* which played 221 performances in London, and opened in Paris in 1925.

During World War I, a profound change began to take place. People sought an escape from the carnage going on around them, and with the US entry into the war, American soldiers brought with them American popular culture. "They wanted singing, dancing, light comedy or even crude farce," says French historian and lecturer Jules Bertaut "and the stimulant of a perpetual rhythm to beat down consciousness."[8] It was the beginning of the jazz age. Historian Jeffrey Jackson writes that "Jazz, the music that 'makes men crazy', was already starting to shape the era that some in France would come to call *les années folles* — the crazy years. Jazz was not just music, it seemed. Rather, it marked the onset of a new and challenging age."[9] The American musical had not yet become the world-beating juggernaut that it was in later decades. American (and other foreign) popular music forms were, to the French, exotic. Even a traditionalist like Messager was an admirer of jazz, as was Debussy.

The Parisian musical comedy emerged into the post-war, modern era of the "années folles" in a quite literal sense, for it was on the day after the armistice was signed that *Phi-Phi* premiered. Originally conceived for the two hundred seat Théâtre de l'Abri, it was moved at the last minute to the much larger Bouffes-Parisiens, which had unexpectedly gone dark. The scene painters and costumiers were offered percentages in lieu of their fees – as it turns out, a lucrative option.

Phi-Phi tells the story of the Parthenon sculptor Phideas in Ancient Greece and his quest to find a model for his statue of Virtue. Having found her, he aims to relieve her of said virtue, but of course complications ensue.

Henri Christiné

The music was by Henri Christiné (1867-1941) a former schoolteacher who was born in Geneva to a French watchmaker and his wife. He rebelled against his strict upbringing by pursuing unconventional interests, marrying a travelling cabaret singer and writing songs for her. He had already written a handful of forgotten stage works before *Phi-Phi*, the show that would make his reputation. His popular songs were performed by Mistinguett, Yvonne Printemps and many others. The book and lyrics for *Phi-Phi* were by former lawyer Albert Willemetz (1887-1964) in collaboration with Fabien Sollar (1886-1982).

Willemetz is credited with more than 3,000 songs, including "Mon Homme", a success for Mistinguett (nee Jeanne Bourgeois, 1875-1956) in 1916 that, in its English form as "My Man" was later a hit for American comedienne Fanny Brice (1891-1951). (This was a case of a song moving from the Folies-Bergère to its American off-shoot, the *Ziegfeld Follies*.) His other collaborators included Arthur Honneger, Maurice Yvain, Vincent Scotto, Moisés Simons and Georges Van Parys. He eventually was made a director of the Bouffes-Parisiens, and was president of the royalty collection agencies SACEM[10] (1945) and CISAC[11] (1956), the only person to serve in that capacity in either organisation who could not read music.

Phi-Phi ran for more than a thousand performances. In May 1919, London producer C.B. Cochran announced that he had acquired the British rights, and that he intended to present it later that season at the London Pavilion.[12] The following year, E. Ray Goetz made a similar announcement for the American rights in New York.[13] Three years later, Londoners were still waiting. *The Daily*

Mirror's gossip columnist "The Rambler" remarked, "In spite of the critics, Mr. Cochran, I hear, is determined to produce another revue, or musical extravaganza, or something of that sort."[14] Evidently, "The Rambler" was taken to task by Mr. Cochran, for only three days later he wrote, "Mr. Charles B. Cochran writes to me to say that I have diagnosed his new production *Phi-Phi* wrongly. I said it was either a revue or a musical extravaganza or something of that sort. Mr. Cochran tells me it is to be an 'operette', with music by Christiné. I must admit that I find it hard to make a definite distinction between Mr. Cochran's revues, musical extravaganzas and operettes."[15]

Alas, when it finally opened on 16 August 1922, it did so in such mutilated form that it surely was not worth the wait. A new English libretto by Fred Thompson and Clifford Grey removed the sauciness of the original, and the score was augmented by Herman Darewski, Nat D. Ayer and even Cole Porter (who contributed a number called "The Ragtime Pipes of Pan"). It starred Clifton Webb, Evelyn Lay and Arthur Treacher, and expired after 133 performances.

The American production fared even worse. A tryout by the Shuberts, with an entirely different book by Glen Macdonough (1870-1924) and Harry Wagstaff Gribble (1896-1981) with lyrics by E. Ray Goetz (1886-1954) and additional music by Arthur H. Guttman (1891-1945) opened and closed at the Globe Theatre in Atlantic City in the same year. It was never seen again in the U.S.

Only the Hungarians seemed to "get" *Phi-Phi*. An adaptation by Jenő Helta (1871-1957) played for more than 200 performances (as *Fi-Fi*) after it opened in Budapest on 7 October 1921.

Phi-Phi may not have changed the world, but it did change the face of Parisian musical theatre. In the 1920s, Paris was presenting forty musicals per year. While French musicals of the twentieth century tend to be lumbered with the label "operetta", it is a misnomer, if you accept Andrew Lamb's definition of a show with "swirling melodies, lush orchestrations, and the romantic doings of palaces and princes". A show like *Phi-Phi* is no more an "operetta" than is *No No Nanette*. The quasi-classical operettas were – in the main – overtaken by the more overtly sexual comedies with modern dances and popular music.

Willemetz and Christiné followed this up on 10 November 1921 with *Dédé*, whose cast included a music hall singer named Maurice Chevalier making his book-musical debut as a profligate dandy named Robert. It ran for nearly three years, although Chevalier biographer Edward Behr dismisses it as "an unbelievably old-fashioned piece of part-spoken, part-sung theater, with a creaking, contrived plot and a host of contrived characters."[16] Kurt Gänzl, on the other hand, praises a score that "rippled with melody and dancing rhythms".[17] Willemetz and Christiné, whom Chevalier would cite as his favourite songwriters, later gave him one of his most popular hits, "Valentine", in 1925, which he also sang in the 1935 Hollywood film *Folies-Bergère de Paris* which was made in both French and English-language versions.

Willemetz worked likewise with André Messager on *Passionnément!* (1926) about an American woman who leaves her jealous, possessive husband for a younger man, and *Coups de roulis* ("Roll of the Waves") (1928), a shipboard romance and Messager's final score.

Reynaldo Hahn (1875-1947), born in Caràcas, Venezuela to a Venezuelan mother and a German father, was also, like Messager, a conductor at the Paris Opéra. A child prodigy, he had already established himself as a serious composer and critic before turning to operettas in the 1920s. Although he was one of many Parisian musicians to show an interest in jazz, his operettas remained doggedly traditional. His first great success was *Ciboulette* in 1923, in which a flower girl seeks to become an actress. Then he teamed with actor playwright Sacha Guitry

(1885-1957) for a series of "comédie-musicales" in which the music played a supporting role to the text. Guitry himself would star in a non-singing role, opposite his second wife, Yvonne Printemps (1894-1977). The first of these was *L'Amour Masqué* (1923) in which a young woman falls in love with the photograph of a young man, not realising that he is the elegant older gentleman who has paid her a visit.

Reynaldo Hahn

In 1925, Hahn took on another musical for Guitry – a story that Messager had turned down – about *Mozart*, starring Printemps in a cross-dressing role as the teenage composer. In 1933, he and Guitry (now divorced from Printemps) turned to a more cynical approach with *Ô mon bel inconnu* ("O My Handsome Stranger") about a married man who joins a lonely hearts club, unaware that the three women he is corresponding with are in fact his wife, his daughter and his maid. American opera historian Richard Traubner says it was "too refined and slight for a public that was slowly nurturing a taste for thumping spectaculars."[18]

Vincent Scotto (1876-1952) was a cabaret songwriter of the belle epoque who eschewed so-called "high culture". An untrained musician who played the guitar by ear, he nevertheless managed to turn out some 4,000 songs and 60 musicals, many of which are still performed in France. Born in Marseilles to Neapolitan parents, his songwriting career began while he was still in his teens. His songs were performed by Maurice Chevalier, Josephine Baker ("J'ai deux amours") and Edith Piaf ("Les mômes de la clouche"). Henri Christiné told him, "Vincent, your songs will be sung in every street and home in France."[19] In 1931, his musical *Au Pays du Soleil* was a big hit. The book was co-written, with René Sarvil (1901-75), by Henri Alibert (1889-1951), Scotto's son-in-law, who also starred as a man falsely accused of murder. All ends happily and he is reunited with his true love. Inspired by Marcel Pagnol's Marsellais plays, this was the first in a series of "Opérettes Marseillaises" that would play Paris's Moulin de la Chanson. Throughout the 1940s, his work became more serious, such as *Violettes impériales* at the Théâtre Mogador in 1948, and he scored some 200 films, including Pagnol's *La Femme du Boulanger* (which formed the basis for Stephen Schwartz and Joseph Stein's 1976 musical *The Baker's Wife*). He was made a Chevalier of the Légion d'Honneur. Kurt Gänzl calls him "one of the most memorable French songwriters of his age."[20] Although his works are sometimes referred to as operettas, like Maurice Yvain, Scotto wrote in the popular music form of the time.

Vincent Scotto

It was Maurice Chevalier who first introduced Albert Willemetz to a composer whom he had known in the infantry a decade earlier, Maurice Yvain (1891-1965). The son of a trumpet player from the Opéra-Comique, Yvain was already a successful cabaret songwriter when he turned to writing musical comedies. It was with Willemetz that he wrote the massively successful *Ta Bouche* in 1922, with a book by Yves Mirande at the Théâtre Daunou for impresario Gustave Quinson (1867-1943). *Ta Bouche* opened on Broadway on 27 November 1923 at the Fulton Theatre as *One Kiss*, for a brief run, with a largely interpolated score. Quinson also controlled the Théâtre des Nouveautés, for which he put Yvain together with librettist André Barde (or Bourdonneaux) (1874-1945) whose *Son p'tit frère* had been a big pre-war hit a generation earlier. The result was the similarly titled *Pas sur la Bouche*, directed by Leon Benoit-Deutsch who, according to Yvain, "seemed not a man of the theatre at first glance"[21], but who nevertheless delivered a hit. Yvain was particularly pleased to be given an orchestra of seventeen musicians – unusually large for that theatre, and for which the front row of seats had to be removed.

The story of *Pas sur la Bouche* is a farce about a woman who discovers that her husband's new business partner is a man to whom she was once secretly married. Yvain describes the show's headliner Régine Flory (1891 or 1894-1926), as "the pet peeve" of wives, having "superb eyes" and "a body you can't take your mind off of"[22]. She was already a star in both Paris and London, but it would all soon come to an end in 1926 when she committed suicide over a failed love affair in the office of the manager of Theatre Royal Drury Lane during the run of *Rose Marie*.

Pas sur la Bouche was "adapted" into English as *Just a Kiss*. Following a tryout at the Princes Theatre in Manchester, it opened at the original Shaftesbury Theatre (destroyed in the blitz on 17 April 1941) on 8 September 1926, produced by Harry Grattan. The setting was changed to Windsor and Mayfair with a new libretto by Frederick Jackson, and Yvain's score augmented by new songs by Vivian Ellis and Phil Craig. *The Times* said that "with a little attention, *Just a Kiss* should be quite a success."[23] Evidently that attention was not paid: it lasted for 93 performances. It played more successfully in Budapest, and toured North America – in its original French.

Unusually, *Pas sur la Bouche* was remade as a feature film in 2003 – almost eighty years after its stage debut (and seventy years after it was filmed for the first time) – by director Alain Resnais (1922-2014), starring Audrey Tautou and Lambert Wilson. Several of Resnais' other films show a strong musical theatre connection: His 1997 film *On connaît la chanson* ("Same Old Song") interpolated popular French songs into the story, and he made a documentary about George Gershwin in 1992. His 1974 film *Stavisky* featured an incidental score by Stephen Sondheim.

In 1923, Yvain and Willemetz collaborated on *Là-Haut* ("On High") which was intended as a vehicle for Chevalier at the Bouffes-Parisiens. However, although it was a hit, Chevalier was upstaged by his co-star Dranem

(1869 - 1935), and left the live stage behind for good after suffering a nervous breakdown.

"Les Six" member Arthur Honneger, the Swiss opera and ballet composer best known for his orchestral work *Pacific 231* was commissioned by Willemetz to write the score for his 1930 adaptation of Pierre Louÿ's 1901 novel *Les Aventures du Roi Pausole*. This was a story about a king with 365 wives whose chaste daughter Aline runs away with a visiting dance troupe. Its frank sexuality insured a long run at the Bouffes-Parisiens. Towards the end of his life, Honneger taught at the École Nationale where his students included future *Baker Street* composer Raymond Jessel.

American popular music was not the only foreign influence on Parisian musicals. During the prohibition era in the U.S., wealthy Americans travelled to Havana to the night-clubs, where they were entertained by Latin rhythms. Cuban composer Moisés Simons (1888-1945) had enjoyed an international hit with "El Manisero" ("The Peanut Vendor"). Aside from writing dance hits, Simons was a composer of zarzuelas, the Spanish equivalent to opéra-bouffe. He had already had works performed in Barcelona before the popularity of such South American dances as the rumba, the samba and the conga brought him to Paris with Rico's Creole Band. His musical *Toi c'est moi* was presented at the Bouffes-Parisiens on 19 September 1934, with a book by Henri Duvernois (1875–1937) and lyrics by Albert Willemetz, Marcel Bertal, André Mouëzy-Éon (1880-1967), Louis Maubon and Robert Chamfleury and was filmed in 1936. The story tells of a Parisian malefactor who is sent to the Caribbean to keep him out of trouble.

Although – with a few exceptions – French musicals of the twentieth century have had a very limited impact outside of their native land, a few French theatrical song writers have enjoyed some international success – even if we may not be aware the provenance of the works in question. I have already mentioned Maurice Yvain's

"Mon Homme" which became Fanny Brice's hit "My Man". Fans of Baz Luhrmann's *Moulin Rouge* may have noticed Canadian singer Rufus Wainwright's rendition of what sounds like an old Parisian street song. It was in fact "Complainte de la Butte", written for Jean Renoir (1894-1979)'s 1954 film musical *French Cancan*. The lyrics were by Renoir, and the music by Georges Van Parys (1902-71), a man with a solid background in cabaret and musical comedy.

Van Parys began as a pianist at the cabaret Chez Fyscher in 1924, and in 1927 he enjoyed his first success with *Lulu* at the Théâtre Danou. This show then travelled to Budapest, and was the first in a series of musicals with lyricist Phillipe Parès and book writer Serge Véber (1897-1976). His wartime musical *Une Femme par Jour* ("A Woman per Day"), with a book by Veber and lyrics by future film director Jean Boyer (1901-65) opened at the Théâtre des Capucines in 1943, and was filmed in 1948. His later works included the spectacular *Les Chasseurs d'images* at the Théâtre du Châtelet in 1947, and *Minnie Moustache*, a parody "western" with a libretto by Jean Broussolle and André Hornez (1905-89) which opened at the Théâtre de la Gaîté-Lyrique in December 1956. In total, he would compose more than sixty scores for the theatre, in addition to some 350 films, beginning in 1930 with the first French screen musical, René Clair's *Les Million*. In recent years, Sudden Théâtre has toured an anthology revue of Van Parys songs called *Comme de Bien Entendu* ("As of Course").

Moulin Rouge

French Cancan offers us a unique contrast to *An American in Paris*, released three years earlier, showing the different American and French approaches to musicals. "Renoir... doesn't do anything as obvious as having a painting come to life", says American director and film scholar Peter Bogdanovich. "It's not studied. It feels like it's in his bones. It's in his blood, and it's just there in every image."[24] Unlike the American musical – according to Bogdanovich – Renoir doesn't sentimentalise his characters. "Danglard [the fictional founder of the Moulin Rouge played by Jean Gabin] is very casual about his affairs. When he's pinned down at the end and [Nini] says 'I want you to myself', he says, 'What, do you want to put me in a cage like a canary?'... It's totally different from the way the Americans would do it. It is, in fact, totally realistic in terms of that kind of person." Although the film has not been widely seen by English speaking audiences, it was a hit on its home turf.

The real Moulin Rouge opened in 1889 on Boulevard de Clichy in Montmartre. It was built as a cabaret by Joseph Oller (1839-1922), who also owned the Paris Olympia music hall. It gained notoriety as the place where the can-can was reborn. Originally a working-class dance, the Moulin Rouge introduced courtesans to perform seductively for male patrons. As the night-club became more fashionable and respectable, the courtesans were replaced by professional dancers, and in its heyday the club was headlined by the likes of Josephine Baker (1906-75), Edith Piaf and Mistinguett. Henri de Toulouse-Lautrec (1864-1901) designed a famous series of posters for the club.

The Folies-Bergère at 32 Rue Richter in the 9th arrondissement is one aspect of Parisian musical theatre that has had an unmistakable influence on Broadway. It was in turn patterned after London's Alhambra music hall in Leicester Square. An announcement in the *Album des Théâtres* in 1867 proclaimed that "the performances to be shown in the new hall will be a combination of various genres: Operetta, lyrical fantasy, pantomime, song and acrobatic display."[25] When it opened on 2 May 1869 as the Folies Trévise, the Duc de Trévise, who did not want his name to be linked to such lewd entertainment, pressured the management into changing the name. On 13 September

1872, the name was changed to Folies-Bergère after a nearby street. (The word "folies" is derived from the Latin "foliae", meaning "leaves", although in this context it means "field", suggesting a place of open-air entertainment, or a place where clandestine lovers may meet.)

It took time for the new venue to catch on. The Franco-German war, the siege of Paris and the Commune had to be endured, but after a decade or so Paris began to experience a renaissance, and the Folies-Bergère was the beneficiary. The first "glamour revue", *Place aux Jeunes* opened on 30 November 1886. This was the template for what was to follow, the world that the novelist Colette knew very well. The stars of the Folies-Bergère later included Josephine Baker and her pre-Carmen Miranda "banana dance", and Maurice Chevalier.

In 1895, Florenz Ziegfeld (1867-1932) was travelling in Europe, looking for a new star. He found one in Anna Held, who was under contract to the Folies-Bergère. After paying $1500 to buy her out of her contract, he took her to New York to star in his production of *A Parlor Match*. It was at Held's suggestion that Ziegfeld presented an American version of the Folies-Bergère. The first edition, which opened on 8 July 1907 at the roof-top Jardin de Paris in New York was called *Follies of the Day*. The title was drawn from librettist Harry B. Smith's newspaper column, thus giving the word "follies" a double meaning, referring to human foibles. These "revues" (Ziegfeld also imported the French spelling of that word) ran in annual editions until 1931. Stars of the *Ziegfeld Follies* included Fanny Brice, who made an American hit out of Maurice Yvain and Albert Willemetz's "Mon Homme" ("My Man").

In the period following World War II, at precisely the same time that the American musical was reaching its apex and was beginning to be taken seriously as an art form, the precise opposite happened to the French musical. "A kind of concensus between artists, politicians and intellectuals chucked light entertainment out", says actor and singer François Raffenaud. "Artists had to be 'serious' and 'philosophically' if not 'politically' committed. A generation of amazing lyricists and performers emerged, but operetta became a symbol of superficiality."[26] According to critic Kim Willsher, musicals had been "long dismissed by Paris' highbrow as low art".[27] It had failed to keep pace with the new developments that were happening on Broadway, and – in my opinion – to fully develop the dramatic potential of their own chanson tradition. This was further complicated by the fact that some artists, including Albert Willemetz and Sacha Guitry were accused of collaborating (and I don't mean in the words and music sense) with the Nazis.

A few, such as Vincent Scotto and Francis Lopez (1916-95) continued to write. Lopez, who trained as a dentist, had a major hit with his first show *La Belle de Cadix* with a libretto by Raymond Vincy (1904-68) that opened at the Casiono-Montparnasse in 1945 and ran for two years. He balanced large scale musicals with intimate shows, including *Quatre Jours à Paris* and *La Route Fleurie*. Kurt Gänzl says, "Unsophisticated though it may often be, the rythmic, sentimental and immsensely singable music of his earliest opérettes is in the happiest tradition of popular light musical theatre."[28] His later works, written without Vincy, were less accomplished, and his final work, *Les Belles et le gitan*, was staged in 1993. But somehow the French writers had failed to move with the times. "With their old-fashioned style rooted in European dance rhythms and their old-fashioned lyricism, Lopez's shows did not stand a chance in New York or London", says Andrew Lamb (1942-).[29]

Although I have argued that the modern musical began in Paris with Offenbach, there is little evidence that the next generation of French musical writers have any consciousness of their heritage. *Nôtre Dame de Paris*, with original lyrics by Canadian-born Luc Plamondon (1942-) and pre-recorded music by Riccardo "Richard" Cocciante

(1946-) enjoyed some success in Paris and in Plamondon's native Montreal, and survived in London despite tepid reviews. According to Kurt Gänzl, "It was equipped with embarrassingly lowest-common-denominator lyrics and a ramming, repetitive score".[30] Still, it "became the most successful of the Gallic-themed shows to open in the West End during 2000."[31] Another show with lyrics by Plamondon and music by Michel Berger (1947-92) called *Starmania* has also had a tough time outside of the French speaking market, in spite of English lyrics by Sir Tim Rice (1944-). (In the Act II chapter "Europe After Hitler", I will examine the success of three post-war French musicals that enjoyed international success: *Irma la Douce*, *Les Parapluies de Cherbourg* and *Les Misérables*.)

Paris may have had an impact on international musical theatre in a very indirect way. It was the haunt of Porter and Gershwin, and although there is scant evidence that French musicals inspired them per se, one must assume that something in Parisian musical culture attracted them. When Gershwin was in Paris working on *An American in Paris*, he consulted with Maurice Ravel (1875-1937), Francis Poulenc (1899-1963) and others. Ravel was something of a mentor, and Gershwin returned to New York with eight bound volumes of Debussy scores in his luggage. Similarly, Porter studied in Paris at the Schola Cantorum[32] with Vincent d'Indy (1851-1931). Porter would be hired to interpolate songs into the English adaptations of *Phi-Phi* and other continental shows. Satie and Ravel were major influences on the work of Stephen Sondheim – just listen to Satie's *Trois Gymnopédies* then listen to "Goodbye for Now" (the theme from the film *Reds*), or to "Someone is Waiting" from *Company*.[33]

While few French musicals have been international successes – not for lack of trying – Paris was the undisputed birthplace of operetta, the Folies-Bergère and the cabaret – three of the most basic building blocks of the modern musical. Yet somehow the notion that the city of lights is a musical dead spot has been allowed to take hold, and little that has emerged in recent years seems likely to change that perception, although Théâtre du Châtelet has made some inroads with their English-language productions of Broadway shows. (One, *An American in Paris* even transferred successfully to Broadway and the West End.) However, the fact that it took other hands – German, British and American – to integrate these elements does not in any way detract from the credit due to their originators.

In my mind – and this is, of course, the view of an outsider – there is one song that sums up the musical voice of Paris. I first heard it sung by Maria Friedman in an English version by her then-partner Jeremy Sams called "Paris in the Rain". Although it comes from the film *French Can-Can*, "Complainte de la Butte"'s pedigree covers all bases: its composer Georges van Parys has written for cabaret, café-concert and musical comedy, and the lyrics by Jean Renoir sum up the melancholy spirit of Montmartre and the Moulin-Rouge. Little wonder that Baz Luhrmann chose it to set the scene for his opus.

Cabaret:
From "Le Chat Noir" to the Algonquin Room

The musical has benefited from many ancillary art forms, such as vaudeville, burlesque, ballet and opera. But there is one that is close to my heart, because for both writers and performers, it has often acted as their proving ground.

While cabaret exists as a separate form in and of itself, it is inextricably linked – aesthetically, commercially and historically – with the worlds of theatre and music, and indirectly with the musical theatre. This is especially true of the French and German cabarets of the early twentieth century. Weimar Kabarett was a theatrical form, which borrowed from Broadway and operetta. Mischa Spoliansky and Friedrich Holländer were cabaret writers who wrote musicals, just as Vincent Scotto and Leo Fall did. In many of its incarnations, it seems that cabaret and revue have been a development ground where writers honed their skills, to be later applied to larger canvases. This is as true in New York as it was in Berlin and Paris.

Of the contribution of "café-concert", music hall and cabaret to the musical theatre, opera historian Richard Traubner says, "Both the music halls and the *bals* [dance halls] had a direct influence on the infant operetta, requiring songs (for the most part) to be accessible to untrained ears. They had to be catchy and, if possible, eminently danceable... Offenbach and his librettists were hardly unaware of the *café-concert*. Many of their stars... were groomed there, and the valuable training in diction, comic values and 'putting across' songs were unmistakable facets of the very first and greatest operettas."[1]

The relationship between cabaret and musical theatre varies widely in different places. In New York, the cabaret repertoire tends to be dominated by show tunes, and many of the performers are "resting" Broadway actors. In Europe, the cabaret has stood as a separate – yet still related – art form, and as often as not is cast as the mother rather than the child.

Yet according to Maximillien de Lafayette, the self-proclaimed "world authority on cabaret" (not to mention UFOs) who claims to have written more than 1200 books, eleven dictionaries and nine encyclopædias, "The overwhelming majority of cabaret goers in the United States misunderstand the real meaning of the world [sic] Cabaret … It disturbs me to see and hear well-established American singers… associating Broadway with cabaret."[2] Surely, if the majority of people "misunderstand" the meaning of something, it is because the meaning has changed. This sort of "puritanism" only muddies the already murky waters, for those who want to treat the word as an "appellation of origin" will have a difficult time.

In fact, "cabaret" has taken on a different form in each one of the many countries it has taken root in. In Paris, it was a place where the bohemian avant-garde met. In Berlin, it was a showcase for political satire and alternative sexuality. In New York, it is a venue for hearing the Great American Songbook. In my native Canada, it sometimes even refers to taverns where Country and Western music is heard, but is also synonymous with small-scale musical theatre.

The word "cabaret" is derived from the Latin "camera", meaning chamber or room, from the Greek "kamárā", meaning "vault" or "arch".[3]

At first, the term "cabaret" was employed in Paris to refer to an early version of what would become the "restaurant", in which wine is sold only with a meal. These did not, at first, include entertainment. However, they gradually evolved into the café-concert, which was all about entertainment.

As a term for the entertainment on offer – as opposed to the venue itself – most histories of the cabaret begin in 1881[4] with the Chat Noir, a lair for bohemian artists in Montmartre. The historian Paul Bourget described it as "a fantastic mixture of writers and painters, of journalists and students, of employees and high-livers, as well as models, prostitutes and true grand dames searching for exotic experiences."[5] Paris was, at the time, the cultural capital of the Western world, and people from the visual and performing arts formed an unofficial alliance of Impressionists, Dadaists, etc.

The Chat Noir was owned by Rodolphe Salis (1851-97), an entrepreneur and would-be artist and poet, the son of a brewer, whom Rhodes College Memphis associate history professor Jeffrey Jackson describes as "something of a publicity genius."[6] He was the master of the promotional stunt. When the Chat Noir moved to larger premises, he staged a funeral procession to the new venue. He also published his own newspaper. "To many observers," Jackson says, "this kind of crass commercialism betrayed the neighborhood's reputation for placing a higher value on artistic expression."

Salis had chosen Montmartre because the rent was lower than in the Latin Quarter, but soon the mixture of criminals, prostitutes, poor workers and eccentric artists made it a focal point for modernism. Among its early patron/performers was the composer Claude Debussy (1862-1918), who became friendly with a number of Impressionist painters. It also became the headquarters of the Hydropathes who apparently took their name from the Hydropathen-valsh ("Waltz of the Hydropaths") by the Hungarian-German musician Joseph Gungl. They described themselves as "those who are afraid of water – so they drink only wine", a group of artists, intellectuals and musicians led by journalist, novelist and poet Émile Goudeau (1849-1906).

Musically, the cabaret was a bastion of the traditional chansons, mixed with a touch of political satire and anything else the avant-garde of the "fin-de-siècle" and "belle époque" could conjur up.

"It is difficult to imagine now the full importance of the song as a medium of public communication in those radio and television free days", says Lisa Appignanesi (1946-), author of *The Cabaret*. "Not only was the chanson a love lyric or mood piece which entertained, but it could function as a reporting vehicle – a performed alternative to the newspaper, which because of its dependence on machinery and finance, was largely controlled by the ruling class... Thus it came to serve as a democratic tool, a satirical weapon for criticism and protest."[7]

The entertainment was, in the beginning, spontaneous and unstructured, with Salis himself as compere. Some of the songs were pastiches of popular arias by Offenbach and others, with satirical lyrics. One might have heard the black humour of Maurice Mac-Nab (1856-89), a French singer of Scottish descent, or the songs of Aristide Bruant (1851-1925), the chansonnier who would eventually open his own cabaret, Le Merliton in the Chat Noir's original site when the latter moved to larger premises in 1885. Bruant would also come to own the nearby Lapin Agile.

In Jean Renoir's 1954 musical comedy film *French Can-Can*, Jean Gabin – a chansonnier in real life – plays a fictionalised character representing the founder of the Moulin Rouge who overhears a serving girl singing what he supposes to be a song of the streets. This is in fact "Complainte de la Butte", written for the film by Georges Van Parys (1902-71), with lyrics by Renoir. Van Parys began his own career as a cabaret pianist at Chez Fischer.

Looking at the list of musical contributors to the early cabarets, you might be forgiven for supposing that this was a hotbed of the esoteric, but you would be only partly right. The idea of drawing on so-called street songs was central to the Parisian cabaret ethos. The group of French composers known as Les Six – a name given in 1920 by music critic Henri Collet (1885-1951) of the trade paper *Comœdia* to Georges Auric (1899-1983), Louis Durey (1888-1979), Arthur Honneger (1892-1955), Darius Milhaud (1892-1974), Francis Poulenc (1899-1963) and Germaine Taillefere (1892-1983), all followers of Eric Satie (1866-1925) and the playwright Jean Cocteau (1889-1963) – drew inspiration from Parisian folklore, music hall and circus. They also frequented the cabarets (although Satie later renounced this). Milhaud and the others incorporated American jazz rhythms into their work. "Les Six wanted to unite jazz techniques with their own French compositions," writes Jeffrey Jackson in *Making Jazz French*. "American jazz (ironically, since it was an imported form) became a way of articulating a seemingly lost vitality within the French musical tradition that [Milhaud] hoped to reconstruct with a more muscular sound."[8]

Early in his career Satie had, through economic necessity, become a cabaret accompanist. Steven Moore Whiting describes him as "the composer whose music bore the most distinctive impression of the Montmartre cabarets... Satie transferred the techniques of parodic quotation and distortion learned in the cabaret to whimsical but disconcerting piano suites, to songs by turn medieval and madcap, and eventually to avant-garde ballets like *Parade* (1917), *Mercure* (1924) and *Relâche* (1924) – leaving it to enraged critics and engaged supporters to argue whether his music was *fumisterie* ["humbug"] or motivated by serious artistic intentions or both at once."[9]

Soon, the cabarets developed a bourgeois clientele who would "slum it" in a sort of radical-chic sense, taking Bruant's verbal abuse on the chin, or listening to the radical polemics of Jules Jouy (1855-97), one of the Hydropathes, or even an elaborate shadow play. Indeed the Prince of Wales managed, on occasion, to slip in anonymously.

Other cabarets of the same period included the still-surviving Lapin Agile, which in its previous guises as "Au rendez-vous des voleurs" and "Cabaret des Assassins" (so called, according to legend, because a gang of thieves had murdered the proprietor's son), had been open as a tavern since 1860 (in a building dating to 1795). People like Pablo Picasso (1881-1973) and André Gill (1840-85) lived a bohemian existence there, playing pranks and somehow avoiding Paris' rather draconian censors. In fact, the Lapin Agile takes its name from the sign that Gill painted for the

entrance: a rabbit jumping out of a sauce-pan – "Lapin à Gill", or "Gill's Rabbit". This later became corrupted to "Lapin Agile", or "The Nimble Rabbit".

One of the most infamous pranks was instigated by the writer Roland Dorgelès (1885-1973), who expressed his disdain for the Cubists – fellow Lapin patrons – whom he deemed to be pretentious. He took particular aim at Guillaume Apollinaire (1880-1918), a poet, chansonnier and spokesman for the avant garde. Dorgelès invented a fictitious artist called Joachim-Raphael Boronali, and submitted a painting called "Le soleil se couche sur l'Adriatique" under that name to the Salon des Indépendants, where "Boronali", who was proclaimed to be the leader of a new artistic school called "Excessivisim", became the toast of the critics.

Of course, there was no such artist as Boronali. So who was responsible for the painting? Lolo, that's who – the donkey who belonged to the Lapin's proprietor, Frédéric "Frédé" Gerard. Witnessed by an officer of the court, Dorgelès tied a paintbrush to Lolo's tail, and submitted the resulting masterpiece.

When I visited the Lapin Agile in June 2008, I found an audience that included Japanese tourists, but the repertoire was all in French. It included standards such as "La Vie en Rose" as well as older songs dating to the Belle

Époque. One assumes that the paintings on the dimly lit walls are mostly reproductions. Gone are the days when Picasso paid his bar tab in canvases – his painting "At the Lapin Agile" has been valued at more than $8 million. The cabaret's fame has been revived in recent years by the Steve Martin play *Picasso at the Lapin Agile*, which concerns a fictional meeting between the artist and Albert Einstein. Now, it's a sort-of living museum of cabaret, where the audiences are encouraged to sing along.

The original Chat Noir closed when Salis died in 1897. After World War I, American jazz became a greater influence, and vied with the more traditional chanson for public acceptance, until the Hot Jazz Club of France promoted a French form of jazz, with musicians like Stéphane Grappelli (1908-97) and Django Reinhardt (1910-53) and the American expatriate singer Josephine Baker (1906-75).

"For some, Josephine Baker's *La Revue Nègre* embodied a transfusion of new blood and energy for a France stultified by tradition and sorely in need of renewal", say African-American author and lecturer Henry Louis Gates Jr. (1950-) and his colleague Karen C. C. Dalton in their introduction to *Josephine Baker and La Revue Nègre*. "For others, who held that the future of civilization itself lay in protecting an untainted French culture from invaders from the jungle, *La Revue Nègre* foretold the disintegration of centuries of classical cultural attainment, achievements of the mind over the body."[10]

The centre for cabaret began to move across the Seine to Montparnesse in the Latin Quarter, where the world of the cabaret meshed with the world of the café-concert and the music hall with the emergence of artists such as Édith Piaf (1915-63), Charles Trenet (1913-2001), Léo Ferré (1916-93) and Jacques Brel (1929-78).

At the end of the nineteenth century, the concept of cabaret began to spread – both through foreign visitors to

Paris, and foreign sojourns by Parisians. By the early years of the twentieth century, Berlin had become the world's third largest city, behind London and New York. Peter Jelavich (1954-) of Johns Hopkins University says, "Germany was a fertile ground for cabaret because it had a very strong theatrical culture going back to the eighteenth century. I also think that imperial Germany [was] not a repressive society but it certainly was not democratic either. And so you had enough freedom to be able to voice criticism but enough structural constraints, both politically and socially, so that there was a lot of aggravation and tension. That's a very fertile mix for cabaret, which flourishes best when people are discontented and yet they have enough freedom to voice that discontent."[11]

Contrary to English prejudices, Berliners did indeed possess a sense of humour – something called "Berliner Witz" – developed in the furnace of a highly cosmopolitan city. (Two centuries earlier, Berlin had welcomed Jewish refugees expelled from Vienna, as well as French Huguenots – ironic, given what was to come.) When Marlene Dietrich (1901-92) returned to Berlin for a concert in 1960, she told her audience that "no matter what madness affects the world, Berliners will keep their sense of humour".[12]

Unlike the Chat Noir and Lapin Agile, Berlin's first cabaret was in a legitimate theatre space. Ernst Von Wolzogen (1855-1934)'s Buntes ("Motley") Theatre – sometimes known as the "Überbrettl" ("superior club")[13] – opened on January 18, 1901 in the Alexanderplatz. His musical collaborators included Oscar Straus (1870-1954), the Viennese composer who would later gain fame for his operettas and musical comedies. Wolzogen, a poet and dramatist with aristocratic breeding who had written the libretto for Richard Strauss (1864-1949)'s *Feuersnot*, started out with lofty ambitions of finding a middle ground between the avant-garde and the banality of popular entertainment, but soon found himself pandering, out of economic pragmatism, to the erotic tastes of his middle

103

class audience. Due to the initial success of this venture, the Überbrettl soon had many imitators, and Wolzogen took his own show on tour.

In many ways, Wolzogen became a victim of his own success. With all the new interest in cabarets, he was forced out of his original premises, and built a spectacular new 800 seat auditorium designed by August Endell. Unfortunately, he had fallen out with some of his artistes, (including Oscar Straus), who were lured away by his rivals. Consequently, the quality of his entertainment – which had never found wide favour with the critics – declined. He had also failed to develop a stable of Berliner writers – much of his material was imported from Munich and other places. The Motley theatre never lived up to its lofty artistic ambitions, and so folded. According to Peter Jelavich, "both press and public realized that they often could find much better entertainment at the more established vaudeville halls."[14]

Almost concurrent with Wolzogen's enterprise was a literary parody called Schall und Rauch (Sound and Smoke), established by a man who would become one of the world's most respected theatrical innovators: Max Reinhardt (1873-1943). Like Wolzogen's, this first incarnation was short lived, but it set Reinhardt on his future course, one that included the production of many revues, (and Sound and Smoke would be revived in 1919). At the same time, Munich's Eleven Executioners, founded by *Spring Awakening* playwright Frank Wedekind (1864-1918) and others, began as a theatrical club in open rebellion against censorship.

In his novel *Goodbye to Berlin* (which formed the basis for both the play *I Am a Camera* and the musical *Cabaret*), Christopher Isherwood (1904-86) describes the character of cabaret singer Sally Bowles: "She had a surprisingly deep husky voice. She sang badly, without any expression, her hands hanging down at her sides – yet her performance was, in its own way, effective because of her startling appearance and her air of not caring a curse what people thought of her."[15] He could easily have been describing Marlene Dietrich or Lotte Lenya.

The composer Rudolph Nelson (1878-1960) helped to move cabaret in the direction of topical revue, both before and after the First World War. In 1907 he opened a cabaret on the Friedrichstrasse that borrowed its name from Paris's Chat Noir, and its entertainment was patronised by the Kaiser himself. Nelson frequently collaborated with Kurt Tucholsky (1890-1935) who wrote in 1913, "If you analyse these cabaret songs, then you find that the bottom line confirms the existence of extra-marital relations."[16] According to Lisa Appignanesi, "[Nelson's] revues had that mixture of the capricious, the racy, erotic and sentimental which Tucholsky was always drawn to."[17]

Suffice to say that cabaret (or kabarett) gained a reputation for Weimar decadence. Whether this was an expression of artistic freedom or commercial pragmatism is hard to say. Did the cabarets really resist Nazism, or did they – albeit accidentally – help bring it about? There is a theory that the cabaret decadence pushed tolerance to the breaking point. Others say that the cabarets failed to actively support the fragile democracy of the republic. When somebody said to English comedian Peter Cook (1937-95) that the Berlin kabaretts were the most powerful satire in history, he replied "Yeah, they really showed Hitler, didn't they?"[18]

The history of Weimar kabarett and its defiance of censorship and moral strictures has been told many times, and there is no need to repeat it in detail here. What I am interested in exploring is its relationship with musical theatre, and especially the development of songwriters.

Perhaps the best known composer was the London-born Friedrich Holländer (1896-1976), who became internationally famous for his score for the 1930 film *The Blue Angel*[19], including the now-standard "Falling in Love

Again" with English lyrics by Sammy Lerner (1903-89). Hollander was the son of Victor Holländer, the composer of the pre-war Metropol Theater revues, and the nephew of Felix Holländer, a member of Max Reinhardt's production staff. Educated at the Berlin Conservatory, by the age of eighteen he had become associate conductor of the Prague Opera House. However, it was lighter music that would prove to be his forté. Having already made a name for himself with songs for Sound and Smoke, Friedrich wrote both songs and scripts for cabaret star Rosa Valetti (1878-1937)'s Cabaret Grössenwahn ("Cabaret Megalomania", modelled on Aristide Bruant's "Le Merliton") in the early 1920s. (Valetti would later play Celia Peachum in the original production of *Threepenny Opera*.) He also wrote for his eventual wife Blandine Ebinger (1899-1993).

Hoping to emulate the success of Weill and Brecht's *Threepenny Opera*, he also wrote at least one book musical: an adaptation of the *Bourgeoise Gentilhomme* called *Bourgeois Bleibt Bourgois* ("Bourgeois Remains Bourgeois") with book by Ernst Toller (1893 – 1939) and Walter Hasenclever (1890-1940), lyrics by Hermann Kesten (1900-96) and directed by Andrew Granowsky. It opened on 2 February 1929 at the Lessing Theatre and lasted only eight performances. "Critics were divided between those who primarily blamed Granowsky and those who blamed the authors... But the text was severely criticised, especially the second part, which one critic called 'shallow repetition'. Holländer thought the text departed too far from Molière. Kesten, writing nearly thirty years after the event, was unkindly dismissive of his former colleagues."[20]

It was Rosa Valetti who first introduced Holländer to the *Blue Angel*'s future star Marlene Dietrich (1901-92). His score for that film included the immortal standard "Ich bin von Kopf bis Fuß auf Liebe eingestellt" which can be literallytranslated as: "I am, from head to toe, ready for love", but better known by its English title, "Falling in Love Again (Can't Help It)".

Following that film's success, Holländer left for Hollywood. There he became "Frederick Hollander" and wrote scores for well over a hundred films, as well as a number of songs in collaboration with future Broadway tunesmith Frank Loesser (1910-69). Some of these were sung by Dietrich in films like *Destry Rides Again* ("The Boys in the Back Room"). He tried to revive Berlin's Tingel-Tangel cabaret on Santa Monica Boulevard, but it was a dismal failure, even when sung in English. He even tried his hand at film directing, with *The Only Girl* (1934), starring Charles Boyer, for which he also wrote the score. In the 1950s, and 60s, he returned to Germany, mounting revues in Munich.

Another of Hollander's colleagues from *Sound and Smoke* was Werner R. Heymann (1896-1961), a child prodigy who had written his first composition at the age of eight. He wrote the music for the stage play *Die Wandlung* ("Transformation") by the expressionist playwright Ernst Toller (1893-1939) in 1919, but is probably best remembered for his song score for the musical film *Die Drei von der Tankstelle* ("The Three from the Filling Station") directed by Wilhelm Thiele (1890-1975), an Austrian. Among the cast were the Comedian Harmonists. It was the highest grossing German film of 1930. A Jew, Heymann left Germany when the Nazis came to power, and worked in Hollywood on films by Ernst Lubitsch (*Ninotchka*, 1939) and Preston Sturges (*The Shop Around the Corner*, 1940). After the war, he returned to Germany, where he scored a stage version of *The Blue Angel*.

Another important composer for the Weimar cabaret was Mischa Spoliansky (1898-1985), who worked on both *Sound and Smoke* and Trude Hesterberg (1892-1967)'s Wilde Brühne ("Wild Stage"). He was born in Bialystock, Russia, the son of an operatic baritone. The family moved to Germany when his mother died in 1905, and Mischa gave his first concert at the age of ten. Like Holländer, Spoliansky was seduced by the cabaret. In fact, it was

Victor Holländer who first encouraged him in that direction, bringing him into the Reinhardt organisation. He was commissioned to write (as well as perform in) a musical called *Victoria* based on Somerset Maugham's *Home and Beauty* which toured to Vienna and Salzburg after a successful run in Berlin. In 1922 he met the lyricist Marcellus Schiffer (1892-1932), a leading humorist whose other collaborators included Friedrich Holländer, Rudloph Nelson and the opera composer Paul Hindemith. Their greatest hit was the revue *Es liegt in der Luft* ("It's in the Air") featuring Schiffer's wife Margo Lion and Marlene Dietrich. The setting was a department store, in a spoof on consumerism. One of the songs "Wenn die beste Freundin" ("When the Special Girlfriend") depicted two women shoppers who decide to "exchange" their unsatisfactory husbands for each other. This song became an unofficial anthem for Germany's lesbian community. (Schiffer was gay, and Lion a lesbian.) A "cabaret opera", *Rufen Sie Herrn Plim!* ("Send for Mr. Plim"), produced at the Kabarett der Komiker (Cabaret of Comedians) in 1932 with a book by Kurt Robitschek and starring Harald Paulsen (1895 – 1954) (who had appeared in *Threepenny Opera*) also had a department store setting, with the management devising a unique way of dealing with customer complaints. Mr. Plim's job was to be "fired", supposedly acting as a scapegoat for all complaints, but in fact undermining his employers by gaining the customer's sympathy.

But Germany was dancing toward disaster. "To the Nazis," Liel Leibovitz and Matthew Miller say in their book *Lili Marlene*, "Berlin's freewheeling culture, dominated as it was by leftists, liberals, and Jews, represented an insidious threat to the pure Aryan culture [the Nazis] wished to see reborn in a Germany cleansed of non-Germans. To them, the playful criticism of the ruling classes that the cabaret shows engendered amounted to treason and the black musicians and American jazz that were celebrated in its rollicking halls were a cancerous tumor rotting the German soul."[21] Within a year, Adolph Hitler would become Chancellor, and the curtain would come down – quite literally – on kabarett. However, Marcellus Schiffer would not live to see it – he ended his own life in 1932 with an overdose of sleeping pills.

Like Holländer, Spoliansky fled Germany when Hitler came to power, settling in London and working in films for Alexander Korda, among others. He also wrote propaganda songs for the German language service of the BBC during World War II (although, as an "enemy alien", his work was banned from the domestic service).

Benny Goodman recorded some of his music, and he could count George Gershwin among his admirers. He never worked in English language musical theatre, but not for lack of trying – his musical version of Shaw's *Pygmalion* was never pursued. Back in Germany he did an adaptation of Carl Zuckmayer's 1928 folk play *Katharina Knie*, set in a travelling circus, with book and lyrics by Robert Gilbert (1899-1978). This opened at the Theater am Gärtnerplatz in Munich on 20 January 1957. *Wie lernt man Liebe?* ("How You Learn Love"), described as a "musical party game" also written with Gilbert, based on Sheridan's *School for Scandal*, was produced on stage and television there a decade later. In 1978, he and Margo Lion accepted an invitation to the Berlin Arts Festival in a performance of his music. It was such a triumph that they were invited back again the following year.

Spoliansky did finally make his posthumous English language musical theatre debut in 1999, when *Send for Mr. Plim* was revived in an English adaptation by actor Julian Forsyth at the Battersea Arts Centre in London. *The Guardian*'s Michael Billington wrote, "The piece is pure joy and a total vindication of the form of cabaret opera: it says more in 60 minutes than most musicals galumphingly say over three hours."[22]

The genesis of this version came some years earlier when Spoliansky's daughter Spoli Mills (1923-2004) came to see Forsyth in Trevor Nunn's stage production of *The Blue*

Angel, which had used some of her father's songs. She then sent him the piano score for *Plim*.

"It's full of pastiche of all sorts of musical styles", Forsyth told me. "It'll switch very quickly from pastiche Richard Strauss or even Wagner or Handelian recitative into a fox-trot or various other jazz rhythms. And it's very fascinating, but I thought, as it stood, for a modern audience, maybe there's a little bit too much of a requirement for audiences to recognise some of the operatic pastiche... Is that going to disengage them from the story if they're going 'oh, there's a little bit of *Rosenkavalier* here', or 'a little bit of recitative that sounds like Handel'? It seemed to me there was more of that than there was of the jazz... It felt to me, at the time, as though we were admiring how clever a composer could be. That worried me slightly."

Then an idea occurred. "As it happened, we made contact with an English vocal group called Cantabile who, amongst other things, do arrangements of German popular songs in the style of the Comedian Harmonists." The latter was a cabaret sextet in Weimar Berlin who had made their film debut in *The Three from the Filling Station*. The original members were Harry Frommermann, Erwin Bootz, Roman Cycowski, Aspurach Leschnikoff, Erich Collin and Robert Biberti. The Harmonists had taken part in another Spoliansky revue, *Zwei Krawatten* ("Two Neckties") which also featured Marlene Dietrich. (Joseph Vilsmaier's 1997 film *The Harmonists* is based on their story.)

Forsyth and his director wife Marguerite decided to bring in Cantabile to play the department store managers. He expanded the roles of the manager and personnel manager in the original version into four, thus forming a vocal quartet. "Cantabile had evolved over a generation or two, and so there was quite an interesting age range", Forsyth explains. "You've got the senior, rather conservative boss, then the next in command is maybe a little bit prickly. He was the one [who], because he could sing counter-tenor as well as tenor, would be the most likely to say something rather dramatic and do it as a kind of Handelian recitative. Then the next one down was the guy who'd worked in Macy's for a year and [is] very astute and always thinking the American way. And then we thought it's interesting to have one guy below him who's got an eye on his job and is younger and will maybe pick holes."

In order to accommodate this, he was able to interpolate other Spoliansky melodies – particularly some originally written for the Comedian Harmonists – into the score. "You would get the feeling that switches in musical style were in some way organically generated by their interaction amongst each other and also whomever else they might encounter." This also resulted in a jazzier, more popular style.

Ultimately, the managers' plan falls apart. "What they don't reckon with is that Mr. Plim turns out to be kind of subversive in the funniest ways. They... give him instructions as to how to behave with these angry customers, and whatever instructions they give to him he takes to its logical extreme. So instead of the customer leaving feeling satisfied that they have actually assisted Wertheim's [Department Store] by getting rid of an unsuitable employee, they end up leaving even more angry. The things they complain about are absolutely ludicrous, but the management kow-tow to them and are terribly obsequious. It just so happens that whatever instruction they give to Plim, whether it's [to] be very apologetic and in fact almost be grateful that your inadequacies have been pointed out to you... He's so grateful for being put on the dole along with millions of other Germans who can barely eat that this lady from the Women's Institute in Leipzig is even more angry when she departs than when she arrives. So they say, 'we obviously got that wrong...you'd better show a little bit of distress'. So of course Plim becomes this wonderful actor. You're never sure whether he just has that mindset – 'Okay, I'll play that to the hilt' and it all just happens to go horribly wrong, or whether there's some subversive element in what he's doing."

Many have taken this to be a critique of capitalism and consumerism, but Forsyth believes it has a more specific target. "The whole idea of the need for a scapegoat – who's to blame for the Wall Street crash that wrecked the German economy – all these loans recalled, the millions of people thrown out of work – who's to blame? Of course, we all know what the Nazi Party's answer to that particular question was."

There were other challenges in adapting *Plim* for an English audience. "A curious thing about cabaret music at that time, which you find in Spoliansky and Schiffer and you certainly find in Brecht and Weill is sometimes the words fit the music in ways you really wouldn't expect. In fact, it's almost deliberately put together in a way that it really doesn't fit. It's anti the normal American way of doing things. Where the music dictates the stress should be is exactly where you wouldn't want it if that person were just saying that sentence."

When the New York Shakespeare Festival mounted a revival of *Threepenny Opera* starring Raul Julia in 1976, translators Ralph Manheim (1907-92) and John Willett (1917-2002) attempted to find an English equivalent to this way of phrasing. The earlier Marc Blitzstein (1905-64) translation had aimed to make the lyrics more singable, but in this case producer Joseph Papp felt "it was evident that the intention of its creators had been to violate the musical rhythms so that the force of the language dominated the hearing of its audience. While I admit that the popular and Americanized treatment of Brecht's lyrics are in some instances more beautiful than what appears to be the clumsier and less manageable text in this more authentic translation, on the whole the deliberately crude artistic texture of the original is clearly diminished."[23]

"I'm inclined to agree with Joe Papp that the 'deliberately crude' juxtapositions of text and music in the

Brecht/Weill originals is something that translations of those works should try to emulate if one wants to capture the flavour and intentions of the originals", says Forsyth. "But I think Brecht/Weill set a trend... and Marcellus Schiffer was to some extent copying that. But Schiffer and Spoliansky are of course much less edgy and groundbreaking than Brecht and Weill, and I just felt that copying the deliberate idiosyncrasies of the *Plim* prologue for example wouldn't do them any favours with audiences who had never heard any Spoliansky music before... I think to a modern ear it would seem quaint to the extent of almost 'whoever's done that translation hasn't done a very good job', because the words don't go with the music. It would probably seem dated in German too."

"I felt you almost need to forget that people were singing. You need to see them interacting almost as if it were a little intimate play. The interaction between characters needs to be organic and therefore any changes in musical style need to be organic. You need to see somebody thinking, 'Oh, I know how to respond to this, but I will choose to respond to it in a fox-trot.'

The critical success of this version has led to some renewed interest in the piece. There were some initial legal complications, as Spoli didn't own the rights, but now that they have been resolved, Forsyth is translating his adaptation back into German, where it will exist as an alternative to the original.

Although they were working in a very controversial field, there was one thing that Holländer, Spoliansky and Weill had in common – they were all highly classically trained. They all were also clearly enamoured of American jazz and Tin Pan Alley. (While Kurt Weill never actually wrote for the cabarets, Bertolt Brecht did, albeit briefly, and that influence can be heard in *Threepenny Opera* and other works).

The first attempt at cabaret in Vienna was in the

cellar of the Theater an der Wien in 1901, when Felix Salten (1869-1945) opened his *Theater zum lieben Augustin* which lasted for only seven performances. Five years later, a more permanent cabaret opened in the same space, called Die Hölle ("Hell"). This was soon followed by Marc Henry's "Fledermaus" in Kärtnerstrasse, whose contributors included future operetta composer Oscar Straus. One of the most successful and long-lasting was "Simplicissimus", founded in 1912 by Egon Dorn as a restaurant with entertainment. One of its emcees was Fritz Grünbaum (1880-1941), who would later establish himself in operettas as a librettist before dying in a concentration camp. "Simpl" – as it came to be known – survived the war, and still exists.

After Hitler came to power, most of the cabarets in Germany closed. Those that survived were converted into so-called "positive cabaret", which presented a pro-Nazi outlook devoid of any real satire.

Lale Anderson (1905-72) was one artist who survived, in spite of her anti-Nazi beliefs and her Swiss Jewish lover. Her story is proof that even a control freak like Joseph Goebbels couldn't stage-manage everything.

In 1938, she recorded "The Song of the Young Sentry", a sentimental ballad composed by Norbert Schultze (1911-2002) as a setting of a World War I poem by Hans Leip (1893-1983). The story concerned a young soldier who yearns for his girlfriend. Leip combined the names of two girls he had romanced, "Lili" and "Marlene". The recording disappeared without a trace – almost. When Radio Belgrade required some fresh light music to fill their daily broadcast to the German soldiers in Eastern Europe and North Africa, they were erroneously given a number of records that had been rejected by the mainstream German broadcasters, including this one. It became a hit with soldiers on both sides of the conflict, and there wasn't anything either Goebbels or Churchill could do to stop it.

Some of the exiled artists took their acts to Austria (until its German annexation), Switzerland, the Netherlands and Britain. After the war, Holländer tried to revive Tingel-Tangel in Munich in the 1950s, and a form of cabaret called Die Distel was tolerated by the East Berlin authorities as a safety valve. It survives to this day in a converted cinema in Friedrichstrasse. Berlin sketch writer Jergen Behrens says, "Cabaret should be a combination of living room and bedroom."[24]

Cabaret of the sort practised in Paris and Berlin was never very big in London, although some indigenous attempts were made. In 1912, Austrian heiress and journalist Frida Strindberg (1872-1943) (nee Uhl), ex-wife of the famous Swedish playwright August Strindberg, established the "Cave of the Golden Calf" in the basement of a merchant's warehouse just off Regent Street. It lasted for just over a year. With the possible exception of Peter Cook's Establishment Club in Soho in the early 1960s, what little cabaret there has been in London has tended toward jazz clubs such as Ronnie Scott's, rather than satire. In recent times, there have been a few nightclubs such as the Pheasantry and the Crazy Coqs that feature theatre artists singing a repertoire of Broadway standards.

In the post-war period, the Netherlands developed its own brand of cabaret. Although it owed much to Weimar, it took on a character of its own. Some of the most famous "cabaretiers" included Wim Sonneveld (1917-74) and Toon Hermans (1916-2000) who mixed political and celebrity satire, music and poetry and movement. Their characters were larger than life, but very real as well. Dutch actor and dancer René Driessen remembers artists like De Mounties, and Snip en Snap. "When I was a kid we used to love watching them and especially around New Years Eve and in the Christmas Holidays they would be shown often on TV and the whole country watched them. We only had one or two channels and nobody looked at foreign channels then, which is completely different now. It sometimes saddens me that those people and those times are gone, because it had a real intimate sense of 'home'".

One Dutch cabaret-writing team turned their hands to writing book musicals. Their biggest hit *En Nu Naar Bed* ("And Now to Bed") which opened in Amsterdam on 5 November 1971 with book and lyrics by Annie M. G. Schmidt (1911-95) and music by Harry Bannink (1929-99), was directed by the Canadian-born, London-based choreographer Paddy Stone (1924-86). (I will talk more about this and other post-war European musicals in the chapter "Europe After Hitler".)

Of course, in recent years, the word "cabaret" has taken on other meanings. When Lisa Appignanesi talks about New York cabaret, she is talking about the stand-up comedy of Lenny Bruce, Mort Sahl and Mike Nichols and Elaine May, and her only musical references are to the jazz of the Beat generation. Yet, that is not the context in which I usually hear the word used today.

In the U.S., there is a monthly magazine called *Cabaret Scenes* with articles on cabaret artists such as Amanda McBroom and John Bucchino. There is no mention of stand-up, and little talk of political satire. Nor is the emphasis on jazz. Many, if not most of the artists listed are in some way connected to musical theatre – either as off-duty actors, or as singers who draw heavily on the Broadway repertoire.

"For a good part of the 20th century, musical theatre songs *were* the majority of the popular songs," says American cabaret singer Karen Oberlin, "so those were the songs being performed in the intimate clubs, even in New York. Everyone performed the theatre songs, including theatrical singers and jazz singers, so I think the infusion of theatre songs was quite natural and continues to be part of the tradition. In an intimate setting, the lyrics have to 'hold up,' and a performer must be living within a song, so theatre songs work well."[25]

"Cabaret has 'evolved' to become 'personal theatre', in other words, the songs are 'acting pieces' that allow the singer to convey something personal to the audience", says singer Anne Kerry Ford.

"Some of the best 'acting songs' naturally come from musical theatre. These are usually the songs with the deepest lyrical content (say, over 'pop' songs). Not always... I mean, I have heard all kinds of songs done well in cabaret shows, but the Broadway material almost demands to be sung out of the context of the show they were written for, because they are so lyrically rich. It is fun for the audience to hear them in a different context from the show they were written for, as they can consider the song as a complete work of art in itself, and they usually hear it afresh without the story of the show around it. These songs are gems in themselves, and often they stand up quite well when taken out of context, if they make sense in the context of the cabaret show. It's like deconstructing a dress (read 'Broadway show') to make a quilt (read 'cabaret show'). Both are valid art forms; the same material is just being used in different ways. I personally look for material that has a lot of emotional content, as these are the ones that resonate with me and allow me to use my acting chops. That's why I have made the music of Kurt Weill my metier."[26]

"I believe that the reason Broadway music ended up in cabaret rooms is that performers who are drawn to musical theatre are interested in telling stories through song", says American actor and singer David Cameron Anderson.

"These people, if they're at all ambitious, have no intention of waiting for someone to tell them, 'You can sing now,' or 'You may sing now, however your 'type' is (fill in the blank – ingenue, leading man/woman, character man/woman) therefore you may only sing songs that we think 'fit' your type' and continuing, 'The public is not interested in the love lives of the less than beautiful – so you can sing the best friend's song or the fathers song or the janitor's song but, God forbid, you should dare to sing to express how you love or how you are loved' and to the beautiful people, 'you're pretty – you don't get to tell the jokes'... So these disenfranchised performers pick music that matters to them and find a place with a piano and a microphone and a place for the audience to sit and then they sing for all they're worth. And Broadway songs are already story songs so there you have it... Then they find that the Broadway trunk, though substantial, cannot possibly fill hour after hour in cabaret rooms without overexposure so they look at others who write story material – folk writers, country and western writers, literate pop writers."[27]

When a song from a musical is performed in a cabaret, it is stripped naked. Usually with only a piano for accompaniment and no more than two hundred people in the audience, this is a friendly communication between artist and audience that plays to the musical theatre's greatest asset: the lyrics. Whether it is Ann Hampton Calloway singing Frank Loesser or Edith Piaf singing Marguerite Monnot, the effect is the same – they are telling stories to an audience hanging on their every note and word. Jacques Brel understood this, which is why his songs were so easily adapted to the revue format. Size isn't everything. "When Sarah McLaughlin sings 'Angel', accompanying herself on a piano, in the Universal Amphitheatre (seating at least 4,000) it is cabaret to me," says Anderson. On the other hand, "Some brilliant theatre singers are lousy in small venues," says Lorna Dallas. "Imagine [Ethel] Merman reigning in her voice for some place like Jermyn Street? Impossible."[28]

Whether by accident or by design, cabaret and revue have long been a proving ground for new writers who then go on to write full scale musicals. This is true in New York, but it was also true in Paris and Berlin. Vincent Scotto, Albert Willemetz and Henri Christiné wrote for the cabarets in Paris, as did Bertolt Brecht in Berlin.

In London, Mark Bunyan began in the late 1970s "where I managed to skilfully fall between any of the available stools." As an outspoken gay artist, he was deemed too radical for the mainstream (one West End management told him, "We can't put that on the *Val Doonican Show*"), but not radical enough for the "soft-soap socialism of many of the alternative comedians who merely replaced the word 'mother-in-law' with 'the fuzz' and alcohol with cocaine." He ended up playing solo acts in theatres before a largely gay audience until he began to reach a "much wider spectrum who just want to be intelligently entertained."[29]

I got to know Mark through the Writing Block, a group of songwriters who used to meet once a month in Covent Garden to try their songs out on each other – much like the Hydropathes of a century earlier. "I suppose it was an obvious step for me as a narrative-writing cabaret writer… to move into writing narrative musical theatre." His musical *Achilles in Heels* was mounted at the Landor Theatre in South London in 2007.

Cabaret works differently in different places. In Toronto, it has traditionally been allied with revue and dinner theatre, where artists like the late Tom Kneebone and Dinah Christie did revues such as *Oh Coward!* There is a great comedy tradition, beginning with the annual *Spring Thaw* revues that ran from 1948-71. Although *Second City* originally began in Chicago, its Toronto offshoot has largely eclipsed the parent, having spawned the long running *SCTV* television series. (It also, indirectly, spawned *The Drowsy Chaperone*.) In fact, while Toronto cabaret has largely gone in the Broadway-writ-small direction, the sort of political satire that Appignanesi has identified with cabaret still exists. Videocabaret was founded in 1976 by Michael Hollingsworth, Deanna Taylor, the "Hummer Sisters", who set out to "invent theatrical vocabulary for the age of information"[30] using video-charicatures with altered footage of real political figures with dubbed voices.

Satire has also prospered – on and off – on TV and radio. *This Hour Has Seven Days*, which ran on CBC television from 1964-66, combined serious public affairs journalism with biting satirical songs (usually sung by

Dinah Christie) and sketches. Former Canadian broadcaster Sandy Stewart describes it as "a lively, provocative and even outrageous program which was required viewing for all intelligent Canadians."[31] It was taken off the air following network attempts to curtail some of its more controversial subjects, although a much more recent series on the same network, *This Hour has 22 Minutes* was inspired by it. The spirit of *Spring Thaw* has also survived in the form of *Royal Canadian Air Farce*, first on radio, then on TV.

In Australia, an annual international cabaret festival has been held in Adelaide since 2001. It has developed an updated form of its own, allied to alternative fringe comedy. "Here, the word 'cabaret' isn't loaded with European and American baggage", says London based performer Barb Jungr. "This is the country that gave the world Robyn Archer, and followed with Caroline Reid's *Pam Ann* and Tim Minchin. There seems to be a fair amount of envelope pushing as far as the genre is concerned."[32] Minchin has more recently enjoyed London success with *Matilda*, his musical adaptation of the Roald Dahl classic, and with *Groundhog Day* (book by Danny Rubin). *Keating*, a highly successful cabaret musical with a political theme, will be discussed in the chapter "Larrikins and Sentimental Blokes: Musicals Down Under".

Declaration of Independence:
The American Musical

That the American musical developed from European operetta and musical comedy is well documented. While the primary thrust of this book is the work that exists away from the centres of New York and London, I feel that it is useful to look at how American (and British) musicals developed their own distinctiveness, so that others may learn from them.

North America is, in a sense, a partitioned country, much as Ireland is. It is divided between those whose loyalty remained with the British Crown (or at least with a European way of life) and those who set out to create a new nation. The former, of course, became Canada, and the latter became the United States of America.

In Canada, for much of the first century of its existence as a nation-state, its mother culture was that of Britain (for the Anglos) and France (for the Francophones). Their evolution (not "revolution") toward democracy mirrored that of Britain, which had begun with the Magna Carta and continued through the English Civil War.

In the United States, on the other hand, deliberate and concerted efforts were made to differentiate themselves from their former colonial masters. They consciously set out to change their language, dropping the "u" from words like "colour", and changing "zed" to "zee"[1]. This was not just natural evolution, but a deliberate effort at nation building. In *The White Jacket*, Herman Melville proclaimed, "We Americans are the peculiar, chosen people... We are the pioneers of the world; the advance guard, sent on through the wilderness of untried things, to break a path in the New World that is ours."[2] They had decided to re-invent themselves, and the year 1776 had become, in their minds, the year "one".

The American musical is not – in my view – a

separate art form from its European parent, any more than American English is a separate language from British English. That said, the development of a distinctively American form of the musical, like the changes in the language, was deliberate. For much of the first century of its existence, American music struggled for acceptance against the much more ubiquitous European forms.

English musicologist Wilfred Mellers defines American culture as "an extreme evolution from the European consciousness"[3]. When America began to import musical comedies from Britain and Europe in the nineteenth century, they were filtered through their own very American sensibilities. *HMS Pinafore* was wildly popular when first produced there, but not for entirely the same reasons as at home. "The Savoy operas were... a somewhat different thing for the Americans than they were for the English," says Raymond Knapp, a professor in the Department of Musicology at UCLA.

> "The political basis for Gilbert's humor created not only a sense of recognition in America, but also an awareness of difference, for political structures and issues, too, had diverged dramatically. And the music itself was distinctly more European than American, with little or none of the diverse African-American inflections, already then present to some extent in American music (in minstrelsy and spirituals), that would eventually develop into idioms of jazz and blues. These subtle shades of difference helped Americans to recognize and appreciate the ways in which their own development had diverged from that of their English counterparts; in conjunction with Gilbert's often pointed critique of English mores, these easily perceived differences encouraged Americans to see themselves in a more favorable light."[4]

It is inevitable, given the radically different milieu that the European immigrants found themselves in, that American music would begin to develop a voice of its own. Mellers says of early American composer Charles Ives (1874-1954),

"If he was to be an honest creator, he had to take his materials from the world around him: which was the provincial community of the hard-bitten farmer, the small business-man and tradesman. Here was a certain measure of pioneering vitality, mixed with a somewhat blighted religious ethic; of refinement or 'culture' there was no trace. In musical terms, this life meant the town band (which Ives's father directed), ragtime, the corny theatre tune, the chapel hymn. All these were crude but full of conviction, since they were aspects of a way of life."[5]

The Broadway sound was established by the generation of Jewish and Irish immigrants who came to New York in the latter half of the nineteenth century. These people were outsiders with something to prove. Much is written about the Klezmer sounds from Eastern Europe (whose improvisational nature made it an easy soul mate for jazz). But the Celtic strains of Irish and Scottish music made their impression as well, eventually emerging as modern bluegrass. Although his music doesn't sound particularly Celtic, George M. Cohan (1878-1942), a second generation Irish American who grew up on the vaudeville stage, gave his work an aggressively patriotic zeal. There was a reason for that aggression: the Irish, like the Jews, had not yet been accepted as true Americans. "The Irish were culturally displaced", says Ethan Mordden (1949-), "a clan in a strange land. Cohan assimilated the Irish. His musicals were not pure Yankee: they were symbolic of a time in which the Yankee melting pot yielded a richer stock from its infusion of races. One of the reasons he got such bad press in his early years is the sociological impact of his shows. They celebrated racial integration: this was a controversial topic in the early 1900s."[6] (I will discuss Cohan further in the chapter "Between the Wars".)

More than anybody, it was Jerome Kern (1885-1945) who brought maturity to the nascent American form. It is important to remember that at this time, London and Vienna were the capitals, and New York was still an upstart. Kern was, in fact, strongly influenced by the central European operetta, for some of his earliest successes had been with songs interpolated into American productions of European musicals. Sometimes this involved travel to London, where he met and collaborated with future *Jeeves* author P.G. Wodehouse (1881-1975). Kern explained to a journalist at the time his understanding of why they had to make these adaptations:

> "In London... the doors open at 7:30 o'clock and the crowd flocks in. At 8 o'clock the curtain rises with not a soul in the stalls. The fashionable part of the audience does not begin to arrive before 8:30, and it is 9 before most of them come. From 8 to 9 then the time is filled in with the most awful stuff in the world. Poor songs, worse comedy and stale jokes are used as padding till the audience in the stalls arrives. Then the play begins in earnest. The result is that when the play is brought to New York it has to be almost entirely made over. The first hour is usually tossed out bodily and scenes from the other acts are brought forward. This leaves holes in the show that must be filled, and the plugging of those holes has been my task.
>
> Sometimes, too, the nature of the music is such as to make it unfit for use here. This is particularly true of the music of the German composers. Their musical comedy singers usually can sing. They sacrifice looks to voice, and it is not uncommon to see a big, buxom woman of thirty-five playing the role of a girl of eighteen. However charming the majority of our musical comedy players may be, not many of them are prima donnas. So a great deal of the score has to be set aside or rewritten."[7]

The Girl from Utah was a 1913 musical from London with music by Paul Rubens and Sidney Jones, a book by James T. Tanner, and lyrics by Adrian Ross, Percy Greenbank and Rubens. It ran for 195 performances at the Adelphi Theatre, but American producer Charles Frohman (1856-1915) felt it had a weak first act. He hired Kern to write five new songs, including "They Didn't Believe Me", with lyrics by Englishman Herbert Reynolds (real name Michael Elder Rourke, 1867-1933), of which composer Alec Wilder (1907-80) says, "The melodic line... is as natural as walking"[8]. This song, says music historian Andrew Lamb, "symbolised the emergence of American theatrical song, in which swirling melodies, lush orchestrations, and the romantic doings of palaces and princes were replaced by simple, gently tripping melodic lines and lyrics that expressed the workaday sentiments of ordinary people."[9]

> And when I told them how beautiful you are,
> They didn't believe me.
> They didn't believe me!
> Your lips, your eyes, your cheeks, your hair,
> Are in a class beyond compare,
> You're the loviest girl that one could see!
> And when I tell them,
> And I cert'nly am goin' to tell them,
> That I'm the man whose wife one day you'll be.
> They'll never believe me.
> They'll never believe me.
> That from this great big world you've chosen me!

It was adapted by a then unknown and uncredited Cole Porter[10] – at the time apparently serving in the French Foreign Legion – as a song in a London revue that eventually found its way into the British trenches of World War I with a powerfully ironic lyric:

> And when they ask us,
> how dangerous it was,
> Oh, we'll never tell them
> No, we'll never tell them:
> We spent our pay in some café,
> And fought wild women night and day,
> 'Twas the cushiest job we ever had.
> And when they ask us,
> And they're certainly going to ask us,
> The reason why we didn't win the Croix de Guerre,
> Oh, we'll never tell them,
> Oh, we'll never tell them
> There was a front, but damned if we knew where.

I'm not sure even Porter forsaw the irony that last line would gain when his version of this song became the finale of *Oh! What a Lovely War*.

Soon after, Kern would solidify his reputation with a series of intimate musicals at the 299 seat Princess Theatre, including *Very Good Eddie*, *Leave it to Jane*, *Oh Lady Lady!* and *Oh Boy!*. All had a book by Guy Bolton (1884-1979) and lyrics by P. G. Wodehouse (1881-1975), both of them English born. Dorothy Parker (1893-1967) wrote:

> Well, Bolton and Wodehouse and Kern have done it again. Every time these three gather together, the Princess Theatre is sold out for months in advance. You can get a seat for *Oh, Lady! Lady!!* somewhere around the middle of August for just about the price of one on the stock exchange. If you ask me, I will look you fearlessly in the eye and tell you in low, throbbing tones that it has it over any other musical comedy in town. But then Bolton and Wodehouse and Kern are my favorite indoor sport. I like the way they go about a musical comedy... I like the way the action slides casually into the songs... I like the deft rhyming of the song that is always sung in the last act by two comedians and a comedienne. And oh, how I do like Jerome Kern's music. And all these things are even more so in *Oh, Lady! Lady!!* than they were in *Oh, Boy!*[11]

Kern's most signifigant contribution would come after the war, thanks to Edna Ferber (1885-1968), a girl born in Kalamazoo, Michigan to a Hungarian Jewish father and a German mother. The inspiration she gained in one night not only changed her life, but would indirectly change the musical theatre forever.

She was part of a famous group of New York literati who met for lunch each day and engaged in repartee that would inevitably wind up in the newspapers. At first they called themselves "the Board" and their luncheons "Board meetings". After the hotel assigned them a waiter named Luigi, they became the "Luigi Board". Finally, they called themselves the Vicious Circle, although the public knew them as the Round Table after a cartoonist published a picture of them sitting around the Algonquin's round table wearing armour.

Through the Round Table, she met and collaborated several times with one of its members, George S. Kaufman (1889-1961). Their first play together was called *Minick* (based on their own short story *Old Man Minick*), and it was while this was in tryouts in 1924 at the Lyceum Theatre in New London, Connecticut that they found the structure had been taken over by bats, which made a right nuisance of themselves in the middle of a performance.

After the show, the producer Winthrop Ames (1870-1937) joked, "Never mind, boys and girls! Next time I'll tell you what we'll do. We won't bother with tryouts. We'll all charter a show boat and we'll just drift down the rivers, playing the towns as we come to them, and we'll never get off the boat. It'll be wonderful!"[12]

Ferber was intrigued. "What's a show boat?" she asked. He told her how the show people "lived and slept and ate and worked right there on the boat. The country people for miles around would hear the calliope screeching and they'd know the show-boat folks were in town."

"I was hot on the trail of show boats", wrote Ferber. "Here, I thought, was one of the most melodramatic and gorgeous bits of Americana that had ever come my way. It was not only the theater — it was the theater plus the glamour of the wandering drifting life, the drama of the river towns, the mystery and terror of the Mississippi itself."

She signed herself on for a four day stint on one of the last of the show boats, the James Adams Floating Palace Theatre, which operated out of Bath, North Carolina from 1913-41. "When April came, I went as eagerly as a lover to meet the show boat." She lived among the performers and crew and even sold tickets in the box office. It turned out that the people who operated the boat were all fans of her novels and short stories. "I spent a year hunting down every available scrap of show-boat material; reading, interviewing, taking notes and making outlines." She turned her experience into a novel called *Show Boat*.

Through critic Alexander Woollcott (1887-1943), a member of the Round Table, Kern and Ferber were introduced. I think you now know where this story is heading, but it took some persuasion for him to convince her that what he intended was not a frivolous musical comedy, but a whole new type of show. He and his collaborator, Oscar Hammerstein II (1895-1960) would merge American popular musical comedy with European operetta in their 1927 hit *Show Boat*.

"Here we come to a completely new genre – the musical play as distinguished from musical comedy", says composer Mark Lubbock (1898-1986). "The play was the thing, and everything else was subservient to that play. Now... came complete integration of song, humor and production numbers into a single and inextricable artistic entity."[13] Director George C. Wolfe (1954-) called it "the first American musical, the first to have the real texture of this country".[14]

A new era had begun. "The four year cataclysm helped to crystallize America's confidence in her own culture", says Lehman Engel of the period following World War I. "Whether in a practical or in a deeper, spiritual sense, the war brought a crucial period of independence to the American theater."[15] Jaded by a war they had fought in only reluctantly, by the 1930s Americans had become more culturally isolationist. Although this may have been, at its heart, a reactionary tendency, it also brought out a spirit of radicalism in the arts. In her biography of Leonard Bernstein, Meryle Secrest writes, "The role of American composers in building a brave new world was to create a uniquely American contribution, based on the New England heritage of hymns, dances and folk songs and on the rich and exploitable vein of Negro rhythmic patterns and tone colors."[16] New Hampshire based composer and educator John Warthen Struble (1952-) writes, "The imagination of America was turned inward during the Depression, toward things American, and foreign musical influences held less power than at any previous time in our history."[17]

One tangible result of this was the Works Progress Administration's Federal Music and Federal Theatre programs. In 1935, composers like Aaron Copland (1900-90) and Marc Blitzstein (1905-64) were given grants to write music in an American style and on American subjects. Blitzstein wrote the left-wing agit-prop musical *The Cradle Will Rock*, which was directed by Orson Welles for the Federal Theatre in 1937 (although, due to its political content, WPA support was withdrawn), with musical direction by Lehman Engel. In 1942, conductor André Kostelanetz (1901-80) commissioned Copland and Kern (among others) to write orchestral pieces based on American historical figures. Kern chose Mark Twain, while Copland ultimately settled on Abraham Lincoln.

Broadway has always prided itself in being a "melting pot", made up largely of immigrants from Eastern Europe or of first-generation Americans. Irving Berlin was born in Russia (as Israel Isidore Beilin, 1888-1989), but arrived in New York when he was a small child. But what of the composers who had already received their training and begun their careers in their home countries?

Victor Herbert (1859-1924) was born in Dublin and at the age of twenty-four became the principal cellist in the court orchestra at Stuttgart before emigrating to the U.S., where he played with the orchestra of the Metropolitan Opera. His first operetta, *Prince Ananius* was a success in 1894. "There were always hints of his Irish heritage in his music", says Alan Jay Lerner (1918-86), "which frequently gave his melodies a wistful tenderness."[18] Broadway conductor Lehman Engel says, "Although his avowed purpose was to further Viennese operetta, he unconsciously succeeded in creating a style that represented the first significant step away from the European models. His melodies were simpler, more easily remembered, and easier to perform. His harmonic sense was less sophisticated, and although he was a highly skilled musician, he chose to shed musical complexities, which had been the hallmark of the Europeans."[19]

Vernon Duke (1903-69) was born Vladimir Dukelsky, in Parfianovka, Russia where he went to school with George Balanchine. After arriving in New York, he worked on *Garrick Gaieties* for the Theatre Guild. He also wrote serious works under his birth name, although according to Alan Jay Lerner, "Duke proved to be more successful than Dukelsky".[20] He wrote revues with E. Y. Harburg (1896-1981) including *Walk a Little Faster* starring Beatrice Lillie in 1932 that featured the song "April in Paris".

Rudolph Friml (1879-1972) studied under Antonin Dvořák at the Conservatory in Prague. He visited the U.S. in 1902 as accompanist to Jan Kubelík before moving there in 1906. In 1912 he met music publisher Max Dreyfuss who encouraged him to write his first operetta, *Firefly*. He had a major hit in 1926 with *Rose-Marie*. "Friml's musical composition and improvisation never departed from the tradition that was his European musical heritage", writes Richard Kislan. "He detested the new music of syncopated rhythms and dismissed the songs of the modern composers as 'freakish, unmusical and exaggerated'. For him, melody blossomed under his fingers and rhythm would never be allowed to get out of control."[21]

Frederick (originally Friedrich) Loewe (1901-88) was born in Berlin to Austrian parents. His father Edmund Loewe played Prince Danilo in the first Berlin production of *The Merry Widow* and also starred in Oscar Straus's *The Chocolate Soldier*. "Fritz" is said to have studied piano in Berlin with Ferruccio Busoni (1866-1924) – who also taught Kurt Weill – and Eugene d'Albert (1864-1932)[22]. He came to the U.S. with his parents to do a show for David Belasco, but Edmund Loewe died during rehearsals. He played piano in a 1931 revival of *Die Fledermaus* on Broadway. After meeting Alan Jay Lerner in 1942, together they would write several of the most enduring Broadway musicals of all time, including *Brigadoon, My Fair Lady* and *Camelot*. "Fritz Loewe's musical sensibilities – unlike those of [George] Gershwin, [Jerome] Kern, [Harold] Arlen, [Frank] Loesser, [Arthur] Schwartz or [Vincent] Youmanns – were untouched by black music", says Lees. "They were entirely European. He did not immigrate to the United States until he was twenty-three, by which time his musical character was formed."[23] He died in 1988.

Sigmund Romberg (1887-1951) was born in Nagykanizsa, Hungary and studied in Vienna. He was sent to the U.S. by his parents in 1909 to discourage him from writing music. (Clearly Europeans didn't regard New York as any kind of cultural Mecca then.) He worked in a pencil factory for $7 a week and played in an orchestra and wrote dance tunes. In 1914, was hired by the Shubert Brothers as a staff composer, where he worked on fourteen musicals in just over two years. According to Alan Jay Lerner,

> "He had assembled over the years a library of all the great operas, operettas, *lieder* and orchestral works that had ever been written. He read them all carefully and made notes next to the hundreds and hundreds of orchestral and vocal parts. Perhaps it would only be four bars, but next to it he would write 'good baritone solo' or 'soprano'. He then kept a catalogue of all his notes. When the time came to sit down to write a score, if he were about to write a baritone solo, he would check his files for a 'good baritone solo', etcetera. Perhaps he would not use it verbatim, but it would give him a start. The wheeze around Broadway during the war was that Romberg's music was suffering because there were no German scores being shipped in."[24]

Richard Kislan says that Romberg

> "understood the stage... [He] saw in operetta a stage medium whose potential for the evocation of deep feeling increased in proportion to the skilful addition of great music... [He] became the most celebrated American

operetta composer to speak out on the importance of the book... Romberg knew that great music in the theater without acceptable dramatic context wastes away or overwhelms the drama altogether. Consequently, he believed it to be his duty to create a complete score with mutually agreed-upon allegiance to the story well before the casting and rehearsal period."[25]

Kurt Weill is one of the most obvious examples of an immigrant coming to Broadway with a pre-existing reputation in the musical theatre. Some critics are divided over Weill's work after he went to New York. Former literature director of the Arts Council of Great Britain Charles Osbourne (1927-2017) says that in New York "Weill became more relaxed politically. In Berlin he would never have considered writing for the established bourgeois theatre. In New York, however, he began to understand the lure of Broadway, and for a time he succumbed to it."[26] (By "for a time", we should read "for the rest of his life".) Osbourne calls *Knickerbocker Holiday* "a Broadway musical... a superior Broadway musical, certainly... but a Broadway show nevertheless." With *Lady in the Dark*, "his capitulation was complete."

That is certainly a fashionable view, but not entirely an accurate one. In Berlin, Weill contacted his publisher frequently to ensure that his music was being played in all the top dance halls. Brecht may have been a Marxist, but Weill's politics were far more nuanced. His biographer Foster Hirsch says, "Weill's American work, judged as compositions for the theatre, is of a quality that is comparable to his European catalogue, and is arguably more diverse."[27]

Other American-born songwriters acknowledge European influences. As a teenager, Jerome Kern (whose father was German) studied in Heidelberg, Germany. "Kern had his musical roots in the fertile Middle European and English school of operetta-writing", says Richard Rodgers, "and amalgamated it with everything that was fresh in the American scene to give us something wonderfully new and clear in music-writing."[28]

Ira Gershwin acknowledges a debt to W.S. Gilbert. "Gilbert was the greatest, no question of that. If he were alive today, he'd be doing good musical-comedy songs."[29] In London, Ira and his brother George contributed to a 1924 revue called *Primrose*, co-produced by George Grossmith Jr.(1874-1935), whose father George Grossmith Sr. (1847-1912) had starred in many of Gilbert and Sullivan's productions, including the original *HMS Pinafore* and *The Mikado* (as Ko-ko). *Primrose* included a song in four-part harmony called "Four Little Sirens We" that parodied Gilbert's "Three Little Maids from School". Grossmith Jr. would also work with Jerome Kern.

The final triumph of Broadway as the primary centre for musical theatre following the Second World War happened for a number of reasons. Since many of the leading composers of European musicals were Jewish (and most of those who weren't staunchly opposed Fascism), there was an exodus of talent, and much of it went to either New York (Kurt Weill) or Hollywood (Friederich Holländer). In England, Vivian Ellis (1903-96) and Ivor Novello (1893-1951) continued to ply their trade, but began to look increasingly tired and old-fashioned next to the more brash work that was coming out of New York. And, of course, in 1943 the operetta world of Oscar Hammerstein II (1895-1960) met the musical comedy world of Richard Rodgers (1902-79), and we've never looked back since.

Thus began what is often referred to as the golden age of Broadway. Nelles Van Loon was a pupil of Lehman Engel, whom he said "believed in a golden age of the American Musical theatre starting roughly with *Show Boat* and continuing through to the best work of Steven Sondheim after which it lost itself somehow."[30] While the social and technological changes of the post-war period brought about a widening gap between musical theatre and popular music, Broadway continued in the evolutionary path that it had begun with *Show Boat* in 1927. However, the seeds of its decline (in influence, if not in quality) had already set in. Whereas popular music had, with the invention of magnetic tape, become something that could happen any time and in any place, the American musical was still firmly centred in New York. Only by touring, or being produced by regional stock companies (or adapted into films) could its impact spread beyond New York. And, as mid-westerners like to say, New York is *not* America.

Entr'acte: A New World Order

The New World(s)

In the first "Act" I have explained how musical theatre developed out of opera in Europe, was influenced by cabaret, vaudeville and music hall, then migrated to New York. It suffered a calamity at the hands of Hitler, and was usurped by the new kid on the block.

It is in Act II, the post-war period, that there was a seismic shift in the popular music industry with the birth of rock. One of the other after-effects of Word War II was the final dissolution of all of the older European empires, especially those of France and Great Britain. With that came a cultural awakening in the former colonies, and a new sense of national identity. There was a sense that smaller countries, long hidden in the shadows of the great powers, were entitled to speak to themselves and to the world in their own voices.

I experienced this "renaissance" myself in my native Canada. After the war, we Canadians gained our own citizenship (1947) and our own flag (1965). The centennial of confederation in 1967, which culminated in Expo '67 in Montreal, awakened a new interest in Canadian culture that is continuing to unfold.

The other countries I have explored tell, to varying extents, similar stories. Just as the Americans declared their independence from European operettas, so are Australians, Canadians and others attempting to break free from the Broadway and West End hegemonies. Some, like South Africa, have overcome oppressive regimes and are just beginning to flower. Other countries such as Japan and Argentina have long held their own traditions. Even the European "motherlands" are slowly returning to musical life. As the economic centre of gravity inexorably shifts towards Asia, countries like Korea, Singapore, the Philippines and China are entering the field. Even in "old" Europe, musical theatre began to spring back to life in places like Italy, Greece and Spain.

At this point, my analysis becomes largely speculative. It is unfinished. In some cases, even "unbegun". I am looking for the seeds that can be planted and watered; the foundations upon which an indigenous musical theatre form might be built. As indicated in the "overture", this is a search for signs of life. Nobody can say with certainty which "seeds" will grow. What we can do is look at the "soil conditions". My belief is that a unique culture exists in every country, but not all have learned how to articulate it. Some countries, such as Japan, Canada, Australia and Argentina, have at least some history with the musical theatre form. Others, like Korea and Singapore, are almost entirely new to the game. The challenges and obstacles they face are vast. This is not so much a survey of past accomplishments as an anticipation of future potential. In most cases, there is not yet a canon of work to be examined. What there is, I believe, is a common principle: each is trying to play to the world by firstly playing to its own audience.

Before we jump into Act II and the new developments by the old world's cultural "offspring", I want to talk about some of the factors that have helped to bring about this new world order.

Between the Wars

Between the old world and the new, between the "parents" and the "offspring", there is a now largely forgotten world in transition in which some appeared to be clinging to something old – i.e., "operetta" – and those who appeared to be trying to develop something new – i.e., "musical comedy". I say "appeared" because in fact the future lay not in the triumph of "new" versus "old" but, as with Rodgers and Hammerstein, in finding ways of accommodating and even merging the best of both. (This continues to hold true today.)

One figure who often seems to get lost in this shuffle is poor old Ivor Novello (1893-1951). The Grove's Dictionary of Music and Musicians claims he was, "until the advent of Andrew Lloyd Webber, the 20th-century's most consistently successful composer of British musicals"[1]. The Welsh-born composer, playwright, actor and all-round polymath first gained fame as the composer of "Keep the Home Fires Burning" (1914) and later as Britain's leading silent movie actor, whose films include Alfred Hitchcock's *The Lodger*. In the 1920s he wrote and starred in a string of very popular West End non-musical stage plays including *A Symphony in Two Flats* and *The Truth Game* which successfully transferred to Broadway. During a brief interlude in Hollywood, he wrote the dialogue for the first *Tarzan* film, but soon returned to London. From then until his death in 1951 he was responsible for an unprecedented string of successful plays and musicals, yet at the end of the war, the English culture changed for good, and it seemed there may no longer be a place for the kind of gentility that he represented. If the Strand theatre (in which he lived for most of his life in an upstairs flat) had not been renamed for him in 2005, he would be almost completely forgotten. Why?

Ivor Novello

Some of the problems are economic. For *Glamorous Night*, his first full-scale operetta, he asked for a forty piece orchestra, and a cast of one hundred and twenty (which you could get away with then). Director and choreographer Stewart Nicholls, who staged a recent revival of Novello's *Gay's the Word* at London's Finborough Theatre says, "From a contemporary perspective, there are four fundamental problems with Novello's shows: the books do not stand up today, and they require a leading man of great presence, a strong operatic soprano as the female lead, as well as expensive scenic effects."[2] Playwright Julian Fellowes, who featured Novello as a character in his screenplay for *Gosford Park* adds, "His librettos are really not suitable to this generation. They are very sentimental. They have very little narrative. They're not very funny. They're not witty. It's mainly some wretched princess sobbing away on a clifftop."[3] Fellowes doesn't believe any Novello shows could be revived professionally unless their librettos were extensively reworked, which the Novello estate shows no interest in doing. "The other problem with the scores: they are almost all ballads."

Even for its time, much of Novello's music was considered old-fashioned. When a 1917 show called *Arlette* to which he had contributed some songs was revived on tour two decades later, he found that the musical director had beefed up the show with more modern numbers. The revived show, now called *How Do, Princess* was a flop, but the point was not lost. In his next show *Careless Rapture*, Novello conceded the need for at least some modernity in the music claiming, "I am sort of betwixt and between; if there was a hymn that was neither ancient nor modern, it would be me."[4] Drama critic Philip Hope-Wallace (1911-79) called him "a master of the shameless cliché."[5]

Novello's best-remembered musical *The Dancing Years* was inspired by an account given by a friend who had visited a music shop in Vienna in the late 1930s where he was unable to find any records of any Jewish composers.

"It occurred to me to wonder what would have happened to me if, as a composer of popular music, I had also been Viennese and of Jewish descent."[6] Ironically, early productions of this show were required to play down this political content in a vain attempt by the Chamberlain government to placate the Nazis.

In the post-war period, even Novello's friend the critic James Agate (1877-1947) warned him against trying another old-fashioned operetta. "They won't like it", he said. "You will find that even a first-class cast, charming music, and a good plot won't save the show. What the modern generation apparently wants is plenty of hot music and transatlantic rhythm."[7] He didn't listen, and in his lifetime at least, he got away with it. To Novello, the American musical was "teaching us to defy convention in our own way... I have always tried in everything I have written to appeal first to the heart... The only thing that remains constant is an emotional quality that you can't nationalise."[8]

It's difficult to gain an accurate representation of Novello from his contemporary biographers due to the attitudes prevelant at the time. Peter Noble's hagiography *Ivor Novello – Man of the Theatre*, the first book to appear on the subject, quotes Novello as saying "My one regret is that I have never married, for I would love to have a family. Now I am too set in my ways to attempt marriage and much too difficult to live with."[9] Of course, what they could not say in 1951 was that his partner of thirty-five years' standing was Robert "Bobbie" Andrews (1895-1976), an actor who appeared in many of Novello's plays and musicals.

Theatre historian W. J. MacQueen-Pope (1888-1960) wrote, "Future stage historians will assign to Ivor Novello a most important position in the theatre of the middle twentieth century. For a time when, through no fault of its own, inspiration and achievement languished under the drain of two world wars, Ivor Novello was there to keep the flag flying, to keep the home fires burning, and to give distinction, quality, and talent to the stage, and joyous, happy memories to millions of playgoers."[10] Author Adrian Wright says, "His presence brought not only the voice, the manner, the profile, the accumulated reputations of brilliant boy composer, film star, playwright, but a sense of taste. A visit to a Novello musical guaranteed spectacle and music, but Novello's presence brought in its train the assurance that he was a man who understood not only spectacle and music but poetry and beauty, the ballet, the opera – a man who in some way was putting his audience in touch with the higher arts. He was not doing so, but there is the hint of that trick being played."[11] And a "trick" is evidently what it was: Novello died during the run of *King's Rhapsody*, in which he starred. After his understudy took over the role, business quickly fell off. A 1978 television production of *The Dancing Years* seems to have been his last professional breath.

Noël Coward also enjoyed success with *Bittersweet*, his 1929 operetta, but even he did not enjoy the kind of consistency that his friend Novello did. The English operetta form had one final gasp with *Bless the Bride* in 1947 with music by Vivian Ellis (1903-96) and a libretto by Sir Alan Patrick Herbert (1890-1971) which appeared at the time to hold its own against *Oklahoma* and *Annie Get Your Gun*.

While operettas by Gilbert and Sullivan, Offenbach and Strauss are still revived professionally, sadly the works of Ivor Novello are not. Although his songs are occasionally heard in concert and cabaret, there has not been a major professional revival of a Novello show in more than thirty years. His name lives on in the Ivor Novello Award, given by the British Academy of Songwriters, Composers and Authors to the composer of the year's best pop song.

In the United States, there were native artists

striving to create a truly native musical. According to musical theatre historian Gerald Bordman (1931-2011), "The leader in this field was unquestionably George M. Cohan."[12] Musically they couldn't be more different: Novello was quasi-operatic, Cohan (1878-1942) was pure Tin Pan Alley, just one generation away from Stephen Foster. They are, in a microcosm, an example of the difference between British and American musical theatre of the period. Both were of Celtic ancestry: Novello was Welsh born (his real surname was Davies) and Cohan was of Irish descent (his name had originally been Keohane). Both had written hit songs from World War I that are still with us: (in Cohan's case it was "Over There"). Like Novello, Cohan was also known as an actor, a producer, a non-musical playwright and above all as a force of nature. Joining his family's vaudeville act "The Four Cohans" and with virtually no formal education, he began writing sketches and eventually left vaudeville for Broadway. According to American theatre critic Ward Morehouse (1895-1966), he "had a crazy dance, a kangaroo walk and nasal, out-one-corner-of-the-mouth talk; he had a giggle, a grimace and a wagging finger. He came into the theater as a kid of the streets, moved right in, and won the homage of millions."[13] Heywood Broun (1888-1939) of the New York *World-Telegram* called him "almost a symbol of brash violence in theatrical entertainment."[14] American historian Laurence Bergreen (1950-) says, "The key to Cohan's larger-than-life reputation lay with his loudly proclaimed patriotism. Many of his best-known shows and songs illustrated patriotic themes and reveled in heartfelt – if shameless – flag waving."[15] Some of this hyper-patriotism may have stemmed from his Irish-American roots, where he had to fight to be accepted as an equal with the Anglo-Saxon mainstream. (This was the era of "No Irish, No Blacks, No

George M. Cohan

Dogs")

Cohan's writing, if not his acting, fell out of favour with the public long before his passing. He was deemed to be old-fashioned. He claimed, "You have to give them filth these days or it's no good."[16] Turning more and more to acting in other people's shows, he still received acclaim, if not satisfaction.

When he starred in *I'd Rather Be Right*, with a book by George S. Kaufman and Moss Hart and a score by Richard Rodgers and Lorenz Hart, he was openly resentful of the younger songwriting team, referring to them as "Gilbert and Sullivan". "His own school of melody was not theirs," says Morehouse, "and he was inclined to think of them as upstarts in a game he had mastered when they were children – or before they were born... frequently saying, 'Tell Gilbert & Sullivan to run over to the hotel and write a better song'."[17]

Novello and Cohan's two songs from World War I provide us with an opportunity to compare and contrast these two writers. Novello's "Keep the Home Fires Burning", which was originally published in 1914 as "Till the Boys Come Home", has lyrics by Lena Guilbert Ford (1870-1918), an American expatriate who had opened her home to care for British soldiers. Its words are plaintive, reflecting public awareness of the danger that their soldiers were facing:

> Let no tears add to their hardships
> As the soldiers pass along,
> And although your heart is breaking,
> Make it sing this cheery song:
> Keep the home fires burning,
> While your hearts are yearning.
> Though your lads are far away
> They dream of home.

On the other hand, "Over There", to which Cohan

wrote both music and lyrics, is nothing more than a collection of jingoistic slogans designed to appeal to a patriotic spirit and recruit potential soldiers:

> Johnny, get your gun, get your gun, get your gun.
> Take it on the run, on the run, on the run.
> Hear them calling you and me,
> Every Son of Liberty…
> Over there, over there,
> Send the word, send the word over there
> That the Yanks are coming, the Yanks are coming
> The drums rum-tumming everywhere.
> So prepare, say a prayer,
> Send the word, send the word to beware –
> We'll be over, we're coming over,
> And we won't come back till it's over, over there.

They even gave him a special Congressional Medal for it. Of course the British response was "over-paid, over-sexed and over here". Even recently, it has annoyed British audiences as the jingle for the "Go-Compare" insurance commercials. While other individual Cohan songs have survived – "It's a Grand Old Flag", "Give My Regards to Broadway"[18], his main contribution to the American musical theatre was the introduction of a brashness which was adopted by later songwriters, including Irving Berlin, to whom he was a mentor. "To Berlin", says Bergreen, "Cohan incarnated American show business: hard sell and soft shoe, emotional, frenetic and relentlessly cocky."[19] One must remember that when "Give My Regards to Broadway" was written in 1904, Broadway was not yet the international theatre capital that it later became, and the United States was not yet a world superpower.

The problem is, when you're there first, everyone who comes after improves on it. Irving Berlin, Jerome Kern, George Gershwin and even Rogers and Hart took Cohan's idea and built on it to the point that the original no longer stands up. Like Novello, Cohan never wrote any shows that are currently revivable in their original form. (The late David Cassidy starred in an ill-fated attempt to revive *Little Johnny Jones* on tour in 1982.)

While Novello was universally loved, Cohan loved his friends and they loved him back; those whom were not his friends often hated him. One person who could not be considered a Cohan fan was Broadway conductor Lehman Engel. "He did send 'our boys' into World War I with 'Over There' on their needlessly dying lips, and Congress rewarded him with a decoration and royalties poured lavishly into his bank account. He was also regarded as an impossibly difficult man to work for and with, a selfish tightwad and a supreme egotist. He also – almost solely – held out against the formation of Actors' Equity (the actors' union) and never did relent or change his opinion as long as he lived."[20]

George M. Cohan's legacy, though, was Broadway itself. "The Man Who Owned Broadway" created much of the mythology upon which the American musical is based. For this reason, he is the only artist – either actor or writer – to be honoured with a statue in Times Square, New York.

The Rock 'n' Roll Syndrome

The arrival of rock music affected musical theatre – and the rest of popular culture – in much the same way that the arrival of a meteor affected the dinosaurs. Everything that came before was swept aside. For popular music, the date was 9 July 1955, when Bill Haley (1925-81)'s "Rock Around the Clock" hit number one on the *Billboard* charts. Some music critics actually cite this as the date when popular music began – apparently dismissing Irving Berlin and Cole Porter entirely.

Of course, it's all nonsense. The Beach Boys' Brian Wilson (1942-) says, "I've always loved George Gershwin. The earliest music I remember hearing is 'Rhapsody in Blue'"[1], while Paul McCartney (1942-) grew up with ambitions to be the next Cole Porter, and his company owns the publishing rights to works by Frank Loesser (1910-69), Jerry Herman (1931-), Meredith Willson (1902-84) (the Beatles once recorded Willson's "'Til There Was You") and Charles Strouse (1928-). In fact, both have released albums that are love letters to the classic American songbook: McCartney's 2012 CD *Kisses on the Bottom* and Wilson's 2010 release *Brian Wilson Reimagines Gershwin*. These pre-baby-boomers grew up in the era of Tin Pan Alley. John Lennon (1940-80) could talk about Buddy Holly, but Hoagy Carmichael (1899-1981) was part of the mix too, as was a whole raft of British folk-music and music hall tradition.

Not so for the generation that followed them. Nowadays, the pop music world's approach to Tin Pan Alley and Broadway resembles the way Christian Creationists rationalise the existence of dinosaur skeletons: they belonged to a mythical earlier world, if indeed they existed at all. For folk music to be heard, it had to be called folk-rock. For jazz, it had to be fusion. So fundamental was the post-war demographic shift for the record buying public that everything without a rock beat was marginalised, if not entirely obliterated. In the theatre, in the post-*Hair* world, *New York Times* critic Clive Barnes

(1927-2008) declared that all future musicals would need to be like *Hair*.[2] He was wrong, but Charles Strouse, to his regret, took him at his word and used rock rythms in *Applause*.

A number of forces came together to create this meteor: some were economic, some technological. The invention of magnetic tape meant that music could be recorded anywhere, not just in the major studios. (Nowadays, music software on computers have brought recording even closer to home.) In the U.S., the establishment of Broadcast Music Inc. (BMI) in the 1940s broke the monopoly of ASCAP on the licensing of music on the airwaves. (The first was controlled by the songwriters and publishers who were concentrated in New York; the second were on the other side of the equation: broadcasters across the U.S.) These two developments brought about a change in whose songs were being sung. Songs about "hillbillies" were now being written by hillbillies, not New York songsmiths. Nashville was on the rise. Impresario Billy Rose (1899-1966) said in 1956, "Not only are most of the BMI songs junk, but in many cases they are obscene junk pretty much on a level with dirty comic magazines… Today it is a set of untalented twitchers and twisters whose appeal is largely to the zootsuiter and the juvenile delinquent."[3] Richard Rodgers was slightly more polite: "Musically, it's repetitive; I don't know why it has to go on for 32 bars in the same way; even the chord structures are '1-5-4-5-1'; it seems to me you could try something else every now and then."[4]

Even before this, there was a kind of class distinction between Tin Pan Alley and Broadway. The former, with songs like "Three Little Fishies (Boop Boop Diddum)", "Flat Foot Floogie (with a Floy Floy)[5]" and "Mairzy Doats" aimed for a less sophisticated audience than the works of, say, Cole Porter. Although Tin Pan Alley briefly morphed into the "Brill building" set with writers like Jeff Barry (1938-), Carole King (1942-)/Gerry Goffin (1939-2014) and Burt Bacharach (1928-)/Hal David (1921-

2012), in the post-Beatles era, most singers were expected to write their own songs. This meant that song writing – and especially lyric writing – became a less specialised art. Since the music tended to be written by guitar players who didn't read music, it seldom existed in a precise enough form to be concerned with marrying individual words to individual notes. When the songwriter is also the performer, it becomes easy to simply shoehorn the words into the melody, rather than carefully crafting the metre to the rhythm or the open vowel to the whole note. Lyrics became, at best, sung poetry (fraught with meaning, but lacking in musicality) and at worst, doggerel.

This has affected the music as well. "At least 150 years ago", says composer Howard Goodall, "the very slowness of making a notated score of a piece of music meant that the creator had to live with it and think about it for a period of time before it was released to the world."[6]

The old guard certainly had their backs up. Tom Lehrer (1928-) famously lumped rock and roll in with "other children's records"[7]. As English pop music historian Ian Whitcomb (1941-)(himself a one-time rock star) says, "It was a cry from the heart, not the pocket-book. Long-held deep beliefs of a civilized way of life were being assaulted by hillbilly songs of fightin', boozin', cheatin'; by rhythm and blues songs about getting' loaded, wantin' a bow-legged woman and rockin' all night long. But worst of all was assault by rock 'n' roll noise, which when coherent seemed to be solely concerned with sex, violence and our own people. All those years of gradual growing away from crude ragtime and jazz towards a disciplined fine art of reticence (with maybe hints of suggestion) all wiped out by our wives and children leaping about to Chuck Berry on the phonograph!"[8]

"Rock had its own sophistication, rhythmic and street-wise, but its shallower harmonic well has never provided even its best songwriters with the abundance of great melodies that Gershwin poured forth in less than two decades of work", argues singer-songwriter Paul Simon (1941-). "Rock critics have consistently derided orchestral or symphonic fusions as pretentious and bourgeois, while exalting the nihilism of punk and alternative bands as the best way to purify and revitalize rock and roll. Perhaps the deeply ingrained oral tradition in rock has left an indelible mark on the psyche of its musicians: beware the written form, the manuscript paper with notes, clefs and musical direction in Italian. It's a credo of rock that raw is true, yet in the adjacent world of jazz no such constraints hinder its composers."[9]

Somewhere along the line we lost Mozart's (and Leonard Bernstein's and Kurt Weill's) notion of elevating the public's taste.[10]

Pop music became – in theory – more democratic. Kids got together in their parents' basements and garages and formed rock bands. They made demo tapes on portable tape recorders. The new music acts came from the working class areas of Memphis, Detroit and Liverpool. On the other hand, the new generation of Broadway writers came from privileged backgrounds. Stephen Sondheim's family owned a major garment manufacturer, while Andrew Lloyd Webber's father was the head of the London College of Music. The musical – which was born alongside democracy – had lost its common touch. Still, it took a few years for Broadway to lose its edge.

In Britain, at around the same time, a similar shift occurred in the legitimate theatre. When John Osborne (1929-1994)'s *Look Back in Anger* opened, it spelled the end for the "well-made plays" of Noël Coward (1899-1973), J.B. Priestly (1894-1984) and Terrence Rattigan (1911-77). However, since it tended to appeal to an older and wealthier audience, the "well-made" musical continued to dominate on Broadway for at least another decade. Alan Jay Lerner said, "As a theatre-goer and theatre lover I somehow cannot find it in my heart to rebel against a well-made play. The great plays of history have usually been splendidly constructed, most often with whopping good parts, and both author and audience have gone home quite contented."[11] Perhaps we need to rid ourselves of the notion that every new thing is there to replace whatever came before it, rather than to augment it.

Until the mid-1960s, Broadway cast recordings were a major force in the record industry. Then, when rock and roll came on the scene, a new youth market was discovered, and the "singles" charts were geared toward transistor radios, meaning that the limitations of guitar-based music were confounded by poor sound reproduction. (The arrival of hi-fi only partly mitigated this; the damage had been done. Rather than allowing for subtlety, it simply made the floor vibrate.) Instead of appealing to a smaller group of people with a lot of money to spend, they began to target an enormous group with pocket money. It wasn't so much that the same people changed their tastes as that they were usurped by a new, younger market and the record companies turned to them, largely to the exclusion of all others. Record stores now had youthful employees with an extensive knowledge of the rock world and little or no knowledge of anything else. The latest music was played in-store at high volumes, and the other clientele gradually fell (or were driven) away.

I've never entirely bought into the whole 1960s myth. (I was there, and I *do* remember it.) The generation that preached peace and love hurled their music as an offensive weapon. For me, the era of great music and radical politics was the 1930s, when you had Gershwin, Ellington and Porter. Rather than being forced against their will to fight Communism in Korea and Viet Nam, young men were being *prevented* from fighting against Fascism in Spain. I know of no more effective protest song than E. Y. Harburg and Jay Gorney (1894-1990)'s "Brother, Can You Spare a Dime?", written for the 1932 Broadway revue *Americana*. (There were attempts by Republicans to ban it as anti-capitalist propaganda.)

> Once I built a railroad,
> I made it run
> Made it race against time
> Once I built a railroad,
> Now it's done
> Brother, can you spare a dime?[12]

The '60s were a time of rebellion; of drugs, sex, peace and social justice. Later on, that generation would say, "Weren't we silly", and then dump the peace and justice and keep the drugs and sex. Small wonder that they grew up to become the neo-conservatives of the nineties, favouring free markets and general hedonism with the odd military intervention thrown in. The irony is that John Osborne became a right-winger, whereas J.B. Priestly remained a socialist. *Easy Rider* actor Dennis Hopper (1936-2010) was a life-long Republican. Rodgers and Hammerstein were outspoken liberals. Andrew Lloyd Webber and Tim Rice are not. Who's a rebel now?

I'm not saying that the rock revolution was entirely bogus. But when I saw the British film *The Boat that Rocked*, I was nauseated by what a self-absorbed lot they all were. I can say this, because it is my own generation that I'm talking about. The film dealt with the explosion of pirate radio stations in Britain in the 1960s, when the BBC confined rock and pop music to one weekly programme. In the end, the film triumphantly claims victory when the British airwaves become overwhelmed by this revolution. What it doesn't say is that the poles were reversed, and the other non-rock forms were ghettoised. If you didn't buy into this totalitarian regime, you were written off as "square". (People with an intimate knowledge of only their own generation's music were now "broad-minded", whereas those with a wider spectrum, who knew very well that 90% of what they were hearing would inevitably be consigned to some future rubbish bin, were "narrow-minded".) When I hear people saying that musical theatre should be embracing this totalitarian culture, it reminds me of a 1985 film called *The Coca-Cola Kid* in which an American executive is sent to investigate a small Australian out-back who have had the temerity to say "no" to Coca-Cola.

That said, I should, for the purposes of full disclosure, state what my own relationship with 1960s pop and rock has been. I feel I expressed it best in the following item which appeared originally in *Musical Stages* magazine under the title "An Epiphany":

> I am undone.
>
> For twenty years, I have dedicated myself heart and soul to writing musical theatre. Not campy gags either, but sophisticated, dramatic stuff. I've studied the greats - Sondheim, Gershwin, Hammerstein - and have entered into erudite discussions of the under-appreciated works of Schmidt and Jones. My record collection includes the works of Brecht and Weill sung in the original German by Lotte Lenya. So why did I risk chucking it all by exposing my dark secret?
>
> It happened by accident. As I felt myself being sucked inexorably into the vortex of cyberspace, I stumbled on a website that would draw me back into my deep and distant past, and force me to confront the truth. My formative influence was not *Anyone Can Whistle*. Nor was it *Candide*. Nor *Porgy and Bess*. It was "Sugar, Sugar" by The Archies.
>
> Yes, I'm out of the closet now. As an eleven-year-old, I gave hours of pleasure to my family as I played that song over and over again, at least twenty times a day. Stigmatised by some as "bubble gum" pop, it was, for me, an act of open rebellion. Not "Born To Be Wild" so much as Born to be Reviled. My idolatry of a pop group whose only public face was as a semi-animated cartoon show in the ghetto of Saturday morning TV certainly set me apart.
>
> Eventually, I put all this behind me, moving on to the concerns of underscoring the nuances of

subtext. Within ten years, the only musical impression the name "Sugar" would conjure up was in the first Broadway incarnation of *Some Like It Hot*. The truth was safely buried - until I stumbled upon www.rondante.com. Suddenly I found myself holding information that, thirty years earlier, I would have climbed over the bodies of old ladies to obtain – such as, who they really were. I could now rejoice in the knowledge that among those clapping their hands and exclaiming "Honey, honey" were Ray "Everything is Beautiful" Stevens and Ellie "Leader of the Pack" Greenwich. And guitarist Hugh McCracken would later grace albums by both John and Paul (of the Beatles - you've heard of them?) Or that the female voice claiming "I'm gonna make your life so sweet" was Toni Wine, who wrote "Groovy Kind of Love". I comforted myself in the knowledge that lead singer Ron Dante would later produce *Ain't Misbehavin'* on Broadway.

I briefly explored the possibility of auctioning my old Archies albums on Ebay as collectors' items. Then I inspected them. With a signal-to-noise ratio of two-to-one, "Sugar, Sugar" came out sounding like "Foofah, ah funny funny..." amid the snap crackle pop of those twenty times a day airings.

Now as I listen to the mp3 files downloaded from the website, I find myself thinking – "Ah, that's how you write a hook song!" Jeff Barry may not have been Larry Hart, but he knew how to get his tunes lodged in your brain.

Now a slightly worrying thought occurs to me. As I struggle to champion a return to melody on the musical stage, is it possible that the bubblegum pop of my youth had a lasting impact?

There go my chances of ever being invited to join the Mercury Workshop.[13]

At least, on the last point, I was proven wrong: I have been a member of what is now Mercury Musical Developments since 2003. Archies lead singer Ron Dante (1945-) himself may have thought this vignette "the funniest I have ever received about my recording of 'Sugar, Sugar'"[14], but I was being serious.

So how does rock (and all the other forms that followed after it) fit in to the musical theatre scheme of things? In 1974, the late choreographer and director Gower Champion (*Bye Bye Birdie*, *Hello, Dolly!*) said, "It's so damned ironic. There's been this incredible proliferation of music, but not one note of it has made it to the Broadway stage. If Joni Mitchell or Carly Simon could only be persuaded to write for the theatre, that would be the fresh input the theatre needs. But those people don't need the hassles, the incredible complications of the theatre."[15] Philip Hedley, former artistic director of London's Theatre Royal Stratford East argues ruefully that *Hair*, the first successful rock musical on Broadway, didn't appear until fourteen years after "Rock Around the Clock" hit the airwaves. Of course, *Hair* wasn't the first musical to employ rock idioms – *Bye Bye Birdie* had done that eight years previously (albeit in a satirical sense), and London's *Expresso-Bongo* was even earlier than that.

In fact, even in the so-called "golden age" of Broadway, few successful musicals drew on just one style, form or fashion. If there were any "ragtime musicals", "jazz musicals" or "big band musicals", they have long been forgotten. Lehman Engel says, "Ragtime is a style or vocabulary, not an all-inclusive language."[16] Even Scott Joplin's *Treemonisha* cannot be considered a "ragtime opera". Engel says the same for jazz and rock – they can be employed as styles, but are not complete forms in themselves.

Shows like *A Chorus Line* and *Company* have incorporated rock music without truly being "rock musicals". "I only use rock where I think it's emotionally justified", Stephen Sondheim said in 1970. "Too many people use it because it's the contemporary sound. There's a mystique about rock that it's an arcane[17] language. One of its salient features is the freedom of form, which I think is terrific."[18] Lehman Engel said, "I am not against rock as such but only against the fact that it is born of 'freedom' more rigid and limiting than anything that ever before existed in music."[19] Mark N. Grant, in *The Rise and Fall of the Broadway Musical*, claims that "the theatre loses richness and power as a narrative and literary medium when it panders to the audience before it serves the play. Such a theatre may well generate a carnal excitement, but it cannot function as an evoker of Aristotelian pity and terror. Paradoxically, heightened engagement of sensation and rhythm alienates the theatregoer from a true emotional engagement."[20]

"Rock 'n' Roll", says American cultural observer John Lahr, "put a premium on energy, not expertise".[21] Traditional musical theatre writing thrives on expertise. Jim Betts, the former artistic director of Toronto's Script Lab once said to me, "With what I've heard recently of the generation of Canadian musical theatre writers that came after the Lehman Engel era, the traditional 'craft' is not something that seems very important any more. I think that's a shame."[22]

Can the craft of the classic Broadway musical be applied to contemporary musical forms – i.e., rock, hip-hop? Of course it can, if people demand it. When Cole Porter was writing, people demanded smart rhymes. Nowadays, pop writers not only aren't fussy about perfect rhymes, they sometimes even actively avoid them, thinking that they sound pretentious. To director Scott Miller, Artistic Director of New Line Theatre, "insistence on perfect rhyming and scansion seems silly in the age of rock and roll. Old school theatre music, including the music of Stephen Sondheim, is about order and control. Rock and roll is about freedom and anarchy. If every rhyme in *Rent* was perfect, it wouldn't quite feel right. If every line scanned perfectly, it would seem considerably less authentic."[23]

However, in the theatre, the audience is lost if they can't understand the lyric the first time they hear it. They can't study the words on the back of a record sleeve. Accurate rhyming helps the listener to anticipate the word, thus aiding clarity. It may be possible that this doesn't go along with the rock and roll ethos. If, as Lahr suggests, rock emphasises energy over expertise, then it would follow logically that this fine technical craft of lyric writing, which I tend to compare to a well-made piece of woodwork in which the nails are invisible, would be abandoned as well.

In the late seventies – early eighties, a shift occurred in musical theatre, similar to the one that had already overtaken pop music (although not as all-consuming). As a new generation began to grasp musical theatre, the values changed. *Jesus Christ Superstar* begot *Les Misérables*, and *Hair* begot *Rent, Spring Awakening* and *Next to Normal*, and the theatrical world hasn't been the same since. London's stage schools began turning out Michael Ball and Frances Rufelle clones. The pop power ballad became, in the theatre, an overwrought catharsis in which sheer volume was equated with emotional intensity. André Previn complains that musicals have "degenerated into the screeching and wailing of the adolescent pop stars of the week, leering with teenage concupiscence and flashing their pimples."[24]

Shows like *The Producers* and *The Drowsy Chaperone* seemed to be a nostalgic counter-attack. The students of Lehman Engel adopted a "if you can't join 'em, beat 'em" tactic, becoming more esoteric, with mixed success. Others struggled to create a "contemporary" musical – *Rent, Spring Awakening* – evidently equating "contemporary" with "under thirty", as if youth culture were somehow under-represented. Musical theatre became polarised between the Sondheim and Lloyd Webber camps – or, perhaps more accurately, between traditional Broadway and something that had not quite defined itself.

But let's be honest. Musical theatre writers are a snobbish lot. The accuracy of our rhyming has become a demarcation point that places us on a higher plain than those untutored, boorish pop writers. That and the fact that most pop musicians wouldn't know a music score from hieroglyphics allows us to believe we can bar the great unwashed from our hallowed halls. (One further bit of disclosure is necessary at this point: I *can* read music. What I *can't* do is play any instrument proficiently.)

Therefore, part Sondheim, part "Sugar, Sugar", I am caught between two poles. I share the anguish of those who long to preserve the craft of the "traditional" musical theatre. I also understand how staid those old musicals seemed to me as a youth. I can remember the excitement when my sister's high school did *Bye Bye Birdie* in the late 1960s. (It didn't hurt that none other than Chita Riveira (1933-) came out to coach the cast.) This was a show with a contemporary feel – and with rock 'n' roll. The following year, my sister groaned when she learned that they would be doing a really corny, old-fashioned 1940s style show – *Guys and Dolls*. Looking back on it, which show seems dated now?

Universality Part 1:
"Do They Understand This Show in America? It's So Japanese!"

Before I begin to talk about the musicals that have been springing up in diverse places, from Sydney to Seoul and from Toronto to Tokyo, I need to pose the question, "What is meant by universality?" What does it mean when some people say that the best musicals have "universal appeal"? Does it mean that they will be perceived the same way, whether they are playing in New York, London or Madagascar?

"Certain musicals play better within their own country than outside", says London producer Sir Cameron Mackintosh. "*Guys and Dolls* has always proved to be the longest running musical in New York when it is revived, whereas in England it would be *Joseph* [*and the Amazing Technicolor Dreamcoat*], *Oliver!* and *My Fair Lady*. *A Chorus Line* and *Hello, Dolly!* are two of the longest running musicals of all time in New York, yet only managed to run a couple of years in London, whereas *Fiddler on the Roof*, *Phantom* [*of the Opera*], *Les Misérables* and *Cats* have proved to be universal long runners. Inevitably, some shows play better in major cities rather than out of town, and occasionally vice versa."[1]

While this book is primarily about indigenous musical theatre outside of New York and London, I believe it's also important to look at how Broadway and West End shows are perceived outside of their natural habitat. What makes a musical universal? Why is it that some musicals play successfully all over the world, when others don't? Obviously, in purely commercial terms, it is desirable for a musical to be a success in all the key markets. But we've already seen that many fine French and German musicals failed to make the transition into English. Also, an Australian political satire such as *Keating* tackles a subject that would be virtually unknown outside of its native country. Does that make it less valid? Just because a show doesn't work globally, does that mean it isn't good?

When *Fiddler on the Roof* opened in Japan for the first time, producer Kazuo Kikuta (1908-73) of the Toho Company asked the show's book writer Joseph Stein (1912-2010), "Tell me, do they understand this show in America?" Perplexed, Stein replied "What do you mean?" "It's so Japanese!"[2]

This statement can actually be read two ways. Many will interpret it to mean that *Fiddler* is so "universal" that it works in even the most remote cultures. On the other hand, it deals with arranged marriages, a concept that exists in Japan's recent history, but not in America's. Koji Aoshika, Vice-president of MTI Asia, says "Japan was the same [as in *Fiddler*]. You had to follow what the father said – arranged marriage, for instance. So, the story of a Jewish father losing power in the family life and girls starting to make their own decisions resonates."[3] Japanese director Amon Miyamoto agrees. "We have a 'so traditional' way. We have to be careful always. Our parents say, 'Tradition! Tradition!'"

Stein said, "We had unwittingly written something very special and apparently universal. The themes of the show are as true to the Japanese experience and Japanese culture as they are to the Americans or English: the breakdown of tradition, the differences between generations, the eagerness to hang on to a religious background. These things are very much a part of the human experience. I think if anything, *Fiddler on the Roof* is even more relevant today, because it talks about a world in turbulence."[4]

"Universality is something that helps to give something longevity, and it helps to reach a broader audience", says Chris Grady, "Fundamentaly, humans have some things that are very similar: a wish for safety, a wish for love, a wish for family, a wish to be safe in your own country… A story which talks about being unsafe or the breakup of a family or the challenges of a family; those become universal elements that resonate with an audience in any country."

Even the most "universal" shows will be perceived differently in each country where they play. Broadway conductor Lehman Engel wrote, "When one thinks of *My Fair Lady* in Turkish, *Man of La Mancha* in French, and *Fiddler* in Japanese, a number of important questions arise: How do a cockney flower girl and her snobbish speech-teacher friend find empathy in a poor country like Turkey? How does a musically very American version of a Spanish classic find favour with super-critical French audiences? How does a show about Polish [sic] Jews at the turn of the century relate to Japan?"[5]

When a Broadway musical succeeds abroad, the circumstances of its success are as unique and individual as they were in its original production. For example, in Paris – a city that is notoriously reluctant to embrace American musicals – *Man of La Mancha* was helped by the presence of the legendary Belgian troubadour Jacques Brel (1929-78) in the title role. (Brel also provided the French translation.)

Engel concludes, "The answers to these questions are to be found in two considerations: the universality of the original material... and the excellence of the transformation based on a profound knowledge and understanding of local people and customs." Please note that in each example Engel cites, it is an American show set in a foreign (i.e., non-American) locale.

Engel had his own experience with cultural exports. He took *Porgy and Bess* to Ankara, Turkey in 1968, where the "Buzzard Song" gave them particular problems:

> Boss, dat bird mean trouble.
> Once de buzzard fold his wing an' light over yo' house,
> All yo' happiness done dead.
> Buzzard keep on flyin' over, take along yo' shadow.[6]

There are no buzzards in Turkey. "So many things were different", says Ira Gershwin (1896-1983). "Idiomatic things like crap game. They had to hunt for its equivalent in Turkish. Very, very difficult."[7] Lehman tried to explain the crap game terminology to the Turkish cast members. "'Box-cars', 'crapped-out', 'nine to make nine', 'Little Joe' and many others had been literally translated as I had suspected and meant nothing to anyone," says Engel. To make matters even more difficult, the translation had been based on a German text, as the translators did not understand English. "I took the singers very slowly and mechanically through the scene indicating precisely where the dice had to be thrown in order to 'suit the action to the word'. Three times through and there was a glimmer of comprehension. However the arduousness of explaining each point to Hassan [Engel's interpreter] who in turn had to explain to Mr. [Aydın] Gün [(1917-2007) the director] who in turn directed the singing actors, was tremeandous... Suddenly, Mr. Gün through Hassan asked me what a buzzard was. I demonstrated by doing a bit of pantomime to explain these kind of scavengers. The Turks said that in the translated lyrics, the bird had been called an owl in one place and in another, a bat! This then was corrected and the entire dramatic intent was clarified."[8] Gershwin later told Engel, "I do sense though you feel that all the discomfort, the sweat and the rage you went through were worth it for the respect and acclaim you finally received."[9]

One question the manuscript does not address is race. Did they use black actors? I very much doubt that any were available in Turkey at the time.

A show's universality can be hampered by ignorance and/or insensitivity. If, in seeking to create a show with "universal" appeal, you also want a show that will withstand the test of time, one should bear in mind that future audiences may be more enlightened about the places and situations in your story than past or present ones have been.

It is very seldom that either Broadway or Hollywood pays any attention to my home country Canada, but it does happen. Most infamous (to Canadians) is *Rose Marie*, the 1924 operetta with musical chores shared by Rudoph Friml (1879-1972) and Herbert Sothart (1885-1949) and a libretto by Oscar Hammerstein II and Otto Harbach (1873-1963) with locations spanning from the Rocky Mountains across the Saskatchewan prairie to the ballroom of Quebec City's Chateau Frontenac. It played for 557 performances on Broadway, two years at London's Theatre Royal Drury Lane, and an amazing 1,250 nights at Paris' Théâtre Mogador. A North American tour included a stop at Toronto's Royal Alexandra Theatre in January 1925.

"American socialisation has not placed a high premium on Canadian knowledge," says Ron Smith of Thompson Rivers University. "The cinematic image of the Mounted Police, therefore, was based on a somewhat romantic representation of the Force, a small detachment of officers decked out in scarlet tunics, who were honest to a fault and clever in a simple sort of way."[10]

The hero was a Mountie of the Dudley-Do-Right ilk. Now, we laugh at the "Indian Love Call" ("when I'm calling yo-o-o-o-o-u") for all the wrong reasons. But it is the even more distorted 1936 film version starring Nelson Eddy and Jeanette MacDonald that has become a buzzword for American misperceptions of Canada (even though it was produced by the New Brunswick-reared Louis B. Mayer.)

"Everybody loved *Rose Marie* when it was first issued because everybody loved Jeanette MacDonald and Nelson Eddy", says Canadian author Pierre Berton (1920-2004). "The idea of a scarlet-coated Mountie carolling his way through the forests in the company of a girl whose brother he is seeking for murder was perfectly acceptable to a nation of moviegoers numbed and dazzled by celluloid make-believe. The joke was only understood years after the event."[11] The film even included one interpolated song – "Some of these Days" – by a Canadian-born songwriter, Shelton Brooks (1886-1975).

The Royal Canadian Mounted Police, who – despite Mayer's concerted efforts – declined to be involved with the film, regarded it as an embarrassment.[12] In the late 1960s, when Prime Minister Pierre Trudeau said Canada was about to shed its *"Rose Marie* image", Friml's secretary replied, "Shame on you! ... The beautiful legend of *Rose Marie* is as much a part of Canadian history and tradition as is the French language in Quebec."[13] Alas, "history" is largely what *Rose Marie* has been consigned to, although it has enjoyed the odd Canadian revival over the years, including some in French. You didn't have to be Canadian to know that the plot was ludicrous: the Germans saw right through it from the beginning, and so it flopped in Berlin. Now, finally, through Canadian-created shows like *Due South*, Canadians have been able to share in the joke.

In spite of its long run at the Charlottetown Festival, where it plays largely in front of American tourists, Don Harron (1924-2015), author of the book for *Anne of Green Gables - The Musical*, has never believed that his show should even be attempted on Broadway. "We learned long ago it's not that kind of show. *Anne of Green Gables* is not *Annie*."[14] He adds, "I have been at many Broadway opening nights and seen the brittle sophistication of the first niters [sic] who were much more interested in being seen than seeing anything on that stage. Londoners were different, in their ratty fur stoles they wanted to see a show and enjoy it."[15]

Harron's conviction has, alas, grown a new wrinkle. Although his version, written in collaboration with Norman Campbell (1924-2004), Elaine Campbell (1925-2007) and Mavor Moore (1919-2006) is authorised by the L. M. Montgomery estate (to which they continue to pay royalties), the Americans now consider the story to be in the public domain.[16] While the name and likeness of Anne is a trademark owned in Canada by the Anne of Green Gables Licensing Authority Inc., American writers are not obliged to seek permission or pay royalties before writing their own versions. So off-shoots such as a musical called *Anne with an E* have proliferated. Most recently, a new version was presented off-Broadway at the Lucille Lortel Theatre by Theatreworks USA. The libretto was by the noted lyricist Gretchen Cryer (1935-) and the score by her longtime composer partner Nancy Ford (1935-), creators of *I'm Getting My Act Together and Taking it on the Road*. Believing it to be a story that transcends national boundaries, their script makes little reference to its setting. In fact, actress Piper Goodeve, who played the title role, was unaware that it was set in Canada. She conceded, in reference to the Charlottetown Festival version, "I can see how it's upsetting that it's not their version in New York."[17]

David MacKenzie, then-Chief Executive of the Confederation Centre, producers of the Charlottetown version, concurs. "I think there's a little bit of jealousy come forward because I'd love for that show on Broadway or off Broadway to be *Anne of Green Gables - The Musical*, the Charlottetown Festival version, and hopefully some day it will be."[18] Canadian independent producer Michael Rubinoff put it more succinctly. "We should protect one of the few musicals that have become a Canadian institution at home and abroad," he told the *Ottawa Citizen*'s Kate Goodloe. "The original has been around for over 40 years. I can only imagine the outrage if I decided to announce a new version of *Les Misérables*."

While others may adapt the novel, they may not produce souvenir merchandise without permission of the Anne Authority, which is jointly controlled by the estate of the author Lucy Maude Montgomery (1874-1942) and the Province of Prince Edward Island. Montgomery herself fumed when an early silent movie of the story showed the Stars and Stripes flying over Avonlea schoolhouse. She wrote in her diary, "It was a pretty little play well photographed, but I think if I hadn't already known it was from my book, that I would never had recognized it. The landscape and folks were 'New England', never P.E Island... A skunk and an American flag were introduced – both equally unknown in PE Island. I could have shrieked with rage over the latter. Such crass, blatant Yankeeism!"[19]

I doubt that any American could conceive of how it would feel if the rest of the world were unaware that *Huckleberry Finn* actually took place on the Mississippi, and not on the Yorkshire Humber. However, to cite an old truism, "the proof of the pudding is in the eating." Those other *Anne*s have come and gone; *Anne of Green Gables – The Musical*™ has now been playing for more than fifty years and is still going strong.

One other Canadian-based story made it to Broadway, but since the success of *The Happy Time* was modest, it is virtually unknown in the land of its setting. When producer David Merrick (1911-2000) originally approached playwright N. Richard Nash (1913-2000) (*The Rainmaker*) to write the book, Nash preferred instead to do an entirely original story. However, Merrick held the rights to a 1950 Broadway play by Samuel A. Taylor (1912-2000) that in turn was based on stories by Robert Fontaine, concerning a Francophone family in the Ottawa Valley in the 1920s. Ultimately, Nash rewrote his story to incorporate some of Fontaine's characters, and moved his setting to Canada. Composer John Kander (1927-) and lyricist Fred Ebb (1928-2004), fresh from their success with *Cabaret*, were brought in to write the score (after Cy Coleman and Dorothy Fields had declined). The only Canadian involvement was star Robert Goulet (1933-2007) who won a Tony award, and Oscar winning filmmaker Christopher Chapman (1927-2015) (*A Place to Stand*), who designed the film projections. It has been revived in a number of American regional theatre productions, including Goodspeed Opera House and Signature Theatre.

What happens when a successful British musical is remounted on Broadway, and "tweaked" for American audiences? There is a British tendency to balk at the very gloss that Broadway prides itself in. Don Black (1938-) was already an Academy Award winning lyricist when he began writing for the West End stage. Then he was asked to write lyrics for *Bar Mitzvah Boy*, a 1978 musical based on Jack Rosenthal's 1976 TV comedy. The music was by Broadway legend Jule Styne (1905-94). Although Styne had been born in London's East End, he grew up in the U.S. and was a New Yorker through and through. Whereas the original BBC teleplay had been low key and subtle, Styne and his fellow American director Martin Charnin (1934-2019) insisted the musical had to be big and brash. "They brought to it this New York veneer," says Black, "this show-stopping polish, that was wrong for it."[20] Adrian Wright says, "Charnin seems to have set his heart on turning the show into another *Annie*, for which he'd been lyricist and Broadway director. *Bar Mitvah Boy* may have been another show about a not grown-up person, but it was a totally different cup-of-tea to Little Orphan Annie's."[21]

Its production at London's Her Majesty's Theatre closed after seventy-seven performances, but it would lead to Black's next assignment, and to a difficult Broadway transfer.

Song and Dance had begun life as a song cycle with music by Andrew Lloyd Webber called *Tell Me on a Sunday*, written as a vehicle for actress Marti Webb (1943-). It told of the romantic misadventures of an English girl set adrift in America. After a successful stage adaptation (combined with Lloyd Webber's Paganini *Variations*), plans were made to bring the show to Broadway, but Lloyd Webber and producer Cameron Mackintosh both felt it needed to be seen through American eyes. Director and lyricist Richard Maltby Jr. (1937-) was brought on board, and Bernadette Peters (1948-) signed to star.

"I knew something was wrong at the beginning," says Black, "when Bernadette... asked me to show her Muswell Hill... 'because I want to see where this girl comes from'... We spent the day there, and she kept asking things like, 'What does the character's Dad do?' And I'd say, 'Well, we don't talk about her Dad'. She needed to know. 'Could he have owned one of those sweet shops?'... she'd persist. And I'd say, 'Er, yeah'. And she'd reply, 'Great. That helps me.' That's when I realised: she was having to consciously motivate herself to get the character. Call it method acting. Whatever. Marti never asked any of that. She *was* the girl, and that was it, and that was why there was a truth to it with her."[22]

"The attempt to Americanise, supposedly authenticate, *Tell Me on a Sunday* for a New York audience, was a dismal failure", says London theatre critic Michael Coveney (1948-), "insensitive to the fact that Black's heroine's absorption of American detail was filtered through her predominantly Muswell Hill persona."[23]

Even with Sandy Wilson (1924-2014)'s *The Boy Friend* (1953), which was a hit on Broadway, there were tensions. While the original Players Theatre production was performed with just two pianos and drums, producer and director Cy Feur (1911-2006) decided that the Broadway production needed to be flashier and broader. He also felt it required an orchestra, with jazzier arrangements and faster tempos. An outraged Wilson became persona non grata at rehearsals. Original London director Vida Hope (1910-63) wrote, "The whole show is performed with all the high gloss and efficiency of the modern American musical... But inevitably, some of the tenderness has vanished."[24] (It's interesting to note that, fifty years later, when the similarly pastiche Canadian musical *The Drowsy Chaperone* was adapted for Broadway by a sensitive director, its original creators appeared to openly embrace the more polished Broadway approach.)

In dealing with this question of "universality" and cultural sensitivity, there is one Broadway show that gives me a great deal of trouble. Not that I dislike it – on the contrary, *The King and I* has, since my childhood, been one of my favourite musicals. Lehman Engel regarded it as one of the fifteen all-time best, and it has been staged successfully in countries as far afield as Japan and Israel – but never in Thailand, the land of its setting. In fact, it has been banned there.

"The Thai people find *The King and I* in its movie and Broadway play forms offensive because it caricatures His Majesty King Mongkut in such a denigrating and condescending manner"[25], wrote the Honourable Nitya Pibulsonggram (1941-2014), then-Thai ambassador to the United States in a 1997 letter addressed to Christopher Cox of the *Boston Herald*. In fact, under their law of Lèse Majesté, defaming, insulting, or threatening the king, queen, heir-apparent, or regent is punishable by three to fifteen years in prison. Amnesty International now considers any person to be held in such a way to be a political prisoner. The current Thai constitution includes this statement: "The King shall be enthroned in a position of revered worship and shall not be violated. No person shall expose the King to any sort of accusation or action."

When Rodgers and Hammerstein adapted Hungarian playwright Ferenc Molnár (1878-1952)'s 1909 drama *Liliom* to become *Carousel*, Hammerstein was uncertain that his audience would accept a foreign locale. "There was no way of knowing how the public would be thinking"[26], he said. They avoided the problem of a foreign culture by changing the setting from Budapest to New England, thereby Americanising it. Clearly, a change of setting would not be possible for *The King and I*.

It was leading actress Gertrude Lawrence (1898-1952) who initiated the project. She had optioned Margaret Landon's 1943 novel *Anna and the King of Siam*, and initially approached Cole Porter, then Noël Coward to write the score. Rodgers and Hammerstein declined at first, deeming Landon's story too episodic in nature, but they were persuaded when they saw Rex Harrison in the non-musical 1946 film of the book.

The novel was in turned based on the highly fanciful memoirs of the Welsh-descended school teacher Anna Owens (1831-1915), who travelled to Bangkok in 1862 to be a teacher for the children of King Mongkut (known officially as Rama IV). Here is where the trouble begins. Owens, (who added her husband's middle name to his surname to become Leonowens in her writings) felt the need to spice up her stories by adding harrowing tales of harem girls and torture. She didn't limit her fantasy to descriptions of the Siamese court – she also re-invented much of her own back story. She was born in India, but she considered herself to be Welsh, even though she had never lived there. (She wasn't the only colourful member of her family: her great nephew William Pratt became the actor Boris Karloff.) Crucially, she also portrayed herself as the king's most trusted adviser, whereas the historical record reveals otherwise: King Mongkut kept extensive journals during this time, in which Mrs. Anna's name occurs only once, and in a very trifling reference. The official opinion is that it is likely that their contact was minimal, if in fact they ever even met.

In 1897, Anna reunited with King Chulalongkorn, Mongkut's heir, during a state visit to London. While he expressed gratitude for all that she had done for him, he was more circumspect toward her literary treatment of his father. "Why did you write such a wicked book about my father King Mongkut? You know that you have made him utterly ridiculous." According to her granddaughter Anna Fyshe, who was with her at the time, she replied that the King had been "a ridiculous and a cruel, wicked man".[27]

However, American audiences and theatre professionals in the 1950s were unconcerned by any of this. This is Lehman Engel's assessment of *The King and I*: "The arrogant King of Siam has sent for a Welsh schoolmistress, Anna, to educate his numerous children and wives. It is the King himself, however, who needs Anna's help – although he doesn't admit it and seldom accepts it without protest.

Anna, a widow with a young son, has needs of her own. The audience's strongest wish is to see both of them helped, and each of them in this situation is the only one who has the power to help the other."[28] Of course, Engel's concerns are for the needs of the Broadway musical, not for the representation of Thai culture.

"In this age of 'political correctness'", counters the Thai ambassador, "it is stunning to sit through a performance of *The King and I* and to see not only the King, but all the Thai people portrayed via an extreme example of ethno-centricity as childlike, simple, and hopelessly unable to cope with the arrival of westerners. The British, however, are portrayed as superior beings, gently trying to uplift their naïve hosts. The wonderful music and the visual treats of the production camouflage the real insult that lies at the core of the play. Imagine if there were a similar caricature of Benjamin Franklin or Abraham Lincoln. Would you find it amusing to laugh at them, particularly if it requires a foreigner to teach them the necessary veneer of civilized behaviour? I doubt Americans would find it funny." Bearing in mind that, under this king's rule, Thailand was one of the only Southeast Asian countries that was able to withstand the assault of Western imperialism in the nineteenth century, he may have a point. If somebody were to make a film or play about the American Revolution in which the redcoats were the heroes and George Washington a terrorist, it might not be banned[29], but it certainly would not be popular stateside.

Still, in the "Occidental" world, *The King and I* is a beloved musical, written by two men with impeccable liberal credentials: both were active supporters of Roosevelt's New Deal who campaigned vigorously against racism in all its guises. I'm sure they would be appalled to find that they had caused offence. Perhaps, though, they should not have been surprised. After all, this was written for American consumption, and at that time you were thought to be very progressive if you portrayed non-whites as sentient beings.

It should be noted, however, that an earlier draft of the score included a song called "Now You Leave" sung to Mrs. Anna by Lady Thiang, the King's premier wife, trying to persuade her to stay. "Lady Thiang is rebuking Anna Leonowens... for not facing the consequences of imposing Western values into Siam"[30], says Dr. Dominic McHugh of the University of Sheffield. This was replaced by the much softer "Something Wonderful". When I asked if this song would have made a difference to the show's acceptability, he answered with an emphatic "No!"[31]

They had already fought a brave battle to retain the interracial romances in *South Pacific*. What is ironic is that it's the reflection of Hammerstein's progressive values that is actually the problem. He believed in the triumph of American-style democracy over what he saw as the tyranny of monarchial rule. If you're going to take that tact, then you have to get your facts straight. Clearly, showing the king of Siam as a cultured, progressive man who was fluent in Sanskrit and Latin (and who impressed westerners with his expertise in astronomy) would not fit that era's idea of an exotic "noble savage".

Rodgers own approach to authenticity is revealing: "It seems more than likely that if one were to attempt to reproduce with accuracy the court of the King of Siam in the year 1860, he might have to show the king as an individual quite unattractive (physically at least) to the Western eye. The palace itself might show a certain weird charm, but there would probably be a strange odour about the palace coming from the kitchen where strange and not entirely palatable foods were being prepared. Continue this technique and let it include the philosophies, the physical discomforts and the appearance of the Siamese women and it seems probable that you would end up repelling completely the Western eye, ear, nose and sense of touch."[32] Clearly Thailand's tourism industry was still in its infancy, and Americans had not yet developed their taste for Thai cuisine. About the music, he wrote in his memoirs:

"Western audiences are not attuned to the sounds of tinkling bells, high nasal strings and percussive gongs, and would not find this kind of music attractive. If a composer is to reach his audience emotionally—and surely that's what theatre music is all about—he must reach the people through sounds they can relate to."[33] World Music was still a few years away.

Viewed as a work of fiction, *The King and I* is a landmark of musical theatre. Viewed as a representation of history, it is a travesty. Sadly, it is all that many Westerners know of King Mongkut.[34]

There is another Rodgers and Hammerstein musical that has run afowl of its Asian subjects, and unlike *The King and I, Flower Drum Song* is now rarely seen, and opinion remains divided over its merits.

Rodgers and Hammerstein had just suffered two flops (*Me and Juliet* and *Pipe Dream*) and were hungry for a hit. They had been approached by librettist Joseph Fields (1895-1966) who had the rights to the novel *The Flower Drum Song* by Lee Chin Yang (1915-2018). It concerned the clash of cultures between the older traditional Chinese immigrants to San Francisco, and their younger more Westernised children. While the title of the novel clearly referred to "flower drum opera", the representative song in the show – "A Hundred Million Miracles" – is pure Rodgers and Hammerstein, albeit employing the "oriental riff" (although real flower drum songs are accompanied by a drum and a gong, as in the show).

While it was very successful at the time it was first staged in 1958 – it ran 600 performances on Broadway and 464 in London – it has since become regarded by some as racist and sexist; ironically, it was the first Broadway musical to feature a mostly Asian cast in sympathetic roles.

I would assert that the real problem with *Flower Drum Song* is not its political incorrectness so much as the fact that Rodgers and Hammerstein seemed to have lost the nerve that they once showed in the days of *Oklahoma!*, *Carousel* and *South Pacific*. They toned down or omitted all of the darker elements of Lee's novel, including the suicide of one person. The characters tended to be wealthy, and virtually all of them – including police officers – are apparently Chinese. Professor Kathryn Edney, former managing editor of the *Journal of Popular Culture*, sees this as evidence of segregation: "Although the show celebrates the idea of the melting pot and assimilation, the narrative ensures that its Chinese Americans are safely contained in Chinatown; they are segregated from the rest of white society."[35] She doesn't explain whether they are segregated by white society or whether they just prefer their own company.

I don't believe that Hammerstein and Fields were being knowingly racist. "However, their faulty sense of authority over their subjects undermines their supposed intention of a fair and genuine portrayal of Chinese America",[36] says Sabina Thalheim, Graduate Research Assistant at Ohio State University. She concedes, however, that "Though by today's standards, the characters in Rodgers and Hammerstein's shows often prove problematic, Hammerstein's musicals were taking significant forward strides in mid-twentieth century America."

In fact, they seemed to portray a San Francisco of the 1950s in which racism was almost non-existant, which may have been an error of omission. They wanted to write a musical comedy. Original director Gene Kelly attempted to compensate for the lack of substance through use of physical comedy, and in removing the dramatic tension, what they were left with was, by default, stereotypical. "At its core, a stereotype is bad writing", says Asian-American playwright David Henry Hwang, "a one or two dimensional cutout devoid of humanity, and therefore prone to demonization. Whether your characters are crooks, laundrymen, computer scientists or gangsters, if they are well written, they will exude humanity, which is ultimately the most effective weapon against stereotypes, and the most visceral measure of humanity."[37] Hwang wrote a new book for the show's 2002 Broadway revival.

Edwin W. Chen of Taipei has his degree in film studies from the Tisch School in New York. He is not offended by the original version of *Flower Drum Song*, but has a lot of issues with Hwang's revised version.

> "First, the overall 'Chineseness.' I am talking about a cultural longing that is strongly associated with Chinese people all over the world – the so-called 'Chinese Diaspora' – the sentimentality that [is shared by] integrated Chinese people living in Hong Kong, Taiwan, the Southeast Asia, North America and so on. In Hammerstein's original, especially in Act One Scene One, ... Madam Liang and Wang Da introduce 'You Are Beautiful' and the oriental romanticism embodied by the poetry Hammerstein created. (The lyric to 'You Are Beautiful' is, honestly, very much like a Chinese poem... The imitation of Chinese lyrics is wonderful... The only part Hammerstein mis-used is in the verse: 'Along the Huang Ho Valley'. Geographically speaking, the Huang Ho (Yellow River) Valley is not suitable for any flower boat's sailing. The location should be changed to the West Lake or other similar places.)
>
> Later in the same scene when Mei Li and her father visit the Wang family and perform the Flower Drum Song ["A Hundred Million Miracles"], there are some very important lines [in the dialogue] illustrating the routes they took from the Chinese Mainland to Formosa to the Philippines and then Vancouver and then San Francisco. This journey draws a map of 'The Chinese Diaspora' that is *vital* to the story of *Flower Drum Song*, and it should not be eliminated in any revival, needless to say a 'revisal.'
>
> Secondly, David Henry Hwang's knowledge of the Chinese Opera is embarrassingly distasteful. He got away with it in *M. Butterfly*, razzle-dazzlling it with gender issues. In the new *Flower Drum Song*, he made it one of the main plots and failed *big time*. It takes years to train a good 'qian-dan' (male actor specializing in portraying female characters on

stage). But in the new *Flower Drum Song*, Hwang writes about a father who owns a Peking Opera theatrical group [and] forces his own son to play female characters to support his own leading man status. He adopts the 'no woman is allowed on stage' formula to tell a story taking place in the early 1960s. I don't even think he understands the difference among Peking Opera, Cantonese Opera and Flower Drum [Opera]…

I always believed the new *Flower Drum Song* is more associated with the immigrants and their lives from People's Republic of China in the 1990s than the world created by C.Y. Lee in his bestseller and fashioned with the late 1950s Broadway lights by Rodgers and Hammerstein. The new production even got the wrong Chinese translated title! *Flower Drum Song* has always been 'Hua Gu Ge' (flower – drum -song). The Chinese characters on the poster were 'Hua Gu Qu' (flower – drum -melody)."[38]

The Hwang revival of *Flower Drum Song* ran for only 169 performances on Broadway.

Yemen-born Canadian journalist Kamal Al-Solaylee (1964-) says that Rodgers and Hammerstein confronted issues like slavery and racism "head on. While musicals like *South Pacific, The King and I*, or *Flower Drum Song* suggest to our more sensitive ears stereotypical treatments of Asians and Asian-Americans, they were inseparable from their creator's progressive, liberationist views. Hammerstein in particular was a crusader for racial justice, a life-long commitment".[39]

A recent film, *Blinded by the Light* by British director Gurinder Chadha (1960-) makes for an interesting comparison with *Flower Drum Song*. It also focuses on the clash of cultures between Pakistani immigrants and their Westernised children. However Chadha's story doesn't shy away from the darker elements and is more three dimensional. Still, I felt myself wondering, if it had been written and directed by white people, would it not be deemed racist, even if it were exactly the same film? Why is *Flower Drum Song* politically incorrect, yet *The Book of*

Mormon is okay?

The film musical *Hans Christian Andersen* also raised hackles in Denmark, even though screenwriter Moss Hart, composer-lyricist Frank Loesser and producer Samuel Goldwyn made no pretentions that this was a biography. Its star Danny Kaye told a Copenhagen press conference that the film was "just another fairy tale, an entertaining film built on an incident which might have taken place in Hans Christian Andersen's life."[40] However, the Danish critics complained that the film reflected a German, rather than a Danish setting: the names "Hans" and "Copenhagen" were given German pronunciations, and the actors dressed in Bavarian costumes. Nevertheless, fifty years later this would not stop the city of Copenhagen from an adopting the song "Wonderful, Wonderful Copenhagen" as the theme song for its tourism promotion.

As we've seen with the examples of *Hans Christian Andersen*, *The King and I* and *Rose-Marie*, it is very seldom that any Broadway musical set in a foreign "exotic" country ever truly works when exported back to that country. Even *Les Misérables* failed in Paris when re-imported from London, and it was originally written by Frenchmen.

One of the few exceptions to this is Lerner and Loewe's *My Fair Lady*. Perhaps this is because it was based on an Anglo-Irish source (Shaw's *Pygmalion*) and because Alan Jay Lerner (1918-1986) was educated in England. (Still, it didn't stop him from writing "*On* the Street Where You Live" instead of "*In* the Street...") Even its director Moss Hart was of English parentage. Actor and writer Steve Nallon (1960-) has a more elaborate theory. "It is difficult to think of a show that is more 'British'", he says.

> "The 'Britishness' of *My Fair Lady* is really found in its 'Englishness', or more specifically 'the cold-blooded murder of the English tongue'. But Shaw's obsession with the way the English speak, perfectly captured in 'Why Can't the English?', is only a means to an end. Higgins

properly hits the nail right on the head when he sings, 'The verbal *class distinction* by now should be antique'... It seems to me that *class distinction* is at the heart of *My Fair Lady*, and indeed the lifeblood of every British musical."[41]

On the other hand, Lerner and Loewe's *Brigadoon* presents a highly romanticised view of Scotland. "Much of this comes from the invented traditions of Scotland, such as kilts and clan tartans", says Jennifer Oates, Associate Professor at Queens College, City University of New York. "The Scots played a role in creating these as a way to recover or assert a national identity after merging with England in the Union of 1707."[42] This is what Colin McArthur refers to as "Scottish Discursive Unconscious" in his book *Braveheart, Brigadoon and the Scots: Distortions of Scotland in Hollywood Cinema*.[43] This image, according to Oates, is not an American view of Scotland so much as an idealised view put forward by the Scots themselves in the literature of Sir Walter Scott, the comedy of Sir Harry Lauder and promotions of Scottish tourism.

Something similar happened more recently with the enormously popular *Riverdance* phenomenon. Laura Farrell-Wortman, who holds a BA in Irish literature from New York University, asserts that its greatest success was in "the creation of a recognizable brand... Coming as it did during the rise of the Celtic Tiger economy, the show was the product of a nation in transition, seeking a new global identity to match their new global economic prowess. *Riverdance* was able to take a traditional, rural cultural form – Irish step dance – and bring it up to date, modernizing it and reimagining the possibility inherent within it."[44]

Andrew Lloyd Webber (1948-) and Tim Rice (1944-)'s musical *Evita*, based on the life of Argentine first lady Eva Perón, has never been professionally staged in Buenos Aires. However, contrary to some claims, it is not banned. It seems more likely that the people of Argentina prefer their own versions of their history. A number of plays and films have dealt with the subject, both critically and favourably, including at least two musicals: *Eva, el gran musical argentino* (1986) and *Evita - Volveré y seré millones* (1989) are both dealt with elsewhere in this book. The Argentine critical consensus of the Lloyd Webber/Rice version seems to be that it is a miscomprehension of Argentina's complex political dynamics. One essayist criticises "*Evita's* oversimplified dismissal of Perónism as simply 'common or garden fascism' (Rice's phrase), with no understanding of or appreciation for the complexities of Perón's Justicialist Party, a political movement that included factions from the Right, the Center, and the Left."[45]

How important is this type of cultural authenticity in a musical? In 1976, Stephen Sondheim (1930-) and John Weidman (1946-) made a concerted effort to make a culturally sensitive portrayal of the Japanese in *Pacific Overtures*, but some critics questioned the decision to try to tell it from the Japanese point of view when surely the Japanese could tell their own story much better. Director Harold Prince (1928-2019) told the *New York Times*' David Oyama, "It would be arrogant and stupid for me to suggest that what we did was Kabuki, but what fascinated me most – and what I did try to infuse into *Pacific Overtures* – was the peculiar energy of Japanese theater and their unabashed enthusiasm for theater itself."[46]

Then this version was seen on television by a young would-be director named Amon Miyamoto (1958-). At the time, he found it rather "weird" seeing a Japanese theatrical form – Kabuki – combined with Western music, but a couple of decades later, in 2000, he was given the opportunity to stage this show at Tokyo's National Theatre when the rights to another play by famed novelist Yukio Mishima (1925-70) fell through. Until then, the National Theatre had never considered doing a musical. "The musical was seen as a kind of cheap entertainment in Japan", says Miyamoto. But the artistic director read the script without the music, and decided it was "good enough".

While Harold Prince had staged the original in a pastiche of Kabuki style, Miyamoto felt that it was better suited to the simpler and less flashy minimalist Noh style, a form that is even older than Kabuki. "Not like a spectacle. Not [the] Kabuki way."

Japanese audiences were sensitive to the perceived historical inaccuracies of John Weidman's script, particularly regarding two of the principal characters. "For example, Kayama [a samurai] and Manjiro [an imprisoned fisherman] never met each other [in real life]", says Miyamoto. "But I don't care, because how the two men go in different directions is more important for me." (In the show, Manjuro becomes fiercely anti-Western, whereas Kayama embraces the new world.)

Miyamoto's version made it to New York in two incarnations. First, his National Theatre production was presented in Japanese at Lincoln Center in 2002, where the *New York Times* said it "has been directed with verve and imagination... In reinterpreting an American musical about their own country, Mr. Miyamoto and company have bestowed a great gift upon New York: a chance to see muscle-flexing Americans as aliens at a moment when it is especially crucial for the United States to understand how it is perceived internationally."[47] Michael Feingold in the *Village Voice* said, "Rumi Matsui's starker sets and Emi Wada's less ornately patterned costumes seemed built out of a whole culture's visual sense, not designed with a distancing specialness born of research."[48]

Two years later, he returned to restage it, this time in English, at the Roundabout Theatre. He found working with American actors required some adjustment. "It was a big shock when I first worked on Broadway in 2004. Japanese casts don't oppose you. They just listen to what you tell them as to a teacher and say 'yes'," he told *CNN Asia*'s William Andrews. "But that's horrible! I want to do work together. We have to communicate and share ideas. I tried to work in the usual Japanese way in America but on the third day of rehearsal the cast told me I had to change."[49] Of this production, Feingold remarked that "Miyamoto's cast demonstrates its success, ironically, by seeming far less rooted in an Asian sensibility than the original. But then, this, too, suggests Miyamoto's approach, which often seems to make Broadwayish what the original strove to make more 'Japanese'."[50] Of course, this is not surprising, given that the original production was by an American "Japanophile", whereas this was by a Japanese-born "Broadway Baby".

There is a song in *The Drowsy Chaperone* that contains the intentionally very Politically Incorrect lines:

> What is it about the Asians
> That fascinates Caucasians?
> What is it about the Asians
> That's so nice?
> Is it the won-tons? The egg-roles? The rice?[51]

This sort of exoticism – and the potential for cultural misunderstanding – has long fascinated writers. "Whenever one culture looks at another, especially from so remote a distance," says Raymond Knapp, Professor of Musicology at UCLA, "it cannot help essentializing differences, so that often what will barely register for an insider stands out in high relief for an outsider, forming the basis for stylistic imitation... Part of the problem is, to be sure, that the point of exoticism is largely *not* to fully understand the Other, but to keep it usefully at a distance so that its foreign flavour might be savoured."[52]

In an article in *Studies in Musical Theatre*, Doctoral candidate Jessica Hillman writes, "Musical theatre, as a popular and populist art form, reflects and absorbs America's highly sensitised identity politics, making issues of ownership and authenticity central."[53] When in 2004 a new revival of *Fiddler on the Roof* opened on Broadway directed by Englishman David Leveux (1957-), some dubbed it "Fiddler with no Jews" or "Goyim on the Roof" because Leveaux cast his non-Jewish compatriot Alfred Molina (1953-) as Tevye, the milkman. Thane Rosenbaum of the *Los Angeles Times* said it lacked a "Jewish soul"[54]. In an attempt to further "universalise" an already internationally successful show, some complained that its ethnic identity was watered down. There were also complaints when another non-Jew, ironically named Norman Jewison (1926-), directed the 1971 film version, in which the ethnic identity was heightened. However, what Jewison did was to return the story to its Eastern European roots – to the world of the Sholem Aleichem (1859-1916) stories and the Marc Chagal (1887-1985) paintings that had inspired the show in the first place. Some felt that it lost some of the humour that it had on stage. If that's true, it certainly didn't hurt the film's international appeal. Perhaps more significant than his being a protestant, Jewison was a Canadian. *Fiddler on the Roof* – as a movie – was no longer being seen from a New York perspective.

In February 2005, I received an intriguing email from a Dubai-based company called Capacity World. It said, "We are now preparing for a great fantasy musical production" and that they were looking for a lyricist and book-writer. Hisham Abdel Khalek, their artistic director, "reaming with all our best regards"[55], asked me to send samples of my work.

Alas, as it turned out, this was to be somebody else's adventure. New York based book writer and lyricist Stephen Cole, whose credits include *After the Fair*, *Night of the Hunter* and *Merman's Apprentice*, also received a similar email, only in his case, it asked point-blank: "We want you write musical. How much?" This show would be performed only once for the opening of Aspire Sports Academy, the world's largest glass-enclosed soccer arena, in the presence of Sheikh Hamad bin Khalifa Al Thani, the Emir of Qatar, and a thousand foreign diplomats. For the music, they ultimately settled on composer David Krane

(1953-), an established Broadway dance arranger and protégé of Leonard Bernstein whose credits included the film versions of *Chicago, Nine, Into the Woods* and *Mary Poppins Returns.*

Krane and Cole had never met before, but they bonded instantly, and soon they were on a flight to Dubai, where they were given their remit: the spoilt son of a Sultan has been locked away in a palace and wants to possess a star from the sky. The settings were to include a desert and a sea, and it must travel in time to Egypt of the Pharaohs, ancient Greece and the Stone Age. The show was to include pearl diving, falconry, a score of camels, ten Arabian stallions and a major sporting star. Cole had to turn these requirements into a coherent plot. He decided, first of all, that the reason why the son was locked in the palace was that his father wanted to protect him from the world. The star that he craved was turned into a magical character who came down from the sky and took him on adventures to ancient Greece, Egypt and pearl diving in Qatar. (They were able to persuade the producers to omit the Stone Age.) Each journey would teach the boy lessons about brain, heart and strength, the qualities of a good sportsman. They had six weeks in which to write it. The show would, like its venue, be called *Aspire*.

Back in New York, they turned out a song a day. "We wrote as if we were writing Broadway's next Tony Award-winning musical", Cole wrote in the *Dramatists Guild Quarterly*. "I did some of my best lyrics and the music was filled with the mystery and beauty of Arabian nights, with a little Broadway and pop thrown in for good measure."[56] They managed to turn it in a week early. "It had everything: camels, soaring stars, singing Sultans, dancing sports celebrities, flying carpets, King Tut, and a small chunk of Homer's *Odyssey*."

There were learning curves: after they auditioned the score for the producers in London, they were met with a stony silence. They were told that they could not use the name of "Allah" in a song lyric – even if it did refer to apple pie à la mode. Krane had, for local colour, quoted one Arab folk tune that he was told could only be played during Ramadan.

These problems fixed, Krane went with orchestrator Larry Blank to Bratislava to pre-record the score with a seventy-piece orchestra. They also tried to pre-record the chorus using Slovakian singers, but the phonetically rendered results were unacceptable, so the chorus was re-recorded in London.

Then they found out, to their stupefaction, that they were not to be included in the casting, nor would they be invited to attend any rehearsals. The director had a background in Italian opera, and had never seen a musical.

They arrived for the final rehearsals to find the show, according to Cole, "in a shambles. The cast was tanned but under-rehearsed. No run-through ever got past the third song. The lights were rented from a local disco, the Russian dancers were choreographed by a kindergarten dance teacher from Boca Raton, the sets were so huge that some of them didn't fit on the stage, the effects (including a wall-to-wall LED screen rivalling Times Square) didn't work, there were flying accidents, backstage fights among the hundreds of Arabs required to push the huge sets around and no one spoke the same language." And it played in English in front of an audience who, without the full Arabic translation in their programs, wouldn't have a clue as to what was going on.

Yet, somehow it all came together, and the Emir gave it a standing ovation. They asked for a Broadway-style musical, and they got one. The only thing that didn't happen was their third and final payment, due upon performance. In Cole's words, "Our producers had folded their tents and tiptoed into the desert, never to be heard from again." He later told me, "It was certainly an adventure and I am glad I didn't miss it."[57]

Since they had always felt like they had been living in a Bob Hope / Bing Crosby "road" movie, they decided that "maybe art imitates Arabs" and conceived a new show about the experience, called *The Road to Qatar*. "We treat the Arabs with affection", Krane told Kathryn Boughton of the *Litchfield County Times*. "You can't make fun of them. I feel we have done a small bit for peace in the world."[58] It opened at the Lyric Stage in Dallas, Texas on 9 October 2009. "It's the company's giddiest yet, with a production as nifty as a terrific band of New York pros can make it,"[59] wrote Lawson Taitte in the *Dallas Morning News*. The *Dallas Voice*'s Arnold Wayne Jones said, "Because it's autobiographical, *The Road to Qatar*... has the immediacy of insane guerrilla theater."[60]

If a show doesn't have "universal appeal", does that mean it's not as good? Norman Campbell, the composer of *Anne of Green Gables - The Musical* once told me, "It is very important that we are able to write musicals that are about we Canadians, and about our own scene. To be inhibited by making it universal just by taking away place names and issues is a mistake."[61] Imagine if the Broadway producers of *1776* had worried about whether it would play well in London? (It didn't.) A show can be well written, well crafted and still be of its time and place. Surely there's nothing wrong with that.

Universality Part 2:
A Sense of Time and Place

The ironic thing about universality in a musical is that it usually requires a very specific milieu in order to work. It's very hard for me to imagine *Anne of Green Gables* without its Prince Edward Island setting. It's when that sense of time and place is so clearly articulated that even a person who has never been there can appreciate its sense of detail that you have a show that transcends borders.

In the mid 1970s Canada's Charlottetown Festival produced a musical based on the film *The Rowdyman*, which told a story set in a Newfoundland out port. Author and star Gordon Pinsent says,

> "There are no excuses for this project to have been less than expected, except to say that I had little preparation time. And the nature of the piece – were it to retain the gritty, natural texture of the film – didn't require twenty-six musicians in the pit. It really was a play with music, needing a half-dozen musician-actors weaving their way through the production, complementing the content in a much more unique way than in the predictable musical comedy sense of your average Broadway show. Cliff Jones did a marvelous job matching music to my lyrics, but in my final opinion the book worked and the music worked, but not together! The tunes seemed as if they had been parachuted into the story, with no connecting sympathy among them."[1]

Jamie Portman of the *Southam News Service* felt much the same way. He complained that "there is no real sense of time and place – despite Pinsent's careful Newfoundland dialect... The idiom is certainly not Newfoundland, only Broadway derivative."[2] Pinsent concluded, "I should have devoted far more time to it than I did... The end result was a lacklustre event for both the Charlottetown Festival and me."[3] Interestingly, his idea of doing it with a small group of actor-musicians would have brought it closer in style to *Come from Away*, which may very well have suited it. It ran for 23 performances in rep with *Anne of Green Gables* in the summer of 1976.

This is one of the problems that I constantly ran up against in my native country. Because the musical is regarded as an American art form, it has not been taken seriously by the Canadian cultural establishment. A part of the problem is that historically there has been no musical-theatrical form that clearly evokes Canada. This was my initial reason for researching the roots of the Canadian musical in my previous book, *Broadway North*. In it, I asserted that one reason that it is so difficult to define Canada in terms of music is that we have been so pre-occupied with appealing to foreign markets that we have failed to develop our own identity. It is there, I believe, beneath the surface. For me, God is in the details.

I once saw a low-budget Canadian film called *My American Cousin* that depicted a place I was familiar with (the Okanagan, where our family had vacationed when I was a child) so vividly that I felt that it was my life up on screen. The funny thing is, Steven Spielberg evidently agreed with me, and hired its ingénue Maggie Langrick (1971-) for a part in one of his films. And I'm pretty sure he didn't grow up anywhere near Penticton, British Columbia. But because writer and director Sandy Wilson (1947-) was writing about what she knew (and managed to impart that knowledge coherently), it worked. More recently, the internationally successful television series *Murdoch Mysteries* has clearly delineated its Toronto setting and its late 19th century period.

There is no formulaic approach to this. John MacLachlan Gray (1946-), the author of *Billy Bishop Goes to War*, told me "a lot of people start thinking of other musicals when they write, and not that space, that theatre, that stage, those actors. The more you have that in mind, the more you are in touch with the form."[4]

I am not arguing that every Canadian musical has

to be set in Canada or be a Canadian story. (Or Australian, or South African.) If Australians write a show – especially if it is aimed at an Australian audience – it will have an Australian point of view. That's not the tricky part. People writing musicals in those places should know how to evoke their own milieu.

That said, musical "authenticity" can be ambiguous. Often the music that we associate with a particular place is not actually from there. The American popular music of the Tin Pan Alley era is largely European and African in origin, but achieved its popular success in New York, and is indelibly linked to that place. The folk music of the British Isles evolved into the folk music of the Appalachians and gave birth to bluegrass. Music does not have to originate in a place in order to be identified with it.

In Broadway's golden age, writers thought nothing of "evoking" Thailand in *The King and I*, Scotland in *Brigadoon* and France in *Can-Can*, safe in the knowledge that few in the New York audience would have ever been to any of those places. In fact, few would have seen any foreign films, and their knowledge of foreign shores would be limited to books that were probably written by American writers. Broadway conductor and teacher Lehman Engel wrote, "Richard Rodgers… set shows in the Oklahoma Territory, the New England coast about 1873, the South Pacific of World War II, Siam, San Francisco, Salzburg, and many other places, but the basic melodic, harmonic and rhythmic style are all quite recognizably Rodgers. Here and there, there are colorations. The melodic style of *Oklahoma!* is unrelated to that of *Carousel*. *South Pacific* has its "Orientalisms" ('Bali Hai,' for example), Salzburg is here and there slightly more 'musical' musically than *Oklahoma!*, but throughout all of it, it is obviously American and Rodgers."[5]

On the other hand, Engel criticised *Cabaret* for trying too hard to sound like Weimar-era Berlin. "I cannot understand why so much of *Cabaret* sounded like Kurt

Weill... In the end, this sort of thing must fail since at best it is only an imitation."

Yet Vincent Patterson, the American director who mounted a revival of *Cabaret* in Berlin in 2006 says, "I am really blown away that [John] Kander and [Fred] Ebb and Joe Masteroff, who wrote the book, had not come to Berlin before they wrote this piece. They did this while sitting in New York... Somehow the muses got inside of them and informed them of not only the story that was so powerful, but the sentiment and the sounds of the music and the dialogue and the way people spoke and the feeling of this time."[6] Composer John Kander had immersed himself in the music of not only Kurt Weill, but of Friedrich Holländer, Mischa Spoliansky and others of that period. Of course, it *is* an imitation – albeit a particularly skilful (and appropriate) one. (Engel later conceded that "*Cabaret* is a far better show than I had at first thought."[7])

Times have changed. Not only are people better travelled now, but the chances are that Broadway shows are not playing strictly to New York (or even American) audiences anymore. Broadway and the West End are now more reliant than ever on tourists, and the centre of gravity is shifting.

Another factor is that people in other parts of the world are getting tired of being portrayed as stereotypes. Brazil is not populated by exotic women who wear fruit bowls on their heads. Canadians do not live in igloos, nor do their policemen ride on horses wearing bright red tunics, and Australians are not all crocodile-hunting bushrangers.

However, that only covers what they are *not*. Discovering what they *are* is a process that is a whole lot more difficult. How do you write a show that is set in Australia and make it instantly recognisable without resorting to stereotypes?

"When you hear Australians sing in their accent,

you know exactly where you are because it's such a remarkably different accent", says Melbourne director Aaron Joyner. "Admittedly, musical theatre style is actually easier to sing in the American accent. The vowel sounds are a lot easier. There are some words that when we're working on a specific song the Australian way to say the words just doesn't really resonate very well, so quite often the temptation is to quickly go back into the American. It can be difficult for our musical directors to hone that in and my ear has become very attuned to it." This means that composers need to be sensitive to the difference in language, and think about how a word is going to scan when they set it to music. It may also be a clue that could lead composers and lyricists to a more comfortable Australian style of scansion.

Søren Møller, the former artistic director of a Danish musical theatre workshop called Uterus and current creative producer at Fredericia Teater says, "I think that [a distinctly Danish point of view] will shine through what we do. I'm not a missionary about that, but I'm hoping that it will shine through that this is a Uterus developed project, that it's developed in Denmark and that it has a certain kind of feel to it that comes from the culture, and defining your own culture is first and foremost. Being part of that organic development of the Danish culture in musical theatre, that's a given that we're part of that. There [are] a lot of Danish composers, and its deep within our soul, and at the same time we've also been under the influence of the same thing by the Americans that everybody else has in the world. I think it's just a big melting pot, but I do think that a Danish composer, being brought up in Denmark, will bring some of Carl Nielsen [composer, (1865-1931)] and the lullabies that we carried as children into the work that we do, and I think that will shine through."

Of course, audiences for musicals like to be transported to some place exotic and unfamiliar – hence the popularity, in the West, of *South Pacific* and *The King and I*. In Japan, on the other hand, the Takarazuka Revue's productions, such as *Rose of Versailles*, are often set in Europe, and of course *Anne of Green Gables*, which is wildly popular there, is set in Canada. I had an illustration of this in Singapore when I met some members of their musical theatre community for dinner in an international buffet called "The Line" at the Shangri-la Hotel. I was only interested in food from Singapore and Malaysia, whereas one of my hosts, Stella Kon, ordered roast beef with Yorkshire pudding. "This, for me, is exotic", she explained.

I even find in London that there is a fascination with all things American. It is, to the British, "exotic" in much the same way as *My Fair Lady* is to Americans. For Kurt Weill and Bertolt Brecht, American culture was seen through the rose-tinted filter of Hollywood. As a result, shows like *Happy End* are America as seen through a Teutonic distortion lens.

There are two American musicals from the so-called "golden age" that have deliberately set out to evoke a peculiar kind of rural Americana. Although they are musically contrasting pieces, the points in common between *The Music Man* (1957) and *110 in the Shade* (1963) are quite striking. For one thing, they each tell the same basic story[8] – that of an outsider, a conman, who comes to a small town, stirs up the population, captures the heart of the local spinster, then finds or brings about some kind of redemption. Of greater significance to me, Meredith Willson (1902-84), the author of *Music Man* was a native of Iowa, where the show was set. Similarly, composer Harvey Schmidt (1929-2018), lyricist Tom Jones (1928-) and book writer N. Richard Nash (1913-2000) were all native Texans.

Musicology professor Raymond Knapp calls *The Music Man* "the most perfect of American musicals".[9] Willson had already established himself as a proud native of Mason City, Iowa in his popular radio appearances as a musician and humorist. It was his friend and fellow composer Frank Loesser who encouraged him to write a musical about his home state.

"Iowans like myself recognize the characters," says Roberta Freund Schwartz, associate professor of historical musicology at the University of Kansas. "Meredith Willson always thought of the musical as a valentine to his native state, albeit one that did not idealize its inhabitants… Iowans have a reputation for being stubborn, pragmatic, direct and sometimes contrary."[10]

Part of the musical personality of *The Music Man* was a product of Willson's having been a flute player in John Philip Sousa's band, but much of it came from his years as a band-leader on various radio shows. Like Paul Shaffer on David Letterman's late night talk show, his talent for comedic banter soon became evident, and he was given the part as the resident Iowa 'hick'. It was then that he developed a technique for writing comedic "speak songs" to be performed by the programme's vocal quartet. These became the prototypes for the stunning "Rock Island" number that opens *The Music Man*, which Stephen Sondheim describes as "surely one of the most startling and galvanic openings ever devised"[11]. Willson says, "I sneaked into this opening speak-song considerable exposition – often a painful part of a play because of the latecomers stepping all over you while you're trying to find out what's going on."[12] He employed a similar technique for the half-sung, half-spoken "(Ya Got) Trouble".

Being the author of the book as well as of the music and lyrics allowed him to play with the rhythm of the dialogue in scenes leading into a song. "Willson's stubborn efforts to emphasize rhythm over rhyme and to create songs with the quality of dialogue were driven by a desire to make the 'River-citezians' [sic] in *The Music Man* sound like Iowans", Schwartz says. "As Iowans do not have a distinct regional accent, Willson used other means to characterize his fellow Hawkeyes." In discussing the song "Iowa Stubborn, she says "The music itself is stubborn: the incessant repetition of a small number of rhythmic motives creates a piece that seems as intractable as the folks who sing it."[13]

Professor Knapp points out that "every problem is solved specifically through music". The townspeople are literally seduced by the power of music, and so is the audience. This has a surprisingly unsentimental effect.

Not that Broadway guru Lehman Engel was impressed: "The makers of *The Music Man* must have felt that they were in trouble when they resorted to an exercise in terpsichore involving a number of fat ladies in Grecian costumes, and the music reached for adrenalin in the form of an old-fashioned American-type march, '76 Trombones'."[14] He used this as an illustration of why that show would not be revivable. Sadly, Engel died before he could be proven wrong.

110 in the Shade, with book by N. Richard Nash (based on his play *The Rainmaker* set in a drought in rural Texas) and music by Harvey Schmidt and lyrics by Tom Jones is not as well known by the general public as *The Music Man*, but it is held by many to be one of Broadway's hidden gems. The music is closer to the ballets of Aaron Copland than to the bluster of Sousa. "[*The Rainmaker*] had a story line about an old maid and a magician that had mythic proportions and cut right through to the heart", says Jones.[15] Schmidt and Jones had both grown up in Texas in the thirties and forties, and knew the setting well. "We searched our own youths and memories of Texas in the summer"[16], Jones says. Like the plays and films of Horton Foote (1916-2009) (*Tender Mercies, The Trip to Bountiful*), there is a soulfulness, an epic quality to it. The original production ran for 330 performances at the Broadhurst Theatre. Of its 1982 revival at York Theatre, John S. Wilson in the *New York Times* said it had "a feeling for the land, for ordinary people, for basic Americana."[17] It was revived again in 2007 starring Audra McDonald (1970-).

Sometimes a show's distinct sense of time and place is a product of its creators' imagination. Frank

Loesser had already mastered the idiosyncratic speech patterns of Damon Runyon (1880-1946) in *Guys and Dolls*. When he attempted to adapt Beatrice Joy Chute (1913-87)'s fantasy novel *Greenwillow*, which is set in an un-specified place and time, he once again gave the characters eccentric phrases such as "Any flimsy-dimsy looking for true love / better smile me no good-deary-good-day".[18]

    The show was not a success; it ran for just 97 performances at the Alvin Theatre in 1960, although Brooks Atkinson of the *New York Times* wrote that "Mr. Loesser has provided a warm and varied score that captures the simple moods of the story... The makers of *Greenwillow* have never faltered. Mr. Loesser has taken care of that by writing music out of personal musical convictions."[19] On the other hand, *Time Magazine* reported, "Whatever the charm of *Greenwillow* the novel, the play is as vague in its storytelling as in its geography. It offers lovers but no proper love story, devils but no improper temptations, and the sort of artificially flavored language that tries to be folk poetry but turns out as horrible prose. Doubtless some people will think it delightful, but anyone with memories of a J. M. Synge must find its whimsies bogus, while people with memories of a J. M. Barrie should find its cuteness grim."[20]

    While *The Sound of Music* is at its heart an American musical, there is still a very definite sense of place. Of course the film version was able to make stunning use of its Alpine setting, but Sarah T. Ellis, a Ph.D. student in Theatre and Performance Studies at the University of California at Los Angeles argues that Richard Rodgers' (1902-79) music constitutes a place in and of itself. "In *The Sound of Music*, the reiteration of music via orchestral and sung reprises continually reinscribes a sense of place for the von Trapp family, regardless of their physical location. The very sound of music encompasses both a nuclear family and value system for the von Trapps – a transportable, or transposable, sense of place... the von Trapp family nests in their nuclear family and ideals of freedom by way of the very sound of music."[21] In other words, it is when they sing together – in harmony – that they are at home.

Of course, *The Sound of Music* is based on a true story, albeit with a very fanciful reworking. While it is purportedly based on the memoirs of Maria Augusta Trapp, in fact it draws a lot from the 1956 film *Die Trapp-Familie* that was West Germany's biggest hit of the decade. The idealised portrayal of Maria comes from the film, as does the scene where the children gather in her bedroom during a thunder storm. About the only things in the musical that were true were the fact that Maria was studying to be a nun, she did marry Baron von Trapp, the family did sing and they left Austria. However, she was never governess to all seven children – only to one – and she and the Baron had been married for nearly a decade by the time they "escaped". He was a loving and attentive father who certainly never forbade his family to sing. (She was the more distant one.) He was in financial difficulty due to a bank failure. He was never drafted into the German navy: because, having been born in Zara, Dalmatia[22], he was an Italian citizen, so the Nazis couldn't force him to do anything. Still, being an opponent of the regime who had refused to sing for Hitler's birthday made life uncomfortable, still their rather routine "escape" was by train. In fact, they rented out their home during their absence, and returned to it at least once during Hitler's occupation.

Even *Grease*, in its original Chicago incarnation, had a definite local feel to it, although much of this was lost when it transferred to Broadway. Its creators, Jim Jacobs (1942-) and Warren Casey (1935-88) met in 1963 as part of the Hull House Theatre, whose prime director Bob Sickinger (1926-2013) was later my collaborator on two projects. The original version of *Grease* opened at a converted streetcar barn, the Kingston Mines Theatre in 1971, where it reflected Jacobs' own memories of Taft High School. Its cast included future *Taxi* star Marilu Henner (1952-) who originated the roll of "Marty", and New York theatre composer Polly Pen (1953-), who would later write book, music and lyrics for *Bed and Sofa*, originated the part of goody-goody Patty Simcox.

"*Grease*, which affectionately spoofed the teen culture of the late 1950s, was determinedly retro", says blogger Albert Williams.

> "Some even found it reactionary, believing the characters' black leather jackets and worker boots smacked of a fascist aesthetic. But most responded positively to the show's cunning blend of irony and nostalgia. It was both a welcome escape from the turbulence of Nixon's America and a wry critique of conformism. The point of the show, after all, is that the cool rebels who populate the story are every bit as obsessed with peer pressure and living up to the status quo as the squares they despise."[23]

The script was riddled with local references to places like Palmer House, Melrose Park and Lakeshore Drive.

Local critics championed the show – Will Leonard of the *Chicago Tribune* called it "one of the most screamingly funny shows in town"[24] – and New Yorkers began to take notice. Producers Ken Waissman and Maxine Fox suggested they would produce it in New York if certain changes were made. "We were told it was necessary to make the characters loveable, instead of scaring everybody", Jacobs told the *Chicago Tribune*'s Chris Jones. "The show went from about three-quarters book and one-quarter music to one-quarter book and three-quarters music."[25] Where the original had been an ensemble piece, the Broadway version shifted its emphasis to the characters of Sandy and Danny.

Alas, some things were lost along the way. "We cut the book to shreds and added more singing and dancing,"[26] says Jacobs. "The forest preserve became the park, and Foster Beach [a popular Lake Michigan summer spot] became the lake… It lost the magic of being a purely Chicago show."[27]

In 2011, something resembling the original version was presented by director P.J. Paparelli, using a combination of the original rehearsal script and some restored cut material, stripping it of most of the songs added for Broadway, including "Summer Nights". "Everyone involved here has made sure that the kids of Rydell High – or, if you peel back the thinnest of disguises, Taft High School circa 1959 – are finally allowed to be kids again," writes Chris Jones, "mocking one another as Polacks and spaghetti benders, obsessing over tattoos, cup sizes and prophylactics floating down the Chicago River, and generally doing what working-class kids did and what parents teachers and ratings-obsessed filmmakers fear."[28]

Instead of "You're the One That I Want", the show ends with Sandy singing to Danny: "If you want my love ever true again, you've got to get down on your knees and kiss it."

And so, as shows move from one place to another, they either adapt to the foreign environment, or else their audiences do. (Or they die trying.) The rules are, I believe, changing. During the period of the so-called "golden age" of Broadway – the 1940s and 1950s – only the very wealthy could afford to travel abroad. Now nearly everybody can do it. Therefore it stands to reason that this change will affect how foreign locales are depicted in musicals. Any sense of "otherness" that is concomitant with the "exotic" will change with it. Before any other cultures can take their place in the new musical theatre world order, they will have to do some soul searching to discover what that place might be; to find their own voice.

"The Lore of It, the Craft of It, the Technique of It"

In the preface, I mentioned learning the craft of writing (and performing) musicals. If you're not an American, and living in New York is not a viable option, you have to find another way. This is what I did.

When I first moved from Vancouver to Toronto in 1983, I became a member of the Guild of Canadian Musical Theatre Writers' workshops based on the teachings of Broadway conductor Lehman Engel. This was shortly after his passing, so I never actually met him, but I was being taught by his followers, few of whom I knew anything about.

Up to that point, I had been praised as a composer with "enormous promise"[1] by no less a figure than Stephen Schwartz, composer of *Godspell*, *Pippin* and (much later) *Wicked*. I really thought I was on my way. Given that nobody in these workshops had ever written a Broadway show, or even had a particularly great regional hit, I fully expected to be a big fish in a small pond and to rise quickly to the top. (Nobody had yet pointed out that a fish rising to the top of a pond was not a good thing.)

Among our earliest lyric-writing assignments was one to write an additional verse to "Oh, What a Beautiful Mornin'" in the style of Oscar Hammerstein. Why, when I'm trying to develop my own voice, would I want to do that? Maybe there were reasons, but I didn't understand them then. (If I were to teach a course like this myself today, I think I would instead begin by asking the pupil to set lyrics to "The Blue Danube" in a way that tells a story or sets a scene, develops character and in which the words fit the scancion and overall arc of the music.)

This first exposure to the establishment's craft of writing musicals was a shocking and gut wrenching experience. If you're going to go into that environment, you had better have a very firm grip on your own individuality, or else there is a major temptation to give in to peer pressure. Although nobody actually said this to me, I felt as if I was regarded as second class because, unlike everybody else, I had not been taught by the great man himself. (While they like to boast that *A Chorus Line* lyricist Ed Kleban had brought that show through the New York Lehman Engel workshops, what they don't say is that this was done over composer Marvin Hamlisch's strenuous objections.)

My work was dismissed as "predictable". They said that the "music is pretty, but still, needs a lyric that is fresh... lyrics need specificity. Perhaps too much vagueness in the lyrics... needs less clichés and perhaps work could be done with much of the writing."[2] Ouch. Who did these people think they were? I mean, they may have been correct, but surely that's not the point.

It may have been easier if the fellow members of the workshop had been people whom I knew and whose work I looked up to. For the most part, they weren't. Not that they weren't good, but I didn't really know their work: few Toronto shows travelled much beyond Toronto then, and so I had only ever seen one show written by workshop members. I knew that the shows they liked were not necessarily the shows I liked: I loved *Man of La Mancha* but they all thought it was "boring" (as did Lehman himself). I was told at the outset that if I wanted to write like Andrew Lloyd Webber, I was in the wrong place. Nothing less than the-Lord-Thy-God Stephen Sondheim would do.

I had grown up accustomed to Vancouver's "Movers and Shakers", and I didn't hear the kind of soaring, glorious melodies coming out of this group that I had expected. They seemed not to care. Follow-the-bouncing-ball-type memorable tunes were deemed passé. In fact, hit songs seldom came out of musicals any more. Some saw this as a kind of liberation, but I had mixed feelings.

Lyric writing is a craft that can, to a certain extent, be taught. Melodic genius cannot be. Possibly as a result, the emphasis seemed to be more on the lyrics than on the tunes, and making them very specific to the dramatic situation at hand. This, in hindsight, was probably good for me, as at the time, music was my strong suit and lyric writing – all those clichés – was where I needed to concentrate. What I didn't realise then was that Stephen Schwartz may have told me I had *"enormous promise"*. He didn't tell me that I had *achieved* it. I was in for a steep learning curve.

Leslie Arden, who would go on to study with Stephen Sondheim in Oxford and to write *The House of Martin Guerre*, found him to be old-fashioned. "He was advocating writing in four-bar phrases and a lot of stuff I really thought we were moving out of; all our stuff had to be verse, A-A-B-A. It was just a step behind the times, but I realised that really early on, so it wasn't a problem. This was like learning your Bach or doing your scales."[3]

I was now in the world of "perfect rhymes", a concept that was new to me. To the students of Lehman Engel, you could not try to rhyme "them" with "when". I rebelled. What's wrong with "Hello darkness, my old friend / I've come to talk with you again"[4]?, I thought.

I once heard Leonard Cohen (1934-2016) talk about how perfect rhymes "delight the ear", but he confessed that he sometimes used false rhymes, because the audience that he wrote for didn't mind. "They are really false rhymes but they are close enough that the ear is not violated"[5], he maintained. Bob Dylan (1941-) adds, "It gives you a thrill to rhyme something [where] you might think, 'Well, that's never been rhymed before'. But then again, people have taken rhyming now, it doesn't have to be exact anymore. Nobody's going to care if you rhyme 'represent' with 'ferment', you know."[6] In the world of pop music, "The Sounds of Silence" sounds just fine.

That said, I certainly wasn't going to write false rhymes, knowing that I was foisting an inferior product on audiences that didn't know any better, although even now, and with established librettists, this argument can stir up deeply held feelings. Vincent de Tourdonette, the Canadian librettist of *Pelagie* (and a Dylan fan) argues, "When almost all popular music contains slant rhyme, you might as well rage against the wind... Slant rhymes, associations, false rhymes, alliteration, consonance etc. [are] all tools I use personally, as do 90% of the lyricists I admire. I've been upbraided for it by critics, and likely will be again."[7]

The disconnect between the generation of the "Great American Songbook" and the current rock/pop generation can be quite profound. (In fact, until Dylan went electric, there was also a similar disconnect between rock and folk.) I would argue that Bob Dylan and Leonard Cohen probably hold equivalent positions in the esteem of rock and folk music fans to what Stephen Sondheim holds to lovers of musicals. I remember hearing Canadian radio journalist Jian Gomeshi trying to engage Sondheim in a discussion of Cohen's work. He received the radio equivalent of a blank stare. (And Cohen was born only four years after Sondheim, so it's not strictly generational.)

"There is nothing 'wrong' with near rhymes:", says Sondheim, "two generations of listeners brought up on pop and rock songs have gotten so accustomed to approximate rhyming that they neither care nor notice if the rhymes are perfect or not. To their ears, near rhymes are not only acceptable, but preferable; as in all popular art, familiarity breeds content (accent on the second syllable)."[8]

He brings up a good point – those who grew up on the perfect rhymes of everybody from Irving Berlin to Oscar Hammerstein II believe they are sacrosanct; those who grew up with Bob Dylan (himself a disciple of Woody Guthrie (1912-67)) or Leonard Cohen as their heroes are not so fussy. You must, however, remember that their songs are written to be heard repeatedly at the listener's leisure on the radio or on a record album. (You might even find the lyrics printed on the record sleeve.) They are not something that exists in character which you hear only once within a dramatic context on stage.

In a perfect rhyme, the vowel sound and the ending consonant sound of two words are identical. In the case of a two syllable (feminine) rhyme, the ending syllables are also identical. The preceding consonants will be different. (If the preceding consonant sound is also the same, it is not a "rhyme" but an "identity".) In a "false rhyme", only the vowel sound (or the ending consonant) is the same. Assonance, on the other hand, when used correctly can be effective: "In only a moment we both will be old/ We won't even notice the world getting cold".[9] The words "only", "moment", "both" and "cold" unconsciously help to propel the lyric forward.

Sondheim dismisses the argument that perfect rhymes allow only a limited emotional range. "The notion that good rhymes and the expression of emotion are contradictory qualities, that neatness equals lifelessness is, to borrow a disappearing phrase from my old counterpoint text, 'the refuge of the destitute'"[10] I would argue that, considered correctly, far from limiting the writer, the craft of good lyric writing unleashes limitless potential. As Sondheim says, "A perfect rhyme snaps the word, and with it the thought, vigorously into place, rendering it easily intelligible."

In live theatre, the audience only has one crack at understanding a lyric. Perfect rhymes make the lyrics easier to hear. Craig Carnelia (1949-), composer-lyricist of *Is There Life After High School?* and lyricist (to Marvin Hamlisch's music) of *The Sweet Smell of Success* says, "True rhyming is a necessity in the theatre, as a guide for the ear to know what it has just heard. Our language is so complex and difficult, and there are so many similar words and sounds that mean different things, that it's confusing enough without using near rhymes that only acquaint the ear with a vowel."[11] They are also considered a mark of craftsmanship, like a piece of fine woodwork with no visible nails.

Just as a former smoker is often the most radical advocate of clean air, once I had learned about the "rules" of rhyming, I began to see a sense of symmetry in a perfect rhyme, and false rhymes became like fingernails on a blackboard. You can't unlearn that. I then went through all my work with a fine tooth comb and removed all my indiscretions.

Shortly after moving to London, I had lunch with the late Dick Vosburgh (1929-2007), the American-born lyricist behind *A Day in Hollywood / A Night in the Ukraine*. Over a meal in Leicester Square, he gave me a lecture on why he thought Alan Jay Lerner's lyrics to "On the Street Where You Live" were sloppy, even though Lerner was a noted perfectionist who would sometimes spend months on a lyric. Ignoring the obvious fact that it should have read "*In* the Street Where You Live", he went straight to the line "People stop and stare / they don't bother me / There is no place else on earth where I would rather be."[12] It was the pairing of the phrases "bother me" and "rather be" that irked him. I suggested that it depended on the accent of the singer, but he told me I had missed the point. "Bother me" and "rather me" would be fine. That is what is called a "triple rhyme". But although, as written, the syllables rhyme individually, they do not rhyme as a unit because of the changed consonant on the last syllable.

It is important, however, when learning about craft, that we don't allow ourselves to become dogmatic. Some will, from a critical perspective, approach shows with a mental "checklist": Do the songs advance the plot? (They do less often than you might think.) Do they establish character? Or set the mood? Do they have a beginning, middle and an end? Are the rhymes clever? Is there a romantic subplot? Do the numbers end with a bang? Are the characters sympathetic? Does it have a hard, brassy edge? While all of these are important things to consider, many shows can work successfully without some or even all of these points.

If you want to teach the craft of writing (or performing), then the first thing you have to do is make people *want* craft; to make them care. It won't make a hoot and a holler difference to much of the audience: people won't be able to tell you *why* something doesn't work. They just know that it doesn't.

Studying dramaturgy does help you to solve some problems, but it's not foolproof. After all, Arthur Laurents (1917-2011) – book writer of both *Gypsy* and *West Side Story* – and Stephen Sondheim, with all their collected wisdom, still managed to come up with *Anyone Can Whistle* which lasted only nine performances on Broadway amid a hostile critical reception. The same team (plus Richard Rodgers) followed it up with *Do I Hear a Waltz* the following year, managing 220 performances.

Do people care about craft any more? In the world of pop music, possibly not.[13] Does it matter? Dave Malloy (1976-), the composer and lyricist of *Natasha, Pierre and the Great Comet of 1812*, is part of the generation that was steeped in rock music.

> "While I love music, and I love theater, I am acutely aware of the stigma of the term 'musical theater,' of all it has come to connote and the kneejerk reactions the genre tends to elicit. My community is largely one of experimental, downtown theater artists and musicians, for whom the love of musicals is either nonexistent, highly qualified, or a shameful secret. The music of musical theatre has evolved into a highly stylized and specific 'genre' of its own, instantly recognizable. And yet this 'genre' has little to do with the rest of the world of creative music-making. Musicals are not reported on by *Rolling Stone*, *Pitchfork* or *The Wire*, or reviewed by music critics, or devoured by people who love music. Instead, they are devoured by

people who love *musicals*, the archetypal 'musical theatre geeks' celebrated in *Glee*."

I view musicals from a different perspective. I neither read *Rolling Stone* nor did I watch *Glee* (too camp for my tastes). This so-called stigma puzzles me, for my knowledge of musical theatre reveals it to be a very broad church, and at its best, it is far more sophisticated, with a much broader musical vocabulary than pop or rock. Malloy continues:

> "The reason so much musical theater sounds bad and 'uncool' to so many ears, particularly when it flirts with rock, is because it lacks authenticity. Because it is being sung by people who aren't rock singers. They are acting. It's an obvious but critical fact; actors perform in fundamentally different ways from musicians."[14]

Yes, that is because this is theatre and they are, of course, acting. They are in character. They may even be triple-threats. If rock music can't accommodate the subtleties of drama, the musical theatre composer will have to find some other form that does. Malloy worries about "authenticity" to the musical form, whereas I am more concerned about authenticity to the culture.

It is true that musicals – especially on Broadway – have, out of necessity, evolved their own genre. That is because they have adapted to suit the needs of the theatre. Of course, if you're an avant garde "experimental, downtown theatre artist" under the influence of massive peer pressure, then being "cool" might be of vital importance to you. To those of us who are serious about our craft, we are more concerned with being "disciplined".

Malloy continues: "We need composers and singers that come from rock clubs, cabarets, basements, not undergraduate musical theatre programs." Yet the score for *Natasha, Pierre and the Great Comet of 1812* actually sounds surprisingly conventional and the singers in it certainly have legit musical theatre voices, no doubt trained in undergraduate programs. It requires a set of skills that you won't learn singing with a garage band. You only need to look at what happened when Cameron Mackintosh tried to hire TV soap star Martine McCutcheon to play Eliza Doolittle in his revival of *My Fair Lady*. She sounded fine in the auditions, but her instrument, which was untrained, could not handle an eight show week. The understudy Laura Michelle Kelly – who was legitimately trained – wound up doing more performances than McCutcheon. That understudy, in turn, ended up becoming a star herself, whereas McCutcheon never did a musical again. A similar thing happened when Andrew Lloyd Webber tried to cast Faye Dunaway in *Sunset Boulevard*.

While I am looking toward the future, I am not prepared to turn my back on two centuries of progress in order to create work that won't last five minutes past its sell-by date. Malloy seems to ask us to adapt to a new set of principles that are not best suited to our purpose.

In the Lehman Engel workshops, more important than perfect rhyming was an increased emphasis on the importance of a strong book. "I had always thought it was the music and the lyrics that were the heart of the show", says Nelles Van Loon, a Toronto pupil of Lehman's. "Lehman convinced me it was the book. I still remember him telling the story of meeting with Richard Rodgers for lunch and listening to Dick lament the fact that the shows he wrote with Lorenz Hart were undoable because the books were so weak, and Lehman concluding the anecdote with, 'If you ain't got a book, you ain't got nothin'."[15] Peter Stone argued, "You can have the best score in the world, but if the book is weak, it won't work. On the other hand, if the book is good, it can carry a mediocre score."[16] In my belief, that's what happened with *1776*, for which Stone provided the book. But, I would argue, if you ain't got a score, then what you have should be a play, not a musical. If a show has a strong score and a weak book, it will probably fail. If it has a strong book and a weak score, it will be lucky if it even reaches the stage. Why would it? After all, they don't call them *booksicals*.

A whole new field of musical theatre dramaturgy has grown up. The book of a musical is not just a play with songs dropped in. The book writer has to understand the role that music will play. This is where the study of the works that have gone before is so helpful. This includes not just the classics, but the failures as well. It also includes shows from the past in your own (and other) parts of the world.

However, in my opinion, nothing should ever come at the expense of the music. I want the songs of a musical to soar and sing. This doesn't mean that they have to be chart hits. It also doesn't mean that the lyrics have to be generic. When asked what the primary requirement of a good lyric was, Alan Jay Lerner answered, "Well, that's easy. The primary requirement is good music. I've heard good music make not very good lyrics sound better, but I've never heard a good lyric really register unless there is the proper music that went with it."[17]

In theatre, pop and classical music, strong melody may have become unfashionable; some might even say sentimental. This may have been, at least in part, a result of the decline in popularity of film musicals, as they reached a broader audience than live theatre did. But if you're going to use leitmotifs, it would be pointless unless they are memorable enough for the audience to recognise them when they occur. To me, melody is to music what plot is to drama. It is the shape of a song. It's what it's about. (Of course, you can write dramas without plots, but you had better know what you're doing.)

"Why is there not a distinctive late 20th century melodic style?" asks British composer Ian Stewart. "The explanation is, I believe, that it would have taken exceptional skill to write melodic music that is quintessentially late 20th century. Composers, instead of facing the problem head on, have decided to ignore it altogether. There is even an unstated view that all melodies have already been written, that there is nothing new in that area."[18] That's a little like announcing that we have reached the end of infinity.

In a musical, the music and the libretto are of equal importance. Neither is more important than the other. It is, I believe, possible to strengthen the one without weakening the other. When John Kander (1927-) and Fred Ebb (1928-2004) wrote *The Scottsboro Boys*, they knew they were taking on a difficult subject (an unjust murder trial of a group of black men), but their first instinct has always been to entertain, so they wrote it in the style of a minstrel show.

"Another of [Lehman's] beliefs was that the score shouldn't call attention to itself as much as it should serve the needs of a show", says Nelles. "The story that illustrated this involved his seeing *Fiddler on the Roof* and being completely carried away by it. At the end [composer] Jerry Bock came up to him and asked him what he thought of the score. Lehman answered, 'What score? I laughed, I cried, I was completely transported', to which Jerry replied, 'That's the greatest compliment I've ever been paid.'" However, with hit songs like "Matchmaker, Matchmaker" and "Sunrise, Sunset", nobody could reasonably argue that *Fiddler on the Roof* doesn't have an outstanding score.

The score by Marc Shaiman (1959-) and Scott Wittman (1954-) for the film *Mary Poppins Returns* has been widely criticised. The duo had already co-written songs for *Smash* and *Hairspray*, among many others. "The songs of *Mary Poppins Returns* are almost shockingly forgettable", says Alissa Wilkinson in *Vox*. "I defy you to hum any of the tunes on your way out of the theater."[19] Director Rob Marshall disagrees. "I think it's a fantastic score, I really do," he told the BBC. "We didn't set out to make them stand-alone songs, because that doesn't work for a musical."[20] But yet Rodgers & Hammerstein and Lerner & Loewe wrote many songs that performed their function in the show **and** were hits outside of it. They saw no contradiction.

I personally found the songs in *Mary Poppins Returns* to be reasonably good. If they were not as 'memorable' as "Chim-Chim-Cheree" or "A Spoonful of Sugar", perhaps it's because their public didn't demand it. The original *Mary Poppins* songs were up against *My Fair Lady* and *The Sound of Music*. Even Frederick Loewe and Richard Rodgers stopped writing their best tunes when the bar was lowered.

Rupert Christiansen wrote in the London *Telegraph*, "The scores of the more recent crop of successful 'original' musicals - *The Lion King*, *Billy Elliot*, *The Book of Mormon*, *Charlie and the Chocolate Factory*, *Matilda*, *Wicked* – are their weakest element. Has one of them yielded a single song which has passed into the general consciousness? All of them seem to prioritise plot and spectacle."[21] (I wouldn't include *Wicked* in this list: it has in fact yielded several songs, including "Popular" and "Defying Gravity".)

The book of *Candide* is widely considered to be problematic. This comes down to the picaresque nature of the novel by Voltaire that it is based on. The composer Leonard Bernstein, who was the most powerful member of the show's original creative team, had written one of the best theatre scores of all time, but the show just didn't work, and ran for only 73 performances. The *New York Times* complained that "the libretto... seems too serious for the verve and mocking lyricism of Leonard Bernstein's score which, without being strictly 18th century, maintains with its gay pastiche of past styles and forms, a period quality."[22]

Twenty years later, it was revived by Harold Prince with Lillian Hellman (1905-84)'s original book replaced by a new one by Hugh Wheeler (1912-87) who had written the book for *A Little Night Music*, and with some very extensive cuts to the score. It ran on Broadway for 740 performances. Since that time, an "opera house" version (also initially directed by Prince) has been created, using the new book but with much of the cut score restored. Nevertheless, it continues, in many people's eyes, to be a great score and a problematic book.

Seattle based librettist Stephen Oles has a problem with all of this. "Theatre music and pop have gone off in their own direction, leaving pop songwriting bereft of craft and intelligence... and theatre composers wandering off into increasingly sterile, etiolated idioms... Virtually every number is medium tempo. Melody is replaced by the repetition of short, uninteresting phrases of four or five notes – in the manner of Sondheim on an off day – and emotion, previously the essence of musical theatre, is eschewed as old-fashioned."[23]

There have been other principles bandied about that I am less certain of, including the virtual ban on one person writing book, music and lyrics – although I am well aware of the problems associated with it. "It is too much for one person to carry," says Tom Jones, librettist of *The Fantasticks*. "And it is too much to expect of one person's talents."[24] Charles Hart (1961-), lyricist of *Phantom of the Opera* and *Aspects of Love* told me that the problems with doing it all yourself were always the same, whereas the problems of working with collaborators were each unique.

In an ideal world – i.e. the so-called "Golden Age" of Broadway – you get the best musicals by putting together the best composer, the best lyricist and the best book writer with the best source material. But we don't always live in an ideal world, and in my own experience, there are so few proven book writers around that you could wait until hell froze over and not write a single word. I list Noël Coward's *Bitter Sweet*, Lionel Bart's *Oliver!*, Frank Loesser's *The Most Happy Fella*[25] and Meredith Willson's *The Music Man*[26] as evidence that successful musicals can be written by a single author. Few and far between, but they do exist.

In the thirty-five-plus years since I was in the Lehman Engel workshops, the world has changed almost beyond recognition. The struggle for "perfect rhymes" has amost been lost.[27] People in the West are better traveled and better read than they were seventy years ago, and they are far more aware of the rest of the world. The days when Rodgers and Hammerstein could write *The King and I* safe in the knowledge that few in their audience would know or care anything about life in Thailand are gone.

Yet, when I visited Singapore, a group of writers there indicated that they were hungry for Western teachers to come over there and mentor them. In this new multi-cultural, multi-national environment, how are we set up to teach the craft of writing musicals to those whose backgrounds are very different from ours?

"The fundamentals of a course are easy to put together, I think", says creative-life-coach Chris Grady. "The fundamentals being: someone who can teach music and someone who can teach words. Every single class needs those two elements in it... But the difference I would make, if I could, would be to find a way whereby it could be taught multilingually, because I think one of the problems with developing musical theatre that is for an audience of a country which doesn't speak English as its first language is that most of the people who want to go and study have to go and study in English. You don't have to be an English-language master to write Polish music."

The Graduate Musical Theatre Writing Program at the Tisch School of the Arts in New York emphasises "tools" over "rules". "Our faculty has set up workshops in several different countries currently including Nairobi[28] and they are able to approach these students the same way we approach ours", says Sarah Schlesinger, director of the Tisch School program.

"I am only qualified to comment on teaching the principles of NYU's Musical Theatre Writing program although I myself went through the BMI Workshop. We have a very different philosophy that assumes a diverse student population. We frequently have students in New York City from the Ukraine, Colombia, Brazil, Chile, Turkey, several provinces in China, Korea, Japan, Singapore, Hong Kong, France, Germany, Norway, Italy, India, Russia etc. What we teach is not writing the Broadway musical. We are teaching how to collaborate to merge words and music. Our students return to their countries or other part[s] of the USA and write in a variety of forms. Although we have an alumni show[29] heading for Broadway in February, students no longer come thinking that they will have Broadway careers. They are preparing to write for Young Audiences, opera, games, software, immersive theatre and numerous other markets around the world."[30]

"The most important part of the craft", says John Sparks, Artistic Director of the Academy of New Musical Theatre in Los Angeles, "is the fact that the musical is, at its heart, a narrative story telling form. So the story matters, and good stories rely on strong characters. In language craft terms this means giving each character a unique speech pattern and honoring that pattern in the dialogue and lyrics, while honoring the stylistic conventions of songs in that language, whatever that may be."[31]

"One of the main reasons for our caring about spreading this art and craft beyond the U. S.", says Schlesinger, "is our hope that other countries will create their own musical theatres, telling their own stories and the stories their own cultures need to hear. There [are] as many possible strategies as there are different cultures."

What sorts of variations in terms of craft might some other cultures and languages demand? One of my major focuses as a composer-lyricist is trying to make the song follow the natural rhythm of speech. I like to give the example of Frank Loesser's *The Most Happy Fella*, in which the transition from dialogue to heightened speech to recititif to song is so smoothe it is virtually imperceptible.[32]

What do you do in a country such as Japan or Finland where the language places more or less equal emphasis on each syllable? Jari Laakso is a Finnish actor, director and musical writer living in London.[33] "Finnish is a strange language as the speech doesn't really have intonations which usually give a rhythm to the speech. So rhythm is free to follow music. If it's writing in verse, sure there is a flow but it's not strict."[34] Chris Grady adds, "You have to work with composers and poets or writers of words in a way that works for their lyrical structure, their syntax, their style of presentation of words. And in some languages like Chinese Mandarin for example, just the simple process of singing a word can change its meaning completely, because of the tonal language."

And how does rhyme work in other languages? "In some languages (French for instance)", says John Sparks, "rhyme is more or less ubiquitous and therefore not so much an issue as it is in English." Sarah Schlesinger adds, "Many languages place no value on rhyme. Their particular musical forms also dictate a lot about organization and content. We teach basic song form and let the students adapt what works to their needs."

Another lesson that I have learned along the way is that it matters what vowel sounds you match to what notes. Singing the word "be" on a high "C" may put your singer in the hospital. (Just ask Michael Crawford, whose high octane rendition of "Music of the Night" in *Phantom of the Opera* did just that.)

In Singapore, Dr. Kenneth Lyen of Musical Theatre Live observes, "Our globalisation is an inadvertent one in that the traditional Chinese, Indian and Malay dramas do not follow the traditional Aristotelian[35] three act structure. It is a little bit more meandering. It's good and bad – it's good in that it's more Asian and has a slightly mystic quality, but it's bad in that it doesn't have the dramatic tension which most Western theatre has – developing, complications and final resolution."

Do we adapt our preconceptions in order to reach across cultures? We certainly haven't always. Susan Cluff was a student of Lehman Engel in Toronto in the 1970s. "Lehman did not adjust his perceptions", she says. "He was what he was. We were learning about writing American musicals. Many writers obviously went on to write 'Canadian' shows but not because of any encouragement of Canadianism from Lehman. He was an American and believed in the American Broadway musical... He taught us from his perspective, which was Broadway... not composers and lyricists who would be fortunate to get small shows produced at small venues, if they were produced at all."[36] Michael Bawtree, who ran the Music Theatre Studio Ensemble at the Banff Centre, says "Yes, he was a child of the American commercial theatre, and did believe that in the end the acid test of the success of a work was whether it attracted an audience. But in another period I believe he would have been just as happy to create work like Mozart etc. - for a patron."[37]

Much of dramaturgy depends on a sense of where the audience's empathy lies. While I regard the book to *1776* as a masterpiece, its failure in London can hardly have been a surprise, given they were in the land of the "enemy". "Interest and empathy cannot be predicted", says Sarah Schlesinger. "We push our writers to write about difficult subjects without artifice."

I believe it is important to have more than one teacher. Stephen Sondheim was, in an artistic sense, raised by Oscar Hammerstein II, who taught him to regard songs as mini-three-act dramas. Only later did he learn about list songs and other things that looked at songwriting in another way. In many ways Sondheim moved the musical beyond the Rodgers and Hammerstein template.

Chris Grady was involved in organising the one-off Highland Quest for New Musicals, which was supported by the government of Scotland and the Mackintosh Foundation. He ran a short course there to try to bring together collaborators and to find and nurture new work.

> "If you mentioned Jason Robert Brown in that room, there was one person there, I think, who happened to live in London but was Scottish, who would have known who that was. No one else knew or cared. They had all heard of Andrew Lloyd Webber, they had maybe heard of Stephen Sondheim, but probably didn't know much of his work. They didn't know the lyrics of Tim Rice particularly, or Don Black or anything else like that. They wrote poetry. They wrote songs. They wrote music. They were steeped in the legends of their forefathers. They were steeped in the music that they played as children, and through ceilidhs and through work right the way through to the contemporary festivals. They came without that baggage... They were completely illuminated by their own music and their own poetry. The most interesting stuff for me came from those people working within their own cultural resonance."

"Universality is the surest way to reach distant audiences," says Sarah Schlesinger. As I have mentioned in a previous chapter, universality is a key element in the development of the musical as an international form. However, universality is not a bland way of stripping a show of all of its specificity. It is the opposite. For a Korean musical to be a success in Canada, it would, I believe, have to be identifiably Korean.

Now I have a serious confession to make. I didn't remain with the Toronto Lehman Engel workshops beyond my first year. Nor did I remain a member of its sponsor, the since-defunct Guild of Canadian Musical Theatre Writers. I allowed my pride to get the better of me. To say that I lacked humility then would be an understatement. I have regretted it ever since.

My advice to the student of musical theatre is to swallow your pride and try to learn from others. You don't have to agree with them. You don't even have to like them. Keep good enough notes that you can restore your work if their advice doesn't pan out, but keep your mind open.

For years I've been thinking that we needed to establish these international classes, but wasn't so certain that I knew how to do it. Now I realise that *nobody* knows. I've spoken of the "rules" of perfect rhyming, but would that apply in French? In Chinese? How can we respond in a way that encourages indigenous work?

People like me can only teach from our own perspective, but we can allow room for other points of view. The only way forward would be by experimentation. If I were doing a class in Singapore, I would try to bring in somebody with an understanding of a Chinese sense of dramaturgy and structure, as well as somebody else to teach the Western version, giving them a choice as to which path to follow. I would examine the idea of music that follows the rythms of Singaporean speech, and Singaporean syntax, whether in English, "Singlish" or Mandarin. I would teach the principles, but not try to impose the Broadway/West End style. It would be taught in English initially, with the idea that as students emerge and qualify as teachers, they could do so in the native languages. It would become a two-way conversation, with lots of trial and error.

It would be an adventure.

ACT II: The Offspring

Europe after Hitler

While British musicals survived and sometimes even prospered, the Second World War decimated continental European musical theatre. Pre-war French musical comedy breathed its last gasp with the operettas of Vincent Scotto and Francis Lopez. In Spain, the zarzuela tradition began to fade out after the Spanish civil war. In Germany (and all the countries it had occupied) Hitler had either killed or driven away the talent pool, and the city of Vienna saw fit to demolish many of its celebrated musical houses. It seemed that not only had the skills and the talent pool been lost, but the whole art form – especially in France and Austria – had been tainted.[38] Yet, three of France's greatest international successes were still to come.

The first French composer since Offenbach to enjoy world-wide success with a book musical was Marguerite Monnot (1903-61) who is perhaps best known as Edith Piaf's favourite songwriter. She trained with Nadia Boulanger (1887-1979), who also trained the Broadway composers Charles Strouse and Marc Blitzstein, as well as orchestrator Robert Russell Bennett, French film composer Michel Legrand and the Argentine tango composer Astor Piazzolla, all of whom in some way contributed to the musical theatre.

Poor health had forced young Marguerite to give up a career as a concert pianist and she turned instead to popular music. After many hits (including "La Vie en Rose", "Hymne à l'Amour", "Milord" and "La Goualante du Pauvre Jean"), she first turned to writing for the theatre with *La P'tite Lili*, an operetta with book and lyrics by Marcel Achard (1899-1974) starring Piaf, Robert Lamoureux (1920-2011) and Eddie Constantine (1913-93) which lasted for seven months in 1951 at the ABC Music Hall in Paris.

Then on November 12, 1956 came her biggest success, when *Irma La Douce* opened at the Théâtre Gramont. The book and lyrics were by Alexandre Breffort

(1901-71). He expanded a short story he had written for the satirical magazine *Le Canard enchaîné* ("The Chained Duck", of which he had been editor since 1934) which he had already turned into a twenty-minute cabaret sketch in 1949 at the Cabaret Chez Gilles for the Compagnie Grenier-Hussenot, *Les Harengs Terribles*. ("Harengs" is an argot slang term for a man who lives off the avails of prostitution.) When he and Monnot expanded it into a full-length entertainment, he was emphatic that it should be a "comedie-musicale" and not an operetta.

Bob-le-Hotu introduces the action: "The story we are about to tell you is the story of a ménage à deux – something you don't see everyday!" The story concerns a naïve member of the Paris underworld (a law student in the English version) named Nestor-le-Fripé ("Rumpled Nestor") who falls in love with a prostitute and becomes her protector. Wanting her to himself, he disguises himself as a wealthy patron named Oscar who buys her exclusive services. When the strain of maintaining this double life becomes too much for him, he "kills" Oscar – and is convicted of murder. (Only through bribery is he able to convince the authorities that he didn't actually "murder" himself.)

The original production was directed by René Dupuy (1920-2009), director of the Théâtre Gramont from 1954-1973, who also played the narrator, Bob-le-Hotu, proprietor of the Bar-des-Inquiets ("Bar for Worried People"). For the leading role of the prostitute Irma, Juliette Gréco (1927-) and Colette Deréal (1927-88) were considered, but the part finally went to Colette Renard (1924-2010), who was married to the show's musical director Raymond Legrand (1908-74). Another sometime Piaf collaborator, Legrand's son Michel was the un-credited co-arranger (for a four piece on-stage band). Nestor was played by Michel Roux (1929-2007), who had also appeared in the original sketch. *Le Figaro* said, "Alexandre Breffort achieved a slight of hand in dealing with a difficult subject without for one second falling into the trap of vulgarity."[39] It transferred to the larger Théâtre de l'Athénée and ultimately played for a total of 962 performances, including a 1967 return engagement.

Irma La Douce managed to achieve what few of even the best French musicals could manage: it was successfully adapted into English. Bandleader Henry Hall (1898-1989) had seen the show in Paris and obtained the rights, which he then sublet to Donald Albery (1914-88) for Donmar Productions, and Binkie Beaumont (1908-73) for H.M. Tennent Ltd.

Monty Norman (1928-), David Heneker (1906-2001) and Julian More (1928-2010) had already collaborated on the music business satire *Expresso Bongo*. On the strength of this, they were approached by the producers to provide an English libretto for this French hit. The director was to be Peter Brook (1925-), whose only previous musical was 1954's short-lived *House of Flowers* with a libretto by Truman Capote (1924-84) and score by Harold Arlen (1905-86).

Translating a musical from one language into another is always a tricky business. Michael Kunze, who in addition to being a successful lyricist and book writer in his own right, has also created German-language translations of *Evita*, *Chicago* and many others. He maintains that it is more adaptation than translation. "I try to become the original librettist and lyricist," he told me, "writing the whole show again in German. It is more important to keep the original intentions and atmosphere than to stick to the words. All my partners saw it the same way, Tim Rice, Fred Ebb, Stephen Schwartz, even Stephen Sondheim. Likewise, I never demand a word-by-word translation from my authors."[40]

It is fair to say that the English version of *Irma la Douce* is an adaptation rather than a translation. The challenge was enormous, for all the elements that had defeated shows like *Phi-Phi* were there in spades: a risqué subject, a distinctly French flavour, and liberal use of slang terms such as "grisbi" (money), "poule" (prostitute), "mec" (pimp) and "millieu" (Paris underworld), and expressions like "dis-donc" (you don't say), not to mention Breffort's penchant for puns. Imagine trying to translate the Damon Runyon dialects of *Guys and Dolls* and you'll get the idea. Even in Paris, a glossary was provided in the programme.

"After several versions had been thrown in the wastepaper basket", wrote Julian More, the principal author of the book, "we eventually hit on the right way to present *Irma* to English audiences: to avoid use of Bronx or cockney slang equivalents[41], so beloved of sub-titlers and so killing to Gallic atmosphere; to use instead a few French argot terms and to adapt the lyrics freely, taking Breffort's thought line but creating our own shapes, and in some cases writing completely new lyrics to Monnot's music."[42] For example, they cut the original opening number "Because" and created a new number, "Valse Millieu", (using the same melody as the title song) in which Bob-le-Hotu introduces the slang terms we are about to hear. In some instances, melodies and the characters who sang them were entirely re-assigned, and the musical structure adjusted. What had originally been "Il a Raison" ("He's Right") sung by Irma became "That's a Crime", sung by Bob-le-Hotu. "Avec les anges" (literally, "with the angels"), with a very slight melodic alteration became "Our Language of Love." (In the English version, what had been a recurring verse is used only as a recitive at the beginning, and the two syllable "an-ges" becomes the one syllable "love".) Because Elizabeth Seal (1933-) was a dancer, choreography by Canadian-born John Heawood (1920-95) was added, which was largely absent in the original.

The collaboraters resisted advice to sanitize the

story and dialogue, and to add more female characters – Irma being the only woman among fourteen men. Director Peter Brook maintained, "The English version was a faithful translation of the original French production – give or take a few score terms in Montmartre argot. We did take liberties there... The story, characters and author's attitude are unalterably French. Our friends advised us to change the locale to London or New York. But we felt the local flavour of the 'millieu' – that is, the community of prostitutes, procuerers and thieves of the back streets around Pigalle, must be maintained."[43]

Of course, in those days, all scripts had to be submitted to the Lord Chamberlain's office (the censor). "He to everyone's surprise passes our script intact", writes Brook in his published journal. "He only cuts, without explanation, one word, '*Kiki*' – and I haven't the heart to tell him that this in Paris slang simply means 'the neck'."[44]

The casting of twenty-five year old Elizabeth Seal also had to meet with the approval of Marguerite Monnot. Seal spoke no French and Monnot no English. Seal remembers,

> "I stood on the Globe stage and sang what became 'The Language of Love'. David Heneker played piano. The More, Norman, Heneker team hadn't even had final approval at that point to adapt and rework *Irma* from the French. Marguerite sat in front stalls, and when I finished the song she got up and kissed me on both cheeks. She didn't want a singer as such, she wanted something more raw from the streets. (I did have to work on this.) However... she liked my cracks... I then had to wait seven months whilst 'the Boys' as they were called translated, changed, adapted *Irma* for English audiences. So that I could turn down other work, Binkie paid me a retainer. I don`t think that would happen nowadays."[45]

"In Paris it was, and is, of its own strange kind, a masterpiece," wrote Harold Hobson in the *Sunday Times*. "One did not notice there the absence of offence. One was conscious instead of the actual presence of virtue, of a love that is, of all quiet things, of generosity and response to kindness... In London, the cast bar their minds against all thoughts of evil, whilst in Paris, the company, with glowing innocence, seem unaware that evil could possibly exist."[46] *Punch* made a similar comparison: "In Paris, one saw the ugliness of Pigalle through a haze of fantasy, and Colette Renard played Irma with such a shining simplicity that one could have almost taken any of one's aunts to see her... This was a trick, I think, that only the French know how to manage... English is a poor language for wrapping squalor."[47]

Following tryouts at the Pavillion Theatre, Bournemouth (where it opened 24 June) and at Theatre Royal Brighton, *Irma la Douce* opened at London's Lyric Theatre on 17 July, 1958, where it ran for a record-breaking 1,512 performances starring Elizabeth Seal (1933-) and Australian actor Keith Michell (1926-2015) (later replaced by Shani Wallace (1933-) and John Neville (1925-2011)). The music was re-orchestrated by another French composer, André Popp (1924-2014), who had arranged many of Jacques Brel's early recordings and would later write the hit "Love is Blue".

The Times wrote, "Treated clumsily, the frivolous anecdote which *Irma la Douce* expands into a musical comedy could only hope to raise sniggers. Happily, the book of M. Alexandre Breffort is adroitly written, and though it goes somewhat heavily into English a special sort of innocence has been retained, and the audience at the Lyric, at any rate in the first half, is kept in a perpetual ripple of open and more or less sunny laughter."[48] The *Manchester Guardian* called it "thin stuff and... it seems paradoxically thinner in this export version because Peter Brook's vigour in production swells the volume of what is more acceptable when left sleazy and frail."[49] Although most critics had nothing but praise for Elizabeth Seal, the *Observer* claimed she was the show's weak link: "vocally too weak and coy to suggest a convincing whore."[50] On the other hand, the *Daily Herald*'s Harry Weaver complained that "Not even Liz Seal's vitality and urchin charm or the hard work of Keith Michell make this an evening to remember. Maybe *Irma* should have stayed in the original French."[51]   However, *Tatler*'s Anthony Cookman wrote, "The delightful thing about the adaptation of *Irma la Douce* at the Lyric is that it somehow contrives to extract the innocent absurdity of the original French musical and make it easy for us to swallow the absurdity neat."[52]

The "prompt book" of the London production reveals that two songs were re-written during the run – "Valse Millieu" replaced the lines :

> Millieu's the name of the underworld mob
> Poule is the girl who goes out on the job
> Mec is the fellow who pockets the cash
> Grisbi's the cash which is lovely to stash

with

> This is the Paris that hides from the day
> Waiting 'til night for the stranger to stray
> This is the world to forget or forgive
> Sinner or saint, we have all got to live.

The lyrics for "Wreck of a Mec" were also entirely replaced. Before opening in New York under the aegis of David Merrick (1911-2000), the show went through yet another transformation. "Très Très Snob" (which in the original version had been "C'est Polyte le Mou", or "It's Spineless Polyte") was rewritten as "Sons of France". A very Broadway sounding overture was added, as were two major dances, arranged by future composer John Kander (1927-) and choreographed by another Canadian, Onna White (1922-2005) .

Irma la Douce opened at the Plymouth Theater (following a two-week tryout in Washington, D.C.) on September 29, 1960 with the same director (and the same three stars) but with additional orchestrations by Robert Ginzler (1910-62) (who had done the same chores on *Gypsy* and *Bye Bye Birdie*), and ran for 524 performances. Peter Brook's future assistant Nina Parry remembers,

> I saw *'Irma la Douce'* in London, many times, when I was very young and I was passionate about the show and the music. This original production had great rough charm and the feeling of a tiny part of Paris. But when I listened to a record of the New York version it had a very different feeling. And what a surprise when what must have been a long, new dance routine somebody suddenly shouted 'Penguins'!!![53] There were no penguins in London!! It felt more like a Broadway idea of Paris. How could it not – the music was re-orchestrated by great Broadway musicians. That was obviously how things were done in those days.[54]

Howard Taubman in the *New York Times* wrote, "Trust the French to make vice as innocent as a fable."[55] *Time* magazine explained that "by putting its bad apples at the top of the barrel and its milk of human kindness inside Pernod bottles, *Irma la Douce* endows its harmless story with a nice tingle of iniquity, even a certain mixture of sweetness and bite… Marguerite Monnot's score has a gay street-music tinniness that can have resonance too, as in the rousing wail of 'From a Prison Cell' or the ring and bounce of 'There is Only One Paris for That'".[56] John Chapman in the *Daily News* declared, "There won't be a more captivating new musical on Broadway all this season than *Irma la Douce*".[57] John McClain in the *Journal American* said, "Here is authentic French atmosphere which will entrance anyone who loves the byways of Paris and harkens to the lilting music of Montmartre."[58] The *New York Post*'s Richard Watts Jr. decided that "its chief virtue as a musical play is that it has taken the materials of cynicism, sentimentality, mockery and what might be termed sexual preoccupation and woven them into an integrated whole that posesses strikingly imaginative style and originality. In this achievement it is greatly aided by Marguerite Monnot's charming score".[59] Only the *Herald-Tribune*'s Walter Kerr seemed not to have been swept away. "It's a pity that someone couldn't have decided that the evening had an impish point to make and then stuck to it, instead of letting it gradually transform itself into a sort of poor man's *Beggars' Opera*, or even, at times, into a beggar's *Beggar's Opera*. There is imagination, and to spare. But there is no staying-power, no hearty filling inside the showy meringue."[60]

Noted New York theatre critic Howard Kissel has said, "What made *Irma* a show of note, though no one sensed it at the time, was that – despite its saucy, endearing score and its 'whore with a heart of gold' plot – it was very much an experimental musical. It used almost no scenery. Its cast consisted of all men except for the title character. At a time when American musicals prided themselves on their psychological subtlety, *Irma* relied on old-fashioned touches from vaudeville and burlesque to tell its story."[61]

A German production opened on 24 January 1961 at the Theater der Stadt in Baden-Baden, and an Australian company opened at Theatre Royal, Sydney on 25 February of the same year. A Hebrew production opened at Habimah in Israel in 1962, and in the same year a Spanish-language version opened at Teatro Insurgentes in Mexico City, starring Silvia Pinal (1931-) and directed by Enrique Rambal (1924-71). In Buenos Aires it opened at Teatro Smart on 23 October 1963, and a Hungarian version opened in Budapest on 4 November 1964.

Following *Irma*'s world-wide success, Monnot was invited to write songs for Walt Disney (interesting, in light of *Irma*'s subject matter), but she didn't want to leave France. In 1960, she and Breffort wrote one more musical together, *L'Impasse de la Fidélité* which starred the music-hall chanteuse Patachou (Henriette Ragon, 1918–2015) at the Théâtre des Ambassadeurs. The following year she died of a ruptured appendix at the age of 58.

The film rights to *Irma* were sold to the Mirisch Corp. two months before the Broadway production had even opened, but they had to wait until the stage show had run its course before they could begin shooting. Director Billy Wilder (1906-2002) then hired Shirley Maclaine (1934-), who had recently starred in the film of Cole Porter's *Can-Can* to play the title role, and Herschel Bernardi (1923-86), who would later star in *Fiddler on the Roof* was cast as Inspector LeFevre. The supporting cast included Bruce Yarnell (1935-73) who had starred in a Lincoln Center revival of *Annie Get Your Gun* opposite Ethel Merman, and Canadian character actor Lou Jacobi (1913-2009), who had appeared in the London productions of *Guys and Dolls* and *Pal Joey*, as Moustache (Bob-le-Hotu in the stage version). Even Jack Lemon (1925-2001) as Nestor has been known to put across a song, and the presence of André Previn as musical arranger certainly pointed toward this being a musical.

Yet, as Wilder and his co-screenwriter I.A.L. Diamond (1920-88) progressed with their adaptation, they gradually reached the conclusion that the songs had to go. "I have nothing against music", he says, "but the more I went into that story, the better I thought it was. And for me, the numbers got in the way. So, first, one of them went. Then another one went. And, one day, I made the decision, and we threw the whole score out and made it a straight picture."[62] Producer Walter Mirisch (1921-) says, "He felt more comfortable doing it as a straight farce. He had done only one musical, *The Emperor's Waltz* with Bing Crosby, and it had been unsuccessful."[63]

Thus Marguerite Monnot's music was relegated to the background (although "Dis-Donc" is virtually staged as a diegetic musical number, even although no lyrics are sung except for a brief exclamation of the title). Monnot and Breffort were both credited as the original authors of the play, without any specific reference to music. André Previn won an Academy Award for his adaptation of her themes, including "Language of Love / Avec les Anges" and "Dis-Donc". Interestingly, in her later one-woman-show, Maclaine performed some of the songs that she would have sung in the role had she been given the chance.

While the film was, at the time, the most commercially successful of all of Wilder's, it is not one of his best remembered. Many feel that by cutting out the songs, he cut out the heart. As Wilder's biographer Ed Sikov writes, "The wonderful ... thing about Hollywood musicals is that characters can tap immediately into their emotional lives by opening their mouths and singing... Love, joy, regret, despair, bliss, triumph – these are the mainstays of musical comedy, but for Billy they're too quick, easy and pretty."[64] For *The Guardian*'s Richard Roud, the film reminded him of the story of Lichtenberg's knife. "As every schoolboy knows, George Lichtenberg was an eighteenth-century German satirical writer who invented the knife without a blade whose handle was then removed. Following what we might call Lichtenberg's law, then, this plotless musical has now had its songs and dances removed. Surely this is madness and the result is pretty disastrous."[65] Interestingly, cutting the songs did not speed the plot along: it still runs well over two hours.

Irma la Douce was adapted for French television in 1972, starring Marie-Claude Mestral as Irma and Jean-Pierre Moulin as Nestor. It was directed by Paul Paviot, and first broadcast on 17 February 1972. The original French stage version has been revived in Paris several times, including a major production at the Opéra-Comique in 2000, directed by Jérôme Savary (1942-). *L'Express* called it "a delight in pictures and song." The *New York Times* said this production "has everything going for it: good singers, good dancers, good costumes, good sets that spin and open up like gigantic dollhouses. It also has Savary's characteristic frenetic pace, busy staging and visual gags, leaving never a dull moment. Here's a chance to spend two hours with some bad guys you can't help but love."[66]

It's hard to know how Breffort and Monnot felt about the English version. After Breffort's death in 1971, Colette Renard said, "You never knew if he was happy or unhappy. He loved to make people laugh, but personally, I never saw him laugh."⁶⁷ There was, for a time, an embargo placed on the English language version because of a (possibly financial) dispute with the estates of the French writers. Greg MacKellan of San Francisco's 42nd Street Moon says,

> "I was told that it started right after David Heneker died - that as long as all three of the English adapters were alive there was no problem, but the death of one of them led to problems with the attorney for Marguerite Monnot and Alexandre Breffort. Year after year we'd ask to do it at 42nd Street Moon, and get turned down, told no one else was allowed to produce it here, either... Toward late 2007, Sarge Aborn at Tams-Witmark told us there was a new attorney representing the French authors, and that we could finally do the show, which we did in Sept. 2008... If one has seen or heard the original French version, it's not so hard to see why Monnot and Breffort had problems with the show. The English version is so different in tone, and many of the songs are used in a completely different way than they are in the French version. When the movie came out, with the songs excised save for underscore, only Breffort was still alive, and he took an even stronger dislike to the piece."⁶⁸

Breffort himself never understood *Irma's* international appeal. "There are feelings that do not make it across borders", he said. "My heroine is so typically Parisian that you couldn't even transplant her from Belleville to Ménilmontant!"⁶⁹ However, foreign audiences don't necessarily have to understand something to be amused by it: Monty Python's Eric Idle was always confused by Americans laughing at the line "Keeble College, Oxford." (I think probably because they heard "Keeble-kolly-joxford".)

Of course, as soon as you move anything outside of its native language you separate it from its culture, but I believe that what distinguishes *Irma la Douce* from *Phi-Phi* and other French musicals that failed in translation is the extent to which Messers Brook, Norman, More and Heneker respected their source material. The fact that they attempted to preserve as much French atmosphere as the English language could accommodate surely counts for something. *Irma la Douce* was revived in concert at New York City Center *Encores!* in 2014.

Irma was not the only French musical on Broadway around the same time. *La Plume de ma Tante* ("The plume of my aunt"), a revue devised by Robert Dhéry (1921-2004) with music by film composer Gerard Calvi (1922-2015) and lyrics by Francis Blanche (1921-74) and Ross Parker (1914-74) which had already run for three years at London's Garrick Theatre, opened on Broadway at the Royal Theater on November 11, 1958 and closed on December 17, 1960 after a total of 835 performances. *Time Magazine* called it "as engagingly French as it is abundantly funny."[70] The ensemble was awarded a special Tony Award in 1959. Calvi and Dhéry also created the 1965 production *La Grosse Valise* with lyrics by Harold Rome (1908-93) and conducted by Lehman Engel which played for twelve previews and seven performances at New York's Fifty-fourth Street Theatre.

Shortly afterward, there came another international success in a most unlikely medium – the cinema. *Irma La Douce*'s uncredited arranger Michel Legrand (1932-2019) had become a world-class jazz musician and film composer. Teamed with French "New Wave" auteur Jacques Demy (1931-90), he created the first in a series of Gallic-flavoured musical films. *Les Parapluies de Cherbourg* ("The Umbrellas of Cherbourg") was a through-sung musical about young love and teenage pregnancy set against a backdrop of the Franco-Algerian war in the 1950s. Although it had an industrial port setting and gritty subject matter, Demy bathed his film in such glowing Technicolor that it was literally seen through rose coloured glasses. The result was a soaring melo-drama which included the Oscar nominated hit song "Je ne pourrai jamais vivre sans toi" ("I will never be able to live without you"), known in English as "I Will Wait for You". Writer and actor Tom Shea calls it "as cinematic a musical as there's ever been; it's a superb application of French New Wave film techniques to the movie musical genre."[71]

Demy explains, "I try to fight the belief that musicals can't make it in France. There've been counter-examples like *West Side Story*. Plenty of Stanley Donan [the director of *Singin' in the Rain*] musicals have done well in France and were superb. We haven't made many in France, but when we've tried... they were charming, done with a sense of lightness and charm that created a dreamy atmosphere." [72]

"It's just love that you send out in a certain manner, a way of communicating that I find more interesting if it's sung", Demy continues. "It can be more tender, more generous, more violent, more aggressive, whatever... That's what interests me. It's a language, my language." Demy and Legrand set out to give their recitative "language" the same rhythm as speech. Although professional singers were pre-recorded, and the songs were later lip-synched by the actors, the two sets of performers worked in close collaboration. The actors, including star-in-the-making Catherine Deneuve (1943-) were present during the recording sessions, working with their singing counterparts on phrasing and intonation. (This also happened when Marni Nixon dubbed Deborah Kerr's voice in *The King and I*.)

I first saw the film when it was re-released in a restored print in the 1990s. My initial reaction was, "I wonder how many times Boublil and Schönberg saw this before they wrote *Miss Saigon*?" I think I got my answer in 2008, when *Marguerite*, which they wrote in collaboration with Legrand, opened in London.

Michel Legrand says, "[Demy] wanted an opera,

he got one. It was entirely sung. He wanted it to be clear, self-evident, he wanted it as a kind of song throughout the film, a single through line, from start to finish... Audiences wept, it was so sad. We'd planned it... Jacques and I wrote on the score: 'First hanky, page 38... Second hanky...' So we had... a scoreful of hankies."[73]

The *Umbrellas of Cherbourg* was adapted for the English-speaking stage in 1979 by Sheldon Harnick (1924-) and Charles Burr (1922-76) (in collaboration with Demy and Legrand) and directed by Andrei Serban (1943-). It enjoyed a brief run of 79 performances in New York at the Public Theatre, and received its Paris stage premiere in the same year at the Théâtre Montparnesse using a small orchestra. The English version opened in London at the Phoenix Theatre on 10 April 1980. It lasted only twelve performances. This version was revived at the Gielguid Theatre in London on 22 March 2011 by Kneehigh Theatre's then-director Emma Rice (1967-). It closed on 21 May of the same year.

The *Guardian*'s Michael Billington decreed: "Watching the stage version is like seeing a Technicolor film rendered in black and white: Lez Brotherston's set, with its partitioned steel structures, seems determined to evoke the reality of Cherbourg, whereas the point of the story is that it is a romantic fairytale... What is lost are the very things that made the film so original. One is the way in which the fluid camera movement matched the seamless recitative of the Legrand score: take that away, and you are left with a show that, with the exception of 'I Will Wait for You', seems strangely lacking in musical or dramatic highlights. The other missing ingredient is the candy-coloured artifice of the film, in which even the wallpaper matched the characters' costumes."[74] *Variety* largely concurred: "Oddly, Rice doesn't appear to have adjusted the lyrics first heard in Sheldon Harnick's translation in a production at Gotham's Public Theater in 1979. Hearing a cast using English accents to sing such American phrases as 'I guess' and 'trimming the tree' is jarring."[75]

Demy and Legrand followed up the original film in 1967 with *Les Demoiselles de Rochefort*, also starring Deneuve as well as her sister Françoise Dorléac (1942-67). It also included American guest-stars Gene Kelly (1912-96), George Chakiris (1934-) and Grover Dale (1935-) and was choreographed by Irish-born Norman Maen (1932-2008), who had worked in Canada with choreographer Alan Lund (1925-92) before becoming a principal dancer on Broadway and a choreographer in the West End.

Although Maen was the choreographer-of-note, Gene Kelly staged all the dances he was involved with. Grover Dale, who would go on to be a Tony Award winning director and choreographer on Broadway remembers,

> "Ten days in...while shooting in the town square...George Chakiris signals me that Gene Kelly has his eyes on us... The one and only Gene Kelly... Within seconds, George and I learn he wants to choreograph and perform a 'dancing-down-the-street' sequence with the two of us... During dinner with the cast and crew, Gene Kelly brings up the new dance he's playing around with. As applause erupts, Kelly laughs, assuring everyone how much better it would feel to hear the director say the number will be included in the film. Jacques Demy squirms in his seat. All eyes turn towards him. Within seconds, Jacques confides he can't justify a way for our three characters to meet face-to-face. Groans erupt. (The ones from George and me are noticeably louder.) 'The plot,' adds Jacques, 'would suffer and the ending won't work....' More groans. Sensing the dance with Kelly is history, George and I slump in our chairs. Jacques Demy apologizes for the decision."[76]

"It's... a musical that periodically defamiliarizes – 'makes strange' – the form of the musical", says American film critic Jonathan Rosenbaum. "Some American viewers may find it difficult to feel their way into such an aesthetic overload... Received wisdom on musicals is that the genre's greatest achievements – such as the entertaining Astaire-

Rogers steamrollers and *Singin' in the Rain* – are triumphs of engineering, co-ordination and expertise... Unless you conclude that the only reason for 'technique' is to express what you want to say, the technical shortcomings of *Les Demoiselles de Rochefort* are bound to be disappointing."[77]

However, for Grover Dale,

"The camaraderie between French, English, and Americans was exceptional. The warmth coming from Jacques Demy, his wife Agnes Varda, Gene Kelly, Catherine, Françoise, George, and the camera crew...added so much to the experience. Menial chores, like 'pulling plugs' from under film tracks was acceptable. If we had a line to say, or an action to perform, we did it... and then ran behind the camera to help the crew with small details. Privileged players didn't exist in Rochefort. A handful of us shared a bed-and-breakfast overlooking the sea. It was a magical time."

Even now, five decades on, Demy's effect is felt in both the theatre and the cinema, especially in the critically acclaimed 2016 movie musical *La La Land*, whose director Damien Chazelle (1985-) told the *Hollywood Reporter*, "No movie has ever hit me more... I remember seeing [*Umbrellas of Cherbourg*] for the first time as a kid and going from annoyed — 'Are they really going to do this much singing?' — to utterly overwhelmed by the end. It was the combination of fantasy and realism that got me."[78]

Since then, Legrand established a major career in both France and Hollywood as a composer. His films include *Summer of '42* and *The Thomas Crown Affair*, for which he wrote the song "The Windmills of Your Mind" with lyrics by Alan and Marilyn Bergman, with whom he would work again on his only English-language film musical, the Oscar-winning *Yentl*.

More recently, Legrand wrote a musical for the stage that was deliberately evocative of Offenbach's "opéra-bouffe" style. "I have always loved Offenbach, so inventive, so droll, with splendid harmonies."[79] The result was *Le Passe-Muraille*, with a libretto by novelist Didier Van Cauwelaert (1960-) based on a short story by Marcel Aymé (1902-67) about a man who can walk through walls. It ran for a year at the Théâtre des Bouffes-Parisiens in Paris in 1997 (where it won the Prix-Moliere for Best Musical), and, with an English adaptation by Jeremy Sams (1957-), transferred to the Music Box theatre on Broadway – for a brief run – as *Amour* in 2002.

The *New York Times* declared, in a mixed review, "even charming is too weighty a word to describe the appeal of *Amour*", a "twinkling trinket of a musical".[80] The critical consensus seemed to be that Van Cauwelaert's libretto – with its intricate wordplay – didn't translate well, and that perhaps it was too small a show for a Broadway theatre. Sams told me that it "mystified Broadway audiences and critics. They said it wasn't like an American musical and they were right!" A revised version was presented at the Royal Academy of Music in 2015, and it received its British professional debut in a 2019 London off-West End production.

Sams argues that "The idea of dramaturgy in a musical is totally absent in Offenbach and all French works, including, fascinatingly, the French (pre Cameron [Mackintosh]) version of *Les Miz*."[81] He argues that this is also true of French drama. "Structure, in the post 1940s sense, has no interest to the French. French shows have nothing in common with, and no influence on the structured American musical." He adds, "I'm personally glad of this, since the 'song shows' of France lead to wonderful things like [Charles] Trenet and [Jacques] Brel, to [Francis] Poulenc and [Arthur] Honegger's operettas, to Michel Legrand's movie musicals – all things I love." But, he adds, "What they don't lead to is Broadway."

Alain Boublil (1941-), lyricist of *Les Misérables* wrote a stage adaptation of *Les Demoiselles de Rochefort*. More recently, Boublil and his partner Claude-Michel Schönberg (1944-) collaborated with Legrand on another project, *Marguerite*, a Second World War updating of Alexandre Dumas' *Our Lady of the Camelias*. Thus Legrand, who has also worked as an arranger with Maurice Chevalier, Jacques Brel and other stalwarts of the French music hall and "chanson" traditions, embodies at least one link between the musical theatre of the Belle Epoch and that of *Les Misérables*.

Of course, the latter would go on to eclipse all that had gone before it. However, unlike *Irma la Douce* or *The Umbrellas of Cherbourg*, it was not really just another French show that had been adapted into English. Beginning as a concept album and then staged in a Paris arena, *Les Misérables* was entirely reconceived by producer Sir Cameron Mackintosh (1946-) and directors Sir Trevor Nunn (1940-) and John Caird (1948-).

Boublil and Schönberg were French pop songwriters who had ventured into the world of theatrical spectacle in 1973 at the Palais des Sports in Paris with *La Revolution Française*. They were enamoured of *Jesus Christ Superstar*, *West Side Story* and *Oliver!* In fact, it was the latter show that would give them their greatest inspiration, for the Artful Dodger's rendition of "Consider Yourself" reminded Boublil of the character of Gavroche in Victor Hugo's novel. "As soon as the Artful Dodger came onstage, Gavroche came to mind. It was like a blow to the solar plexus. I started seeing all the characters of Victor Hugo's *Les Misérables*—Valjean, Javert, Gavroche, Cosette, Marius, and Éponine—in my mind's eye, laughing, crying, and singing onstage."[82] Boublil wrote the original French libretto in collaboration with poet Jean-Marc Natel (1942-).

He and Schönberg recorded *Les Misérables* as a concept album at CTS Studios in Wembley, London in 1980, with orchestrations by John Cameron (1944-) who would remain involved with the project throughout its development. It was staged by director Robert Hossein (1927-) at the Palais de Sports where it ran for three months. A tape of this production found its way, via Hungarian director Peter Farago (1946-), to Mackintosh. "It was an instant combustible decision", he told Sheridan Morley and Ruth Leon. "By the fourth track I had already decided that I had to do it."[83]

Rather than simply assigning the rights, Boublil and Schönberg became part of the creative team. RSC Casting director Siobhan Bracke provided a literal translation of the original libretto. "I was credited in programmes for some time"[84], she told me. From this an initial set of lyrics were to be written by English poet James Fenton (1949-), but Mackintosh found his words to be uninvolving. He was replaced by South African-born lyricist Herbert Kretzmer (1925-), although Fenton retains a credit for his contribution to the structure.

"The project was probably too patrimonially French for anyone else to have done it in a way that would be what the show is today"[85], says Boublil. The show would ultimately be expanded from one hour to three, and only about a third of Kretzmer's lyrics were direct translations of Boublil's originals.

The original Royal Shakespeare Company production at the Barbican Theatre received tepid notices. Francis King in the *Sunday Telegraph* called it "a lurid Victorian melodrama produced with Victorian lavishness", while *The Observer*'s Michael Ratcliffe called it "a witless and synthetic entertainment". Nonetheless, Mackintosh proceeded with a transfer to the West End, and he hasn't looked back since. (Ironically, given that Gavroche was their starting point, one of the cuts made during the transfer was "Little People", Gavroche's answer to *Oliver*'s "Consider Yourself".)

In 1992, Vienna's Theater an der Wien housed the most successful post-war German language musical, *Elisabeth*, with book and lyrics by Dr. Michael Kunze (1943-) and music by Sylvester Levay (1945-). The story concerns the life of Austro-Hungarian Empress Elisabeth (1837-98), wife of Emperor Franz Josef (1830-1916). In this show, her "leading man" wasn't the emperor, but a young man who is the embodiment of Death. Kurt Gänzl calls it "a landmark in the history of the European stage."[86] The original production ran for six years. *Variety*'s review by Larry Lash said, "*Elisabeth* is never less than entertaining as it tells its tale of a tragic life, but when it takes on history, it truly soars."

Michael Kunze was born in Prague in 1943 to Austrian parents and grew up in Munich. He studied law, history and philosophy, and in the late sixties turned to writing pop lyrics, becoming the first German ever to win a Grammy award. In the early seventies he met Sylvester Levay, a Hungarian composer who had worked in Hollywood, providing the theme music for television series such as *Airwolf*. His hits included "Fly, Robin, Fly" and "Get Up and Boogie".

Initially, Kunze was not a fan of musicals – "my idea of a Broadway show was people dancing with a straw hat"[87] – until some New York colleagues took him to see *The Wiz*. "I was excited because it was contemporary, and it told a story with my kind of music."

"I don't feel at all linked to the tradition of the Viennese, German or French operetta", he explained to me. "But I did like the *Threepenny Opera* of Brecht and Weill and most of their other works, and I may have been influenced by them."[88]

He was asked by Andrew Lloyd Webber to translate *Evita* into German. This led to further adaptations of *Follies, Aspects of Love, Cats, A Chorus Line, Phantom of the Opera, Company, Little Shop Of Horrors, Into The Woods, Kiss Of The Spider Woman, Sunset Boulevard, The Hunchback Of Notre Dame, The Lion King, Aida, Mamma Mia!!* and *Wicked*.

Then he began writing his own original shows with Levay. *Elisabeth* was their first hit, but they have also written *Mozart* (1999), *Rebecca* (from the Daphne DuMaurier novel, 2006) and *Marie Antoinette* (2006). An English version of *Rebecca*, adapted by Christopher Hampton was in the works, but collapsed amid allegations of fraud on the part of the producers. His first venture into English-language musicals was a similarly unhappy occasion.

Dance of the Vampires, with music by American pop songwriter Jim Steinman (1947-), who wrote Meat Loaf's *Bat Out of Hell* album, was based on a Roman Polanski comedy that was released in 1967 under the more farcical title *The Fearless Vampire Killers (or, "Pardon Me But Your Teeth are in my Neck")*. Although he wrote it in English, it was first produced in German in Vienna in 1997 where it ran for two years in a production directed by Polanski himself. Five years later, it opened at the Minskoff Theatre on Broadway, starring Michael Crawford.

The New York producers brought in playwright David Ives (1950-) to Americanise the dialogue. At the time, Kunze told Ellis Nassour, "I'm completely happy with it... I'm not able to write in the 'Broadway' style... There're people here who can do this type of thing so much better."[89] However, seven years later, he would tell me "The *Dance of the Vampires* Broadway version was not an authorised adaptation of my musical. It was rather a mutilation." Needless to say, the Broadway run was short and the reviews scathing. He explained to me, "I gave that interview at a time when I knew that David Ives and Jim Steinman had mutilated my book and lyrics. I wouldn't have been professional nor practical to complain about it to the press. I had to keep smiling, but I was not 'completely happy', quite the opposite. If you know Broadway and the Rialto[90] gossip, you don't want to feed bad rumours before an opening. I've learned from that experience to make sure I have contracts that cannot be circumvented."[91]

In Amsterdam, two writers with a background in cabaret created a book musical called *En Nu Naar Bed* ("And Now to Bed") which opened at the Carré Theatre on 5 November 1971. The book and lyrics were the work of children's author Annie M. G. (Maria Geertruida) Schmidt (1911-1995), and the music was by Harry Bannink (1929-99). The director was the Canadian-born, London-based Paddy Stone (1924-86), who had worked with Japan's all-female Takarazuka Revue and who later choreographed the film *Victor/Victoria*. It told the story of Frans, who since birth has been presided over by a good fairy played by Mary Dresselhuys (1907-2004) and a bad fairy by Conny Stuart (1913-2010), who guide the course of his life, taking on different human forms: as a teacher, as a checkout lady, as a customer in a shop, as a psychiatrist. The show ran for 345 performances, and produced the hit song "Vluchten kan niet meer" ("There is no more escaping it").

Bannink and Schmidt began their collaboration in 1965 with *Heerlijk duurt het Langst* ("Delicious lasts the longest") which, like *En Nu Naar Bed*, starred Stuart and was directed by Stone. Schmidt had been a popular columnist with the newspaper *Het Parool* ("The Password") and had written songs for cabaret artist Wim Sonneveld (1917-74) and a radio series called *De familie Doorsnee* ("The Average Family"). Sonneveld, known to English-speaking audiences for his role of Boroff in the film of Cole Porter's

Silk Stockings, had starred in a very successful Dutch-language version of *My Fair Lady*. After this, Schmidt was much in demand as a translator of lyrics, but finally she told producer John de Crane, "As long as I still have as many new ideas, I won't translate anything." At this point, de Crane replied: "If you still have so many ideas..."[92]

She teamed with former dance band pianist Bannink, who had been Sonneveld's tutor on *My Fair Lady*. "The first one is most precious to me", says Bannink. "We both made beginners mistakes, but we were convinced it would be good. That wasn't overconfidence, but a sacred naiveté. We've become addicted to this genre, but that huge feeling became a lot less strong later on. More professional and thought through. With each next show we knew exactly when the intermission had to come and that's a pity, because you have to retain your child-like innocence."[93]

Coming from a Dutch cabaret tradition, and working with one of the Netherlands' most famous authors, the lyricist was queen. "Holland is the country of the church, so of the word", says the composer. "When I hear that seven applicants for the Cabaret Academy [in Amsterdam] sang Bannink songs at the audition, then I'm very satisfied."[94] Bannink and Schmidt worked together for the next twenty years. Their other shows included *Foxtrot*, *Wat een planeet* ("What a planet", 1973) and *De dader heeft het gedaan* ("The culprit did it", 1984).

Schmidt disliked the slickness of American musicals. Neither did she moralise like her Dutch cabaret contemporaries. "I don't answer the question: What is good, what is bad? I say in every song: Look at the lunacy of this. What do you think about that?"[95] Bannink, who is said to have written some three thousand songs, also eschewed the standard reprise form structure of a Broadway score, leaving it to director Stone to provide a unifying visual concept. Bannink later became the chief composer for the Dutch version of *Sesame Street*, and has a theatre named in his honour in his home town of Enschede. Schmidt was awarded the Hans Christian Anderson award for her children's literature. She ended her own life in 1995, and Bannink passed away four years later.

Jos Brink (1942-2007) was an actor, lyricist and comedian who came into musical theatre via cabaret. In 1972 he teamed up both professionally and personally with Frank Sanders (1946-) to form the cabaret group Pierement. Their musicals together included *Masquerade* (1979), *Madame Arthur* (1985) and *Max Havelaar* (1987). Later in his life he became a Protestant minister and campaigner for gay rights.

The first Dutch musical ever to open on Broadway was *Cyrano*, based on the play by Edmond Rostand (1868-1918). The original Dutch book and lyrics were by Koen van Dijk (1959-) and the music composed by Ad van Dijk (1959-), who is no relation. The English adaptation was by Peter Reeves and Sheldon Harnick (1924-). Producer Joop Van den Ende (1942-) told Marlise Simons of the *New York Times*, "I try to be in step with or ahead of a trend. But an American audience can be quite different from ours. The United States is sometimes far behind us and sometimes far ahead."[96] It opened at the Neil Simon Theatre on 21 November 1993 and, although it was nominated for Tony awards for Best Musical, Best Book, Best Score and Best Costume Design, it closed after only 137 performances. Ben Brantley in the *New York Times* wrote that the music "recalls the mechanically propulsive score of *Les Misérables*"[97]. *Variety*'s Jeremy Gerard dismissed it as "a thundering mishmash of unspectacular spectacle, non-musical music and anti-romantic romance."[98] The director Eddy Habbema and leading actor Bill van Dijk (1947-) (again, no relation to the writers) were both responsible for the extremely successful Dutch language production in Amsterdam the previous year. The composer and lyricist later collaborated on *Joe*, a musical based on the 1944 film *A Guy Named Joe*, (which had already been remade by Steven Spielberg in 1989 as *Always*), about a pilot who comes back from the grave to mentor a young protégé.

While none of these shows have had a successful life much beyond their native country, I believe that a more recent Dutch musical may have international potential. *Ciske de Rat* ("Ciske the Rascal") is a trilogy of children's books begun in 1941 by Piet Bakker (1897-1960). It has been adapted for film twice, in 1955 and 1984. The leading actor of the latter version, Danny de Munk (1970-) later became a musical theatre star, playing Marius in *Les Misérables* in Amsterdam in 1991. He returned to the story that made him famous, playing the older Ciske in a massively successful musical version, which opened in Amsterdam on 5 October 2007.

Ciske de Rat
©Joris-Jan Bos Photography

The book and lyrics of the musical were written by André Breedland and Maurice Wijnen and the music was by Henny Vrienten (1948-), one time member of the 1980s Dutch ska/reggae band Doe Maar and a protégé of Harry Bannink. Vrienten had also scored a number of Dutch films, including *The Vanishing* and *Left Luggage*, and contributed one song to the Bannink and Schmidt revue *Foxtrot*.

The story of *Ciske*, set in Amsterdam in 1934, concerns eleven year old lonely street urchin Franciskus "Ciske" Vrijmoeth, a sort of "arse-kicking" Oliver Twist, who has no friends. After pouring ink over his teacher's head, he is forced to change schools, but he is befriended by his new teacher Bruis. He would rather live with his father Cor, a fisherman who is absent much of the time, but instead he is stuck with his alchoholic mother Marie and her abusive new boyfriend. During a heated altercation, he stabs her and is sent to prison. The story is told from the perspective of the older Ciske, who has been drafted into the army of occupation in 1940.

The show was directed by Paul Eenens and presented by Dutch theatrical giant Stage Entertainment, owned by former carpenter turned billionaire media mogul Joop Van den Ende (1942-), who was also a major player on Broadway and in the West End at the time and produced both the Dutch and English incarnations of *Cyrano*. *Musical Stages*' Sebastiaan Smits says, "It's been a long time since I've been enthusiastic about a Stage Entertainment musical, but after such disasters as *Three Musketeers* and *The Wiz* they finally got it right."[99]

I asked director Paul Eenens if they have considered adapting it for export. "*Ciske* is so very typically Dutch in every way", he explained.

> "The story is Dutch heritage, the music is composed with typical Dutch influences, the political and social context of the story is very Dutch, the characters are very Dutch etc. As you mentioned, *if* the show would be brought to another country that would ask for intelligent adaptation and an answer to the question *how* this story can/should be told in a specific country. We are not saying that adaptation is not possible or that the show will not be adapted for another country in the future. The story is strong enough and has universal elements in it. But until now the focus was/is completely on the Dutch run and success of the show that is now in its second year with more than 500 shows... And we are proud of the fact that an original brand new Dutch musical creation and story is so incredibly successful amidst and next to lots of originally foreign musicals with foreign topics."[100]

I would argue that its unique Dutch character is what might make it interesting to a foreign audience, provided that it is adapted intelligently and that they retain its Dutch millieu. The score is tuneful and well-shaped, the story is heart rending without being mawkish, and if any Dutch musical has a chance in the English speaking world, this may well be it. "I'm quite fond of *Ciske* too," says Jeremy Sams. "It has some nice stuff, among the ordinary. But at least it's not... merely an imitation of a UK or US model."[101]

Sweden's Benny Andersson (1946-) and Björn Ulvaeus (1945-) have been extremely successful with *Mamma Mia!!*, derived from the back catalogue of their former band "Abba", and to a lesser extent with *Chess*, the pop opera written with Tim Rice that ran for three years in London and about that many weeks in New York. However, these shows were all originally written in English, and were first mounted in London.

Kristina från Duvemåla is another matter. It is based on Vilhelm Moberg (1896-1973)'s 1949 novel *Utvandrarna* ("The Emigrants") which was filmed in 1971 starring Max von Sydow and Liv Ullmann, as was its sequel *Nybyggarna* ("The New Land"). The story follows a Swedish family as they emigrate to the new world. A hit when first mounted in Sweden in 1995, an English version called *Kristina* with lyrics by Herbert Kretzmer received a concert performance in New York at Carnegie Hall starring Louise Pitre in 2009. "Major asset is Andersson's music," says *Variety*'s Steven Suskin, "which on first hearing is more impressive than *Chess*. Trouble is, there's way too much of it – song after song after endless song."[102]

Another concert version was performed at London's Royal Albert Hall in 2010. As of this writing, it has yet to receive a full staging in English.

One of the reasons why *Mama Mia!!* is such a success is that while it is a jukebox musical, I believe that Benny and Bjorn wrote those songs with a theatrical sensitivity. They live and breathe on stage. They don't even need Frida and Agnetha singing them – they are damn good songs.

During an award acceptance speech in New York in 2010, Andersson reflected on the influence of the "melancholy belt" of European traditional music: "If you live in a country like Sweden, with five, six months of snow, and the sun disappears totally for like two months, that would be reflected in the work of artists... It's definitely in the Swedish folk music, you can hear it in the Russian folk songs, you can hear in the music from Jean Sibelius or Edvard Grieg from Norway, you can see it in the eyes of Greta Garbo and you can hear it in the voice of Jussi Björling [(1911-60), a Swedish operatic tenor with the Metropolitan opera]... and for those who are observant enough, they might even spot it in the odd Ingmar Bergman movie."[103]

In addition to its tradition of Zarzuelas, Spain has been known to create a few musicals. The most successful has been a jukebox musical called *Hoy no me puedo levantar* ("Today I Can't Get Up") by the band Mecano, telling the story of a couple of impoverished musicians struggling to be a part of Madrid's "La Movida Madrileña", the pop culture that emerged following the end of the regime of Generalisimo Francesco Franco. After a successful run in Madrid in 2005, it was produced in Mexico City in 2008 and has been seen by over three million people.

Sancho Panza had an original score by José Luis Morán (1963-) and lyrics by his wife Inma Gonzáles and Morán, written for the four hundredth anniversary of the publication of *Don Quixote* by Miguel de Cervantes. It was produced in Madrid in 2005 then toured Spain. Alas, Iñigo Santamaria, author of *Guía Ilustrada del Teatro Musical en España* ("Illustrated Guide of the Musical in Spain"), dismisses it as "a completely irrelevant childish musical".[104]

Mar i cel ("Sea and sky") is a 1987 musical with a libretto by Xavier Bru de Sala (1952-) and music by Albert Guinovart (1962-) based on a play by Àngel Guimerà (1845-1924). It is set in seventeenth century Spain after the expulsion of the Moors, and tells of the illicit relationship that develops between a Muslim pirate and his Christian captive. In 2007 it was presented in Germany in translation by the Halle Opernhaus. Guinovart is a classical composer and conductor whose other musicals include *Gaudi* (2002, with libretto by Esteve Miralles and Jordi Galceran), *Flor de nit* (1992, libretto by Manuel Vázquez Montalbán (1939-2003)) and *Scaramouche* (2016, libretto by Joan Lluís Bozzo, David Pintó and Joan Vives).

Italy is also more than just a centre for opera. In fact, it had its own internationally successful book writing duo, Pietro Garinei (1919-2006) and Sandro Giovannini (1915-77). According to *The Guardian*, they created "the most popular revues and musical comedies seen on Italian stages since 1945"[105], many of them in Rome's Teatro Sistina, which they ran themselves.

Their first musical in 1952 was *Attanasio cavallo vanesio* which is commonly regarded as the first true Italian musical comedy, with music by Gorni Kramer (1913-95). It was filmed in the following year.

In 1956, they worked with Kramer again on *Buonanotte Bettina* ("Goodnight Bettina"), based on the 1954 novel *Bonjour Tristesse* by the then-eighteen year old Françoise Sagan (1935-2004). In 1960 it transferred to London's Adelphi Theatre under the title *When in Rome*, starring Dickie Henderson (1922-85). The same show was translated and produced in Hungary, Spain, Poland and Argentina. It was filmed in 1967.

Their musical *Enrico 61*, written for the centennial of Italian unification in 1961 told the story of Italy's first hundred years through the eyes of a Roman hatter born in

1861. It debuted at the Teatro Lirico in Milan with music by (and starring) Renato Rascel (1912-91) with musical arrangements by future film maestro Ennio Morricone (1928-). Following its initial three month run in Milan, it played four months at the Sistina in Rome and, two years later, eighty-six performances at the Picadilly Theatre in London, with English lyrics by Ronald Cass (1923-2006) and a man whom Ron Moody called the "enfants terribles"[106] of revue writers, Peter Myers. Milton Shulman of the *Evening News* found Rascel "an amiable little man with a mildly endearing comic style and little else. He sings and dances too, but I hardly think they are counted among his major talents."[107] Others complained that Rascel's Italian accent was impenetrable.

In the same year came another celebration of Italy's centennial, *Renaldo in Campo* ("Rinaldo in Arms") with music by (and also starring) Domenico Mudugno (1928-94) which told the story of an Italian Robin Hood in the Sicily of 1860. Gabriele Bonsignori, who teaches at the Bernstein School of Musical Theatre in Bologna, says "The finale is not a real happy ending, but [an] open end: Rinaldo leaves his girlfriend Angelica (played by Delia Scala) [to] join the battle of Giuseppe Garibaldi for the unification of Italy."[108] Bonsignori explains that "Modugno composed epic and dramatic songs, power and romantic ballads". The choreography was by future Hollywood director Herbert Ross (1927-2001). A hit in Italy, it also played in Serbia and Russia, and was televised in 1961 and again in 1987.

In 1962 *Rugantino* with music by Armando Trovajoli (1917-2013) was presented, which *The Guardian* deems to be their greatest achievement. It also impressed American producer Alexander Cohen enough to bring it to Toronto and then New York for a sold-out 28 performance engagement on Broadway, where it played in Italian with subtitles. "There's an Italian abundance in 'Rugantino,' said *The New York Times*. "Mixed into it like a rich sauce for a tasty pasta are impudent and bawdy comedy, maudlin melodrama, songs with soft, swaying Latin rhythms, scenery that moves clockwise and counterclockwise simultaneously, gaudy costumes, lively actors, pretty ragazzine (that's what Romans call cute dishes) and a laughing, brooding affection for the spirit of old Rome."[109] In Italy, it has been revived six times, most recently in 2013, and was filmed in 1973.

In 1964, they gave us *Il Giorno Della Tartaruga* ("The Day of the Turtle") with music by Renato Rascel (1912-91), who also starred in this two hander about a married couple, anticipating the later *I Do! I Do!* It was also a hit in Paris in 1965.

Marcello Mastroianni (1924-96) made his musical-comedy debut with them as Rudolph Valentino in *Ciao, Rudy* in 1966, with music by Trovajoli, who would score all of their remaining shows. According to *The Guardian*, it "benefited from a scintillating, Rex Harrison-style song-and-dance performance by the star."[110]

Their 1974 musical *Aggiungi un posto a tavola* ("Add a seat at the table") based loosely on the novel "After Me, the Deluge" by David Forrest (the pseudonym of David Eliades and Robert Forrest-Webb), also enjoyed a London transfer. The plot concerns a latter-day Noah who is asked by God to build an ark. It ran for three and a half years in Rome and, as *Beyond the Rainbow*, with English lyrics by Leslie Bricusse (1931-), it played for 238 performances at the Adelphi Theatre in London in 1978. It was also produced very successfully in Mexico, where it was known as *El Deluvio Que Viene* ("The Flood That is Coming"), and where it was the first musical seen by musical theatre historian Fabian de la Cruz Polanco. "I do not completely remember what I felt then", he wrote in his book *Magia pura y total* ("Pure and Total Magic"), but what he sensed was "the taste for musical theatre, a genre despised by many, but from my perspective, as well as that of others, the expression more complete than the scenic art can offer."[111] It was recorded for RAI television twice; once in 1978 and again in 1990.

Tania Piattella, who starred in the 1990 revival at the Teatro Carcano in Milan, remembers Garinei as "a great white bear... a lot of authority but also a lot of sweetness. A professional and a unique man! I remember that he had renamed me 'the hurricane', because of the fact that I never stopped for a moment."[112]

In 1970, Tito Schipa Jr. (1946-), son of the noted opera singer Tito Schipa (1889-1965), composed what is regarded as Italy's first rock opera, *Orfeo 9*. It was filmed in 1973. Bonsignori describes it as "a sort of 'hippie flower power' version of the ancient legend Orpheus and Eurydice with a cast of young rock singers."

Hollywood - Ritratto Di Un Divo ("Hollywood – Portrait of a Star") is a through sung musical first produced in 1998 with a score by Gianni Togni (1956-), lyrics by Guido Morra and book by Morra and Giuseppe Patroni Griffi (1921-2005). It is inspired by the legendary figures of Greta Garbo and John Gilbert, whose lives are intertwined at the thresholds of sound cinema: her star on the rise, while his, as a silent movie actor, was in decline. It was produced in 2002 in Sweden under the title *GG*. In this version, the plot was restructured to give more emphasis to Garbo, whereas Gilbert was the star in the original Italian version.

Togni followed this up with *Poveri Ma Belli* ("Poor but Handsome"), based on a 1957 film by Dino Rissi (1916-2008). The book was by Massimiliano Bruno (1970-) and Edoardo Falcone, based on an idea by (and dedicated to) playwright, actor, and lyricist Pietro Garinei.

In 1994, actor turned director Saverio Marconi (1948-) created, with Ugo Chiti, a musical called *Fregoli* based on the life of Leopoldo Fregoli (1867-1936), the world famous "quick change artist". The music was by Bruno Moretti (1957-), who studied with famed film composer Nino Rota (1911-79). The lyrics were by Michele Renzullo, who was also the executive producer, and the choreography was by Baayork Lee (1946-), one of the original Broadway cast members of *A Chorus Line*.

A few years later, Marconi achieved greater success with *Pinochio* with music by the Italian pop band Pooh and book by Marconi and Pierluigi Ronchetti, based upon the popular novel of Carlo Collodi. The original production ran for nearly two years at Teatro della Luna in Milan. It has been revived four times, most recently in 2014. It made Manuel Frattini (1965-) a star of Italian musical theatre.

Among the more contemporary Italian musicals is *Giulietta e Romeo* with music by Riccardo Cocciante and lyrics by Pasquale Panella (1950-) with a cast consisting mostly of teenagers. (Panella had also worked with Cocciante on the Italian version of *Notre Dame de Paris*.) It premiered in Verona in 2007 and has toured Italy.

If any country in Europe ought to have a strong tradition in musical theatre, it's Ireland. This is, after all, the birthplace of Victor Herbert, and the ancestral home of George M. Cohan. It is the land of Oscar Wilde and George Bernard Shaw. Celtic music and dance permeates the Irish soul – and yet, they have seldom managed to put all these elements together into an integrated whole. Until recently, the nearest Ireland had come to a successful piece of musical theatre has been *Riverdance*, with an original score by Bill Whelan (1950-) and choreography by Michael Flatley (1958-). However, *Riverdance* was a dance spectacular with a loosely defined theme, but no book or characters as such.

There have, however, been some recent attempts. Alastair McGuckian (1936-)'s *Ha'penny Bridge* is what is euphemistically referred to in the business as a "vanity project". McGuckian, a farming systems designer who financed the show himself, had the initial idea while stranded in Saudi Arabia during the first Gulf war. He also wrote the book, music and lyrics. The story concerns love and divided loyalties during Ireland's 1922 civil war. It was initially produced at the Cork Opera House in 2000, then remounted in an expanded version at The Point, Dublin, in June 2005. "It's the first time that West End production values are really being brought to bear on a musical premiered here; the kind of production values that audiences expect after *Riverdance*," McGuickan told *The Sunday Times'* Michael Ross. "We went to London to get the people we needed. It's very expensive to stage. It's certainly running into big money now. There are about seventy people working on this, it would be impossible to recoup the investment in Ireland."[113]

"This could have been Ireland's answer to *Les Misérables*", wrote Patricia O' Callaghan of Radio Telefis Eirreann. "Their revolution, our civil war. It could have been great. But, judging by the finished production, our civil war was the lesser exciting of the two."[114] The *Village*'s Colin Murphy wrote, "As drama, this musical is awful, though probably marketable. Each scene looks like a set piece from some kind of theme park, cabaret numbers perhaps for a Las Vegas 'Irish Experience'."[115]

Still, McGuickan didn't give up. A CD was produced, and he hired noted Broadway orchestrator Larry Blank to rework the score for a proposed North American premiere at the Princess of Wales Theatre in Toronto in May 2008 before travelling to San Francisco's Golden Gate Theatre on a pre-Broadway tour. The director was to be Stratford Festival veteran Donna Feore (1963-), and American actress Anika Larsen (1973-) (*Rent, Xanadu*) was announced to star. Then, five weeks before rehearsals were due to start, producer Garrett McGuickan – the composer's son – announced, "Despite the outstanding job our creative staff has done reshaping the book, music and lyrics of the show, we, as producers, feel the production is not yet commercially ready."[116] It seems that not enough American cities signed up to make a tour viable, and no Broadway theatre was able or willing to take the show in. "I've given two years of my life to the project", Feore told Richard Ouzounian. "I'm angry for myself, but I'm disappointed for my creative team and my cast, who have given so much to the show."[117] In 2009, I asked Larry Blank if there had been any further progress. His answer was one word: "History"[118].

Improbable Frequency, a musical satire with book and lyrics by Arthur Riordan and music by Conor Kelly and Sam Park, (calling themselves "Bell Helicopter") received a warmer critical reception when it opened at the Dublin Theatre Festival in 2004. It was remounted at Dublin's Abbey Theatre in March 2005. The story concerns some suspicious calls to a Dublin radio request show in 1941 that catch the attention of Britain's MI5, resulting in a meeting between the English poet John Betjeman and the physicist Erwin Schrödinger, calling into question Ireland's claimed neutrality. The *Irish Independent* described it as "slick and seamless throughout, with touches of brilliance...a landmark achievement". *The Village* called it "the first great Irish musical." When it opened in December 2008 at New York's Off-Broadway 59E59 Theatre, the *New York Times'* Charles Isherwood found it to be "a bit like early Stoppard crossed with a Gilbert and Sullivan operetta. Most unexpected is how consistently this strange concoction entertains..."[119]

In 2006, an Irish musical film called *Once*, made on a budget of €130,000 was enthusiastically received by both the critics and public. The score was written and performed by its two leading actors, Glen Hansard (1970-) and Markéta Irglová (1988-). The story concerns the burgeoning relationship between a Dublin busker and a young Czech woman. The song "Falling Slowly" won an Academy Award for best original song. A stage adaptation directed by John Tiffany (1971-) with a new book by Irish playwright Enda Walsh (1967-) opened at the New York Theatre Workshop on December 6, 2011, and transferred to Broadway's Bernard P. Jacobs Theatre on March 18, 2012, where it played for 1,167 performances. Ben Brantley in the *New York Times* wrote:

> "In translating *Once* into three dimensions, the playwright Enda Walsh and the director John Tiffany haven't steered clear of what were probably inevitable excesses. The script is now steeped in wise and folksy observations about committing to love and taking chances, most of which are given solemn and thickly accented utterance by Girl (played by Cristin Milioti), who is Czech. Guy, played by Steve Kazee, has been transformed from a shaggy nerd into a figure of leading-man handsomeness, while Girl has turned into a full-fledged version of what she only threatened to be in the film: a kooky, life-affirming waif who is meant to be irresistible ... But a merciful reversal occurs when *Once* breaks into music, which is often. Characters become less adorably overwrought and more genuinely conflicted, with distinctive personalities instead of standard-issue ones. The songs (written by Mr. Hansard and Ms. Irglova) soar with rough-edged, sweet-and-sad ambivalence that is seldom visited in contemporary American musicals."[120]

It won the 2012 Tony Award for Best New Musical. It opened at the Phoenix Theatre in London's West End on 9 April 2013 and played until 21 March 2015.

Even Portugal has produced at least one musical of note: In 2000, writer, producer and director Filipe La Féria (1945-) created *Amália*, a tribute to Amália Rodrigues (1920-99), the "Queen of the Fado singers", referring to a Portugese song form full of sombre melodies and lyrics, songs about the sea or the life of the poor, and with a melancholic feeling of resignation. *Amália* toured to Paris and other cities in France and Switzerland, and was seen by over sixteen million people.

Russia has also produced a few musicals in the post-war era. *Junona i Avos* ("Juno and Avos") was a rock opera with music by Alexey Rybnikov (1945-) and libretto by noted poet Andrei Voznesensky (1933-2010) from 1981. It takes its title from two ships of Russian explorer Nikolai Rezanov's expedition, and concerns a love story between Rezanov and Concepción Argüello, a 15-year-old daughter of José Darío Argüello, the colonial governor of Spanish California whom he met while he was seeking provisions for Russian settlements in Alaska. Unfortunately, Rezanov died while travelling home, and Argüello lived the remainder of her life under a vow of silence. It is is based on Voznesensky's poem *Avos!* written in 1970, which in turn is based on a true story. It has been televised twice and has been seen more than seven hundred times on stage.

Nord-Ost, composed by Aleksei Ivaschenko (1958-) and Georgy Vasilyev (1957-) (known collectively as Ivasi), is based on the novel *The Two Captains* by Veniamin Kaverin. It is a historical drama concerning the 1913 discovery of the Severnaya Zemlya archipelago in the Russian Arctic. A former ball-bearing factory was converted into a theatre at a cost of the equivalent to 4 million dollars. It claims to have played over 400 performances, but alas it has a more unfortunate claim to fame.

"At first it seemed like part of the show", Peter Baker and Susan Glasser say in their book *Kremlin Rising: Vladimir Putin's Russia and the End of Revolution*.

> "The second act of the musical *Nord-Ost* had just opened, and a troupe of actors in olive drab World War II uniforms had just tap-danced its way across the stage. They were singing about the derring-do of Soviet pilots, the thrill of the narrow escape. No-one thought much of the masked-man dressed in camouflage and toiting an assault rifle entering from stage left. Even after he let loose a burst from his Kalashnikov into the air, some theatregoers still considered it part of the performance."[121]

In fact, he was the first of some forty to fifty armed Chechen rebels who took the entire theatre hostage on 23 October 2002. Three days later, at around five o'clock in the morning, the theatre was stormed by Russian special forces, after gas had been pumped in through the ventilation system. The official death toll from the gas was given as 130, although some estimates go up to 300. Only two people were actually killed by the terrorists. The producer and co-author Georgy Vasilyev was among the hostages.

Even Serbia has one theatre devoted entirely to musicals. The city-owned Terazije Theatre opened in Belgrade in 1949. Its founder and initial director Radivoje Lola Đukić (1923-95) also wrote one of the earliest Serbian musicals, *Kill or Kiss*. Since then it has endured the breakup of Yugoslavia, the dictatorship of Slobodan Milošević and the adaptation to a market-led economy. Since its thorough renovation in 2005, it has produced Serbian versions of *Chicago* and *The Producers* as well as *Tabor ukhodit v nebo* ("Queen of the Gypsies"). They even secured former Bob Fosse collaborator Chet Walker to conduct a two-week workshop with their dancers.

In Kosovo, which broke away from Serbia in 2008, members of the Serbian minority mounted a musical called *The Lift: The Slobodan Show* by Belgrade-based writer Jelena Bogavac in 2018. This certainly created controversy as it was mounted in Gracanica, where the Serbs are a majority in an otherwise Albanian dominated country. Director Nenad Todorovic, a Kosovo Serb says, "If you ask me what I think about Milosevic, I don't believe it will be for newspapers. Too many bad words." Nevertheless, the show was criticised for not incorporating any Albanian viewpoints, but Todorovic was anxious to break what he calls the last Serbian taboo. "We don't speak about our problems. If we don't have catharsis, we don't have healing."[122]

Greece is, of course, the birthplace of theatre – and

that theatre included music. Without newspapers or television, the theatre was the arena for political discourse. Like the musical, the birth of theatre itself coincided with ancient Athenian democracy, and was an active part of it.[123] The meaning of the Greek word "hypokrisis" (ὑπόκρισις) refers to "play-acting", and actors were known as "hypocrites" before that word took on its more negative connotations.

While ancient Greece is now considered to be the bedrock of Western civilisation, that was long ago and for much of their history they have been occupied, first by the Romans, then the Byzantines and much later (from 1453-1827) the Ottoman Empire. This has created a mixed cultural identity in which some have identified themselves as "Romeic", descending from the Ottoman occupation and the East, and others as "Hellenic", relating to ancient Greece and the West. Rebetiko, a broadly based form of urban folk music now played mainly on a bouzouki and sometimes known as the "Greek blues"[124], is considered to be Romeic because it is largely derived from Ottoman roots. Author Tassos Vournas (1913-90) once described it as the art of the oppressed masses.[125] Those of the "Hellenic" persuasion would look to modernity and try to maintain a distance from what was regarded as a "barbaric" past.[126] On the other hand, some scholars refer to the "Western" influence on Greek culture, as if it were an outside force and not the very foundation of the country. It is tempting to think in terms of "low brow" and "high brow", although that is probably over-simplifying it.

Within the past couple of centuries, a couple of Greek musical theatre forms have developed out of this cultural mix. "Epitheorisi" literally means "the inspectorate", but in its theatrical context, it is a form of revue which falls roughly between "vaudeville" and French/German cabaret, with a bit of zarzuela thrown in. While the first epitheorisi was presented in the 1880s, they drew on comic traditions going back two and a half thousand years. Anna Stavrakopoulou, assistant professor at the Faculty of Drama in Thessaloniki's Aristotelian University says, "The comedies of Aristophan[e]s were far blunter in their censure and formed the basis for the contemporary epitheorisi."[127]

In 1894, an Italian company presented the zarzuela *La Gran Via* which captivated the Athenian audience, and inspired the early versions of epitheorisi. According to academics Thodōros Chatzēpantazēs and Lila Maraka, the public were "at a stage of total rejection of their traditional self and the pursuit of a new identity".[128]

In the beginning there was a definite dramatic structure, although by the 1960s it had evolved into a more fragmented, sketch driven revue format in which numbers were added or dropped according to their topicality. "As a form, *epitheorosi* provided the opportunity for a show of wealth and stability, so desirable to an aspiring middle class", says Prof. Aliki Bacopoulou-Halls, former President of the Hellenic Centre of the International Theatre Institute. "It also appealed, however, to audiences with its topicality, and, initially, with its messages of freedom from rules and conventions, both social and artistic."[129]

Operetta was also a popular field in the early twentieth century. *O Vaftistikos* ("The Godson") with both music and libretto by Theophrastos Sakellaridis (1883-1950) based on the French farce *Madame et son filleul* by Maurice Hennequin (1863-1926), Pierre Veber (1863-1926) and Henry De Gorsse (1868-1936) was premiered in 1918 by the Ioannis Papaioannou Theatre Company. Set during the Balkan Wars, a young housewife has her "godchild" come to live with her, unaware that he is in fact an imposter who has assumed the identity in order to make love to her. It remains the most popular of Sakellaridis' eighty operettas, five operas and various epitheorisi songs. Filmed in 1952 and presented on Greek public television in 1984, it is still in the repertoire of the Greek National Opera. Of his own work, Sakellaridis has said, "I write with Athenian inspiration. When we listen to an operetta by Lehar we exclaim 'It has the scent of Vienna'. If tomorrow it is said that my works have the scent of Athens, allow me to consider this as my artistic dream coming true."[130]

Lydia Papadimitriou, senior lecturer in screen studies at Liverpool John Moores University says, "Failing to modernize in theme or style, the appeal of the operetta was mainly nostalgic, and as a result the genre has declined since the 1960s."[131] That said, the operetta and the epitheorisi influenced each other.

Manos Hatzidakis (1925-94) is from a different background. Classically trained, he was one of the main proponents of "éntekhno", which could be described as the urban folk art song. He is probably best remembered as the Oscar-winning composer and lyricist of the song "Ta Pediá tou Pireá" ("The Children of Piraeus") from the film *Pote tin Kyriaki*, (better known to English-speaking audiences as *Never on Sunday*) in 1960. The original Greek lyric translates as:

> If I search the world over
> I'll find no other port
> Which has the magic
> Of my Port Piraeus

The film concerned the adventures of a carefree and good-natured prostitute in Piraeus. This, in turn, became the 1967 Broadway musical *Illya Darling* with music by Hatzidakis, lyrics by Joe Darion (1917-2001) and book by Jules Dassin (1911-2008), the author, director and co-star of the original film. It played for 320 performances at the Mark Hellinger Theatre, based on the drawing power of its star, Melina Mercouri (1920-94). John Chapman of the *Daily News* called it "A big, splashy and unusually tuneful musical"[132]. *St. Petersburg Times* critic Jack Gaver said, "It is a fact that any commercial success this new musical may have depends largely upon public interest in its Greek star. Tuesday night's arrival at the Mark Hellinger Theatre lacks solid, over-all appeal, so the international reputation of

Miss Mercouri as a movie star with a tremendous sex image and a volatile acting style is really on the line... there is exuberance in the several dance numbers, the score has some rousing numbers and there are excellent portrayals in top roles."[133]

Hatzidakis also wrote a musical in his native country and native language: *Odós Oneirwn* ("Street of Dreams") opened in 1962 at the Metropolitan theatre in Athens. In its opening number, the narrator tells us "the dreams of so many children are born and die, until the moment when their breath becomes one with the springtime breeze of Easter time Epitaphios [funeral oration] and then is lost. And yet, at night they cannot sleep and whenever they're not dreaming, they sing."[134]

In 1966, Hatzidakis composed the music for a stage adaptation of the novel *Captain Michalis* by Nikos Kazantzakis (1883-1957), thus bringing together two legends of modern Greek music and literature. The novel, written in the vernacular Demotic Greek, concerns the 1889 rebellion on the island of Crete against the Ottoman Empire. Hatzidakis took selections of Kazantzakis' prose and set them to music. This included the song "Den Itan Nissi" ("It wasn't an island, it was a monster that you could see in the sea"). This was later made popular by Nana Mouskouri, who would introduce the song saying,

> "Legend says that Alexander the Great had a sister mermaid living in the waters around Crete. She never admitted to her brother's death, and to convince herself she used to ask the sailors of the ships passing by whether he were still alive or not. If the answer was 'no', she cried so many tears that the swell of the waters sank the boats. But if they replied 'Alexander the Great is still alive and conquers the world', then she'd happily blow into their sails, to send them safely home."[135]

At the same time as Hatzidakis was presenting his *Street of Dreams*, in the nearby Park theatre, Greece's other legendary songwriter **Mikis Theodorakis (1925-)** opened his own epitheorisi written with lyrics by his younger brother Yannis and book by Mentis Bostantzoglou (1918-95), known by his pen name "Bost". The title song "Omorphi Poli" ("Beautiful City") would later be recorded by Edith Piaf. Outside of his homeland, Theodorakis is best known as the composer of the music for the film *Zorba the Greek*.

The epitheorisi and operetta both influenced the Greek movie musical, which prospered for two decades beginning in 1954 with *Charoumeno Xekinima* ("Happy Beginning"), directed by Dinos Dimopoulos. The plot concerns three male musicians and three female singers who are all rivals – in both work and love. According to Papadimitriou, "*Charoumeno Xekinima* has many formal similarities with American musicals and a carefully balanced narrative structure. It nevertheless conveys a strong sense of Greekness due in part to its location shooting and its links to the Greek musical theatre."[136]

Diplopennies (known in English as *Dancing the Sirtaki*, 1967) was directed by George Skalenakis (1926-2014). It tells of a house painter who leaves his wife when he achieves success as a singer. The wife, not to be bettered by her unfaithful husband also becomes a star, but wanting him back, falls pregnant. Skalenakis said, "I always had the ambition to make a national musical – I mean Romeic. Why should we make musicals of an American kind when we do not have the means of American productions and when our films will be pale imitations of theirs? Such a film is *Diplopennies*. I tried to convey the local colour (of Greece) in a film inundated with music, dance and *kefi* [fun]."[137]

Greek-born translator and actor Anthony Burk says, "I think that we have a long history in musical theatre and it is very appealing to the Greeks, whether it's an operetta or an 'epitheorisi'... At first there were a few producers making musicals but now that's not the case. Big theatres choose big productions and a musical is a big production. I think that if creators commit to it and they start training people for musicals, there would be an audience."[138]

Turkey had been the centre of the Ottoman Empire from the fourteenth until the early twentieth centuries. As it controlled territories in both Asia and Europe, it was seen by many as a cultural crossroads. The first public Turkish translation of a European opera – *Belisario* by Gaetano Donizetti (1797-1848) – was published in 1842. It was just a matter of time before Turkish writers would attempt their own work.

Just as the Broadway musical has tended to be dominated by an ethnic minority, the Jews, so were the arts in Turkey at this time dominated by ethnic Armenians. A Turkish operetta called *Leblebici Horhor Ağa* ("Good old Horhor the Chickpea Seller") by Istanbul-born Armenian composer Tigran Tchoukhajian (1837-98) with a libretto by Takvor Nalyan premiered in 1876 at the French theatre of the Palais de Cristal. It is often referred to as the first original Turkish operetta, although the same composer had already produced at least one other work. While the score for *Leblebici Horhor* was written in a very Western style, it still managed to incorporate Turkish elements.

The story concerns a chickpea seller from Anatollia whose daughter Fatime falls in love with Khourshid who takes her off to Istanbul to live with him. The poor father Horhor rushes after her but has difficulty adjusting to life in the city and is ultimately unable to stop the wedding. It has been filmed three times, and was revived in an English adaptation at the Arcola Theatre in 2015.

Author and playwright Halid Ziya Uşaklıgil (1866-1945) has said that, after a full serving of imported Italian operettas, seeing an operetta with a local setting, he thought he was dreaming. In fact, he said, it drove the people mad.[139] It actually captured London in 1897 under its new title *Yashmak*, although its entire score and most of the book were ultimately replaced by other hands.

World War I spelt the end of the Ottoman Empire, and ultimately led to the establishment of the secular Republic of Turkey in 1923 by Mustafa Kemel Atatürk (1881-1938). As part of his cultural and political revolution, he adapted the Turkish language to use the Latin alphabet.

Lüküs Hayat ("The Luxurious Life") was premiered in 1933 at the Şehir Tiyatrosu ("City Theatre") with music by Cemel Reşit Rey (1904-85) and a libretto by his brother Ekrem Reşit Rey (1900-59) in which a thief named Riza Bey is mistaken for a wealthy man with the same name. What follows is a satire on the nouveau riche and their indifference to the circumstances of the average Turk.

It was revived in 1985 to even greater effect at the Istanbul Şehir Tiyatroları ("Istanbul City Theatre") and has been continually revived and toured since then.

Yedi Kokalı Hürmüz ("Seven Husbands for Hürmüz") was a 1980 musical based on a 1967 comedy by Sadık Şendil (1913-86) with music by Attila Özdemiroğlu (1943-2016). Set in the nineteenth century when women had few rights, Hürmüz sets out to marry seven different men in order to achieve financial security. Complications ensue when the seven begin to find out about each other. A more recent 2009 film version of the same story had a new song-score by Ender Akay and Sunay Özgür (1968-).

While there have been a number of European shows in the post-*Les Miz* "Europopera" mode, few of them have succeeded beyond that continent. Perhaps the prospects are better for shows like *Improbable Frequency* and *Ciske de Rat*, which make a virtue of their specific milieux.

"Who Will Buy?"
Lionel Bart and the Post-war British Musical

For much of the twentieth century, the impact of European popular music on the rest of the world – the United States in particular – had been pretty laughable. "Since the heyday of Gilbert and Sullivan and the demise of the Viennese operetta, the leadership in musical theatre has belonged to the Americans," said *Time*'s Michael Walsh in 1988. "British musicals, when they were considered at all, conjured up images of ageing vaudevillians with straw boaters and canes barking strophic ballads at nodding pensioners."[1] The days of Vivian Ellis and Ivor Novello had passed, leaving little impact on the world scene. Then two things happened. One was in the sphere of pop music, the other in the theatre.

I don't think I need to tell you much about John, Paul, George and Ringo. The Beatles and the British invasion that they led are common knowledge. However, it had implications for musical theatre that cannot be overerstated. It wasn't just the beat. It may not have even been the music at all. It was the fact that four working class lads from Liverpool had captured the world's imagination.

The real change, of course, goes back a little further. In 1945, despite the fact that Winston Churchill had led Britain through the war, the British people decided they wanted a change – a new social contract, really. They elected Clement Attlee (1883-1967) and the Labour party. This was a part of a massive social upheaval that accompanied post-war austerity. There was, of course, the sexual revolution and the rock revolution. But more fundamentally, the class system finally began to break down, and it became fashionable to speak in a working-class accent. In the so-called straight theatre, the "angry young man" John Osborne (1929-94) supplanted the "well-made plays" of Noël Coward (1899-1973) and Terrence Rattigan (1911-77).

In London, all social classes attend the theatre (including pantomimes) at some point in their lives. In New York, it is largely the domain of the upper middle classes. According to a survey commissioned by the Society of London Theatre in back in 2008, the average West End theatregoer then earned £31,500 per year, while the average Broadway audience member earned a whopping $195,700.[2] (Another more recent survey by The Broadway League gives a similar figure for the Broadway audience.)

In many ways, Lionel Bart (1930-99) exemplifies the post-war British musical. Unlike any of his American counterparts, he actually moved into musical theatre from the rock 'n' roll world. He continued to straddle both spheres: his circle of friends included Coward and Rattigan as well as The Beatles and the Moody Blues. Although he began his career writing revue material for the left-wing agit-prop Unity Theatre, it was as a songwriter for Tommy Steele (1936-) ("Rockin' with the Cave Men") and Cliff Richard (1940-) ("Living Doll") that he achieved his first success.

While Bart is credited as the sole author of the book, music and lyrics for *Oliver!*, actor Ron Moody (1924-2015), who originated the role of Fagin writes in his memoirs that he substituted many of Bart's lines with the original Dickens, changing for example "How d'ya do?" to "I hope I shall have the honour of your intimate acquaintance?" "Bart's script seemed rather too evenly spaced, even sparse, with short bursts of dialogue alternating with a page or two of lyric. We soon discovered, however, that this simple balance played incredibly well."[3] At the time, Moody wrote in his diary, "[Bart] is no marvel and all his tunes are derivative, some incredibly so, but he is workmanlike and clear cut in his decisions", although he more recently commented, "How strange to read that opinion fifty years later, when the entire score has been enshrined in the archives of musical comedy greats."[4]

"It's hard now to realise how thoroughly he transformed the British musical", wrote Michael Coveney in London's *The Independent*. "He mined an entire semi-submerged territory of music hall, parlour songs and cockney anthems and filtered them through an idiosyncratic gift for rhythm, phrase-making and song construction."[5] Within a very short time, Bart would achieve the kind of prosperity that would only be overtaken by Andrew Lloyd Webber. In 1959, he had two shows – *Fings Ain't Wot They Used T'Be* opened at Theatre Royal Stratford East on 17 February, while just over three months later, on 28 May, *Lock Up Your Daughters* (for which Bart contributed only lyrics to Laurie Johnson (1927-)'s music) opened at the Mermaid Theatre. Over the following year, both shows would successfully transfer to London's West End, and on 30 June 1960, he would make it a hat trick with the show that would seal his reputation – *Oliver!*

Bart learned from the American musicals and applied their principles to British culture. It is in this way that he serves as an example to people in other parts of the world who want to create indigenous musicals. Like the Broadway writers of the golden age, he learned to use street vernacular in his lyrics. While he was writing *Blitz* he said, "I've gone back to English folk groups and based things on English street cries and English nursery rhymes. And I'm a Jew, so there are Jewish things in it, too. I use jazz where it comes in… I'm not a musical scholar but I have a good ear and I've gone into musical origins. Jazz, real African jazz, isn't far from Jewish music, which is quite close to Gregorian, and leads on to Celtic music and then to English folk songs and Cockney street chants."[6]

In London, *Oliver!* was produced by Sir Donald Albery (1914-88) at what was then the New Theatre, now called the Noël Coward Theatre. In New York, it was presented by David Merrick (1911-2000), and the song "As Long As He Needs Me" was already on the charts. Its first tryout was a seven week run in Los Angeles, followed by another seven weeks in San Francisco, then three weeks in each of Detroit and Toronto, before opening on 6 January 1963 at the Imperial Theatre in New York. Merrick had to book some heavy advertising to make up for opening during a newspaper strike.

Compared to other British shows, *Oliver!* survived its transfer relatively unscathed, although Merrick did ask *Irma la Douce* veteran Clive Revill (1930-), whom he had cast as Fagin, to tone down the "Jewishness" of the character. He also enlarged the show's orchestra from the chamber-sized one used in London, for the simple reason that the Musicians Union required twenty-five people in the pit, and Merrick wasn't going to pay anybody to **not** play.

Oliver! inspired a rash of imitators – *Pickwick*, *Scrooge*, even Andrew Lloyd Webber's early work – but Bart was determined not to repeat himself. His theme song for *From Russia With Love*, for instance, sounds nothing like anything in *Oliver!* Although *Oliver!* is perhaps the only Bart musical to withstand the test of time, *Blitz!* (1962) and *Maggie May* (1964) were modest successes, and only the catastrophic failure of *Twang!!* (1965) and the still-born *La Strada* have blighted his reputation as Britain's greatest post-war musical writer.

Bart was not alone in his desire to drag the post-war British musical into the modern era. Nor was he the only person trying to create a distinctive British form of musical. Author and playwright Wolf Mankowitz (1924-98) declared in 1965: "Those of us who have been working for the musical theatre for some years would like to make it categorically clear we are not concerned to create pastiche American musicals. We are driving towards a specifically British musical theatre."[7] His efforts included the pop music satire *Expresso Bongo* (1958) and *Make Me an Offer* (1959) and his co-conspirators – Monty Norman (1928 -), Julian More (1928-2010) and David Heneker (1906-2001) would dominate the British musical from the late 1950s through the early 1960s. (Heneker would achieve his own international success in 1963 with *Half a Sixpence*.)

They and others pioneered what theatre historian Adrian Wright calls the "verismo"[8] musical, which should "offer an accurate reflection of real life... Verismo holds up the glass to life, the unflattering light of day, sordidity, pans across the drawing room with its chintzy cheeriness to the kitchen sink."[9] (This is similar to the principal of "putting the audience on stage" put forward by Gratien Gélinas and Mavor Moore in the chapter "Canada – Still Deciding What it Will Be".)

The Crooked Mile (1959) with book and lyrics by Peter Wildeblood (1923-99) and music by sometime Noël Coward accompanist Peter Greenwell (1929-2006) depicted Soho's gangs and prostitutes, albeit sweetened with sentimentality. Its score included the ballad "If I Ever Fall in Love Again", sung by the American expatriate Elisabeth Welch (1904-2003).

However, after *Oliver!*, the trend turned toward chirpy, nostalgic literary adaptations (*Pickwick*, *Half a Sixpence*) and, according to Wright, "The British musical was almost done with holding a mirror up to life".[10] (For a detailed account of the more obscure post-war British musicals, see Wright's book *A Tanner's Worth of Tune*.)

Andrew Lloyd Webber may ultimately have turned to Puccini-esque quasi-operatic romantic schmaltz with *Phantom of the Opera*, but his first un-produced collaboration with Tim Rice, *The Likes of Us* sounds like he'd slipped into a coma with the *Oliver!* cast album on auto-repeat. Still, by the time *Jesus Christ Superstar* rolled around – actually their fourth collaboration – he had found a way to combine the form of a Broadway musical with the kind of quasi-symphonic rock heard in the final tracks of The Beatles' *Abbey Road*.

"The urgent and forceful nature of the rock idiom was there," says Kurt Gänzl, "but the bones that lay under the surface of the score were of a more thoroughly classical shape. Just as the jazz and ragtime idioms had been adapted for song and, eventually, for show music, here was the rock idiom being modified into a theatrically acceptable and dramatically effective style of music by being cross-bred with the solid tenets of a more regular style of theater music."[11] "Influences abound," writes Alan Jay Lerner, "but they are filtered through a very distinctive musical personality, which gives his music a sound of its own... [He] speaks in the popular musical language of the day, more literate but, nevertheless, contemporary through and through."[12]

The musical theatre establishment has been reluctant to embrace Lloyd Webber. They complain that his music is bombastic, that his scores are all interchangeable, and that he is more interested in being theatrical than in being dramatic. It may also be that he is a victim of his own success, and that, as with Rodgers and Hammerstein before him, over-familiarity breeds contempt.

Aside from Andrew Lloyd Webber, successful British musicals have been thin on the ground. The landmark critical successes have been even fewer. Therefore, the two shows I'm going to examine here were not commercial successes, but were nevertheless highly regarded. (Although Adrian Wright doesn't mention them, I wonder if they might not fall into the verismo category?)

Musically, *The Hired Man* (1984) would appear to be as far away from *Oliver!* as you can get, although I believe that composer Howard Goodall (1958-) had taken some of the same lessons on board. Telling a love story set among a Cumbrian coal-mining community in the years leading up to World War I, based on a book by Melvyn Bragg (1939-), Goodall combined English folk music with the sort of choral sounds he learned as a chorister at Oxford. Michael Coveney, writing in the *Financial Times*, said "a marvellous succession of chorales, operatic duets and vigorous foot-stomping rhythms — an altogether thoroughly vital score by Howard Goodall — interspersed with dialogue and rustic historical tableaux that would not disgrace *Emmerdale Farm* in an average week. *The Hired Man* is, all the same, an engagingly different kind of musical, the sort of thing perhaps Andrew Lloyd Webber (who presents the show) was thinking of when he hoped to establish a British musical academy at the Old Vic. Lyrics and libretto, as Mr Lloyd Webber knows only too well, are the great problem with contemporary musicals. No one is very good at either. Certainly not Mr Bragg and Mr Goodall, who come seriously unstuck the minute the music stops."[13]

He set out to be a serious composer – and he has several choral works to his name, but it is his work with Rowan Atkinson and the *Not the Nine o'Clock News* team that defined Goodall's early career. Even now, he is probably best known for the theme from the TV sitcom *Red Dwarf* (Jenna Russell singing "I want to lie shipwrecked and comatose, drinking fresh mango juice...") and his work on *Blackadder* and *Mr. Bean*. In fact, what sets him apart is his ability to write richly textured music that is also highly melodic. "Goodall caught the English choral tone magnificently", says Kurt Gänzl.[14] Although he has continued to write musicals, including *Girlfriends* (1987), *Days of Hope* (1991) *Love Story* (2010) and *Bend It Like Beckham* (2015), he has never fully embraced the values of Broadway. Instead, he has been in demand as a presenter of television programmes *about* music. In this way, like Mozart, Weill and Bernstein, I count him as a composer who aims to elevate popular tastes. Although it ran for only 164 performances at London's late Astoria Theatre, *The Hired Man* raised great hopes in some people's minds.

When I first heard that somebody had written a musical about Viv Nicholson, a woman who won the pools in the early 1960s and then lost everything, I thought, "Who cares?" However, a number of people whose opinions I trusted were raving about it, so I finally went to see *Spend, Spend, Spend* by composer Steve Brown and author Justin Greene, which opened at the Picadilly Theatre on October 12, 1999 following an initial production in 1998 at West Yorkshire Playhouse.

Ian Shuttleworth in the *Financial Times* had declared it "the most glorious new musical I can ever recall seeing". Ian Bradley, in his book *You've Got to Have a Dream*, called it "a classic example of a musical based on a subject which would previously have been treated via a kiss-and-tell biography or a television documentary. At the end I was left asking the question what was added to the story by making it a musical?"[15] While I was still not entirely won over by its principal character, the score was, alongside *The Hired Man*, probably the best in any British musical of the last three decades.

It won the *Evening Standard* award for Best Musical, and star Barbara Dickson managed to capture an Olivier Award. She told journalist Piers Ford, "It really speaks to me, which is important for an artist. I always feel that if you're not moved when you read something, there isn't much point in doing it. She is a fascinating character, and I think it's because of the subject matter. She was a poor woman who won money that they spent like water, and then her husband died. [Greene and Brown] just went headlong at it."[16] It managed to hold on for the better part of a year before going on tour, and was revived at the Watermill Theatre in Newbury, Berkshire in the summer of 2009. Brown also wrote the score for the unfortunately titled *I Can't Sing!* which closed quickly in 2014.

Brown, whose TV work includes *Spitting Image, The Ant & Dec Show* and *I'm Alan Partridge*, had previously attempted a musical version of *Elmer Gantry* but was spurned by the rights holders. His *It's a Wonderful Life* played at the New Wolsey Theatre in Ipswich in 2009.

For a couple of decades now, in many people's

minds, the great hope of British musical theatre has rested on the shoulders of lyricist Anthony Drewe (1961-) and composer George Stiles (1961-). They differ from Brown and Greene or from Goodall in that, unusually for European writers, their forté is musical comedy.

They met at Exeter University in the early 1980s, and won the first ever Vivian Ellis Prize in 1985 with *Just So*, a musical based on stories by Rudyard Kipling. Under the auspices of Sir Cameron Mackintosh, it was produced first at the Watermill Theatre in Newbury, then at London's Tricycle Theatre. The rights were optioned by Steven Spielberg, but the proposed animated film never materialised, and neither did a West End production. *Honk!*, their update of the ugly duckling tale, also began at the Watermill, where I saw it in December 1993 when it was called *The Ugly Duckling (or, The Aesthetically Challenged Farmyard Fowl)*. It was later produced at the National Theatre, and has since been seen more than a thousand times at regional theatres around the world.

When Cameron Mackintosh acquired the stage rights to *Mary Poppins*, one of the conditions dictated by the late author P.L. (Pamela) Travers (born Helen Lyndon Goff 1899-1996) was that the writers must be British. Mackintosh knew that audiences would expect to hear the songs by Richard M. Sherman (1928-) and Robert B. Sherman (1925-2012) from the Walt Disney movie – which Travers loathed – so he asked Drewe and Stiles to rework them. Following a tryout at the Bristol Hippodrome, *Mary Poppins* opened at the Prince Edward Theatre in 2004, directed by Sir Richard Eyre.

In spite of that show's success – both in London and New York – Stiles and Drewe have yet to emerge as the bankable household names that many people believe they have the potential to be. Yet they are two of only a small handful of people in Britain who make a full-time living from writing musicals. *Betty Blue Eyes*, with a book by American writers Ron Cowan and Daniel Lipman based on

Alan Bennett and Malcolm Mowbray's 1984 satirical screenplay on postwar rationing *A Private Function*, opened at London's Novello Theatre on 14 April 2011. The *Evening Standard*'s Henry Hitchings called it "a production with heart and an unusual mixture of gentleness and naughtiness. Though not an instant classic, it's satisfyingly meaty."[17] *The Guardian*'s Michael Billington said, "This is a rare show in several ways. It is a genuine 'musical comedy' rather than a through-composed pseudo-opera... The success of this show relies on the fact that the songs grow out of, and are always proportionate to, the situation."[18]

It closed after seven months, but this has not curbed Stiles' optimism. "I don't want to come over as a Pollyanna", he told *The Stage*, "but I have good reason to think we might be entering a pretty rich vein of British musical theatre. It's a staggeringly broad church... and I would rather celebrate that than harp on about great work not having longer runs."[19] Since then, they have written new songs for a short-lived revival/revisal of *Half a Sixpence*, again for Cameron Mackintosh.

More recently (and successfully), Roald Dahl's *Matilda* was adapted by English playwright Dennis Kelly (1970-) and Australian comedian and songwriter Tim Minchin (1975-) at the Royal Shakespeare Company, which transferred to the Cambridge Theatre in London's West End in 2011. "Dennis Kelly's adaptation grips from the start", said *The Times*. "Jokes and numbers come thick and fast...Tim Minchin's lyrics, to his own music, are so good that the temptation to write them down could, at any point, make you miss some extraordinary sight."[20] "The Royal Shakespeare Company has struck gold with this wildly entertaining musical", wrote *The Independent*. "Dennis Kelly's clever adaptation and the witty, intricate songs by Aussie comic Tim Minchin create a new, improved version of Dahl's story."[21] The *Evening Standard* said, "In this lovingly created show, *Matilda*'s magic positively sparkles. There's a cleverness in the writing which ensures that, while it appeals to children, there is plenty for adults to savour... It's blissfully funny... There's a playfulness throughout that proves intoxicating."[22] The RSC produced the transfer itself, and it is estimated that it recovered its £2.6 million investment in early 2012.[23] It won seven Olivier awards, including Best Musical. As of early 2019, it is still running in London.

At the far end of the spectrum from *Betty Blue Eyes* and *Matilda* is *London Road*, a music-theatre piece by documentary playwright Alecky Blythe and composer Adam Cork, developed with director Rufus Norris (1965-) at the National Theatre Studio. It opened at the Cottesloe Theatre on 7 April 2011.

Blythe recorded testimonies from those who had been affected by a series of murders of prostitutes in the London Road area of Ipswich. The verbatim accounts were then set to music by Cork, retaining the rhythm of the original speech. "The presence of music alters how we hear these words, forcing us to pay attention to the exact intonation used in the act of reproduction", says Sarah Whitfield of University College Falmouth. "*London Road* does something remarkable, in occupying this troubled space between song and spoken dialogue. It opens a different road for music theatre, not at the expense of the musical, but by demonstrating the possibilities for collaborations between unlikely practitioners, and the benefits of the kind of institutional support and protection the National Theatre is able to give new work."[24]

Critic Mark Shenton found the result to be "totally absorbingly different... bursting into arresting, affecting life... an innovative and challenging show".[25] Perhaps this is a return to verismo?

Canada –
"Still Deciding What It Will Be"

To some people, my home country Canada is the very incarnation of ennui, and Toronto, its economic and cultural epicentre, doubly so.

Once upon a time, Toronto was a very puritanical, Presbyterian city – hence the epithet "Toronto the Good". There used to be a joke that a competition offered a first prize of a week in Toronto. Second prize was two weeks. And how many Torontonians does it take to change a lightbulb? Two: one to hold the bulb, the other to fly down to New York to see how they do it there.

On the other hand, "Born to be Wild" was written by a Torontonian named Dennis Edmonton (1943-), under the pseudonym Mars Bonfire, and first recorded in 1968 by a Toronto band called Steppenwolf. More recently, Toronto has claimed itself to be the third largest centre for English speaking theatre, behind New York and London. It is one of the most cosmopolitan cities in the world, an exciting and vibrant home to some six million people in its metropolitan area.

Still, it struggles with its past reputation. There are some who seem to feel that it should not get ideas above its (colonial outpost, branch plant) station. For others, it's the dour wallflower that longs to soar and sing.

A few years ago the Toronto Transit Commission unveiled its remodelled Museum subway station, giving it a theme and décor related to the neighbouring Royal Ontario Museum, and hoping to purge its reputation for resembling the world's longest public lavatory. There were the inevitable reactionaries who objected to this desecration of its heritage, claiming it would spoil the system's uniformity. Fortunately, the TTC didn't listen. (No doubt these Philistines objected to Toronto native architect Frank Gehry (1929-)'s reinvention of the Art Gallery of Ontario, too.)

The journalist Robert Fulford (1932-) once said,

"Canada remains a place without final definition, a place whose inhabitants have not all made a total commitment to its existence, a country that is forever reshaping itself... We have no 'foundation myth,' as the anthropologists say. Canadians did not emerge slowly from the mists of time, far back in unwritten history; nor did we, like the Americans, found our state on Enlightenment principles inscribed in a sacred constitution; nor can we, like the Israelis, look for national legitimation through either ethnic history or a covenant with God. We lack ethnic, religious, and ideological identity. We came slowly together, gathering in sparse settlements on the Atlantic coast and later the Pacific coast, and along the way slowly filling the arable land between."[1]

Then again, Rudyard Griffiths (1970-), co-founder of Historica Canada, asserts that "History shows that ours is a political community built on shared democratic values and institutions rather than on ethnicity, region or language." Griffiths maintains that, for Canada's founders, "loyalty to Canada meant a lifelong commitment to the idea of a free and equal citizenry engaged in a great democratic experiment... to advance a single goal: the establishment of a new nation, Canada, as an egalitarian, democratic, economically ambitious and less sectarian society – a wholly Canadian vision that was consciously distinct from Britain's and America's."[2]

I believe that, to some extent, both are correct. "Canada is way more of an idea than it is an ethnic identity or even a collection of myths", says Fulford's son-in-law, novelist and academic Stephen Marche (1976-). "Multiculturalism really does have that power as a binding agent."[3] It's signifigant to note that Fulford and Griffiths are of different generations. Fulford's impressions were formed in Canada's first century, while Griffiths came from its second.

There is a bridge across Vancouver's First Narrows that could stand as a metaphor for Canadian culture. The Lions Gate Bridge was, when it opened in 1938, the highest suspension bridge in the British Empire. However, it is not internationally famous in the way that the Sydney Harbour Bridge and San Francisco's Golden Gate are. I had always wondered why this was, until a recent visit to Vancouver. As my plane flew over the city, I looked down on Stanley Park and the North Shore mountains, yet I could not see the bridge. Painted a deep green, it was invisible against the water. Standing at the entrance to one of the most spectacularly beautiful harbours in the world, it compliments its environment, but does not dominate it. Instead, it is a quietly graceful structure. (However, it hasn't gone entirely un-noticed: a major film studio, Lionsgate Entertainment, is named after it.)

Canadians have tended to eschew mythology altogether, preferring their heroes to be merely life-sized (Paul Bunyan notwithstanding). Putting aside visions of Mounties and beavers, it's hard to find a Canadian stereotype. In order to have one, we would have to at least be known for *something*.

In 1971, when asked why his music sounds so southern American, Toronto-born First Nations rock musician Robbie Robertson (1943-) said, "There's no Canadian music... It's North American music – different countries, but you hear the exact same music, from blues to cowboy."[4] (Robertson, whose titles include "The Night They Drove Old Dixie Down" and "Up on Cripple Creek", is considerd one of the founders of something called "Americana music".) Sadly, the Canadian cultural identity has, in the past, been largely either stifled or absorbed into the larger (and louder) American one.

Singer k. d. lang offers a differing perspective. "The landscape, sparse population, long winters and proximity to nature all contribute to a very introspective, melancholic (and I use that word not in a negative sense) kind of spiritualism – they contribute to an openness and humility."[5] (Robertson later conceded, when asked what makes Canada such a fertile ground for talented artists, "Must be something in the water."[6])

Take away the mythology from art and you are left with journalism. It's a recipe for blandness. But then, I would argue that the notion that Canada has no mythology is in itself a myth.

A century ago, playwright Jessie Edgar Middleton declared in *Canada and Its Provinces*, "There is no Canadian Drama. It is merely a branch of the American Theatre, and, let it be said, a most profitable one."[7] Around the same time, an article in *Canadian Magazine* said, "Canada is the only nation in the world whose stage is entirely controlled by aliens. She is the only nation whose sons and daughters are compelled to go to a foreign capital for permission to act in their own language on the boards of their own theatres. The only road to applause of a Toronto theatre audience is by way of Broadway."[8]

Until the late 1960s, what we saw on stage, TV and the cinema and what we heard on the radio were almost entirely under foreign control. There was no indigenous Canadian music industry, and professional theatre was just developing.

A few isolated songs emerged, such as Ruth Lowe (1914-81)'s "I'll Never Smile Again", first performed by the Percy Faith Orchestra on CBC Radio in 1939 and later made famous by Frank Sinatra, and Elizabeth Clarke (1911-60)'s "There's a Bluebird on Your Windowsill", originally written in 1947 for the patients of a Vancouver children's hospital. However, artists like Hank Snow (1914-99) and Wilf Carter (1904-96) were lured to Nashville, and their Cape Breton Celtic roots became subsumed into country and western. Similarly, light music composer Robert Farnon (1917-2005), an early member of radio's *The Happy Gang*, left for Britain.

(Tony Bennett once said, "The people of Canada should build a statue to Robert Farnon for his unparalleled and magnificent contribution to music this century".[9])

Then something magical happened. Canada celebrated its centennial of confederation in 1967 and it has not been the same since. The alternate theatre movement came into being. Canadian content regulations made a Canadian-based popular music industry possible. (And St. Paul, Alberta built a flying saucer landing pad.)

Pierre Berton called it *The Last Good Year*.[10] That year, my parents took my two sisters and I on a road trip across the country, and that was the best decision they ever could have made. Canada's then Secretary of State Judy LaMarsh (1924-80) said, "We cast off the bonds of our conformity, and slipped out of our cloak of grey anonymity forever."[11] This was, I believe, the dividing line between the Canada that Fulford described and the one that Griffiths laid out. When, in 2017 Canada celebrated its sesquicentennial, it was not so much 150 years of confederation as it was the fiftieth anniversary of the nation's biggest party.

It has taken a long time, but this change has eventually trickled down to the creation of distinctly Canadian television shows. *Due South* and *Being Erica* broke new ground, and prepared the country for the enormously (even internationally) popular *Murdoch Mysteries* and *Anne with an E*.[12] The latter was created by Moira Walley-Beckett, a former musical theatre performer who was a veteran of the Charlottetown Festival's production of *Anne of Green Gables*, based on the same source material. Like *Due South* creator Paul Haggis, Walley-Beckett had spent most of her career in Hollywood, but came back to Canada to do something uniquely Canadian. In the same sense, *Come from Away* would not exist without *The Drowsy Chaperone*, and none of them would exist without *Anne of Green Gables*, which in turn built on the foundations of *Spring Thaw*.

I lived in Toronto from 1983–91. During that time, some important events happened. Throughout the 1970s, Toronto had a very active cabaret and dinner theatre scene, including a lot of original work created by the members of Lehman Engel's workshops. Then along came Marlene Smith and Tina Vanderheyden's all-Canadian production of *Cats*.

I arrived just as this scene was drying up. Until *Cats*, there had been very little large scale professional musical theatre in the city. *Cats* began a wave of imported shows including *Les Misérables, Miss Saigon* and *Rent*. At the time, not everybody in the theatre community saw this as a positive development. Even some of the press opined that it was inconceivable that any of these stages would be taken up with original work – we just don't do that sort of thing.

An organisation was formed called the Cabaret and Musical Theatre Alliance with the objective of preserving "cabaret and small-scale musical theatre". I joined its board of directors soon after its formation, where my one and only contribution was to have them delete the words "small-scale" from its objectives. A small change, but as it turned out, a propitious one: thirty years later, the cabaret and small-scale scene remains moribund. Instead we have the Canadian Music Theatre Project and we're transferring shows to Broadway and the world.

Canada is in a transitional phase. We've had a few successes, as I will outline in this chapter. We've also had a few setbacks. This is something that I believe that every successful culture goes through, but after two Broadway hits, I keep hoping that Toronto will get a bee in its collective bonnet. Yet Toronto's commercial theatres seem to spend a lot of time in sleep mode.

It has become very fashionable to be negative. The 2007 edition of the *Time Out Toronto* guide said, "For the past 20 years, Toronto has been passing itself off as the third largest theatre centre in the English speaking world, after London and New York. This holds true in terms of the number of venues and independent theatre companies in the city, but is debatable in terms of quality or government support."[13] A friend of mine complained of the depressing state of Toronto theatre a few years ago until I reminded him of the Canadian show *The Drowsy Chaperone* that was at that very moment a hit on Broadway.

It has often been claimed that the market is too small to support a viable commercial theatre, but Garth Drabinsky (1949-) claimed that his ten-year production of *Phantom of the Opera* drew on a market of twenty million people from a 250-mile radius of the city.

Historically, Canadian musicals have also struggled to find acceptance within their own theatre community. "To this day, musicals are excluded from most literary and playwriting competitions and prizes," said S. G. (Sharolyn) Lee in 2010, at that time Executive Director of the Imperial Theatre in St. John, New Brunswick. "There has been little serious academic study of musical theatre, and within many of our 'legitimate' actor training institutions there is still considerable prejudice against musical theatre."[14]

This brings me to the stigma that once existed regarding Canadian culture. We called it our "National Inferiority Complex". Back in 1986, Robert Fulford told me, "Most Americans react with total indifference to Canadian culture - except in those cases (such as a Jewison film or a Plummer performance) when they don't know or care that it's Canadian."[15] This was before a Canadian named Chris Hadfield emerged as the world's coolest astronaut. Although we are still haunted by its shadow, following the success of *Due South*, *Murdoch Mysteries* and *Anne with an E*, as well as the musicals described herein, this stigma has now largely been made irrelevant, if not forgotten. I will also argue that by the time you realise that you have put something like this behind you, you will learn that the seeds of its destruction go back to at least twenty years earlier.

In 1985, I began working on what would eventually become my book *Broadway North: The Dream of a Canadian Musical Theatre*. I worked on it for a year, travelling to the Charlottetown Festival, and interviewing people like Mavor Moore and John MacLachlin Gray. I stopped when I failed to get either funding or a publishing deal, but the fact was that the timing was not right. Canadian musical theatre had not yet reached that plateau of maturity from which we could profitably reflect. Twenty years later, conditions had changed somewhat radically: a hit Canadian musical – *The Drowsy Chaperone* – had just opened on Broadway. The seeds for it were all there in 1985, but they had yet to ripen. The timing was right in another unfortunate sense, too – a number of my interview subjects, including Norman Campbell, Marian Grudeff and Tom Kneebone, passed away before the book was even finished.[16] Things have continued to mature since then, with another even bigger hit.

However, we still have to deal with the remnants of that National Inferiority Compex which continues to (mis)inform our psyche. Traditionally, the phrase "Canadian musical" had always been treated as an oxymoron. Playwright and humorist Eric Nicol (1919-2011) joked that a Canadian musical was "built around one girl who can play the harmonica while tap-dancing."[17] Back in 1948, the future Canadian novelist Margaret Laurence (1926-87), then a newspaper columnist at the *Winnipeg Citizen*, wrote:

> "It seems to be very difficult to capture the much more rugged atmosphere of Canada in a musical comedy... They must deal in subtle wit, and the wit of this country is not generally found in the super-civilized repartee. They must be gay, and while this country has great potentialities for humorous writing, it is not basically gay... I feel that the Canadian scene simply does not lend itself to good musical

comedy. Just as great tragic drama flourished in Elizabethan England, the time and the tone of a country almost always sets the pattern of its artistic creation. Until musical comedy actually fits in with the life of our people, and until it can be written with more spontaneity than at present, I think we would be better to forget about it for a while."[18]

Ironically, this was written in the same year that *Spring Thaw*, the world's longest-running annual professional satirical revue first appeared. This was the show that would begin the long process of proving that Margaret Laurence was wrong. In fact, "fitting in with the life of our people" was what *Spring Thaw* was all about.

Founder Mavor Moore took his inspiration from *Les Fridolinades*, the Montreal revues conceived in 1937 by Gratien Gélinas (1909-99). Toronto critic Christopher Hoile says, "For students of Canadian theatre *Les Fridolinades* is essential viewing. Gratien Gélinas, the father of Québecois theatre, created the character of Fridolin for the radio in 1937. The next year saw the first of many stage revues based on these radio pieces that were the first to reflect everyday Canadian life on stage in everyday language."[19] According to Moore, Gélinas "deserves the credit for insisting that Canadian theatre had to start putting its audience on stage."[20] Among the shows that *Spring Thaw* in turn influenced are *Rowan and Martin's Laugh-in*.

Moore later adapted this approach to include book musicals. When he founded the Charlottetown Festival, he set out to commission new Canadian musicals, and *Anne of Green Gables - The Musical*™, with book by Don Harron, music by Norman Campbell and lyrics by Campbell, Harron, Moore and Campbell's wife Elaine, was their first great success. It began life when Campbell, a television producer with the Canadian Broadcasting Corporation, had a ninety-minute slot to fill. Actor Don Harron was reading *Anne of Green Gables* to his daughters Martha and Mary[21]. "I suggested to the Campbells that it would make a good TV musical", says Harron, "because the heroine has such an imagination that the only way to render her expressive outbursts in a dramatic form would be to set them to music."[22] Of Lucy Maude Montgomery's original book, Robert Fulford says:

> "Everyone has an imagination, and everyone is encouraged to deny it – or at least fence it in. The world teaches us early that our imaginations are dangerous or frivolous. The world tells us to stop dreaming and be serious... Anne's unique ability to invest her surroundings with world-shaking, heaven-storming possibilities – this is what gives her story the power of enduring myth. That's also what makes her such a peculiarly Canadian heroine – like the best Canadian artists, she turns an unpromising landscape into a proper home for the imagination."[23]

Anne of Green Gables, Theatre Under the Stars, Vancouver, 2004
(Photo courtesy Roger Smith)

Anne has been playing in Charlottetown every summer since 1965, and has played well over three thousand performances. It is the world's longest running seasonal musical. Until the recent Broadway successes of *The Drowsy Chaperone* and *Come from Away*, it was Canada's best-known stage show, and the first Canadian book musical to receive world attention.

Anne essentially went through three major stages of development. Firstly, it was adapted as a ninety-minute live television special in 1956 starring Toby Tarnow (1937-) as Anne and John Drainie (1916-66) as Matthew. This version was repeated in 1958 with Kathy Willard as Anne. Then, in 1965, Alan Lund staged it at the Charlottetown Festival. However, between 1965 and 1969, it remained a work in progress. For the first season, the orchestra consisted of two pianos, percussion and trumpet. A number of new songs were added – including "Open the Window", "Did You Hear?" and "The Words", which had lyrics by the Festival's founder Mavor Moore, because Don Harron was tied up with filming commitments. After the success of the first season, musical director John Fenwick re-orchestrated the score, and since that time Campbell and Harron secured a contractual commitment for a minimum of nineteen players in the pit (now supported by the Norman and Elaine Campbell Legacy Fund). At one point, during negotiations, somebody suggested that, if the Festival really wanted to save money, they could change all the half notes to quarter notes, and thereby go home earlier. In subsequent seasons, more numbers were added, including "General Store".

In 1969, Canadian-born London impresario Bill Freedman (1929-) brought the show to London's New (now Noël Coward) Theatre, where it opened on 16 April starring Polly James (1941-). For the first time, a Canadian book musical was on foreign turf. "Bill Freedman didn't want the critics to know that it was a Canadian show in any way"[24], says Norman Campbell. *Mame* was about to open in London starring Ginger Rogers. It had songs called "Bosom Buddies" and "Open a New Window". *Anne* had "Bosom Friends" and "Open the Window". The latter was easily solved by changing the title to "Learn Everything", a hook in the original lyric. "Bosom Friends" was another matter – this required an entirely new song. However, Don remembered that a recurring line in the book was "Kindred Spirits". And so, with the help of a piano loaned by none other than Liberace, "Kindred Spirits" was added to the London score, and eventually to the Charlottetown version as well. However, Freedman also wanted a more up-tempo number for Hiram Sherman (1908-89), as Matthew, to sing in the first act. "(I Can't Find) The Words" was replaced by "When I Say My Say", while a reprise of "The Words", sung by Marilla, played by Barbara Hamilton (1926-96) in the second act after Matthew's death, was retained as a stand-alone number. (This change was never incorporated into the Charlottetown version of the show, although it remains as an appendix to the published script.)

While it was generally warmly received by the London critics, *Anne* closed after a respectable but loss-making 319 performances. "I was very unsophisticated in 1969", says Freedman. "I should have toured it. I would not have done it today without two stars."[25]

In Japan, *Anne* (the novel) has been a phenomenon since it was published in 1952 as *Akage no An* ("Anne with Red Hair") in a translation by Hanako Muraoka (1893-1968), who had been a student of Tōyō Eiwa Jo Gakkō, a girl's school founded by the Women's Missionary Society of the Canadian Methodist Church. Muraoka began work on her translation in 1939, just before the outbreak of World War II. She had been given the novel by a New Brunswick missionary named Loretta Leonard Shaw (1872-1940) with the urging that she translate it into Japanese. During the war, she had to keep her work – which was in the language of the "enemy" – hidden. After the war, a ravaged Japanese population identified with the story of a perky but unwanted orphan. A 1979 animee version on television spiked its popularity, and a Canadian-themed park opened with a replica of Green Gables. Since then, every year thousands of Japanese have made a pilgrimage to Prince Edward Island.

Anne the musical has been presented several times in Tokyo in a Japanese language production by the Shiki Theatre Company. Aside from the translation into Japanese, according to Harron, the script is the same as the Canadian version. "There was no strangeness", says Norman Campbell. "Everyone thought we should react to a Japanese girl wearing red pigtails, but it was perfectly natural... The cast was excellent, all of them being good musicians and having great schooling in theatrical arts."[26]

Since then, Canada has developed a handful of musicals that have earned international reputations. John MacLachlan Gray (1946-) and Eric Peterson (1946-)'s *Billy Bishop Goes to War* – an enormous hit to this day at home – played briefly on Broadway and in the West End in the

1980s, but it would take another two decades before Canada would have its first unqualified Broadway hit.

In 2006 *The Drowsy Chaperone*, with book by Bob Martin (1962-) and Don McKellar (1963-), and music and lyrics by Greg Morrison (1965-) and Lisa Lambert (1962-), opened at the Marquis Theatre on Broadway, where it broke box office records after winning five Tony Awards (including best book and best score.) The musical, in which a lonely divorcee sits in his apartment listening to the cast recording of his favourite "1920s" musical, had begun on the fringe in Toronto in 1998, and graduated through many incarnations before making its move south.

Bob Martin attended Lawrence Park Collegiate (folk singer Neil Young's alma mater) with two of his future collaborators, Lisa Lambert and Don McKellar. Even then they dreamed up mock musicals. The late Marian Grudeff, a veteran of *Spring Thaw* who co-wrote the score for the Broadway musical *Baker Street* with Ray Jessel, remembered Don as an English student at Victoria College. "He looked like a rabbinical student", she told me in 2004. "He played Hysterium in *A Funny Thing Happened on the Way to the Forum*. He had a lot of charisma on stage. He's a very musical man. He'd come over and sit beside me on the piano and we'd go over a whole book of different songs."

McKellar and Lambert recalled their friendship with Grudeff to Sandy Thorburn, musical director of a production of *The Drowsy Chaperone* at Thousand Islands Playhouse in Gananoque, Ontario. "I'd never sung in public before", says McKellar, "and I felt hopelessly nervous and out of place, until the accompanist [Grudeff] beckoned me over to her piano and privately, gently, probed the limits of my voice. 'Not much there', she confided, 'but what voice you have is musical and has character'... With humour and inexplicable generosity she taught me Hysterium's song 'I'm Calm'. I performed it for the director and I got the part. I still have no idea why she took the time to draw me out of my shell, but the next year, when I was asked to helm the annual Vic musical *Salad Days*, I accepted on the condition that Marian was the musical director."[27]

Lambert and Martin were also in that production. "At that time I was obsessed with musicals," says Lambert, "and when I learned of Marian's history I was beside myself. Don and I started spending time at her house – a little Broadway haven in the middle of polite North Toronto... It wasn't long before she was mentoring me; I would bring her rough lyrics and confused melodies and she would show me how to turn them into real songs. And when Bob Martin and I started creating musical revues at the Fringe of Toronto Festival, Marian was an integral member of the troupe. Together we wrote such bizarre routines as 'We're the Only Tulips on the Track Team', 'Le Chef Grotesque' and 'That Haircut Doesn't Suit You, Mr. Green'. (And not only was Marian an inspired collaborator, she had a way of directing and accompanying singers and non-singers so that they sounded better than they had a right to.)"

McKellar says, "We never would have written a musical if we hadn't met Marian. It's inconceivable. She simultaneously glamorised and demystified Broadway. Her affectionate and irreverent anecdotes made it irresistible and somehow within reach. Heaven for 'Man in Chair' would have been an evening with Marian Grudeff: trading tidbits of musical comedy arcana, laughing himself silly and singing into the night."[28]

It was their work with Grudeff that led to the creation of *The Drowsy Chaperone*. "Her influence is all over it", says Lambert. "She and I often discussed creating a strange, archaic show with, as she put it, 'first-rate second-rate songs'. One of my big regrets is not thanking Marian in my Tony acceptance speech. She's why my dreams came true."

When Bob asked Lisa to be the "best man" at his wedding to Janet Van de Graaff, the wheels of *The Drowsy Chaperone* were set in motion. Lisa and Don, together with Greg Morrison, a composer whom Bob had introduced them to, began to write a forty-minute pastiche 1920s musical about the marriage of two people (who happened to be named Robert Martin and Janet Van de Graaff) as a stag night entertainment. This very first incarnation was performed on 9 August 1998 at the Rivoli on Toronto's Queen Street. It was open to the public, and was advertised in the newspaper. The show, at that point, contained a half-dozen songs, of which two, "Aldolpho" and "An Accident Waiting to Happen" survived into the Broadway production. "It was broader at first", composer Greg Morrison told an American Theater Wing symposium *Working in the Theatre*. "The original score spanned greater periods – a forties song, a thirties song, a twenties song – and as the show developed, that was one of the things that the score honed more into – developing specifically as a twenties show."[29] Among the titles that didn't survive was one called "Hey, Sourpuss". That first book, which contained the basic plot of the musical within the show, was written by McKellar in collaboration with Matt Watts and the actors.

They decided it shouldn't end there. Bob Martin joined the team as a co-writer, and the character of the Man in Chair was born – a would-be raconteur, an obsessive show-nerd who can – and does – recount every detail about his favourite 1928 musical, *The Drowsy Chaperone*. "I would say one of the greatest evolutions was the character of the Man in Chair", Don McKellar told the *Working in the Theatre* symposium. "We realised early on that he was really the lead character and in a way his story is the real story arc of the script." Lisa Lambert told me, "It's all about the private place – the bedrooms where musical-theatre-fan teenagers record their YouTube renditions, etc."[30]

Lambert herself played the title role, and McKellar played the Latin lover, Aldolpho, while Janet Van de Graaff played her own namesake. Also in the cast was Jonathan Crombie (1966-2015), who would later replace Martin as the Man in Chair on Broadway and on tour. A new song, "It's an Over-rated World (With Seven Underwhelming Wonders)" was created for the title character to sing. This version, now an hour long, opened on 2 July 1999 at the 181 seat George Ignatief Theatre as a part of the Fringe of Toronto Festival, directed and choreographed by Steven Morel. (I have seen a video of this hour long version, the first to include the Man in Chair. "Aldolpho" and "Accident Waiting to Happen were still the only songs to survive into the Broadway version, although the basic plot and much of the dialogue remain.) Robert Crew of the *Star* pronounced it "so much fun it's barely legal." John Karastamatis, director of communications for Mirvish Productions, waited in line for one of the half dozen sold out performances.

On 24 November 1999, with backing from Mirvish Productions and a $120,000 budget, Karastamatis presented the show for a three week run at Theatre Passe Muraille, directed by Sandra Balcovske, a director from Second City. Two more songs were added for this version: "Cold Feet" and "I Do I Do in the Sky". It won the "Pretty Funny Comedic Play" and "Pretty Funny Director of a Comedic Play" awards at the Canadian Comedy Awards.

By this time, Matt Watts' name was no longer included among the collaborators. "It hurt", Mr. Watts told Susan Dominus of *The New York Times*, "but I'm still very close to them all."[31] He was not left out entirely. While in its transition from fringe comedy to Broadway musical the improv performers were necessarily replaced by singing and dancing triple threats, the creators made sure their friends received a share of the royalties. "If anything, they've been overly concerned and caring about it." There is still something of Watts' contribution left in the final script: "All that monkey imagery that's still in the play, that came from my obsession."

On 7 June 2001, Mirvish Productions presented a full-scale production directed by Daniel Brooks (1958-) – artistic director of Necessary Angel Theatre Company – at the Winter Garden Theatre. "Show Off", "Bride's Lament", "Message from a Nightingale" and "I Remember Love" were added for this version. The set consisted of a bare stage with six doors and a chair. "I think the design was supposed to support a big farce section that got pared down later in the rehearsal process", explained Lambert. Martin told the *Working in the Theatre* symposium, "We had to make a choice as to whether we allow the show to be an evocation of the musical – in other words, do we have a neutral place where both worlds co-exist like a metaphor for the theatre of a blank space where anything can happen? Basically that decision was made for us by our very small budget at the Winter Garden to be perfectly frank, but we knew that there was something unsatisfying about that, so we wrestled with the idea of fully realising the real world."

Xtra!'s Gordon Bowness called it "a delightful combination of high camp and low shtick that often leaves you breathless with laughter."[32] But Richard Ouzounian, theatre critic for the *Star*, was apparently underwhelmed. "This is probably a musical for people who hate musicals, and secretly think they're all silly and trivial. I don't, and so I was less than amused by most of the proceedings. There are people who will enjoy this, and I wish them well. I just don't agree with them. But most of all, let us hope this is where the expansion of *The Drowsy Chaperone* ends. I really don't want to see it further 'improved' a year from now at the Hummingbird [now Sony] Centre, or – heaven forbid – Skydome [now Rogers Centre]." His comments seem strange in light of two things – firstly, it has since been described as a "valentine" to the musical; secondly, in his former guise as host of CBC Radio's *Say It With Music*, Ouzounian himself bore an uncanny resemblance to the

Man in Chair. Lisa Lambert swears the character wasn't based on any real person, although Bob Martin told *NOW Magazine* that he "is based on someone with [Ouzounian's] enthusiasm, someone who's maybe a little bit too much into the show, someone who bores people by talking about their original-cast albums. Basically it's what Richard Ouzounian would have become if he weren't successful."[33] And, of course, *The Drowsy Chaperone* certainly didn't end there. (And Bowness added, "Richard Ouzounian hated *Drowsy*, so it's got to be good.")

American producer Roy Miller saw the show at the Winter Garden, and with Paul Mack, presented a showcase of it at the National Alliance for Musical Theatre's Festival of New Musicals in New York in 2004. (Among the cast was Broadway veteran Christine Ebersole (1953-)). Co-producers Kevin McCollum (1962-) and Bob Boyett (1942-) came on board at this point.

The show's title was a cause for some concern. McKellar and Lambert had originally seen it as a plausible title for a forgotten twenties musical. In fact, they deliberately wanted a bad title. At one point they considered changing it to *The 'Oops' Girl* (a reference to the Janet Van de Graaff character), but ultimately the title remained unchanged.

A new director was brought on board. Casey Nicholaw (1962-), who had been nominated for a Tony award for his choreography of *Spamalot*, would make his Broadway debut as both director and choreographer. "We knew that in order for the show to be truly effective, the musical within the show had to be fully realised, with great voices, great dancers, great costumes," Martin told the *Working in the Theatre* symposium. One of the first decisions made was to ditch the six doors. Instead, a realistic setting of the Man in Chair's apartment was created, which could be magically transformed into the settings for the musical within the show. "We were excited when we thought about the idea of a director-choreographer, because the show is not just about dancing, it's about movement, and the set itself is almost like another character in the show. It's constantly transforming, and it's absolutely crucial that we had somebody at the helm who knew how to move the action around with the characters in and out of these two worlds that we're presenting."

So many shows from other countries have gone to New York and lost their souls to producers who had no understanding of their original concepts. "It was certainly something we were really scared of", McKellar told Phil Hahn of CTV News, "but it never entered into that territory where we sold out or betrayed our initial impulse… At first, when we had our American partners involved we were sure that was going to be an issue, and it would lose its irony… but fortunately we had, in our producers and our director and our creative team, collaborators who were able to understand the importance of the tone, and the irony that we came with – and encouraged us to stick with that."[34] Of course, this is a show that benefited from Broadway gloss, as opposed to one smothered by it (as others have been). However, having seen it play so successfully in its original pared-down incarnation, the American producers knew that they mustn't throw the baby out with the bath water.

A tryout production was arranged at the Ahmanson Theatre in Los Angles. Three new songs, "Fancy Dress" (the opening number), "As We Stumble Along" (replacing "Over-rated World") and "Toledo Surprise" were written. For the Broadway opening, "I Remember Love" was replaced by "Love is Always Lovely in the End".

"'I Remember Love' seemed to come out of nowhere", Larry Blank, the orchestrator, remembers. "It didn't land very well in L.A. and it was decided that a new number would help. The new number seems to work much better in the general scheme of the show… but I always thought 'I Remember Love' was the better, more fun song. And I had more fun with the orchestration as well."

There were other changes – a ballet in the second half, following the "Bride's Lament" was also lost. "*Drowsy* was a very good show in L.A.," says Blank, "and it became much more polished and focused in N.Y. Once in previews in N.Y., the most attention was paid to cleaning up 'Accident Waiting To Happen' and smoothing all of the 'best man' transitions. Like most successful shows, this one was positive from the go, and the fixes were mostly cosmetic. A lot more credit should go to Casey Nicholaw who really pulled it together."[35]

Associated Press' Michael Kuchwara called it a "disarming, delightful soufflé".[36] Howard Kissel of the *New York Daily News* found "cause for rejoicing. It's full of wit and high spirits".[37] The all-important *New York Times* critic Ben Brantley said "The gods of timing, who are just as crucial to success in show business as mere talent is, have smiled brightly upon "The Drowsy Chaperone," the small and ingratiating musical that opened last night at the big and intimidating Marquis Theater." But he added that, "Though this revved-up spoof of a 1920's song-and-dance frolic, as imagined by an obsessive 21st-century show queen, seems poised to become the sleeper of the Broadway season, it is not any kind of a masterpiece."[38]

Still, on the night I attended – two days after the opening – the audience was warm and healthy. The show won seven Drama Desk awards, including Best Musical, best book and best score. It also won the Best Musical award from the Drama Critics Circle, and was nominated for thirteen Tony awards, including every category for which it was eligible.

The first Canadian show since *The Dumbells* (a First World War comedy troupe that played on Broadway in 1920) to be an unqualified Broadway hit, it repaid its $8 million cost within thirty weeks before finally closing at the end of December 2007 after 674 performances. The London production didn't fare quite so well; starring Elaine Paige in the non-starring title role, it finished after only eight weeks at the Novello Theatre, although it managed to be nominated for five Olivier awards (alas, losing to *Hairspray*). It has since enjoyed a successful pared-down revival at Upstairs at the Gatehouse, one of London's fringe theatres.

I was amazed to find that some people in the musical-loving community took serious offence to *The Drowsy Chaperone*. What is even more amazing is that these were some of the real life "Men in Chairs" – the people I would have expected to be the show's biggest fans. On an on-line discussion group, I heard some object – with no apparent sense of irony – to the portrayal of a stereotypical "show queen" as a lonely, neurotic obsessive-compulsive with no apparent social life – then proceeded to lambaste the show for its "inaccuracies" – the belting voices, the brassy orchestration, and the obvious fact that there were no cast-recordings in 1928. This actually turned into a heated argument about the "willing suspension of disbelief". I wondered if the show had simply cut too close to the bone.

There were great hopes for a triumphant homecoming, but an opportunity was missed when it was decided that it would not have a sit-down Toronto production. Mirvish Productions decided to pass, thinking that it was too soon after its original run. (Also, they had lost heavily on *The Producers*, *Hairspray* and *Lord of the Rings*.) Instead, a new company, Dancap Productions decided merely to open its North American tour in Toronto (with an all-American cast, save for its star Bob Martin).

It received a rapturous reception at the Elgin Theatre (which is downstairs from the Winter Garden, where Mirvish presented the first full-scale version). Even Richard Ouzounian re-evaluated the show. "It's interesting to see how the show has changed over the years. When it first started out, everyone was thrilled that four local authors (Martin, Don McKellar, Lisa Lambert and Greg

Morrison) had succeeded in conveying their unique sense of musical comedy hijinks to a theatrical audience. But as the work got closer to Broadway, the glitter got a little blinding and the sizzle sometimes threatened to overwhelm the steak. Well, a year on Broadway, a largely new touring cast and a return to this city where it all started has done wonders. In many ways this is probably the best, most balanced and most ultimately satisfying of the show I have ever seen. What makes it special? I call tell you that in two words. Bob Martin. He's always been *The Drowsy Chaperone*'s secret ingredient."[39]

Still, I believe that an open ended Canadian production would have been a greater triumph. It has, however, found a home among Canada's regional theatres, having been staged at the now-defunct Vancouver Playhouse in Christmas 2008, and at Edmonton's Citadel Theatre and the National Arts Centre in Ottawa in 2009. Playhouse artistic director Max Reimer told *Equity Quarterly*'s Matthew Hays, "Even though it has less name recognition than something like *The Sound of Music*, I wanted to put it on here. We had amazing success with it. It was great to put on a Canadian show that the audiences took to so strongly. I really hope that there are more musicals like it."[40] It was revived again in Vancouver in 2017 at Theatre Under the Stars.

An Australian production opened in 2010 in Melbourne – where it broke box office records – starring Geoffrey Rush (1951-). It has even been presented in Tokyo, directed by Japan's top musical man, Amon Miyamoto, who had brought his Japanese production of *Pacific Overtures* to New York in 2000. "I love this Canadian focus", he told me. "This is how they loved musicals long distance. That's good for me. It's all in his imagination, his own creation. This is a Canadian viewpoint. That's what made me very excited when I saw it on Broadway. It touched my heart. I cry a lot. Japanese people looking at Broadway and Canadian people looking at Broadway, the distance is similar."

Anne of Green Gables - The Musical and *The Drowsy Chaperone* actually have one very important thing in common. Both were originally created by a group of people who had been drilling together for a long time. In the case of *Anne of Green Gables*, Don Harron, Mavor Moore, Director/choreographer Alan Lund, Barbara Hamilton and much of the ensemble came from *Spring Thaw*, whereas *The Drowsy Chaperone* came out of Toronto's Second City and other improv comedy traditions.

How "Canadian" is *Drowsy Chaperone*? It has often been described as a love-letter to the American musical – but, as the Japanese director observed, that letter was definitely post-marked Toronto. "We've always felt that there is a Canadian angle," says Don McKellar, "which is sort of the Man in Chair, that he has this perspective outside of Broadway. In a way, he's watching as we watched from across the border and imaging what it's like and being titillated by it, and also critical."[41]

Co-author Bob Martin is a former artistic director of *Second City*, and co-creator of the superb TV mini-series *Slings and Arrows*, and Don McKellar is an actor, writer and film maker of some note in Canada. (He directed the film *Last Night* and was made a member of the Order of Canada in 2016.) Through the character of the "Man in Chair", it possesses that detached irony that has long been a trademark of Canadian humour. Although few foreign observers pick up on this, it is clear to me that the Man in Chair's apartment is in Toronto. The souvenir programme that was sold at the theatre makes it clear that he visits New York *as a tourist*. He views Broadway from a distance. In fact, crucially, he has never actually seen his favourite 1920s musical of the title; he simply knows it by its cast album –

the same way I first became acquainted with the great Broadway shows. (I didn't see a musical in New York until 1996, after I'd been writing them for twenty years.)

Lisa Lambert told me, "For me, the apartment is my bedroom in the North Toronto house I lived in growing up in Toronto – my crappy record player and Broadway cast recordings I stole from my mother's collection."[42]

In its transition from Toronto to New York, the show did lose one joke – expressing his hopes for a good evening's entertainment, the Man in Chair originally prayed, "If it must be a Canadian play, please don't let it be a *Canadian* play." There was even talk of a movie, to be directed by an Australian, Fred Schepisi (1939-) and starring Geoffrey Rush, although to date nothing has happened.

Since *Drowsy*, Nicholaw and Martin have collaborated on *Minsky's*, with music by Charles Strouse (1928-) and lyrics by Susan Birkenhead (1950-) based on the 1968 film *The Night They Raided Minsky's*, which tried out at the Ahmanson Theatre in Los Angeles, opening 6 February 2009, with a plan to transfer to Broadway. (To date, that transfer has not happened.) He also collaborated with the late Thomas Meehan (1929-2017) on the book for the 2010 Christmas show *Elf*, also directed by Nicholaw, with music by Matthew Sklar (1973-) and lyrics by Chad Beguelin (1969-).

The Drowsy Chaperone was not the only Canadian success in New York that year. Three graduates from Queens University brought their camp fringe show *Evil Dead – the Musical* from Toronto's Tranzac Club to New York's off-Broadway New World Stage, where it opened on November 1, 2006.

The idea was first conceived in a bar in 2002 when comedy writer George Reinblatt (1977-) was enjoying a drink with fellow Queens alumni Christopher Bond, who was appearing in a production of *The Rocky Horror Show* at the time. They decided that they too could create a cult horror musical, based on Sam Raimi's *Evil Dead* series. With Raimi's blessing, they brought in composer Frank Cipolla along with Melissa Morris and Rob Daleman and put it together on the fly.

They thought they were doomed when it opened on the night of the great Toronto blackout, when even the streetcars were left – quite literally – dead in their tracks. But then a strange thing happened. Line-ups began forming for tickets. People were willing to wait ten hours just to get in. Word spread, and *Evil Dead* fans from all over North America began to congregate. This attracted the attention of producer Jeffrey Latimer, who had presented the Toronto production of *Forever Plaid*. He booked it in to the Montreal *Just for Laughs* festival, which then attracted American interest. Multiple Tony award-winning choreographer Hinton Battle (1956-) signed on as a co-director for the New York production. It played for 126 performances and 34 previews before shuttering on 17 February 2007. A cast recording was issued by Time Life Music. It then moved back to Toronto where it enjoyed another run of four months at the Diesel Playhouse. A Korean production opened in Seoul in 2008.

In the same week in Autumn 2006 that my book *Broadway North: The Dream of a Canadian Musical Theatre* came out, Canadian Stage presented a charming new Canadian musical called *The Story of My Life* with songs by Neil Bartram and book by Brian Hill, starring Brent Carver and Jeffrey Kuhn.

Bartram, from Burlington, Ontario, and Hill, from Kitchener, met in Toronto while performing in the revue *Forever Plaid* in the early 1990s. Their previous musical *Somewhere in the World* ran for five seasons in Charlottetown.

The Story of My Life tells of a lifelong friendship

between a writer (Carver) and his childhood friend and muse, told in flashbacks after the latter's death.

I considered this lovely little show to be a shining example of all that was right with Canadian musical theatre, but alas the Toronto critics had other ideas. The *National Post*'s Robert Cushman said it was "close to unbearable", and even made reference to the title of my book in saying, "This isn't the dream of a Canadian musical, and it's too mild even to be the nightmare of an American one."[43]

However, that was not the end of the line for *The Story of My Life*. On February 19, 2009, it opened at the Booth Theatre on Broadway in a production directed by Richard Maltby Jr. (1937-), starring Will Chase (1970-) and Malcolm Gets (1964-). Still, for reasons that are inexplicable to me, the critics (or most of them, at least) didn't get it. Ben Brantley in the *New York Times* wrote: "In addition to jettisoning the usual excesses of tourist-trapping extravaganzas, they have tossed away such niceties as originality, credibility, tension and excitement."[44] *Variety*'s David Rooney said, "This flavorless new musical is not exactly terrible, but it's not terribly interesting, either."[45]

At least Michael Kuchwara of Associated Press disagreed. He called it "a heartfelt little musical that has the courage of its sweet-tempered, low-key convictions."[46] Peter Filichia, in his *Theatremania* blog, concluded that "it deserved far more respect than it got."[47] In a personal email to me, he cited author Ethan Mordden's assessment of the decline of the Broadway musical, saying that "stupid people like stupid things"[48]. Perhaps "sweet-tempered" and "low-key" is just too Canadian for New York. It closed after only five performances, although the New York production received four Drama Desk Award nominations for book, music, lyrics and outstanding production of a musical. (One of the reasons for the early closure was that the producers decided to spend the money they saved on recording a cast album. As I have always contended, the cast album is almost as important to ensuring a show's future as the production itself.) It has been successfully mounted in Korea, and appears to have a future in regional theatre productions. Brian Hill told me, "The Broadway production of *Story* was quite beautiful and benefitted greatly from having the CanStage tryout. As for the critics, we don't read or care about reviews so we can't really comment."49

Of course, there was other activity. In 2007, the Shaw Festival in Niagara-on-the-Lake, Ontario, presented the world premiere of *Tristan*, a musical by Jay Turvey, an actor with the company, and Paul Sportelli, the festival's musical director. Based on a story by Thomas Mann, the show opened at the Courthouse Theatre on 28 July 2007, directed by Eda Holmes. Turvey and Sportelli had previously collaborated with librettist Morwyn Brebner on the Dora Mavor Moore award-winning *Little Mercy's First Murder* at Toronto's Tarragon Theatre in 2003, so hopes were high. The *Hamilton Spectator* called it a "brave and beautiful evening of theatre"50, and the *Niagara Falls Review* proclaimed, "Instead of just staging excellent musicals, [the Shaw Festival]'s now creating them."51 Alas, the Toronto papers were less generous. Richard Ouzounian of the *Toronto Star* found it to be "a well-intentioned disappointment"52, while *Now*'s Jonathan Kaplan wrote, "The composers' songs are often elegant and moving, alternately simple and richly textured, their lyrics clever. The narrative, however, with its talk of art and love, is too stretched-out to hold our interest."53

In 2011, they followed it up with *Maria Severa*, starring Julie Martell as Maria, which opened at the Courthouse Theatre on August 5, 2011, directed by Jackie Maxwell. "The score is a considerable achievement", said *Variety*'s Richard Ouzounian. "Unfortunately, the book Turvey and Sportelli have concocted doesn't have the weight or the originality of their songs. It's a pretty predictable affair about an aristocratic bullfighter, Armando (Mark Uhre), who falls in love with the lowly Maria (Julie

Martell) but loves her for her art as well as her physical charms."[54] In a similar review in *The Star*, he elaborated that "their story of the poor Portuguese prostitute who invented the art song form known as *fado* demands a score of passionate depth and they provide it. Haunting melodies, unexpected harmonies and ever-changing rhythms are just a few of the things they do to make their music soar. And the lyrics fit smoothly and often powerfully to fill in the feelings underneath."[55] "The songs they've written for Maria herself," says the *National Post*'s Robert Cushman, "are melodically moody and rhythmically complex; a number that she shares with a street-walker friend, titled 'Bread and Butter', comes over like Portugal's answer to Brecht and Weill. Sometimes the score strays further afield, or maybe that should be closer to home; the ensemble number "At the Bullfight", is high-end contemporary Broadway, and so, even more, is the beautiful love-duet 'I Can't Touch You with Words'. The lyrics can be pungent, though they can also, too often, sound earnestly explanatory."[56] Like Ouzounian, he found the weakness to lie with the book, which he felt was strong on atmosphere but weak on structure.

In 2009, Tarragon produced *Mimi, or A Poisoner's Comedy*, a musical about French serial killers with book and lyrics by comic actors Nick Roberts and Melody Johnson and music and additional lyrics by Allen Cole, whose previous scores have included *Pélagie* and *The Wrong Son*. Richard Ouzounian of the *Star* wrote, "When this show is good, it's very, very good, but when it's bad, it's better."[57] Robert Cushman of the *National Post* wrote, "The delight of *Mimi*... is that it's written by people who know how. That makes it a phenomenon among new musicals, Canadian or other."[58] Only Christopher Hoile of *Eye* didn't quite agree: "A musical so ineptly written and directed it is a waste of the considerable talents of all those involved."[59]

When *The Drowsy Chaperone* opened on Broadway, Bob Martin said "In terms of creating shows for Broadway, I would hope that *Drowsy Chaperone* shows that it is possible."60 My belief is that we will know that Toronto has arrived as the major theatre capital that I have always believed it could be when a Canadian-written show transfers to a commercial theatre for an indefinite run before ever attempting Broadway or the West End. It hasn't happened yet, but there has been progress.

Recently there has been a promising development in the creation of Sheridan College's Canadian Music Theatre Project, which like Denmark's Uterus workshop, is attached to an established musical theatre school, in this case Sheridan College in Oakville, Ontario.

"Establishing a permanent headquarters for the development of new musicals is a culturally significant event in Canada"61, says Michael Rubinoff, Associate Dean of Sheridan's performing arts school. As Mr. Rubinoff explained to me,

> "I certainly believed in our Canadian writers and our Canadian musical theatre but one of the biggest challenges we had was [we had] never institutionalised a development process. Of course we had the Lehman Engel workshops and we had ScriptLab and Jim Betts' work in terms of turning ScriptLab's focus to musical theatre which I was involved in, but theatre companies weren't taking on the responsibility in the country to do it, and we had a really good opportunity because Sheridan's music theatre program was transitioning from a three-year advanced diploma to a four year honours bachelor's degree. We needed a capstone project so we needed a project in fourth year where students applied the skills from the previous three years to something... For us, the belief was it should be working on a new musical... What the Canadian Music Theatre Project was initiated to do was to focus on development. The entire purpose was you'd have five weeks to work on any part of the show that you wanted to work on, and your only performance obligation was a forty-five minute reading with books and stands, not a full production."

They began with two projects: *Central Park Tango* is

a musical about two male New York penguins who want to start a family. It was written by Robert Gontier (a Sheridan faculty member) and Nicky Phillips.

Come from Away at Sheridan College

The second was *Come from Away* about the people of Gander, Newfoundland who took in the airline passengers stranded after the World Trade Centre attacks with book, music and lyrics by the husband and wife team David Hein and Irene Sankoff. These were both showcased at Toronto's Panasonic Theatre on 10 April 2012.

Rubinoff explains,

"I've always believed you need two things for a musical: you need a compelling story and a compelling reason to musicalise it. When 9/11 happened... there's a Canadian lens from our media, and the lens looked towards places like Gander as we now know, and the planes when US air space was closed, hundreds of planes were grounded across Canada but there was something really special that happened in Gander, Newfoundland. Learning about that story, immediately and then the aftermath, I was quite moved. I was proud to be a Canadian. I was very emotional reading the stories. This was an amazing story. The other benefit was – and I had never been to Newfoundland and Labrador – but I knew... that the way Newfoundlanders tell their stories and record their stories is through music. Story telling, kitchen parties; that is so much a part of their culture. I did believe that we had a compelling story; we had a compelling reason to musicalise it. I'm not a composer or writer. A creative producer, certainly. How do you find somebody to write the show?"

He tried several teams who all turned him down. Then he saw a show called *My Mother's Lesbian Jewish Wiccan Wedding* by the married team of David Hein and

Irene Sankoff.

> "I didn't know David and Irene... I loved the show. They were both in it. I thought they were fantastic. We went out for dinner and hit it off. I just sent them a Facebook message saying 'We should know each other'. At the end of that three hour dinner I said I'm trying to find people to write a musical about the events in Gander, Newfoundland on 9/11. They said 'That sounds interesting'."

David Hein explained to me,

> "We talked about musical theatre in general, and he introduced us to the story of Gander over 9/11. We then dove into researching it like crazy and found out there was a commemoration ceremony that was going to be happening in Newfoundland on [the tenth anniversary of] 9/11, and all of these passengers who were stranded there were returning to commemorate the kindness they had seen, and to reunite with the friends they had made there ten years earlier. So we applied for a grant from the Canada Council for the Arts and were able to travel out there for almost a month. We got to extend it a little while because the people in Newfoundland wouldn't let us stay in a hotel. They would say, 'Oh, no, no, no, here are the keys, come stay with us.'"

In support of their grant application to the Canada Council, Michael Rubinoff wrote,

> "There is a significant Canadian story to be told here and using the medium of musical theatre that story can be told in the most compelling fashion. It is an opportunity to find a way to share such a moving and important story with audiences at home and around the world. I believe a musical based on this event can appeal to so many and be a cultural ambassador for Canada around the world."[62]

What was their background?

> "We're married, so we can't keep each other out of each other's business, so we share everything," Hein continues. "I used to be a singer/ songwriter and my wife is still an

actress. The reason we started writing musicals together was between our day jobs and our night jobs we never had time to see each other. We wrote an entire first draft of [*My Mother's Lesbian Jewish Wiccan Wedding*] that was all fictionalised. It was based on a song I had written which was called "My Mother's Lesbian Jewish Wiccan Wedding". The humour of it was that I essentially said those words over and over again. People seemed to like the song and it was based on a true story, so we thought we would write a musical about it. And we wrote a full musical but then a friend of Irene's said what she was so excited about was that it was based on a true story, and Irene came home and said 'I think we need to scrap it all.' I said, 'Are you crazy? We just wrote an entire musical!' She said, 'Let's just try it'. So I tried it, and it's actually just so much better to base it on our real family stories, and that's what we put on stage. We did it in the Toronto Fringe Festival in a small theatre called Bread and Circus which holds about eighty people. It's in Kensington Market. It used to be a skate shop and I think it may now be something else, a restaurant or something. I had played there before as a singer/songwriter so we sort of knew the space."

It was this show that put them on Michael Rubinoff's radar.

Knowing of their experience on their previous show, I asked David if *Come from Away* had been fictionalised at all. He shook his head. "It is all true." He continued,

"At the same time, we sort of went out there and we interviewed as many people as we possibly could. We did interviews for hours at a time. So we sometimes joke about how there were seven thousand people on the planes and nine thousand people in the town, so we're trying to tell sixteen thousand stories in a hundred minute musical. We wanted to get every possible detail we could in there but what it meant was that we had to combine some characters and amalgamate some story lines. Our goal was for the people we interviewed to come to the show and say, 'You got it right, that's exactly how it happened.' We've been really fortunate to have had that been true. At the same time, it's not a documentary so if you point out that there's only two teachers at Gander Academy, that's obviously not true. Even Beverly Bass [American Airlines' first female captain], a story that's very true to her, is an amalgamation of her and other captain's stories. If it was predominately based on one character with some amalgamation and poetic licence we would use their full name. Often if it was based on two characters or we're trying to express that it was a composite character then we would use someone's first name then another person's last name."

What were their backgrounds in musical theatre?

"I performed in theatre in high school and I got a degree in set and lighting design. I'd seen a couple of musicals: *Phantom*, *Les Miz* and *Cats*. I didn't know musicals very well. Irene introduced me to musicals. She comes from old school black-and-white movies, seeing *Les Miz* at the Royal Alex countless times. That's what she grew up on. I grew up on Newfoundland music and folk music and rock music. [We] pretty quickly fell in love with it together and became *Rent*-heads and lined up in New York to see *Rent* and would go on long car trip with the cast album and challenge each other to who could sing a song from a new musical, and then the next song would have to be from another musical. Twelve hour car ride without stopping; just devoured it all."

Come from Away opened on Broadway at the Gerald Schoenfeld Theatre on 12 March 2017, attended by Prime Minister Justin Trudeau, who addressed the audience. Ben Brantley, chief theatre critic for *The New York Times*, wrote "Try, if you must, to resist the gale of good will that blows out of 'Come From Away,' the big bearhug of a musical that opened on Sunday night at the Gerald Schoenfeld Theater. But even the most stalwart cynics may have trouble staying dry-eyed during this portrait of heroic hospitality under extraordinary pressure."[63]

A new open-ended production began its run at the Royal Alexandra Theatre in Toronto on 13 February 2018, following a sold-out run at the Royal Manitoba Theatre

Centre in Winnipeg. (What I had hoped would happen with *The Drowsy Chaperone* finally did happen with *Come from Away*.) Once more, there is talk of a movie, which will of course be filmed in Gander.

The London production opened on 18 February 2019 at the Phoenix Theatre, following a run in Dublin. The *Evening Standard* said "there are moments when *Come from Away* feels like an advertisement for Canadian decency and its capacity to improve the lives of malcontent Americans... But in the end its defining features are charm, energy and a real generosity of spirit, and audiences are left with a nagging question: in a situation like the one the people of Gander faced, would we do the same?"[64]

It opened at the Comedy Theatre, Melbourne on 20 July 2019. Catherine Lambert in the *Sunday Herald Sun* wrote, "Of all the jewels in the musical theatre crown, few shine as brightly as newcomer *Come From Away*. Not only does it present a perfect example of how intricate and skilled musical theatre can be, it goes further by breaking the mould and moving the medium into new directions."[65]

Another project commissioned by the Canadian Music Theatre Project was *The Theory of Relativity* by Neil Bartram (music and lyrics) and Brian Hill (book), the creators of *The Story of My Life*. The premise was to show the interconnectedness of people's lives. It was later produced at Goodspeed Festival of New Musicals in East Haddam, Connecticutt and at the Iris Theatre in London.

They are more recently working on another commission for Sheridan called *Senza Luce* which tells the story of a remote village in the Alps that has lived for centuries without sunlight, and of the brave individual who has a plan to change all that.

While Toronto has yet to emerge as the major

theatre capital I believe it could potentially be, it is making good progress. *We Will Rock You* and *Dirty Dancing* may not have been Canadian shows, but they did give Toronto one advantage: American tourists could come to Toronto to see a show that was not (yet) playing in New York. And their nationally televised search for a new Maria for Andrew Lloyd Webber's production of *The Sound of Music* did raise the profile of Toronto as a centre for musical theatre.

This trend began when Mirvish Productions hosted the North American premiere of *Buddy – the Buddy Holly Story* which had been selling out in London. They then transferred this production for a short-lived Broadway run. They had greater success with *Mamma Mia!*, which originally settled in for a 26 week Toronto run in 2000. When that show transferred to Broadway (with its Canadian star Louise Pitre (1957-) in tow), they recast the Canadian production, and it continued for another four years.

With *Dirty Dancing*, a new precedent was established that I think could have interesting implications. This production, a stage adaptation of the film, originated in Australia, then transferred to London. Producer Amber Jacobsen told the *Globe and Mail*'s Kamal Al-Solaylee, "We Australians feel that we're quite like Canadians. We did think about that. We're part of the Commonwealth."[66] Since then, the Mirvishes have also hosted the North American premiere of *Priscilla, Queen of the Desert* prior to its Broadway engagement. It might be interesting if shows were to start moving directly between Melbourne or Sydney and Toronto, before trying their luck in London or New York.

So, does all this make Toronto "Broadway North"? Like Melbourne, Toronto has a central theatre district containing several legit commercial houses. Primary of these is the Royal Alexandra Theatre, the oldest continuously operating legitimate theatre in Canada, and

North America's first theatre to be built with a cantilevered balcony. Built in 1907 by architect John McIntosh Lyle (1872-1945) for a syndicate headed by Cawthra Mulock (1886-1918), it operated in stiff competition with the nearby Princess Theatre, controlled by the powerful New York-based Theatrical Syndicate that held a near monopoly on touring shows. The Princess was gutted by fire on 7 May 1915, the same day as one of the Theatrical Syndicate's principals, Charles Frohman (1856-1915) went down with the RMS Lusitania.

In 1963 the Royal Alex was purchased by Edwin Mirvish (1914-2007) who then turned some nearby derelict buildings into restaurants. This would prove to be a shrewd move, as it helped to develop the infrastructure that is essential to attracting audiences.

In 1981, the Ontario Heritage Foundation (now the Ontario Heritage Trust) purchased the Elgin and Winter Garden Theatres, the world's last remaining Edwardian stacked theatres. Built in 1913 as vaudeville houses for American impresario Marcus Loew, it was designed by Thomas W. Lamb, who would also design the nearby Ed Mirvish Theatre. The upstairs Winter Garden had sat idle since 1927, and still preserved its ancient vaudeville scenery. In 1985, the lower Elgin Theatre was the scene for the two year run of *Cats* and since then, following a thorough renovation, has hosted *Rent*, *Tommy* and a new Canadian musical *Napoleon* which was later seen briefly at London's Shaftesbury Theatre.

The Ed Mirvish Theatre was originally built in 1920 as the Pantages, another vaudeville house. Although it spent most of its life as a cinema, in 1989 it re-opened as a live theatre, with Garth Drabinsky's production of *Phantom of the Opera* running for more than a decade. Following Drabinsky's fraud and forgery conviction, it ultimately fell into Mirvish hands.

At the same time, Mirvish also acquired what was

then called the Panasonic Theatre. Originally opened as the Victory cinema in 1919, it had been through a number of names before its 1993 conversion to live theatre. In 2005 it was almost entirely rebuilt as the Panasonic Theatre and has housed productions of *Forever Plaid* and *We Will Rock You*. As part of a sponsorship deal, it is currently known as the CAA Theatre.

The Princess of Wales Theatre was built for the Mirvishes and opened in 1993 with a production of *Miss Saigon*. Since then it has also hosted *The Lion King* and *The Lord of the Rings*, among others. At one point, Mirvish had planned to demolish it and replace it with a new development designed by Frank Gehry, but due to negative public reaction, they came up with a revised plan that reprieved the theatre. The name has a triple meaning: it was named for Diana, Princess of Wales, but also refers to the fact that Princess Alexandra, namesake of the Royal Alex, was also a Princess of Wales, and is a tribute to their old competitor, the nearby Princess theatre.

I've argued that Toronto's theatre district needs a brand. Like Broadway and the West End, the area on King and Yonge Streets where these theatres are located needs an identity. The potential is there: these theatres, in addition to the Sony and St. Lawrence Centres and the Four Seasons Opera House, as well as Roy Thomson and Massey Halls are all in easy walking distance of each other, and are close to the top hotels and restaurants. In *Broadway North*, I proposed calling this area "The Core". Perversely, since then, the area that has advertised itself as the "Entertainment District" does not include the theatres of Yonge Street, nor the St. Lawrence Centre. This is the equivalent to Broadway not including the theatres on Forty-Second Street, or the West End ignoring Shaftesbury Avenue. I received the following "explanation" from the office of the Toronto Entertainment District Business Improvement Area: "Our mandate is to support and promote the businesses located within our boundaries only... I believe it would be the responsibility of the City of

Toronto and Tourism Toronto to promote Toronto theatres as a whole."[67] I beg your pardon? I know that we Canadians like to shoot ourselves in the foot, but do we have to actually shove our big toe up the barrel of the gun?

Of course, Ontario is not the only part of Canada where musicals are being developed. In Winnipeg, there is a group calling itself White Rabbit Productions (formerly the Canadian Musical Theatre Development Group) that aims to develop new work through workshops and showcases. Although it is a small city, it has always been a place of cultural importance. In the 1950s, the Manitoba Theatre Centre became Canada's first regional theatre, and the Royal Winnipeg Ballet is world-renowned.

Winnipeg writer and composer Danny Schur has taken an independent road to success, and managed against the odds. Already known as the composer of the theme song for the 1999 Pan Am Games, his musical *Strike!* managed to achieve a certain degree of national attention, largely due to its historic subject matter. Based on a 1919 general strike in which a Ukrainian immigrant was killed by the Mounties, *Strike!* was workshopped privately in 2003, and mounted independently at an outdoor theatre in Kildonan Park two years later with backing from the labour movement and the Ukrainian community (of which Schur is a member).

CBC Radio's Robert Enright said, "It's a story that fills your heart with goodness and hope and expectation for the future. Whether or not the specific aspects of this particular moment in history... will travel – I don't know."[68] The *Winnipeg Free Press* said, "*Strike!* is not so impressive that it takes the art of musical theatre anywhere it hasn't been before. But it is intelligent and curiously touching."[69] A revised version played at Saskatoon's Persephone Theatre, and, inspired by the chapter on "radiophonic" musicals in my book *Broadway North*, Schur successfully pitched it to CBC Radio, where a concert version was broadcast nationally in 2007.[70] It was filmed in

2018 under the new title *Stand!*

Vancouver also has a company dedicated to treating musical theatre as an art form. Patrick Street Productions presented Adam Guettel and Craig Lucas' *The Light in the Piazza* in September 2011, winning the Jessie Richardson award for outstanding production. "We have a huge creative community in the theatre, and they all go 'I want to do it my way'", Artistic Producer Peter Jorgensen told *The Georgia Straight*'s Janet Smith. "That's the way [wife] Katey and I started too. I had a certain idea of how musicals should be done, and I wanted to see if I could make that happen."[71] In 2015, they presented the premiere of *The Best Laid Plans*, a political satire based on the novel by Terry Fallis with book by Vern Thiessen, and music and lyrics by Benjamin Elliott and Anton Lipovetsky.

In 2011, Touchstone Theatre, together with the Arts Club Theatre presented the first *In Tune Conference – Creating the Great Canadian Musical*. Among the guest speakers were composer-lyricist Jim Betts, who was a student of Lehman Engel. Their purpose, according to their press release was to "engage in a community-wide consideration and celebration of how we currently develop new musicals in Canada, and what kind of scenarios might encourage more work and greater success and profile for work created." The next one, which I addressed, was held in 2013, and there were subsequent events in 2015, 2017 and 2019.

Canada has long had excellent training facilities for performers, beginning with the musical theatre program at the Banff Centre, to the one at Toronto's Sheridan College, where a course on Canadian musicals was taught, based in part on my book *Broadway North*. Vancouver's Capilano University also offers a musical theatre program.

Canadian performers have long been a staple of Broadway and the West End, from Robert Goulet (1933-2007) to Victor Garber (1949-).

In 2012 the Stratford Festival's hit production of *Jesus Christ Superstar*, directed by Des McAnuff (1952-) opened on Broadway at the Neil Simon Theatre on 1 March 2012. Composer Andrew Lloyd Webber has described this production as "definitive", saying "I've never really been happy with it before... now it's right."[72] Alas, although it was nominated for a Tony award for best musical revival as well as for best featured performer Josh Young (1980-) as Judas, it closed on 1 July 2012 after only 116 performances. During the awards broadcast, presenter Ben Vereen evidently didn't know the name of North America's premier classical theatre company, calling it the "Stamford Festival". "That was really the last straw, wasn't it?"[73] says *Toronto Star* critic Richard Ouzounian.

Although founded by Mavor Moore with the intention to develop new Canadian musicals, inadequate funding has led the Charlottetown Festival to the decision to mount imported shows like *Buddy*, *Hairspray* and *Ring of Fire*.

The Centre was established in 1964 with a mandate to "inspire Canadians to celebrate the creative vision of Confederation and Canada's evolving nationhood by showcasing the nation's visual and performing arts and artists."[74] At one time, the Festival presented up to four original Canadian musicals a year on its main stage, but that was long ago.

Former artistic director Anne Allan is said to have waged losing battles with the board over her artistic plans, but incoming Director Adam Brazier told Richard Ouzounian, "I will work endlessly with the board and the executive to make the right decision that we can all agree on. But if it's something that I don't believe in, I just won't let it happen."[75]

Shows like *Ring of Fire* and *Mama Mia!* may keep the box office ticking over merrily, but they do nothing for the development of the indigenous form. Then again, perhaps Prince Edward Island and its largely American tourist audience is not the best development ground for Canadian theatre – musical or otherwise.

Artistic Director Adam Brazier says,

> "Although we are very proud of the festivals growth artistically," "it still exists in a very financially unstable marketplace. Tourism on Prince Edward Island is very much based on the weather and the value of both Canadian and American dollar and oil. If the weather is poor or the price of gas too high, Atlantic Canadians won't come. Should the Island have a poor tourist season, the entire Centre suffers as well. Since the festival carries the majority of The Confederation Centre of the Arts yearly revenue, when the festival has a poor year of sales, the entire organization stalls until it has the opportunity to produce again, the following summer. This kind of box office risk is not ideal for an 1100 seat theatre in a population of 37,000."[76]

Given this privation, the Festival has still managed to pull the odd miracle out of its hat. In 2013, in the last year of previous artistic director Anne Allan's tenure, the Festival presented Ted Dykstra (1961-)'s adaptation of Henry Wadsworth Longfellow (1807-82)'s 1847 epic poem *Evangeline*, telling of an Acadian girl and her search for her lost love Gabriel, set during the time of the Acadian expulsion.

Dykstra was already well-known on the international scene as the co-creator of *Two Pianos, Four Hands*, a play with music that had successful engagements both in London and off-Broadway. *Evangeline* had been developed over the previous decade with some financial assistance from Mirvish Productions. "David Mirvish went crazy for it, but then his team got around him and said, 'Very good, but we think it needs to be edgier,'"[77] Dykstra told Jane Taber of *The Globe and Mail*. After an unsuccessful pairing with a Broadway librettist, they amicably parted company. With encouragement from Adam Brazier and Anne Allan, he brought it to the Charlottetown Festival.

The show was huge by Canadian standards, with a cast of more than thirty, including Chilina Kennedy as Evangeline and Adam Brazier as Gabriel, and a fourteen piece orchestra, with a budget of $1.5 million. It was revived in 2015 in a co-production with Edmonton's Citadel Theatre, directed by Bob Baker.

The *Globe and Mail* said, "Evangeline remains a moving symbol of the resilience of all displaced people – and Dykstra's show a reminder that the land we live in has not always been a place of refuge."[78] Richard Ouzounian in the *Star* said, "It's taken 10 years for this show to reach the stage and it seems a shame that a work so melodically rich, emotionally profound and dramatically challenging had to languish for a decade before Charlottetown stepped up to the plate and had the guts to stage it."[79] As of this writing, there are plans for a New York workshop.

"The Charlottetown festival has renewed and recharged its commitment to producing and creating new and exciting Canadian theatre," says Brazier. "Over the past four seasons we have produced, with the exception of our yearly production of *Anne*, twenty shows; Seventeen of which were Canadian and eight of which were world premieres."

During his term, the Festival has also produced *Jesus Christ Superstar*, *Mama Mia* and *Million Dollar Quartet*, although the second stage season in their cabaret theatre has done some original work, including *A Misfortune*, adapted from a short story by Anton Chekhov. "As the Confederation Centre of the Arts continues to pursue stronger funding opportunities, so will the opportunities for more new work to be properly developed and produced, within it's walls."

The late Cathy Elliott (1957-2017) was a status

member of the Mi'kmaq from Nova Scotia's Sipekne'katik First Nation who was also a well-established composer, lyricist and book writer based near Toronto. Her previous works included *Fireweeds: Women of the Yukon*. She was the principal writer behind *The Talking Stick*, a presentation by the Confederation Centre's Young Company for the Summer 2011 Charlottetown Festival. A free forty-five minute lunchtime outdoor presentation, it included First Nations stories and legends from across Canada, using music, dance and spoken word. The finale from this show was performed before the Duke and Duchess of Cambridge in 2011. As an actress, Elliott also appeared in Corey Payette's musical *Children of God* at the National Arts Centre in 2017. This show examined the problems of Cree and Anishnabek residential schools in Northern Ontario.

This is one area in which Australia is ahead of Canada: the encouragement of aboriginal musicals, although there have been some recent developments in this regard. Thomson Highway (1951-), Canada's pre-eminent native playwright collaborated with composer Melissa Hui (1966-) on *Pimootewin (The Journey)*, an opera written entirely in Cree and based on First Nations legends. The story tells of how the Trickster and the Eagle, who miss their friends who have died, visit them in the land of the dead, and attempt to bring them back to life. It received its world premiere on 15 February 2008 at the St. Lawrence Centre in Toronto then mounted a regional tour. "When culture is alive, it's dynamic and relevant," director Michael Greyeyes (1967-) told CBC News. "Our culture, Cree culture, is exactly that – it's always being redefined, reinvented, reinvigorated and so for us to in effect hijack the form of opera to tell our stories, Cree stories, I think is a really crucial lesson that we share with these communities."[80] Highway, himself a classically trained pianist, is the author of the hit plays *The Rez Sisters* and *Drylips Ought to Move to Kapuskasing*.

Beyond Eden is a show written by two white men

that tells the true story of an attempt to save the totem poles of the ancient Haida village of Ninstints, a United Nations World Heritage site in Northwestern British Columbia. Bruce Ruddell, a composer of choral and chamber music and Bill Henderson (1944-), a former member of the rock band Chilliwack worked together on the show that premiered during Vancouver's Cultural Olympiad in 2010. It was the culmination of thirty years' work for Ruddell, who was inspired by his friendship with Bill Reid, the late Haida carver who was involved in the original rescue attempt. After first trying it as a choral composition, it was Broadway director Harold Prince who suggested he turn it into a musical. *The Vancouver Sun*'s Peter Birnie wrote, "While this story of a real-life expedition in 1957 by Victoria anthropologists to recover (steal?) totem poles on Haida Gwaii is gorgeous to look at and lovely to listen to, it's also a genuinely compelling and largely successful attempt to blend 'white' and 'Indian' sensibilities."[81]

With all of this activity, you would think that Canada's cultural leaders would take notice. You would be wrong. These mandarins act as a sort-of control valve to turn off the flow of oxygen whenever something looks like it might be in danger of getting too interesting. Since cancelling Richard Ouzounian's Sunday afternoon series *Say It With Music* (from which the creators of *The Drowsy Chaperone* are said to have gained some of their inspiration), CBC Radio has virtually expunged show music from its national airwaves, claiming that the world's most popular theatrical form does not appeal to a wide enough audience. In April 2012, as a result of a $3 million cut in funding, all drama was eliminated from CBC Radio One.[82] To be fair, a regional program called *North by Northwest* featured *Broadway North* five years after its publication. But the one organisation with the resources to nurture musical theatre writers is just plain not interested.

So Canadians with talent and ambition leave. Not just to earn more money, but to earn more respect. Film director Norman Jewison has said, "Artists need to feel that their work is appreciated. They need approval. When the encouragement to produce their best work doesn't exist in their own country, they go somewhere else."[83] This problem is not unique to Canada. In Australia, they call it the "cringe factor". If it's home grown, it can't be good. And if it becomes too successful, the "tall poppy syndrome" will soon cut it down to size.

As a centre for commercial theatre, Toronto remains a city on its way up. Its history hasn't happened yet. Novelist Nino Ricci has said, "Toronto is still deciding what it will be. We're still finding out what it means to be Torontonian. Our mythology has yet to be written."[84] I think this applies to the rest of Canada as well. Or, to quote one of the first hit Canadian show-tunes, it's still "waiting for the sunrise". The artists are ready. They just need to bring the government and the public onside. Maybe the success of *The Drowsy Chaperone* and *Come from Away* will make the world finally take notice.

Larrikins and Sentimental Blokes: Musicals Down Under

When Mark Twain visited Sydney in 1895 he described the Australians as "English friendliness with the English shyness and self-consciousness left out."[1] Until my own visit, all of my perceptions of Australia came from the films of Peter Weir, Bruce Beresford and Gillian Armstrong. *Picnic at Hanging Rock*, *Breaker Morant* and *My Brilliant Career* were my touchstones. For many other people – especially in Britain – Australia is the land of Kylie Minogue and of the TV soap opera in which she once starred, *Neighbours*. (Two of my colleagues who assisted me with this book, Peter Pinne and Ray Kolle, were writers for that show.) My introduction to Australian musical theatre came through *Once in a Blue Moon*, a CD made in 1994 by the Australian Broadcasting Corporation featuring the Melbourne Symphony Orchestra with guest soloists in a television concert of songs from Australian shows.

I had always suspected that if my homeland were to be twinned with any other country, it would be our antipodean cousins. Both are former British colonies, with relatively small populations spread over vast territories, much of which is barely fit for human habitation. Both are also under foreign cultural domination, from which they have sought liberation and validation. Australia has one advantage over Canada – its isolation from the rest of the world. That is also its disadvantage. (Similarly, Canada's proximity to the United States is both its advantage and its disadvantage.)

Also, strange as it may seem, because they don't see very many of Broadway's flops, they've missed out on a great learning curve. According to Neil Gooding, director of New Musicals Australia, "We get to import into Australia the global hits. We don't see many of the flops that don't work, because by the time we're bringing *Phantom of the Opera* and *Les Miz* and *Wicked* and *Jersey Boys*, they've been hits in at least one if not two of the major markets of the world." This actually causes a problem. "Even the funding bodies don't understand the kind of success rate and the failure rate of new musicals."

When I travelled from London to Sydney in November 2008, I flew across Russia and India, taking a gruelling twenty-one hours (not including my nine hour stop in Singapore). I had flown to the other end of the world to be in a country that was culturally so similar to my own. I was there to see a production by Kookaburra, Australia's National Musical Theatre Company, and to witness OzMade Musicals, a showcase of new Australian musical theatre. Neither of these exists anymore.

Wanting to gain a feel of the countryside, I travelled by train from Sydney to Melbourne. The 962 km journey took just over eleven hours, calling at stations with names like Wagga Wagga and Cootamundra. Although we grazed the Southern Highlands of New South Wales, most of the journey was relatively flat and extremely dry. My fellow passengers informed me that it hadn't rained in seven years. Less than three months later, Victoria and parts of New South Wales would be devastated by bush fires, destroying 1,800 homes and killing 173 people, including the actor Reg Evans (1928-2009) who had appeared in *Mad Max* and *Gallipolli*. In fact, part of one of the rail lines I had travelled on was damaged.

In Melbourne I was a guest on a radio show called *Broadway at Bedtime*, presented by Will Conyers and P.J. Buchanan. Part of my initial impression had been that Australians projected a more confidant image than Canadians did, but I soon learned that they also suffered from something called the "Cringe Factor", similar to Canada's "National Inferiority Complex". I saw an illustration of this when I attended OzMade Musicals: Coming out of the theatre, I got into a conversation with a local woman. When I explained that I had come from London specifically to see this, she immediately answered, "Oh, you must be so disappointed!"

Our two countries certainly had much in common – especially in our pursuit of a cultural identity. Will told me about the Australian actress Jill Perryman, M.B.E. (1933-), who worked in the business for some forty years, playing leading roles in shows like *Hello, Dolly!* before finally having a chance to sing in her own accent in *The Boy from Oz*.

Comedy and Her Majesty's Theatres, Exhibition Street, Melbourne

Dr. Peter Wyllie Johnston, a theatrical historian at the University of Melbourne, and author of a number of articles on the history of Australian musicals, was one of those struck by the similarities between our countries. "You've got the physical commonality with a huge country spread over big distances... The creative people aren't all concentrated in one place... We have Melbourne and Sydney forever as rivals and neither of them really co-operating."

Of those two cities, it is Melbourne, with a population of about three and a half million – slightly smaller than its rival – that comes the closest to having a Broadway-style, clearly defined precinct known as the East End Theatre District, bounded by Spring Street, Flinders Street, Swanston Street, and Lonsdale Street. Actor John O'May told Will Conyers, "When you are performing at Her Majesty's and something's on at the Comedy and something's at the Princess and the Regent is going all of a sudden the city ... is lit up ... and it is one of the most exciting things... it becomes a part of what a city's life is." [2]

You can stand in front of the Athenaeum Theatre

in Collins Street and look over the road to the Regent. Both of these theatres have long histories: the Athenaeum dates from the 1830s, while the Regent – which has a ballroom attached beneath the 3,500 seat main auditorium – was built in 1929 as a cinema with live entertainment. Similarly, the Comedy and Her Majesty's Theatres are directly opposite each other in Exhibition Street, while the Princess is nearby in Spring Street, near the Victoria Parliament House. All were built on the sites of earlier nineteenth century theatres from the Victorian gold-rush era.

Sydney, on the other hand, has a less coherent infrastructure, having lost most of its historic theatres. There is no entertainment precinct per se. While there are several major venues, including both commercial and non-profit, they are spread out. The Sydney Lyric in Darling Harbour, where I saw *Priscilla, Queen of the Desert*, is attached to the Star casino complex, whereas the Seymour Centre, where Kookaburra performed most of their shows, is part of the University of Sydney campus near Central Station, and lacks a street frontage and the nearby restaurants and coffee bars that support audience development.

In the past, both Canadian and Australian actors worked freely in Britain in the days when a Commonwealth passport meant open borders. Cyril Ritchard (1898-1977), Keith Michell (1926-2015), Michael Blakemore (1928-) and Sir Robert Helpmann (1909-86) were among a large Australian Diaspora in London, just as Christopher Plummer (1929-), Cec Linder (1921-92) and Bernard Braden (1916-93) were from Canada.

In the beginning, the Diaspora was long on talent and short on national identity. The Australian-born actor and playwright Oscar Asche (1871-1936) created the musical *Chu Chin Chow* as a reworking of the story of *Ali Baba and the Forty Thieves* in 1916, with music by Frederic

Norton (1869-1946), an Englishman. In 1920, the Tivoli circuit brought it to Australia. The London production ran until 1921, making it one of the most popular musicals of that period.

John Stange Heiss Oscar Asche was born in Geelong, Victoria in 1871. His Norwegian father had practised law in Oslo, but had become an innkeeper after moving to Australia. Young Oscar was educated at Laurel Lodge, Dandenong, and travelled to China as a teenager. Upon his return, he articled for a short time with an architect, then lived in the bush and worked as a jackaroo[3] on a sheep station before announcing to his parents that he wanted to become an actor. His father sent him to study in Norway, but the playwright Henrik Ibsen told him he should return to his own country and work in his own language. Instead, he went to London and worked to lose all trace of his Australian accent. As a result, "Oscar Asche... was regarded as British," says Dr. Wyllie Johnston, "and if you look up a lot of English books on the musical, it's claimed as a British musical of course, and there's no reference to the fact that he was Australian."[4]

Such was the fate of any Australian who wanted to write musicals (or act in them, for that matter). Not only did they have to leave Australia, but they had to stop being Australian. There was no infrastructure at home to support them, and the commercial producers of the day took precious little interest in developing local talent. Again, something any Canadian could relate to.

The process of developing an indigenous Australian musical theatre has been a slow and laborious one. Among the first entirely Australian shows to be professionally staged was the mysteriously titled *F.F.F.*, an "Australian Mystery Musical Comedy" with libretto by Clement John "Jack" De Garis (1884-1926) and music by Reginald Stoneham (1879-1942) that opened at the Prince of Wales Theatre in Adelaide on 28 August 1920. De Garis was a dried-fruit magnate with considerable charm as well as artistic ambitions. Stoneham had already written the World War I hit "Heroes of the Dardinelles" and together they had previously collaborated on *Sun-Raysed Waltz* as a promotional piece for the Australian Dried Fruits Association in 1915. On his own De Garis had published a four-act military drama called *Ambition Run Mad* in a bi-weekly newspaper called the *Murray Pioneer*. According to impresario Claude Kingston (1886-1978), in "one of those blinding mental flashes which he mistook for inspiration"[5], he conceived a musical comedy with a title whose significance was known only to himself (if even that). He managed to sell it to the Tivoli circuit's owner Hugh D. McIntosh (1876-1942), partly by flattering him by naming one of his characters "Hugh D. Collins". (This was a man who was reputed to be so persuasive that he managed to sell a piece of real estate to a police officer who had just arrested him for writing bad cheques.)

Although the Adelaide production lost money, the *Advertiser* claimed it opened to a "capacity house" which "thoroughly enjoyed one of the best shows seen in Adelaide."[6] De Garis posted a guarantee against losses of up to two thousand pounds, allowing it to open in Perth on 29 September, where according to Claude Kingston, "takings hardly met the cost of lighting the theatre". Still, it moved on to Melbourne, where De Garis claimed "a record box office success"[7] when it opened at the King's Theatre on 9 October. It was "enthusiastically welcomed by a large audience"[8] according to the *Sunday Times* (a newspaper owned by Hugh McIntosh). The *Melbourne Herald* said, "There seems to be no adequate reason why Australian song-writers should not find as much inspiration in Croajingalong as the Americans have found in Dixie."[9]

With debts of £420,000, De Garis ended his own life in 1926.

Hugh McIntosh had taken over the Tivoli circuit in 1911 following the death of its founder, Harry Rickards (1843-1911), who had emigrated from his native England to

Australia in 1871. Forbidden to attend the theatre by his puritan parents, Rickards became a singer of comic songs, even performing before the Prince of Wales. In 1893 he bought the Garrick Theatre in Sydney and renamed it the Tivoli. He also bought theatres in Melbourne and other cities, and brought in acts such as Harry Houdini and Marie Lloyd.

After Mackintosh purchased Harry Rickard's Tivoli Theatres Ltd. for £100,000, he continued to expand the chain, adding theatres in Adelaide and Brisbane, becoming an effective competitor to the J.C. Williamson and Fullers chains. He sold it to Musgrave Theatres in 1921, and it became part of the Williamson stable in 1924. Its scantily clad chorus line was known as "Tivoli Tappers". As a victim of television, the last Tivoli show was in 1966.

Australia's southern neighbour, New Zealand, was also trying to establish its identity on the world stage. Established as a British colony in 1840, "English-speaking theatre became an integral part of its culture almost immediately", says Julie Jackson-Tretchikoff, a Ph.D. student at Auckland University, "although the predominantly English/Scottish European population in Auckland numbered only 2,000 compared with approximately 20,000 indigenous Maori."[10] The first musical theatre production, an evening of songs, was performed in a men's pub in 1841. Amateur operatic societies were formed, in part, because "the new migrants needed a sense of identity, of belonging to a community where the music was familiar in the harsh, frontier society so far from Great Britain".[11]

Although most of this activity involved amateur productions of British, European and, later, American musicals, some New Zealanders longed for the big-time, and to express their own voices. Poet and journalist Arthur Adams (1872-1936) teamed with Australian-born, Leipzig-trained composer Alfred Hill (1869-1960) to write an operetta called *Tapu, or a Tale of a Maori Pah*. When Adams showed this to Australian impresario J. C. Williamson in 1898, he bought it immediately, and hired Adams as his literary secretary.

The original Australian constitution had left a provision for New Zealand to join the Federation as a state, and at the time that *Tapu* was written, this was seriously under consideration. The plot is set in a Maori village, where an Australian delegate is awaited to discuss New Zealand's entry. At the same time, an acting troupe arrives on the scene, and their actor-manager is mistaken for the Australian diplomat. The title refers to a Polynesian concept of spiritual restrictions, and is the origin of the English word "taboo". *Tapu* received its world premiere in Wellington's Opera House on 16 February 1903.

J. C. Williamson saw the show in Wellington. This renewed his interest, and he mounted a tryout production in Auckland before moving it to Melbourne, Brisbane and Sydney. The *New Zealand Times* announced that, "For the first time on any stage there was produced an opera which essentially belongs to New Zealand".[12] However, the critics reserved all of their praise for Hill, and Adams had evidently abandoned the book to other hands long before the opening. The late New Zealand broadcaster Peter Harcourt wrote, "Adams had simply failed to get the mixture right. His theatre people, with their posturings and protestations, were figures of fun who amused him and gave him an opportunity to mock their blurring of fantasy and reality. The Maori characters were another thing altogether, and the use of more or less authentic Maori poi dances and the haka never failed to bring an ecstatic audience response. In short, the component parts of Adams' libretto were like oil and water and no amount of shaking and stirring would ever have caused them to blend."[13] His play *Mrs. Pretty and the Premier* was presented by Melbourne Repertory Theatre in 1914 and at His Majesty's in London in 1916.

After *Tapu*, Hill teamed up with another journalist,

the American-born John Youlin Birch (1872-1951) to write *A Moorish Maid* (1905). While its initial productions in Auckland and Wellington were well received, an attempt to bring it to London ultimately collapsed. Hill would go on to become one of Australia's leading composers, and was appointed to the Order of the British Empire and a Companion of the order of St. Michael and St. George. Both Adams and Hill would make their careers in Australia.

For much of its history, commercial theatre in Australia and New Zealand – and especially musical theatre – was dominated by one company: J. C. Williamson Ltd., known to people in the business as "The Firm". At one point it even claimed to be the largest theatrical firm in the world. James Cassius Williamson (1845-1913), or "Handsome Jimmy" as he was known, was actually an American who had come to Australia on tour as a dialect comedian under contract to English-born actor, entrepreneur and politician George Coppin (1819-1906). Four years later, he acquired the Australasian rights to *H.M.S. Pinafore* for £300. To Williamson, "A good play should appeal to the eye, to the heart and to the mind, in that order."[14] For the next thirty years, he built up an empire that included the Princess and Her Majesty's theatres in Melbourne and Her Majesty's in Sydney (among others), for which he imported stars such as Sarah Bernhardt. He fought – successfully, for a time – against the formation of an Australian actors' union. The company was often accused of behaving like a monopoly, and of taking little or no interest in the development of indigenous Australian theatre, claiming that Australian audiences did not want to see themselves on stage. "The commercial theatre has, at times, resembled the last bastion of colonialism", wrote lecturer, actor and director Malcolm Robertson (1933-2016) in 1977, "as it has sought desperately to preserve its dependence on the English theatre and, to a lesser extent, the American theatre, for its continuous existence, seemingly oblivious to what was happening around it."[15]

When Williamson died in 1913, the control of "The Firm" passed to five brothers, Charles (1868–1933), John (1871–1955), Nevin (1876–1961) , E. J. (1878–1947) and Frank Tait (1883–1965), who in conjunction with other partners – including Williamson's former associates Sir George Tallis (1869-1948) and Ernest C. Rolls (1890-after 1937) – guided the company for the next half century. Some of their successes included the D'Oyly Carte Opera Company, the Borovansky Ballet and, in 1947, a tour of *Annie Get Your Gun* that heralded a stream of imported Broadway musicals.

At first it was the Australian performers, rather than writers, who managed to break through and light up the stages, both at home and abroad. "We became known as a sort-of glorified summer stock out here", says actor Tony Sheldon (1955-), whose grandmother Stella Lamond was a leading lady in the Tivoli variety circuit. At the beginning of the twentieth century, companies such as J. C. Williamson would import the entire original casts of shows from England and America, including silent film star Harry Langdon in *Anything Goes*. Gradually, they began sending out the second string casts – the understudies who would still invariably be billed as 'Direct from Broadway', with Australians playing supporting roles.

Then the Second World War began, and the ships carrying the imported stars stopped coming. "Rather than not do anything, we started a series of revivals of shows like *No, No, Nanette*," Sheldon explains. "We became very, very good at reproducing Broadway musicals using Australian performers. Rather than creating original works, we cultivated the performers. We became known for our energy, for our commitment, for being triple threats: we have very good dancer-singer-actors in Australia – a lot more than in England. All the way through to the sixties and seventies, we compared very, very favourably against English performers who were known as being wishy-washy in comparison to the very robust Australian style of performing, which came from our culture. We're a beach culture; we're an outdoor culture. The dance teachers were tougher... We suddenly realised, 'yes, we are capable of performing leads'."

In September 1956, commercial television broadcasting arrived in Sydney, with one very indirect benefit to Australian musicals: a few local actors began to establish familiarity with audiences, leading to their eventually overtaking some of the foreign talent on stage. Then in 1957, *The Pajama Game* was presented with an all-Australian cast. This happened because a proposed tour by Margot Fonteyn had been postponed, leaving theatres in Melbourne, Sydney and Adelaide dark. The star was Sheldon's mother, Toni Lamond (1932-), half-sister of singer Helen Reddy. "J. C. Williamson took a bit of a risk with that", says Sheldon. "It went through the roof. It ran two and a half years." The cast also included Bill and John Newman and Tiki Taylor (John Newman's wife), who sang "Steam Heat".

Although J. C. Williamson returned to their old practice of importing leads for *My Fair Lady*, the precedent had been set. Jill Perryman got the lead in *Funny Girl*, and Nancye Hayes (1943-) played *Sweet Charity*.

Today, Australia still produces top-drawer musical theatre performers, including Caroline O'Connor (1962-), Philip Quast (1957-) and Hugh Jackman (1968-). Unusually, the leading school for musical theatre, the Western Australian Academy of Performing Arts (part of Edith Cowan University) – of which Jackman is an alumnus – is located in Perth, at the opposite end of the country from the two leading theatre centres of Sydney and Melbourne. Sheldon is on the faculty there. Over seven hundred people a year audition for eighteen places (nine men and nine women). Other major programs include the National Institute of Dramatic Art in Sydney and the University of Ballarat in Victoria.

Of course, for Australia to really have a vibrant

musical theatre scene, they would have to create their own shows. *Collits' Inn* with book by Sydney journalist Thomas Stuart Gurr (1884-1967) and music and lyrics by Isobel Varney Monk (1892-1967) was the result of a 1932 Light Opera and Revue Competition sponsored by Sydney singing teacher Nathalie Rosenwax. The setting for the story was the historic inn built in 1823 by Pierce Collits, an Irish convict who had been transported to New South Wales twenty-two years previously. The story was a highly romanticised account of Collits' daughter's marriage.

Although it failed to win first prize, Rosenwax decided to mount a production of *Collits' Inn* with her students in Sydney in December 1932. The opening was attended by the New South Wales governor. There was a repeat performance at Mosman Town Hall in March 1933, and in June an abridged version was broadcast nationally on the Australian Broadcasting Commission's radio network. They then submitted it to J. C. Williamson Ltd., but were told that it was no good. Then, when they were ready to give up, Melbourne-based film producer Francis William Thring (1882-1936) came forward, saying that "a country which could produce a [Nellie] Melba, a Florence Austral and many other world-famous names, should surely possess individuals capable of providing the material for musical productions equal to those from abroad."[16] He had equally ambitious plans for the Australian film industry, having in 1931, written, produced and directed *Diggers*, the first successful Australian sound feature.

Hoping that it would be the first in a series of Australian musicals, Thring opened *Collits' Inn* at the Princess Theatre in Melbourne on 23 December 1933 starring Gladys Moncrieff (1892-1976), Australia's most popular star of light opera who had made her name in the English operetta *The Maid of the Mountains* in Melbourne in 1921. This expanded version of *Collits' Inn*, which employed Australia's first revolving stage, contained the "corroboree ballet", said to be a transcription of an authentic aboriginal chant that Monk heard in Kiama which she hoped would rival the "totem" dance in *Rose-Marie*. According to Wyllie Johnston, Monk's transcription of the chant was pretty accurate in its original version. "Unfortunately, the musical director of the Thring production took it upon himself to change the [time] signature. It's in 9/8 in the original, but [he changed it] to 3/4. It suddenly becomes rather conventional."

The Age said that "the most uproarious enthusiasm with which the play was received from start to finish, and the gasps of amazement and admiration that resounded through the theatre as that ingenious novelty a revolving stage revealed several scenes of spectacular colour and beauty left no doubt at all as to the success of the show." *Smith's Weekly* said, "It's Australian — and it's good". The Sydney *Daily Telegraph* said, "It was with a distinct shock that the audience realised that this play was Australian; that some one had had the audacity to use gum trees (magnificently reproduced gum trees) as a setting; that someone had realised the potentialities of a corroboree for ballet. Something for even New York to become excited about." The Melbourne *Argus* proclaimed, "It satisfies as no *Rose-Marie* or *Lilac Time* can satisfy." It ran for sixteen weeks in Melbourne before moving to the New Tivoli Theatre in Sydney for eight weeks.

Thring had ambitious plans to make a film of the show, but they were never realised. Only a sound recording (on nitrate film) was ever made, and this is now preserved in Australia's National Film and Sound Archive. Thring produced a second Varney Monk musical, *The Cedar Tree*, which opened 22 December 1934 at the Princess Theatre in Melbourne, also starring Gladys Moncrieff. According to Dr. Wyllie Johnston, "J. C. Williamson, the huge theatre chain in Australia... were very upset that Thring was being so successful, and so when *The Cedar Tree* moved from a successful season in Melbourne to another season in Sydney, they gave it the worst theatre in town, and it closed after three or four weeks in the middle of a summer heat wave." Thring died in 1936.

Collits' Inn sparked a brief flurry of activity that would include *Blue Mountain Melody* for J. C. Williamson with music and lyrics by Charles Zwar (1911-89), (whom Thring had hired to augment the *Collits' Inn* score, adding the song "They're in Love") and a book by cartoonist J. C. Bancks (creator of the *Ginger Meggs* comic strip) and starring Cyril Ritchard which opened on 22 September 1934 at Sydney's Theatre Royal.

"A lot of Australian stuff was terrible," Sheldon says, referring to some of the other nameless product that ensued. "We deserved to have the cringe factor."

As in Canada, many of those who had talent left for greener pastures. Zwar moved to London, where he played piano for revues at the Gate Theatre near Charing Cross. He contributed songs to *Sweet And Low*, *Sweeter And Lower* and *Sweetest And Lowest* with Hermione Gingold and had a modest hit in 1952 with *Bet Your Life* starring Arthur Askey, Julie Wilson and Sally Ann Howes. In New York, where Gingold had already used some of his songs in *Murray Anderson's Almanac*, a revue of his songs – *From A to Z* – ran briefly at the Plymouth Theatre, and back in London, his musical *Marigold* (with lyrics by Alan Melville) was staged in the West End at the Savoy for seventy-seven performances in 1959.

Edmond Samuels (1895-1973) was a Sydney pharmacist (and proprietor of the "world-famous headache bar") who also "dabbled" in writing popular songs. Many of his customers were theatre people – he touted himself as a "hangover expert" – and as a result he managed to have one of his songs performed at the Tivoli variety theatre. As a regular first-night theatre-goer, he became particularly enamoured of musicals such as *Show Boat* and *Rose Marie*. "I studied the production methods, becoming deeply immersed in this type of show", he later wrote. "Being so very Australia-minded, I felt it was time someone created a musical with an Australian flavour, using our natural scenery for its setting."[17] Encouraged initially by F. W. Thring, he wrote *The Highwayman*, but found no takers in his native country. With English book writers Guy Bolton (1884-1979) and Clifford Grey (1887-1941)[18], he rewrote it as *At the Silver Swan*, the "first attempt by a young, super-patriotic and ambitious Australian to present a musical play with an Australian background on the London stage."[19] It opened at the Palace Theatre, London starring Alice Delysia (1889-1979) on 19 February 1936 (after a tryout in Glasgow) and closed after fifty-three[20] tortuous performances.

Fourteen years later, Samuels would try again, this time in his own country. He even managed to interest the theatrical giant J. C. Williamson in backing his venture under its original title, *The Highwayman*. This was no mean feat; Williamson's were notoriously disinterested in local talent, on or off stage. However, what they actually did was to encourage him to death (almost). Samuels had seen it all before in London, where it appears that some "angels" hadn't quite earned their wings: his backer's auditions for *Silver Swan* exposed him to the quasi-criminal machinations of some theatrical financiers. In Australia, Williamson's kept stalling on signing a contract, and shortening the length of booking they could promise him.

Finally, he joined with expatriate American director Carl Randall and managed to snatch the "resting" cast of the recently closed *Annie Get Your Gun* from under the Williamson's noses. He booked the King's Theatre in Melbourne, controlled by the Fullers' group, JCW's competitors, where it received a warm reception. Perhaps too warm: Melbourne was in the throes of the worst heat wave in half a century, and the King's Theatre had no air conditioning. Still, it ran for three months and was seen by 100,000 people.

They decided to transfer the show to Sydney, where Samuels secured another Fullers' theatre, the Palace. Only a five-week slot was available, and the theatre was small, but Samuels preferred to stay out of the Williamson's stable. The Australian Broadcasting Commission aired a condensed version of the show on radio, and EMI eventually made a recording of excerpts from the score.

"There [were] key people spread around the place at different times who created musicals seemingly, sometimes, out of nothing", says Dr. Wyllie Johnston. As was the case in Canada, "when you do the research you find there's actually a big background there. In many cases [we find] people with a lot of depth of knowledge and understanding who've done a lot of work about how to write shows and eventually have at least one success." Although, unlike Canada, Australia never had any equivalent to either the Lehman Engel workshops or the Charlottetown Festival, "we did have a few people who went to the West End and came back determined to try to create something of a good standard." However, distance was always a problem – not just the distance between centres, but from the rest of the world and the creative communities. "If they had a success, it came, it went, people forgot about it. There was nothing that really kept the whole tradition alive."

The Phillip Street Theatre, established in Sydney by the Scottish-born former Old Vic stage manager William Orr (1924-ca.92) and his partner Eric Duckworth (1915-2013) in 1954, was one of the first regular outlets for writers. John McKelllar (1930-2010) created the *Phillip Street Revues* (1954-71), which, like Canada's *Spring Thaw*, "for the first time held a mirror up to Australian culture, particularly suburban culture," according to Tony Sheldon. Even the expatriates were persuaded to return: Charles Zwar contributed to 1964's *Is Australia Really Necessary?* Other productions included *A Cup of Tea, A Bex and a Good Lie Down* (1965). Among the acts to emerge from these revues was "Dame Edna Everage", the brainchild of actor Barry Humphries (1934-).

This led to other offshoots: *Revue '60* was a television show whose English-born head writer Chris

Bearde (1936-2017) later went to Toronto and wrote for *Nightcap*, the *Spring Thaw*-influenced CBC local satirical show that would inspire *Rowan and Martin's Laugh-In*. When the latter show began in 1968, Bearde teamed with Canadian writer Allan Blye (1937-) to join that show's writing staff in "beautiful downtown Burbank".

Lola Montez: Frank Wilson and the Ladies of the Town
Photo by Fred Carew from Elizabethan Theatres Trust production courtesy Peter Pinne

Lola Montez (1958), with music by Peter Stannard (1931-2018), lyrics by Peter Benjamin (1930-2008) and book by Alan Burke (1923-2007), told the story of the Irish-born Spanish dancer's time in the mining village of Ballarat, Victoria. It was originally tried out by the Union Theatre Repertory Company (now Melbourne Theatre Company) in Melbourne where it opened on February 19, 1958. The Australian Elizabethan Theatre Trust, established in 1954 as a nurturing body for the performing arts, then chose it for a full production. "Things happened thereafter beyond the authors' control",[21] Stannard told me. George Carden (1913-1981), an Australian expatriate who had choreographed the variety shows at the London Palladium for many years, was engaged as director-choreographer. He brought over one of his English dancers, Mary Preston, to play the lead role. Preston was then in her early twenties, while the real-life Lola had been thirty-seven when she came to Australia. "And Mary didn't have much of a voice", says Stannard.

Brigid Lewisham (Lola) performs her Spider Dance in ABC-TV's production of *Lola Montez*, telecast nationally on May 7, 1962.
Photo courtesy Peter Stannard

What the composer calls the "blown-up" version opened under their auspices on 1 October at Her Majesty's Theatre in Brisbane, where it ran for five weeks. While the critical reception was warm, the audiences were small, and things did not improve when it opened in Sydney on October 22. Still, EMI produced a cast album – the first stereo recording to be made in Australia, and so the show's reputation grew. One song, "Saturday Girl", was touted as Australia's first hit show tune. It was later produced on both radio (1959) and television (1962). A revised version opened December 3, 1988 at the Playhouse Theatre, Canberra. "The show still bobs up somewhere in the country every now and again," Stannard says. "Even Japan plays some of the music on radio and the trickle of royalties is welcome!"

The same writing team were later commissioned by the ATN7 network to write a musical for television called *Pardon Miss Westcott*, which was broadcast nationally on Christmas Eve, 1959. After that, Stannard largely returned to his day job as an advertising executive, with occasional forays into music and theatre.

"The trap we fell into was trying to emulate the Broadway musical, and we just weren't good at it", says actor Tony Sheldon. "It was strange to do a show about Lola Montez coming to the gold fields in about 1850, which is about miners. Everybody goes, 'let's make it like *Paint Your Wagon*', but Australians don't want to see a bunch of gold miners getting up and doing dance numbers because it's not in the Australian character." Peter Stannard maintained that George Carden's "dance routines were bawdy, verile – *very* Australian."[22]

While *Lola Montez* seemed to be following the American model, *The Sentimental Bloke* by Albert Arlen (1905-93), Nancy Brown (1909-2003) and Lloyd Thomson (1919-2015), revealed an English influence. Peter Wyllie Johnston calls it "our most successful original score of the twentieth century".

Arlen had worked as a musician and composer in London, where his *Alamein Concerto* (1944) had been recorded by Mantovani. He began working on *The Sentimental Bloke* in 1950, based on C.J. Dennis (1876-1938)'s poems *Songs of a Sentimental Bloke*, (which had also been made into a silent movie in 1919) but it took more than ten years for it to reach the stage.

This show managed to tap into Australia's "larrikin"[23] humour of defiance of authority and irreverent self-deprecation. He tried to interest managements in both Australia and London, but with no success. Finally he and his wife Nancy Brown mounted it themselves with an amateur cast at Albert Hall in Canberra on 7 March 1961.[24] This came to the attention of theatrical giant J. C. Williamson, who presented it in what was meant to be a limited six week season at Melbourne's Comedy Theatre on 4 November 1961.[25] Edwin Ride played the title role, as he did in the original amateur production. This was extended to five months, then a tour was mounted to Adelaide, Brisbane, Sydney and New Zealand. Nancy Brown later complained, "Not one management asked us if we had anything else we could show them. Our work went as if for nothing."[26]

At this time, there were a handful of Australians who were having some success abroad. Queensland-born Ron Grainer (1922-1981), now best remembered as the composer of the *Dr. Who* theme, collaborated with English librettist Ronald Millar (1919-98) on *Robert and Elizabeth*, based on *The Barratts of Wimpole Street*, which enjoyed a healthy run of 948 performances at the Lyric Theatre in London's West End in 1964. Producer Garnet H. Carroll later brought this home to Australia.

In parallel to the Canadian experience, Australia also began to develop a more nationalistic "alternate" theatre. Both countries were influenced in this by London's Unity Theatre and by Joan Littlewood's Theatre Workshop.

"By the 1950s", explains Dr. Wyllie Johnston, "you had a grass-roots movement that grew up that was strongly connected to the trade union movement, which was very concerned to depict other parts of Australian life."

Reedy River, which premiered at Melbourne's left-wing New Theatre on 11 March 1953, had a book by Dick Diamond (1906-89) about a shearers' strike in the 1890s that made use of traditional folk songs. "This was considered very radical and not terribly okay by the establishment and by the prevailing political forces of the 1950s when the conservative government was in power under [Robert] Menzies. Yet it had tremendous popular support and went right around Australia and travelled to London where it was also successful."

Robyn Archer (1948-), Australia's leading interpreter of the songs of Brecht and Weill and of the Weimar cabaret says, "One can stage a biting anti-government satire which will be guaranteed to appeal to at least half the population, simply because no matter how the gerrymander works in favour of a Liberal Party [i.e. conservative] victory at elections, at least half the population always votes Labor."[27] Dr. Wyllie Johnston says, "This was the beginning of a separate tradition of musical theatre which really took off a lot more in the late seventies and into the eighties when Nick Enright [(1950-2003)] and Dennis Watkins came into their own and began to write musical theatre."

The Ballad of Angel's Alley was a 'pocket opera' concerning thieves and prostitutes by television writer Jeff Underhill (1927-78) and composer Bruce George (1913- ?). It was first tried out at Melbourne's New Theatre on Boxing Day in 1958 as a co-operative venture, because no commercial producer would take it on. "Most managements in this country can't even read a score", said Underhill at the time. "They have to go to New York or London to find a musical that they can put on here."[28] In 1962, it was successfully remounted by the Melbourne

Theatre Company. Frank Murphy in *The Advocate* (Melbourne) called it "a delicious extravaganza, written in a mock serious style that capitally captures and sustains the old ballad melodramas"[29].

Beginning on 14 May 1966, Melbourne's Emerald Hill Theatre presented Australia's first rock musical, *A Bunch of Ratbags*, with music by Peter Pinne (1937-) and lyrics by Pinne and Don Battye (1938-2016). The book by Battye was based on a novel by William Dick about gang warfare in Melbourne in the 1950s. Pinne says, "When Don Battye and I first started writing we deliberately eschewed going the 'gumnuts and wattle' route (period works about the bush and searching for gold etc.), which up until that time had been the subjects of the only Australian musicals we had seen. We wanted to write something about contemporary Australia."[30] Leonard Radic in *The Age* wrote, "This is an all too rare venture in Melbourne's theatrical life – a locally written and commissioned musical which holds up the mirror to aspects of Australian life. On these grounds alone it is worth applauding... It has its deficiencies and its weaknesses, granted; it also has vitality, colour and a measure of authenticity."[31] Jean Battersby in the *Canberra Times* added, "The potential of this musical for large scale professional production is impossible to ignore."[32] Pinne and Battye would collaborate on several more musicals, including *Caroline, Red, White and Boogie* and *Prisoner Cell Block H*, which played in London's West End in 1995, starring Lilly Savage.

Another milestone in the progress toward a distinctly Australian musical style was *Flash Jim Vaux*, a ballad opera presented by Nimrod Theatre, where it opened 28 April 1972 with book and lyrics by former radio producer Ron Blair (1942-) and music by Terrence Clarke (1935-) and Charles Colman based largely on traditional tunes. Based on the true story of a prisoner who had been wrongly transported to Australia three times, "It worked because it was intrinsically Australian", says Tony Sheldon. "It suited the material. It wasn't imposing a sort of

Broadway sensibility."

Reg Livermore (1938-), a veteran of the Phillip Street Revues who had appeared in the Australian cast of *Hair*, wrote a rock musical – with a score by Patrick Flynn (1936-2008) – about *Ned Kelly*, which opened at the Adelaide Festival Theatre on 30 December 1977.

Grahame Bond (1943-) and Jim Burnett (1947-)'s *Boy's Own McBeth*, about a forty-two year old man who contrives to stay in school in order to secure free room and board, opened on 11 July 1979 at Kirk's Gallery in Sydney, and has, according to Peter Pinne, "been one of the most performed original Australian musicals playing over 600 performances around the country. It also played a gig in Los Angeles."

One of Australia's best known writers – both of musicals and straight plays – was the late Nick Enright, who may be best known internationally as the screenwriter of the film *Lorenzo's Oil*. "Nick in particular began to steer the musical in a more self-consciously Australian direction", says Dr. Wyllie Johnston, "but also one that had a bit more political substance in it." Some of Enright's shows as book writer and lyricist included *The Venetian Twins*, a two-act musical comedy based on Carlo Goldoni's 1747 play *I due gemelli veneziani* ("The two Venetian twins"), in turn based on the *Menaechmi* of Plautus, which was also the source for Shakespeare's *The Comedy of Errors*; *Orlando Rourke* (1985) with music by Alan John (1958-), produced at the Adelaide Festival Centre by the State Theatre of South Australia; *Summer Rain* – about a travelling tent show in the outback in post-war New South Wales – with music by Terrence Clarke, first produced by the National Institute for Dramatic Arts at the Parade Theatre in Sydney on 19 October 1983 and later by the Sydney Theatre Company; and *Mary Bryant*, with a score by David King, which opened at the Ensemble Theatre, Sydney, on 5 September 1988 after a production at the Western Australia Academy of Performing Arts in Perth. (He also wrote the book for

The Boy from Oz, which we will come to later.)

Then, Australian musical theatre suffered one of its greatest box office setbacks. *Manning Clark's History of Australia – the Musical*, based on the six-volume history by Professor Manning Clark (1915-91), opened at Melbourne's Princess Theatre on 16 January 1988. The book was by Tim Robertson (1944-), John Romeril (1945-), and Don Watson (1949-), with music by Martin Armiger (1949-) and George Dreyfus (1928-), and it was produced by John Timlin.

It was mounted to commemorate the bicentennial of the establishment of the first permanent British settlement in Australia (which was, of course, a penal colony). "This was a musical which attempted to put a particular point of view about the history of Australia", says Dr. Wyllie Johnston, "which accorded with Manning Clark's view, and which had tremendous support from the government at the time under Bob Hawke and a lot of other people but sadly, the public didn't buy it." The *Sun News-Pictorial* declared it "A tawdry and tacky affair, enough to give the Bicentennial a bad name".[33] It ran for five weeks and then closed. "It's only been produced a couple of times since in amateur productions, and once in America by a Jewish guy from Melbourne who was a drama teacher who took it there to show the people in Texas and Arkansas and places like that the history of Australia from a rather left-wing point of view," says Wyllie Johnston. "One can't imagine how it went down."

Also a Bicentennial project, Dr. Wyllie Johnston says that *Seven Little Australians* "would be the closest thing we have to *Anne of Green Gables*." The story, based on a novel by Ethel Turner (1873-1958), is about a dour widower with seven children, and his efforts to have them accept his child bride. "It's a perennial part of Australian culture," says Dr. Wyllie Johnston. It was "clearly influenced by Rodgers and Hammerstein, especially *The Sound of Music*." David Reeves (1943-) wrote the music, and the lyrics were by John Palmer (1940-), with Palmer and Peter Yeldham

(1927-) sharing credit for the book.

The show opened on 22 June 1988 at the Comedy Theatre, Melbourne, although its life actually began more than a decade earlier at the Armidale, a (then) independent boys' school in rural New South Wales. In 1976, Desmond Lyle "Jim" Graham (1933-2016), a history teacher obtained the musical rights to Turner's novel from her son. The following year Reeves became the school's director of music. Graham, who had already written and produced various shows for the school, asked Reeves to write the music. Reeves had worked as a jazz pianist and written scores for documentaries but never for the theatre.

It opened in 1978 as a co-production with the nearby University of New England. It played for five nights, and then was revived for one night only at the Seymour Centre in Sydney. *The Armadilian* reported enthusiastically,

> "In the frantic weeks of rehearsal which led up to the performances at the end of April, boys and staff who were involved on stage, in the orchestra, or on stage-crew, worked with a dedication and enthusiasm which did credit to the best traditions of theatre. For the 'back-stage boys' the experience gained by working with professionals, and in a theatre such as the Arts Theatre at U.N.E., was to prove invaluable... particularly when it became known that the play would also be presented at the Seymour Centre in Sydney. All rose to the occasion, and the result was a triumphant and spectacular evening, with many Old Boys and their families in a capacity audience. The proceeds of the evening were directed towards the Sheppard Centre for deaf children."[34]

Producers Malcolm Cooke and Mike Walsh (1938-) showed interest in it, but this is where it gets complicated. As early as September, 1979 Ray Stanley's "Whispers, Rumours and Facts" column in *Theatre Australia* mentioned "There's whisper of a musical version of *Seven Little*

Australians."[35] They booked theatres in Sydney and Melbourne. They then announced in the February 1980 issue of *Theatre Australia* that "Malcolm Cooke and Hayden Price Attractions [Walsh's company] will present the world premiere of a musical based on *Seven Little Australians*"[36].

However, at this point, there was a veritable revolving door of writers, directors and even composers. They brought in, at various times David Mitchell, Richard Wherrett (1940-2001), Eleanor Whitcomb (1923-) (who had written a non-musical adaptation for the Australian Broadcasting Corporation a few years earlier), and Rodney Fisher to work on the book and lyrics. David Mitchell told me, "Malcolm C. Cooke and Mike Walsh were planning it and Oscar winner John Truscott designed a set. I went to Armidale to work with the then composers and we wrote one or two songs. Then suddenly it was all off!"[37]

They even tried to replace Reeves' score with a new one by Jeff Hales, arranger of *In Melbourne Tonight*[38], and when that came to nought, Cooke and Walsh washed their hands of the project, and used their bookings in Sydney and Melbourne to present *The Best Little Whorehouse in Texas* instead.

In the meantime, the relationship between Reeves and Graham had soured, and Reeves – back on board as composer – obtained the services of John Palmer, a writer and lyricist of such animated films as *Dot and the Kangaroo* to do the libretto.

Then Sydney Festival director Stephen Hall (1936-2014) entered the scene and, with the support of building materials manufacturer James Hardie Industries, set out to raise a budget of a million dollars. They then approached Noel Ferrier (1930-97) at the Australian Elizabethan Theatre Trust, who arranged a workshop. However, it languished further after the Trust, due to internal divisions, then bowed out of any further involvement. In the end, James Hardie Industries, in attempt to improve an image tarnished by their extensive involvement in asbestos mining, agreed (by arrangement with impresario Paul Dainty) to produce the show for the Australian Bicentennial.

Alas, the revolving door still was not quite fixed in place yet. Evidently dissatisfied with the book, in March 1988 – just three months before the opening – Reeves brought in noted playwright and screen writer Peter Yeldham. At this point, future Queensland Theatre artistic director Christine Johnson walked out and American expat John O'May – who was already playing the father – became the director.

It opened at the Comedy Theatre in Melbourne on 22 June 1988. In an attempt to pre-sell the show, "Look for a Rainbow" was commercially recorded as a single by Julie Anthony (1949-). Only two songs, "Discipline" and "Catching the Central Express" remained from the original Armidale production.

Leonard Radic in *The Age* called it "a comfortable family-style show: warmhearted, sentimental and ever so wholesome".[39] *Variety*'s review by rock journalist Debbie Kruger (1962-) possibly reveals more about Australia's notorious cringe factor – not to mention civic rivalry – than it does about the show: "Producers of new indigenous works have enormous courage, and despite a natural Aussie cynicism, ingrained particularly in the theater industry, nobody really wants to see such ventures fail. Which could explain why 'Seven Little Australians' has been well received, despite its glaring inadequacies. This stage version… trivializes the subject and sets Aussie legit back 90 years... Chances are this musical will best succeed in Melbourne, appealing as it does to a conservative, undemanding audience. First-nighters were in raptures. Families in search of old-fashioned idealism and innocuous entertainment will be pleased. More discerning folk in Sydney, however, might be less likely to pay top prices for something the likes of which they could see free of charge at their local shopping center any lunchtime."[40]

It ran for about four months in Melbourne, then played a week at the Theatre Royal in Hobart, then eleven performances in Launceston, Tasmania, from whence it travelled to Adelaide for twenty-four performances over Christmas. Nine months later, a new and revised version opened at the Footbridge Theatre in Sydney, where it played sixty-four performances in a seven hundred seat auditorium at the University of Sydney.

Its initial presentation at the Comedy had an orchestra of twenty-two musicians, but by the time the revised version opened in Sydney, this was reduced to just nine. A new song "Back, Back to Sydney" was added, and they re-instated "Soldiers of the Lord" and "Have a Hearty Meal" which had been previously cut. The program included all of the song lyrics, and O'May was credited as co-lyricist. Until this time the programmes said it was "based on a concept by Jim Graham", but this testimony had now disappeared.

In all, it grossed around three million dollars. Dan Crawford of the King's Head Theatre proposed a London production under the title *Judy* but this never happened. It was revived by the Royal Queensland Theatre Company in 1991 by director Alan Edwards (1925-2003), using the Sydney revised script, and has been popular with amateur companies since then.

"I like the score", says Peter Pinne. "It's old fashioned Broadway, and by [that] I mean Broadway of the fifties and sixties. It satisfied, and it was emotional and it had some heart. It certainly was one of the better scores of Australian musicals of the period, and it still stands up today."[41]

The show that has probably achieved the highest international profile would be *The Boy from Oz*, with a book by Nick Enright telling the story of Australian singer and songwriter Peter Allen (1944-92), using Allen's own songs. Directed by Gale Edwards (1954-), it opened on 5 March 1998 at Her Majesty's Theatre, Sydney.

Jill Perryman told me, "It took me fifty years of singing and acting in musicals from the U.S. before *The Boy from Oz* came along in which I was overjoyed to play the mother of Peter Allen who was such an icon in our musical history, and it *was* a strange feeling singing in a broad Australian accent."[42]

"The authors went to great pains to work out what was Peter Allen's demon", says Tony Sheldon. "This man whose stage persona was this camp, devil-may-care, let's have a good time, 'I Go to Rio' thing, yet all his songs were about loss and loneliness. The author, Nick Enright, spent nine drafts trying to pin down what was the demon that drove this man. He pinned it down to his father's suicide. Peter Allen's father shot himself in front of Peter... when he was a child, and Peter and his mother were left to clean the blood off the walls. This was something that scars a person terribly. What they chose to do, through many drafts, was to not mention this – you just knew there was something dogging him until the end of the show. They kept the suicide off-stage, then it all built to the song 'Tenterfield Saddler', which he wrote about his father, which is Peter Allen's most personal song. It's what *The Boy from Oz* hangs on."

Sheldon draws a big breath. "The first thing that happens when they take the show to America is they cut the song. They cut the entire suicide as a plot point, and they finish with 'I Go to Rio' instead. And the producer gave an interview and said, 'Peter Allen never had a dark side.' So you've immediately emasculated the entire project in one fell swoop."

The original Australian production sold around a million tickets and grossed about sixty million Australian dollars. The Broadway production, starring Hugh Jackman, had a new book by Martin Sherman (1938-) (author of *Bent*) and a new American director, Philip William McKinley. It ran for a year – the duration of Jackman's contract. Ben Brantley of the *New York Times* called it an "indisputably bogus show".[43]

Director Gale Edwards followed *The Boy from Oz* in 2004 with *Eureka* (a musical about the 1854 Eureka stockade miners' rebellion) with book and lyrics by Maggie May Gordon, Gale Edwards and John Senczuk and music by Michael Maurice Harvey, a show which, according to Edwards, "celebrates our national story and I think that, as Australians, the audiences will want to stand up and cheer."[44] When critics failed to do that, she told Will Conyers, "*Eureka* is an interesting example of a show that drew on a tremendous wide range of Australian resources, and was very close to being fantastic, but was completely destroyed by the critics. I think Germaine Greer ... gave it 'zero'. You can't give it 'zero'. Not acceptable. You can say that you didn't like this and this and this about it, but you can't actually give a show which cost five million dollars and drew on that kind of power and had that sort of expertise and was such a valiant and noble effort – you can't give it zero because that is actually contempt."[45]

One of the cast members was Nancye Hayes, who told broadcaster Peter Thompson, "It's been a hard road to hoe with the Australian musical, but we will not give up, we are determined to get one up there."[46]

In recent years, the creation of new Australian musicals was supported by a biannual prize established by Jeanne and Richard Pratt ($50,000 to the winners, plus $30,000 towards a workshop by Pratt's own The Production Company). "The purpose of this award is to stimulate the creation of music theatre," said Jeanne Pratt in a press release dated November 28, 2002.

"When we began advertising for entries... we expected we would get perhaps a dozen or two. With six weeks to go before entries closed – June 30 – we had 10 or 12. But in the following final weeks, another 132 entries came flooding in! Clearly, this award has been a powerful creative catalyst."

The first Pratt Prize was awarded to *Sideshow Alley* by Paul Keelan and Gary Young. The story tackled themes of acceptance and prejudice in a touring sideshow in 1950s Australia. Following a workshop directed by Gale Edwards, the show was picked up by Melbourne based producer Jim McPherson, whose massively successful tour of *Menopause – The Musical* had been directed by Young.

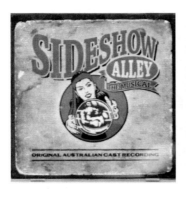

A full stage production of *Sideshow Alley*, under Young's direction, opened at the Playhouse in Brisbane in 2007. The authors aimed for a distinctly Australian feel to both the music and words. "I think it's time musicals became more Australian," said Gary Young. "Plays have become much more localised but musicals are late off the mark dealing with Australian stories. And this is an original story, script and score, set in Australia with Australian slang, about Australians."[47] He elaborates, "Where else in the world but here is any one going to say to you, 'Sorry mate, I was flat out like a lizard drinkin!' or 'I was off like a bride's nightie!' or 'Crikey love, you're all dolled up like a Mungandai squatter!'"[48]

Many people's hopes were riding on this show – not just those of the creative team. It opened on February 3, 2007 following ten days of previews. "At last the arrival of a new musical that isn't strung together from a back catalogue of popular tunes", said the *Herald-Sun*. "*Sideshow Alley*... is that rarest of things in today's conveyor-belt culture – an unashamedly Australian tale replete with larrikins, show people, dry humour, slang and sentimentality."[49] Rosemary Duffy of *State of the Arts* wrote, "The show's good-natured, unrestrained larrikinism reminds us just how distinctive preglobalized Australia was."[50]

Yet, in spite of some very vocal support, audiences simply didn't turn up in sufficient numbers, and in fact some performances were aborted due to poor ticket sales. Planned engagements in Melbourne and Sydney were cancelled. Alas, the last Pratt Prize was awarded in 2008.

The Pratt Prize was not the first attempt at this sort of thing: in 1991, Jim Sharman – the director best known for *The Rocky Horror Picture Show* – set up the Australian Musical Foundation based at the National Institue for Dramatic Arts. The final show to be developed by them was *The Emerald Room* with music by Chris Harriott and libretto by Dennis Watkins which bombed at the Playhouse in Adelaide in 1994.

"Here, we call it 'Australiana'", says producer and director Neil Gooding. "That kind of old version of everything being very, very Australian and very 'Ocker' we call it here... We have matured a bit as a country. Australia tends to do two things: even the new musicals that people write, Australia was so heavily defined by that kind of larrikin old Australia, or by war. They're the two things we default to to identify ourselves. Some of the people are still producing shows that I just think don't have an audience any more because they're so 'Old Australian'".

Melbourne-based Magnormos Productions began producing an annual festival in 2002 called OzMade Musicals. Artistic director Aaron Joyner explains, "The idea was to have a production company that could produce Australian work, as well as key international work... There wasn't really anything happening for Australian writers."

Beginning with a concert on Australia Day (January 26), he presented a concert of songs from Australian-written musicals. Finding that it was hard to attract an audience on a public holiday when many people were away, he later moved the show to November, but the idea remained the same, "to create pathways for writers to get their work demonstrated, developed and presented in front of an audience of people that includes media and producers and practitioners and the general industry, and actually get the work showcased in a classy presentation."

He had the same funding problem that people with similar plans have in the U.K. and Canada. "Unfortunately, musical theatre is problematic to the Australia Council because it's a multi-discipline art form. Therefore, when you go to apply, you have to choose between applying for music, dance or theatre or even literature, depending on what stream it is. So, it's very confusing when you speak to one board and they say, 'well, you really should speak to *this* board'."

Neil Gooding of New Musicals Australia agrees.

"Historically they have a very poor track record of supporting anything that looks like a musical theatre piece. Within the Australia Council there was a theatre board, and there was a music board and there was a dance board, but the music and theatre boards could never decide which one of them was dealing with musical theatre. Some would apply to both of them, and then nobody was getting funded. There was a chairman of the music board called Paul Mason who kind of pro-actively put up his hand and said 'We acknowledge that musical theatre is being badly represented by us, and so to clarify for everybody we are going to put musical theatre pieces through the music board' and [they] found this discretionary core funding which was what led to the first funding of New Musicals Australia. So, that was a big game changer for us. It's still limited support and it doesn't solve all the problems of Australian musical theatre but at least it's a start."

OzMade did receive corporate sponsorship from companies like Yamaha Music, who provided musical instruments, and the BMD group, a Brisbane-based construction company who set up a cultural fund. The performers and musicians worked for nothing, but as Joyner explains, it was a chance for them to "work in their own accent, which is something that rarely happens in Australia for musical theatre performers."

They sent one show, *Joe Starts Again* (2004, book by Martin Croft and Mark Fletcher, music by Dean Lotherington and lyrics by Martin Croft) to the New York Musical Theatre Festival, whose then Artistic Director Kris Stewart was an Australian. They would have sent *All Het Up* the following year but, although it had been accepted, they were unable to raise the financing. Other shows developed by Magnormos went on to be short-listed for the Pratt Prize.

Sadly, OzMade Musicals has since folded. "Yes I did suspend OzMade Musicals in 2013," Aaron Joyner told me. "Unfortunately nothing has yet taken its place in the same way, but hopefully in the future something may continue the legacy. Development is so important as you know, but our commercial producers in Australia and (unfortunately) our arts funding bodies don't exhibit much respect or understanding for its performance."[51]

A unique development in Australia is the aboriginal musical. When Jimmy Chi (1948-2017)'s semi-autobiographical *Bran Nue Dae* opened at the Festival of Perth in the Octagon Theatre on February 22, 1990 following a tryout in his hometown of Broome, a dam broke. "Australia has always had a big issue with its native heritage", says Dr. Wyllie Johnston. While shows like *Collits' Inn* and *The Highwayman* featured Aboriginal "corroborees" as an exotic feature, *Bran Nue Dae* was the first musical to be written from the native perspective. This led to the foundation of Black Swan Theatre Company, under the patronage of Janet Holmes à Court, the then-owner of London's Stoll Moss Theatres chain.

"*Bran Nue Dae* is a musical in the Western European popular stage tradition", says Paul Makeham, drama professor at Queensland University of Technology. "It is clearly influenced by the Hollywood musical film genre as well. Yet the play amalgamates the generic conventions of the popular musical with those of Aboriginal oral culture, including those formalised in the tradition of the song cycle. Thus the structural motif of the journey in *Bran Nue Dae* is overlaid onto the specifically Aboriginal form of the song cycle, a type of ritual journey of re-enactment which, like Chi's play, is also 'a musical journey' and a renewal of origins. For the landscapes encountered by the play's travellers are to a large extent sung; through a combination of words, music and images, these landscapes embody aspects of Aboriginal philosophy and consciousness."[52] The musical styles, which incorporate reggae, gospel and country-and-western as well as Broadway, stem from the imported music and films Chi was exposed to in Broome as a young man.

However, to non-Australian ears, *Bran Nue Dae* did not *sound* Australian, and this was a problem for former Theatre Royal Stratford East director Philip Hedley who remarked, "It's a wonderful show, an important show, but it was a mystery to me as to how it arrived at its shape, particularly why it had so many Western borrowings in it."[53] Another Melbourne critic, Catherine Lambert, complained that "although the music explores a range of styles from country to rap, many of the songs are overly simplistic and trite".[54] Wyllie Johnston counters, "The interesting thing about the community in Broome is that it's been a very multi-cultural society for a long, long time. We've had a tremendous number of influences coming and going... via radio, TV, stereo, but also with people visiting there. Jimmy Chi said that he grew up with all these eclectic influences around him musically, and this is why his own music has that kind of feeling... He didn't go for the cliché things, which you can easily do."

"Aboriginal Australia's triumph in survival has been its easy ability to appropriate any cultural tool it needs to make strong statements", says Robyn Archer, who was artistic director of the 1998 Adelaide Festival. "Jimmy Chi and his collaborators appropriated a further form, the popular musical, to make a new kind of statement in the widely travelled and televised *Bran Nue Dae* and, subsequently, *Corrugation Road*."[55]

This raises an interesting problem for those wishing to export their shows. They don't always live up to our stereotyped expectations. A friend of mine's father was a well-known Scottish-born jazz trumpeter who had emigrated to Canada. When somebody sent him a recording of bagpipes he said, "I left Scotland to get away from that stuff!" We non-Australians may have a mental picture of what an Aboriginal musical ought to be that won't necessarily tally with contemporary reality. I believe that the same principal will also apply to other countries. In Argentina, they do tango shows for the tourists, but the domestic audiences have other ideas.

Bran Nue Dae was made into a film in 2009 starring Ernie Dingo (1956-) and Geoffrey Rush (1951-), directed by Rachel Perkins (1970-). It has led to other shows written, at least partly, by Aboriginal writers and composers. Wesley

Enoch (1969-), with composer John Rodgers (1962-) wrote *The Sunshine Club*, about a native serviceman returning from World War II and encountering racism in the dance halls. *The Australian*'s Veronica Kelly hailed it as "a brilliant new landmark in Australian musicals".[56]

The birth of the Adelaide Cabaret Festival in 2001 has encouraged the development of a new, distinctly Australian form of cabaret musical. *Shane Warne – The Musical* opened at Melbourne's Athenaeum Theatre late in 2008, about the Australian cricket star, written by and starring cabaret artist Eddie Perfect (1977-). The director, Neil Armfield (1955-), was responsible for another hit cabaret musical, Casey Bennetto (1969-)'s *Keating*, about the former Labor Prime Minister.

"The joy of Eddie Perfect's *Shane Warne* musical is that it absolutely acknowledges that sport is the obsession in Australia", says Tony Sheldon. "There is no interest in culture, really, from a very high level. We've had Prime Ministers who have never set foot in a theatre in their entire term. And so the opening number of *Shane Warne* is three families at a back yard barbecue in the sixties, and they're all out there in their thongs with their stubbies, their beers, and they're saying, 'How's young Kevin going?' 'Oh, he's great. He won footie this week.' And then, 'How's young Kaylene?' 'She's a champion swimmer'. Then they go, 'How's young Fred?' and his parents say, 'Oh, he's wonderful. He's just got a scholarship to medical school where he's developed a theory on brain surgery.' And they all just stare. 'Oh yeah, that sounds nice.' And they all go back to talking sport. It sets the tone for what the show is going to be about, which is hero worship of a man whose great skill is he can throw a ball… It sums up the Australian character so well."

At first, Warne was angry about this unauthorised musical, but once he saw it, he was evidently won over. So was the Australian cricket establishment: Eddie Perfect was invited to sing the national anthem on the opening day of the test match against South Africa on Boxing Day at the Melbourne Cricket Ground. The show was a hit in Melbourne, but sadly closed after a mediocre three week run in Sydney. It won the 2009 Helpmann Award for Best New Australian Work. Perfect has since written new songs for the Broadway production of *King Kong* (based on the 1933 classic movie) and for *Beetlejuice* (which, as of writing, had not yet opened).

Tony Sheldon invited me to see a show that he was the star of in Sydney. *Priscilla, Queen of the Desert* is, to date, the most commercially successful stage production in Australian history. Based on Stephan Elliot (1964-)'s 1994 film about a trio of Sydney drag queens who become stranded in the desert when their bus ('Priscilla') breaks down, with a score made up of 1980s disco hits, it has grossed more than A$90 million and been seen by a million people on its home turf.

There was a point in the show's early workshops when the question was raised – should it be a 'jukebox' musical, or should it have an original score? "I must confess I was one of the people who said, 'I think you're in very, very dangerous territory there," Sheldon told me. "I mean, I look at *Thoroughly Modern Millie*, that score, and you think, what is it? It falls between two stools. I am concerned about that mixture. I don't know how that works. Still, after two years with *Priscilla*, the reviewers say, 'We wish the songs were more specific.' But I don't think we would have run two years without the songs that we have. It's what people relate to. The minute that overture starts, and the first notes of 'I Love the Night Life', people scream in the audience. So I understand why people rush to the jukebox as an alternative form now. It will die out I'm sure, but it seems to be what people want to hear now. The pre-sold title seems to be all now. Base your show on a famous film or a famous book and half your work is done."

Once more, a lot of hopes were riding on this

show. "That, as a musical, I think could be the un-locking of a door for a new generation for Australia, even though it's a jukebox", said Aaron Joyner in 2008. "It's still created by Australians... If they do good box office success like they are, then it allows producers to have a bit more confidence in what the next product could be."

On 24 March 2009 it opened at the Palace Theatre in London with Sheldon in the role of Bernadette (created in the original film by Terrence Stamp), starring alongside former soap star Jason Donovan. Sheldon told the *Australian Times*, "To play an Australian character in an Australian musical on Broadway or the West End has always been my dream. And now, after 45 years as an actor, my dream has come true."[57]

London News said, "It's difficult not to be swept away by this riotously enjoyable show."[58] *London Lite* called it "a real dazzler".[59] Simon Edge in the *Daily Express* said, "All wrapped up as a shiny, pink bowed package, this sumptuously dressed show works gloriously, with its parade of ever more jaw-dropping costumes an utter feast for the eye."[60] Nicholas de Jongh of the *Evening Standard* said, "At a time when escapist musicals are all the rage, here's a rare one that takes you happily out of yourself and into daring places your wildest fantasies might never have dreamed of visiting."[61] But for the *Guardian*'s Michael Billington, "Given the unexplored riches of Australian theatre, it's a pity that artistically buoyant country should now be represented in the West End by this garish throwback in which camp is determinedly overpitched,"[62] while Michael Coveney in the *Independent* declared, "Donovan, it has to be said, seems to have lost what little stage personality he had developed as Joseph in the dreamcoat, and turned, well, rancid – while the long-standing Australian drag queen Tony Sheldon, who starts off promisingly as a dead-ringer for Kim Cattrall and descends into big-mouthed anonymity, and Oliver Thornton as the wicked Felicia – look like Friday night acts at the long-ago Vauxhall Tavern."[63] Rebecca Jones of the

BBC decided, "You could pick this show apart if you wanted to – it isn't subtle and the content is a bit thin, but if you want a fun night out with toe-tapping tunes, you'll love it."

Co-writer Allan Scott (1940-) said, "It is curious the way in which a show, no matter its history, doesn't seem to exist or be considered 'real' unless and until it plays in London. The fact that *Priscilla Queen of the Desert – The Musical* has been seen by over a million Australians is, as it were, no more than a bagatelle of Commonwealth trivia. Apparently it is only when we open in London to be seen and judged by British audiences and British critics that we really exist."[64]

Its next stop was Toronto, where it opened at the Princess of Wales Theatre on 26 October 2010, prior to a Broadway transfer. Richard Ouzounian in *Variety* said it was "light years superior to the London production in terms of production standards, pacing (it's 30 minutes shorter) and the emotional honesty of the leading players."[65]

One of the producers of the North American incarnation was actress Bette Midler, and she conceded that some changes have been made to appeal to middle-American sensibilities. "You still get the flavor that has always been part of *Priscilla*, but it's not quite as down and dirty, not as in your face so much so that you might pull back," she told the *New York Times*' Patrick Healy. "It manages to have all the fun of camp without too much of the dark side of camp and drag. Which for Broadway, I think, is a good thing."[66]

The story has also been restructured to shift emphasis onto Tick, the drag queen looking to reunite with his estranged son Benji. "The thinking was that in America having a child say he needs his father would convey the stakes of the road trip immediately to an audience,"[67] said Simon Phillips, the director.

Priscilla opened at Broadway's Palace Theatre on 20 March 2011. *The New York Times'* Charles Isherwood wrote, "While it is performed with gleaming verve and infusions of bawdy humor – Tony Sheldon, who has been with the show from its Australian debut, is particularly winning as the gracious-lady transsexual Bernadette – Priscilla feels monotonous and mechanical... Like Priscilla the bus, *Priscilla* the musical moves in fits and starts under Simon Phillips' direction, trundling along as a series of interchangeable, aggressively rambunctious dance routines interspersed with catfights and scenes of moist sentiment in which bonds are forged and secrets revealed. (The choreography by Ross Coleman is mostly uninspired music video-style callisthenics.) It doesn't help that the songs are often awkward fits for the dramatic situation."[68] The Broadway production lasted 526 performances.

"I do know we're capable of producing work that can stand up in an international landscape", director Gale Edwards told Will Conyers. "I lament the fact that we have to be told that something's been a big hit on Broadway or the West End before we quite trust it. I think money is a big problem in getting shows produced. For a country the size that we are, and cities as big as Melbourne and Sydney, there are fewer commercial producers than there should be, and therefore fewer opportunities because fewer shows get done. I think we have some of the best musical talent – musical performers, particularly – in the world... but they're largely unemployed... I long for a time when musical theatre really comes to the fore... because I think musical theatre's terribly important and often looked down upon for all the wrong reasons."[69]

The Hatpin, with music by Peter Rutherford and book and lyrics by James Millar received its world premiere on 27 February 2008 at the Seymour Centre in Sydney, produced by Neil Gooding. It told the horrifyingly true story of a home for orphans in which the charges were murdered by their supposed guardians. Neil Litchfield in

Stage Whispers wrote, "It's premature to say step aside *Les Miz*, but Australia's 19th century downtrodden get their turn at musicalisation in this show. *The Hatpin* was quite riveting, despite some musical and dramatic unevenness, not unexpected in a brand new work. Occasionally, the score was only solid, but it also reached genuine heights."[70]

"I went to one of the first workshops of it when it was in its purest form, and it was the Australian *Sweeney Todd*," says Tony Sheldon. "I mean, you just sat there going, 'This is a knockout!' I went to a meeting at a leading Australian theatre company the next day, [talking to] somebody that had been there. I said 'Wasn't that the most thrilling experience?' and they said, 'Yeah, pity it's never going to get on'. My heart dropped to my boots because I knew that these people were just looking at the economic viability of putting on a dark show like this. Anyway, the show was then workshopped considerably over the next two years and I watched it get worse and worse with every successive reading. It was like, 'You've got to have a big number to close act one' or 'We need an up tune here'. Suddenly the show became this little bastardised piece. I don't like the current version of *The Hatpin*, and the one that opened commercially starring Caroline O'Connor – all my friends whom I trust said, 'Oh, God, it was a hard night to get through. It was really boring'. Well, that's not the show I saw two years [earlier] in its purest form when it should have been allowed to just go on then without anybody tampering with it. It came from the writer's heart, and they knew of what they wrote at the time, and then they listened to far too many people."

Peter Cousens (1955-), who appeared in the original production, says "Originally it was much more of a whodunnit, and you never really knew who, out of that family [committed the murders] but the way it was redone, it became reasonably obvious early on who were the culprits. It became a kind of a thriller, really, about how they were finally entrapped. You knew where you were heading as an audience." It was presented for six performances at the New York Musical Theatre Festival, but received a cool critical reception. David Finkle of Theatremania.com complained of "agitated melodic lines and... quasi-poetic lyrics"[71].

In 2006, Cousens launched a new company, Kookaburra, with the bold ambition to be "Australia's National Musical Theatre". Their offices were in Australian Hall, one of the former homes of the Phillip Street Revues. "The company is committed to the art form, and developing the art form", Cousens told me in November 2008. "What that means is not only developing new work, but it's developing audiences to be educated to what other sorts of musicals there are, and also giving opportunities to people who work in the industry in this country who usually get locked out of musicals because they're directed, produced, choreographed and designed overseas. Even the actors are basically told what to do, in terms of what an actor did in London and in America." This is a business that Cousens knows very well, having acted in franchised shows such as *Les Misérables*.

"As a company, it's never been about 'Australian musicals', whatever that is. The company is committed to the art form, and therefore the programming needs to come from anywhere that's good... We're about doing musicals that wouldn't necessarily be produced by commercial producers... We have to balance a way of doing work that is reasonably artistically motivated but also has an opportunity to support us in terms of being able to sell it."

One of their initiatives was to be called The Nest, a development programme for new works, managed by Clive Paget, former Associate Director of the Bridewell Theatre in London. There were also school tours of Stephen Schwartz's *Emperor's New Clothes* and Jason Robert Brown's *Songs for a New World*. When I met them in November 2008, they were developing a new educational show with Craig Christie, co-author of *Eurobeat*, an Australian show that enjoyed a summer run at London's Novello Theatre in 2008.

Cousens informed me that they had workshopped six works in 2008, with a view to taking one forward to production in 2009 – "as long as we can get it funded".

Alas, Kookaburra's initial offerings met with mixed results. *Pippin* was neither a commercial nor a critical success. "Audiences couldn't cope with *Pippin* because it was so out of left field", says Cousens. "It had a backpacker who blew himself up at the end. It had resonances with terrorism and all sorts of things."

Their second show, *Company*, was helmed by Australia's most internationally celebrated director of musicals, Gale Edwards. The opening at Sydney's Theatre Royal was attended by the show's composer Stephen Sondheim, and both reviews and box office were promising. But then, something happened that would haunt the company for the rest of its short existence. A couple of weeks into the run, actress Christie Whelan (1982-), who played the supporting role of April, came down with pneumonia. On this particular evening, one of the company's sponsors was in, and there was no room in the budget for understudies.

When contacted by telephone, Cousens decision was, rather than to cancel the performance, to simply cut the scenes and songs that Whelan was involved in. (This included the songs "Barcelona" and "You Could Drive a Person Crazy".) "I was trying to put a very positive spin on the fact that all was well [and] that nothing had gone on at the theatre that was a problem for the public to be made aware of,"[72] he told the *Sydney Morning Herald*. Unhappy with this decision, one member of the cast got in touch with the composer, who had not been consulted, and who demanded an immediate public apology, or else face the withdrawal of the rights for subsequent performances. The following evening's performance was cancelled while a replacement was found for Whelan.

The company issued a statement saying,

"Kookaburra celebrates the work of Stephen Sondheim and [book writer] George Furth and apologises for interfering with the integrity of their work".[73] Cousens told me, "With a five week run, the last thing you want is an understudy running around and paying for. Yes, we had an incident on *Company*, but it didn't affect the show."

Aaron Joyner says, "That was a sad day for the company and a sad day for Australia's theatre industry really, to have pissed off one of the art form's legends. It was not a great thing to happen, for a company that had made a big splash about being the saviour of the art form."

The story soon travelled around the world. In London, *The Stage*'s Mark Shenton described it as a decision "so dumb that it beggars belief"[74]. As a part of their settlement with Sondheim and Furth, they added a charity performance in aid of Oz Showbiz Cares and the Actors' Benevolent Fund.

Alas, the problems didn't end there. The company's next scheduled production, Adam Guettell's *Floyd Collins*, was cancelled due to poor ticket sales – "a disastrous piece of programming on my part", says Cousens. "It probably needed to be in a theatre that held a hundred people." A proposed Sydney transfer of the new Australian musical *Sideshow Alley*, which had opened in Brisbane, was also cancelled. "*Sideshow Alley* is a wonderful Australian musical," Cousens told *The Australian*, "but we want to protect it from the crowded 2008 season."[75] A co-production with the Really Useful Group of Andrew Lloyd Webber and Don Black's *Tell Me on a Sunday* received tepid reviews, and while their production of the American musical *Little Women* (which I saw) was well received, it lost money.

Sadly, Australia's recession-ridden economy could not sustain them, and several major sponsors pulled out. While they did receive some emergency funding from the New South Wales government, they subsisted largely – in

Cousens own words – on "a wing and a prayer and an overdraft." In late December 2008 – one month after I met Cousens – Kookaburra's staff was laid off, and Artistic Producer Peter Ross accepted a job with another company.

The musical theatre community were hardly sympathetic. One comment from a former theatre critic dismissed Kookaburra as "a time whose idea never came."[76] Another said, "Kookaburra shits in its own gum tree /cutting songs and scenes from "Comp-any" /laugh everybody, laugh everybody, dull our lives must be!"[77]

David Spicer in *Stage Whispers* feels that Kookaburra lacked adequate financial oversight. Their administrative overhead and promotional budgets were, say industry sources, disproportionate to their potential revenue. "Who was monitoring Kookaburra and giving Peter Cousens guidance?... Is there any surprise that if you have a board of directors of a music theatre company filled with people who appear to have limited experience in music theatre that they are not going to be able to provide much assistance? Does Macquarie Bank [one of their sponsors] have a Board made up of people in the main with no merchant banking experience?"[78]

Why was the response from the musical theatre community so virulent? "I think it's very sad for a company that is announcing themselves as the country's national music theatre that in the first two years of programming they haven't staged an original Australian work", says Aaron Joyner. "And they did make the announcement to do so – *Sideshow Alley* – and unfortunately made another media announcement to say they were not going to do it, which I don't think gave much confidence to the form or to their programming choices."

Neil Gooding says, "I guess the lasting lesson out of Kookaburra is that producing theatre is risky, and that most companies are only a few programming decisions away from losing enough money to cease operating."

When it comes to getting sponsorship and government support, you first need both the chicken and the egg.

The scheduled-to-be-last production of their season, the off-Broadway hit *I Love You, You're Perfect, Now Change* was cancelled. The company collapsed, having amassed debts of A$1.6 million.

"Starting a musical theatre arts company in Sydney meant sailing uncharted waters", Cousens wrote in the *Sydney Morning Herald*. "Brisbane, even Melbourne, may have been easier. Sydney is a tough, parochial city determined to prove itself and terrified of failure. If you really walk on the world stage, the potential for failure is just part of the action."[79] However, one unnamed sponsor told the *Herald*, "It was great to see opportunities open up for performers, but no one seemed to make informed or inspired choices."[80]

Certainly, important lessons are to be learned from Kookaburra's experience, but one hopes that Cousen's original vision of a company "committed to developing the art form" will survive. Perhaps if the company had begun more modestly, worked in co-productions with established companies, and allowed itself to grow organically, it may have survived. That seems to be what Hayes Theatre Company is attempting to do.

Named in honour of Australian musical theatre legend Nancye Hayes, the Hayes Theatre Company was established in 2014 at the former Darlinghurst Theatre in Sydney with a revival of *Sweet Charity* that transferred to the the Sydney Opera House and toured the country. The company also manages New Musicals Australia, a development program that has so far given us three new musicals: *The Detective's Handbook* with book and lyrics by Ian Ferrington and music by Olga Solar, *Melba – A New Musical*, book & lyrics by Nicholas Christo, music by Johanns Luebbers, and *Evie May A Tivoli Story*, book and lyrics by Hugo Chiarella, music and lyrics by Naomi

Livingston.

When *Evie May* opened in October 2018, Deborah Jones in *the Australian* said, "Director Kate Champion draws emotionally complex performances from the impressive cast."[81] Cassie Tongue in *Time Out Sydney* said, "With a solid book and the biggest heart in the world, it's hard not to love the characters. There are moments that shine, notes that hang in the air like crystal."[82]

New Musicals Australia was actually established a couple of years before the Hayes by Kris Stewart (1974-) and Neil Gooding.

"When the Hayes was formed and we got that venue," says Gooding, "it seemed to make enormous sense to house that within the Hayes structure." He continues, "The Hayes is only one hundred eleven seats, but it's a very good room to develop in, and to do workshopping and to test productions in a smaller form. One thing Australia has never done well: we tend to throw musicals into 2,000 seat venues with nothing in between. Part of our brief with the Australia Council, which is our national funding body, is that we are committed to staging one if not two original Australian musicals a year at the Hayes and the aim of that is, we hope, that one of these is going to start transferring and become a bigger show."

"We have an open submission process", he continues. "We can receive somewhere between fifty to a hundred musicals per year. We have an industry panel of some of our most experienced directors, and writers and musical directors. We'll get some of them to assess and we'll get their feedback. From that it's short-listed to ten. And those ten works are given a little bit of money to come and present twenty consecutive minutes of their show."

What are the prerequisites for submissions?

"It has to have an original score. We don't accept jukebox

musicals. And it has to have an Australian writer. We can collaborate with international writers, but we're not accepting submissions from English writers and American writers unless they're collaborating with an Australian writer. And the third one is if they've based it on a film or a book they have to show us that they have the rights. We don't even put restrictions on cast size. If you're writing about thirty people, obviously that's not what we'll be able to stage at the Hayes, but still submit that show and then this is the version that will be reduced then should be allowed to grow into a bigger form when it needs to."

What lessons have they learned from the demise of Kookaburra, OzMade and the Pratt Prize?

"The other schemes that have been set up in Australia and disappeared are really a reminder about how under-resourced the development of musical theatre in Australia is. High energised individuals can set up schemes, and they can operate effectively for a period of time, but until organisations and schemes are better resourced, most of these programs have found it hard to have any consistency or longevity once the individual driving them has either moved on, or lost some of their drive. This is where I hope that Hayes Theatre Company and New Musicals Australia may break this trend. The aim is to have a succession plan in place, and enough resources to allow the organisation to continue and to attract great individuals and teams to run the organisation into the future."

In 1958, drama critic Bruce Grant said, "The important fact is not the success in London or the failure in New York but the first success in Australia… the important thing now is to get plays on and to get Australian people to see them."[83] Like their Canadian cousins, the Australian creative community are ready. They just need to bring the Australian public with them.

Africa: Freedom is Coming

One of the questions often asked in creating a new musical is, "What are the stakes?" With whom is Laurie going to go to the box social – the nice guy or the sociopath? What if the stakes were higher?

Alan Jay Lerner once said, "It is highly unlikely that any spectator from the days of stone seats to the present has ever learned anything from the theatre. He may experience the entire lexicon of emotions; be tickled to laughter or moved to tears; be stimulated, mystified or exalted by the grandeur of language. But leave the theatre genuinely intellectually changed? Never."[1] But what if theatre was the only avenue of communication open to you?

Nelson Mandela said that "music is one of the best methods of communication, reaching, as it does, people who attend no meetings, read no newspapers, and whose only interest in TV and radio [is] no more than entertainment."[2] In South Africa, music and theatre are credited with helping to bring down the apartheid regime.

Western-style music was first introduced to South Africa by European missionaries, but this quickly became intertwined with indigenous folk rythms and harmonies. This and the introduction of the gramophone led to the spread of American jazz with a distinctly African flavour. In the 1920s, a Lesotho-born school teacher named Griffiths Motsieloa, who studied at Trinity College of Music in London, led a series of variety ensembles including the Pitch Black Follies. He also acted as a talent scout and producer for Gallo Records.

In 1940 the Anglican Bishop Trevor Huddleston (1913-98) arrived in Sophiatown, a black suburb of Johannsburg where he became active in the anti-apartheid movement in a place where murders and beatings rivaled those of Chicago in the days of Al Capone. Anthony

Sampson, former editor of *Drum* writes, "In its crowded and narrow streets walked philosophers and gangsters, musicians and pickpockets, short-story writers and businessmen. Sophiatown embodied all that was best and worst of African life in towns."[3]

Huddleston encouraged the cultural development of the area, and arranged for one young student — Hugh Masekela (1939-2018) — to receive the gift of a trumpet from the legendary Louis Armstrong.

In 1952, with Bishop Huddleston's encouragement, the Union of Southern African Artists was formed, according to critic Lewis Nkosi, to fuse "African native talent with European discipline and technique."[4] Its founding fathers included Alf Herbert, Solomon Linda and Ian Bernhardt. At first it was greeted with suspicion by the community, who thought it might be just another money-making project. However, this led to a series of Township Jazz concerts that included such luminaries as Yehudi Menuhin (1916-99) and Johnny Dankworth (1927-2010) performing before black audiences.

In 1953, Huddleston presented a concert to raise money to build a community swimming pool. On the bill was a choral work called "Makhalipile" ("The Dauntless One", Huddleston's African nickname) by a composer named Todd Tozama Matshikiza (1921-68).

Human rights lawyer-turned-novelist Harry Bloom (1913-81), future step-father of actor Orlando Bloom and author of the British Authors Club Award winning novel *Episode*, became involved with Union Artists after receiving a letter from New York folk singer Pete Seeger (1919-2014) in 1954 trying to track down a songwriter and musician named Solomon Linda (1909-62). One of Motsieloa's talent discoveries, Linda had recorded an improvised song in 1939 called "Mbube" (or, "The Lion") for which he was paid just £5. Seeger's group The Weavers had recorded a version of Mbube retitled Wimoweh (because they misheard the actual word being chanted, "uyimbube", which means "you are the lion").

They wanted to pay him $1,000 for the use of the song, correctly believing that he would get nothing from the publisher. "[Linda] turned out to be an old man, illiterate and simple," says Bloom, "with snuff boxes stuck in his pierced ear-lobes, and rough shoes cut out of an old tyre – very different from the suave type I had been expecting. But, as I discovered afterwards, he was a big name in the world of African music."[5]

A few years later, "Mbube" went through yet another transformation, becoming the basis for the American pop song, "The Lion Sleeps Tonight".[6] Because South Africa did not have a copyright agreement with the United States, Linda was not paid the royalties he was due, and in fact died unaware that he had written a hit. Only some forty years later were his heirs able to rectify this injustice.

Leadership of Union Artists soon passed to a young advertising consultant with an interest in show business named Ian Ephriam Bernhardt (1930-94), who produced an all black version of *A Comedy of Errors*. According to Bloom, "He not only built it into a powerful force in the South African entertainment field (one achievement, for example, was to persuade the British Actors and Musicians Union[7] to insist on their membership playing to audiences of all races when touring South Africa); but he brought African music and musicians out of obscurity, and... into the view of the whole world."[8]

In 1956, they commissioned Matshikiza to write *Uxolo*, a major work for choir and brass band (because they didn't have access to a full orchestra).

Todd Matshikiza was born to Samuel Bokwe Matshikiza and Grace Ngqoyi Matshikiza. His father was a church organist and his mother a noted soprano. Growing up in a musical family, he received his diploma in music at Adams College in Natal, but also took a teaching diploma at Lovedale Institute, where he later taught English and Mathematics. While his main love was for jazz, he also developed an appreciation for Bach, Beethoven, Mozart and Chopin.

Bloom and Matshikiza were looking for a subject for an "African opera". It was English writer Wolf Mankowitz (1924-98), book writer of *Pickwick* who first planted the suggestion of turning the life of the then-recently deceased black South African boxer Ezekiel "King Kong" Dhlamini (1921-57) into a musical. King Kong, who was reputed to have taken his name from a movie poster, had been convicted of murder, but became a folk hero for his defiance of white rule. Having killed his girlfriend in a jealous rage, he begged the court to execute him. Instead, he was sentenced to twelve years hard labour, but he drowned himself (some say he was murdered[9]) after only two weeks in prison. As the show's publicist Margot Bryant said, "He was a bully and a braggart... yet they cheered him. He brought colour, vitality and excitement into their lives."[10] "When I read of the trial of King Kong", Bloom wrote in the programme, "I saw that here was the story I had been waiting for."

Jazz musician and journalist Todd Matshikiza was a "small, dapper man with a wonderfully bright smile that wrinkled his entire face"[11], according to Mona Glasser (1928-2001), musical director Stanley "Spike" Glasser (1926-2018)'s wife. As a reporter for a black newspaper called *Golden City Post* he had covered the trial of King Kong. According to his son, actor and journalist John Matshikiza (1954-2008), Todd "came up against Kong's gangster cronies and rivals in the black underworld. These guys, naturally, didn't wish to have the details of their intrigues, as unfolded in court, exposed to the public through the newspapers. So they unceremoniously kidnapped the scribe, relieved him of his notebook, which they burned in front of him, and told him to keep his nose out of things he knew nothing about."[12]

"I saw King Kong one day coming out of court, coming down the steps surrounded by thugs", says Todd Matshikiza. "He looked big... He suggested *big* musical sounds. King Kong walked like he meant to dig holes in the pavement... heavy, falling. As I remembered how he looked, I just went up to the piano and played his theme song – the music for him starts high and falls to a low note. I just sat down and played it and knew it was complete."[13]

"Music flowed from within", Mona Glasser continues, "and his varied experience enabled him to appreciate the struggles of King Kong, and to translate them into melody."[14]

Matshikiza was immersed in the jazz scene of the "shebeens" (speakeasys) of Sophiatown, where from the 1930s until the 1950s, a multiracial and multicultural music scene had been allowed to flourish, but which was by then facing demolition and forced removal by the government. From this vibrant scene, artists such as Hugh Masekela and Miriam Makeba (1932-2008) emerged, and the highly rhythmic Mbaqanga (Zulu for "cornmeal porridge") music was born of a fusion between American jazz and traditional African harmonies. (Both of these artists would figure in *King Kong*; Masekela as a musician and Makeba as an actress, and that show's eventual international success brought both of them to a new audience.)

At first, Bloom saw the show as a sort-of revue, with sketches interspersed with a guitar-playing calypso singer. He and composer Matshikiza were invited to use the studio of Clive Menell, (1931-96), a business executive with Anglovaal Group, and an amateur painter. He brought painter and architect Arthur Goldreich[15] (1929-2011) as a designer, and under Menell's influence the show grew from a revue into a full-blown musical.

Menell and his wife Irene (1932-) together drafted

the original outline of the script. This would then be developed by lyricist Pat Williams (1931-) because book writer Harry Bloom was away working in Cape Town. Bloom eventually completed the final draft, and received sole credit for the book, although much of Williams' work remains. (Matshikiza also made contributions to the lyrics.) Ian Bernhardt would later join as producer.

Nathan Mdledle (King Kong) with Miriam Makeba and Joe Mogotsi
Photo courtesy Percy Tucker

"Their indigenous movement is most virile and rhythmic, and their dance potential is magnificent," explained choreographer Arnold Dover (1914-97?) a Sheffield born dancer who immigrated to South Africa in 1936. "Unfortunately there is *no* training whatsoever, and this limits a choreographer tremeandously. One of the difficulties, of course, is that they are used to *ex tempore* expression."[16]

The director Leon Gluckman (1922-78) had worked in England as resident director at the Nottingham Rep, and as an actor at the Old Vic, having trained in the U.S. at Yale University and Pasadena Playhouse. Pat Williams describes him as "a handsome, charming and sensitive man with a brilliant theatrical track record and a prodigious talent as both actor and director."[17] Matshikiza's son John described Gluckman as "a wonderful, passionate and compassionate director".[18] Miriam Makeba, who played King Kong's love interest says, "In the theater, we do not have to call the director *'baas'* because he is white. (We call him 'boss' because he's the director!)"[19] According to impresario Percy Tucker (1928-), Gluckman "felt strongly that black and white would have a great deal to give each other if only they were free to do so".[20]

"In a musical," says Gluckman, "one can go for the big effect. The emphasis is on the visual concept rather than on the interpretation of a single line."²¹ Harry Bloom explains that "township people live in the idiom of musicals. There is nothing artificial about African people breaking into song or dance, or doing so in chorus. They sing when they are sad as well as when they are happy. Musicals are an old tradition of the European and American stage, but really they properly belong to the African."²²

Leon Gluckman was working under enormous restrictions due to the inexperience of the cast, most of whom had never been inside a theatre. Dialogue was limited by the actors' grasp of spoken English. One man, a boxer, felt that he should have been cast as Kong. "But you don't sing", he was told. "Neither did King Kong," came the boxer's reply. During rehearsals, when fights were staged, onlookers had to be stopped from stepping in to break them up, not understanding that it was all "make-believe". Gluckman says, "There was no time to sit back and seek fine interpretations. What was needed was not creativity but staying power."²³

While the script for *King Kong* was not explicitly a political statement, the fact of its existence certainly was. The creative team were highly aware that they were breaking the law simply by attempting to mix black and white, although John Matshikiza says the police "could never pin on the enterprise any real infringement of the country's myriad rules and regulations that could have put a stop to the whole thing."²⁴ Cultural anthropologist David Coplan of the University of the Witwatersrand writes, "Its creators consciously intended it to be a model of fruitful cooperation between blacks and whites in the international entertainment field and a direct challenge to apartheid."²⁵ For Hugh Masekela, this was "a new experience, a combination of talented people of different races working united in the creation of an exciting project."²⁶

Because he was working with so many people who were new to theatre, Leon Gluckman surrounded himself at the top with collaborators with whom he had worked before, including chief orchestrator Stanley Glasser, who would later head the music program at Goldsmiths, University of London[27]. Glasser, in turn, delegated some of the work to members of the band, including saxophonist Kippie Moeketsi (1925-83). "We sat with Glasser for a coupla months", says Moeketsi. "I think two months if I'm not wrong - arranging the score, at Dorkay [House, headquarters of Union Artists]. At times we would go to Glasser's home in Orange Grove or Yeoville, spend some nights there. Or, go back home in the early hours of the morning at about three o'clock - with a bottle of whisky! This was to keep stimulating us, let me put it that way."[28]

All of the creative team, except Matshikiza, were white and of those, all except Arnold Dover were Jewish. Working with a mostly white creative team would create a problem for Matshikiza. He said to set designer Arthur Goldreich, "Tell them to stop writing me in the register from the bottom, and having meetings without me although it's about my music."[29] They agreed, but the meetings often took place in hotels that were barred to blacks, and required evasion of house detectives. "They won't touch you", said Goldreich. "Harry will be there and he's a lawyer."

"Todd's disappointment and sadness had to do with the fact that the production team - of which he, ironically, was a vital part - had not allowed him, at the time the original production was being worked on, to participate in the orchestrating process", says his widow, Esmé Matshikiza. "Granted that he was not formally trained in orchestrating but he could at least have been allowed to make comment or to offer advice. This at one time led him to consider withdrawing his music from the production but he was ultimately persuaded not to do so."[30]

"Every night I dreamed I was surrounded by pale-skinned, blue veined people who changed at random from humans to gargoyles", Matshikiza wrote in his memoir.

"I dreamed I lay at the bottom of a bottomless pit. They stood above me, all around, with long, sharpened steel straws that they put to your head and the brain matter seeped up the straws like lemonade up a playful child's thirsty picnic straw. I screamed, yelled myself out of the nightmare, and fell off my bed each night I saw the brain straws. I dreamed Black names were entered from the bottom of the register and White names from the top. And when a black man told a white man to go to hell, there was no hell. And when a white man told a black man to go to hell, the black man did go to hell... I am on the brink of a nervous collapse because I have been watching my music go from black to white to purple"[31].

Charl-Johan Lingenfelder, who restored the arrangements for a 2017 revival, says "Todd was unhappy with the beefed up arrangements that were done for the London season. The producers and creatives knew they were going to go head to head with all the new big shows in London – which included the original *West Side Story*. So a decision was made to expand on the sound of the show and also include more traditional material which they thought an audience would want to hear."[32] Actually, according to his widow, he was unhappy with the original South African version as well. Esmé Matshikiza says, "The London production only added insult to injury."[33] According to Pat Williams, "the final sound didn't have the depth and richness he had heard in his mind when he was writing his music."[34] Esmé Matshikiza says, "In my view, the producers of the revived version did a good job but their version was what was reflected by the producers of the original production."[35]

With a three-month rehearsal period – not a long time for a cast of sixty-three performers with little or no professional experience – Gluckman set about his near impossible task. Many of the actors were cooks, nannies, gardeners and delivery boys by day, while working as equals with their white creative team by night. Percy Tucker was one of those charged with arranging safe transport for them, delivering them back to their servant quarters. "I was much affected by this anomaly and could only guess at how the people concerned coped with their schizophrenic existence."[36]

On 2 February 1959, *King Kong* opened in Witwatersrand University Great Hall – one of the few venues where a "mixed" creative team would be permitted – on 2 February, 1959. The Johannsburg press responded enthusiastically. *The Star*'s Oliver Walker wrote that *King Kong* was his "greatest thrill in twenty years of South African theatregoing", while the *Sunday Express* said, "There is such boundless vitality in all the acting, the dancing and the mime that you will want to leap from your seats."

"What's it like to be in King Kong?" wrote Todd Matshikiza in the April 1959 issue of *Drum*. "'It's like dreaming all your life, one day I'll be important an' useful an' happy'. Suddenly that dream comes true, an' you're singing an' acting an' passing important ideas to over a thousand people in the University Great Hall, Johannsburg. The lights are bright, the handclaps loud. There are bow ties an' mink. Dresses posh, black an' pink. It's delirious but not dementing. But boyo, let's take a peep into the 'headaches' department. That's where you, the public, don' see what goes on worrisomely backstage."[37]

Pat Williams, the lyricist, kept it all in perspective: "Even though *King Kong* never totally met accepted professional standards for a musical, I doubt whether any of its shortcomings were even noticed on that triumphant night, and indeed were seldom noticed thereafter."[38]

The show became popular with black audiences, including a young Nelson Mandela, who saw it four times. Novelist, playwright and poet Lewis Nkosi wrote, "For so long, black and white artists had worked in watertight compartments, in complete isolation, with very little contact or cross-fertilization of ideas. Johanessburg seemed at the time to be on the verge of creating a new and exciting Bohemia."[39]

Percy Tucker's company Show Service handled the box office. "An unwelcome view of human nature was revealed by those customers who came to the box office and said, 'Of course, I'm not a racist, and I've got nothing against them, but I really don't want to sit next to a black person.' In those cases, I made sure whenever possible that they would be sitting next to a black person."[40] Leon Gluckman said, "Any white person who has seen the show will think twice now before he pushes an African out of the way on a street corner. It's not politics, but a question of human relations."[41]

Following a five-week run, *King Kong* then embarked on a South African tour, although the Pretoria city council refused permission for the show to play in the administrative capital, in spite of a press campaign, saying "Bantu things should be performed in Bantu areas".[42] Across the country, the show was seen by over 120,000 people, over two-thirds of whom were white.

Edward Stanley, 18th Earl of Derby (1918-94), an associate of London bandleader and impresario Jack Hylton (1892-1965) saw the show. In April, Hylton sent his right-hand man Hughie Charles (1907-95) (composer of "We'll Meet Again" and "There'll Always Be an England") to Johannsburg. A West End transfer was soon underway.

In February of 1960, Gluckman travelled to London to finalise arrangements. Uncertain as to whether the South African government would issue passports to the cast – they did, with the "encouragement" of anti-apartheid MP Helen Suzman (1917-2009) – he auditioned British-based black artists as a back-up. He also announced that the show would be re-worked for Anglo audiences, with some rewrites, new songs and traditional costumes. The actors were also sent for elocution lessons.

As the cast gathered at the airport for their departure on 7 February 1961, they burst into a chorus of "Nkosi Sikelel' iAfrika" (God Bless Africa), a then-banned hymn composed in 1897 by a teacher named Enoch Sontonga (1873-1905)[43] which had become the anthem of the freedom struggle and eventually would become the national anthem of a democratic South Africa.

King Kong was presented at the Princes (now Shaftesbury) Theatre in London, opening on February 23, 1961 for a run of more than eight months. Author Kurt Gänzl told me that "they couldn't sell the front rows of the stalls because of flying bodily fluids".[44]

According to John Matchikiza, the composer's son,

"The show was carried along by the music and lyrics, the staging, and the verve of the cast. But as theatrical storytelling it was cumbersome: a group of gossipy narrators, led by Gwigwi Mrwebi, had the task of repeatedly jump-starting the story in between sequences. The dialogue and characterisation that should have been the lifeblood of the play left much to be desired... It had as much to do with the exoticism of an all-black cast jiving their hearts out in the middle of London as with any artistic merit."[45]

The British critic Angus Wilson wrote, "The European applause was not patronage, the African applause was not partisanship, both were responding to the genuine laughs and thrills of a first-rate performance".[46] The *Times* wrote: "We come to realize in the course of the evening that this is a show to which strict standards of professional slickness cannot be applied. Stemming from an amateurish impulse and retaining most of its original character, *King Kong* must be taken on its own terms; and it is then very enjoyable. On any other terms there is much fault to be found... Against all these faults which American professionalism would be swift to remedy can be set virtues rare in the musical light theatre. The authors are so steeped in the special ways of life in the gang-ruled shantytowns of South Africa that the material may be said to infuse the style in which it is treated... They seem to be conditioned by the particular locality to which the characters belong; and it is perfectly easy to take what appear to us as stage clumsiness in our stride and to yield ourselves up to the rhythm and the vitality. Mostly the dances are frankly erotic..."[47]

Bernth Lindfors, Professor of English and African Literatures at the University of Texas at Austin, says the critics "yielded to the temptation to fasten on what seemed to be the crudest aspects of an animated performance."[48] Pat Williams claims that "Most people who had seen the Johannsburg production were a little disappointed by the London one."[49] Percy Tucker believes that its adaptation to English tastes "watered down the magic".[50] Compared to the later *Sarafina!*, *King Kong* sounds much more like the American jazz of Duke Ellington, although its African roots come out in some splendid a capella singing.

A thirteen year old musicals aficionado and *West Side Story* fan named Steven Demetre Georgiou whose parents owned a restaurant nearby, became one of the show's "groupies", seen frequently hanging around stage door. A decade later he would become known by the stage name Cat Stevens.

The programme carried a curious note saying, "In staging the production of *King Kong* in London, Jack Hylton has received every courtesy and co-operation from the Union Government and wishes to record his appreciation." This "courtesy and co-operation" was evidently lacking when book writer Harry Bloom was charged in Capetown with making a false statement while applying for a passport, although Bloom maintained, "I am here quite legally"[51]. In fact, many of the cast members and creative team would seek political asylum in Britain. (Makeba, who had already moved to the U.S., did not join the cast in London.)

A proposed Broadway production (rumoured to star Muhammad Ali) fell through. Half of the company chose to stay in Britain – for better or worse – and the rest headed back to South Africa on 7 December.

Unsurprisingly, the success of *King Kong* inspired a number of would-be successors. In 1960, the Sharpeville Massacre occurred, in which sixty-nine people were killed by police for protesting against the pass laws, sparking international outrage and leading to South Africa's expulsion from the Commonwealth. A little more than a week later, *Mkhumbane*, a three-act a capella musical opened at Durban City Hall on 29 March 1960 with a book by Alan Paton (1903-88), author of *Cry, the Beloved Country*, and with music by Todd Matshikiza. The next day the government declared a state of emergency. The story of the musical focused on the forced removal of black people from Cato Manor. Of the play, David Coplan in *In Township Tonight* says: "Though production difficulties, police harassment and mixed reviews combined to allow *Mkhumbane* only a short run, its particular uses of theme and musical dramatics made it an important forerunner of the popular working-class township theatre of the 1970s."[52]

"It is impossible to overstate either the impact or the significance of *King Kong* in apartheid South Africa of the period", says Tucker. "It gave dignity to the black population of the country and brought recognition of black talent. For white theatregoers it was an eye-opener, and for the theatre itself, a triumphant vindication of the efforts to promote its development and widen its horizons."[53] Pat Williams says, "One or two reviewers, while liking it, felt that the political edge they were hoping for was lacking…

Having lived in a freer society themselves, they didn't understand that *King Kong*'s very existence was a political statement in itself."[54]

Todd Matshikiza settled in London in 1960, where he tried to break into the jazz scene. He contributed a column to *The Drum* called "Todd in London". In 1964, he moved to Zambia where he worked for the Zambian Broadcasting Corporation, but he still felt oppressed in his ability to express himself musically. In 1967, he became music archivist for the Zambian Information Service, where he was able to travel extensively to build up their collections. He died there in 1968. His son John became an actor and his grand-daughter Lindi is now a theatre actress and director.

Ian Bernhardt had long planned a revival, and in the mid-seventies Pat Williams teamed up with playwright and director Fatima Dike to do revisions, but these were rejected sight unseen by the backers who wanted somebody with Broadway clout. It was finally revived – unsuccessfully – in Johannsburg in 1979 by African American director Joe Walker (1935-2003), with ambitions of a Broadway transfer.

The music was "re-arranged" beyond recognition, prompting a threatened lawsuit by Todd Matshizia's widow Esmé. "To sit there and watch this insulting travesty of the original was a nightmare", says Tucker. "It was the only occasion when I rejoiced in a show's failure."[55] Irene Menell said that "the extraordinary distortion of the story, the music and the blatant ignorance of the real context, which was an urban and not a rural one at all, left us completely stunned."[56]

"The crux of the matter," said producer Ian Bernhardt, "is that Joe Walker failed to realize his grandeur ideas. He undoubtedly is a big talent, but in Johannsburg he was not amenable to reason and ultimately became impossible to deal with because he made production promises he was unable to fulfill."⁵⁷ (This was evidently compounded by the director's frequent drunkenness.)

The original creative team considered legal action to prevent the show's opening, but were persuaded that the show would sink under its own weight. They were right. Following Walker's departure, Bernhardt made attempts to salvage the show, even appointing a new director – Corney Mabaso (1934-2009) – but to no avail.

London-based, South Africa-born composer Frank Lazarus (*A Day in Hollywood/A Night in the Ukraine*) says, "*King Kong* was a real landmark in South African theatre and music... it was also a chink in the granite wall of South Africa's political situation."⁵⁸

In 2017, a much more successful revival was mounted by Eric Abraham at Cape Town's Fugard Theatre under the title *King Kong: Legend of a Boxer*. This was staged by English director Jonathan Munby (assisted by Mdu Kweyama) with musical direction by Charl-Johan Lingenfelder which attempted to restore the sound to something closer to what Todd Matshikiza had intended. They even managed to add a couple of "new" songs, based on audio recordings of Matshikiza supplied by his widow Esmé. The book was revised by William Nicholson, an English writer of South African descent who had also done the screen adaptation of *Sarafina*, another South African musical we will discuss later in this chapter.

The satirical revue *Wait a Minim!*⁵⁹ opened in Johannsburg on 17 January 1962 in a small theatre in a YMCA. Leon Gluckman had built this entertainment around the talents of two multi-instrumentalist brothers, Andrew (1936-) and Paul Tracey, whose father Dr. Hugh Tracey (1903-77) was an acknowledged expert on African music. Gluckman soon learned that, however versatile they may have been, they were not seasoned thespians, so he rounded out his cast by adding six more performers, including actor and comedian Kendrew Lascelles (1935-)

and English-born folk-singer Jeremy Taylor (1937-), who would provide most of the original songs.

The revue, which Percy Tucker describes as "a *mélange* of music, mime, song, satire, dance and general craziness"[60] was, at first, a sleeper. It was only when Taylor made a hit recording of one of the songs, "The Ballad of the Southern Suburbs" (or, "Ag, Pleez Deddy"), that the show took off.

"I really didn't think anybody could take exception to this", says Taylor.

> "I was teaching at a school in the southern suburbs of Johannsberg and I was entranced, enchanted really by the way they spoke English, so I wrote them a song… in their patois. It had some strange effects because a lot of people were offended, particularly the parents of some of them who said to me, [in a thick patois dialect] 'Listen, Mr. Taylor, our [boy] used to speak very nice English until he heard your bloody song.' The government didn't like it either because it was mixing the languages. They didn't want black and white to mix, but they didn't want English and Afrikaans to mix either. They wanted purity."[61]

> Ag pleez Deddy
> Won't you take us to the fun-fair
> We wanna have a ride on the bumper-cars
> We'll buy a stick of candy floss
> And eat it on the Octopus
> Then we'll take the rocket ship that goes to Mars[62]

It ran for seventeen weeks in Johannsburg before mounting a national tour. "At that time, we had no censor to pass on scripts", Gluckman told Rex Reed in 1966. "For every person in the government we angered, we pleased ten more. We always played to integrated houses. The blacks loved it as much as the whites… We didn't hide from anything."[63]

A sequel, *Minim Bili* (Nguni for "two") opened in April 1963, followed by *Minim Export*, which combined the best of the two. It was this version that transferred with its all white cast to the Fortune Theatre in London's West End on 10 April, 1964 under its original title, *Wait a Minim*.

The *Times* wrote: "Following the disappointments of *King Kong* and *The Blood Knot* [a play by Athol Fugard, also staged by Gluckman] one has learned to be wary of shows that arrive from South Africa loaded with the honours of their own country and heralded by the organs of British liberal opinion". Nevertheless, they concluded that *Wait a Minim* was "much the best of the lot"[64].

It played in London for two years before moving on to New York, where it enjoyed a run of 456 performances at the John Golden Theatre beginning in March, 1966. Stanley Kauffman wrote in the *New York Times*: "although it is sometimes unfunny and its topical satire is weak, *Wait a Minum* has a congenial spirit."[65] An excerpt from the revue was performed on the popular *Ed Sullivan Show* on March 20, 1966.

Gibson Kente (1932-2004), another Union Artists protégé, began his writing career with the township musical *Manana, the Jazz Prophet* in 1963. Percy Tucker calls him "a substantial force in building a theatre audience in the townships."[66] His next show, *Sikalo* came two years later and even became popular with white audiences. Most of his works centred around the shebeens and the characters who frequented them.

Although Kente eventually fell out of favour because his later works were deemed to be "counter-revolutionary", and most of his work had little direct impact on audiences outside of the South African townships, he trained a great number of black actors and writers, including Mbongeni Ngema, the creator of *Sarafina*.

In the early 1970s, composer Bertha Egnos (1913-2003) was approached by American singer Eartha Kitt who was performing in South Africa and wanted to use some

African music. She didn't use the songs that Egnos offered to her, but in 1973 they appeared on a concept album called *The Warrior*. This was later turned into the musical *Ipi-Tombi*, (sometimes called *Ipi Ntombi*, a corruption of the Zulu "iphi intombi", "where is the girl?") which told the story of a young black man who leaves his family to work in the mines of Johannsburg. The lyrics were by her daughter, Gail Lakier.

It opened initially in Perth, Western Australia, where the backer disappeared with their money. Back home in Johannsburg, Brian Brooke, whom Percy Tucker describes as "a man of immense charm, urbanity and good looks"[67], presented it in his own theatre, where it opened 31 March 1974, and played for three years. With a white creative team and an all-black cast, it was required to play before segregated audiences. Again, Percy Tucker's Computicket handled the box office. "It was impossible to run a colour check at the Computicket terminals, nor did we wish to. In addition, every visitor to Johannsburg rushed to buy tickets, and many locals didn't bother to check which performances were designated for which racial group. The result was a chaotic, illegal and thoroughly amicable breaking of the colour bar which, surprisingly, was ignored by the authorities."[68]

On 19 November 1975 it opened at Her Majesty's Theatre in London. *The Times* described it as, "all ulating leaps, steatopygous flourishes, and tableaux of warriors framed in russet skybroth silhouette... an evening of exotic escape."[69] The *Sunday Times* called it a "thrilling production, presented with a verve, an *éclat*, a technical brilliance, a richness of voice in the singing, an excitement and a precision in the dancing which I do not believe that even the best American musical could rival. It is a riot of colour and movement, yet it is as controlled as the changing of the Guard. Every member of the huge cast is superb."[70]

It ran for about four months. It would later tour Europe, the U.S. and Canada. In New York, it was greeted by anti-apartheid protests when it opened at the Harkness Theatre on 12 January 1977. *Time* magazine wrote that the dances "illustrate how close to nature some Africans apparently still are. The gestures, the rhythms and the sounds indicate an unbroken totemic relationship with animals... This is all done with an agility, grace and energy that is breathtaking."[71] It closed on 13 February.

In 1981 it returned to London for a one-month run at the Cambridge Theatre, and it has been revived many times, in revised forms, on its home turf. According to Mbongeni Ngema's biographer Laura Jones, these shows "were aimed at white audiences, with almost no appeal to the black communities in South Africa".[72]

In 1971, Welcome Msomi, founder of the Zulu Dance Theatre collaborated with Professor Elizabeth Sneddon of Natal University on a Zulu adaptation of *Macbeth* called *Umabatha*. This was invited to London's Aldwych Theatre in 1972 as part of a World Theatre Season organised by Sir Peter Daubeny (1921-75). The *Times* reported, "The effect is as stunning visually as it is to listen to: a mass of moving skins and weapons transforming separate members into a single indomitable animal, bent on celebration, joy, or killing, but unstoppable no matter what its objective."[73]

Kwazulu, another London export, began life as *Isintu*, created by Cocky Thlotothlamaje for Phoenix Players. Canadian producer Clarence Wilson redeveloped it as *Meropa* ("drums") and toured it to Japan and the Far East. Then it was restaged and expanded by Joan Brickhill-Burke and opened in Johannsburg on 3 December 1974 where it ran for three months. Finally, it was brought to the New London Theatre, where the title was changed to *Kwazulu*. (The earlier title was thought too similar to the name of Aristotle Onnasis' sister, Merop.) *The Times*' Irving Wardle said, "If the London stage must carry advertisements for South Africa, the job could hardly be done more plausibly than it is in this production... *Kwazulu* depicts the homelands as a tribal paradise where nothing disturbs the rhythm of man and nature and the only cloud in the sky is that of approaching locusts. The picture is unreal, but there is no denying that an atmosphere of unfaked happiness comes across."[74]

In 1994, when the first democratic elections were held in South Africa, a friend of mine, Dr. Theo Shippey, at the time the rector of the Cape Technikon in Capetown, told me that the country's first priority – ahead of housing and poverty – should be to promote education. *Sarafina!*, Mbongeni Ngema's 1987 musical, also says that education is the key to liberation. It tells the story of an inspiring teacher in a Soweto[75] high school and her relationship with her brightest pupil, Sarafina. At the time, the pro-apartheid government insisted that black pupils be educated in Afrikaans rather than in English. This provoked riots in which a number of students were killed by the security police. Through the course of the show, this teenage girl becomes radicalised through exposure to violence. To Ngema, liberation was now in the hands of children.

The music for *Sarafina* was written by Ngema in collaboration with exiled South African trumpeter Hugh Masekela, who saw this as an opportunity to return to his roots. "All the years I've been living [in the U.S.], I've never been able to get down with the real musical vernacular of the township", he told the *New York Times'* Robert Palmer in 1987. "This show has been a real opportunity for me to do the real thing, not the hybrid."[76]

For Ngema, it was important that his show be accessible to an international audience. "The important thing about life is that when someone says something in their language, you can understand it because the feeling comes before the word", he told Rina Minervini of Johannsburg's *Sunday Star*. "If someone says 'I love you', you will understand it in any language. Sometimes we get stuck in words and lose the feeling, because you want every word right, everything to be grammatically correct and in real life, people are not always correct."⁷⁷

Sarafina
©Ruphin Coudyzer FPPSA

Sarafina! originally opened 12 June 1987 at the Market Theatre of Johannsburg in what South African impresario Percy Tucker called, "an electrifying and unforgettable evening."⁷⁸ The Johannsburg *Sunday Times* reported that "at rehearsals, one could not help feeling the raw texture, colour and beat of the townships. *Sarafina!* vibrates with joy and energy."⁷⁹ It played for ten weeks before a pre-arranged transfer to the Lincoln Center's Mitzi E. Newhouse Theatre in New York, where it opened in October. In his review of the show for the *New York Times*, Frank Rich wrote: "So potent are the songs, the performers and Ndaba Mhlongo's hard driving band that one can usually tolerate Mr. Ngema's considerable sloppiness in other areas. As drama, *Sarafina!* is an attenuated, if well-meaning, grab-bag."⁸⁰ The *Christian Science Monitor*'s John Beaufort wrote: "*Sarafina...* throbs with an energy that reinforces the urgency of its message. The message, of course, is freedom."⁸¹

Then in February 1988, it moved to Broadway's Cort Theatre, where it settled in for the next two years and was nominated for five Tony Awards.

While in New York, discipline became a problem for the cast, according to Hugh Masekela. "They played their new stereo sets at peak volume with their doors open and their televisions turned up loud while they visited one another's rooms at night and raced up and down the corridors and emergency exits, banging on doors, talking and laughing aloud, screaming on the telephone when calling home, and generally partying all night. These were young kids, fresh from South Africa's troubled townships. Maintaining any kind of discipline was almost impossible."[82]

It then toured North America, and came to London's Hackney Empire in 1991. In 1992, white South African director Daryl James Roodt turned it into a film starring Whoopi Goldberg, and produced by Anant Singh.

Towards the end of the shoot, Singh called the entire cast and crew together to meet Nelson Mandela. The late Miriam Makeba, who was starring in the film, was called on to sing. She introduced the song as "My Beautiful Mother", but it was actually an adaptation of the old Sophie Tucker hit, "My Yiddishe Momma". The film was a massive hit on its home turf, but passed largely unnoticed elsewhere.

"The show contravenes every rule of the dramaturg's craft," wrote Wilborn Hampton in the *New York Times*. "For example, what is perhaps the most emotional scene in the show — the funeral of several classmates killed by riot police during a demonstration — comes toward the end of the first act. Ninety-nine directors out of 100 would put that moving scene at the end of the show. But in *Sarafina!*, the show, like life, goes on... It has been suggested that the rousing and evocative Mbaqanga music — the street music of South Africa's black townships — is what keeps people lining up for tickets... But that is only part of the reason the Cort Theater is sold out nearly every night. Perhaps the main reason the show strikes such a chord of unity with its audiences is the young men and women in the cast... When the cast scatters across the stage and up the aisles in the face of police submachine-gun fire and tear-gas canisters, the audience knows it is seeing young men and women who have actually faced bullets and groped through a fog of tear gas on a school playground."[83]

South African journalist Mark Gevisser wrote,

"One way or another, *Sarafina!* became the benchmark musical of the time... The play defines the way most Americans think about South Africa, and it defines the way most young black South Africans think about theatre... The pastiche of political anger and comic burlesque, fused into a form of struggle-minstrelsy, has become the almost inescapable formula for how to make black South African theatre: liberating in the possibilities of success it presents, oppressive in the limitations of style it imposes."[84]

Sarafina is now sometimes criticised for its sentimentality. "One thing the play was, was entertaining", says actor and director Jerry Mofokeng (1956-). "One thing it wasn't, was illuminating of the South African situation."[85]

However, seen in the context of its time, it had a very specific job to do. When his company arrived in New York in 1988 for the Lincoln Centre production, Ngema told his cast that they were ambassadors for the black people of South Africa, to tell a story that the newspapers either couldn't or wouldn't tell. It may appear to be sentimental because of their tendency to smile and laugh through adversity – simply because they know no better way of dealing with it. When asked how he wanted Americans to respond to the show, Ngema replied, "Racism is the problem of the whole world."[86]

When engaged in a struggle, never underestimate the importance of a cheerleader. "By singing a song... you bring a lot of confidence to the soldiers"[87], says freedom fighter Peter Dimba. Fellow activist and later Minister of Small Business Development Lindiwe Zulu (1958-) adds, "Even when we're dying, the feeling was that when people have died, if you mourn them for too long, it demoralises your spirit. So as a result, even when we used to go bury some of our comrades who had been ambushed along the way, we never used to cry. We used to sing."[88] When activist and musician Vuyisile Mini (1920-64) was hanged in 1964, he went to the gallows singing.

In fact, South African musicals provide a unique challenge to Western audiences. In African culture, people really do break into song in real life situations. The challenge in playing to international audiences is that the Africans do not feel the need to justify singing psychologically in the way that, say, American or British creators do. To some, this creates a feeling of awkwardness or naiveté. On the other hand, perhaps Western writers could learn lessons from this apparent ease in musicalising their emotions.

Ngema's background couldn't be further from that of a conventional musical theatre writer. He was born in Verulam, near Durban in 1955. According to his biographer, "While the conventions of European drama and spectacle existed completely outside of Ngema's orbit, he was exposed from the earliest possible age to a form of theater directly related to the dramatic enactments presented at the courts of the great Zulu kings before the undoing of the sovereignty – a pageantry both solemn and joyous, in which he took part every weekend until he was ten years old."[89]

While English director Peter Brook (1925-) and Polish director Jerzy Grotowski (1933-99) were important influences, the musicals of Mbongeni Ngema exist almost entirely without reference to the American/European conventions of musical theatre. "In an American musical like *Fiddler on the Roof*" writes former Lincoln Center Director of Special Projects Laura Jones, "each musical number advances the story or defines some aspect of the character singing the lead vocal. But the structure that supports *Sarafina!* is based on rules of musical composition, orchestration and harmony, and not on Aristotle's *Poetics* or any concept of the 'well-made play'. Each song is an abstract, spiritual expression, arising organically, as songs do in South African life, out of group experience and feeling. The audience becomes intimately involved with the characters moving about before them, living onstage for nearly three hours, displaying every shade of pathos and humor."[90] (This approach is not unheard of in American musicals: see *Godspell*.) To say that *Sarafina!* is primitive is not in any way derogatory. Singing and dancing as an act of defiance is musical theatre in its purest and most heightened form.

Ngema ran into a problem when in 2004 he mounted a revival to celebrate ten years of South African democracy. "The first time I did *Sarafina*, I didn't have to explain anything," he told the *Boston Globe*'s John Donnelly. "The kids experienced it first-hand. But these kids in this new production didn't have a clue about what it was like. I ask them, 'Do you know what a state of emergency is?' They say no. I tell them what it means, and you see their faces change and their eyes open."[91]

A 1996 sequel, *Sarafina 2*, attempted to deal with the AIDS crisis, but was aborted with the loss of its entire 14 million Rand budget (over $3 million US), which had been supplied by the South African health ministry. Health commissioner Dr. Nkosazana Zuma allegedly used funding from the European Union that had been earmarked to combat aids to commission the new show from Ngema, bypassing the State Tender Board. Money also allegedly changed hands even before the contracts were signed. On top of this, the actual depiction of AIDS was highly inaccurate. "It was a genuine scandal", says theatre historian Professor Michael Simpson. "Funds were misused, and for a show with low-paid inexperienced performers, it was unbelievably expensive, and with little to show for all the expenditure."[92]

In 2008, Ngema was in the spotlight again when he was commissioned by the Mpumalanga provincial government to create *Lion of the East*, a musical which celebrated the life of African National Congress activist Gert Sibande (1907-87), who led a successful boycott of potato farmers. Defending its enormous 22 million Rand budget, Ngema told the *Mail & Guardian*, "Like all great musicals, like *The Lion King*, I'm taking you to a world standard... There will be a large cast, a big set, costumes, sophisticated lighting, everything will be done on that large scale."⁹³ However, the artistic director of Grahamstown's National Arts Festival, Ismail Mahomed maintains that the same amount of money "would keep a number of festivals running for a number of years and create work for thousands of people... this level of miscalculation and mismanagement is standard operating procedure there."⁹⁴ This kind of carelessness seems to have been rife; in 2008 a play commissioned by the Department of Human Settlements from TV personality Mpho Tsedu also cost R22 million before being cancelled after only sixty performances.

Kat and the Kings told the story of a mixed-race singer in 1950s Capetown, loosely based on the memoirs of Salie Daniels (who appeared as narrator), with book and lyrics by David Kramer (1951-) and music by Taliep Petersen (1950-2006). It opened in London in 1998 where it won the Laurence Olivier award for Best Musical, then transferred to the Cort Theatre (the same Broadway house where *Sarafina!* had moved a decade earlier) the following year. While the *New York Times* praised the cast's talent, "Yet for all their innate appeal and exuberant energy, there is a sense that they are as confined as genies in bottles, hemmed in by the formulaic cartoonishness of the show in which they appear. And by the evening's end, their exertion in trying to turn period pastiche songs into showstoppers is so visible that you find yourself sweating in sympathy. Talent of this caliber should never have to go begging."⁹⁵ Sadly, Petersen was murdered by burglars in 2006.

Two women who had toured in *Ipi Tombi*, Todd Twala and Thembi Nyandeni, formed their own dance company called *Baobab* (after an African tree that grows robustly in spite of difficult conditions). This eventually evolved into *Umoja*, a show that opened at London's Shaftesbury Theatre on 15 November 2001. The *Daily Mail* found it "totally irresistible", while the *Times* said it "exudes a sincere populist commerciality that is hard not to like", and the *Guardian* called it "A breath of fresh air".

Umoja was forced to close on 6 February 2002 because of noise complaints from neighbouring flats. It returned in the summer to the Queens Theatre for a two-month run, and was back in London again the following year at the New London.

This was not the last time *Umoja* would find itself in trouble. A five-month Canadian tour was curtailed because of complaints from the promoter of irresponsible behaviour by cast members. "Many people come to watch this show because they want to learn more about Africa", co-creator Thembi Nyandeni told South Africa's *Saturday Argus*, "and it is embarrassing when these cast members are falling down drunk on stage — they are an embarrassment to our entire nation."[96]

More recently, it is *Impempe Yomlingo*, an African re-interpretation of Mozart's *The Magic Flute* that has impressed London audiences. It was an Englishman living in Capetown, Mark Dornford-May (1955-), who assembled a cast drawn from the townships, schooled, not in opera but in church singing. The music was adapted for an all percussion ensemble, including specially designed marimbas and African drums. It was two South African expatriates, Eric Abraham and David Lan (1952-) who backed the project. Lan was the artistic director of London's Young Vic, and Abraham a film producer whose credits included *Birthday Girl* (starring Nicole Kidman) and the television series *Dalziel and Pascoe*. The Queen of the Night was played by the director's wife, Pauline Malefane.

The *Independent* declared, "This updating of *The*

Magic Flute to South Africa offers such a miraculous glimpse into a possible musical future that it's hard to watch without a lump in the throat. It speaks directly out of the townships, yet it's entirely true to Mozart."[97] It's that "possible musical future" that I'll be watching for.

It transferred to the Duke of York in February 2008 for a strictly limited two-month engagement. Then it toured to the Tokyo International Forum.

Lwanda, Man of Stone is a 2004 musical theatre piece by leading Kenyan pop musician Eric Wainaina (1973-), a graduate of the Berklee College of Music in Boston. He followed that up in 2007 with *Mo Faya*, first staged at the GoDown Arts Centre in Nairobi, Kenya, directed by John Sibi-Okumu. In 2009 it travelled to the New York Musical Theatre Festival. In 2016 he wrote *Tinga-Tinga Tales* with Claudia Lloyd and Sheba Hirst. In 2017 he established a working relationship with the Tisch School's Graduate Musical Theatre Writing Program, and *Tinga-Tinga Tales* was presented at the New Victory Theatre in New York in 2018.

Although Egypt is an ancient country and the Greeks brought theatre to the Ptolemaic Kingdom, the Arabs were more interested in philosophy and medicine than they were in drama, and so theatre in its modern sense only arrived in the late nineteenth century. One of the earliest creators of an Egyptian operetta is believed to have been Yaqub Rafail Sanu (1839-1912) (also known as James Sanua), a multi-linguist who is considered to be the father of Egyptian theatre and satire. Having studied the works of Carlo Goldoni (1707-93), Molière (Jean-Baptiste Poquelin, 1622-73) and Richard Brinsley Sheridan (1751-1816), he wrote a piece that *may* have been called *Lu'bat Râstûr wa Sheykh al-Balad wa al-Qawwâs* – in about 1870. I say *may* have as details about the show are sketchy: it has been described variously as an operetta or a vaudeville and appears to have used existing songs; it played in one act and in colloquial Egyptian.

Aside from the author's memoirs, there is scant documentary evidence that it ever existed. It may not have, but it seems more likely that censors destroyed all trace of it. Based on Sanu's memoir, Iraqi-American Historian Matti Moosa (1924-2014) provides a description of the opening at the Azbakiyya Garden Theatre:

> "More than three thousand people – Egyptians, European visitors and residents, the Khedive [Ottoman governor]'s retenue and members of the foreign diplomatic corps – gathered to watch the novelty, an operetta in the Arabic language. The hall was packed with spectators, most of whom remained standing, when Sanu and his company faced an audience for the first time... Collecting his courage, Sanu introduced the actors, briefly explained the benefits of the theater... Sanu asked the audience to bear in mind that this was the first experiment of an Arab troupe in Egypt. Apparently, the performance was so successful that the audience asked that it be repeated."[98]

A fierce critic of both Ottoman and British rule in Egypt, Sanu ended up in exile in Paris, and his operetta was banned.

In 1884, a Syrian playwright and composer named Abu Khalil Qabbani (1833-1902), who is regarded as the founder of Arabic operetta, arrived with his troupe, took up residence and performed in the Zizinya Theatre in Alexandria. They were so successful that they expanded, playing in Cairo and other towns until 1900, when his theatre was burned down and he retired to Damascus. He didn't actually create any new Egyptian works himself, but he certainly helped to create the demand for them.

It took a while for a tradition to be established. "The plays of al-Qabbani, like those of Marun Naqqash [Lebanese author, (1817-55)] and other nineteenth century playwrights, are history", says Matti Moosa. "They have no appeal to contemporary audiences in the Arab world, primarily because of their rhymed prose style and their ineptly manipulated plots."[99]

Sayed Darwish (1892–1923) is often described as the father of Egyptian music and one of the bards of the 1919 revolution. He began as a singer, then learned to play the oud (a lute-type stringed instrument) but soon came under the influence of Shaykh Salama Higâzî (1852-1917), a singer and pioneer of the Arab lyric theatre. He attached himself to the troupe of Naguib el-Rihani (1889-1949), the father of Egyptian comedy[100], for whom he wrote seven operettas. In what remained of his short life he composed *Al-Ashra Al-Tayeba* ("The Ten of Diamonds", 1920), an adaptation of *Bluebeard* with overtones of nationalism, *Kullaha Yumayn* ("A Matter of Days", 1920) written for singer and actress Munira El-Mahdiyya (1884-1965), *Scheherazade* (1921) and *Al-Balrouka* ("The Wig", 1921) which were – less successfully – staged by his own company. In total he wrote twenty-six musicals before his death at the age of thirty-one. He also wrote the music for what would become Egypt's national anthem, "Biladi Biladi".

According to Frédéric Lagrange, faculty member of the Sorbonne, "Darwîsh's stage production is often clearly westernized: the traditional takht[101] is replaced by an European ensemble... Most of his operetta tunes use musical modes compatible with the piano, even if some vocal sections use other intervals, and the singing techniques employed in those compositions reveal a fascination for Italian opera, naively imitated in a cascade of oriental melismas. The light ditties of the comical plays are, from a modern point of view, much more interesting than the great opera-style arias."[102]

"Sayed Darwish is *the* seminal figure in Egyptian musical theatre history", says translator and Cairo University lecturer Sarah Enany. "It is impossible to speak of it without including him." Although his work was not accepted by the musical establishment in his time, according to *Al-Ahram Weekly*, his operettas and other works "scaled the depths and breadths of the Egyptian identity... many contend that his music was the first purely Egyptian contribution to the Arabic canon, drawn as it was from the sounds and rhythms of the streets and their inhabitants. His dream was to cross the Mediterranean to Italy, learn classical music and compose a homegrown opera."[103] At the time of his death, he had begun an opera, *Cleopatra and Mark Anthony*, which would be produced posthumously in 1927.

Egypt also began to produce movie musicals, beginning in 1932 with *Onshoudat el fou'âd* ("Song of the Heart"), which was among the first Egyptian sound films. Music was by Neguib Nahas and the script by Khalil Motran (1872-1949), Edmond Nahas and Estafan Rosti (1891-1964). It was directed by Rosti and Mario Volpe (1894-1968), both Italians. Because Egypt did not yet have sound recording equipment, the soundtrack had to be recorded at Gaumont in France at great expense. It was not considered a success, and is believed to be lost.

Because the directors of *Onshoudat el fou'âd* were not born in Egypt, *Al-Warda al-Baida* ("The White Rose") which came the following year is sometimes named as the first true Egyptian film musical. This was one of the first films to poke satirical fun at Egypt's upper classes. It was written and directed by Mohammed Karim (1896–1972), who had also directed Egypt's first (non-musical) sound film, *Awlad al-Thawat* ("Sons of Thieves") in 1932. The songs were by Mohamed Abdel Wahab (1901–1991) who also stars. Abdel Wahab would compose the national anthems of Libya, Tunisia and the United Arab Emirates as well as composing eight French-influenced musical films between 1933 and 1949. Translator Mark L. Levinson describes Abdel Wahab as having "invented the Arabic film musical".[104] He was one of the first to bring Western instrumentation into Arabic popular music. According to Linda Mokdad, Visiting Assistant Professor at Michigan State University, he "borrowed from European art music while discovering ways to make Arab music more compatible with it, thus gaining fame for modernising Egyptian songs."[105] This was his film acting debut, in a story loosely inspired by his own life, in which a young man desperately looking for work ends up in a relationship with his employer's daughter. At the point where he is deciding to pursue a music career, he is seen looking at portraits of various Egyptian musical figures, including Sayed Darwish.

Abdel Wahab also contributed the songs for 1949's *Ghazal al-banat* ("The Flirtation of Girls"). The film tells of an older Arabic teacher, played by Naguib el-Rihani, who is hired to help an attractive young woman to pass her exams. Although he is falling for her, he soon realises that he must let her go, making way for a younger suiter. It was directed by Anwar Wagdi (1904–1955) and co-written, with longtime collaborator Badie' Khayri (1893 – 1966), by its leading actor Naguib el-Rihani, the same man who had, many years earlier, engaged Sayed Darwish as a composer. El-Rihani was educated at a French school in Cairo and was noted for integrating aspects of the French boulevard into his Egyptian work.[106] Like El-Rihani, Mohamed Abdel Wahab was greatly influenced by the French. This would be the last film for both of them: el-Rihani was to die before the film's release, and Wahab would largely devote the rest of his life to patriotic music.

Wagdi also directed *Dahab* in 1953, co-written by Wagdi with Abo El Seoud El Ebiary (1910-69) and with music by Bayram al-Tunisi (1893-1961), Mounir Mourad (1922-81) (Wagdi's brother-in-law) and Ezzat El Gahely. The story tells of a poor street musician, played by Wagdi, who discovers an abandoned baby and raises her as his own. As a ten year old, the child is played by Fayruz (Perouz Artin Kalfayan, 1943-2016), a powerhouse who is considered to be Egypt's answer to Shirley Temple.

Ayyam wa layali ("Days and Nights") (1955),

directed by Henri Antoine Barakat (1914-97) and produced by Mohamed Abdel Wahab with music by and starring Abdel Halim Hafez (1929-77), concerns a woman who leaves her alchoholic husband and raises her son with a rich man and his son. As they grow up, the two sons find themselves in love with the same woman. Tragedy ensues.

Kull daqqa fi qalbi ("Every Beat of my Heart") (1959), directed by Ahmed Diaa Eddine (1912-76) with music by Mohamed Fawzi (1918-66), stars Samiya Gamal (1924-94) as a dancer who meets and falls in love with an aspiring singer, but complications ensue when a rival tries to frame the singer.

Mahmoud Reda (1930-) had no formal training as a dancer, but was an Olympic gymnast who incorporated dance into his athletic routines. He created his first choreography for the operetta *Ya ain, ya lail* ("Oh Eye, Oh Night") in 1957. At the time, dance was equated with prostitution in Egypt, so he replaced the overtly sexual with a more subtle and athletic approach (for example, sanitising the belly dance). A fan of Hollywood musicals, and especially of Fred Astaire and Gene Kelly, his work was part of the nascent nationalism that came with the revolutionary republican government of Gamal Abdel Nasser (1918-70). His older brother (and fellow dancer) Aly Reda wrote and directed *Gharam fi al-Karnak* ("Love in Karnak"), to tell the fictionalised story of the founding of their company Firqah Reda, Egypt's first professional folk-dance troupe. Music was by Ali Ismail, who also composed for their stage shows.

Youssef Chahine (1926-2008) directed *Al-massir* ("Destiny") (1997) about the medieval philosopher Averroes (1126-98) in then-Islamic Spain who dedicated his life to preserving the works of Socrates, Aristotle and other Greek scholars at a time when Europe was in the throes of enforced ignorance. Music was by Yehia El Mougy and Kamal El Tawil.

In more recent years, stage musicals have been advanced, against all odds, by a small cadre of dedicated fanatics. "It does not give you any good revenue", says composer Ibrahim Maurice. "We don't have here the thing that people can pay a lot of money in a ticket to go and watch a musical. If you want to make such a production you have to put [up] a lot of money. Also the producers... If they have this amount of money they would go to put it or invest in soap operas, in movies with famous actors. They put one million, and in a couple of months, they have against it four/five millions and quick money. So that's why the business of musical theater isn't a good investment in Egypt from the producer side and from the audience side."[107]

In recent years, a school has been established to teach both opera and musical theatre. "Fabrica" is the brainchild of renowned soprano Neveen Allouba. They have performed shows ranging from *Les Misérables* to *The Magic Flute* in Sarah Enany's translations into colloquial Egyptian Arabic (as opposed to classical Arabic) as a way of bringing opera and musical theatre to a popular audience. Allouba studied Opera Performance and Vocal Pedagogy at the Hochschule fur Music and Theater in Hannover, Germany. "In over two decades of teaching singing, I realised that there is a lot of potential among young Egyptians," she says. "Only very few have the ability to pursue singing by studying abroad, a few depend on the Trinity Guildhall or London's Royal College of Music curriculums and exams in Egypt. What those young singers always need however is the actual chance to develop professionally and gain recognition inside Egypt."[108]

They produced *Les Misérables* in conjunction with the American University of Cairo. "Creating this musical within the university walls was a good option for many reasons. We needed someone to produce it, at minimal costs, and with a very basic set. We gathered music department students and other good voices at the university interested in joining the production, then we launched auditions which brought students from the German University in Cairo and Cairo University and other young people along." They even toured it to the United States in 2014. "Due to limited funds, we managed to take only twelve cast members with us to the USA and many actors had to play several roles. We performed in a few universities and schools across the country where we were very well received, particularly by the Egyptian community of Boston. It was also in Boston that we were joined by over 100 choir singers from the music department. In New York, we were hosted by a community theatre on Broadway, and we performed for 10 minutes at the opening ceremony of Vermont's new Senate season."

Next, in 2014 they revived what is considered to be a classic Egyptian musical: *El-Leila El-Kebira* ("The Grand Night") with book and lyrics by Salah Jahin (1930-86) and music by Sayed Mekawy (1927-97). It was originally staged in the 1960s using puppets to depict the last night of the moulid (or celebration of the birthdate of the prophet Muhammad), in a humorous fashion, from the perspective of the food stall vendors, jugglers, clowns and circus performers. "I was looking for a musical theater piece that was typically Egyptian and that didn't need too much orchestra or dancing,"[109] said Allouba.

In April 2017, what was billed as the first ever Broadway style musical in Cairo opened at the 1,656 seat Marquee Theatre. *Leila* tells a love story in a sea-side town that is haunted by a witch. It was written and co-produced (with actress Mona Zaki) by Ibrahim Maurice, directed by Hani Afifi and choreographed by Dalia Farid Fadel. The score, played by the Nile Symphony Orchestra, combined elements of rock, jazz and hip-hop with Arabic music.

Maurice told *EniGma Magazine*, "While we are proud of our success and consider our run of five weeks on stage, a very good start for our first musical, we know there are things we can improve."[110] Finding qualified cast members in a city with very little tradition of Broadway-style musicals turned out to be a challenge. "While there were a few graduates of the Conservatoire, so many were young people from other professions, engineers, lawyers, etc... who were eager to enter this field."

The Hebrew word for musical is "mahazemer", a compound of the words "mahazeh" ("play") and "zemer" ("song"). Some claim the biblical "Song of Solomon" to be the first "mahazemer", claiming that it was written to be performed in front of an audience with musical accompaniment.

There is a great tradition of Jewish lyric theatre going back to Leone de' Sommi (1525-1590) and to the Yiddish theatre of Abraham Goldfaden (1840-1908). However, the first musical in the modern sense to actually come out of Israel was called *Manufactured in Eretz-Israel* (the title referred to the "buy local" policy then in effect) with book and lyrics by Emmanuel Harussi and music by Moshe Wilensky (1910-97). It was presented in 1935 by Hamatateh ("The Broom"), a satirical theatre company that was founded in 1928.

While there would be other attempts at creating new Israeli musicals, it was not until the 1950s-60s when the popularity of American imports really created a market for them. Giora Godik (1921-77) had already enjoyed some success with *My Fair Lady*, *The King and I*, *Man of La Mancha* and especially with *Fiddler on the Roof*, but he decided he wanted to do something home-grown.

In 1967, he engaged Dov Seltzer (1932-) to write the score for what remains the most successful Israeli musical of all time, *Kazablan*. Based on a 1954 play by Yigal Mossinzon (1917-94), it is a variation on *Romeo and Juliet*. In the show, Kazablan is the nick-name of a Sephardic Jew from Morrocco (he is named for his birthplace, Casablanca) who falls in love with Rachel, an Ashkenazic Jew from Europe. It has a book by Mossinzon and Yoel Silberg (1927-

2013) and lyrics by Haim Hefer (1925-2012), Amos Etinger and Dan Almagor (1935-). In its original production at the Alhambra Theatre in Tel-Aviv it played for 606 performances, lasting almost two years. It has been revived several times, most recently playing 350 performances at the Chamber Theatre beginning in 2014. It was also turned into an extremely successful film by Menahem Golan (1929-2014), who a few years previously had staged a Hebrew production of *The Fantasticks*.

Dov Seltzer has composed several other shows on his home territory, including *The Megileh* in 1966 based on a play by Shmuel Bunim and the song cycle *Songs of the Megileh* by lyricist Itzik Manger (1901-69) which in turn was based on the Scroll of Esther. This show broke an Israeli taboo against Yiddish in the theatre. Both Golda Meir and Teddy Kollek were among the audience. It played for 550 performances at home, and also played (as *The Megilla of Itzak Manger*) at the Golden Theatre in New York in 1968, where it ran for ninety performances. Richard Shepard in the *New York Times* called it "light as a quality matzoh ball and as sparkling as seltzer".[111]

In the same year, he also produced *Revisor* which is based on the classic play *The Inspector-General* by Nikolai Gogol (1809-52). The book was by Nissim Aloni and the lyrics by Haim Hefer.

In 1968, he and Hefer also wrote (with Godik producing) *I Like Mike* with a book by Yoel Silberg, based on a play by Aharon Meged (1920-2016) about the efforts of a middle-class Tel-Aviv family to marry off their daughter to a rich American. It ran for about a year at the Alhambra.

After making some disastrous miscalculations in business, Godik would flee Israel in debt and end up selling hot dogs for the rest of his life at Frankfurt station. "The collapse of Godik's empire profoundly affected Israeli producers", says lyricist Dan Almagor, who provided many of his Hebrew translations. "For years, no one dared consider staging a big musical."[112] It was not the end of original Israeli musical theatre. It was, however, the end of its golden age.

For many people – especially New Yorkers – their first impression of an Israeli musical might be a show that has never actually played in Israel. *To Live Another Summer, To Pass Another Winter* opened on Broadway at the Helen Hayes Theatre on 21 October 1971. Dov Seltzer, the composer, explains "*To Live Another Summer* is definitely not the most important musical of the Israeli stage. It was never played in Israel. It was conceived for the American public."[113] The book and lyrics of this revue were by the Polish-born Hayim Hefer, translated into English by David Paulsen. Music was by Seltzer, with additional music by David Krivoshei and Alexander Argov (1914-95), and additional music and lyrics by Naomi Shemer (1930-2004). It was directed by Jonaton Karmon (1932-), and tells the story of Israel becoming a nation.

Clive Barnes in the *New York Times* said it "has an endearing vitality and an enduring spirit. It is a simple musical garland of the old brave new world of Israel—a little wry, a little sentimental, a little joyous, a little nationalist, a little humorous and altogether gently life assertive. Even its propaganda has a certain selfmockery to it that only an Arab could hate."[114]

On the other hand, John Simon in the *New Yorker* claimed it was all secretly an Arab plot, saying: "What a Machievellian masterstroke it was to concoct a pseudo-Israeli musical out of the most revoltingly unmusical clichés, occasionally leavened with Levantine modalities, and lyrics that are so gruesomely simplistic as to give goose-pimples even to Mother Goose, plus, by way of a non-book, a slapped-together bunch of Jewish jokes culled from the sere leaves of an ancient Anti-Semite's Manual. To this were added rudimentary scenery and costumes ranging from bad to dismal."[115] And he goes on. It managed a run of 173 performances.

"Down South American Way" – Musical Theatre in Latin America

Whenever the English speaking musical theatre has attempted to represent Latin America on stage, it has veered from the kitsch stereotype of Carmen Miranda to a Jackie-Kennedy-with-claws called *Evita*. Neither image would appear to square with how Latinos see themselves. Given the cultural vibrancy of Brazil, Argentina, Peru, Cuba and Mexico, this seems inexplicable. Each one of those countries has a long musical theatre heritage of its own.

Although Broadway director and choreographer Graciela Daniele (1939-) is a native of Buenos Aires, Argentina's contributions to musical theatre may not be well known in the English-speaking world. The commercial theatres line Corrientes Avenue, with their own traditions dating back to the late eighteenth century, brought over by Spanish and Italian immigrants. One of the earliest was a "sainete" (lyric farce) entitled *El amor de la estanciera* ("The Love of the Rancher's Daughter", ca. 1787). Written by an anonymous author, it is Argentina's oldest piece of theatre. The Argentineans also developed their own localised form of the zarzuela, called the "zarzuela criolla" that lasted in popularity from the 1880s until the 1920s.

Some describe the Tango as the "anthem of the proletariat". It has been a popular feature of the English-speaking musical theatre since the 1950s, and has been celebrated in several Broadway revues, including *Tango Argentino*. What many people probably don't know is that the musical theatre of Buenos Aires is where the Tango first attained popularity. It has come full circle.

Tango is a cocktail of European and African music and dance forms brought to Argentina and Uruguay by immigrants in the nineteenth century. Some say that it is related to the Flamenco. Buenos Aires' earliest Tango, "Tomá, matte, che" by Santiago Ramos was first heard in a play called *El gaucho de Buenos Aires* at the Teatro de la Victoria in 1857. However, the real history of Argentine musical comedy begins when the zarzuela *Justicia Criolla* with a libretto by Ezequiel Soria (1873-1936) and music by Basque-born Antonio Reynoso Compuesto (1869-1912) opened at the Teatro Olimpico on 28 September 1897. It featured the famous Tango "Soy al rubio Pichinango".

After that followed a number of shows which integrated the Tango into their plots. "Many of the most famous Tangos were part of musical comedies," says Pablo Gorlero, a journalist with *La Nacion* and the author of *Historia de la Comedia Musical en la Argentina*, a comprehensive multi-part history of Argentine musical theatre. "In general, people don't know about that. But many famous Tangos like 'Los amores con las crisis', 'La muchachada del Centro', 'Adiós, Pampa mía' or 'Se dice de mí' are a little piece of a musical play. The particularity of many of those Tangos (such as the milongas[1]) is that each of them reflects a little story or situation."[2]

In 1926 came the first show in Buenos Aires to call itself a musical comedy, *Judía*, a romantic mystery set in Russia and starring Iris Marga, which opened at the Teatro Porteña on 8 July. The book and lyrics were by Ivo Pelay (1893-1959) and the music by the Italian-born Ermanno Andolfi (?-1940). That began a wave of shows with Tango, milonga, valsecito (waltz) and fox trot as the principal rhythms.

Composers and authors worked together to try to forge a distinct Argentine identity in the musical theatre, but over time these were eclipsed by the imports from Broadway and the West End. However, from the 1920s through to the early 1960s, Corrientes Avenue was illuminated by up to fifty home-grown productions a year which drew on many traditions – zarzuela, music hall, café-concert, revue, variety shows, operetta as well as foreign musicals.

One of the founding fathers of the Argentine musical was the playwright Ivo Pelay who wrote *La canción de los barrios* ("Song of the Streets", 1925). His musicals, many written with the composer Francisco Canaro (1888-1964), helped to popularise the Tango. Canaro's 1932 hit *La muchachada del Centro* ("The girl in the middle") ran for over nine hundred performances in two years at the National theatre. In 1957 he celebrated his Golden Tango jubilee with a spectacle at the Alvear Palace Hotel, *Tangolandia*.

Some of the other key figures of this time include composer and onetime actor Enrique Santos Discépolo (1901-51) whose Tango hits included "Que vachache" and "Esta noche me emborracho". Within days of its first performance, the latter song earned him notoriety for its lyrics: the title means "Tonight I'm getting drunk".

Así se ama en Sudamérica ("That's love in South America") which opened 29 March 1950 at the Teatro Presidente Alvear with a book and lyrics by Sixto Rios Pondal (1907-68) and Carlos Olivari (1902-55) and music by Bert Rosé and the Brothers Ábalos poked fun at foreign stereotypes of Latin America. Other titles from this period included *El otro yo de Marcela* ("The other face of Marcela"), *Luna de miel para tres* ("Honeymoon for three"), *Yo llevo el Tango en el alma* ("I've the Tango in my soul"), *La cumparsita*, *Rascacielos* ("Skyscraper") and *El Tango en París* ("Tango in Paris").

Buenos Aires even attracted expatriates. Turkish-born French composer Paul Misraki (1908-98), who had worked with such legendary singers as Sarah Vaughan and Josephine Baker, was a refugee from the German occupation of France in 1943 when he wrote *Si Eva se hubiese vestido* ("If Eva would be dressed") with Olivari and Pondal. It opened at the Teatro Astral on 7 July 1944.

However, in 1956, an American invasion began with an Argentine production of *Plain and Fancy* ("Simple y Maravilloso"), a Broadway hit from 1955 set in an Amish community with a book by Joseph Stein (1912-2010) and Will Glickman (1910-83) and a score by Albert Hague (1920-2001) and lyrics by Arnold B. Horwitt (1918-77), translated by Christopher Cooke Cotton and Gaiza Guillermo Paz. (Hague later became familiar to a younger audience in his role as music teacher Professor Shorofsky in the film and television series *Fame*.) This was followed over the years by *My Fair Lady*, *Kiss Me Kate*, *Fiddler on the Roof*, *Hello, Dolly!* and many others.

A few Argentine writers and composers were able to respond to this challenge with independent work. Composer Astor Piazzolla (1921-92), whose "Tango opera" *Maria de Buenos Aires* with a libretto by Horacio Ferrer (1933-2014) premiered on 8 May 1968 at the Planeta, was a Tango moderniser. Piazzolla had spent part of his youth in New York City, where he was exposed to both jazz and classical music. "He was a great innovator", says percussionist and artists' manager Guillermo Masutti. "Rhythmically he broke the **1**-2-3-4, **1**-2-3-4 etc... He wrote putting accents in some weak moments of the bars... in a sort of jazzy oriented rhythm, although he couldn't evade... accenting the first beat of each bar, such as jazz music has: jazz can evade falling on the 'one', Tango can't."[3]

In 1954 he moved to Paris to study under Nadia Boulanger. According to his memoirs, the legendary teacher looked at his manuscripts and told him, "It's very well written... Here you are like Stravinsky, like Bartók, like Ravel, but you know what happens? I can't find Piazzolla in this." Then she began to grill him about his private life. "I was ashamed to tell her that I was a Tango musician", he says. "Finally I said, 'I play in a *night club*'. I didn't want to say *cabaret*... Finally, I confessed and she asked me to play some bars of a Tango of my own. She suddenly opened her eyes, took my hand and told me, 'You idiot, *that's* Piazzolla!'"[4] (However, while Piazzolla is one of Argentina's greatest composers, and he did write one "tango opera", according to Masutti, "he was not a musical theatre composer".)

Like the European musicals, the Argentine scene suffered a loss of momentum under Fascism. The 1970s, during the military rule, marked a dark period in Argentine history, and the theatre suffered for it. *Hair*'s run was suspended shortly after opening, and the Teatro Argentino, where *Jesus Christ Superstar* was to open, was firebombed. New forms of alternative theatre began to spring up, including the café-concert, a form of cabaret. Pablo Gorlero describes it as "a small bar with a small stage, and a solo number. The same actor/actress made differents characters and little plays, generally with songs between them. The most notorius stars of the café-concert [are]: Nacha Guevara [(1940-)], Enrique Pinti [(1939-)], Carlos Perciavalle [(1941-)], Edda Díaz [(1942-)], Antonio Gasalla [(1941-)], Cecilia Rossetto [(1948-)] and 'La' Pavlovsky [(1941-)]."[5] There were other variations on this type of cabaret show. "Our 'varieté' is the synonym of vaudeville or burlesque or variety, in Europe and North America. The Revista Porteña was an adaptation of the brilliant French revue. I think they are siblings of the musical comedy."

By 1976, mainstream musicals with social or political comment were banned, until the restoration of democracy in the mid 1980s. "In the 80's the Argentinian musicals were about the freedom, the modernity, the oppression," says Gorlero. One of the results of the period of censorship was that Argentine theatre was cut off from much of its heritage. "A Berlin Wall was felt in Argentina [in] those years."

When people in the English speaking world think of musical theatre in Argentina, they probably will mention *Evita*, unaware that the Andrew Lloyd Webber – Tim Rice tuner has never been professionally staged there. Not that the subject is taboo – there are several Argentine-written shows about their notorious former first lady – but it seems that Buenos Aires audiences prefer to see their leaders with their own eyes rather than through foreign ones. "We considered Lloyd Webber's *Evita* as a fake history", says

Gorlero. According to him, when Tim Rice came to Buenos Aires, he spoke only to the upper class people who hated Peronism. According to Gorlero, "He didn't [do any] historical research about Evita."

Eva, el gran musical argentino opened at the Maipo Theatre in 1986 with a score by Alberto Favero (1944-)and a libretto by Pedro Orgambide (1929-2003), in collaboration with director and star Nacha Guevara (1940-), a veteran of Buenos Aires café-concerts, with a cast of twenty-one. Another unrelated version of Eva Perón's life appeared three years later: *Evita – Tango Popular Opera* (also known as *Evita - Volveré y seré millones* – "Evita - I'll come back and shall be millions") was written by composers Roberto Pansera (1932-2005) and Domingo Federico (1916-2000) with librettist Miguel Jubany (1938-).

Cuban-born lyricist José "Pepe" Cibrián Campoy (1948-)'s first musical, *Universexus* with music by Oscar Lopez Ruiz (1938-) was first presented at the Teatro Municipal Sarmiento on 22 June 1971. His breakthrough came seven years later when he was inspired to write *Aqui No Podemos Hacerlo!* ("You Can't Do That Here") after seeing *A Chorus Line* in London. It opened on 6 October 1978 after six months of workshops. Although they received a fifteen-minute standing ovation on opening night, the audiences were small until Daniel Lopez, critic for *La Opinion*, proclaimed it "the first major Argentine musical". The music was by Luis Maria Serra (1942-), and the choreography by Ana Itelman (1927-89), with Cibrián directing a cast that included Graciela Pal (1947-). His greatest successes would come after meeting a one-time piano salesman who called himself Angel Mahler (1960-).

Angel Pititto was born in Buenos Aires in 1960, and studied piano with Evi Swillinger and orchestration with Manolo Juárez (1937-). He adopted the surname of the noted Austrian composer Gustav Mahler as his stage name. In 1982, he met Cibrián, and together they wrote *Dracula*, a pop opera based on the Bram Stoker novel. It originally opened at Luna Park Arena in Buenos Aires on 29 August 1991. Australian composer and TV producer Peter Pinne saw a production in October 1997. "The show is very good, with accessible music, spectacular costumes, a large physical production, and in this version, the most wonderful voices... The set was mainly scaffolding, on several trucks, which were mounted on castors and moved around the stage to form various locales... I'm surprised no-one has translated it ... a la *Les Miz* because it has the same potential." It has toured nationally four times, as well as to Chile, Brazil, Uruguay and Barcelona, Spain. Their other works together have included *El Jorobado de Paris* ("The Hunchback of Paris") (1993) and *Caligula* (2002).

La Fiaca ("lazy") with book and lyrics by Ricardo Talesnik (1935-) and music by Gabriel Goldman was based on Talesnik's 1967 satirical play of the same name that was also made into a film by Fernando Ayala in 1969. The story concerns a worker who, bored by his daily routine, decides one day not to come in to work. He is declared "lazy", but is having what we would now understand to be a nervous breakdown. The musical was directed by Valeria Ambrosio. *Clarin*'s Olga Cosentino wrote that the music "speeds up the drama... to get a dramatic synthesis [at] times more potent than dialogue. And the music brings colour and volume to the description of a city that is both home and prison lair."6

Dracula
Photo courtesy of Angel Mahler

Playing the protagonist's wife was a young woman named Elena Roger (1974-) who would soon come to international attention when Andrew Lloyd Webber cast her in the title role in his revival of *Evita*, directed by Michael Grandage (1962-). Two years later, she won an Olivier award for her portrayal of *Piaf* at the Donmar Warehouse, a role that she repeated in 2009 at the Teatro Liceo in Buenos Aires and in Madrid in 2010. She began her career in 1995 in *El Jorobado de Paris II* ("The Hunchback of Paris II") and *Dracula*, both by Cibrian and Mahler. Other credits included playing Bess (Houdini's wife) in *Houdini, una ilusion musical* (2005) at the Metropolitan Theatre with book, music and lyrics by Gonzalo Demaria (1970-), and in the Argentine versions of *Les Misérables, Nine, Saturday Night Fever* and *Beauty and the Beast*. In 2003 she toured Europe in *Tango por Dos*.

Peter Pinne spent eight years in Santiago, Chile during the 1990s, where he was overseeing adaptations of Australian soap operas. A musical theatre writer himself, he managed to take in some of the local offerings.

> "The emphasis on classical music is huge. Fifty percent of the stock in any record store was classical. You would get into a taxi and find the drivers listening to classical music, and even my local supermarket had a string quartet playing in the foyer at Christmas. Opera is very popular, and some of the top singers in the world appear there. On the popular music front, they have a lot of rock bands, and cover bands (they play a lot of Beatles), and of course tours of Latin American pop stars. Buenos Aires is similar. They love opera. But I did see some shows like the Casino de Paris type of show there, headed by a local comic. They love farce, as do Peru. In Lima there is always some hugely

popular farce playing with local comics, most are known from TV, and they love dressing up in drag. So do the Argentinean performers."

La Pergola de las Flores ("The Framework of Flowers") with music and lyrics by Francisco Flores del Campo (1907-93) and book by Isidora Aguirre (1919-2011) opened at the Teatro de Ensayo at the Catholic University of Chile in April, 1960. The story was based on a true incident in which flower sellers appealed to the public to help them save the Pergola de San Francisco in the flower market of Mapocho in Santiago in 1929. It was written to commemorate the sesquicentennial of Chilean independence. Peter Pinne saw a revival in 1996. "The story gave ample scope for some stylish costumes, and the odd – if rather incongruous in the setting – Charleston routine... There was far too much book, not helped by expansive physical business, but the music was pleasant, particularly a first act duet by the young lovers."

Brazil has a long musical history and has exported many popular songs to the English speaking world. Now it is one of the world's fastest growing economies. As Reed Johnson wrote in the *Los Angeles Times*, "Perhaps in a country where irresistible rhythms are always pulsing somewhere and the interplay of tanned bodies along the Copacabana beach can seem as carefully choreographed as a Jerome Robbins ballet, the notion of people breaking into spontaneous song and dance doesn't appear all that far-fetched."[7] Like Argentina, some of this music started out in the musical theatre or the "teatro de revista" (cabaret revues).

On 13 June 1930, a revue called *É do Outro Mundo* opened at the Teatro Recreio in Rio de Janeiro. The music was by Ary Barroso (1903-64), the lyrics by noted cartoonist and illustrator José "J." Carlos (1884-1950), and the book by Margarida Max. Although it was well received critically, audiences didn't really take to it, and it closed within a matter of days. It would have been forgotten, except that a young samba composer named Lamartine Bablo (1904-63) saw the show and fell in love with one of Barroso's melodies, "Esse Mulato Val Sê Meu" ("This Mulato Val Be Mine"), although he detested Carlos' lyric. Evidently without the authors' permission, he wrote his own lyric with a new title, "No Ranch Fundo" ("No Ranch Fund"), which he presented on a radio show with Bando de Tangarás. It was first recorded in 1931 by Elisina Coelho, and went on to become a standard. Bablo and Barroso wrote many more hits together. On the other hand, José Carlos never forgave what he considered to be Barroso's betrayal.

Another song by Barosso would achieve even greater international fame. "Aquarela do Brasil" ("Watercolour of Brazil") also first appeared in a stage musical, *Entra na Faixa* ("Enter the Strip") with book by Luis Iglesias which opened on 10 June 1939 in Rio. Like "No Ranch Fundo", it was not an immediate hit. In fact it was only after it was included in a Walt Disney animated film *Saludos Amigos* that it became popular, becoming the first Brazilian song to be played over a million times on American radio in a recording by Xaviar Cugat. It even formed the musical inspiration for the 1985 Terry Gilliam film, *Brazil*.

Another leading Brazilian samba composer was Noel Rosa (1910-37), whose 1935 operettas *O barbeiro de Niterói* ("The barber of Niterói") and *Ladrão de Galinhas* ("Hen thief") written in collaboration with Arnald Gluckman were musical parodies of Rossini. He also contributed a number of songs to "chanchada"s, Brazil's own form of movie musical.

"Chanchada" was a somewhat derisive term coined by journalists to describe these cheaply made films. (Although the quality improved, the name stuck.) Radio stars were employed to tell backstage stories in a revue or carnival setting. One such film, *Alô, alô, Brasil!* (1935)

starred Carmen Miranda (1909-55). The military dictatorship that ruled for twenty years from 1965 – 1985 put a stop to the teatro de revista, and the chanchada declined in popularity. As in Argentina and Chile, it was on the fringe where those with the courage to stand up to the authorities flourished. Once democracy was restored, the public's appetite for light entertainment returned.

Like Argentina, Brazil has been dominated in recent years by the major Anglo/American blockbusters, mostly presented by the Mexican entertainment giant La Corporacion Interamericana de Entretenimiento. But they have also developed a few shows of their own.

Opera do Malandro, a salsa and jazz reworking by Chico Buarque (1944-) of Weill and Brecht's *Threepenny Opera* (itself a reworking of *The Beggar's Opera*) first opened in 1978, during the country's twenty year military dictatorship. (Buarque was an outspoken critic of the regime.) It was revived in a hit production in 2004.

South American Way, produced and directed by Miguel Falabella (1957-) in 2001 from a script by Falabella and Maria Carmen Borbosa (1947-), tells of Carmen Miranda's rise from the slums of Rio to Hollywood stardom. Although she has been the heroine of cross-dressers throughout the world, her image has not always been so popular on her home turf. "Lots of people here still think she was nothing but a caricature"[8], Falabella told the *New York Times*' Larry Rohter. For one thing, she was born in Portugal, and never did become a Brazilian citizen. But worst of all, Hollywood imposed a kind of Pan-American image on her that was more Mexican than Brazilian. "Brazilians don't always value their own culture," actor and singer Tuca Andrada (1964-) told *Newsweek International*'s Mac Margolis. "What's gratifying is discovering just how much Brazilians like Brazil."[9] The show ran for two years in Brazil and toured to Buenos Aires. It won a Shell Prize in 2002.

Although Brazil and Argentina have successfully exported both their music and their cinema (*Black Orpheus, City of God, The Official Story, Nine Queens, The Motorcycle Diaries*), no musical from either country has successfully penetrated the English speaking market – yet.

Peru can, however, lay claim to one of the most popular Latin American "show tunes" of all time – although it is not generally known as such. "El Cóndor Pasa" ("The Condor Goes by") is the wordless title theme from a zarzuela with music by ethnomusicologist Daniel Alomía Robles (1871-1942) and libretto by Julio Baudouin. Set in a mine in Cerro de Pasco, *El Cóndor Pasa* tells of the struggle between the native workers and their European bosses. The condor is used as a metaphor for freedom. It premiered at Teatro Mazzi located in Lima's Plaza Italia in 1913 and was performed over 3,000 times.[10] When Simon and Garfunkel recorded a version of the show's namesake finale in 1970, it was incorrectly credited as an eighteenth century Andean folk song. Shortly afterwards, film maker Armando Robles Godoy (1923-2010) – the composer's son – successfully sued to assert his father's copyright,[11] and subsequent reissues of the recording have corrected the error.

Lin-Manuel Miranda, the creator of *Hamilton*, has claimed that the "next big thing" may come from Mexico.[12] Jaime Lozano is a native of Monterrey, and has been a composer, musical director, orchestrator and vocal coach. Initially planning to study criminology, he earned his BFA in Music from the Universidad Autónoma de Nuevo León, and was the first Mexican to be accepted into the Tisch School's Graduate Musical Theatre Writing Program in New York.

Among his earlier works produced in his home country was *Tlatelolco* in Monterray in 2001, about an infamous government crackdown on a student protest in which hundreds of people were killed or wounded during the run-up to the 1968 Olympics in Mexico City. "It is a very Brechtian work, a monologue based on real testimonies. The scenography is very simple and is essentially based on the bodily work of the dance body and the projection of real photos and videos of the massacre."[13] This was revived twice: in 2002, and again in 2004.

Next came *Mitos Kamanalis* ("Myths"), which premiered in 2012. "It was a very interesting experiment because we are used to narrating a single story in a musical", he says. "*Mitos Kamanalis*, which I wrote with one of my lyricists in New York, Sara Cooper, is divided into three 20-30 minute acts based on three Jewish myths: Lilith, the first woman, Behemoth, mentioned in the book of Job and Golem, all three adapted to the Mexican context."[14] It has additional lyrics by Jorge Castilla.

Since attending the Tisch School, he has been based largely in New York, where he has presented *The Yellow Brick Road* with lyrics by Tommy Newman and book by Mando Alverado, and *Children of Salt*, presented at the New York Musical Festival in 2016 with book and lyrics by Lauren Epsenhart.

"The truth is that many times we believe that musical theater must necessarily be futile, light and with happy endings. We think that the form, the sequins of the costumes, the brightness of the scenery, and the content are more important. But it's not like that. The musical theater is a genre that allows [you] to tackle any subject."

What is it like to try to write musicals in Mexico?

"There is no economic support or infrastructure for local productions and many times those who stage musicals are very talented people but with little technical training... Very different from what happens here in the United States where people study and prepare for this genre. As for the public, those who attend the musicals want to see the most famous Broadway productions, which I call McDonald's productions because they are an exact copy of those presented in New York. At this moment *Lion King* is happening, and it is a great success. We say colloquially that Mexicans are 'malinchistas', referring to La Malinche, an indigenous woman who helped Hernán Cortés as a guide and interpreter during the conquest of Mexico. What they do abroad always seems better and we do not appreciate or value our culture and our intellectual productions."[15]

He explained to me, "There's not a lot of original musical theatre in Mexico. Producers and audience are more interested in the great blockbuster titles (*Phantom*, *Les Miz*, *Wicked*, *Lion King*, etc)."[16]

"I am convinced that an artist should be a mirror of the times she or he is living", he says. "I tell stories related [to] me and everything around me. Definitely everything I do is in some way dedicated to my country, to my city, to my people; because I'm telling our stories. My country and everything good or not good happening there is gonna be always a part of my storytelling. I can't run away from who I am and where I am from. And I am so proud to be Mexican and tell our stories."[17]

However, Mexico does have its own musical theatre heritage, whether or not its people are aware of it. Mexican zarzuelas date back to the productions of the sisters Genera and Romualda Moriones in the late nineteenth and early twentieth century, which included *El Rataplàn*, *La gatita blanca* and *Mi querido capitàn*. However, as historian and theatrical journalist Fabian Polanco points out, "the theatre of... zarzuela and operetta have no relation to the musical genre, since they were shows that consisted of several musical numbers and jokes that had no relationship between them, unlike the musical comedy that, as you know, is a story told with music and original songs."[18]

Later, Roberto "el Panzón" Soto (1888-1960) established a tradition of revues, including some of

Mexico's earliest political satire. Soto established an early revue, *Rayando el sol*, in which Leopoldo Cuatezón Beristain made what is thought to be the earliest political jokes. Mario Villanueva says, "On stage he was the synthesis of the astute, ignorant and stupid rancher."[19]

Like other countries, Mexico also produced film musicals. One of the earliest and most notable was *Allá en el Rancho Grande* ("Out on the Great Ranch") in 1936. Most of the music was by Lorenzo Barcelata (1898-1943), while the screenplay was by Antonio Guzmán Aguilera and Guz Aguila, from a novel by Luz Guzmán Aguilera de Arellano. It was directed by Fernando de Fuentes, who had previously directed *Vámonos con Pancho Villa*, and its success kickstarted a revival of a moribund Mexican film industry, leading to some twenty similar "canción ranchera"[20] musicals per year. *Allá en el Rancho Grande* is now regarded as Mexico's first movie classic.

Another film musical was *El Gran Casino* set in Tampico during the boom years of oil exploitation directed by the legendary Spaniard Luis Buñuel (1900-83) in 1947. This starred the Argentine ex-patriat Libertad Lamarque (1908-2000), who would also later star in such stage roles as *Hello, Dolly!* By this time, the Mexican film industry was at its peak.

Victimas del Pecado ("Victims of Sin"), a 1951 potboiler directed by Emilio Fernandez (1904-86), starred Ninón Sevilla (1929-2015) as a cabaret singer who discovers an abandoned baby and raises it as her own. The baby's criminal father then discovers her and makes her life a living hell. The music was by Antonio Díaz Conde (1914-76) and Víctor Cavalli Cisneros (1907-2000).

Other composers who worked in Mexican film musicals included Agustín Lara (1897-1970) and José Alfredo Jiménez (1926-73).

Most historians date the modern Mexican stage

musical to 1952, and *Ni Fu, ni fa* ("Okay, Nothing Special") produced by and starring Edmundo Mendosa and directed by the "official chronicler of Mexico City"[21], Salvador Novo (1904-74) at the Teatro Pardavé (formerly known as the Teatro Sullivan). It was written by Mendosa and co-star Beatriz Querol, and included a song called "el complejo de inferioridad" ("The Inferiority Complex") by Sergio Magaña.

"I was studying at the school of Fine Arts and at the Academia de la Danza Mexicans", recalls cast member Armando Pascual. "I received an invitation from Edmundo, who told me that he had a project together with Beatriz Querol – a very beautiful and talented actress who unfortunately committed suicide – to make a musical comedy very close to the original style of the genre and how it was done in the United States… *Ni fu ni fa* was the first musical comedy that was presented in Mexico. However, production was very poor and everything fell under the responsibility of Edmundo Mendoza… we were only in theatres for two weeks, mainly because, due to this shortage, there was no advertising and people did not attend the theatre,"[22] in spite of positive reviews.

The following year popular film comedian Mario "Cantinflas" Moreno (1911-93), best known in the English-speaking world for his supporting role in the film *Around the World in Eighty Days*, opened in *Yo Colón* ("I, Columbus") at the newly-built Teatro de los Insurgentes. Falling asleep at the base of the statue of Christopher Columbus in Mexico City's Paseo de la Reforma, he brings the statue to life, offering his comedic commentaries on contemporary Mexican society. "Each night, the jokes changed according to what happened in the country allowing the Mexican Mime to use their games of words and double meanings to attack politicians"[23], says Fabian Polanco.

The original idea was by J. Montes de Oca, with libretto by Alfredo Robledo and Carlos Leon and music by

Federico Ruiz (1889-1961). Actor and producer Miguel Ángel Morales says: "Cantinflas discovered and knew how to take advantage of the stage fright that invades all theatre people; that white grace, that entanglement with words, that much talking without saying anything, was what characterized him and differentiated him from the other comedians"[24]. Fabian Polanco says, "He has realized his dream of mounting a totally Mexican musical comedy similar, both technically and argumentative, to those presented in North America. It was represented with songs created deliberately for history, dances that supported congruently a plot sequence and that justified what was seen on stage and, thus, allowed the development of the characters and their story coherently and defying the musical conventions."[25]

Sergio Magaña, who contributed to *Ni Fu, ni fa*, also wrote *Rentas congeladas* ("Frozen Revenues") in 1960 which considered the problems of those living under rent control. Martha Rangel, who was in the cast, says "It was a very human work, a magnificent musical comedy, which is a pity that has not been revived because, truthfully, it's really worth it."[26] Actor Héctor Bonilla remembers the show: "I think that the more they reflect who we are and move us, they will have enormous success. That depends on having something in your hand to tell and tell it well."[27]

The majority of shows presented since then have been Spanish-language versions of popular Broadway or London shows, from *My Fair Lady* (in which a very young Plácido Domingo (1941-) understudied the role of Freddie Eynsford-Hill) to *Phantom of the Opera*, *Cats* and *Wicked*.

Actor Manolo Fábregas (1921-96) turned to producing in the late 1950s, and his successes included Spanish-language versions of *My Fair Lady, Hello, Dolly!, Man of La Mancha, No, No Nanette, They're Playing Our Song, Promises, Promises, Crazy for You* and the Italian musical *El Deluvio Que Viene* which ran for six years. Fabian Polanco says, "Manolo Fábregas was and is for many the best producer of musical theatre in Mexico."[28]

Like Fábregas, Silvia Pinal (1931-) was an actress on both stage and film who turned her talents to producing in 1958 with *Bells Are Ringing*. She later presented *A Chorus Line*, *Cats* and *La Cage Aux Folles*.

Julissa (Julia Isabel de Llano Macedo, 1944-) began her career in 1961 as the lead singer of a rock band called The Spitfires with her younger brother Luis de Llano Macedo (1945-). Her father was Luis de Llano Palmer, a television personality who also translated the lyrics for *My Fair Lady*, *The Fantasticks* and others. In the 1970s, she turned to producing Mexican versions of *Grease*, *Jesus Christ Supertar* and *Pippin*. Fabian Polanco says about *Grease*,

> "It was one of the first works mounted in our country that focused directly on the young public and that brought together in its cast youth figures of the time: Julissa, Benny Ibarra Sr., Adrian Ramos, Sylvia Pasquel, Rocio Banquells... The success was overwhelming among the young people of that time. Years later, the children of her followers saw it and, recently, the sons of the children and their followers did the same... what more could be asked? Thanks to the impulse of her mother, Rita Macedo, Julissa found her true passion in the theatre. Besides acting and singing, she ventured as a producer and became one of the main importers of the international theatre for Mexico City."[29]

Her son Benny Ibarra was a member of the pop band Timbiriche[30], which became the basis for a successful jukebox musical conceived by Pedro Damián and written by Martha Carrillo (1963-) and Cristina García (1958-).

Mexico has produced many of its own musical theatre stars, beginning with María Conesa (1892-1978), known as "La Gatita Blanca" ("The White Kitten") after her most famous Zarzuela role. She arrived in Mexico from her native Spain in 1901 and established a reputation as a playful dancer singing suggestive lyrics. According to

Fabian Polanco, her shows "addressed social and political issues, seasoned with good music and lyrics, costumes and dynamic choreography."³¹

Qué Plantón! ("What a sit-down!") by Memo Méndez, an ecological musical, was first presented in 1989 at the Teatro San Rafael and was revived two decades later at Telmex Cultural Center. The book and lyrics were written in collaboration with Maria del Campo. Méndez also created *Catalina Cruel*, also known as *Anjou, el sueño que si sucedió* ("Anjou, the dream that did happen") in 1992. Book and lyrics were written with Lupita Sandoval. This latter show was later presented at the New York Musical Festival in 2009.

El Retrato de Dorian Gray ("The Picture of Dorian Gray") opened on 13 January, 1997 at the 100 seat Centro Cultural Roldán Sandoval and ran for more than 200 performances. It was written by actor and composer Citlalixayotl (Sergio Citlalixayotl Orozco Lara) in collaboration with Agustin Morales Carbalho. It starred Citlalixayotl in addition to producer Fred Roldán, known as "Señor Teatro".

Peter Pinne saw this production.

> "It was surprising what they achieved on the pocket-handkerchief sized stage. My only problem with the piece was that the guy who played the lead was unattractive, which therefore defeated the story somewhat. There was no portrait, but a lit frame over red velvet. It was a very effective and imaginative way of conveying the aging of the portrait. The highlight of the second act was a sexual orgy, which wasn't done completely nude, but near enough to it... At the end of the show the lead talked to the audience for a while, and then they brought out a guy from backstage who spoke English and he came over to me and asked what I thought of the show... Fortunately I had a positive reaction and conveyed those feelings which seemed to please the audience because they gave me a round of applause."³²

It was revived twenty-one years later with its title shortened to *Dorian Gray*.

Citlalixayotl and Carbalho also wrote *Esos invertidos amores* ("Those inverted loves"), presented in 1999.

"I think theater is always in crisis," says José Manuel López Velarde, the writer and director of the '80s jukebox musical hit *Mentiras* ("Liars") which opened in 2009. It has played more than 600 performances to date in Mexico City and toured the country, with productions in Colombia, Panamá and Perú, making it one of the most successful Mexican musicals of all time, having been seen by more than a million people. The story concerns four women who are attending the funeral of a man that each was involved with. *Mentiras'* score was made up of 1980s Mexican pop hits and was produced at Teatro Mexico by Ocesa Teatro, a division of La Corporacion Interamericana de Entretenimiento, Latin America's largest entertainment conglomerate. "Making theatre is betting,"[33] says López Velarde.

For him, its success was a mixed blessing, as his fellow thespians were put off by its commercial success. "That medium is very elitist and does not forgive the success of the *Mentiras* type, which has a very personal theme, it speaks of something profound and important to me: identity!"[34]

Si Nos Dejan ("If they let us") was another jukebox musical of his with mariachi music which ran for 600 performances in Mexico with two seasons in Bogotá Colombia.

Now he runs his own theatre, Teatrería in the Roma area of Mexico City, which he opened with his own musical, *El último teatro del mundo* ("The last theater in the world"), with music by Iker Madrid. This show ran for four seasons in different theatres.

"As a director I learned that the theater is made from the accident that happens in the rehearsal", López Velarde says. "I thought it was as predesigned by me. Yes, there are many things that should be done, but what happens in the rehearsals and that the actor discovers, is something very rich to be taken advantage of, that come out of the error of the imagination, without leaving behind the professional side that the public deserves."[35]

More recently he has written the book and lyrics for *The Name of the Game* with music by Hannah Kohl which premiered in Mexico City in 2018. It follows five children as they travel beneath the earth in search of their identities, while deciding who - and what - they want to be. Funded by the Public Theater's New York Voices series, it brings together puppetry, song and storytelling as we "step away from what is expected and explore what is true".

Carmen Salinas (1939-) is a revue performer, actress and sometime politician who starred in *Aventurera* ("The Adventuress"), which opened in 1997, written by Carlos Olmos from the screenplay of the 1949 film written by Alvaro Custodio. *Aventurera* tells the story of a young girl namef Elena who is left alone when her mother runs off with another man and her father commits suicide. She eventually becomes a cabaret star, but not before complications ensue.

It ran for more than fifteen years, touring Mexico and even into New York and Los Angeles, where it played the seven thousand seat Nokia Theatre. According to Fabian Polanco, it "broke all the parameters since its premiere and will be remembered because it turned a musical into a product capable of filling auditoriums with more than twenty thousand people, either inside or outside the country."[36]

Even now, there is little in the way of formal musical theatre education in Mexico. "Actually I am the only Mexican who has... professional training [for] writing musical theatre," says Jaime Lozano, "and I'm trying to do my best to keep doing originals works down there besides my projects in the States."[37] According to director Rosa Alicia Delain, "In Mexico, we don't have a place where you can go and get a degree in musical theatre... You have to take dance, acting and voice lessons separately where you can find them, and there is no guarantee that you´ll get a good teacher."[38] As a result, Delain studied at the American Musical and Dramatic Academy in Los Angeles. After she returned to Mexico, "I founded a musical theatre school in Mexico City a few years back, Re-Crea Teatro. We can´t offer a degree there yet, but other grads and I give tons of master classes, workshops and classes to share a bit of what we know with the aspiring actors."

"Now it is a little easier to teach everything that surrounds the musical theatre, because there are already several schools in which we do musical theatre", says producer and choreographer Ana Maria Collado who, along with Oscar Acosta is a director of the Broadway Mexico Estudio academy. "Before, if we wanted to learn the discipline of musical theatre, we took ballet classes in one place, from jazz in another, and we did the same with acting and singing, so we combined all these things and applied them when we worked. We did it as we could."[39]

According to actor and director Jose Antonio Lopez Tercero, when people say to him "I do not like musical theatre because it seems absurd to me to sing or to dance to say things that can be expressed speaking, as we do in reality", he replies "Musical theatre is as absurd as painting an Expressionist or cubist painting, or making science fiction novels on themes and characters that cannot exist." He explains, "For more than a century we have had great artists and creatives of Opera, Zarzuela, Operetta, Revue and also, in recent decades, of musical theatre of the North American style, not only with the big hits of Broadway or London, but with original works that [are] close to our culture."[40]

I have asserted that the birth of modern musical theatre co-incided with the birth of or struggle towards democracy, and nowhere is this more evident – if nuanced – than in Cuba. Although they may never have enjoyed what we might call open democracy, the musical's earliest manifestations there were marked by the country's struggle for independence from Spain, and its later neo-colonial relationship with the United States.

Cuban popular music has long had a strong influence on music in the United States, Mexico, Argentina and elsewhere. Dances like the habanera and the bolero have made tracks both north and south since the nineteenth century, but popular musical theatre in Cuba actually goes back at least a century earlier.

While some theatrical performances date back to about 1730, Havana's first proper theatre (and its first wood and masonry building), the Coliseo, was opened in 1775, under the initiative of the Colonial Governor Field Marshall Felipe Fondesviela y Ondeano, Marqués de la Torré (1725-85) and designed by Antonio Fernández Trevejo. Thirty-two years later, the first-known Cuban opera was staged there, *América y Apollo* by an unknown composer but with libretto by Cuba's first poet, Manuel de Zequera (1764-1846), by which time the theatre had been renovated and renamed the Teatro Principal.

Francisco Covarrubias (1775-1850), known as the "caricaturist", is regarded as the father of Cuban theatre for his development of Teatro Bufo ("Theatre of Buffoons"), the name of which reflects the influence of Offenbach's Bouffe-Parisienes. This was a kind of comic musical revue with a veiled criticism of those in authority. Bufo included the "danzón" written in 2/4 time as a slow dance with a partner and syncopation, evolved from English and French folk roots brought to Havana by the Spaniards, combined with complex African cinquillo and tresillo patterns. It's now the country's official dance and its popularty is attributed to bandleader Miguel Faílde (1852-1921)⁴¹. The Bufo's other musical forms also included the guaracha with its rapid tempo and comical lyrics, and other semi-indigenous Cuban forms such as the rumba, the mambo and the son.

Bufo grew to include, among others, the stock characters "Negrito" (a little black person, played by a white actor in blackface), a roguish character who generally ridiculed the greedy "Gallego" (a native of Galacia), "Mulata" (a person of mixed race), a flirt who would also take advantage of Gallego and "Guajiro", a poor white farmer.

All of Cuban culture seems to have been informed by its multi-ethnic, multi-racial make-up, which in turn drove its impetus toward independence and "liberation".

In the early days, African slaves or those descended from them comprised a majority of the Cuban population, and so the elite, both middle and upper class, lived in fear of them. In order to justify their privilege, the Spanish elite deemed the black populace to be of low intelligence and inferior moral character. "Playwrights depicted *negritos* as ignorant, laughable, childlike, something less than human", says Robin Moore, professor of Ethnomusicology at the University of Texas at Austin, and editor of the *Latin American Music Review*. "Even in the 1880s and beyond, authors ascribed lust, greed and other base motivations to most of their black and mix-raced characters... However, some blackface stage plays simultaneously contained other messages of a more populist sort. The *teatro bufo*'s use of local character types, local forms of speech, and uniquely Cuban music and dance resonated with the public in the 1860s and beyond as they begun struggling for an end to Spanish rule."⁴²

Any satire had to be subtle, and did not always successfully evade the authorities. In fact, Bufo was banned for nine years after an 1869 incident at the Teatro Villanueva in which some audience members shouted out "Viva Cuba Libre!" and other pro-independence slogans, provoking a response from the pro-colonial volunteer military force in the vicinity. In the resulting mêlée, several people were killed. Among those present was future Zarzuela composer Raimundo Valenzuela.

Following its introduction to Cuba in 1853, Zarzuela also evolved into a commentary on Cuban politics and social life, although it tended to appeal to a largely conservative clientele.

In 1890,[43] the Alhambra Theatre opened at the corner of Consulado and Virtudes in Havana, and by 1900, under the direction of Regino López (1861-1945), it began what would become a thirty-five year reign of bufo and zarzuela. One of the impresarios behind it was the journalist, librettist and comedian Federico Villoch (1868-1954), who with composer Raimundo Valenzuela (1848-1905) wrote the Zarzuela *La mulata María* in 1896. After a long run and many successes, the Alhambra closed in 1935 after a bomb apparently caused its roof to collapse.[44]

Building on the farcical tradition of an earlier Spanish form known as the sainete (literally, "titbit"), some other Cuban composers at the Alhambra included Jorge Anckermann (1877-1941) whose zarzuelas and bufos *La isla de cotorras* ("The Island of Parrots"), *Un bolero en la noche* ("A Bolero at Night"), *El quitrín, Flor de Yumuri* ("Flower of Yumuri") and *El arroyo que murmura* ("The Babbling Brook") inaugurated a new form known as the Guajira, a model that was adopted by other Cuban zarzuela composers. Unlike Spanish zarzuelas, the Cuban variety tended to have tragic endings.

Others included *La Virgen Morena* with music by Eliseo Grenet (1893-1950) and libretto by Aurelio Gutiérrez Riancho which opened 30 November 1928 at Teatro Regina, and *Cecilia Valdés* with music by Gonzalo Roig (1890-1970) and libretto by Agustin Rodriguez and José Sánchez-Arcilla, based on a novel by Cirillo Villaverde (1812-94) about love and revenge in early 19th century Cuba which premiered at Teatro Marti in 1932. As in South Africa, as an outlet for satire, both Zarzuela and Bufa are believed by some to have played small parts in various Cuban revolutions.

The Teatro Martí, the "theatre of a hundred doors" (in reference to the many French windows that adorn its exterior), is a Romanesque style building. First opened in 1884 as Teatro Irijoa, in 1900 it was renamed after Cuban poet and patriot José Martí (1853-95), author of what would become the original words to the Cuban revolutionary song "Guantánamera" ("Woman from Guantánamo"), with music attributed to Joseito Fernández (1908-79). It became the home to many zarzuelas and bufos, and was restored in 2014 after four decades of dereliction.

One of the song hits to emerge from Cuba in the 1920s was "El Manisero" ("The Peanut Vendor"), a "son pregón" (a song based on a street vendor's cry) by composer Moisés Simons (1888-1945). This song was sung in Spanish by Rita Montaner (1900-58) and in English by Antonio Machin (1903-77), the first million-selling record for a Cuban artist. It was also performed by Louis Armstrong and Duke Ellington, and decades later an excerpt was sung by Judy Garland in the film *A Star is Born*. In addition to the zarzuelas Simons created in his native Cuba, he was also a success in Spain and in France.

Ernesto Lecuona (1895-1963), possibly the most internationally known of Cuba's theatrical composers, wrote his first piece of music – a two-step for military bands – at the age of eleven. He studied in Paris under Maurice Ravel. Because he elevated popular music to classical status, he is often referred to as the Cuban George Gershwin. (In fact, he and Gershwin became good friends, and the latter evidently thought that Lecuona's interpretation of "Rhapsody in Blue" was among the best.)

He was prolific: on one occasion, he is said to have written four hits songs in one evening. Some songs were translated into English and became North American hits. For example, "Dame tus dos Rosas" became "Two Hearts That Pass in the Night", a hit for Guy Lombardo (1902-77). His music was also championed by fellow Cuban Desi Arnaz (1917-86).

His zarzuelas included *La Niña Rita* ("Young Rita"), written with Eliseo Grenet and produced at the Teatro Marti in 1927 and *María de la O* with a libretto by Gustavo Sanchez Galarraga (1893–1934) which premiered in 1930. The latter was unofficially inspired by the same source material as *Cecilia Valdés*.

Set in Havana during the 19th century, the plot of *María de la O* concerns a free mulata woman named Maria who is pursued by men of different social and racial backgrounds, leading to a tragic conclusion. An English translation was presented in 2010 by Chamber Opera Chicago, whose Artistic Director Barbara Landis says, "When I first heard the music, I was utterly seduced by it! ... The melodies are so rhapsodic and sensuous, and they sit atop an Afro-Cuban beat. Some of the songs sound like Gershwin... very Fred Astaire-Ginger Rogers. There also are dramatic numbers straight out of grand opera."[45]

He wrote eleven film scores for MGM and Warner Brothers, one of which included a song nominated for a 1942 Academy Award, "Always in My Heart" ("Siempre en mi Corazón"), from the American film of the same title. Alas, it lost to Irving Berlin's "White Christmas".

Lecuona had been made cultural-attaché to the Cuban embassy in the US by Cuban dictator Fulgencio Batista (1901-73) in 1943, and so when Fidel Castro (1926-2016) overthrew Batista, Lecuona left Cuba for the US and apparently vowed never to perform again until Cuba was free. He died three years later, and while he is buried in

New York State, his will dictates that his remains will be transferred back to Cuba once the Castro regime is gone.

The 1953 staging of Lecuona's decade-old work *Rapsodia Negra* ("Black Rhapsody"), employing unique Afro-Cuban instruments, was choreographed by another figure who would make his mark on Cuban musical theatre, Alberto Alonso (1917-2007), who had previously danced in the US for George Balanchine (1904-83) and Jerome Robbins (1918-98).

In 1963 the Teatro Musical de la Habana emerged on the site of the Alhambra with an objective to create "a Cuban musical theatre that breaks with the canons established by traditional North American musical theatre; that is, a musical theatre that in some way reflects the idiosyncratic and sociological character of the Cuban people."[46]

Among their productions under artistic director Alberto Alonso, was a 1964 Spanish translation of Sandy Wilson's *The Boyfriend*. Director Humberto Arenal (1926-2012) wrote in the programme, "Except *teatro bufo* and the Spanish *zarzuela*, there is no tradition to guide the creation of a type of popular musical spectacle... This work and others that we are offering in this first stage, tries to summarize the principal scenic experiences that determine the creation of musical comedy."[47] The company survived until 1988.

In about 1963, Alonso created a ballet called *El solar* ("The Slum") which toured to Paris, where one critic labeled it the Cuban *West Side Story* (without the tragic ending). Although Alonso had worked with Jerome Robbins, it may also be that any resemblance between *El solar* and *West Side Story* could be due to the fact that Leonard Bernstein used Cuban musical forms, rather than Puerto Rican in that show. In 1965 it was made into a musical film called *Un día en el solar* ("A Day in the Slums"), directed by Eduardo Manet (1930-) and with music by

Tony Taño (1938-). It aimed to portray people of different socio-economic and racial backgrounds on the eve of Castro's revolution. Under state censorship, the depictions of prostitution and homosexuality were either toned down or removed altogether from the film version. This time, he had reduced control. Not entirely pleased with this, Alonso then adapted the film as a stage musical *Mi Solar* which premiered in March 1965.

The 1959 revolution caused a fair number of artists to leave Cuba. Concerns over their ability to agree their own wages, own their own property and hold their own copyrights were primary. Many of them settled in Miami, causing a brief period of increased international exposure to zarzuela. Sadly, their exile has meant the loss and possible destruction of many musical scores.

Although in the early 1960s the Cuban government initiated a program of encouraging talent and producing zarzuelas in both the cities and as free performances for rural workers, in more recent times the severe economic crisis has meant that when these works are seen at all, they tend to be done with added glitz and often shorn of their libretti to try to appeal to much needed foreign tourists.

Amid a political thaw, in more recent years, there has been some interest in the United States in musicals written by Cuban immigrants. Bookwriter Carlos Lacámara and composer-lyricist Jorge Gomez brought their show *Cuba Libre* to Portland Oregon's Artists Repertory Theatre in 2015. This show employs a more recent Cuban music genre, the timba, which dates from the 1980s and uses some elements of salsa while emphasising rhythm over melody in aid of telling the backstory of recent Cuban immigrants to the United States. It neither glorifies nor demonises the Castro revolution; it merely tells the story of young people struggling to get by following the collapse of the Soviet Union and the continuing American sanctions.

The 1959 Fidel Castro-led coup has continued to rule the country. As a young revolutionary, he and his followers were brutalised by the Batista regime, and since taking power, with opponents who have behaved like gangsters, they have felt it necessary to pass that same brutality on. Sadly, as a result, Cubans have yet to fully achieve the freedom that they have been fighting for. Little of the foreign intervention that they have endured has truly been on the side of democracy, but while Cuban liberty may remain a work-in-progress, its music continues to dazzle the world.

"The Theatre Is Alive"
– Musical Theatre in Asia

Forbidden City. Rose of Versailles. Magnificat. Lunatic. Beauty World. Ang Larawan. The Last Empress. These are all the titles of successful Asian musicals, even although, unless you are Asian yourself, you have probably heard of few, if any of them. But make no mistake, musical theatre here is in its ascendancy, and companies in Korea, Japan, China, Thailand, the Philippines, Taiwan and other Asian countries are investing in the development of new works, both local and foreign, and for audiences who actually do think they're "cool". The musical theatre writing programs at both the Tisch School in New York and Goldsmiths in London have been full of students from Korea, China and Thailand. The Philippines has long had a great reputation for its performers, including Lea Salonga. Even Singapore, long considered a cultural wasteland, is trying to get in on the "act".

On the other hand, in the West, ignorance of this development, even among theatre professionals, is astounding. When I searched Google for "Asian musicals", the list that came through included *The King and I, Flower Drum Song, South Pacific, Miss Saigon, Pacific Overtures* and *Bombay Dreams.* Just to be clear: with the qualified exception of the last one, these are *not* what I mean when I say "Asian musicals". These are Western fantastical notions, an exotic vision of Otherness, whereas I want to talk about musicals that were created in Asia, by (for the most part) Asians and (primarily) for an Asian audience.

The Asian country with the longest tradition of staging more-or-less Western-style musicals is Japan, and that tradition is based at least partly on its own ancient theatrical practices.

The Kabuki Theatre was founded in 1603 by a woman – Izumo-no-Okuni, (born in about 1572 and died anywhere between 1614 and 1658) – and was originally all-female. The word Kabuki is usually translated as "the art of singing and dancing", although a more literal translation gives us "bizarre theatre", while "kabukimono" refers to their unusual dress. Although she was possibly a "Miko" or Shinto-Buddhist shrine maiden, Izumo-no-Okuni was sent to Kyoto as a performer to raise money for the shrine. Here she became known for her performances of "nembutsu odori", an ancient dance in tribute to Amitābha Buddha, although by her time it had become a rather sultry and secular folk dance. This, and the fact that she recruited prostitutes as her actresses, caused some disquiet. It was determined in 1629 under an edict from shogun Tokugawa Iemitsu (1604-51) that actual females were banned from the stage, and their parts in the Kabuki were to be played by "onnagata", or male actors with a female form. These artistes sometimes carried this pretence into their private lives. This rule was not repealed until 1890.

In 1913, railway, baseball and department store magnate Ichizō Kobayashi (1873-1957) conceived of a plan to revive the notion of all-female musical performances in what was originally called Takarazuka Shōjo Kageko ("Takarazuka Girls Opera") in the emerging spa-town of Takarazuka ("treasure mound"), near Osaka, as a way of boosting failing passenger revenues on what would become his Hankyu Railway. Here, in a semi-rural resort environment, people could stay in a Western-style hotel, eat Western food, and enjoy Westernised entertainment. An academy was established where young recruits from affluent families were drilled with militaristic discipline. All of this was intended to prepare them to be *ryousai kenbo* ("good wives, wise mothers") in accordance with the Meiji Civil Code[1] then in effect. The young women must be single, and even today, must leave the company if they ever get married. Ironically, this ultra conservative ideology unwittingly gave birth to a form that has been embraced by radical feminists.

It was after the Takarazuka Grand Theatre was

completed in 1924 that the show began to assume its revue format. "There was a dramatic change in the physical appearance of its performers on stage, from childish 'school play' participants to sexually alluring young women,"[2] says Leonie Stickland, who wrote her doctoral thesis on the Takarazuka Revue at Murdoch University in Perth, Western Australia in 2004.

Takarazuka Kagekidan ("Takarazuka Revue") staged the first ever Moulin Rouge-style revue in Japan, *Mon Paris*, on 1 September 1927. After the Tokyo Takarazuka Theatre was opened in 1934 their school adopted the motto "kiyoku, tadashiku, utsukushiku" ("be pure, be proper, be beautiful"). They toured Europe, China and North America in the years immediately before World War II at the behest of the Japanese government in an attempt to improve Japan's image with the Western powers, appealing to both men and women.

As the Second World War approached, they were co-opted by the government to promote "Japanization" in the occupied Far East. During this time, all foreign loan words were banned from the lexicon, and their emphasis shifted from the exotic to the militaristic, sometimes at the expense of its female audience base. Although Kobayashi was a member of the totalitarian Taisei Yokusankai ("Imperial Rule Assistance Association") and was Minister of Commerce and Industry in the wartime government of Prime Minister Fumimaro Konoe (1891-1945), following disagreements with future Prime Minister Nobusuke Kishi (1896-1987), he resigned after less than a year. After the war he was initially purged by the American occupiers for his political activities, although he was eventually acquitted by the Allies of any wrongdoing.

Toyokichi Hata (1892–1956), who had, among other things, translated Erich Maria Remarque's *All Quiet on the Western Front* and Goethe's *Faustus*, was president of the Tokyo Takarazuka Review and had conducted their 1938-39 European tour. After the war (and his release by the allies from prison as a war criminal), he organized a dancing team at the Nihon Theater (commonly known as the "Nichigeki"), which was then temporarily under Takarazuka control while their main theatre was being used by the occupation forces. They imitated what he had seen in America and specialized in small-scale burlesque and variety shows. He produced a revue in 1947 called *Meiga Arubamu* ("Collection of Painting Masterpieces") at the 420 seat Teito-za in which women, standing still, posed nude within a picture frame as if they were famous paintings. This was perhaps similar to some of the burlesque tableaus staged at the Windmill Theatre in London.

The present-day Takarazuka Revue has five troupes: Hana (flower), Tsuki (moon), Yuki (snow), Hoshi (star) and Sora (cosmos). In a variation on the traditional kabuki form, all roles are played by women; the actors who play men are known as otokoyaku (male role) and those who play women are called musumeyaku (daughter's role). The acting style fuses Japanese elements such as kabuki with western techniques.

Their fan base is now overwhelmingly female, and some can become quite obsessive. In fact, although they deny that it is homoerotic, the management has always encouraged a kind of platonic-romantic fantasy. Opinion is divided as to suggestions of lesbianism. Some argue that the otokoyaku defy gender stereotyping by, in effect, showing women in positions of power. On the other hand, British director Jeremy Sams tells me, "My spies told me that the company itself was a hotbed of institutionalized lesbianism... and there was only one way to get on in the company!"[3] In any case, the otokoyaku do not attempt to become fully masculine – rather, they represent highly idealised representations of man and woman.

Jennifer Robertson, an American cultural anthropologist who has studied the revue in detail writes, "Whereas Kobayashi sought to use the actor as a vehicle for introducing the spectacular artistry of the theater into the home, some Takarisiennes and their fans used the theater as a starting point for an opposing strategy, which included the rejection of gender roles associated with the patriarchal household."4 Dr. Stickland, who teaches at the University of Western Australia and has acted as a translator for the Revue, says that "Takarazuka is a shared fantasy of not only fans, but of the performers, too, who 'live' the dream of portraying beautiful people in their everyday work, and even perpetuate this fantasy after the curtain is down, in an environment considerably removed from regular society."5

Kobayashi wanted his Takarazuka actresses to be "more suave, more affectionate, more courageous, more charming, more handsome and more fascinating than a real male,"6 but this idealised and exotic vision of masculinity is not for Amon Miyamoto (1958-). "[Takarazuka is] not my type", says the man whose critically acclaimed minimalist revival of *Pacific Overtures* was remounted in English on Broadway. "It looks beautiful, but for me it is like a cartoon... more kitsch." He believes the Japanese "ladies dream about men like that... It's a fantasy for them," but he believes that real men frighten them.

The repertoire of Takarazuka is now a mixture of Western musicals such as *Flower Drum Song, Elizabeth* and *Grand Hotel,* as well as their own adaptations of classic novels, such as Edith Wharton (1862-1937)'s *The Age of Innocence* or Leo Tolstoy (1828-1910)'s *War and Peace,* and some original stories, mostly with foreign and exotic settings. The company have also adapted works from Japanese fiction, including *Osaka Samurai,* based on a short story by Ryōtarō Shiba (1923-96).

Other musicals with a foreign setting have included *Kiri no Mirano* ("Milan Wrapped in a Fog"), a tale of political intrigue set in Italy under Austrian rule in the 1850s with a book by Yukihoro Shibata and music by Kohji Nishimura and Shinichi Kuratomi, produced in 2005.

Higher than the Sky of Paris (2006) with music by

Yuko Yishida is based on *Flowered Port* by Kazuo Kikuta, and tells of love and larceny set against the backdrop of the building of the Eiffel Tower.

Canadian-born choreographer Paddy Stone (1924-86) was the first of many Western artists brought over since the 1960s to try to raise their standards, which had declined from the pre-war period. He was followed by American directors and choreographers such as Gemze de Lappe (1922-2017) – a protégé of American ballet choreographer Agnes de Mille – who in turn brought a more Broadway style. De Lappe's production of *Oklahoma* stressed realism in its depiction of masculinity, to the consternation of some of the troupe's fans.

When Takarazuka Revue did *Grand Hotel*, they brought the original Broadway director/choreographer Tommy Tune (1939-) to create a revue, *Broadway Boys*, for them to perform in tandem with it in 1993. Tune describes working with them as one of his greatest achievements.[7]

"I saw *Grand Hotel* and its attendant revue in Tokyo," says Sams, "and have never forgotten it – the sheer numbers and the faultless routines – kind of like synchronised swimming on stage. But, no connection with real emotion"[8], an opinion that Miyamoto shares.

Sams found Takarazuka to be "deeply puritanical. No one kisses for real. At one point a girl took her stockings off, to reveal another pair of stockings underneath (oddly quite sexy!)... Also, the 'negro' bartenders had their faces painted red to show 'otherness'."

As with *Grand Hotel*, many of Takarazuka's other shows are accompanied by a pre-or-post-show revue. For example, their 2008 revue *Miroirs* ("Endless Dreams of the Mirrors") was created by director Satoru Nakamura and choreographers Risa Wakao, Satoshi Hirasawa, Anju and Yumino Miori to accompany the Snow Troupe's production of *Je T'aime*. Using both original music and popular standards such as "Johnny Angel", "Night and Day" and "The Way We Were", the show explores the power of mirrors, including the story of Snow White.

"Takarazuka has always seemed to be a very obvious dialogue between Western and Japanese cultures", says Ben Whaley in his blog *A White Boy in Japan*. "This dialogue is by no means confined to the stage; it permeates nearly every aspect of modern Japanese culture."9

Long before Disney began to adapt their animated features for the stage, Takarazuka was adapting works from their manga (comic book) and anime (animation) traditions. Takarazuka has, in turn, influenced anime. Leading cartoonist and animator Osamu Tezuka (1928-89), known as the "father of manga", grew up in Takarazuka and his mother was friendly with many of the troupe members. It is said that their visual sense influenced his art style.

Berusaiyu no bara ("The Rose of Versailles") was a 1974 adaptation by Shinji Oeda (with music by Irie Kaouru, Hirao Masaaki, Kuratomi Shinchi, Terada Takio, Kawasaki Tsuneo and Yoshida Yuuko) of a 1972 comic book by Riyoko Ikeda (1947-) about a young woman named Oscar who is raised as a boy. (Although she has a masculine name and dresses in male clothing, it is common knowledge among those who know her that she is in actuality a woman. In fact, she inspires a fashion for cross-dressing.) She grows up to be Marie Antoinette's personal guard, but becomes disenchanted with what she sees and ultimately joins the revolution.

The success of *Rose of Versailles* prompted Takarazuka to commission new scripts, which emphasised different sub-plots of the original story. Some dwelled on the romance between Marie Antoinette and her lover the Swedish Count Axel von Fersen. Others concentrated on the relationship between Oscar and her servant and best friend André Grandier. More recent versions have developed side stories about some minor characters, including Victor-Clément de Girodelle, the man whom Oscar is intended to join in an arranged marriage. (When the Revue adapted *Gone With the Wind*, they also created a "Scarlett version" and a "Rhett version".)

In total, the various Takarazuka versions of *Rose of Versailles* have been seen by some four million people. The same story also formed the basis for Jacques Demy's 1979 English-language film *Lady Oscar*. An anime television series appeared in the same year.

In 2006, American composer Frank Wildhorn (1959-) worked with librettist Shuichiro Kolke on *Never Say Goodbye* (2006), set in the Spanish Civil War. This was the first time that a new show was commissioned from a non-Japanese composer.

The Viennese musical *Elisabeth*, with book and lyrics by Michael Kunze and music by Sylvester Levay, has been performed several times by Takarazuka under the title *Erizabēto - ai to shi no rondo* ("Elisabeth: the rondo of love and death"). The revue claims that *Erizabēto* has played to over fifteen million people, making it by far their most successful import. This version turns the relationship between Elizabeth and Death (her desire to die is anthropomorphised) into a sort-of romance.

It has also been done in a more conventional version by the Toho Company. In fact, Maki Ichiro, the otokoyaku who played the androgynous male lead in the Takarazuka production, was later cast in the (female) title role in the Toho version. This is not entirely coincidental. Toho was founded by Kobayashi in 1932 to run the Tokyo Takarazuka Theatre, and both are now part of the Hankyu Hanshin Toho Group, including the famous Toho film studios, makers of *Godzilla* and presenters of the Tokyo run of *Les Misérables*.

"When you get used to the strange fact that all characters are played by women you find that the production works quite well"[10], says Kunze. "The audiences obviously love the Takarazuka version of *Elisabeth*. As a Japanese production, I prefer the one of the Toho Company."

With playwright Kazuo Kikuta (1908-73) as its head, the theatrical division of Toho introduced open ended runs in the 1950s, presenting both indigenous Japanese musicals such as *Morugan Oyuki* ("Oyuki Morgan") about a Geisha who marries into the J.P. Morgan family, as well as imported musicals like *My Fair Lady* in 1963,[11] the first major production of a Broadway musical in Japan. Kikuta is credited by some for revolutionising the presentation of musical theatre in Japan.[12]

In 1966, he wanted to create a stage adaptation of *Gone With the Wind* and secured permission from Stephens Mitchell (1896-1983), brother of author Margaret Mitchell (1900-49). This was to be a two-part non-musical (but with incidental music by Koseki Yūji) of which part one, opening on 3 November at the newly rebuilt Teikoku Gekijō ("Imperial Theatre") ended with the destruction of Atlanta. This was achieved in a spectacular fashion by using film projections made at the Toho film studios. The concluding half opened in the summer of 1967.

A few years earlier, David O. Selznick (1902-65), the original film's producer, had approached Broadway composer Harold Rome (1908-93) – composer-lyricist of *I Can Get it for You Wholesale* – about writing it as a musical, but was turned down. Kikuta invited Rome to see his non-musical version, with the same objective. This time Rome said "yes".

For the show now called *Scaretto* ("Scarlett"), their original plan had been to employ an American book writer, then have his work translated into Japanese, but the writer they had in mind turned out to be unavailable, and they were left with a less-than-ideal arrangement.

Kikuta became the de-facto author of the book, but as he also had the responsibility of running the Toho theatrical division, and he spoke no English, there was little collaboration in the conventional sense. Florence Rome, the composer's wife wrote a memoir of the experience entitled *The Scarlett Letters* in which she remembers:

> "What *he* was doing on his side, we never learned. My fears at the time were that, as the Japanese had never done an original musical[13], they were totally unaware of things which we all took for granted – one of which is that whatever you write is expendable. The most beautiful song ever written, the wittiest bit of dialogue – if it does not fit the mood of the show, it must go. It was difficult to explain to Kikuta that Harold was aware that certain of the songs he was playing did not necessarily represent the finished product, that they might be changed or entirely eliminated if they were inappropriate. Nor did we know for sure whether his compliments were sincere or simply a manifestation of Japanese politesse."[14]

In any case, they saw very little of Kikuta. Joe Layton (1931-94), who had won Tony Awards for his work on *No Strings* and *George M.!* was hired as director and choreographer. Layton had his own concept for the show: "A broad, sweeping view which would do away with the conventional staging of musicals of the past," according to Florence Rome.

> "There would be no set scenes, songs or ballets, each stopping the other. With so much already familiar story to tell, Joe felt that an orthodox approach would be death, for it would simply be the movie all over again, with songs and dances added... He described his plan to Mr. Kikuta, laying it out scene by scene as he wanted it. As Mr. Kikuta left for Japan, we all sat back and hoped for the best."[15]

Lehman Engel would be the Musical Director. "Lehman was Rome's MD of choice", remembers Ed Weissman, a participant in the BMI workshop. "The Romes were good friends with Lehman."[16] "This production was different from all others", says Engel.

> "The differences took two forms. The songs were imbedded in an almost endless musical texture that became underscoring for the dialogue between sung phrases and music for dancing and pantomime. Second, the dramatic scenes were generally acted down in front (in 'one'), while frequently behind these was continuous ballet. Then too, while most music was played by the live orchestra of thirty-five, some was pre-recorded and heard phantom-like. Three times the live and recorded music was heard simultaneously and contrapuntally, producing a nightmare effect. Layton seldom allowed a song to end, an effect appropriate for Tokyo audiences, who applaud infrequently except at the end of the show, but frustrating for Western audiences deprived of self-expression and given no clear idea of the songs themselves."[17]

Layton and Rome set to work from a literal English translation from the Japanese script. They fought over casting: Toho wanted to use the people whom they already had under contract, whereas Layton and Rome wanted open auditions. Only when the latter two threatened to pull the plug did Toho relent. Lehman Engel was shocked to learn that, in a country where neither the actors nor the musicians were unionised, the four hour musical would play twice a day, with a six day week, and only three-quarters of an hour between shows.

There were many misunderstandings between the American creative team and the Japanese producers. Florence Rome remembers,

> "It sounded suspisciously as though Toho, having brought over all that high-priced talent in order to learn how to do a musical, was now tirelessly blocking every effort to let them do it... It was nothing of the sort, of course. It was simply a total incapacity to understand each other – not just the language, but the method of working and the attitude toward that work."[18]

This Asian notion of "saving face" was something that I later encountered in my experience touring Taiwan with a circus. In Chinese it was known as "Guanxi", a sort-of "I scratch your back..." kind of protocol in which you are expected to show gratitude for whatever your host comes up with, even if it does not precisely meet your needs. (We asked for a six-ton forklift. They didn't have one, so instead they gave us a four-ton and a two-ton.)

Florence Rome continues, "We all knew there was simply no *time* for protocol and face and bowing and all that jazz, but the Japanese could not function without them. If the proper forms they used were not observed, it threw them into a tailspin."

The show opened in January 1970 and ran until the end of March. Florence Rome sums up:

> "Reflecting on these things as we were packing to leave Japan, I decided that 'incomprehesible' was the clue word in our dealings with Toho. The thing we did not comprehend clearly, or perhaps had forgotten about, was that Toho had not simply brought us there to do a show. They had bought knowledge, and they were determined to wrest every ounce available. The assistants with whom they had supplied us were there to learn from us as much as to help us, and this dual role of teacher-worker was one which our people had not counted on or had time for. Had it not been for the fact that the learners were so alert and intelligent, so tireless in their efforts, I doubt they'd have gotten the show on at all – but the fact remains that they were all these things."[19]

The Japanese version ultimately entered the Takarazuka repertoire. It was also presented two years later in London by Harold Fielding (1916-2003) under the title *Gone with the Wind* with an English book by Horton Foote (1916-2009) where it ran for just under a year. While this version made it as far as Los Angeles and San Francisco in 1973 where it starred Leslie Ann Warren, its scheduled Broadway opening was cancelled. A 1976 revised version toured to Dallas, San Francisco, Miami and Kansas City, but still no Broadway. It would prove to be Harold Rome's final musical.

Of course, there are other major players in the Japanese market. Gekidan Shiki ("Four Seasons Theatre Company") was founded in 1953 by artistic director Keita Asari (1933-2018), and like Takarazuka, they provide a training regime for their actors. Their original shows have included *Yume Kara Samete Yume* ("A Dream Within a Dream") based on a novel by Jirō Akagawa, and *Yuta to Fushigina Nakama-tachi* ("Yuta's Enchanting Friends") based on a novel by Miura Tetsuo. They have also presented Japanese adaptations of West End and Broadway shows such as *Cats, A Chorus Line* and *Wicked*, as well as *Anne of Green Gables* from Canada and *Le Passe Muraille* from France (produced on Broadway as *Amour*). When *Anne* opened in Tokyo, its composer, the late Norman Campbell told me, "There was no strangeness. Everyone thought we should react to a Japanese girl wearing red pigtails, but it was perfectly natural... The cast was excellent, all of them being good musicians and having great schooling in theatrical arts."[20]

Their first original musical was *The Emperor's New Clothes* in 1964, presented as part of the first Nissay Masterpiece Theatre, a programme sponsored by the Nissay Culture Foundation to bring first class theatre to school children. Their first mainstage original show *Ri Kōran*, about a Chinese-born Japanese singer, premiered in Tokyo in 1991, then toured four cities in China in 1992 as part of celebrations of the twentieth anniversary of restoring diplomatic relations. *Ikoku-No-Oka*, presented in 2001, dealt with post-war prisoners in Siberia, and *Southern Cross* (2004) told the story of innocent Japanese soldiers accused of war crimes. *Ri Kōran* and *Southern Cross*, together with *Foreign Hill* make up the *Showa Trilogy*. Shiki Theatre Company employs about eight hundred people with around 2,800 performances a year.

Most Japanese musical productions differ from their Western counterparts in two ways. Few shows – even hits – have their runs extended, due to the lack of available theatres. Instead, most are remounted – often months or even years later. Also, few engage a live orchestra, most employing recorded music.

Amon Miyamoto collaborated with the noted Singapore composer Lee Peng Boon (1956-) (popularly known as Dick Lee) on *Hong Kong Rhapsody* (1993), which tells the story of a Japanese photographer covering the Tian-an-men massacre. He delivers a letter from a dying man to his daughter in Hong Kong.

The inspiration came when, as a student in London, Miyamoto saw the massacre on the news. When he and a friend went to a pub in Leicester Square, he was mistaken for Chinese. Until that time, he considered London and New York, rather than China, to be his neighbours. "I have a confidence about the Japanese culture, but I didn't have a confidence about another Asian culture" he told me. "So I went back to Japan and did research about China where this happened. And in Japan, they said, 'Don't talk about that'. It's so forbidden, because Japan and China still have a distance. Politically they don't really get on." At first, Lee was reluctant to get involved. "It's so dangerous for him." However, he was anxious to explore the crossover between Western and Eastern music, and he agreed to do it.

Miyamoto is often cited as Japan's leading director of musicals, and was the founding artistic director of the Kanagawa Arts Theatre in Yokohama which opened at the beginning of 2011. His production of *Pacific Overtures* (for which he was nominated for a Tony award) has played in New York in both its Japanese and English versions. (Kanagawa is the setting for the opening scene of *Pacific Overtures*.) Interestingly, when his Japanese-language version visited New York, he included a projected image of an atomic bomb and the American reaction was positive. When he did the same thing in New York two years later in the English-language version, it received an angry reaction:

one person said "Remember Pearl Harbor". "Those two theaters are only a few blocks apart," Miyamoto told *Japan Times*, "yet they could accept the A-bomb scene in a Japanese guest program, but not in English with an American cast."[21]

His other Sondheim productions include Japanese versions of *Sweeney Todd* and *A Little Night Music*. His English language production of *The Fantasticks* (a show that had great early resonance for him) played in London's West End in 2010. He cites directors Peter Brook, Robert LePage and Simon McBurney among his influences.

He was born Ryoji Miyamoto on 4 January 1958. His parents ran a coffee shop which became the haunt of actors from the Embujo Theatre across the street in the Shambashi area of Tokyo. His mother had been a dancer, entertaining American troops after World War II, but she gave it up when she married his father, who didn't approve of the "showbiz" lifestyle. Still, she encouraged her young son in his love of musicals, and coached him as he worked out his own dance routines on tatami mats in their flat.

At one point, as a teenager, he became a *hikikomori* (social recluse), stayed at home, committed *toko kyohi* (refusing to go to school), and shut himself in his room for a year with his beloved cast albums. (Small wonder that, many years later, he should identify himself with the Man in Chair character in *The Drowsy Chaperone*.)

While his mother understood, his father reputedly came at him with a samurai sword. "At the time, I'm looking – why [do] I grow up? How can I live from now? I wanted an answer."

A production of *The Fantasticks* was a major influence, because "I was the same age as [its ingenues] Matt and Luisa, and so [I'm] trying to find [out] 'How can I grow up? What is my future?' That's the kind of guy I was." Tom Jones, who wrote the book and lyrics for that show, cites Peter Brook's book *The Empty Space* as a major influence, and Amon followed in the same footsteps. "I fell in love with Peter Brook's *The Empty Space*, and this is my most important thing at the moment, because what is real for me is always looking for something. It has to touch the heart." One record he listened to was *A Little Night Music*. He told *Japan Times*, "Sondheim's music sounded superb to me, as it deeply expresses the human soul and his tunes represent people's multi-layered and complicated thoughts."[22]

"And when I read *Empty Space*," he told me, "this is for real. I decided to myself, I want to be a director some day. I can communicate more with people. How I can live honestly to myself. That's why I choose this theatre." In 1987, upon his return to Japan after studying in England, he legally changed his first name to Amon, which means "Asian gate".

"In Japan, I think audiences are a little bit getting lazy. They sit waiting – what is next? – like a film. They don't want to use [their] imagination. The theatre is alive. Audiences and casts are connected with creation. We are not animals, right? Human beings can make a creation with each other. This is a great moment for me – why I like theatre." He told Hideo Nakamura of *Chopsticks New York*, "We Japanese are people who appreciate the spirit behind things, in my opinion. We are people living in a culture that treasures things, no matter how small they are. I think that's what we can let the world know."[23]

While *Pacific Overtures* may have been the first Japanese musical production to play on Broadway, it was not the first to play in New York City. In 1969, a young student named Yutaka Higashi (1945-2000) left Waseda University with a plan to form a company of actors called the Tokyo Kid Brothers to present his own musicals. One of their first shows, *The Golden Bat*, with book and lyrics by Higashi and music by Itsuro Shimoda came to New York's La MaMa Experimental Theatre Club[24] (where *Godspell* was originally developed) in 1970, and then transferred to the Sheridan Square Playhouse. A second show, *The Moon is East, The Sun is West* toured Europe, and they returned to La MaMa with *Coney Island Play* and *The City*.

A decade later, *Shiro*, with book and lyrics by Higashi and music by Takashi Yoshimatsu (1953-) told the story of a group of teenagers who travel back in time to 1623 and the great Shimbara Revolt, the greatest peasant uprising in Japanese history. *New York Times* correspondent Henry Scott-Stokes describes Higashi's work as "the right mixture of blatant sentimentality and deliberate *kitsch*. It's an echo of the old Kabuki tradition. There is lots of colour, noise, action – and tears, with elaborate tableaux and gorgeous costumes adjusted on stage by kuroko (black-clad stage hands)... If all this sounds risky, the entire show is a gamble befitting the theatre, a great throw of the dice. No one else in Japan but Mr. Higashi would risk the spectacle of fully armoured samurai trundling about the stage in horned hats to music from a tiny rock combo, reinforced by the magical *shakuhachi*, or bamboo flute."[25] Mel Gussow in the *New York Times* wrote, "*Shiro* is sumptuous in its design but in other respects it is a mixed blessing... The confrontation between contemporary street kids and medieval warriors is a promising idea, but the issue is confused in the telling. The dialogue is in long bursts of Japanese, followed by an often indecipherable bullet of English."[26] He added that Yoshimatsu's score "has an exotic Japanese flavor". Following its New York engagement in 1981, it transferred to the Kennedy Center in Washington, D.C., then toured the U.S. and Canada.

To the best of my knowledge, only one musical by a Japanese composer has ever played in the West End, and sadly it was cited in one blog as No. 12 in their list of the twenty Worst Musicals in History.[27] I saw the show and while I might have concurred with that opinion at the time, having heard director David Gilmore's unrealised designs for it, I'm not so sure now.

Out of the Blue, a musical about the atomic bomb dropped on Nagasaki in 1945, lasted for only twenty performances at the Shaftesbury Theatre in 1994. It had a score by Japanese film composer Shun Ichi Tokura (1948-) whose film scores include *Code Name Black Cat*, *Barrow Gang BC* and *Memories of Matsuko*. The libretto was by an English poet, actor and singing teacher named Paul Sand (1951-), whose CV includes more than thirty musicals and operas, including the more successful *Mad and Her Dad*.

The musical, initially called *Light Years*, was workshopped in London in early 1994. The creative team were well aware that the subject matter was a tough sell in Britain, probably tougher than it would have been in Japan. However, the show's mostly Japanese backers had placed a time limit before which the show had to be staged, a condition the composer regretted agreeing to. "I was rushed,"[28] says Tokura.

Following its catastrophically short run, director David Gilmore says:

> "It was interesting that I've read a number of things in the time after it has closed which were much more objective, and indeed recognised what it was trying to do in quite a different way than those overnight reviews written at the time... My feeling, very very strongly, is that Shun and his backers should [have done] the show in Japan first. They should [have opened] it there to an audience to whom it would speak in a very, very different way. As soon as you say you're putting on 'a musical'... an awful lot of expectations are raised about 'what is a West End musical?' If you're a practitioner, it can be anything you want it to be, but if you're an audience and a critic, all sorts of expectations come up: romance, comedy, spectacle, whatever it might be. But if something had opened abroad, and then indeed the book and the lyrics had been translated from another language into what I would have hoped was a heightened linguistic style, it could come carrying with it shades of Japanese theatre and be seen through a different set of spectacles. Opening in London raised these preconceptions which I was at pains to get rid

of… I went to Japan and went to Kabuki theatre and Noh[29] theatre and watched traditional fighters – immersed myself fairly thoroughly in Japanese culture and traditions – and I became convinced it should be done in stylised clothes to some extent, and indeed with masks. We rehearsed it as a piece played behind masks. And in the rehearsal, and into the final run-throughs and into the previews, I personally thought that made the show work. Preview audiences responded very, very favourably – it was like watching something in one of the Old World theatre seasons."

However, it was not to be.

"I came under a lot of pressure… to at least try one preview without the masks and given that I was being asked by the people whose show it was – the producers, I could hardly refuse… And we did one, and they all came to see me and said, 'We would like the show to remain like this, to be played without the masks. We feel there is a more direct relationship between the audience and the characters with no masks on'. Well… I reluctantly agreed, and that was the show we did. To this day, my feeling is I would have liked the critics to have seen the production behind the masks because it was a different kind of theatre."[30]

The *Independent* wrote, "*Out of the Blue* never established its right to the pretensions it kept inflating",[31] but the show they were seeing was not the one that director David Gilmore envisaged.

Since then there has been interest, but nobody has bitten. "After it closed in London," says Tokura, "I had so many inquiries from the U.S., especially in the West Coast, San Francisco area… all these regional theatres showed interest. In fact, I did some showcases, one in New York, one in Oakland. Of course it didn't go into any major theatres."

However, he is realistic in knowing that it needs work. "If we are going to remount this musical, we do have to rewrite the book. There are some loose ends that we do have to tie together..."

Japan also imports musicals from other Asian markets, including Korea, Singapore and India. *Muthu* was an Indian musical that was exported to Japan by Indian Productions and Min-On Japan based on the film *Muthu, Dancing Maharaja*. "In the end of the show, all the audience stood up and most of them started to dance with the music," say Hiroko and Yoshihisa Honda, Japan correspondents to *Musical Stages*. "Both of us stood up without any hesitation and were very surprised to see young and old people were equally happy to dance with the performers. As you can imagine, the costumes were very exotic and beautiful."[32]

It is easy to see why Andrew Lloyd Webber was so anxious to draw on India's own well established, vibrant tradition of film musicals, especially with a large Indian diaspora in Britain. According to Indian journalist Mihir Bose, "Songs had been part of Indian films since the days of the talkies, reflecting the enormous part music, song and dance play in Indian daily life."[33] The tradition of Hindi musicals can be traced back to Sanskrit "natya", or dance-dramas described in an ancient treatise called the *Natya-Shastra*, and to later Indian folk traditions and Parsi theatre, in which for example they would create an Indian folk version of a Shakespeare play and add songs to it. Elaborate and colourful dance numbers feature in many Hindi films, with leading actors usually lip-synching to recordings of professional singers. This form became especially popular after India achieved its independence in 1947. However, since classical Indian music is largely improvised, some Western conventions – such as music notation – had to be adopted in order to make filming practical.

Bose explains, "The Bombay film song had become the Indian song, with a song for every situation – romance, laughter, sadness, cabarets, eroticism – important in a country where the censor did not allow kissing on the screen... The songs lived on long after the films had been forgotten and Indian movie-goers had made it clear that a film without song was not worth going to."[34]

While the films were influenced by the early Hollywood musicals, they departed from them in several important ways. "Indian filmmakers, while enhancing the elements of fantasy so pervasive in Indian popular films, used song and music as a natural mode of articulation in a given situation in their films", say K. Moti Gokulsing, K. Gokulsing and Wimal Dissanayake in their book *Indian Popular Cinema: a Narrative of Popular Change*. "There is a strong Indian tradition of narrating mythology, history, fairy stories and so on through song and dance... Whereas Hollywood filmmakers strove to conceal the constructed nature of their work so that the realistic narrative was wholly dominant, Indian filmmakers made no attempt to conceal the fact that what was shown on the screen was a creation, an illusion, a fiction. However, they demonstrated how this creation intersected with people's day to day lives in complex and interesting ways."[35] In turn, Australian director Baz Luhrmann (1962-) says that Hindi musicals inspired his film *Moulin Rouge*.[36]

Only occasionally does the Bollywood form interact with its Western counterpart. In India, Disney's *High School Musical* was promoted through a series of "My School Rocks" dance competitions, which produced some interesting localised results. "They are moving beyond those American-oriented movements and meanings to produce cohesive, hybrid, original dances,"[37] says Kristin Rudisill, Assistant Professor of Popular Culture at Bowling State University in Ohio. "This contest is not about careful viewing or even careful imitation of *High School Musical*, but about bringing Indian kids' own experiences and cultural capital to this American product and claiming it through their bodies and movement." The competitions were so popular that Disney repeated the idea in Malaysia, Singapore and Taiwan. More recently, in 2016, Disney brought its *Beauty and the Beast* to Mumbai and Delhi with an all-Indian cast.

Adapting the Indian form to the West End stage proved to be a daunting challenge. Producer Andrew Lloyd Webber began by approaching noted Indian film director Shekhar Kapur (1945-), who suggested the composer A. R. Rahman (1967-), a Bollywood legend who had scored the Oscar nominated *Lagaan*. Then he hired English comedienne Meera Syal (1961-) to write the book, and Don Black (1938-) – the only person with a non-Asian background on the creative team – to do lyrics. Here the cultural gap was felt. Rahman, who had never seen a stage musical, was accustomed to improvising his music on synthesisers in a recording studio. "Getting full-length songs out of him was very difficult", Black told his biographer James Inverne. "It was a long, laborious job to get actual shapes of songs that could be right for the West End and Broadway. And I had to remember the whole time to tread that delicate line, getting the theatricality we needed and yet keeping Rahman's own distinctive voice."[38] *Bombay Dreams* enjoyed a modestly successful London run at the Apollo Victoria Theatre, although it disappeared quickly on Broadway.

Although not noted as a breeding ground for musicals, even Taiwan came up with *Qiwang* ("The Chess King") in 1987, based on a novel by computer scientist and science fiction author Chang Shi-Kuo (1944-). The story concerns a successful advertising executive who uses a young boy's powers of clairvoyance to make him a chess prodigy. *Asia Weekly* had proclaimed this to be one of the top 100 Chinese novels of the century.

The novel was first published in 1975, the same year as Taiwan's dictator Chiang Kai-shek died. The period immediately following it was one of great transition, in which Taiwan went, in a very short period of time, from being a third world country to being one of the Asian Tiger economies while also evolving a nascent democracy.

The Chess King was produced on a makeshift stage in the China Sports and Cultural Center by composer-turned-impresario Hsu Po-yun (1944-) and his company, New Aspect.[39] The libretto was by Chang and fellow novelist Sanmao (Chen Mao Ping) (1943-91), and the music by aboriginal Taiwanese composer Li Tai-hsiang (1941-2014). It was directed by American academic Dr. Stanley Waren (1919-?). His wife Florence (1917-2011), a South African Jew who had danced before Nazis while aiding the French resistance in occupied Paris, was the choreographer.

According to Hsu, "both he and his wife read an English language edition of the novel and said they were immediately stirred by Chang's characters, their problems, and the almost dizzying rhythmic pattern presented of a Taipei undergoing rapid industrial, financial, commercial, and social changes."[40] He added, "Dr. Waren said that he would try his best not to superimpose any Broadway or overwhelming American form on the work."

Designer Nieh Kuang-yen responded to the challenges of working in a less than hospitable environment when their intended venue, the Sun Yat-sen Memorial Hall was unavailable and they were forced to stage it on a badminton court in a gymnasium. Its well-below-par acoustics were addressed through the use of cordless microphones, and he suspended three giant screens over the audience, showing slides of "Taipei Impressions" by eight local photographers, in addition to lasers.

The music, Hsu explains,

"is an interplay between the so-called academic and the popular, and is jointly performed by both opera singers and pop singers. But the lyrics properly expressed the theme of the play. For example, the enthusiastic theme song 'Taipei Is Alive' has sarcastic connotations... Li Tai-hsiang's impressive music captures the spirit of change and excitement, but the lyrics add a sometimes disconcerting dimension to the story line. Beyond the play itself, however, this is another of Li's efforts to upgrade the quality of popular songs in Taiwan. For the last few years he has been fighting against the often senseless lyrics that make up most of today's contemporary music."

The Chess King encountered a mixed reception from the Taiwan news outlets, one of whom called it "a rehearsal of American cultural imperialism"[41]. "I can't agree", says Hsu. "The musical of course is an American creation. Therefore, it's impossible for us to create and produce the musical form first. It already exists. But we can adapt the form in Chinese ways. And if this is called a cultural invasion, then operas and movies imported from abroad can also be criticized the same way... Art has no nationality. To refuse exotic products can only slow the pace of progress. If we argue against 'importing' Western culture, how can we then 'export' the philosophy of Confucius, the art of Chang Tai-chien, or any other part of Chinese culture?"

Noted Taiwanese feminist writer Li Ang (1952-) wrote in a newspaper editorial, "In Taiwan's current level of social development, there are many audiences who think ordinary TV programs are too shallow, and classical music or opera are too lofty. Therefore, my opinion is that this musical provides both proper entertainment and an upgrading spiritual activity."[42] Financial problems caused its run to be cut short.

Other subsequent works included *Lingdai yu gaogenxie* ("Neckties and High-heeled Shoes", 1994) by Greenray Theatre Company which, like *The Chess King*, also examined Taiwan's emergence into the world of capitalism.

More recently, I saw my first Taiwanese musical as part of the Daegu International Musical Festival in Korea. *One Fine Day*, which was in Mandarin with Korean subtitles, had a libretto and direction by Chang Yang-Shuan and music by Chang Hsin-Tzu. It tells the story of a dying mother's wish to spend her remaining time nurturing her six-year-old daughter.

Filipino film director Pepe Diokno (1987-) has said, "When you watch films from, say, Hollywood – your perception of the world becomes according to the way Hollywood dictates… That's why we have a pretty twisted culture because we don't have a formation of what our identity is. It's important for us to see ourselves on the big screen. It's our projection of who we are and who we want to be."[43] The same principals can be applied to the musical theatre.

The Philippines is an Asian country that was under Western occupation (first Spain, then the U.S.) for four hundred years. There are two official languages, English and Tagalog.[44] These are only two out of some 187 different tongues and dialects spoken, and Tagalog, the "national" language is native to only a third of the population.

The Philippines was cobbled together by the Spaniards out of numerous divergent peoples. Many Filipinos have Spanish names, although few can speak the language. While it is considered to be a recently industrialised nation rich in natural resources, parts of it – especially the non-Tagalog speaking outer islands – remain very poor. In fact, the indigent still make up more than a fifth of the population.[45] This presents problems in trying to fashion a single, unified culture, making it easy to see why identity is a big issue.

In spite of all this, the Philippines has managed to develop its own nascent form of musical theatre going back more than a century. Sir Anril P. Tiatco, an academic from Singapore who is an associate professor of theatre arts at the University of the Philippines, says "The [Original Filipino Musical] is a contemporary genre in the Philippines that is often viewed as a combination of three traditional theatrical forms: the *komedya*, the *sarsuwela*, and the *bodabil*. These traditional forms include dances and songs, which are of course defining features of the musical theatre."[46]

The Asia Pacific Database on Intangible Cultural Heritage defines the term "komedya" as "a colorful theatrical tradition in Christianized Philippines whose plot generally revolves around the social, political and religious conflicts of Muslim and Christian heroes dramatized in colorful romantic and stylized acting, and in exotic costumes, presented usually during community festivals with the support and patronage of the community."[47]

The zarzuela was brought to the Philippines from Spain in the late nineteenth century initially for the benefit of the Spanish colonisers. As also happened in places like Cuba, native writers soon began to create their own indigenous works called "sarswela"[48]. "Although their models for the form, the Spanish zarzuelas, dealt with mythology, royalty, nobility, Dons and Doñas and other characters of Spanish life," says teacher and author Doreen G. Fernandez (1934-2002), "the native sarswelistas focused on Filipino situations, domestic and social: marriage, family, vices, elections, feasts. Staged drama in the Philippines, which had before then been mainly religious or been drawn from European metrical romances, had finally found the form in which it was possible to present native day-to-day life on stage."[49]

Another Filipino musical form was the Kundiman, which some describe as a form of folk serenade that developed into an art song, but which Filipino composer Ryan Cayabyab says has a deeper meaning:

"In my case, and from oral tradition (from the words of one of my composition teachers in the university) musically, the kundiman is in 3/4 and takes on a binary form: part A is in minor and part B is in major (normally the parallel major). The importance of this dichotomy is in the marriage of the lyrical content with the mode. Part A speaks of sadness and longing while Part B speaks of hope, joy. And the theme is always about love: love for a person or love for country, and even if it is not about the country, there seems to be a personification of country in the lyrics. It could be from bondage (minor) to freedom (major); from loss of a loved one, to finding the loved one; from the darkness of night to the breaking of dawn (still talking about a man 'in the dark' with his relationship to a woman he is trying to woo, wishing that dawn comes soon) etc."[50]

One of the best known Tagalog-language sarswelas was *Dalagang Bukid* ("The Country Girl") which opened at the Teatro Zorrilla in 1917, written by librettist Hermogenes Ilagan (1873-1943) and composer Leon Ignacio (1882-1967). *Dalagang Bukid* concerns a young flower girl, Angelita, played by Atang de la Rama (1905-91), the Queen of the kundiman. Betrothed by her parents to a wealthy, old man, Don Silvestre, Angelita secretly loves Cipriano, a law student.

Dalagang Bukid toured the islands, playing more than a thousand performances, and produced the hit song "Nabasag ang Banga" ("The Jar was Broken") which says in translation:

> Watch what you're doing, said the maid
> Have pity on me, was his answer
> Don't pester me so, the lass decried
> But I am in love, the man replied.

It didn't end there. In 1919, this was to be the first locally produced Filipino silent film. For *Dalagang Bukid*, original star Atang de la Rama was engaged, during the film's Manila run, to stand behind the screen and sing "Nabasag ang Banga", accompanied by a violin, coronet and piano.

Believe it or not, this idea of silent movie musicals actually caught on. The idea may sound to our ears like an oxymoron, but there was a precedent: *Carmen* had already been filmed in 1915 in Hollywood, starring famed soprano Geraldine Farrar. According to filmmaker Nick Deocampo, "During the silent era that came during the early years of the American occupation, the Spanish-inspired *sarsuela* served as the major source and inspiration for the musical film. Popular musical plays were turned into motion pictures, enthralling audiences despite their lack of a soundtrack. The live voice accompanying the screening, along with the live orchestra providing the musical score, were enough to entertain the film audiences and keep musicals popular for years to come."[51] Alas, this film of *Dalagang Bukid* is now believed to be lost.

Vaudeville first appeared in the Philippines in the early 1900s as entertainment imported for the benefit of the occupying armies, but an indigenised "bodabil" soon caught on with the native population, putting a Filipino spin on a popular Western entertainment form, combining music with comedy, acrobatics and even magic acts. It reached its peak during the Japanese occupation (during which Allied movies were banned), and lasted right through the 1960s – twenty years later than its American parent.

Thus komedya, sarswela and bodabil formed the basis for the Original Filipino Musical. "Significantly, OFM producers draw on a range of local source material, from popular culture to social issues," Prof. Tiatco explains, "and consequently inscribe a genre that simultaneously entertains and critiques the Philippine social sphere."[52]

Since the American occupation in the first half of the twentieth century, the intellectual elites were being educated in English. "The colonizers who came to establish the American Insular Government in the Philippines came upon a theater scene they could not understand", says Doreen Fernandez. So they just replaced it.

> "There was the change of language, first of all, which inferentially made vernacular theater fit only for the provinces, the fiestas, for the unschooled, and English the language of the schooled and eventually the learned. Certainly *sinakulo*[53] and komedya would not be performed or mentioned, much less studied, in schools... The images of musical theatre held by the schooled and the young were generally not sarswela and [Filipino matinee idols] Rogelia de la Rosa - Carmen Rosales romances, but the Broadway musical as typified by *Oklahoma*, *Carousel* and *South Pacific* and the Hollywood musical extravaganza, as exemplified by the musicals from Busby Berkeley and the Ziegfeld Follies to *Singin' in the Rain* onward... The idea of theater, its form and content, and its social function of education and entertainment were thus, for the schooled Filipinos of the first half of the twentieth century, according to the American model. Because of the gap between vernacular and English theaters, there was no consciousness of the community base of Philippine theater, or of the forms it had taken before the advent of English and the educational system."[54]

As a former American possession, they were inculcated with American culture (and, to a lesser extent, with British). The elites now looked to Shakespeare and Eugene O'Neill as their dramatic gods. To them, the Sarswellas were embarrassingly twee, naïeve and simplistic, and so began to lose favour among the middle classes. Filipinos were introduced to the musical via their Hollywood adaptations. At the same time, Philippine nationalism became a popular theme.

They fought their first revolution – against the Spanish – in 1896 and declared the first Republic on 23 January 1899. The Republic then fought a two year war against the Americans, which they lost. They did not give up however, and the American occupation was relatively short-lived. In fact, the Americans didn't really want the Philippines per se, they just wanted Manila harbour.[55] They remain the only former American colony to be given its independence: Philippines finally became a self-governing nation immediately following the Second World War.

There was even some revival of interest in sarswela in the 1970s as nationalism and resistance to the martial law imposed by President Ferdinand Marcos took hold and brought forth a new, modern version. But, then came the British megamusical…

Joy Virata (1936-), wife of former Prime Minister Cesar Virata (1930-), wrote a musical in English in 1998 with director Freddie Santos (1956-) based on the life of her husband's grand-uncle Emilio Aquinaldo (1869-1964), the president of that first Republic. Called *Miong*, it had music by Ian Monsod, a former rock musician who became managing director of Warner Music Philippines.

Virata explains, "I've used the meter of the 'Balagtasan'[56] which is an old form of entertainment which meant two men pitted against each other in a poetic war (something like present day rap) or merely as a poetic form. I've also incorporated the 'pabasa'[57] which was a chant commonly done on Holy Week by old ladies in the neighbourhood and the martial beat of marching bands which all barrios[58] had at that time."[59] *Miong* has been revived twice, most recently in 2019 at Repertory Philippines.

"The Filipinos have inherent musical talent", says Virata.

> "For some reason we have a very good ear - both for music and speech. This is why we are very adept at picking up music and speech (hence our huge outsourcing industry as well as our export of musicians). We also have a history of music. We have the gongs and bamboo instruments of pre-Spanish days, we have the influence of Spanish Music (400 years) which included many stringed instruments, hence the zarzuela and the various kind of string ensembles, then we have the American influence - roughly fifty years of

colonisation - leading into movie and pop culture. Broadway came in with the movies. There were performing arts theatres in every small town (now replaced by movie houses), there were marching bands in every town. These have continued in the form of pop music groups. Music has always been a vital part of life... I know there are those who think that we have no 'identity'. But in my own personal opinion it is our mixture of races brought about by our own, very unique, history that makes us very Filipino. This is who we are now, this is our identity, and to me this is our cultural strength, not our weakness. Of course I can be accused of feeling this way because I am half British – my mother was British – but there is some mixture in most Filipinos — Chinese, American, Indian, Spanish, British, European, Japanese — along with our basic Malay ancestry — and thus we have been influenced by different cultures. After all we are an island archipelago!"

Ever since Lea Salonga won the title role in *Miss Saigon*, the country has been noted for the quality of its musical theatre talent. In 2017, Miss Salonga released a CD, produced by Ryan Cayabyab, called *Bahaghan*, made up of folk-songs in several Filipino languages.

Another English-language musical, *The Silent Soprano* with libretto by Ricardo Saludo, a drama teacher and former chair of the Philippines Civil Service Commission, and music by Vincent de Jesus (1968-) and Arnel de Pano was about a Filipino domestic worker in a Hong Kong office of a pop music producer. It is discovered that she can sing, but can only be successful if they can pass her off as Chinese. It was produced in 2007 by Dulaang Unibersidad ng Pilipinas, which is affiliated with the University of the Philippines.

Most successful of the indigenous musical writers is Ryan Cayabyab (1954-), a pop musician known as the "Leonard Bernstein of the Philippines" (although he says, "I don't think I am an iota of the Leonard Bernstein kind, nor a Stephen Sondheim kind", calling himself "a work in progress") and to people in the business as "Mr. C." who also crossed over into the classical world as a composer, arranger and conductor of the now-defunct San Miguel Philharmonic Orchestra.

"My mother was an opera singer and a faculty member of the [University of the Philippines] College of Music", says Cayabyab. "I grew up listening to her opera arias, French art songs, Neapolitan songs, German lieder and Filipino art songs."[60]

When his mother died, his ears opened up to pop music, citing the Beatles, Jimmy Webb, Burt Bacharach and Motown as influences, but also including Rogers and Hammerstein musicals: *South Pacific, the King and I, Carousel* and *Oklahoma*. "The very first musical I ever saw on Broadway was *They're Playing Our Song*... Of course, my all time favorite would still be *West Side Story* - also because of the film."

He began as a pop, jazz and choral arranger, then earned his Bachelor of Music degree and worked as a musical director for local productions of *Godspell, Two Gentlemen of Verona, The Fantasticks* and the rock opera *The Survival of St. Joan*. "In the seventies we jammed Sondheim musicals (*Company, Follies, Sweeney Todd* etc) together with songs from *the Wiz*, and Stephen Schwartz's *Pippin* whose music I fell in love with."

The first large-scale theatre work he completed was a pop-ballet-musical in 1980 entitled *Rama-Hari*, which used pop singers and classically trained ballet dancers to present a version of a Hindu epic, the *Ramayana*.

"Fresh off college, my music was very eclectic, blending western orchestra with an indigenous Kulintangan[61] ensemble with pop ballades and rock rhythms." The libretto was written by Bienvenido Lumbera (1932-).

"In the 80s when I began teaching composition

and music theory in the university, I completely lost interest in musicals. I wasn't even into *Les Miz*, until I heard *Miss Saigon* in the late 80s."

His first true musical was *Katy* in 1988, with a libretto by Jose Javier Reyes (1954-) based on the life of bodabil torch singer Katy Dela Cruz. "The music has strong period influences", he says. "This is probably the musical that more people remember me for." His other musicals, mostly in Tagalog but with Western-style music, have included *Noli Me Tangere* (1994, libretto by Lumbera) and *El Filibusterismo* (1996, libretto by Jovi Miroy) both based on novels by Filipino patriot Dr. Jose Rizal (1861-96), which toured Japan and Malaysia in the 1990s.

In 1997, Cayabyab collaborated with librettist and director Rolando Tinio (1937-97) on *Ang Larawan* ("The Portrait") a through-sung musical which was in turn based on an English-language play by Nick Joaquim (1917-2004) called *A Portrait of the Artist as Filipino*. Set in Manila on the verge of the Second World War, the story concerns two sisters who live in genteel poverty in a grand house in Intramuros, the old walled city of Manila while caring for their ailing father, a painter whose self-portrait gives the play its title. Death and decay hang in the air: of a way of life, and literally of Intramuros and the sisters themselves as the devastation of the war is imminent. They are being pressured to sell this painting, but they resist, and the central conflict of the story is the stress which this places on the family. It becomes a metaphor for post-colonial life in the Philippines.

In 2017, the musical was adapted as a film produced by Girlie Rodis and Celeste Legaspi (1950-), directed by New York-based scenic designer Loy Arcenas (1953-) and starring Joanna Ampil (1975-) (who played Mary Magdalene in the 1997 West End revival of *Jesus Christ Superstar*) and Rachael Alejandro (1974-) as the sisters. While the stage production was through-sung, the film mixes spoken and sung dialogue. KQED in San

Francisco called it "a lustrous gem of a film" and wrote, "The movie can be appreciated as a period piece rife with nostalgia for a high-minded, Spanish-influenced culture that was rapidly eroding under the crass, free-wheeling mercantilism under the American regime."[62] *Broadway World* called it "a lavish, absorbing family drama"[63], while the *National Catholic Review* called it a "transcendant gem of global cinema" [64].

The People Power Revolution of 1986, which saw the overthrow of President Ferdinand Marcos, brought changes to the theatrical industry as well. Old regimes fell in some of the major cultural institutions, and Rodis and Legaspi were part of the incoming. They formed a company – originally called Musical Theatre Philippines Inc. – that produced the original incarnation of *Katy* among many others. Gibbs Cadiz, theatre editor of *Inquirer* said that it was "a unique undertaking in that it was the only local theater company exclusively dedicated to commissioning and mounting original Filipino musicals."[65] They have now renamed themselves Culturtain[66] Musicat Productions Inc., and their first major project is the film version of *Ang Larawan*.

Repertory Philippines was founded in 1967 by two women – Carmen (Baby) Barredo and Zeneida (Bibot) Amador (1933-2008) – who had gained theatre degrees in the U.S. (Barredo had studied voice in the University of Indiana, and then went on to complete Drama in the American Conservatory of Dramatic Arts in New York. Amador studied a post-graduate course in Drama at the American Academy of Dramatic Arts in New York.) Its objective was to bring good English-language theatre to Manila. Seven of the fourteen Filiponos recruited for the original production of *Miss Saigon* – including Lea Salonga and Monique Wilson – were from this company.

One thing that has restricted the flow of commercial theatre in Manila is a shortage of suitable venues. The principal subsidised venue is the Cultural

Center of the Philippines, opened in 1969 by the central government, which includes four auditoria. Although criticised during the Marcos regime as an elitist establishment, after the 1986 revolution it catered to "a Filipino national culture evolving with and for the people"[67], according to Nicanor Tiongson, Professor Emeritus of Film and Audio-visual Communication at the College of Mass Communication in University of the Philippines Diliman.

In the private sector, the Solaire resort and casino complex includes a 1700 seat theatre presenting Broadway shows. In all there are over thirty auditoria including university theatres. However, few can accommodate an indefinite run.

In recent years, a style of Filipino pop singing called "Birit" has found its way into musicals. "Birit" consists of singers belting out sustained high notes, with coloratura-like improvisations to denote emotion.

South Korea is a country with a stand-alone language and writing system that, until the beginning of the twentieth century, had no indoor theatres. Although records show itinerant outdoor performances dating back to the sixth century, only after a strong merchant class began to emerge at the end of the nineteenth century was there a commercial demand for this type of entertainment. However, its people are resourceful, determined, and not afraid of completely re-inventing themselves. Since then they have made up for lost time with a vengeance.

In 1902, the Hùidae theatre (after 1908 known as the Wòn'gaksa ("circle") theatre) was opened with the largely unrealised intention of hosting King Kojong (1852-1919)'s fortieth anniversary celebrations. Its operations were overseen by an office of the royal court known as the Hyòmnyulsa ("musical company"), so that they could present traditional Korean opera to foreign diplomats. This was the first indoor theatre to be built for Korean music and drama.[68] It was round, with a thrust stage, much like an English Elizabethan theatre. Given that just over a century has passed since its creation and destruction, information on this theatre is surprisingly vague: its capacity has been variously described as anywhere between four hundred to two thousand people. Within a few years, the theatre was overtaken by other more successful ventures, and it burned to the ground in 1914. Nevertheless, its brief existence gradually led to the development of an indigenous Korean form of music-theatre originally called Sinyeongeug ("New Theatre") but now known as Ch'anggŭk, or "singing play".

This is an account written by one British Major Herbert H. Austin in which he refers to the Wŏn'gaksa as the "Theatre Royal":

> Desirous of seeing Korean life in all its different aspects, we paid a visit after dinner to the Theatre Royal, close by, and derived no little entertainment from watching several acts of a Korean play, performed mainly by men and boys. The building in which it took place was one of some size, the seats in the body of the hall being raised in steps until they reached the level of the gallery or promenade, on which we had our seats in a private box on the right-hand side. There were four or five boxes on each side of the hall; those on the left, reserved for Korean ladies, being all full. Not understanding a word of the language, we were, of course, unable to fathom the plot—if there was one at all—though a gigantic paper or cardboard pumpkin, which was repeatedly being cut, seemed to be the chief cause of interest in this highly sensational drama. Most of the dialogue was chanted to the accompaniment of a drum played by a man on the stage, and from time to time supers strolled across the scene as though they regarded themselves as invisible for theatrical purposes. The music was by no means discordant, and the high falsetto voice so commonly heard in India appeared to be considered worthy of commendation in Korea, as applause occasionally broke out when a peculiarly high note had been successfully grappled with. At the end of each scene a red-and-white curtain, running along a wire, was pulled across the stage from one side, and a member of the

company would come before the footlights and hold forth to the audience, whom he was apparently informing what might be expected in the scene about to follow.⁶⁹

The "pumpkin being cut" refers to the story of Hùngbo, one of the traditional plots of P'ansori, or dramatic narrative singing, out of which Ch'anggŭk developed, and which dates from the late seventeenth century. In P'ansori, a solo singer is accompanied by a round drum called a puk. Originally the performances would take place outdoors, in a market or a green. Influenced by Japanese, Western and Chinese forms, the Ch'anggŭk expanded on this by distributing the parts among a number of singers, adding sets and a larger ensemble of traditional instruments, performed in a theatre.

However, P'ansori purists looked on Ch'anggŭk as a dilution of their form, and with its short history, it has struggled to firmly establish itself. Kim Seung-hye of *Joongang Daily* says it "has long been considered a genre of Korean traditional music that's boring, difficult to follow, and appeals only to highly patriotic audiences."⁷⁰

"I wouldn't say that Ch'anggŭk has influenced Western-style musicals in Korea as far as I know," says Dr. Andrew Killick, senior lecturer in ethnomusicology at the University of Sheffield, "though the reverse is certainly true and Ch'anggŭk itself often tries to combine traditional Korean music with elements of modern Western musical theatre. In fact, some recent productions have been advertised as 'musicals with traditional music'."⁷¹ As if to illustrate this point, musical theatre writer Jang Yoo-jeong (1976-) (*"Finding Mr. Destiny"*) recently adapted the traditional P'ansori story of *Chunhyang* (about a young woman who risks death by refusing to be the concubine of a corrupt magistrate) as a Ch'anggŭk.

When asked if there was any potential to use Ch'anggŭk in modern musicals, Dr. Killick replied "I don't think that's very likely except for occasional scenes of 'diegetic' P'ansori singing in musicals with a historical Korean setting."[72]

Korea has been through a lot over the past century. From 1910 until 1945, they were occupied by the Japanese. Since 1948, they have been an independent state, or more acurately two states: the Communist ruled People's Democratic Republic of [North] Korea has stood as a law unto itself since that time, and its spectre haunts the south to this day. The Republic of [South] Korea has, in the past, had its own struggles over the meaning of "freedom", although it has since the 1970s progressed from being a third world economy into a world-beating juggernaut, while also evolving into a democracy.

Although Koreans had been exposed to American musicals and revues since the 1920s, the history of modern Western-style musicals in Korea can be traced to 1961 when Yegrin Akdan ("Yegrin Musical Company") was conceived as South Korea's first publicly funded arts organisation. It had a specific mandate to mix traditional Korean music with western forms, including the creation of a South Korean version of the Western-style musical. This would show the kind of "vitality" that founder, spymaster and future Prime Minister Kim Jong-pil (1926-2018) believed was essential to combat the North Korean influence, although he denied that his motives were political.[73] "Just as I believed it was important to have sound political and economic systems to rebuild the country," says Kim, "it was equally important to have an arts infrastructure for the country. After all, we wanted to modernize the country and improve the livelihoods of the people through industrialization. Flourishing cultural activities was an essential element for improved livelihoods."[74] This was shortly after a military coup had seized power, and was very much a part of the Cold War mindset.

The name Yegrin (sometimes transliterated as "Yegreen") is a neologism that suggests remembering the past but looking forward to the future. Because of the perceived political nature of its inception, it led a somewhat chequered existence.

In 1966, a rather truncated production of *Porgy and Bess* was commercially mounted in Seoul, the first ever professional staging of an American musical in that city. In the same year, Yegrin sponsored a two-day symposium on musical theatre, investigating means by which traditional shows could be brought up to date, and the creation of an indigenous Korean musical theatre. They concluded that American and British forms could be used as a guideline only.

The result was *Saljjagi Obseoye* ("Sweet, Come to me Stealthily") which, although there were other less successful progenetors,[75] most Korean experts cite as the first true Korean musical. Premiered in 1966 at what was then the 3,000 seat Seoul Citizen Center (now the Sejong Center for the Performing Arts) by Yegrin, it was based on a folk-tale of the Joseon Dynasty (1392-1897) called *Baebijangjeon*[76] ("The Story of Bae Bijang") about a petty official named Bae Geol-deok-swe who is sent to an island where, faithful to his late wife, he has sworn he will never be seduced. The local magistrate wants to test him, and arranges for a gisaeng (roughly the Korean equivalent to a Japanese Geisha) to attempt to seduce him. The book was by novelist Kim Young Su, the lyrics by company director Park Young Gu and the music by classically trained Choi Chang Kwon (1929-2008).

The title song was recorded by the leading actress Patti Kim (1938-) and played on local radio, leading to a sell-out in its admittedly short run. "It was really cold and we had this stove on to keep the rehearsal room warm", Patti Kim remembers. "We practiced for more than three months for a week run, but had to wrap up in five days because the government needed the theater for the visit of then-U.S. President Lyndon Johnson."[77]

Over the next thirty years, musicals – now

branded "K-musicals" (in the same manner as their pop music is branded "K-pop") – became very big business in Korea. It has been part of what they call Hallyu ("Korean Wave"), a great interest in Korean culture that has enveloped south-east Asia and beyond.

The Last Empress, with music by Kim Hee Gab and lyrics by Lee Moon Roel based on a novel by Yi Mun Yol, tells the story of Empress Myeongseong (1851-95) (commonly known as "Queen Min"), wife of King Gojong (1852-1919). Min fought a futile struggle to maintain Korea's independence, and was eventually assassinated by Japanese agents.

Director Yun Ho Jin explains, "The form is Western-style, the sets are Western, but the songs carry a lot of Korean rhythm and emotion." [78] The show premiered in Seoul on December 30 1995, and was brought to New York's Lincoln Center three years later in a translation by Georgina St. George. It has since played Los Angeles, London and Toronto, and played to its one millionth customer in Seoul in 2007.

"The Korean musical is going to boom," predicted the show's American-born and educated musical director Kolleen Park (1967-) in 1998. "We are the frontiersmen. That's why we shed tears and blood. We've been working on this show for seven years. The musical is here to stay."[79]

At first, the beneficiaries of this new market were the usual suspects – *Phantom of the Opera*, *Mamma Mia!* and *Miss Saigon*, but then a few more original ideas began to creep in.

In 1999, producers found a way around the language barrier by creating *Nanta* which combined *slapstick* with "samulnori" percussion (literally, "four objects play", meaning it is played with four traditional instruments: a "Kkwaenggwari" or small gong, a "jing" or larger gong, a "janggu" or hourglass-shaped drum, and a "buk", a barrel drum similar to a bass drum) in a nonverbal show. *Nanta* played at the Edinburgh Festival in 1999 and ran off-Broadway in 2004 for 642 performances under the English title *Cookin'*.

In 2009, on the 100th anniversary of the assassination of Ito Hirobumi the Japanese governor of Korea by independence fighter An Jung-geun (1879-1910), composer Sang Joon Oh and lyricist A Reum Han created *Hero: The Musical* celebrating what they called An's "sacrificial death" by execution in 1910. This was a big hit in Seoul, and in 2011 was brought to Lincoln Centre in New York for a brief visit, playing in Korean with English surtitles.

The *New York Times* wrote: "As drama, 'Hero' has the problems of a patriotic story in which good and evil are too clearly defined... Toward the end, the villain, Ito, is given some complexity; he may want to experiment on bodies, but he also wants peace and prosperity for a Japanese-led Asia. An, though, remains a paragon, a hero first, last and always... If the story sags, the staging never does. The director, Ho Jin-yun, and his design team want to wow you, and frequently succeed."[80]

Between 2000 and 2002, musical grosses in Korea jumped from 34 billion South Korean Won (US$30 million) to over 125 billion SKW ($110 million), or roughly half of all live performing arts takings. More than a thousand musicals were produced in Korea in 2005. However, since that time, there has been a five-fold increase in production costs. Because of the relatively small talent pool, name actors are able to command the equivalent to more than 10 million SKW (or $9,000 USD) per performance. This means that in order to keep the cash flowing, producers need to have multiple shows in production, and often use the profits from one show to pay off the debts of another – which, from an investor's point of view, can be a recipe for disaster. It is estimated that the Korean musical has an audience pool of just over five million people.[81] Whereas

London and New York play to international tourists, Korea – due to the language barrier – can only count on its domestic market.

By 2006 the income had nearly doubled again. This has made the country's moribund film industry sit up and take notice. "These days, audiences are responding much better to musicals than films," says Kim Mi-hee of film company Sidus FNH. "The musical industry has huge possibilities insofar as it attracts talent and money."[82] Goh Jung-min of the Samsung Economic Research Institute says, "The musicals sector is slowly becoming one of the areas with the brightest prospects."[83] Thus film producers began to adapt their own catalogues to the musical stage, and a number of investment funds have been created to back new ventures.

One of these "movicals", *Nae maeumui punggeum* ("The Harmonium in My Memory") is based on a 1999 film of the same name, which in turn was based on a novel called *Female Student* about a sixteen year old girl who falls in love with her teacher in rural 1960s Korea.

Another movie-to-stage adaptation was *200 Pound Beauty*, about a singer who undergoes plastic surgery to lose weight, in order to improve her career prospects. The show combined some songs heard in the original film with a score by American composer Tim Acito (1968-). It opened in Seoul in January 2009 at Chungmu Art Hall.

Comedian Baek Jae-hyun created an adaptation of Neil Simon's *The Good Doctor* called *Lunatic* that has been seen by more than 600,000 people since its debut in 2004. For his follow-up creation, *Skywalk*, he is aiming even higher. "With the experience and know-how I gained doing *Lunatic*, I hope to make the show popular across Korea first, and ultimately on Broadway"[84], he told Han Aran of Korea.net. Another musical of his, *Steam-Family*, about the Korean martial art Taekwondo enjoyed an off-Broadway run in October 2008.

Some Korean musicals tackle serious subjects. Jung Sung San's *Yoduk Story* is set in a North Korean prison camp, featuring song titles such as "If I Could Walk Freely" and "All I Want Is Rice." Faced with resistance to his difficult subject matter, Jung at one point borrowed money to finance the show from a loan shark, putting up his kidney as collateral. "Even a dark and tragic story can be beautiful," he told *Los Angeles Times*' Barbara Demick. "It will make them realize what happy lives they have here".[85] Jung defected from the North in the early 1990s, after being imprisoned for listening to South Korean radio. His father, a highly placed civil servant, was later executed.

Since 2006, every year the city of Daegu has held the Daegu International Musical Festival for three weeks from mid-June until early July. In its first few years, they worked in partnership with the New York Musical Festival, exchanging productions. According to their website, "It was born to enjoy musical together with Daegu citizen and global people and to grow it up as an industry."[86] In some ways, this can be seen as a continuation of the process that began with the symposium held by Yegrin in 1966.

Given the emerging importance of Asia as a musical theatre market, I set out to attend the thirteenth annual festival in 2019. I arrived in Seoul on 19 June, and travelled by train to Daegu the following day. The city was filled with nearly identical high-rise apartments, few of which appeared to be more than a decade old. This scene was broken by small hills – mounds, really – that had very little development on them. Several of these had been made into parks, and I managed to explore a few of them. Its central core was noted for having several "heritage" buildings surviving from the era of Japanese occupation from 1910-45. Much rarer was any vestige of old Korea, although there were a few examples if one knew where to look.

Having never been to this part of the world, I

sought to aclimatise myself by visiting the Daegu National Museum, the Daegu Museum of Modern History, the ancient burial tombs of Bullodong and the shrine of General Sin Sung-gyeom (which commemorates a battle in which said general died defending his King in 927). I was trying to imbue some sense of the history of the place, although in terms of musical theatre, everything was new.

While it was as ancient as Europe, Korea had, in a very short period of time, changed beyond all recognition. The population of Daegu was now ten times what it had been at the end of the Second World War, and as a consequence, they had little use for anything old. They had even, to a large extent, gone from being a Buddhist country to being Christian, if they had any religion at all. Aware of the risk of becoming soul-less, in recent years they have invested enormous amounts on culture: not so much on preserving the existing one as inventing a new one.

There are many publicly-owned arts centres spread throughout the city. These have all been built within the past three decades. Some of these were built in a style once popular in the West in which they seem to want to keep the audience a safe distance from the stage. Few of them posess any form of catering facilities, as if to say you're not there to to relax, but to witness Art. If at the interval you want to drink anything other than water, you will have to fend for yourself. (Buddhist temples, on the other hand, generally have Coca-cola vending machines.) The front-of-house staffs also expect audiences to behave themselves – I was scolded for leaving my jacket over the back of my seat and instead told to place it on my lap.

What is this "festival" about? It's not a conference, nor is it really a trade fair. It is a festival in the same sense as Cannes. There were shows from the UK, France, Spain, Russia, mainland China, Taiwan and Thailand, as well as Korea. (While they had previously included works from the U.S., in recent years the focus has clearly shifted to Asia.) Until a couple of weeks before the event, the lineup had not been finalised, and I had no way of knowing what I would be in for.

Its intention is to bring the best in the world to Daegu, its program describing it as "the Mecca of Asian Musical!" aiming "for the popularization of Korean musical and activation of musical industry." Their English may be idiosyncratic, but their intentions are serious.

What sort of thinking is driving this venture? Since achieving independence in 1948, Korea has been obsessed with the need for success in virtually every field. "The desire to measure up is a result of Korea's troubled history", says former *Economist* writer Daniel Tudor. "For the South under [former dictator] Park Chung-hee, it meant pursuing economic growth... A surprisingly high number of Koreans know the size of the national GDP, and how this stacks up against other countries. They know that Korea is the number one country in shipbuilding and semiconductors. They also know that the Korean Olympic team's medal table rank has been consistently improving, and that [pop star] Psy's[87] 'Gangnam Style' hit number two in the US pop chart. In fact, 'Gangnam Style' not making number one was itself a story. When will Korea have its first US number one, ran the headlines?"[88] The Korean government even put him on a series of postage stamps.

So the powers that be decided that Daegu was going to become a music city. Not just any music city, but in terms of musical theatre, they aimed to be third behind New York and London. (Or at least, for three weeks out of each year.)

Bae Sunghuck, the chairman of DIMF's executive committee, describes it as an "art market that introduces works from all over the world in Korea and introduces excellent domestic works abroad."[89] Most of the attendees whom I saw seemed to be ordinary members of the public. Korean pop star Suho (Kim Jun-myeon), who had starred in a Korean production of Frank Wildhorn's *The Man Who*

Laughs, was its ambassador. Apart from the participants in some of the guest shows, I appeared to be almost the only Westerner there.

The shows that I saw during the 2019 festival were *The Wedding Singer*, a UK-based production of a show that had a modest run on Broadway in 2006; *Tevye and his Daughters*, a Russian re-telling of the same Sholem Aleichem stories that inspired *Fiddler on the Roof*; *The Twilight of Springtime* from Shanghai; *Montand and the French Lover*, a French jukebox musical based on the life and loves of Yves Montand; *La Calderona*, a bit of Spanish history set to hip-hop; *In the Mood for Sorrow*, a juke-box musical based on the highly theatrical and narrative songs of Taiwanese composer Huang Shu-Jun (1966 -); *One Fine Day*, also from Taiwan; *Turandot, Lee Jung Seop's 'Memory'*, *Song of Yoon-A* and *Song of the Dark*, all from South Korea, and *Amelia* from Thailand. Most of these shows were subtitled, but not always in English.

From Shanghai came *The Twilight of Springtime*, with a libretto by Yu Rongjun, the chief director of ACT Shanghai International Theatre Festival and music by Zhao Guang, a graduate of the Shanghai Conservatory of Music. It tells a nostalgic love story of life in Shanghai in the 1990s, told by a group of friends meeting on the verge of the millenium. "The musical is both a love letter that I write to 1990s China and a youth declaration for the new era of Shanghai"[90] says Yu.

The choreography was by Wang Yabin, whose international renown has brought commissions from the English National Ballet among others, and whom *Dance Magazine* says "converts movement into liquid that spills across the stage."[91]

"Firstly, my choreography helps to portray the story in a better way", she says, "showing off the dancer's vitality and youthfulness. Moreover, I hope to create moves filled with nostalgia, while giving people a sense of modernity at the same time which matches the city very well."⁹²

Koreans Seo Sookjean and Jeong Jiajin created one of the most stunning scenic designs I have ever seen, incorporating virtual scenery with computer generated animation. It was directed by Zhou Xiaoquan.

Memory is a Korean musical by writer-director Lee Myungil and writer-composer Yoon Jeongin based on the tempestuous life and work of Korean national painter Lee Jung-Seop (1916-56). The production used simply animated versions of Lee's paintings as a scenic backdrop. It was choreographed by Lee Sunkyoung and Kim Wanwook.

The festival itself produced a Korean reinvention of the Puccini opera *Turandot* with a libretto by Lee Haeje and music by Jang Soyoung and Hwang Gyudong. It first opened in 2011 and has travelled to China as well as Eastern Europe. Ingrid Faisiang, the Director-General of New Stage Theatre in Bratislava, Slovakia says, "I had the opportunity to see this musical directly at the DIMF Festival in Daegu in 2016 when we performed with the musical *Madame de Pompadour*, and [it] immediately caught me with [its] magnificent, European-style music, [its] naivety, and [its] theme – the story of Princess Turandot is our close and European viewer, especially thanks to the great opera work. I believe that such an exclusive Asian title will greatly enhance the offer of our theater and bring the audience a new and contemporary theater experience."⁹³

On the final day of the festival, I stayed around to see if I might have a chance to meet some of the people behind the shows. The front of house staff, believing I was trying to crash the party, tried to persuade me to leave but I was spotted by one gentleman who had seen me at several of the events. He turned out to be Lee Jangwoo, the festival's chairman. Thus, serendipity (or a higher power) intervened again: what I had always hoped would happen, but was unable to plan, happened. When I explained what

I was doing, he invited me back to their offices, where I also met Bae Sunghuck, chairman of the festival's executive committee.

Bae said (through an interpreter) "I understand the system of Broadway and West End and we hope to have that type of run-through system as well, but the market is completely different from here and there, and then for us it's really the cost of creating those musicals is more expensive than making musicals there because we don't have enough people to come and watch." He suggested that I return again in five years. "There are high possibilities of releasing some musicals based on K-pop and very successful musicals, not really Broadway-style musicals, but Korean-style musicals."

Given their success in using K-pop stars in musicals, it tempted me to think the unthinkable: could it be that, in this country at least, musicals are actually "cool"? The two chairmen left me with a bag of gifts to take back as I found a taxi back to my hotel, and prepared to return to London.

Korean producers have begun to look beyond their own domestic market, exporting both homegrown musicals and Korean productions of Broadway and West End shows. "It shows the growth of the Korean musical that a Korean troupe is staging a Broadway musical hit in our native language in Japan, a nation which is so proud of its long performing arts history", says Eric Song of Shownote, whose production of *Hedwig and the Angry Inch* toured in 2006. They have also sent home-grown works there. *Winter Sonata* based on a Korean TV drama with music by Kim Kyong Suk, toured to Sapporo, Tokyo and Osaka. In fact, in recent years their emphasis has shifted from New York and London to Japan and China.

It was when a proposed co-production agreement between the Chinese authorities and British producer Sir Cameron Mackintosh fell through that an opening appeared for Korean producers, which they have since exploited, in spite of the fact that their languages are unrelated, to make themselves the gateway to China. How were they able to do this? Apart from simply jumping at an opportunity when it arose, the Chinese market is very complex for Westerners to manoeuvre in. Even without the ideological baggage, as we have seen already, there are cultural differences that Koreans and other Asians would have a better chance of understanding than Westerners would.

China has its own early history with a kind of musical theatre. Li Jinhui (1891-1967) is considered to be the father of Chinese popular music, although during his lifetime his work was frowned upon by both the Kuomintang ("Nationalists") and later by the Communists. He established the Bright Moon Song and Dance Troupe in the 1920s, and through them contributed to a kind of fusion of Chinese folk music with American jazz called Shidaiqu. Inspired in part by the Huagu Xi ("Flower Drum Opera")[94], he inaugurated a form known as Gewuju, or "dance drama".

In 1982 came what is considered to be the first modern Chinese musical: *Women xianzai de nianqingren* ("We the Young People Today") by the Xiangtan Opera Company and the National Opera. Composer and lecturer Sissi Liu says, "Chinese musical theatre practitioners have continued to explore new ways to incorporate western (especially Broadway) style into a form that accommodates Chinese taste, reflects Chinese cultural values and, more recently, embraces the international musical theatre market and resonates with the current practice and philosophy of transnational collaboration."[95]

A New York-based company called Broadway Asia International with extensive involvement in Chinese performing arts brought a show called *Reel to Real, the Movies Musical* to the 2010 Edinburgh Fringe Festival. The multi-million pound show with a cast of twelve but a backstage crew of 32 used cutting edge projection technology to allow its live actors to interact with characters from classic Warner Brothers, MGM and 20th Century Fox movie musicals. The show, which was performed in English, used interpolated songs drawn from the catalogues of Rodgers and Hammerstein, Stephen Sondheim, Frank Loesser, Irving Berlin and others. It was originally commissioned to open the Huairou Theatre in a suburb of Beijing. "There's a huge renaissance in Mainland right now in terms of incorporating culture into the development of the socio-economic system", producer Simone Genatt Haft told *The Stage*. "It's a shift in perspective from when they were a country where culture was primarily for the purposes of propaganda."[96] Their next project, a contemporary adaptation of the traditional Kunqu opera *The Peony Pavilion*, by a team of Broadway artists, opened in Beijing in January 2012.

Broadway Asia has been involved in China since the government opened the market up to foreigners in 2005. Their productions have included *The Sound of Music*, *Cinderella*, *42nd Street*, *West Side Story*, *Cookin'* (a percussion show from Korea) and *Hairspray*.

They have also worked with the Shanghai Conservatory of Music on a student production of *Carousel* and with the Shanghai Dramatic Arts Centre to train local performers. With the latter, they co-produced the first Mandarin language production of the off-Broadway hit musical, *I Love You, You're Perfect, Now Change* starring a Chinese pop star named Lin Yu-lin. In the last few years, Broadway Asia has toured shows in thirty-five cities throughout Mainland China. Gennatt told me they "have always focused on a two-way cultural bridge, bringing the best of Broadway to Asia and developing new shows with Asian artists."[97]

Similarly, Nederlander Worldwide Entertainment, who presented *Aïda* in Beijing in 2008, has worked with both Central Academy of Drama and Peking University to develop localised adaptations of Broadway shows, including a Mandarin version of *Fame*.

Singapore is full of contradictions – an Asian country where English is the common language. Its name translates from Malay as "lion city", although lions have never been native to this city state of just under five million people. Originally a Malay fishing village, the East India Company founded it as a British trading fort in 1819. It has four official languages: English, Mandarin, Tamil and Malay, of which Mandarin Chinese form the largest ethnic group. The working language is English, which everybody learns in school. Since gaining independence in 1965, the city-state has concentrated on economic development, and until the late 1980s, paid scant attention to the arts. That has now changed, and the government is actively promoting it as a "Renaissance" city.

"I used to go to pantomimes when I was a kid, because I grew up in colonial Singapore with a very colonial grandmother", says composer Dick Lee. "My father used to work with a lot of British and Dutch people in Shell Petroleum, so my upbringing was pretty Western."

Two shows, *Makanplace* and *Beauty World* both premiered in 1988 and claim to be the first Singaporean musical. "Yet our forebears were enjoying fusions of music and drama long before that, in multiple forms: Chinese opera, Malay *bangsawan* theatre, British pantomimes, assorted vaudeville acts and variety revues", says Singaporean critic, playwright and librettist Ng Yi-Sheng.

"The Golden Age of Malay Cinema in the 1950s and '60s was chock full of musical films, overlapping with the genres of horror, history and social commentary. Similarly, the tradition of Tamil dance drama has thrived since colonial times, with original works influenced by Bollywood, Kollywood [Tamil cinema] and therukoothu [an ancient Tamil art with dance and music and storytelling]. In the end, it's probably safest to define the Singaporean musical as any performance that advertises itself as such. Under those terms, it's generally—but not always—a homegrown interpretation of American Broadway fare, with all the pageantry and light comedy associated with the form."[98]

Makanplace, with music and lyrics by Saedah Samat-Alkaff and Jasmin Samat Simon, additional music by Varian Lim, Jerome Quek and Eugene Ryan Chionh and book by R. Chadran opened in March 1988, produced by Act 3 Theatrics Pte Ltd. The story focuses on two teenagers working at a "hawker centre" (food and drink concession). It was revived in 2012.

Beauty World, with a book by Michael Chiang (1955-) and music and lyrics by Dick Lee premiered on 4 June 1988 as part of the Singapore Festival of the Arts. It tells the story of a young woman who returns to Singapore and a cabaret called Beauty World in the period after World War II in search of her family. The title refers to an actual amusement park and market that began during the Japanese occupation and continued until the 1970s which had areas for performance as well as for gambling. Its initial production by Theatreworks ran for eleven sold-out performances, seen by nearly 10,000 people. It has been revived three times and toured Japan. There have also been student productions abroad, one at the University of Chicago in 2006, and another at King's College London in 2009.

Malaysian-born actress Claire Wong was in the original production in 1988. "Before that I was doing a lot of Western plays, where locals would go up on stage and use blonde wigs and speak with an English accent, because they were playing these white characters," she told the Kuala Lumpur *Star*. "*Beauty World* was, in fact, one of the first early plays created and told by people who were close to us – who were us. It was the first time I went on stage and spoke normally as a local person would. It was a very exciting period."[99]

"*Beauty World*'s success, with its secrets, cabaret girls and themes of rape and Japanese love, has been popularised by Singaporeans because it is something to which they can relate", says Dr. Aaron Hales of the University of Western Australia. "As such, Chiang and Lee have written about these themes using history, humour and song that draws upon clichéd Singaporean characters reminiscent of the 1950s and 1960s..."[100] Although *Beauty World*'s music is largely the Latin-based pop that was popular in Singapore in the late 1950s, it is also influenced by Cantonese melodrama, and uses such localised Asian entertainment forms as *getai* ("song-stage") and *gamelan* (a type of performance associated with the Hungry Ghost Festival, which is rooted in Buddhist and Taoist culture and happens during the seventh month of the Lunar calendar), both of which featured in the real Beauty World park.

"*Beauty World*, intended for tourist consumption and composed with Western techniques, has actually used Asian music genres that are either specific or geographically related to Singapore itself", says Dr. Hales. "It is interesting to note that in his pursuit of creating a West End or Broadway-styled musical, my analysis suggests that Lee has, whether it be a conscious or unintentional choice, done so using musical composition structures and performance genres very much rooted in Southeast Asia and Singapore itself."[101]

Forbidden City (2002) has been, to date, Lee's – and Singapore's – biggest success. Chosen to open the Esplanade Theatres, it tells the story of China's last empress through the eyes of an American woman who has been hired to paint her portrait. "Everything that I'm doing, I feel that I'm laying some kind of foundation", Lee says. It has been revived three times since opening in 2002.

Forbidden City: Hossan Leong and Sebastian Tan.
Photo Sealey Brand courtesy Singapore Repertory Theatre

"Being Asian working in a Western medium, I'm always faced with this issue of East meets West… There's a true, very real sense of fusion from Singapore, because we speak English… It does confuse us writers because … I am Chinese doing things in English in a Western medium using mainly Western influences and yet being Asian". As a result, even his perceptions of Asia are westernised. "All my references have been from *Madame Butterfly* to *Turandot*. All the big, major interpretations of Asia I've seen have been from the West… All of us in the arts are trying to find our own voice."

Lee is seventh generation Peranakan (Malay for "descendants") Chinese, a minority group whose ancestors settled on the Malay Peninsula and became assimilated into Malay culture, and his first language is English. "My relatives all speak Malay… The irony is that eighty-percent of our population is Chinese, so there is the problem in terms of racial harmony. The Malays were outnumbered by… Chinese. A few thousand of us Peranakans were in between. We were once the bridge, but we ended up being more British than anything else. The new Singapore has got a lot more tradition infused from the different ethnic groups because so many more immigrants came in. Most of the Singaporeans you see are second generation. They are still very Chinese. They bring a strong Chinese culture, which is why there are many pop stars from Singapore in the Chinese market. This coupled with the way the colonial past mixed with this new thing, I think that's creating something very interesting."

"All my music writing in my career has touched somewhat on the subject of identity—Singaporean, Asian, Peranakan, or otherwise—and my musicals have been wonderful platforms to expound my ideas,"[102] Lee told Clarissa Oon of the Esplanade Theatre in June 2017.

Lee wrote a pop song in 1974 called "Fried Rice Paradise" as "a way of expressing my Singaporean-ness right, but you know, Radio and Television of Singapore, in those days, banned the song. Because of the Singaporean-ness. After that happened, I decided to bury my Singapore identity. I decided to become international... There was no interest from Singaporeans about being Singaporean. Nobody cared at all... So, in '88, when *Beauty World* happened, and the Arts Festival was starting to become a Singaporean thing and the audience was starting to feel Singaporean... everyone was ready to accept it. And so, that freed me."[103]

While Lee has been a pioneer, and is so far the most successful writer of Singaporean musicals, there are others who are trying to develop new work. Another Singapore musical that has travelled to Malaysia, Thailand and China was *Chang and Eng* (about the original "Siamese" twins) which received its world premiere in 1997 at the Festival of Asian Performing Arts, with book by Ming Wong and music and lyrics by Malaysian-born Ken Low, the director of the brand management division of the Singapore Tourism Board. It starred Robin Goh as Chang, Sing Seng Kwang as Eng and Selena Tan as their mother Nok. The cast included a mixture of Singaporean, Thai, Filipino, Malaysian and Australian talent (including one-time *Neighbours* star Nathalie Basingthwaighte). The director, from Thailand, was Ekachai Uekrongtham.

Malaysian Business magazine wrote, "The depth and myriad emotions that the audience experienced just from watching the musical is testament to the level of talent and expertise involved in the Asian production."[104] After playing in Malaysia, Thailand and Beijing, China, it was revived in Singapore in 2001.

"Singapore is at the cross-roads between the Far East and the West", says Dr. Kenneth Lyen, a noted paediatrician, composer and vice-president of Musical Theatre Live, a development group for original Singapore musicals. "Our musical theatre influences are from England and the USA on the one hand, China and Japan on the other, and perhaps to a lesser extent, Southeast Asia and India." Lyen studied medicine in England in the 1970s, where in his free time he saw shows like *A Chorus Line*. He became hooked. He says, "The average Singapore audience prefers low-brow humour and melodic songs, and tends to avoid intellectual or deeply emotional themes. Knowing this, the creative teams write accordingly."

Stella Kon, Dr. Kenneth Lyen and Desmond Moey of Musical Theatre Live

Beginning in October 2004, Musical Theatre Live has been running a programme called "Beat By Beat" to "incubate" new musicals, by presenting them in a no-frills environment as part of the Singapore Festival of the Arts fringe. Seven playwrights were teamed with seven composers, and assigned mentors. In February 2005, a director was assigned to each team. In April, performers were brought in, and each musical was read in front of all the participants. According to Lyen, "a community of collaborators, producers, directors and actors was created." These shows were presented in front of an audience in June 2005, as part of *Five Foot Broadway*, in collaboration with the United Artistes Network and the Next Stage Performing Arts Academy. "The general public's response was overwhelmingly positive", says Lyen. "Not only did we have full houses every night, but we received a heavy demand for tickets, and eventually had a waiting list of 150 members of the public who were unable to get tickets." In August 2005, Creative Community Singapore became involved. Since that time they have staged 22 new musicals. The mentoring programme has also been bolstered. Only shows that receive a positive dramaturgical report go on to the next stage. While they have yet to produce any world beating successes, it is still early days, and they know they have a long way to go. Part of their aim is to create training programmes and workshops for composers, lyricists and book writers.

Unlike Lee, Dr. Lyen doesn't feel the "dislocation between East and West". Like the majority of Singaporeans, he is second generation Chinese.

"We embrace both Eastern and Western cultures quite naturally. We lapse into English and Chinese with ease, and hardly notice anything out of the ordinary... most Singaporeans, especially those who are more recent immigrants, retain their Chinese cultural heritage, whereas the Peranakans who are a much older vintage, have almost totally forgotten their Chinese culture. They cannot even speak Chinese. This makes them feel culturally dislocated. It is observed that many prominent personalities in the performing arts are Peranakans (a far greater proportion than expected given their relatively small population size), and I have often wondered if it is because of their sense of dislocation that makes them feel like 'outsiders'. The theory is that artists tend to be people who do not fit in with their society or culture."

Until the *Report of the Advisory Council on Culture and the Arts* recognised the importance of cultural investment in 1989, Singapore had been a virtual wasteland. "Countries all over the world are recognising the positive impact of the arts on the economy"[105], wrote the report's author, Ong Teng Cheong, at the time the country's second Deputy Prime Minister. Lyen believes that the arts and the creative industries are vital to Singapore's continued prosperity. "Government policy has a great influence on the arts. The Government suddenly realised that in order to get brilliant people to come and live in Singapore, they have to diversify. They have to tolerate different religions, different viewpoints, and so now suddenly they've woken up and they now want to have musical theatre as one of the many art forms." According to William Peterson, who helped establish a theatre programme at the National University of Singapore, "No cultural terrain in Singapore has received more conscious engineering on the part of the government or prominent individuals in the arts community than the Singaporean Musical."[106] The Singapore government has invested some S$600 million in developing the Esplanade, a complex of theatres, concert hall and a performing arts library that opened in October 2002 with Dick Lee's *Forbidden City*, co-produced with Singapore Repertory Theatre. Since then, a major casino and entertainment complex has opened at Marina Bay Sands, where BASE Entertainment Asia staged a smash hit production of *The Lion King*. Thien Kwee Eng, Executive Director of the Economic Development Board hopes that producers "can find in Singapore world-class performing venues, as well as forge collaborations with our creative talent and theatre groups."[107]

Esplanade Theatres on the Bay

Lily Kong, Associate Professor in the Department of Geography at the National University of Singapore says, "I will suggest that, despite the rhetoric about the importance of the arts in developing a 'gracious society', the major motivation behind cultural policy is economic; indeed, often, the economic works through the socio-cultural. Certainly, despite fears about the potential threat to the development of 'Singaporean' artistic and cultural forms posed by cultural development policies which appear to privilege foreign talents over local ones, such presumed challenges to the construction of a 'Singaporean idiom' are dismissed by the state whereas in other arenas, it has been vigorous in efforts to construct a 'nation' and build national identity."[108] Between 2005 and 2010, government investment in the arts rose by 82%, with the hope that the arts would contribute 6% of gross domestic product by 2012. "If they want vibrancy," says Dr. Lyen, "they've got to pay for it."

Lee adds, "Singapore is striving to be a global city. Singapore has been criticised for its stringent, old-fashioned ways and they need to open up. They realise that, but they don't quite know how to do it… You can't just let loose. Personally, I think some kind of governance is good, because we don't really know where to go. Being born and bred in Singapore, I cannot try and replicate Western values the way I'd like. I think it would be chaotic. It has to come one step at a time."

For some people, those "stringent, old-fashioned ways" have been a stumbling block to the musical's progress. If musical theatre developed alongside democracy, then how does it fare in a place where democracy is still somewhat constrained? While, since obtaining full independence from Britain in the 1960s, Singapore has become one of the most prosperous countries in Asia, it is looked on by many Westerners as being highly authoritarian. The U.S. based Freedom House classes it as "partly free". Homosexuality is frowned upon. Party political films are banned. Although it regards itself as a parliamentary democracy, ever since home rule was established it has been ruled exclusively by the People's Action Party, and is effectively a one-party state.

"Singapore writers and composers are not bound by West End or Broadway traditions", says Lyen. "One might have expected them to look at the musical from a fresh perspective and to be more experimental in their efforts. However, they tend to be rather conservative. There may be many Asian stories to tell, and indeed the Singapore musical does well in telling these stories, but the stories chosen tend to be rather bland and without intellectual or emotional depth."

"The rise of musical theatre requires a democracy, and also economic well-being," says Lyen. "Our government, which has been very successful economically, has been less successful in terms of the arts, in part because of their fear of the Communist element, and also civil unrest due to racial conflict. Censorship was very heavy. Shows were not allowed to have any racial or ethnic conflict in it, nor could they have anything to do with overt politics – especially left-wing politics – and gay movement, same-sex relationships were also frowned upon... All we could do was write romantic comedies. You run out of ideas after a while. This really deterred a lot of people from writing." About *Beauty World*, Dr. Aaron Hales of the University of Western Australia says, "The fact that Chiang and Lee are able to write about contentious issues such as race and class within Singapore is a testament to the genre of the musical. Practitioners of the arts, for fear of censorship, generally avoid issues of race within their representations, as such subject matter is heavily scrutinised by the government."[109]

Librettist Stella Kon, Musical Theatre Live's chairperson, told me of a rather blatant example of censorship in a play called *Trial*, in which Socrates is on trial in Singapore: "It came back with one line cut. The line was where a student gets up and shouts, 'There is no freedom of speech in Singapore!' You're not allowed to say there is no freedom of speech in Singapore!" The play went on, minus that one line. "It was crafted such that everything was said between the lines." Lyen adds, "We write fairy tales, we write folk tales, but actually we are writing about Singapore. So when we write [in] *The Magic Paintbrush* [2000, with music by Lyen and book and lyrics by Brian Seward] about the dictatorial emperor, it is actually about Singapore... We defy the government in our own very subtle way, and they don't seem to have noticed." (Singapore's neighbour Malaysia also suffers from censorship. "No musicals that have elements of dissent or put the government in a bad light are allowed," says librettist Teng Ky-Gan. "Ever." More about that later.)

Although things in Singapore have been liberalised in recent years, the legacy of repression has resulted in a kind of arrested development. Aaron Hales says, "I would argue it is impossible to sustain and expand culture if it is illegal to comment upon almost every cultural aspect of society in which you live."[110] "If we were allowed, we could have explored all these issues, the controversies and the emotional depth," says Dr. Lyen. "We could have produced really world-class plays and musicals... One of the problems I find now with the younger generation of writers is that they don't want to tackle these subjects. They shy away from them, which to me is a tragedy... To me, the best writers are the rebels."

Aaron Hales wrote his doctoral thesis on the influence of censorship on Singapore's indigenous musical theatre. In it, he discusses three musicals by Dick Lee: *Beauty World* (1988), *Mortal Sins* (1995) and *Forbidden City* (2002). Hales argues that it is *Mortal Sins*, one of Lee's least known works, which is most interesting. The book by Michael Chiang is openly critical of Singapore's censorship regime. "The musical was far too confronting for Singaporean audiences – it was not a comedy with light-hearted music. Instead, its narrative was serious, tackling the serious problems that underpin Singapore, such as censorship and suggestions of corruption in the civil service – themes that are generally located in 'niche' theatre representations and not large scale musical theatre representations."[111] It played for a week to full houses, but has never been revived, and Lee doesn't even include it in the biography on his website.

However, Lee claims that he has not suffered from censorship. "They used to censor local works but now most theatre companies practice self-censorship. They trust us. I'm with the Singapore Repertory Theatre, so I know we don't have to submit our scripts anymore." Dr. Lyen adds, "Funnily enough, when you are immersed in the Singapore system, you are less consciously aware about the effects of censorship... And to be fair to the Singapore government, the days of heavy censorship is largely over, and nowadays there is considerable freedom of expression... with the one proviso that if you are seeking Government funding for a controversial show, you may sometimes find yourself inexplicably unfunded."

Singapore also lacks a sufficient pool of trained actors, musicians, technicians, directors and choreographers. "We had to more or less start from scratch," says Lyen.

"Singapore is quite dated in its content", says Amanda Colliver, an Australian-born former singing teacher at the LaSalle College of the Arts, "but you have cultural things that you don't want to leave behind in the name of Western progression, and I think that's a very challenging mixture."[112] However, according to Colliver, Singapore has yet to develop triple-threats – actors who also sing and dance with equal proficiency. "The level is quite low here, but the potential is here." Dr. Lyen says, "We do have good performers here, but you can count them on one hand. We often import a lot of singers. The Philippines is blessed with quite a large talent pool... We are training our directors, we are training our singers, choreographers, dancers, the whole lot. It's a team effort."

Dick Lee has frequently worked with British and American collaborators. "I had been in Japan for about five or six years, and I'd done three musicals in Japan. The Japanese tradition for theatre and musicals is so strong. It's so professional, so developed. When I was considering doing a musical in Singapore, I wanted the same standards. The Singapore Repertory Theatre was an offshoot of a theatre group called Stars – the American community theatre in Singapore. The man who ran it, Tony Petito [(1950-2018)], when he came to see me, I got the sense that he wanted to have a very high standard, and that meant bringing in and collaborating with people from Broadway and the West End."

His first show written this way was *Sing to the Dawn* (1996), with London based South African-born director Steven Dexter (1962-), who had previously staged *Little Shop of Horrors* for SRT. "Tony Petito wanted the musical to be properly constructed with the right production values that a musical should have." He brought in lyricist Anthony Drewe (*Honk!*, *Mary Poppins*, *Betty Blue Eyes*), with whom he would also work on *A Twist of Fate* the following year.

A few years later, he teamed up with Dexter again, along with lyricist Stephen Clark (1961-2016) (*Martin Guerre*, *Zorro*, *Love Story*) to write *Forbidden City* for the opening of the Esplanade Centre in 2002.

Dr. Lyen feels that more could be done to develop Singapore's own writing talent. "Dick Lee realizes that book writing and lyric writing is relatively weak here in Singapore, and so he collaborates with English book writers and lyricists. While it gives him instant credibility and brings his works up to international standard via the express stream, it raises a few thorny questions... The look and feel of his musicals are very British. Indeed, you would not realise they are from Singapore, despite the fact that the subject matter is Asian... His works are not really representative of Singapore in language and 'soul'... Having said that, Dick Lee deserves a place in the hall of fame of Singapore musical theatre writers."

Although Singapore speaks English, it has its own unique dialect known as Singlish, a pidgin English which borrows words from Malay, Hokkien[113], Tamil, Cantonese and other south-east Asian languages. Lyen says that use of Singlish in the theatre is "mildly subversive". Singlish has always been frowned on by the government, who want to promote Standard English. "We do it when we're talking to our friends and our children and our neighbours," says Dr. Lyen. "It's colloquial English spoken, and some of the songs, especially songs written by Dick Lee, contain a lot of Singlish. Some of the words, like the word 'kiasu' is actually a Hokkien term." It refers to fear of failure, in which you modify your behaviour so you do things that are not necessarily socially acceptable. For example, at a buffet, you take more than you need because you are afraid that when you come back later the food will be gone. "We do borrow a lot of phrases from other dialects – Malay, Chinese, Indian... In a sense this has affected our theatre because it's less able to travel. If people cannot understand lyrics in Singlish, it is less likely that these shows will travel overseas." To illustrate, he says, "It is relatively cheap to employ a rickshaw puller, it is therefore a 'cheap buy', meaning an inexpensive purchase, but 'cheebye' is also a Hokkien very fowl word. Your grandmother will kill you if you use that word."

Dr. Lyen adds, "When Dick Lee's *Beauty World* came out in 1988, it was chocker-block full of Singlish. Only Singaporeans could understand it. But that was fine because only Singaporeans watched it." Lee said, "We were very concerned that when you sing, it cannot suddenly be Queen's English, and then when you talk, it's different. So, we carried (the Singlish) through (into the music and lyrics) and that made it sound very Singaporean, I think."[114]

Lee himself felt that the results were mixed. "There's a very fine line between it sounding comical and a bit over-the-top. Even with Singlish-speaking Singaporean actors, when they do Singlish on stage, it sounds forced. I don't know why, they can't speak naturally. They're only just now starting to do that... [The audiences] don't laugh anymore. Now a lot of theatre has gone very natural."

"Therefore we are caught in this awful dilemma", says Lyen, "should we write for an international audience with the hope that our shows can travel abroad? Or should we write something that reflects our culture? ... You can see why musical theatre has trouble finding its own voice here in Singapore because of our conflicted use of English."

For Dr. Lyen and his group, developing a strong sense of Singapore identity is important. "We are in the business of discovering and nurturing new talent, and to carve out a unique Singapore voice, influenced by but different from Broadway and West End", says Dr. Lyen. "Indeed we have a lot of young raw talent. My job now is to find a way to help them develop further, and if necessary, to invite people from Broadway and the West End to help in this process. Our mission at Musical Theatre [Live] is not only to build up our creative team and performers, but we are also trying to increase our audience size. Our core objective is to get people writing, and we do 'demo' staged readings. Also we are actively involved in community and school musicals."

Ken Lyen says, "A large percentage of the population speaks Chinese as a first language. The segment that speaks English well and attends English-language theatre remains relatively small." Although most Singapore musicals have been in English, there has been a recent trend toward shows in Mandarin. "Everything seems to have come together over the past three years", Goh Boon Teck, chief Artistic Director of the Toy Factory told the *New York Times*' Sonia Kolesnikov-Jessop in 2010. "The few Mandarin musicals that have been put on so far have done well at the box office."[115] These have included *December Rains*, a musical written in the Xinyao[116] form which is unique to Singapore, with a book by Liang Wern Fook and songs by Liang and Jimmy Ye, first presented by Toy Factory Productions in 1996, and revived at the Esplanade Centre in 2010. It tells the story of an idealistic young woman who falls for a political activist in 1950s Singapore. "Such familiarities have a stronger pull"[117], says J. P. Nathan, director of programming at the Esplanade. Other Toy Factory musicals have included Raymond To Kwok-Wai's *Shanghai Blues* (2007).

It is the stated aim of the Singapore government to

develop a "renaissance" city, but they face a number of obstacles. "In a nation built upon the necessity for financial success", asks Aaron Hales, "where is the space for artistic failure if every artistic product has to be considered an economic miracle?"[118] Dr. Hales does not believe that shows like *Forbidden City*, which seem to him tailored to gain official approbation, are the answer. "*Forbidden City* is a safe, reliable spectacle – highly colonialist – with clichéd depictions of Western music and imagery. It is colourful and bright and contains stereotypical Chinese costumes for colonial viewing. The production adheres to all the stage conventions for a European and American audience. At the same time, Singaporean audiences appreciated these themes and the musical sold out repeatedly. It is the perfect production for the selling of an Asian stereotype." But, says Hales, it "defines everything wrong with the Singaporean arts – all of Singapore is removed from the narrative… The local Singaporean public does not endorse works that challenge the audience and push theatrical boundaries in Singapore. Therefore, no 'endorsed' musical theatre product from Singapore is going to make a mark on the global arts scene."[119]

Dick Lee counters, "Nowadays the problem we're facing is sponsorship. A musical costs so much to stage. You have to sell so many tickets at such high prices to recover, which is why *Beauty World* could only be staged [in revival] because it had been staged three times before. But to do a new show with a new title would be – I wouldn't even take that risk. Not now."

Like its neighbour, Malaysia has a nascent musical theatre culture. Playwright and lyricist Teng Ky-gan (1982-) began in 2006 by collaborating with composer Lim Chuang Yik on *Broken Bridges* about a young man who returns to his home town of Ipoh (Teng and Lim's home town) in the 1950s. "He comes home with bright ideas," says Teng, "but the people of the town hate him for bringing change."

Broken Bridges
Photo courtesy Teng Ky-gan

The following year the same team created *Tunku*, a historical epic. However, censorship in Malaysia is even more restrictive than in its neighbour. "I'm surprised it got through," says Teng. "It was about a racial riot in 1969. The official government version is that the opposition started the riot. My musical showed the government starting the riot (to cut the very long story short). I was surprised it escaped banning, but my guess is that the person who read it couldn't read English very well, especially if it's in verse form... If you keep your lines ironic or sarcastic, they usually can't see further than what is written. Many political plays have been let through this way."

Like Dick Lee, Teng's first language is English. Just as Singapore has "Singlish", so Malaysia has its own native form of pidgin English called Manglish. Teng's ethnic background is Chinese, which makes him part of a minority in this Islamic, Malay dominated country.

More recently, in collaboration with composer Chuang Yik, he has presented *Paper Crane* about the rise and fall of a famous Chinese opera star, Ah Kit which was presented in 2012 at the Kuala Lumpur Performing Arts Centre. This show set itself a difficult challenge: to tell the story of a Cantonese opera star in the English language. According to librettist Teng Ky-gan,

> "The musical is set at the back stage of a Chinese opera. Hence, making them speak 'proper English' would be extremely out of place (while wearing Chinese opera costumes). Many lines are direct translations from

Paper Crane

Malaysian English/ Cantonese and here the audience would easily know what they mean; although to an American it would sound very strange. I would say that the language in *Paper Crane* is exactly how a Malaysian/ Cantonese speaker would expect it to be."[120]

According to Teng, the government encourages musicals that advance its own agenda. "Anti west/ anti colonialism/ anti Jew musicals or musicals with these elements are a big favourite. Stories of Malay rebels slaughtering evil white colonizers are also big."

The official performing arts centre in Kuala Lumpur is the Istana Budaya ("Palace of Culture") which presents classical music, opera and musical theatre. One Malaysian musical that was presented there to great success was *Puteri Gunung Ledang* (2006) a fifteenth century tale of love among the Malay aristocracy and royalty with music by Dick Lee and book by Adlin Aman Ramlie (1972-), Saw Teong Hin and Zahim Al-Bakri based on a 2004 Malaysian film of the same name also directed by Saw. It also travelled to Singapore's Esplanade Centre.

Author John Lahr says that the American musical "celebrates two things: abundance and vindictive triumph."[121] Singapore, Korea, the Philippines and no-doubt other Asian countries seem to equate musical theatre with prosperity. Whether it is through the importation of Broadway and West End shows or the encouragement of indigenous works, it is popular because it represents Western-style affluence.

As in Korea, Thai people have only recently become interested in musical theatre. They have imported productions like *Lion King*, *Phantom of the Opera*, *Miss Saigon*, as well as creating original Thai musicals. Peevara Kitchumnongpan, the managing director of the Southeast Asia division of British producers Selladoor Worldwide dates this development to 2005, when the 1,495 seat Muangthai Ratchadalai Theatre opened. "That really marks a huge leap in our culture," he says.

Eight years later, he appeared as an actor in a Thai production of *Miss Saigon*. "Because of my English, I shadowed Cameron [Mackintosh]'s licensing quality control person here in Bangkok, and it was discussed that it was one of the best reproductions of *Miss Saigon* that's ever been done in the world, and that production never made back its money. If *Miss Saigon* doesn't work in Bangkok, what will?"

Ever since then, Peevara has been searching for an answer to that question. As a passionate devotee of musical theatre, as well as a patriotic Thai, he has been trying to find a way of educating Thai audiences. "You have to look at the state of the country in a fluctuating, developing world in order to tell the right story at the right time. I would say that back when *Miss Saigon* was on, the society just did not need a tragedy. It needed a comedy, and without the word of mouth of people having such a great time – 'Oh my God! You need to come and see the show' – this show would never really take off... That's part of the reason why I personally felt that *Miss Saigon* failed even though it is one of the best things that has ever been produced in this country."

Peevara came to London and obtained his Master's degree in musical theatre creative producing from Mountview Academy of Theatre Arts. He has since then partnered with Selladoor, running their Bangkok office.

"Now we're one and a half years running, and we're slowly building up our ecology in how to make theatre works... For example, last year we produced *Little Shop of Horrors* fully in Thai and that was very successful critically. We weren't successful commercially, but we were able to find out the Thai production's capability through our experience... Thailand is a very, very unique market and very niche. It needs a very specific content, so our next production is going to be programmed for developing a brand new Thai musical. We're in the middle of that process now, which is very exciting."

One of his projects is a show called *Klong* which is the Thai word for 'drums'. "We want to create a rhythm show that is specifically and uniquely Thai with a little bit of traditional references but we want to create [a] show that is competitive in price and quality and work with our partners in the U.K. to send our shows the other way around."

Peevara is up against an audience climate that is in its infancy.

"I would say that the area of the appreciation of the arts is not as strong as in other countries such as South Korea or Japan. The audience sophistication is not as high culturally as those places. It doesn't mean that the city doesn't feel like it's progressive: It is high tech, it is multicultural, it is Westernised, but you have to take into consideration as well the sophistication of people on the inside, and not on the capitalism or materialism, because all those areas are very progressive, but unfortunately, appreciation for the arts is really not there. Otherwise, theatre would have a much easier time being produced here."

Although Thailand is still considered to be a developing country, Peevara doesn't believe the problem is primarily economic, but cultural.

"In Thailand, for a mass audience, that hasn't been fully introduced and fully embraced the idea of live theatre, they would often say to me, 'what makes your show more worthwhile than spending the same amount of money to buy that ticket and see *Avengers* five times in the cinema?' The answer for theatre people is that you can't possibly compare the value of going to cinema to the live theatre. But that understanding is very, very difficult to get across to a Thai mass audience, and that is mainly the problem."

Peevara also believes the problem is educational: "The lack of theatre arts in schools. So therefore people who want to go into theatre can only study and experience it from university and up."

In fact, university is where much of it is happening. For the past twelve years, Napisi Reyes has taught the history of musicals and directing at her country's first and so far only full-time musical theatre program, at Mahidol University in Bangkok. She and her composer husband Krisada have also used this program to create some of their original musicals. The one I saw was called *Amelia*, in which the role of American flyer Amelia Earhart was played, at different stages of her life, by six actresses, who also doubled up playing the other supporting roles, both male and female. While the story was American, it was written and performed in Thai.

Thai musical theatre employs both traditional and Western styles. Kresida Reyes' background is mostly Western, "But I also have some works that were influenced by Thai classical music… The mainstream ones still use pop music as a core or as a form, and the idea of making a musical is a reference to Broadway. But there are still some small theatre groups that are different. We are between. We are… not in the mainstream but try to make something different."

Napisi did another musical for children, called *Dearest Moon*. "It's a story about the moon… who came to earth to see why people didn't respect him anymore… and we did use some Thai elements. For example, [Kresida] would compose using the pentatonic scale, but that was a Thai story."

They have also done some original musicals at Bangkok University. One with a Thai theme was *Dear Death* (2009), which Kresida and Napisi wrote with a book writer and director Punnasak Sukee from that school's own Performing Arts program. It is about an encounter with the god of death, expressing Buddhist philosophy. In it, a young man is coming to terms with the imminent passing of his grandmother, and learns to see this as a natural and beautiful experience.

Other Thai composers occasionally working in musical theatre include Anant Narkkong (1965-), a noted composer of Thai traditional music whose works for the Patravadi Theatre (established in 1992 by Patravadi Meechuthon) have included *PraLor* (2008-11), *WiwahPrasamut* (2012) and *Rocking Rama* (2013). Another one is Rapeedech Kulabusaya, a graduate of Mahidol University who is very productive. His works include *"Klaikungwon" Musical on the Beach* as well as Dream Box's production of *Mae Nak*.

There are other companies besides Selladoor who do commercial musical theatre: Scenario Company Limited, owners of the Muangthai Ratchadalai Theatre have, under president Takonkiet Viravan, been involved as a producer both in Bangkok and New York. Their productions in Thailand, which Pawit Mahasarinand, a teacher at Chulalongkorn University, describes as "middle to lowbrow",[122] have included *Thawiphop: The Musical*, a historical romance based on a novel by Thai national artist Thommayanti (Wimon Chiamcharoen, 1937-) about a woman who travels back in time and helps defend Thailand against the French and British. They also presented an adaptation, directed by Viravan, of *La Cage Aux Folles* that was reset in Thailand. In New York, they were co-producers of *Lysistrata Jones* and *Nice Work if You Can Get It*, and the revivals of *On a Clear Day You Can See Forever*, *How to Succeed in Business Without Really Trying* and *Promises, Promises*. They even tried to bring one Thai musical to

Broadway. *Waterfall,* based on a novel called *Khang Lang Phap* ("Behind the Painting") by Siburapha (Kulap Saipradit, 1905-74), with its original Thai score replaced by a new one by Richard Maltby Jr. and David Shire, got as far as tryouts in Seattle and Pasadena, starring Thai pop singer "Bie" Sukrit Wisetkaew (1985-).

Dream Box is Thailand's oldest professional theatre company, established in 1990 by Daraka Wongsiri and Sangarun Kanjanarat, who both graduated in drama from Chulalongkorn University, and Suwandi Chakraworowut, who graduated from Thammasat University. They use M. Theatre as their home, where their musicals have included *Koo Kam* ("Soul Mate") (2003), *Mae Nak* (2009), *Nam Sai Jai Jing* ("True Sprit") (2011) and *Prissana* (2012).

Other smaller scale companies worth mentioning include Be Musical (*Love Game*). Institutions that produced musicals also include Rangsit University, Chulalongkorn University, Burapha University and Kad Theatre in Chiangmai province.

Pradit Prasartthong, a friend of Napisi's, is a Thai playwright with an interest in promoting and defending Thai democracy. *Mangkorn Slad Gled* ("Dragon Heart"), which premiered at the Bangkok Theatre Festival in 2013, tells the story of Puey Ungphakorn (1916-99), the Rector of Thammasat University who was forced to resign and flee the country following the 6 October 1976 massacre of student protestors. The music by composer and actor Gandhi Wasuvitchayagit is based on melodies by the late Sudjit Duriyapraneet and is in the style of Lakorn Rong, a form of traditional Thai musical theatre developed by King Mongkut's son Prince Narathippraphanphong (1861-1931) that is, in turn, based on Bangsawan, a type of Malay opera.

"Even though he always paints these men and women as unequivocally good and heroic, Pradit's intention is to humanise and entertain rather than provoke,"[123] says Amritha Amranand in the *Bangkok Post*. "The student massacre scene involving the right-wing groups and the police, as imagined by the artist, felt real and true, especially for an event that no governments since have considered worthy of an official death toll." In addition to Lakorn Rong, other traditional Thai musical theatre forms include Lakorn Nok (performed by males) and Lakorn Nai (performed by females).

Knowing that in recent years Thailand has alternated between being a democracy and a military dictatorship, I asked if Thailand is subject to censorship. Peevara says, "I'm not particularly a political person, but the easiest way to describe being in Thailand now is that it feels like a democracy, but it's not. I don't feel like I'm being watched or anything like that... I don't feel like it's the military dictatorship in the worst of ways that we know throughout history. It's more like the political world here feels a little bit unprogressive... I feel that, over time, even though we have been dealing with democracy for ages, sometimes when the military has to step in to our country to stop two opposing forces or political parties from killing each other and return peace to the society by dictatorship, you're starting to really wonder whether the people here are really as well developed as we think in the first place." A new government was elected on 24 March 2019 under a new constitution that had been proclaimed by the military government in 2017, and the National Council for Peace and Order which ran the dictatorship was technically dissolved on 16 July.

Like Chinese, the Thai language is tonal, meaning that a word changes meaning depending on the pitch it is spoken at. "It's like a musical language", says Napisi. "There are five intonations... like a melody. If you use the wrong intonation, the meaning will change." Kresida says, "If I compose in Thai, I have to think about – especially when I'm combining words – we have to modify melodies to match."

Of her students, Napisi says that "Ninety percent of them would still work in the musical theatre field, but not all of them would be able to work as a performer. Most of them would teach at the studio, and teach the children to sing musical songs. They would perform in a production as their part time job. They cannot do it full time. We cannot survive by doing productions alone, so they would have to teach or do something else." Some of her students have come to London, and at least one person worked in the West End revival of *Miss Saigon*.

Peevara Kitchumnongpan says, "Our landscape is different in Thailand, as you may know. It's a lot harder to make work happen. It's a foot-on-the-ground to starting to build up a future economy that not-quite exists as in the West just yet."

For commercial musical theatre, touring in Thailand is virtually non-existant. Bangkok is the sole market. I asked him what would improve the scene in Bangkok. "We lack medium sized theatres, around three hundred to five hundred seaters would immensely help the kind of shows that should be produced right now in terms of engaging younger audiences, smaller crowds and build up a much faster culture."[124] Most commercial theatres in Bangkok work on a "four walls" rental basis, meaning that box office and front of house staff have to be provided by the producer, making it very expensive. "They take zero risk on any kind of projects made in their venue at all." As this book went to press, his company were seeking control of their own performing space.

As they are at the beginning stages of developing a musical theatre culture, I believe that the Asians could benefit from the guidance of visiting foreign artists, but only if those artists are sensitive to the local idiom. While they do have a few composers with potential, they have yet to develop world-class lyricists and book writers. However, a teacher who wants merely to impose West End and

Broadway values would not benefit them, unless they can also help to nurture their own nascent voices. They have a long road ahead of them. With the right nurturing – and some master classes – who knows?

New Musicals:
"You Have to Kiss a Lot of Frogs"

In the late-1970s, I had a conversation with Jennings Lang (1915-96), who was then a vice-president of Universal Pictures. We were talking about who we thought might advance the musical into the twenty-first century. I mentioned Andrew Lloyd Webber and Tim Rice to the man whom, a few years previously, had green-lit the film version of *Jesus Christ Superstar*. He shook his head. "One hit wonders", he said.

Lang was not alone in this assessment; Richard Kislan's book *The Musical*, published in 1980, doesn't even mention Lloyd Webber by name, and dismisses his potential impact on musical theatre by saying, "Not surprisingly, the rock opera frenzy initiated by *Tommy* and *Jesus Christ Superstar* declined simultaneously with the popularity of those productions."[1] (And *Evita* had already been running for a couple of years when he said this.) Critic Mark Steyn writes, "To Broadway folk, Lloyd Webber was just one of many writers who had emerged in the peace and love era, turned out one rock musical and then disappeared."[2]

Yet, three decades later, Lloyd Webber and his contemporaries are equally dismissive of the next generation. "There is a great misconception in the heart of the musical theatre industry that the world is littered with Cole Porters and Irving Berlins", says lyricist Don Black. "It is not. They are not out there and Andrew Lloyd Webber is always saying he wishes he had more competition from younger people. There is not a bunch of new people writing."[3] His fellow lyricist Sir Tim Rice concurs. "Where is a single young team or young writer writing fresh new musicals that are successful? I can't think of one."[4]

I have another theory. There are not many people writing the kinds of musicals that Lloyd Webber, Rice, Black and Mackintosh *want to see*. In the post Lehman

Engel era, everybody wants to be Sondheim, but there is only one. Even producers who have grown up in the era of subsidised theatre want to produce Adam Guettel, Jason Robert Brown and Michael John Lachiusa, all of them talented, but none of whom has written a major hit.

On the other hand, there have been successful shows – from *Matilda* to *Everybody's Talking about Jamie* – that don't fit the paradigm of a traditional musical. That is what I would call a "glass half empty" approach. Writers have to be nurtured. For that to happen, producers must be able to take a chance, to invest in the person, without any guarantee of making a quick buck.

Cameron Mackintosh maintains, "There have never been that many really good musicals... We can all probably agree on the top dozen, but then we'd all have a huge argy-bargy about the next twenty. And that's about all there is."[5] Of the many musicals he receives from unknown writers, "Ninety percent are terrible. They're untalented and shouldn't write musicals... There's also a group of people out there who are talented, who can write terrific songs, good lyrics. But only rarely do you find people who can write a good *musical... What you write about* is as important as what you've written... A lot of these scripts – there is no reason for people to see these shows." I know that it takes a lot more effort to persuade me to go to the theatre now than it did twenty-five years ago.

But when somebody complained to American director Harold Prince that "there are no composers anymore", he replied, "That's nonsense! There are not enough serious, creative producers."[6] By way of contrast, in the late fifties-early sixties, Frank Loesser actively nurtured the careers of Meredith Willson, Jerry Herman, Adler and Ross and many others.

"I think that the majority of producers are incredibly complacent about new work", says performing arts manager and consultant Georgina Bexon. "They think the really hot musical is just going to land on their desks. They don't accept the challenge of going out and searching." "For my mind", says Chris Grady, former head of international licensing for Cameron Mackintosh, "we have to do a lot of development work first to see that there is cream to rise to the surface." In other words, you have to feed and milk the cow.

History has taught us that the more shows that get produced, the more successful shows there will be; the fewer that get produced, the fewer hits. It's as simple as that. While we want to learn our craft from the masters, it's important that we don't set the bar so high that success becomes inattainable.

The next "big thing" might be the latest hip-hop show, it might be an old-fashioned musical comedy, or it might even be an esoteric piece of music theatre. I'm naïeve enough to believe there might be some producers out there who still do it for love, or who just have a gut feeling. Or perhaps there's somebody who is smart enough to know that in order to write or produce a hit show, we have to be prepared to produce a few that might not be hits. We can make educated choices, but we cannot make guarantees.

The real misconception is that you can always spot a diamond in the rough. Few people who heard "We're Six Little Nieces of Our Uncle Sam" back in 1917 thought to remember the name of the composer – somebody called George Gershwin.

Writers do not appear out of the woodwork like magic. They must be trained and nurtured. Even *My Fair Lady* was not an obvious hit in its developmental stage – when Lerner and Loewe auditioned their score for Mary Martin, she reportedly said, "These dear boys have lost their talent!"[7] And they weren't alone – Rex Harrison was not initially won over by the score either.[8]

Musicals are not initially heard accompanied by

orchestras and professional singers. They are often heard in dark rehearsal halls played on pianos which may – or may not – be in tune. There is a (possibly apocryphal) story in which Irving Berlin is auditioning a new song for a producer. The producer listens patiently, and when Berlin has finished, he thinks to himself, "That was really awful. What will I tell him? Wait a minute. Get him to play 'Puttin' on the Ritz'." He plays "Puttin'on the Ritz". "That was awful too!"...

Mackintosh concedes, "Most of what we look back on now as the great classics of musical theatre were basically shows that everyone else in the theatre thought was [sic] going to be crap and thrown out of town. I mean, *Romeo and Juliet* with street gangs?"

"Nowadays the terrible thing is that young people don't get a chance to be heard," said Stephen Sondheim back in 1973. "And therefore they get discouraged and say, 'Screw it,' and they start writing stuff for movies, or they try to start a rock group. It's awful. A terrible shame – nobody gets a chance to learn what he's doing."9 Things have not improved much since then.

In the U.S., where the development of new musicals has always been taken more seriously, there is a trend toward workshopping at universities. Tracey Moore, who played Emma Goldman in the national tour of *Ragtime*, became the head of the Musical Theatre program at Western Kentucky University. "Spending so much time in the presence of musical theatre writers in my career as a musical theatre performer meant that many become close friends, so it was a natural consequence that I would start a new musical development series at my university, twenty years later," she wrote in *Studies in Musical Theatre*. "I call it 'Before Broadway'. And mine is not the only one. I've noticed a surprising groundswell of new musical performances – in small schools like mine and in Banner Elk, North Carolina, and in larger ones like Penn State, Yale and Northwestern. University theatre programmes have become a new, safe place for writers, a place where they can make mistakes and learn from them – in front of an audience."[10] Oklahoma City University's Bass School of Music started a similar program, "OCU Stripped", in 2006.

However, outside the U.S., new musicals are not being so widely supported. In 2003, the British parliament's Culture, Media and Sport Committee held a series of hearings into the state of funding for musical theatre development in the UK. This coincided with a funding crisis that had engulfed both the Bridewell Theatre and the National Youth Music Theatre. The transcripts of these hearings were published in 2005, and they make interesting reading.

"We should be asking ourselves why there are so few brand new musicals by British writers in the West End", said the written submission from Mercury Musical Developments,

> "and to answer that question, one has to look behind the successful gloss of West End musical theatre at the structure that lies behind it, or, rather, the lack of any kind of funded structure. It is easy to conclude that, because of the success of certain West End musicals, plenty of money is floating around the industry. Unfortunately, however, this income is returned to private investors ('angels') and to the producers as profit (once costs are recouped) and is not being fed back into the grass roots level of development, to the very area where it is most needed. West End producers can and will happily continue to stage revivals and pop shows but these shows say little about the world we live in and are doing little to advance an art form which is the most popular live art form in the world. We need to create a proper structure for new musicals to be developed and flourish."[11]

This then raises the thorny spectre of public funding. "I had a conversation about twenty years ago with the head of music at the Arts Council of Great Britain", says Chris Grady, "and I had tried to get some funding for a project on developing musical theatre."

"I was told by the head of music that, no, they couldn't fund it. Why not? 'Well, because if you'd called it 'music theatre' we could have funded it.' So if I'd taken the 'a' and the 'l' off the words, then they might have funded it. That's rubbish. So I said, 'well what do you mean by 'music theatre'? 'I mean, if it was by serious composers.' Okay. So what do you mean by 'serious composers'? 'Well, opera. Through-composed.' Okay. So, *Magic Flute*, which, if I'm not mistaken, has got dialogue in it. 'Oh, yes, that's serious music.' Okay, that's by Mozart. Fair enough. So if you've written a requiem, would that be all right? 'Of course.' Okay, so Andrew Lloyd Webber's written a requiem. Are we now suddenly moving him into serious music? You just go round and round in circles. But there was a perception at that point that if it was 'music theatre' done by a 'music theatre' company with a kind-of opera singers, potentially, then that's fine, that can be funded by the Arts Council, but if it happened to have singers who could belt out a rock song or could also play in the West End, then that was not deemed to be fundable."

What is this "music theatre"? How is it different from "musical theatre"? God help the person who wants to try to explain that one. Some, like the Canadian Music Theatre Project, just use the words as synonyms for musical theatre, but back in the 1980s, things were quite different. Stephen MacNeff, one-time Associate Director of the Banff Centre Music Theatre Studio Ensemble says, "The simplest definition, really, is any kind of lyric stage activity that has music and where the dramatic component is as important as the musical component."[12] But doesn't that describe *Oklahoma!*? MTSE's founder Michael Bawtree says it aims "to combine the virtuosity of opera with the vitality of Broadway".[13] In practice, it seems that the term "music theatre" has been used to describe the less commercial type of show, such as *Nixon in China* or *Floyd Collins*. It reminds me of a rejection letter I received – without any intentional irony – from the artistic director of a Canadian "music theatre" company:

"We are interested in works which are unusual, often a new work which pushes out the traditions of operatic presentation, or a twentieth century piece which has not been presented to the Canadian audience. We are a so-called serious music organisation, recognising that everyone who creates music considers their work serious. I don't think we will find ourselves in the commercial musical comedy field in the near future and if we did I would look for a very innovative piece, I suppose ideally Sondheimesque."[14]

In any case, beginning in 2011, Arts Council England has given grants to Mercury Musical Developments as well as to two other development groups, Perfect Pitch and Musical Theatre Network. (From this, MMD and MTN have jointly sponsored BEAM, a bi-annual series of workshops and showcases of new work.)

There are a number of helpful organisations in different countries aiming to create an environment conducive to the creation of new musicals. In New York, there are musical theatre workshops started by both ASCAP and BMI, and the Tisch School of the Arts at New York University has a training programme for musical theatre writers, and in London, Goldsmiths has an MA in musical theatre meant to develop both writers and producers. (I am a graduate of that program). London also has both Mercury Musical Developments and Musical Theatre Network. (I should say, at this point, that both Don Black and Tim Rice have, in the past, supported some of these organisations.) Toronto has the Canadian Music Theatre Project at Sheridan College. In Singapore, Musical Theatre Live has their "incubation" programme. In Fredericia, Denmark, there is a programme called Uterus run by Søren Møller as part of Fredericia Teater, which develops two to six shows per year, a third of which are aimed at the international market.

Yet, when I participated in a series called Musical Futures at Greenwich Theatre (London), there was nary a producer to be found in the audience. It seems that the only way that new work can be produced is if the writer has the wherewithal to mount it himself. (And unless you're Adam Guettel and your grandfather was Richard Rodgers and you have a trust fund to live off of...) Only in the US are there well-funded workshops to develop new writers. And guess what? They're finding them.

Chris Grady complains, "We don't have a network of theatres yet that are funded or supported to do musical theatre... The writer needs to see it up on its feet so that they can see what works and they can see what doesn't." London's Bridewell Theatre had hoped to fill this void, but the funding crisis forced them out of their venue in 2005. Although the Arts Council England has begun to take musical theatre seriously, it is not treated as a separate form from either music or drama, and the higher development costs for musicals have discouraged most regional theatres from taking them on.

In Denmark, Uterus does not have that problem. "Uterus is mainly government money", says Søren Møller. "I give credit to the Danish Ministry of Culture for being brave with that, but actually it's the only sane thing to do. Musical theatre is the stage art that brings in the most audience. It's the most viewed art form, and it's the only art form that doesn't have development at all." As the principal of the Danish Musical Theatre Academy (now merged into the Danish National School of Performing Arts), he knew he was in the best position to move this idea forward. "I realised that, us being the only musical theatre institution in the country, we should do something about that. Having taken that initiative, they've only backed us from the beginning, and that's great."

One of the shows developed through Uterus was *Steam*, a musical reworking of *A Midsummer Nights' Dream*, re-set in New York in the 1950s. The music and lyrics are by Helle Hansen, with book by Mads Abeløe and Thomas Bay Pedersen, all Danish, based on an idea by American-born, Germany-based director-choreographer Tim

Zimmermann. They began developing it on their own initiative in 2007, and it was showcased at Uterus in April 2008.

The showcase, for two performances, included Act One and a "slap-on" ending. (To North American ears, the Danish actors' versions of a Brooklyn accent took a bit of getting used to.) Then it played the Edinburgh Fringe in August 2008.

"It's very intended as an off-Broadway sort of thing," said Møller. It was showcased at Penn State University in the US in 2010. "Not the greatest performance of the show," says the composer Helle Hansen, "but we learned that the bulk of it worked, but needed to be trimmed a lot - and move a lot faster - toward the end, and – partly as a result of this – would be better served in a one act format... After Penn State... we rewrote some of the ending, then let it rest a while. A long while. Doing other stuff separately in different countries."[15]

Then Søren Møller invited them to do a production in Danish (it was originally written in English) at Fredericia Teater in 2016. "This time the production would be at the harbour front, outside, using big metal containers, which was both a challenge (sound, weather, making entrances, changing clothes, crossing the back stage unseen), but also gave unique possibilities of designing the stage container setup... We agreed that this was the final version (with the option of adding ensemble, dancers for bigger festival productions)."

Møller explains, "There are three phases that you go through when you submit."

> "Anyone from anywhere in the world can submit work. Having done that, when you get selected, which happens from both us that run the centre and we have a committee of external readers – a producer, two musical directors, a composer and a lyricist that read and give feedback which

we of course listen to, but ultimately we take the decision. Getting selected, you get a three week workshop. There's a pre-phase to that where we give feedback to the writers where we say what we see is lacking or how this would benefit most from a workshop would be to hire such-and-such. Hopefully they agree to that. We've had projects where we've had to stop at that phase. Sometimes a composer or a writer does not really want their work developed or doesn't want the feedback, and I completely respect an artist's right to say, 'I don't want that.' We give, I think, very constructive critique upon the work, very caring and nurturing critique, but we will say what we see the problem is. Maybe we don't know, and then we will call somebody – maybe abroad – and say, 'this work has this problem – do you know a really good arranger for this style?' It could be an arranger, it could be a dramaturge or it could be a director... Having agreed upon what we are going to do, we will then cast it as we would cast a professional show. You will have either a pianist, a combo or a full orchestra, depending on what the piece needed and where the focus should lie. Then they dive into that three week workshop of development. Mid-way through that three-week period, we will sit down and find out whether we will take it to phase two, which is a showcase. So we might actually do a three-week workshop and not showcase it. We will still invite a few business people to come and watch a reading or whatever at the end, but we will not do the showcase if we do not think that the work is ready for it. It doesn't mean we've killed it – we might have to take it back and do another pre-phase and say this needs further development."

Uterus pays the full development cost, in exchange for 1.5% of the show's future royalties.

The correct conditions for the nurture of talent need to be in place. Canadian journalist and cultural commentator Malcolm Gladwell writes, "The sense of possibility so necessary for success comes not just from inside us or our parents. It comes from our time: from the particular opportunities that our particular place in history presents us with."[16] Writers need to achieve a critical mass – an environment in which the more peers achieving success, the better – to prosper in. It is common for people in the theatre to jokingly say that they hope their colleague's show is a flop, but it really doesn't work that way. One of the lessons that I learned from my research for *Broadway North* was that the more people who are writing good, successful musicals there are, the easier it becomes for the rest of us. Success breeds success. My belief is that if *The Drowsy Chaperone* had not succeeded, there would likely have been no Canadian Music Theatre Project and thereby no *Come from Away*. Not only does it make it easier to raise financing, but also the artists inspire each other. (In the pop music world, it was after John Lennon heard the Beach Boys' pioneering *Pet Sounds* album that he and the other Beatles set to work on *Sergeant Pepper's Lonely Hearts Club Band*.)

They also need to be allowed to fail. British comedian John Cleese (1939-) says,

> "People must lose their inhibitions. They must gain the confidence to contribute spontaneously to what is happening. Inhibitions arise because of the fear of looking foolish, the fear of making mistakes. People are held back by this fear; they go over each thought they have six times before expressing it, in case someone will think it's 'wrong'. While this is going on, nothing useful can happen creatively. A positive attitude towards mistakes will allow them to be corrected rapidly when they occur."[17]

I will argue that any culture that is successfully adapting the musical – or any other art form – as their own will end up passing through a number of phases, and it may help to understand this in advance. Firstly, they will import the form intact, just as America imported European operetta. They will then begin to produce their own imitations of varying quality. Perhaps some of those imitations will eventually begin to take on local characteristics, in the way that Cuban zarzuela did. Of course, since under even the best of circumstances eighty percent of new shows fail, they will probably develop a stigma or inferiority complex as the local imitations are compared to the real thing. I know this happened in Canada. Even the Americans had their suspicion that they were "Rome to Britain's Greece".

Then somebody may even emerge who has distilled the "rules" of how things work, and a group of disciples will slavishly follow them. Some of the resulting work will be promising, others hopelessly derivative. Then some other people will want to throw out the rule book and produce new work from scratch. The failure rate may rise to ninety-nine percent, although once again the odd promising work may make it through. Then another generation will come along and play mix and match, combining some of the old with a bit of the new. Some of these shows may be successful. A few may even achieve great success. Some people will then sit up and take notice.

Only twenty or thirty years after this has happened may we expect the stigma to disappear. If this sounds negative, it is not meant to be. When *Anne of Green Gables* was first produced, Canada was deeply ensconsed in the National Inferiority Complex. Now, fifty years later and with two Broadway hits in addition to numerous domestic successes, we are beginning to become confidant that we might actually be good at something.

The point is to keep your eye on the ball and never fear failure – it is just a stepping stone to success. Approximately one show in six on Broadway is successful, and that doesn't include the 99% that don't make it that far. That's how it has always been. In the so-called "golden age", the ratio of flops was just as high, but there was so much more product being turned out that more hits were created. While many critics will complain about a string of flops, the fact is that you have to kiss a lot of frogs to find the one that will turn into a handsome prince.

Minimising the risk is the function of workshops and try-outs. Beginning in 1961, Broadway maestro Lehman Engel, who began his career as musical director of

Marc Blitzstein's *The Cradle Will Rock* in 1936, established a workshop in New York under the auspices of Broadcast Music, Inc. to teach the craft of writing for the musical theatre. While Engel was not known as a composer of musicals himself, he had waved his baton in front of enough of them – including *L'il Abner*, and *Destry Rides Again*, among many others – to have developed a few theories about what makes them tick. Members of his New York workshop went on to create hits like *A Chorus Line*, *Nine* and *Little Shop of Horrors*. Eventually, more workshops were established in Nashville, Los Angeles and Toronto. (Leslie Arden, from the Toronto workshops, was also a student of Stephen Sondheim. When her *The House of Martin Guerre*, produced in Chicago and Toronto in 1996, was compared with the bigger and more famous Boublil-Schönberg *Martin Guerre*, it prompted American author Tom Shea to opine, "smaller is better".[18])

After Lehman died in 1982, the workshops carried on, led by former pupils. In Toronto, Jim Betts taught them, first through the Guild of Canadian Musical Theatre Writers, and later through Script Lab. The New York workshops were led for a time by *Nine* composer Maury Yeston, and in Los Angeles, the current artistic director of the workshop is John Sparks.

"It's a bastard art," says *Annie* composer Charles Strouse (1928-) "and there are those who want to make it into some kind of a lady. I think the workshops, all of the workshops — and I started one [for ASCAP] — I'm not sure they do any good. But on the other hand, I don't know what the alternative is."[19]

An example of the advice Engel would give can be heard in this anonymous account by one of his students from the New York workshop's newsletter:

> "'To make 'em cry, write optimistically... because self-pity only makes 'em laugh. Learn to find comedy in pathos; tragedy in optimism. Remember, we weep for those who

do not weep for themselves'... Lehman discussed the dramatic device of what he called 'misplaced optimism,' comparing two songs from *Porgy And Bess*: 'We cry more at 'Oh Lord, I'm On My Way' than we do at 'My Man's Gone Now'. [In the latter] we just hope she hits the high notes.' Lehman also had cautionary advice on the subject: 'Beware of adding sentiment to sentiment. Just adding *music* is adding sentiment.' Finally, he insisted that, 'Genuine emotion is not corny,' and on at least one occasion admonished a writer that '[The] ending [of your song] is straight from a can of Niblets.'"[20]

I joined the workshops in Toronto in 1983, one year after Engel died. At the time, they were being carried on by the Guild of Canadian Musical Theatre Writers, an organisation that aimed "to encourage and promote the development of composers, lyricists and librettists in musical theatre across Canada"[21]. When I was researching my book *Broadway North: The Dream of a Canadian Musical Theatre*, I spoke to four of my former colleagues – David Warrack, Nelles Van Loon, Jim Betts and Susan Cluff – about their memories of the man.

Toronto composer and musical director David Warrack (1945-) took part in both the Toronto and New York workshops. "They were an inspiration"[22], he told me. Jim Betts adds, "He brought a great enthusiasm about musical theatre to those of us who met with him over the years. It was wonderful hearing him talk about what was going on in New York City, getting caught up on the latest shows, learning about who was writing what, etc. He gave those of us in Toronto a feeling of being a part of the greater musical theatre community."[23]

"Indeed, the uncompromising nature of his personality put a lot of people off", says Warrack. "After one of the showcases in which [Martin] Short was a performer, Marty informed me in no uncertain terms that he would never do it again, because of the way Lehman treated him. Fair enough. But I saw Lehman in so many different circumstances that I believe it gave me some perspective on his mercurial moods." Another Toronto participant, Nelles Van Loon, says "In my view, Lehman was a great teacher and great teachers have a way of being dogmatic, not just out of arrogance, but because they have earned their stripes and acquired their convictions through many years of study."[24]

"At the root of it all," Warrack explains, "was his insistence on the highest professional standards and his immense love for the theatre. He positively glowed with that elfish smile on his face when he encountered a magnificent song, or scene, or performance. It wasn't easy to get him there, but anybody who did received tremendous encouragement."[25]

Engel's advice wasn't always correct. Susan Cluff remembers, "He told us not to worry about getting the rights to source material, which, in at least one writer's case, was not good advice. Lehman felt that if you wrote a good show that you or the producer would be able to [obtain] the rights."[26]

Nor were his assessments of shows always universally accepted. He claimed that, during the so-called "golden age" of the Broadway musical, only one show – *Bye Bye Birdie* – with an original book (as opposed to an adaptation) had been an enduring hit. Yet, he cites *Brigadoon* as one of the all-time greats. What was it based on? Alan Jay Lerner says it was an original.[27] And what of *Finian's Rainbow*? And *The Music Man*[28]? None of those shows were based on existing material. And I'm sure that many producers – and even authors – would have balked at his suggestion that "On the Street Where You Live" should have been cut from *My Fair Lady*.[29]

"I would also say that Lehman's students taught each other a great deal," says Van Loon. "I can remember Jim Betts saying it was quite possible for one person to write book, music and lyrics, or I might never have tried it... So, the disciples ... have altered the principles in various ways, but for my money, Lehman had an (almost) unerring instinct for what was at the guts of a show."[30]

In November 2006, Script Lab presented its first ever Festival of Canadian Musical Theatre in Toronto. The festival included songs from established Canadian hits such as *The Drowsy Chaperone* and *Billy Bishop Goes to War*, as well as a reading of *Turvey* by Don Harron and Norman and Elaine Campbell, the creators of *Anne of Green Gables - The Musical*. Although I wasn't there for the festival, one of my songs – "Something in the Air" (from *Perfect Timing*) was included in a showcase of new writing, sung by Elizabeth Rose Morriss.

Still, as in London, it has been difficult to get the industry to back indigenous musicals, and a subsequent Festival had to be cancelled when a sponsor withdrew. Still, Toronto has managed to foster such talents as Neil Bartram and Brian Hill, whose *The Story of My Life* played – briefly – on Broadway.

A "Graduate Musical Theatre Writing Program" was established at New York University's Tisch School of the Arts in 1981, the only programme of its kind in the world. Its founding mentors included Jule Styne (1905-94), Leonard Bernstein (1918-90), Lee Adams (1924-), Sheldon Harnick (1924-) and Arthur Laurents (1917-2011). The early instructors included Betty Comden (1917-2006) and Adolph Green (1914-2002), Stephen Sondheim (1930-) and Richard Maltby Jr. (1937-). One of the first students was George C. Wolfe (1954-) (*Jelly's Last Jam, Bring in da Noise, Bring in da Funk*). Under the leadership of Deena Rosenberg (1951-), a curriculum evolved until, after 1991, a permanent faculty was assembled, all drawn from the professional theatre community. In 1996, Sarah Schlesinger, librettist of *The Ballad of Little Jo* replaced Rosenberg as programme head.

The admissions process is extremely competitive. "We don't want people who aren't ready to collaborate",

Schlesinger told playwright and journalist Lee Davis. "The one thing they have to have in common is the desire to be a collaborative artist." [31]

For the first year, they concentrate on the basics of structure and craft. "We use the past to inform the present", says Schlesinger. They learn by doing, writing simple songs and scenes, culminating in a twenty minute musical and seeing it performed by professional guest artists. In the second year, the focus is on developing a finished "thesis" piece, which is critiqued at each stage of its development. The students now come from all over the world, including Europe and Asia. "It's a big world out there."

However, there is a big caveat: with tuition in the six figures, unless you either get a very generous scholarship or your Daddy's in the Forbes 500, you ain't gonna get in. Goldsmiths in London, the only other permanent MA program in musical writing, is considerably less expensive but also less comprehensive.

In recent years, London's Theatre Royal Stratford East has initiated a programme to develop musicals specifically for their ethnically diverse audience. One of their first successes was *The Big Life*, a version of Shakespeare's *Love's Labours Lost* transposed to Britain's Caribbean immigrant community of the 1950s. The book and lyrics were by Paul Sirett and the music by Paul Joseph. The *Independent*'s Adam Scott wrote, "The emergence of a strong, original-book musical into the London stage wilderness of cut-and-paste, back-catalogue plundering was always going to be welcomed. That when it arrived it would be as joyous an affair as Paul Sirett and Paul Joseph's *The Big Life* is more than the jaded musical theatre-goer could have dared hope for... Amid the fun, the social comment laced through the evening gains power from its understatement. The racist hostility the characters endure is met with a confusion and pain that Sirett's clear lyrics convey without rancour. Indeed, for all the show's verve and exuberance, every element - from performers, band, laughs and social comment to the economical and witty set - is perfectly balanced in an irresistible whole."[32]

Founded by Joan Littlewood (1914-2002) as Theatre Workshop in 1953, the theatre has always nurtured working class writers and composers, including Lionel Bart, whose *Fings Ain't Wot They Used T'Be* opened there on 17 February 1959, then transferred to the Garrick for a two-year run. Three years later, *Oh, What a Lovely War!* transferred to both the West End and Broadway and was made into a film. More recent successes have included *Five Guys Named Moe*.

"We did more black, Caribbean and South Asian new work than any other theatre in the country," says Kerry Michael, who stepped down as Artistic Director in 2017 to be replaced by Nadia Fall. "That was all because the area was changing, and those immigrants were now finding themselves in East London. All that kind of work had a popular, accessible feel to it, and often used comedy and music to kind of tap into an audience that connected with them."

In 1996, then-Artistic Director Philip Hedley initiated a development programme for "urban musicals", drawing on East End hip-hop and Asian music. He felt the theatre was "well-placed to achieve this, with its famous history in musical theatre and its deep roots in its own urban community."[33] In 1999, he brought over Fred Carl and Robert Lee from the Tisch School for what became an annual four-week summer workshop, working with writers who would have had neither the funds nor the academic standing for the NYU course. Hedley "began a process of developing the Urban Musical, while not excluding or disparaging the creation of new musicals in the classic Broadway tradition."

How adaptable is the classic Broadway model to new cultural environments? John Sparks says, "I think that the Lehman Engel style workshop could work in any cultural setting, because it emphasises how the craft of the writing affects the communication in the theatre," he said. "In other words, whatever one is trying to communicate, at whatever level of theatrical abstraction, a writer must remember that the words and music are a means to an end – therefore, the music and lyrics must work together in a way that clearly communicates to the audience at which the piece is aimed."[34]

"The variations in rap fascinate me", Hedley told Tim Saward. "I am no expert in rap, but even I could see how easily blank verse raps. Just as Shakespeare would vary the blank verse or just do half a line for some emotional reason, or he would suddenly rhyme two lines and give you a couplet for good reason, that rap had all its rules and had its grammar and so on. The youngsters listening to it understood what was going on, and I was of that generation where it's all terribly loud and I can't understand the words, and they can perfectly understand them. Their ears are trained for it."[35]

This plan has been met with some resistance by advocates of the "classic Broadway tradition", who feel that hip-hop is not "theatre music". Interestingly, however, Stephen Sondheim disagrees. "Of all the forms of contemporary pop music", he writes, "rap is the closest to traditional musical theatre (its roots are in vaudeville), both in its vamp-heavy rhythmic drive and in its verbal playfulness."[36] The nearest thing to a mainstream success with a hip-hop influence has been *In the Heights* by Latino composer-lyricist Lin-Manuel Miranda (1980-), which opened on Broadway in 2008 and was nominated for thirteen Tony Awards. This was followed in 2015 by the enormously successful *Hamilton*. Of Miranda's work on *In The Heights* Sondheim says, "Rap is a natural language for him and he is a master of the form, but enough of a traditionalist to know the way he can utilize its theatrical potential."

Many critics complain that few recent musicals deal with contemporary issues – but this criticism is not new. Most of Rodgers and Hammerstein's (and all of Lerner and Loewe's) works are set either in the past or in a fantasy locale. Rodgers and Hammerstein's only real successes with a then-contemporary time period – *South Pacific* and *Flower Drum Song* – had either an exotic setting or a sense of "otherness".

Critic Mark Steyn, a musical theatre specialist who also doubles as a right-wing political commentator, dismisses rap and hip-hop out of hand. "Rap is the logical consequence of promoting social over musical content: the reduction of the tune to a banal stationary backing track, the debasement of lyric-writing to a formless pneumatic laundry list of half-baked hoodlum exhibitionism."[37] On the other hand, it could be argued that William Walton and Edith Sitwell's 1921 "entertainment" *Façade* was an early form of rap.

In 2003, Stratford East was given permission to do a hip-hop adaptation by DJ Excalibah and MC Skolla of *The Boys from Syracuse* called *Da Boyz*. For *British Theatre Guide*'s Jackie Fletcher, it was an "invigorating blend of dance, song and comedy".[38] "That was for a very specific kind of audience who completely got it", says Michael, although some clearly didn't: "My review of *Da Boyz* could be condensed to 'Worst Fears Confirmed'", wrote Rhoda Koenig in *The Independent*. "The men are portrayed as either fools or hustlers, the women as robots or sluts, and the exquisite waltzes, punchy duets, and impish comedy numbers either altered by simple perversity (in 'This Can't Be Love,' for instance, by failing to resolve a chord) or, more often, bludgeoned and broken by constant pounding and thumping… *Da Boyz* has more in common with a pop concert or a TV variety show than a musical. The libretto has been slashed to the barest minimum, and is literally sidelined onto large screens flanking the stage on which the actors, behind the scenes, mug their way through brief comic bits. The mood of the music, either angry or glumly earnest, is not up to conveying more than a limited number of emotions, and rather unpleasant ones at that."[39]

Attempts to bring contemporary popular music into the theatre since the time of *Hair* have been fraught, and success has been rare. The reasons are partly economic – the young people to whom the music would appeal can't afford Broadway and West End ticket prices. There are also practical reasons. When it can take a decade to get a show on, following trends can be pretty futile. But it may also be that few pop writers have taken the care to learn the craft of writing for the theatre. This is where Stratford East feel they have an edge. "I think that rap and hip-hop are more easily accessible to musical theatre by far than rock and roll", Hedley told Saward.

"[The Tisch instructors] talk about principles as opposed to rules," says Michael. "But the nature of the kind of students who went to the Tisch School were being filtered because they had to pay to do that course. You get a certain kind of person who can afford to do that, and another kind of person, for whatever reason, falls by the wayside. What we were able to do here was give them a whole raft of kinds of artists who they weren't particularly working with in America. That's what excited them in terms of coming over here every summer and doing the course. What we did was put them in a room and talked about collaboration and partnership and how musicals aren't written, they're rewritten, and also why does this story need music for the story to be told."

By 2004, over a hundred writers had been through the programme: 60% of them were black, 20% Asian and the rest were white. "It is greatly to the advantage of the originality of British pop music that this mixing of styles of music from different racial backgrounds happens more readily in London than in, say, New York," says Hedley. "There is an advantage too that no country has the particular mix of cultures that Britain has from its colonial history, and so the contemporary musicals developed in

Britain will by definition be different from those developed in the USA."

"We did a piece by Jonzi D (a black, British hip-hop artist) called *Aeroplane Man* which was a dance musical", says Kerry Michael. "He goes back to find who he is as a hip-hop artist and he goes from London to America to find if that's where he belongs. Then he goes back to Jamaica, to Jamaican influences on hip-hop, and then from Jamaica he goes to Africa. From the gum-boots to reggae to hip-hop, there are links there in terms of the musical form. That's how he worked out what he was about." Jonzi D explains, "For once I heard a culture that actually celebrated this environment and used it creatively. I enjoy the fact that we use walls and pavements as our arenas of expression. That's cool. That makes a bit more sense to me than going to dance school and wearing tights... Can you imagine how embarrassing it is when you tell your friends what you are up to? As far as I am concerned, classical ballet was a bit camp for me, and hip-hop culture is a truer way of expressing myself."[40]

"Hip-hop is so broad now", says Michael. "You have British hip-hop, French hip-hop, R&B, R&B jazz. When you look at the spectrum of where hip-hop spans, it's quite broad. It's just about tuning your ears to the complexity. I think hip-hop is far more complicated, far more broad than Sondheim is. If anything, Sondheim's the same thing for two and a half hours."

Hedley contends, "There are comparatively few black and Asian writers and composers concentrating on musical theatre, partly because they can see so few role models to encourage them to do so." Michael continues, "They're bringing their music, they're bringing their words, they're bringing their stories. The basic challenge we have with all that is the structure of two-hour story telling. A 'well-made play' has a Western model to it. That's how we perceive something to be good or bad in this part of the world. What we want to do is kind of break free from that."

Michael was carrying forward Hedley's legacy, although they had to discontinue the summer Tisch programme due to withdrawal of funding.

Whether the hip-hop musical is the wave of the future, or just one faction in a many-faceted new way of looking at musicals remains to be seen. What is clear is that there are people in different parts of the world working to develop new and unique forms.

"I believe and I hope that musical theatre can become part of the present culture," says Søren Møller. "At a certain period in time, it seemed like musical theatre had become a musical style of its own, and I actually don't think that is the case. I do believe that musical theatre is a stage art form that contains a million different musical genres beneath it. So I am very much about trying to stay true to the genre that you're writing in, and I don't want to develop one kind of musical genre. I really want it to be different. We are all under the influence of everything that's run through the water until this very day."

I believe that the potential exists to combine the expertise and craft of the classic Broadway musicals with indigenous forms. "How any particular audience hears and simultaneously understands songs in the context of their culture is certainly a factor in shaping the craft of song writing for that culture", says John Sparks.

> "In the theatre, regardless of cultural differences, one thing remains the same – it is not like listening to music in other forms because there are competing elements. Sets, costumes, movement, aspects of character, linguistic anomalies... the song in the theatre must cut through all the competition and communicate directly to the audience with no need to process the information. The audience must be able to understand it without thinking about it. If, however, you are in a culture where the music and words are not part of the drama, but more of a decoration, more like scenery than content, then of course, that craft would not be so important. The American musical does have

impact in other cultures, first by being performed in translation, and ultimately by imitation. But as other cultures adopt and adapt the form, it changes and becomes suitable to the culture borrowing the style. This is how European operetta morphed into the American musical in the first place, being infused with jazz and variety, taking bits from African American music styles, from vaudeville and other influences that were at the time rather uniquely American."[41]

At Stratford East in 2008, they were aiming to reinvent the form. "But I don't know whether we'll call it a musical", said Kerry Michael at the time. "Is *Cirque du Soleil* a musical? In our terms it's not, but from other points of view they're doing as many of the common traits you'd find in a more conventional musical. It's just that we have to think about what we mean by the word 'musical' and how we define what a musical is. As far as I'm concerned, it's just something that fuses music, lyric and word. So a pantomime's a musical as much as *West Side Story* is."

Finale: Are We Up For It?

If I had known when I was starting out as a musical writer in the late 1970s just how difficult a road it was going to be, I might very well have given up. I say this because I am actually grateful that I didn't know then what I know now. On the other hand, when Stephen Schwartz told me back then that I showed "enormous promise", that kept me going through many a dark night. I say this not to blow my own horn, but to stress the importance of *nurture*. (Now, through his ASCAP and Disney workshops, Schwartz has similarly encouraged hundreds of other promising writers.)

When I hear course leaders telling their students to lower their expectations, something inside me rebels. Like the students in the opening scene of the original Broadway version of *Merrily We Roll Along*, I want to scream, "Give us a break, Mr. Shepard!" Not that I'm naïve about the reality behind the musical theatre business, but I would never discourage anybody with talent from aiming for the Big Brass Ring. After all, nobody chooses to write musicals for a living unless they're at least a little bit delusional. As the noted Basque writer and poet Miguel de Unamuno (1864-1936) said, "Only he who attempts the absurd is capable of achieving the impossible."[1] It is unlikely that you will hit higher than you aim.

However, thinking "outside of the box" dictates that we must consider the possibility that the exact whereabouts of that brass ring may have changed.

"I can categorically state that myriad musicals are being developed in America with no thought of Broadway", says John Sparks, Artistic Director of the Academy of New Musical Theatre in Los Angeles. Stephen Sondheim certainly believes that Broadway – and the commercial theatre – is in terminal decline. "There is an anodyne homogeneity that governs Broadway musicals, so I don't see many. There's nothing wrong with having a lot of commercial crap as long as you have something else. You want a supermarket. Unfortunately, nearly everything on Broadway is commercial crap. The same is true of the West End. When I scan what's on, my heart sinks into my boots."[2] But, says lyricist and director Richard Maltby Jr., "All it takes is one new voice with talent and a fresh vision and a hot sense of entertaining people."[3]

How then shall we shape the musicals of the future? In the words of poet W. H. Auden, "No opera plot can be sensible, for in sensible situations people do not sing".[4] How then is it that in so many musicals, songs are used to reason through a problem? (E.g., "Reviewing the Situation" from *Oliver!*) My belief, different from Auden's, is that musicals can potentially be even more realistic or naturalistic than non-musicals, in the sense that a song gives the audience an inside track into how a character is thinking.

Music is not literal. I have said before that good music lifts lyrics up to heaven. There is no inherent artifice in doing that. With the exception of the odd diegetic songs, we do not imagine that one character is really singing to the other, nor that they are really making up clever rhymes on the spot. No drama, musical or non, is naturalistic in its absolute sense: even so-called verbatim theatre is edited. If you've ever set up a stationary video camera in a room full of strangers, then watched the tape, you'll know that the result is pretty uninvolving. In a musical, we remedy this through song which, on the surface may appear to be abstract, but which gives us the pure, uncorrupted version of what the character is thinking.

Director Scott Miller makes a distinction between "realistic" and "naturalistic". "Rodgers and Hammerstein figured out, even before they started working together, that musicals can be realistic. Hammerstein's *Show Boat* dealt with alcoholism, inter-racial marriage, gambling addiction, domestic abuse and more. Rodgers' *Pal Joey* was about a two-bit night-club singer who uses women until they figure out he's using them. But both R&H seemed to think that musicals could be naturalistic too. They were wrong."5

Or perhaps it's all in the perception. Audiences in the 1940s seemed to be able to accept this convention in a way that modern audiences have difficulty with. Maintaining the fourth wall in a musical presents a challenge to the observer's personal space. Music connects them directly to the emotions of the character on stage. Possibly, they have become so cynical that they have forgotten how to accept this.

"All their shows (except *Allegro*) used the Fourth Wall, and this created a dilemma when it came to solos, musical soliloquies. If a character is just going to stand there and tell us what he or she is feeling, how do you justify that in a naturalistic world with a Fourth Wall?"

On the other hand, Sarah Green wrote in the blog *A Younger Theatre*,

> "It is not just the deep-rooted use of music that makes a show naturalistic, but its structure. On 31 March 1943, Rodgers and Hammerstein opened their first show and it was revolutionary – the audience knew it was groundbreaking from the moment the curtain went up. Musical theatre tradition dictated that a show open with a big chorus number and dancing girls. Instead when the curtain rises on *Oklahoma!* the first image the audience sees is an old woman on stage churning butter, which she does for a few minutes before you hear an unaccompanied voice sing the opening lines of 'O What A Beautiful Mornin'' from offstage. This is straight out of the naturalistic movement and has echoes of *Miss Julie* by August Strindberg. In this opening you almost don't have to suspend your belief because Curley is aware that he is singing as well, even saying to Aunt Eller: 'I've come a singin' to ya' – for him,

he is singing a folk song he knows or has just made up as he wanders across the farm. Hammerstein knew that if he could make the audience believe these characters were real, then the singing parts would be believable too."[6]

It's true that some musicals since that time have shied away from this direct expression of emotion. "I get antsy watching musicals in which people are singing as they walk down the street or hang out the laundry", says director and choreographer Bob Fosse. "In fact I think it looks a little silly."[7] However, my belief is that naturalism can work when it is employed skilfully and, most importantly, with honesty.

There is no question that Rodgers and Hammerstein completely re-invented the musical. There is also little question that the Broadway musical has moved on from there, but right now it is in a strange place in the western theatre. It is the most popular theatrical art, yet even with the cinematic success of *Chicago*, *Mamma Mia!!* and *Into the Woods*, it remains "uncool".

"In the old days," Sir Tim Rice says, "musical shows that you wax nostalgic about, were aiming for a very middle class, elitist type of audience. Now musicals are for anybody. Everybody's got their record player, their radio, their CD. The sort of music most people want is not the very sophisticated, twee, *Anything Goes* type of musical. They want raw chunks of emotion in three-minute slabs and they want it now and they want it hard. That's very hard for people brought up on the rather privileged diet of forties and fifties musicals to take." He adds, "I happen to come from a very cushy background, to have been brought up on those musicals, to like them very much, but I also love and enjoy more emotionally, if I'm honest, a great Mick Jagger performance."[8]

Film and theatre producer Scott Rudin (1958-) says, "Why would musical theater be the only culture that resists newness? It doesn't make sense. Bands become successes on [social networking site] tumblr. Where's the tumblr of musical theater? [The problem is] older people are willing to pay for it, and they're the same audience that's not going to want something new. It's a self-fulfilling prophecy. I'd rather go see our future than most musicals. The theater is simply not democratized in any way, and other art forms are. And that's even more true of musicals."[9]

Since the musical theatre came into being alongside democracy, does this mean it is no longer a viable cultural expression? To some people, art is meant to be a reflection of society. Others want it to go boldly forward, and to actually influence society. Do we really want musical theatre to pander to the lowest common denominator? Do we not want shows that are aimed at grown-ups? In the Lehman Engel workshops, stress was placed on the notion that a great musical should be built to last. The economics of the musical are such that creators need to aim for longevity in a way that film makers and pop songwriters don't have to. A musical that is part of a passing trend will not be likely to have a long shelf life, and as such be less likely to recoup.

As of this writing, the current world-wide hit is *Hamilton* with book, music and lyrics by Lin-Manuel Miranda, a rap and hip-hop artist of Puerto Rican descent. What relevance does conventional musical theatre have to *Hamilton*? Quite a lot, actually. While he is undoubtedly steeped in rap, hip-hop and R&B music, Miranda also has a thorough foundation in musicals.[10] Stephen Sondheim, who worked with Miranda on the 2009 revival of *West Side Story* says, "The wonderful thing about Lin-Manuel's use of rap is that he's got one foot in the past. He knows theatre. He respects and understands the value of good rhyming, without which the lines tend to flatten out."[11]

In *Hamilton*, Miranda actually cites the 1969 Broadway historical hit *1776*, quoting its opening number "Sit Down, John!" in reference to the same character, John Adams. He also cites Gilbert and Sullivan's "The Modern Major General" from *Pirates of Penzance*, and was influenced by Sondheim's *Assassins* ("a master class in, okay, how are these people similar, how are they different, what do they want, what story are we telling in this one song?"[12]) Jason Robert Browne's *The Last Five Years* also gets a look-in: ("At the end of Hamilton's affair with Maria Reynolds; he sings, 'Nobody needs to know,' and Jason wrote the ultimate infidelity jam called 'Nobody Needs to Know.' The moment I had the idea, I called Jason and was like, 'Ahhhhh, I need to make this reference!'") And of course *Les Misérables*: ("I learned a lot from *Les Miz* about compression and returning to themes.")

I am not going to try to speculate on what *Hamilton*'s influence will be – not since Clive Barnes infamously suggested that all post *Hair* musicals would be rock[13] has anybody done something that misguided. Besides, so much of *Hamilton* is so specific to its subject that it is hard to imagine how anybody else could employ the same techniques (although I know we are going to be subjected to hundreds of would-be imitators). Sondheim says, "*Hamilton* is a breakthrough, but it doesn't exactly introduce a new era. Nothing introduces an era. What it does is empower people to think differently. There's always got to be an innovator, somebody who experiments first with new forms."

However, what is most significant about *Hamilton* is not its music – much of which is not actually rap or hip-hop – or even its form, but its notion of inclusiveness. Its story of American history is told by a largely non-white cast using musical and theatrical forms that they are comfortable with but that would be anachronisms if taken literally. Many of the lyrics are narrative, making it at times more like an oratorio than a musical.

Just as Stanley Kubrick achieved his stunning effects in *2001: A Space Odyssey* by, in part, choosing only to do that which he could do very well, Miranda limits his use of rap and hip-hop to appropriate situations as a narrative device, often with humorous results. There is little in *Hamilton* that could be described as "naturalistic". By doing this, he allows the audience to accept the notion that the story is being relayed through the media of "modern" people. Not only does it help modern audiences to accept it, but it also conveys the notion that they are, or at least can be, a part of it. In this sense, the musical's relationship with the development of democracy is preserved.

Miranda would not be able to do this had he not had a full musical and theatrical vocabulary. No one musical form – be it rock or ragtime – has the emotional range by itself to tell a great story. Just as Stephen Schwartz, a generation earlier combined his new-found love of folk and Motown with his existing respect for the work of Leonard Bernstein and of Harnick and Bock, Miranda is a merger of two worlds. This is, and always has been, how the musical moves forward. Both the performers and the writers need to have a broad background. Study everything. Pop, classical, musical theatre – it all goes together into the great mix, but a musical, more than any other form, requires eclecticism.

The musical falls into that awkward slot called "middle-brow", meaning it is neither fish nor fowl. It does not meet some people's mandated criteria for "high art", nor should it appeal to the lowest common denominator, and so it slips between the cracks. Hence, so far as the mass media is concerned, it does not exist – *High School Musical*,

Smash and *Glee* notwithstanding.

"For some reason, unfathomable to me, musicals are a much maligned form," says Arden Ryshpan, Executive Director of Canadian Actors' Equity Association. "People complain that they are maudlin, but I suspect that it is because they found themselves swept up in the emotion of the music. Folks scoff at the notion of characters suddenly breaking into song, rather than seeing the musical numbers as a way of telling us more about a character than dialogue ever could, or in some circumstances, actually advancing the plot."[14]

Jessie Thompson in London's *Evening Standard* writes: "When it gets it wrong, it can be cringeingly heavy-handed and formulaic. But when they're good, there's something transcendent about them – that involuntary shiver you get when emotion is conveyed through music in a way dialogue alone can't express."[15]

For some, musicals are inspiring – a barometer of the human spirit. Ian Bradley, a Presbyterian theologian writes that "Nostalgia, retreat from reality and sheer simple uncomplicated entertainment value, as well as massive commercial calculation and hype, all undoubtedly play their part in the continuing appeal of musicals but perhaps they also speak to that deeper sense of yearning which is part of the human condition, particularly in times like our own where so much seems frightening, uncertain and hopeless."[16]

I love musicals for what they are capable of being, not for what they necessarily are. Most of what Broadway and the West End are turning out right now is admittedly pretty banal. But then I hear a score like *Grey Gardens* (2006, music by Scott Frankel, lyrics by Michael Korie) and I feel rejuvenated.

I have my own vision of the kind of musicals I

want to see in the future, and I believe I have set some of that out here. However, in this newly globalised world, I have accepted that others may have different ideas, and the musicals of the future may well be something very different from anything that I (or you) could have anticipated.

If the development of the musical coincided with the emergence of democracy, then what will happen as new democracies emerge? Creative-life-coach Chris Grady asks, "Should we in the developed-musical-theatre-world then be looking at the composers and markets coming through in the wake of the Arab Spring? ... Is the North Korean musical theatre market the next one to keep an eye on?"[17]

As the arts become more polarised, it is the middle ground that invariably loses out. In my native country, the Canadian Broadcasting Corporation has revamped its English network radio format. Classical music has been cut back. "Indie" rock is in. They have disbanded the last of their once-proud local orchestras, and what passes for "arts" programming is somewhat redolent of the MTV generation. What little interest they do show in musical theatre is strictly after the fact news reporting, and even that can be pretty weak-kneed. As for nurturing of musical theatre, there is none.

It has not always been this way. Time was when CBC Radio actually commissioned original musicals. One of them, *Rockabye Hamlet*, even made it to Broadway. (Well, for a few performances, anyway.) But alas, those days are well behind us.[18] In 2009, in an episode of their flagship daily "arts" show *Q*, then host Jian Gomeshi interviewed an American journalist about the current state of Broadway, without ever mentioning the Canadian musical – *The Story of My Life* – that had opened on the Great White Way that very week. The CBC television network cancelled a major performing arts showcase series called *Opening Night*[19], although *North by Northwest*, a highly-regarded regional arts radio program out of Vancouver, did do a feature on

Canadian musicals in 2011, to which I was a contributor.

This is not a problem unique to Canada, never mind the CBC. In Britain, where the BBC's *Culture Show*, which ran from 2004-15, occupied a similar jejune turf to *Q*, *The Stage* complains of "a palpable dumbing down" in arts journalism. "Now the squeeze is on space and the demand is going to be for more glamour-based coverage to compete with the consumer-led material arts editors are going to be obliged to schedule. Arts correspondents will be appointed for their 'compatibility' with the wishes of news desks, not for their knowledge and judgement of the cultural sector or for their skill with concise prose, but for their aptitude for getting alongside stars and their agents."[20]

As has been discussed previously in this book, we have a similar problem with funding agencies. However, there are encouraging signs. While development programmes for writers and composers are thin on the ground, musical theatre courses for performers are a growth industry. From Buenos Aires to Singapore, schools are cropping up to train singers and dancers for all the cloned musicals that New York and London can supply. Some of these schools are taking a proactively internationalist stance. The Musical Theatre Educators Alliance (to which I belong) has members from across North America, Europe and Australia.

I have shown that there are people in many different countries struggling to create indigenous musical theatre. These people are facing many of the same problems, and often finding very creative solutions to them. In several places, there are organised workshops to develop new, indigenous work. It seems to me that the next step would be to borrow a page from the Musical Theatre Educators Alliance and to form an international network. While Mercury Musical Developments in the UK has fraternal relations with the Academy of New Musical Theatre and the National Alliance of Musical Theatre Producers in the U.S., I believe it would be useful to expand that group to include Sheridan College's Canadian Music Theatre Project, Teater Fredericia in Denmark, Musical Theatre Live in Singapore and New Musicals Australia. For example, all could learn from the kind of showcases that Aaron Joyner once produced for OzMade in Melbourne. They could also benefit from the expertise of the Academy of New Musical Theatre and the Lehman Engel workshops. Musical Theatre Live have expressed the desire to bring in outside mentors to help to develop their own writers. Such an alliance could facilitate this.

The next step would be an International Festival of New Musical Theatre. While this was tried to some extend with the Global Search for New Musicals in Cardiff, I believe it should be truly internationalised and hosted by a different country each year.

I have already seen that shows from Austria (*Elisabeth*) and Canada (*Anne of Green Gables*) have been very successful in Japan without having been Broadway hits. Toronto has transferred two shows from Australia, via London (*Dirty Dancing*, *Priscilla Queen of the Desert*). Perhaps soon a show will move directly between Canada and Australia. Maybe we'll even have international co-productions. (We've had them for years in the non-musical theatre.)

One thing that I, personally, would ask is that we resist the temptation to "dumb down" our musicals. All too often, I hear producers claiming that in order to appeal to a younger audience – apparently wanting theatre to resemble the pop music industry in aiming for the under fourteen market – musicals need to be written by off-duty pop stars, rather than by people who have dedicated themselves to mastering a difficult form.

On the other hand, let's also resist the temptation to do nothing but tuneless quasi-operas. While it is true that a strong book is of primary importance, musicals need memorable songs. So let's reclaim that middle ground by reaching out to a populist audience and then raising their aspirations without pandering, just as Mozart and Schikaneder did with *The Magic Flute*. Let's become as aware of the international community in musical theatre as we are in cinema and world music. That way, we can re-invigorate the musical. Who knows – we may even make it "cool" again.

Bibliography:

Appignanesi, Lisa, *The Cabaret*, Yale University Press, New Haven, CT, 2004

Arundell, Dennis , *The Story of Sadler's Wells*, David & Charles, London, 1978.

Atkey, Mel, *Broadway North: The Dream of a Canadian Musical Theatre*, Natural Heritage Books/Dundurn Press, Toronto, 2006.

Baillie, Joan Parkhill, *Look at the Record: An Album of Toronto's Lyric Theatres 1825-1984*, Mosaic Press, Oakville, 1985.

Baker, Richard Anthony, *British Music Hall – An Illustrated History*, Sutton Publishing, Stroud, Gloucestershire, 2005

Bawtree, Michael, *The New Singing Theatre*, Oxford University Press, New York, 1991.

Behr, Edward, *Thank Heaven for Little Girls – The True Story of Maurice Chevalier's Life and Times*, Hutchinson, London, 1993

Berton, Pierre, *Hollywood's Canada: The Americanization of Our National Image*, McClelland and Stewart, Toronto, 1975.

Bordman, Gerald, *Jerome Kern: His Life and Music*, Oxford University Press, New York, 1980.

Bradley, Ian, *You've Got to Have a Dream: The Message of the Musical*, SCM Press, London, 2004.

Brett, David, *Piaf – A Passionate Life*, Robson Books, London, 1998

Castle, Charles, *The Folies-Bergère*, Methuen, London, 1982.

Cate, Phillip Dennis and Shaw, Mary, *The Spirit of Montmartre – Cabarets, Humor, and the Avant-Garde, 1875-1905*, Jane Voorhees Zimmerli Art Museum, New Brunswick, NJ, 1996

Cherlin Michael, Filipowicz, Halina and Rudolph, Richard L., *The Great Tradition and Its Legacy – The Evolution of Dramatic and Musical Theater in Austria and Central Europe*, Berghan Books, New York, 2003.

Clements, Jonathan and McCarthy, Helen, *The Anime Encyclopedia – A Guide to Japanese Animation Since 1917*, Stone Bridge Press, Berkeley, California, 2001.

Collerick, George, *Romanticism and Melody*, Juventus, London, 1995.

Collerick, George, *From the Italian Girl to Cabaret*, Juventus, London, 1998

Coplan, David, *In Township Tonight! South Africa's Black City Music and Theatre*, Jacana Media (Pty) Ltd., Auckland Park, 2007

Creekmur, Corey K. and Mokdad, Linda Y., *The International Film Musical*, Edinburgh University Press, 2013.

Damase, Jacques, *Les Folies du Music-Hall*, Anthony Blond Ltd., London, 1962

Dieho, Bart (editor), *De Nederlandse musical – Emancipatie van een fenomeen*, Uitgeverij International Theatre and Film Books, Amsterdam, 2018.

Drabinsky, Garth (with de Villiers, Marq) *Closer to the Sun*, McLelland and Stewart, Toronto, 1995.

Druxman, Michael B., *The Musical From Broadway to Hollywood*, A.S. Barnes and Company, Cranbury, NJ, 1980.

Engel, Lehman, *The American Musical Theater*, Collier Books, New York, 1975

Engel, Lehman, *The Making of a Musical*, MacMillan Publishing Company, New York, 1977

Engel, Lehman, *This Bright Day*, MacMillan Publishing, New York, 1974.

Engel, Lehman, *Words With Music*, Schirmer Books, New York, 1981.

Flinn, Denny Martin, *Musical! A Grand Tour – The Rise, Glory and Fall of an American Institution*, Schirmer, Belmont, CA, 1997.

Freund, Philip, *Oriental Theatre*, Peter Owen Publishers, London,

2005

Gänzl, Kurt, *Musicals*, Carlton Books, London, 2001.

Gänzl, Kurt, *The Musical – A Concise History*, Northeastern University Press, Boston, MA, 1997.

Goodall, Howard, *Big Bangs – The Story of Five Discoveries That Changed Musical History*, Chatto & Windus, London, 2000.

Gorlero, Pablo, *Historia de la comedia musical en la Argentina : desde sus comienzos hasta 1979*, N. H. Oliveri, Buenos Aires, 2004.

Harcourt, Peter, *Fantasy and Folly – The Lost World of New Zealand Musicals 1880-1940*, Steele Roberts, Wellington, 2002

Harron, Don, *Anne of Green Gables the Musical – 101 Things You Didn't Know*, White Knight Books, Toronto, 2008.

Hawthorn, Tom, *The Year Canadians Lost Their Minds and Found Their Country*, Douglas & McIntyre, Vancouver, 2017

Hirsch, Foster, *Kurt Weill on Stage – From Berlin to Broadway*, Limelight Editions, New York, 2003.

Holloway, Peter, *Contemporary Australian Drama*, Currency Press, Sydney, 1987.

Honolka, Kurt, *Papageno – Emanuel Schikaneder, Man of the Theater in Mozart's Time*, Amadeus Press, Portland, Oregon, 1990.

House of Commons Culture, Media and Sport Committee, *Theatre – Fifth Report of Session 2004-05 Vol. III Oral and Written Evidence*, The Stationery Office Ltd., London, 2005

Inverne, James, *Wrestling with Elephants – The Authorised Biography of Don Black*, Sanctuary Books, London, 2003.

Jackson, Arthur, *The Best Musicals*, Crown Publishers, New York, 1977.

Jackson, Jeffrey H., *Making Jazz French*, Duke University Press, Durham, North Carolina, 2003

Jenkins, John and Linz, Rainer, *Arias – Recent Australian Music*

Theatre, Red House Editions, Melbourne, 1997

Johnston, Peter Wyllie, *From the Melburnian*, Ellikon Publishing, Fitzroy, Victoria, 2011

Jones, Tom, *Making Musicals*, Limelight Editions, New York, 1998.

Jortner, David, McDonald, Keiko and Wetmore, Kevin J., *Modern Japanese Theatre and Performance*, Lexington Books, Lanham, 2006.

Kaiser, D.J., *The Evolution of Broadway Musical Entertainment, 1850-2009: Interlingual and Intermedial Interference*, Washington University in St. Louis, 2013. Electronic Theses and Dissertations, paper 1076.

Kennedy, Michael and Joyce, *Oxford Concise Dictionary of Music*, Oxford University Press, Oxford, 2007

Killick, Andrew, *In Search of Korean Traditional Opera: Discourses of Ch'angguk*, University of Hawai'I Press, 2010.

Kislan, Richard, *The Musical: A Look at the American Musical Theatre*, Prentice-Hall Inc., Engelwood Cliffs, NJ , 1980.

Knapp, Raymond, *The American Musical and the Formation of National Identity*, Princeton University Press, Princeton, NJ, 2005.

Kracauer, Siegfried translated by David, Gwenda and Mosbacher, Eric, *Offenbach and the Paris of his Time*, Constable, London, 1937.

Lahr, John, *Automatic Vaudeville*, Alfred A. Knopf, New York, 1984.

Lamb, Andrew, *150 Years of Popular Musical Theatre*, Yale University Press, New Haven, CT, 2000.

Larkin, Colin, *The Virgin Encyclopædia of Stage and Film Musicals*, Virgin Books, London, 1999.

Leibovitz, Liel and Miller, Matthew, *Lili Marlene – The Soldiers' Song of World War II*, W.W. Norton & Co., New York, 2009.

Lerner, Alan Jay, *The Musical Theatre: A Celebration*, McGraw Hill, New York, 1986.

Lewis, David H., *Flower Drum Songs – The Story of Two Musicals*, McFarland & Co., Jefferson, North Carolina, 2006.

Lindfors, Bernth, (editor) *Africans on Stage: Studies in Ethnological Show Business*, University of Indiana Press, Bloomington, 1999.

Mandelbaum, Ken, *Not Since Carrie: 40 Years of Broadway Musical Flops*, St. Martin's Press, New York, 1991

Mariel, Pierre (translated by Peter Munk), *Paris Revue*, Neville Spearman, London, 1962

Maslon, Laurence, *Broadway to Main Street – How Show Tunes Enchanted America*, Oxford University Press, 2018.

McBride, Jason and Wilcox, Alana, *UTOpia – Towards a New Toronto*, Coach House Books, Toronto, 2005.

McHugh, Dominic, *Alan Jay Lerner – A Lyricist's Letters*, Oxford University Press, 2014.

Mellers, Wilfred, *Music in a New Found Land – Themes and Developments in the History of American Music*, Alfred A. Knopf, New York, 1964.

Moore, Mavor, *Reinventing Myself*, Stoddart, Toronto, 1994.

Moorehouse, Ward, *George M. Cohan – Prince of the American Theater*, J. P. Lippincott, New York, 1943

Mordden, Ethan, *Open a New Window – The Broadway Musical in the 1960s*, Pagrave, New York, 2001.

Most, Andrea, *Making Americans – Jews and the Broadway Musical*, Harvard University Press, Cambridge, Mass, 2004.

Münz, Lori (Editorial Director) *Cabaret Berlin – Revue, Kabarett and Film Music Between the Wars*, Ear Books, Hamburg, 2005.

Noble, Peter, *Ivor Novello*, The Falcon Press, London, 1951.

Papadimitriou, Lydia, *The Greek Film Musical*, McFarland & Company, New York, 2006.

Patullo, Heather Ann, *Positively Canadian*, Tellwell Talent, Vancouver, 2017

Platt, Len, Becker, Tobias and Linton, David, *Popular Musical Theatre in London and Berlin – 1890 to 1939*, Cambridge University Press, Cambridge, 2014.

Pinne, Peter and Johnston, Peter Wyllie, *The Australian Musical – from the Beginning*, Allen & Unwin Book Publishers, Sydney, 2019.

Polanco, Fabiàn de la Cruz, *Magia pura y total (Historia del Teatro Musical en la Ciudad de Mexico 1952-2011)*, Samsara Editorial, Mexico City, 2012

Previn, André, *No Minor Chords*, Doubleday, New York, 1991.

Raymond, Jack, *Show Music on Record*, Washington, DC, 1998.

Robertson, Jennifer, *Takarazuka – Sexual Politics and Popular Culture in Modern Japan*, University of California Press, Berkeley, 1998.

Rome, Florence, *The Scarlett Letters*, Random House, New York, 1971.

Rubin, Don and Solórzano, Carlos (eds), *The World Encyclopedia of Contemporary Theatre – The Americas*, Routledge, London, 2001.

Salys, Rimgaila, *Laughing Matters: The Musical Comedy Films of Grigorii Aleksandrov*, Intellect, Bristol, 2009.

Salz, Jonah (Editor), *A History of Japanese Theatre*, Cambridge University Press, Cambridge, 2016.

Samuels, Edmond, *If the Cap Fits*, Modern Literature Co., Sydney, 1972.

Schneider, Jason, *Whispering Pines – The Northern Roots of American Music from Hank Snow to The Band*, ECW Press, Toronto, 2009.

Secrest, Meryle, *Somewhere for Me: A Biography of Richard Rodgers*, Bloomsbury, London, 2001.

Shay, Anthony, *The Dangerous Lives of Public Performers: Dancing, Sex, and Entertainment in the Islamic World*, Palgrave MacMillan, 2014.

Steyn, Mark, *Broadway Babies Say Goodnight*, Faber & Faber, London, 1997.

Stickland, Leonie, *Gender Gymnastics: Performing and Consuming Japan's Takarazuka Revue*, Trans Pacific Press, Melbourne, 2008

Struble, John Warthen, *History of American Classical Music*, Checkmark Books / Facts on File, New York, 1995.

Tait, Viola, *A Family of Brothers – The Taits and J. C. Williamson; a Theatre History*, William Heinemann, Melbourne, 1971.

Thomas, Susan, *Cuban Zarzuela – Performing Race and Gender on Havana's Lyric Stage*, University of Illinois Press, Urbana, 2009.

Traubner, Richard, *Operetta: A Theatrical History*, Routledge, New York, 2003.

Trevin, J.C., *Peter Brook – A Biography*, Macdonald, London, 1971.

Tucker, Percy, *Just the Ticket!*, Jonathan Ball Publishers, Johannsburg, 1997

Vermette, Margaret, *The Musical World of Boublil and Schönberg*, Applause Theatre and Cinema Books, New York, 2006.

Whitcomb, Ian, *After the Ball – Pop Music from Rag to Rock*, Limelight Editions, New York, 1972/1989.

Whitehouse, Edmund, *London Lights – A History of West End Musicals*, This England Books, Cheltenham, Gloucestershire, 2005.

Whiting, Steven Moore, *Satie the Bohemian: From Cabaret to Concert Hall*, Oxford University Press, 1998.

Wright, Adrian, *Must Close Saturday – The Decline and Fall of the British Musical Flop*, The Boydell Press, Woodbridge, 2017

Wright, Adrian, *Tanner's Worth of Tunes – Rediscovering the Post-War British Musical*, Boydell Press, Woodbridge, Suffolk, 2011.

Discography:

N.B. Many cast recordings are independently produced and do not have catalogue numbers or record labels.
N.B. While books are listed by author, videos and recordings (which have many creators) are listed by title.

Anne of Green Gables Charlottetown Festival Cast Music by Norman Campbell Book by Don Harron Lyrics by Don Harron, Norman Campbell, Elaine Campbell, Mavor Moore Attic ACDM1225

Amour Broadway cast album Music by Michel Legrand English Lyrics by Jeremy Sams Original French Lyrics by Didier Van Cauwelaert 2002 Sh-K-Boom CD 4003-2

Aqui No Podemos Hacerlo!, Music by Luis M. Serra, Lyrics by Pepe Cibrián Campoy, Teatro Nacional Cervantes 1994 Argentine Cast CD 672

Belle Époque, La – The Songs of Reynaldo Hahn Susan Graham Sony Classical CD SK 60168

Berlin Cabaret Songs, (English Version) Uta Lemper, 1997 London 452 849-2

Berlin Cabaret Songs, (German Version) Uta Lemper, 1996 Decca 452 601-2

Best That We Can Be Various composers Musical Theatre Limited 2008 CD

Big Bang Music and Lyrics by Kenneth Lyen and Desmond Moey 1995 Rainbow Music/Serenip Productions

Billy Bishop Goes to War 20th Anniversary Recording Book, Music and Lyrics by John Gray 1999 CD

Boy from Oz, The Music and Lyrics by Peter Allen (& others) Book by Nick Enright 1998 EMI 7243 4 95660 2 6

Bunch of Ratbags, A Music and Lyrics by Peter Pinne, Book and Lyrics by Don Battye 2005 RNBW033

Chang & Eng, Music and Lyrics by Ken Low, Action Theatre, 2000

Cheminds de l'amour, Les Jean Stilwell, CBC Records MVCD 1135

Ciske de Rat, Music by Henny Vrienten, Book and Lyrics by *André* Breedland and Maurice Wijnen, 2007, Universal CD 1751114

Come from Away, Music and Lyrics by David Hein and Irene Sankoff, 2017 Original Broadway Cast

Como in la Gran Cuidad ("Like it is in the Big City") Music and Lyrics by Pancho Flores, Book by Herman Letelier, 1971 LP EMI SLDC-41002

Csárdás Fürstin, die ("The Gypsy Princess") Music by Emmerich Kálmán, CD B00PBN39ZE

Cyrano de Musical, Music by Ad Van Dijk, Lyrics by Koen Van Dijk, Original cast 1992 CD DICD 3797

Dracula Music by Angel Mahler, Lyrics by Pepe Cibrián Campoy 1992 CD Luna Park CD-9791

Driegroschenoper, Die Berlin 1930 1929-30, Telefunken Legacy 0927 42663 2

Drowsy Chaperone, The Broadway Cast recording Music by Greg Morrison Lyrics by Lisa Lanbert, Book by Bob Martin and Don McKellar Ghostlight CD 7915584411-2

Elisabeth Music by Sylvester Levay, Lyrics by Michael Kunze Vienna cast 2004 Hit Squad

El Alma Secreta de las Cosas ("The Secret of the Soul and things") Music and lyrics by Juan del Barrio, Argentina, 1993, CD Ciclo-3-50043

El Jorobado de Paris ("The Hunchback of Paris") Music by Angel Mahler, Lyrics by Pepe Cibrián Campoy, 1993 CD 669/2

El Locos de Asis ("The Madman of Assiswi"), Music by Martin Bianchedi, Book and lyrics by Manuel Gonzalez Gil, 1985

El retrato de Dorian Gray, Citlalixayotl / Carbalho, Mexico 1997.

En Nu Naar Bed Original Cast, 1970 Phillips LP 8410046

Evil Dead – The Musical Music by Frank Cipola, Christopher Bond,

Melissa Morris, George Reinblatt, Book and Lyrics by George Reinblatt Time Life M19407

Evita – Tango Popular Opera, Roberto Pansera, Miguel Jubany and Domingo Federico, Argentina 1989 CD Music Hall MH 10.021-2

Field of Stars: Songs of the Canadian Musical Theatre, Betts, Jim (editor) Northern River Music, Toronto, 2005.

Five Foot Broadway Various Composers Musical Theatre Limited CD

Fledermaus, Die Metropolitan Opera Music by Johann Strauss Book by Garson Kanin Lyrics by Howard Dietz CD PACO 030

Forbidden City Music by Dick Lee, Lyrics by Stephen Clark, Book by Stephen Clark and Dick Lee 2006 Singapore repertory Theatre

Foxtrot Music by Harry Bannink, Lyrics by Annie M.G. Schmidt 2004 CD: Brommerpech PCD 505039 2

French Operetta Arias Susan Graham Erato Disques CD 0927-42106-2

Gitano – Zarzuela Arias, Placido Domingo (conductor) Rolando Villazón (tenor) 2007 CD Virgin Classics LC 7873

Ha'penny Bridge, The, Book, Music and Lyrics by Alastair McGuckian. Original cast 2005

Hatpin, The Original Cast Recording Music by Peter Rutherford, Book and Lyrics by James Millar CD NGP01 9 369999 007645

Hired Man, The Music and Lyrics by Howard Goodall, Book by Melvyn Bragg TER CD CDTER2 1189

Hong Kong Rhapsody, Music by Dick Lee, CD B00005HF4R

Ipi Ntombi Music by Bertha Egnos, Book and Lyrics by Gail 7 Lucille Lakier CDSGP0577

Irma la Douce Music by Marguerite Monnot, Book and Lyrics by Alexandre Breffort, 1967 Paris cast, VEGA CD 465 826-2

Irma la Douce Music by Marguerite Monnot, English Book and Lyrics by Monty Norman, David Heneker and Julian More, London Cast, SEPIA CD 1120

Irma la Douce Music by Marguerite Monnot, English Book and Lyrics by Monty Norman, David Heneker and Julian More, Broadway Cast Sony Broadway CD SK 48018

Joe de Musical, Music by Ad Van Dijk, Lyrics by Koen Van Dijk, Original cast CD, Endemol ENCD 7111

Kabarett Jean Stilwell CBC Records MVCD 1162

Kat and the Kings, West End Cast Book, Music and Lyrics by David Kramer and Taliep Petersen First Night CD CASTCD 67

King Kong Music by Todd Matshikiza, Lyrics by Pat Williams Book by Harry Bloom CDZAC 51 R

La Pergola De Las Flores, ("The Pergola of Flowers") Chilean musical comedy with music by Pancho Flores, lyrics by Isidora Aquirre, Presented by "Teatro de la Universidad Catolica de Chile" with Ana Gonzalez, Silvia Piñeiro, Carmen Barros, Hector Noguera and original cast. Phillips LP 630 500 issued in 1960.

Lapin Agile, Au – Le doyen des cabarets de Montmartre EPM CD 980122

Lola Montez Music by Peter Stannard, Lyrics by Peter Benjamin, Book by Alan Burke Bayview CD RNBW003

Magic Flute, The (Impempe Yonlingo) Original Cast recording Young Vic Production CD

Magic Paintbrush, The Music by Kenneth Lyen, Lyrics by Brian Seward

Mama es una Estrella ("My Mother is a Star") Music by Angel Mahler, Book and Lyrics by Jorge Mazzini 1997 CD-675

Marguerite Original London Cast recording Music by Michel Legrand Lyrics by Herbert Kretzmer, Original French Lyrics by Alain Boublil, Book by Alain Boublil, Claude-Michel Schönberg and Jonathan Kent First Night CAST CD102

Maria la O, Music by Ernesto Lecuona, Libretto by Gustavo Sánchez Galarraga, CD B003ID8CLK

Mkhumbane, Music by Todd Matchikiza, libretto by Alan Paton, B01F5MIZ0Y

Morphium und Widerstand Music by Mischa Spoliansky Klein aber Kunst CD KK-003/4

Musicals from the Land of Oz Various composers Bavview CD RNBW012

Opérettes Marseillaises Music by Vincent Scotto Universal CD 476 2107

Out of the Blue, Music by Shun Ichi Tokura, Lyrics by Paul Sand, Stage Door records, CD B0042FXIKS

Phi-Phi Music by Henri Christiné Book and Lyrics by Albert Willemetz and Fabien Sollar Universal CD 465 886-2

Re:mix Music by Dick Lee, Book by Dick Lee, Cheek and Paul Tan Singapore repertory Theatre 2002 Teflon Music CD YM-REMIX003/EA70099

Rob Roy Book, Music and Lyrics by David Warrack 2006 WPRR-1

Sentimental Bloke, The ABC Television Production Music by Albert Arlen, Book and Lyrics by Nancy Brown and Lloyd Thomson LP

Seven Little Australians, Music by David Reeves, CD B01G47RCT4

Sideshow Alley Original Australian Cast recording Music by Paul Keelan, Book and Lyrics by Gary Young CD

Spend, Spend, Spend Music by Steve Brown, Book and Lyrics by Steve Brown and Justin Greene 2000 Garforth Records GAR001

Street of Dreams Music by Manos Hadjidakis, Lyrics by Manos Hadjidakis, Alexis Solomos, Iakovos Kambanelis, Nikos Gatsos and Minos Argyrakis. EMI 50999 516433 2 4

Strike! Music and Lyrics by Danny Schur Book by Danny Schur and Rick Chafe 2006 CD

Toi, C'est Moi, Music by Moisés Simons, Book by Henri Duvernois, Lyrics by Albert Willemetz, Marcel Bertal, André Mouezy-Eon, Louis Malbon and Robert Chamfleury. Les Brigands CD

Tourdillon

Tristan Book, Music and Lyrics by Jay Turvey and Paul Sportelli 2007 JPCD04

Twist of Fate, A Music by Dick Lee, Lyrics by Anthony Drewe, Book by Steven Dexter and Tony Petito 1997 Singapore repertory Theatre

Ute Lemper Sings Kurt Weill, 1988 Decca CD 425 204-2

Veronique Music by André Messager, Book and Lyrics by Albert Vanloo and Georges Duval CD EMI Classics 7243 5 74073 2 3

Wait a Minim! Music by various, London Records, B005CRF0EC

Videography:

Amandla! A revolution in Four-Part Harmony Directed by Lee Hirsch 2002 Artisan DVD

Billy Bishop Goes to War Directed by Barbara Willis Sweete Brightspark Productions DVD BSPK779

Blue Angel, The ("Der blaue Engel") Directed by Josef Von Sternberg, Music by Friedrich Holländer 1930 Ufa Kino International DVD

Bran Nue Dae – a film about the musical by Jimmy Chi and Kuckles Directed by Tom Zubrycki, Bran Nue Dae Productions Aboriginal Corp., Broome, Western Australia, 1991.

Broadway – The American Musical Directed by Michael Kantor 2004 Granada DVD

Chasing the Tango High, Written and Directed by Shel Piercy, Infinity Filmed Entertainment, 2006

Dancing Years, The, Book and music by Ivor Novello, lyrics by Christopher Hassall, Associated Television, 1976.

"Drowsy Chaperone, The", *Working in the Theatre*, American Theater Wing, City University Television, April 2006

French Can-Can Directed by Jean Renoir, Music by Georges Van Parys 1954 DVD The Criterion Collection

Keating! The Musical Directed by Neil Armfield, Book, Music and Lyrics by Casey Bennetto 2008 Australian Broadcasting Corp. DVD

Not on the Lips ("Pas sur la Bouche") Directed by Alain Resnais, Music by Maurice Yvain, Book and Lyrics by André Barde 2003 Wellspring DVD FLV5452

Oh Rosalinda! ("Die Fledermaus") Music by Johann Strauss Lyrics by Dennis Arundel Directed by Michael Powell and Emeric Pressburger

Rose of Versailles: Girodelle side story Written and directed by Shinji Ueda, plus *Miroirs* ("Endless Dreams of the Mirrors") Book by

Nakamura Satoru, Music by Nishimura Kouji, Kuratomi Shinichi, Kai Masato and Nakao Tarou Takarazuka Snow Troupe, 2008 DVD TCAD-216

Sarafina! Directed by Darrell James Roodt, Book, Music and Lyrics by Mbongeni Ngema, Additional Music and Lyrics by Hugh Masekela DVD Buena Vista 26283

Umbrellas of Cherbourg, The ("Les parapluies de Cherbourg") Directed by Jacques Demy, Music by Michel Legrand (DVD includes documentary *The World of Jacques Demy*) 1963 Optimum Releasing DVD

Voices of Sarafina! Directed by Nigel Noble Music by Mbongeni Ngema and Hugh Masekela New Yorker Video 1988 NYY 58091

List of Interviewees

Georgina Bexon, London, 4 November 2008
Peter Cousens, Sydney, 14 November 2008
René Driessen, Arnhem, 12 May 2009
Julian Forsyth, London, 27 October 2009
Neil Gooding, Sydney, 5 July 2018
Chris Grady, London, 31 October, 2008
Chris Grady, London, 10 January 2019
David Hein, New York, 17 May, 2018
Peter Wyllie Johnston, Melbourne, 17 November 2008
Aaron Joyner, Melbourne, 18 November 2008
Dick Lee, London, 2 December 2008
Kenneth Lyen, Stella Kon, Desmond Moey, Singapore, 11 November 2008
Kerry Michael, London, 27 October 2008
Amon Miyamoto (with Yuriri Naka, interpreter), London, 7 June 2010
Søren Møller, Hamburg, 12 September 2009
Peevara Kitchumnongpan, Bangkok, 5 August 2019
Krisada and Napisi Reyes, Daegu, 4 July 2019
Michael Rubinoff, Toronto, 4 May 2018
Tony Sheldon and Ray Kolle, Sydney, 13 November 2008
Bae Sunghuck and Lee Jangwoo, Daegu, 9 July 2019

Mel Atkey

Mel Atkey has been writing musicals ever since he was in high school in his native Vancouver. He possesses an MA in Musical Theatre from Goldsmiths, University of London. He was a finalist for the Musical of the Year competition in Aarhus, Denmark, and his work has been short-listed for the Vivian Ellis Prize, the Quest for New Musicals, the Ken Hill Prize and Musical Stairs. His first musical, *Shikara*, was produced on radio in Canada. A single was released by singer Janice Jaud of one of the songs, "Far Away", and received airplay across Canada and the U.S.

Mel spent two years as a theatre critic in Vancouver before moving to Toronto to pursue his career as a musical theatre writer. He was commissioned to write songs for CBC Radio, and was a member of the Guild of Canadian Musical Theatre Writers' Lehman Engel Workshop. He was a director of the Cabaret and Musical Theatre Alliance until he moved to London in 1991. He made his New York debut in April 2001 with an off-off-Broadway showcase of *O Pioneers!* with book by Robert Sickinger. This show was then a finalist for "Stages 2002" at the New Tuners theatre in Chicago. Their second musical, *A Little Princess* was presented at Wings Theatre in New York in 2003, and his two character musical *Perfect Timing*, for which he wrote the book as well as music and lyrics, was showcased in 2005 to great acclaim as part of Greenwich Theatre (London)'s Musical Futures series. He wrote the opening number for Janie Dee's critically acclaimed one-woman show.

His first two books, *When We Both Got to Heaven* and *Broadway North: The Dream of a Canadian Musical Theatre* were published by Natural Heritage Books/Dundurn Press in 2002 and 2006 respectively. *Running Away with the Circus – or – "Now is the Winter of our Missing Tent"* was published by Friendlysong Books in 2013, and *Breaking into Song – Essays, Articles and Interviews on Musical Theatre* was published by Friendlysong in 2015. He has contributed to the Oxford University Press Handbook on the Global Musical and the Brock Revue (an academic journal published by Brock University in Canada) and has lectured internationally on the subject of musical theatre.

www.melatkey.com

Index

A Comedy of Errors, 369
"A Misfortune", 315
A Portrait of the Artist as Filipino, 468
Abbey Theatre, 252
Abbott, George, 13
ABC Music Hall, 217
Abeløe, Mads, 519
Aborn, Sarge, 228
Abraham, Eric, 382, 394
Academy of New Musical Theatre, 536, 545
"Accident Waiting to Happen, An", 288
Achard, Marcel, 217
Achilles in Heels, 119
Acito, Tim, 477
Acosta, Oscar, 427
Actors' Benevolent Fund, 362
Adams, Arthur, 325
Adams, Lee, 527
Adelaide Cabaret Festival, 354
Adelaide Festival Centre, 340
Adelaide Festival Theatre, 340
Adiós, Pampa mía', 407
Adler, Gusti, 70
Adler, Richard, 513
Aeroplane Man, 533
Aeschylus, 68
Afifi, Hani, 402
After the Fair, 181
"Ag, Pleez Daddy", 383
Agate, James, 140
Age of Innocence, The, 440
Aggiungi un posto a tavola, 248
Aguila, Guz, 420
Aguilera de Arellano, Luz Guzmán, 420
Aguilera, Antonio Guzmán, 420
Aguirre, Isidora, 414
Ahmanson Theatre, 292, 297
Aïda, 238, 485
Akay, Ender, 262
Alamein Concerto, 337
Al-Ashra Al-Tayeba, 397
Al-Balrouka, 397
Albery, Donald, 219
Albery, Sir Donald, 265
Aldolpho, 288
Aldwych Theatre, 386
Aleichem, Sholem, 181
Alejandro, Rachael, 468
Aleksandrov, Grigorii, 49
Alhambra, 91
Ali Baba and the Forty Thieves, 322
Ali, Muhammad, 380
Alibert, Henri, 86
All Het Up, 351
All I Want Is Rice, 478
All Quiet on the Western Front, 438

Allá en el Rancho Grande, 420
Allan, Anne, 313, 314, 315
Allen, Peter, 346, 347, 555
Allouba, Neveen, 401
Almagor, Dan, 404
Al-massir, 400
Alô, alô, Brasil!, 415
Aloni, Nissim, 404
Alonso, Alberto, 433
Al-Solaylee, Kamal, 175, 308
Alsop, Marin, 17
Alvear Palace Hotel, 408
Alverado, Mando, 418
Al-Warda al-Baida, 398
Always (film), 241
"Always in My Heart", 432
Amador, Bibot, 469
Amália, 253
Ambrosio, Valeria, 412
Amelia, 481, 506
América y Apollo, 428
American in Paris, An, 90, 94
American Theater Wing, 288, 561
Americana, 150
Ames, Winthrop, 127
Ampil, Joanna, 468
An Jung-geun, 476
"An Over-rated World (With Seven Underwhelming Wonders)", 292
Anckermann, Jorge, 430
Andersen, Hans Christian, 176
Anderson, David Cameron, 117
Anderson, Lale, 114
Andersson, Benny, 244
Andolfi, Ermanno, 407
Andrada, Tuca, 416
Andrews, Robert, 140
Andrews, William, 179
Ang Larawan, 436, 468, 469
"Angel" (Sarah McLaughlin song), 118
Anjou, el sueño que si sucedió. See Anjou, el sueño que si sucedió
Anna and the King of Siam, 168
Anne of Green Gables – the Musical, 1, 3, 14, 27, 32, 163-5, 184-6, 190, 278,282, 296, 341, 448, 523, 527, 546, 550, 555
Anne with an E, 164, 278, 280
Annie Get Your Gun, 47, 141, 226, 328, 333
Ant & Dec Show, The, 270
Anyone Can Whistle, 152
Anything Goes, 328, 539
Aoshika, Koji, 159
Apollinaire, Guillaume, 101
Apollo Victoria Theatre, 457
Appignanesi, Lisa, 99, 105, 116
"April in Paris", 130
"Aquarela do Brasil", 415

Aqui No Podemos Hacerlo!, 411, 555
Aquinaldo, Emilio, 465
Aran, Han, 477
Arcenas, Loy, 468
Archer, Robyn, 120, 338, 353
Arden, Leslie, 199, 524
Arenal, Humberto, 433
Argov, Alexander, 405
Arlen, Albert, 336-7
Arlen, Harold, 131, 219, 559
Arlette, 139
Armfield, Neil, 354, 561
Armiger, Martin, 341
Arms and the Man, 61
Armstrong, Gillian, 319
Armstrong, Louis, 73, 431
Arnaz, Desi, 432
Around the World in Eighty Days, 421
Arts Club Theatre, 312
Arts Council England, 518-9
"As Long As He Needs Me", 265
As We Stumble Along, 292
Asari, Keita, 448
ASCAP, 147, 518, 524, 536
Asche, Oscar, 322, 323
Así se ama en Sudamérica, 408
Askey, Arthur, 332
Aspects of Love, 209, 238
Astaire, Fred, 232, 400, 432
Astoria Theatre, 269
At the Bullfight, 301
At the Silver Swan, 333
Atatürk, Mustafa Kemel, 262
Athenaeum Theatre (Melbourne), 321, 354
Atkinson, Brooks, 24, 193
Atkinson, Rowan, 269
Attanasio cavallo vanesio, 246
Attlee, Clement, 263
Au Pays du Soleil, 86
Auden, W. H., 537
Aufricht, Ernst Josef, 72
Auric, Georges, 100
Austin, Herbert H., 471
Austral, Florence, 330
Australia Council, 350
Australian Broadcasting Commission See
Australian Broadcasting Corporation, 319
Australian Elizabethan Theatre Trust, 335, 344
"Avec les anges", 220
Aventurera, 426
Awlad al-Thawat, 398
Axel an der Himmelstür, 63, 74
Ayala, Fernando, 412
Ayer, Nat D., 84
Aymé, Marcel, 234
Ayyam wa layali, 399

Aznavour, Charles, 31, 77-8
Bablo, Lamartine, 415
Bacharach, Burt, 147, 467
"Back, Back to Sydney", 345
Bacopoulou-Halls, Aliki, 257
Badura-Skoda, Eva, 36
Baebijangjeon, 474
Baek Jae-hyun, 477
Bahaghan, 466
Baily, Leslie, 40, 45
Baker Street, 28, 89, 286
Baker, Josephine, 86, 91, 92, 102, 408
Baker, Peter, 254
Baker's Wife, The, 87
Bakker, Piet, 242
Balanchine, George, 69, 130
Balcovske, Sandra, 289
Ball, Michael, 156
Ballad Of Angel's Alley, The, 338
Ballad of Little Jo, The, 527
"Ballad of Mack the Knife, The", 73
Bancks, J.C., 332
Banff Centre, 312
Bannink, Harry, 116, 239, 240, 241, 242, 557
Banquells, Rocio, 423
Baobab Umoja. See
Bar Mitzvah Boy, 166
Barakat, Henri Antoine, 400
Barbican Theatre, 236
Barbieri, Francisco Asenjo, 47
Barcelata, Lorenzo, 420
"Barcelona", 361
Barde, André, 79, 87, 561
Barnes, Clive, 146, 405, 541
Barratts of Wimpole Street, The, 337
Barredo, Baby, 469
Barrie, J. M., 193
Barroso, Ary, 414, 415
Barrow Gang BC, 453
Barry, Jeff, 147, 153
Bart, Lionel, 31, 47, 263-6, 529
Bartók, Béla, 409
Bartram, Neil, 298, 307, 527
Basingthwaite, Nathalie, 490
Bat Out of Hell, 238
Batista, Fulgencio, 432
Battersea Arts Centre, 109
Battle, Hinton, 298
Battye, Don, 339, 555
Baudouin, Julio, 417
Bäuerle, Adolf, 55
Bawtree, Michael, 213, 517
Bearde, Chris, 335
Beatles, The, 146, 153, 467
Beaufort, John, 388
Beaumont, Binky, 219
Beauty and the Beast, 64, 413

Beauty World, 436, 486, 487, 488, 490, 495, 496, 499, 501
"Because", 220
Beethoven, Ludwig von, 56
Beggar's Opera, The, 22, 46, 72, 225, 416
Beguelin, Chad, 297
Behr, Edward, 85
Behrens, Jergen, 115
Being Erica, 278
Belasco, David, 130
Belisario, 261
Benatzky, Ralph, 60, 63, 65, 67, 74
Bend It Like Beckham, 269
Benedix, Roderich, 57
Benjamin, Peter, 335, 558
Bennett, Robert Russell, 217
Bennett, Tony, 278
Bennetto, Casey, 354
Beresford, Bruce, 319
Berger, Michel, 94
Bergman, Alan and Marilyn, 233
Bergreen, Laurence, 142
Beristain, Leopoldo Cuatezón, 420
Berkeley, Busby, 464
Berkoff, Steven, 24
Berlin, Irving, 17, 39, 129, 144, 146, 200, 432, 485, 512, 515
Bernard P. Jacobs Theatre, 252
Bernardi, Herschel, 226
Bernauer, Rudolf, 61
Bernhardt, Ian, 368, 369, 372, 381
Bernhardt, Sarah, 327
Bernicat, Firmin, 81
Bernstein, Leonard, 17, 23, 42, 65, 128, 149, 182, 208, 269, 433, 466, 527, 542
Berry, Chuck, 148
Bertal, Marcel, 89, 559
Bertaut, Jules, 82
Berton, Pierre, 162, 278
Berusaiyu no bara
  Rose of Versailles. *See*
Best Laid Plans, The, 312
Best Little Whorehouse in Texas, The, 343
Bet Your Life, 332
Betjeman, John, 252
Betts, Jim, 155, 312, 524, 525, 526
Betty Blue Eyes, 271, 273, 498
Bexon, Georgina, 513, 563
Beyond Eden, 317
Beyond the Rainbow, 248
Biberti, Robert, 110
Big Life, The, 528
"Biladi Biladi", 397
Billington, Michael, 109, 231, 272, 356
Billy Bishop Goes to War, 186, 285, 527, 555, 561
Billy Elliot, 208
Birch, John Youlin, 327

Birkenhead, Susan, 297
Birnie, Peter, 317
Birthday Girl, 394
Bittersweet, 47, 141
Bitter-Sweet, 43
Bizet, Georges, 41-2, 77-8
Black Crook, The, 30
Black Orpheus, 417
Black Swan Theatre Company, 352
Black, Don, 166, 362, 457, 512, 518, 550
Blackadder, 269
Blair, Ron, 339
Blakemore, Michael, 322
Blanche, Francis, 229
Blank, Larry, 183, 251, 292
Bless the Bride, 47, 141
Blitz, 265, 266
Blitzstein, Marc, 73, 112, 129, , 217, 524
Blood Knot, The, 384
Bloom, Harry, 368, 379, 558
Bloom, Orlando, 368
Blue Angel, The, 105, 106, 110
Blue Danube, The, 197
Blue Mountain Melody, 332
Blye, Alan, 335
Blythe, Alecky, 273
BMI, 147, 518, 524
Boat that Rocked, The, 151
Bock, Jerry, 207, 542
Bogavac, Jelena, 255
Bogdanovich, Peter, 91
Bolten-Bäckers, Heinrich, 67
Bolton, Guy, 61, 126, 333
Bombay Dreams, 436, 457
Bonbonnière, 74
Bond, Christopher, 298, 556
Bond, Grahame, 340
Bonsignori, Gabriele, 5, 247
Book of Mormon, The, 176, 208
Bootz, Erwin, 110
Borbosa, Maria Carmen, 416
Bordman, Gerald, 45, 142
"Born to be Wild", 274
Borovansky Ballet, 328
Bose, Mihir, 455
"Bosom Buddies", 284
"Bosom Friends", 284
Bostantzoglou, Mentis, 260
Boublil, Alain, 76, 78, 230, 235, 236, 524, 554, 558
Boughton, Kathryn, 184
Boulanger, Nadia, 217, 409
Bourgeois Bleibt Bourgois, 106
Bourgeoise Gentilhomme, 106
Bowness, Gordon, 290
Boy Friend, The, 167
Boy from Oz, The, 321, 346, 347
Boy's Own McBeth, 340
Boyer, Charles, 107
Boyer, Jean, 90

Boyett, Bob, 291
Boys from Syracuse, The, 531
Bozzo, Joan Lluís, 246
Braden, Bernard, 322
Bradley, Ian, 270, 543
Bran Nue Dae, 352, 353, 561
Brantley, Ben, 241, 293, 299
Brazier, Adam, 5, 313, 314, 315
Brazil (film), 415
Bread and Butter, 301
Breaker Morant, 319
Brebner, Morwyn, 300
Brecht, Bertolt, 67, 72, 73, 74, 106, 112, 113, 118, 132, 152, 190, 237, 301, 338, 416
Breedland, André, 242, 556
Breffort, Alexandre, 217, 219, 220, 222, 225, 226, 227, 228, 557
Brel, Jacques, 31, 77-8, 102, 118, 160, 222, 234-5
Brentano, Felix, 69
Brice, Fanny, 83, 90, 92
Brickhill-Burke, Joan, 386
Bricusse, Leslie, 248
Bride's Lament, 290, 293
Bridewell Theatre, 360, 516, 519
Brigadoon, 131, 177, 187, 526
Bright Moon Song and Dance Troupe, 484
Bring in da Noise, Bring in da Funk, 527
Brink, Jos, 241
Bristol Hippodrome, 271
British Academy of Songwriters, Composers and Authors, 141
British Broadcasting Corporation, 109, 151, 166, 357, 545
Broadway Asia International, 484
Broadway at Bedtime, 28, 320
Broadway Boys, 441
Broadway North: The Dream of a Canadian Musical Theatre, 27, 281, 298
Broken Bridges, 501
Brook, Peter, 6, 219, 221, 224, 391, 450, 451
Brook, Sir Peter, 222, 229, 451, 554
Brooke, Brian, 385
Brooks, Daniel, 290
Brooks, Shelton, 163
Brother, Can You Spare a Dime?, 150
Brothers Ábalos, 408
Broun, Heywood, 142
Broussolle, Jean, 90
Brown, Jason Robert, 214, 360, 513
Brown, Nancy, 336, 337, 559
Brown, Steve, 270, 559
Bruant, Aristide, 99, 100, 106
Bruce, Lenny, 116
Bruno, Massimiliano, 249
Buarque, Chico, 416

Bucchino, John, 116
Buchanan, P.J., 320
Buddy -- The Buddy Holly Story, 308, 313
Bunch of Ratbags, A, 339
Bunim, Shmuel, 404
Buntes Theatre Überbrettl. *See* Buñuel, Luis, 420
Bunyan, Mark, 118
Buonanotte Bettina, 246
Burk, Anthony, 260
Burke, Alan, 335, 558
Burnett, Jim, 340
Busch, Charles, 347
Busoni, Ferruccio, 71, 130
Buzzard Song, 160
Bye Bye Birdie, 154, 157, 224, 526
CAA Theatre, 310
Cabaret, 104, 165, 187, 188
Cabaret and Musical Theatre Alliance, 279, 564
Cabaret Chez Gilles, 218
Cabaret des Assassins Lapin Agile. *See*
Cabaret Grössenwahn, 106
Caesar, Irving, 74
Caird, John, 235
Caligula, 412
Calloway, Ann Hampton, 118
Calvi, Gerard, 229
Cambridge Theatre, 272, 386
Camelot, 131
Cameron, John, 236
Campbell, Elaine, 3, 163, 282, 527, 555
Campbell, Norman, 27, 163, 184, 281-2, 284-5, 448, 527, 555
Canadian Broadcasting Corporation, 119, 277, 282, 290, 311, 316, 317, 335, 544, 545, 555, 558, 564
Canadian Music Theatre Project, 279, 302, 307, 517, 518, 522, 546
Canadian Stage Company, 298
Canaro, Francisco, 408
Can-Can, 78, 187, 226, 561
Candide, 65, 152, 208
Cantabile, 110
Cantinflas, 421, 422
Capilano University, 312
Capote, Truman, 219
Captain Michalis, 259
Carbalho, Agustin Morales, 424
Carden, George, 335
Careless Rapture, 139
Carl, Carl, 56
Carl, Fred, 529
Carlos, José "J.", 414
Carltheater, 56, 64
Carmen, 30, 41, 42, 78, 92, 406, 416, 426, 463, 558

Carmen Jones, 42
Carmichael, Hoagy, 146
Carnelia, Craig, 201
Caroline, 339
Carousel, 168, 173, 187, 464, 467, 485
Carré Theatre, 239
Carrillo, Martha, 423
Carroll, Garnet H., 337
Carter, Wilf, 277
Carver, Brent, 14, 298, 299
Casey, Warren, 194
Casiono-Montparnasse, 93
Cass, Ronald, 247
Cassidy, David, 145
Castilla, Jorge, 418
Castro, Fidel, 432, 435
"Catching the Central Express", 344
Cats, 10, 63, 158, 238, 279, 306, 309, 422, 423, 448
Cattrall, Kim, 356
Cave of the Golden Calf, 115
Cayabyab, Ryan, 6, 461, 466
Cecilia Valdés, 430, 432
Cedar Tree, The, 331
Central Academy of Drama, 485
Central Park Tango, 303
Chadha, Gurinder, 175
Chadran, R., 487
Chagal, Marc, 181
Chahine, Youssef, 400
Chakiris, George, 232
Chakraworowut, Suwandi, 508
Chamfleury, Robert, 89, 559
Champion, Gower, 154
Champion, Kate, 365
Chang and Eng, 490
Chang Hsin-Tzu, 460
Chang Shi-Kuo, 457
Chang Tai-chien, 459
Chang Yang-Shuan, 460
Chaplin, Sir Charles, 49
Chapman, Christopher, 165
Chapman, John, 224
Charell, Erik, 63
Charles, Hugh, 377
Charlie and the Chocolate Factory, 208
Charlottetown Festival, 27, 163, 164, 185, 278, 281, 282, 283, 313, 315, 316, 334, 555
Charnin, Martin, 166
Charoumeno Xekinima, 260
Chase, Will, 299
Chat Noir, 78, 96, 98, 99, 102, 103
Chat Noir (Berlin), 105
Chatzēpantazēs, Thodōros, 257
Chazelle, Damien, 233
Chen, Edwin W., 5, 174
Cherlin, Michael, 52
Chess, 244
Chess King, The, 457

Chevalier, Maurice, 77, 85, 86, 87, 88, 89, 92, 235, 548
Chez Fischer, 99
Chez Fyscher, 90
Chi, Jimmy, 352, 353, 561
Chiang Kai-shek, 457
Chiang, Michael, 487, 496
Chicago, 14, 24, 74, 119, 182, 194, 195, 196, 219, 255, 539, 564
Children of Salt, 418
Chionh, Eugene Ryan, 487
Chiti, Ugo, 249
Chocolate Soldier, The, 61
Chocolate Soldier, The, 68
Chocolate Soldier, The, 130
Choi Chang Kwon, 474
Chorus Line, A, 64, 154, 158, 198, 238, 250, 411, 423, 448, 491, 524
Christiansen, Rupert, 208
Christie, Craig, 360
Christie, Dinah, 119
Christiné, Henri, 31, 83, 84, 85, 86, 118, 559
Chu Chin Chow, 322
Chuang Yik, 502
Chulalongkorn University, 507, 508
Chulalongkorn, King, 169
Chungmu Art Hall, 477
Churchill, Sir Winston, 114, 263
Chute, B.J., 193
Ciboulette, 79, 85
Cibrián Campoy, Pepe, 411, 555, 556
Cinderella,, 485
Cipolla, Frank, 298
Circus, 49
Cirque du Soleil, 535
Ciske de Rat, 242, 243, 262, 556
Cisneros, Víctor Cavalli, 420
Citadel Theatre, 295
Citlalixayotl, 424, 425, 556
City of God, 417
City, The, 452
Clair, René, 90
Clark, Professor Manning, 341
Clark, Stephen, 498, 557
Clarke, Elizabeth, 277
Clarke, Kevin, 67
Clarke, Terrence, 340
Clarke, Terry, 339
Cleese, John, 522
Cleopatra and Mark Anthony, 398
Cluff, Susan, 213, 525-6
Coca-Cola Kid, The, 151
Cocciante, Riccardo. *See* Cocciante, Richard
Cocciante, Richard, 93
Cochran, C.B., 83
Cocteau, Jean, 100
Code Name Black Cat, 453
Coelho, Elisina, 415

Cohan, George M., 123, 142, 250
Cohen, Alexander, 247
Cohen, Leonard, 199, 200
Cold Feet, 289
Cole, Allen, 301
Cole, Stephen, 181
Coleman, Cy, 165
Coleman, Ross, 358
Colerick, George, 43, 53
Colerick, George, 71
Collado, Ana Maria, 427
Collerick, George, 36
Collet, Henri, 100
Collin, Erich, 110
Collits, Pierce, 330
Collits' Inn, 32, 330, 332, 352
Colliver, Amanda, 497
Collodi, Carlo, 250
Colman, Charles, 339
Comden, Betty, 527
Come from Away, 5, 31, 185, 278, 283, 303, 305, 306, 307, 318, 522, 556
Comedian Harmonists, The, 110, 111
Comedy Theatre (Melbourne), 321, 322, 337, 342
Comme de Bien Entendu., 90
Company, 94, 154, 238, 361, 362, 467
Complainte de la Butte, 90, 95, 99
Comte, Charles, 22, 35, 77, 79, 102, 107
Comte, Louis, 22, 78
Conde, Antonio Díaz, 420
Conesa, María, 423
Coney Island Play, 452
"Consider Yourself", 235, 236
Constantine, Eddie, 217
Conversation Piece, 47
Conyers, Will, 320, 321, 347, 358
Cook, Peter, 105, 115
Cooke, Malcolm, 342, 343
Cookin', 485, See Nanta
Cooper, Sara, 418
Coplan, David, 373, 380
Copland, Aaron, 129, 192
Coppin, George, 327
Cork Opera House, 251
Cork, Adam, 273
Corporacion Interamericana de Entretenimiento, 416, 425
Corrugation Road, 353
Cort Theatre, 388, 389, 393
Cosentino, Olga, 412
Cottesloe Theatre, 273
Cotton, Christopher Cooke, 409
Coulter, John, 28
Coups de roulis, 85
Coups de Roulis, 80
Courthouse Theatre, 300
Cousens, Peter, 359, 363, 563
Covarrubias, Francisco, 428
Coveney, Michael, 167, 265, 356

Cowan, Ron, 271
Coward, Sir Noël, 43, 46, 47, 141, 149, 168, 209, 263, 265, 267, 284
Cox, Christopher, 168
Cradle Will Rock, The, 129, 524
Craig, Phil, 88
Crawford, Dan, 345
Crawford, Michael, 238
Creative Community Singapore, 492
Crémieux, Hector, 38, 40
Crew, Robert, 289
Croft, Martin, 351
Crombie, Jonathan, 289
Crooked Mile, The, 267
Crosby, Bing, 184, 226
Cryer, Gretchen, 164
Cuba Libre, 430, 434
Cugat, Xaviar, 415
Culture Show, 545
Cup of Tea, A Bex and a Good Lie Down, A, 334
Cushman, Robert, 299, 301
Cuvillier, Charles, 79
Cycowski,,Roman, 110
Cyrano, 241, 243
d'Albert, Eugene, 130
D'Oyly Carte Opera Company, 328
Da Boyz, 531
Daegu International Musical Festival, 6, 460, 478
Dahl, Roald, 120, 272
Dainty, Paul, 344
Dalagang Bukid, 462, 463
Dale, Grover, 6, 232-3
Daleman, Rob, 298
Dallas, Lorna, 118
Dalton, Karen C. C., 102
Daly's Theatre, 60
Dalziel and Pascoe, 394
Dame tus dos Rosas, 432
Damián, Pedro, 423
Dancap Productions, 294
Dance of the Vampires, 64, 238
Dancing Years, The, 139, 141
Daniele, Graciela, 406
Daniels, Salie, 393
Danish Musical Theatre Academy, 519
Dankworth, Johnny, 368
Dante, Ron, 153, 154
Darewski, Herman, 84
Darion, Joe, 258
Darwish, Sayed, 397, 399
Das Gefängnis, 57
Das Pensionat, 57
Dassin, Jules, 258
Daubeny, Sir Peter, 386
David, Hal, 148
Davis, Lee, 528

Day in Hollywood / A Night in the Ukraine, A, 202
Days of Hope, 269
de Crane, John, 240
De dader heeft het gedaan, 240
De Garis, Jack, 323, 324
De Gorsse, Henry, 257
de Jesus, Vincent, 466
de Jongh, Nicholas, 356
de la Rama, Atang, 462
De Mounties, 115
de Munk, Danny, 242
de Pano, Arnel, 466
de Sivry Charles, 100
de Tourdonette, Vincent, 200
Dear Death, 507
Dearest Moon, 506
Debussy, Claude, 76, 82, 94, 98
December Rains, 500
Dédé, 85
"Defying Gravity", 208
del Campo, Maria, 424
Dela Cruz, Katy, 468
Delain, Rosa Alicia, 427
Delerue, Georges, 76
Delysia, Alice, 333
Demaria, Gonzalo, 413
Demick, Barbara, 478
Demy, Jacques, 229, 230-1, 232, 443, 562
Deneuve, Catherine, 232
Dennis, C.J., 337
Deocampo, Nick, 463
Der Rosenkavalier, 68
Deréal, Colette, 218
Desert Song, 68
Desplat, Alexandre, 76
Destry Rides Again, 107, 524
Deutsch, Diana, 16
Deutsch, Leon Benoit-, 87
Deutsches Theater, 69, 70
Dexter, Steven, 498, 560
Dhéry, Robert, 229
Dhlamini, Ezekiel "King Kong", 370
Diamond, Dick, 338
Diamond, I.A.L., 226
Díaz, Edda, 410
Dick, William, 339
Dickens, Charles, 264
Dickson, Barbara, 270
"Did You Hear?", 283
Die Csárdásfürstin, 61
Die Distel, 115
Die Dreigroschenoper
   Threepenny Opera, 72
   Threepenny Opera, The. See
Die Fledermaus, 42, 43, 58, 59, 62, 69, 70, 131, 561
Die Hölle, 60, 114
Die Trapp-Familie, 194

Diesel Playhouse, 298
Dietrich, Marlene, 103, 105, 106, 108, 110
Dietz, Howard, 58
Diggers, 330
Dike, Fatima, 381
Dimba, Peter, 390
Dimopoulos, Dinos, 260
Dingo, Ernie, 353
Diokno, Pepe, 460
Diplopennies, 260
Dirty Dancing, 308, 546
Discépolo, Enrique Santos, 408
Discipline, 344
Dis-Donc, 226
Dissanayake, Wimal, 456
DJ Excalibah, 531
Do I Hear a Waltz, 203
Dollar Princess, The
   Die Dollarprinzessin. See
Dollar Princess, The, 60
Domingo, Plácido, 48, 422
Dominus, Susan, 289
Don Quijote, 48
Don Quixote et Sancho Pança, 37
Donan, Stanley, 230
Donizetti, Gaetano, 39, 41, 57, 261
Donmar Warehouse, 413
Donnelly, John, 392
Donovan, Jason, 356
Dorgelès, Roland, 101
Dorléac, Françoise, 232
Dorn, Egon, 114
Dornford-May, Mark, 394
Dos Passos, John, 67
Dot and the Kangaroo, 343
Dover, Arnold, 372, 374
D'Oyly Carte, Richard, 81
Dr. Who, 337
Drabinsky, Garth, 280, 309
Dracula, 411, 413
Drainie, John, 283
Dranem, 89
Dreiser, Theodore, 67
Dresselhuys, Mary, 239
Drewe, Anthony, 271, 498, 560
Dreyfus, George, 341
Dreyfuss, Max, 130
Driessen, René, 115
Drowsy Chaperone, The, 5, 15, 31, 119, 156, 167, 180, 278, 280-1, 283, 286-8, 290-1, 293-7, 301, 307, 317-8, 450, 522, 527
Drylips Ought to Move to Kapuskasing, 316
Dublin Theatre Festival, 252
Duckworth, Eric, 334
Due South, 163, 278, 280
Duffy, Rosemary, 349
Duke of York Theatre, 395

Duke, Vernon, 130
Đukić, Radivoje Lola, 255
Dulaang Unibersidad ng Pilipinas, 466
Dumas, Alexandre, 235
DuMaurier, Daphne, 238
Dumbells, The, 293
Dunaway, Faye, 205
Dunayevsky, Isaak Osipovich, 48, 50
Dupuy, René, 218
Durey, Louis, 100
Duval, Georges, 81, 560
Duvernois, Henri, 89, 559
Dvořák, Antonin, 74, 130
Dykstra, Ted, 5, 314
Dylan, Bob, 199, 200
É do Outro Mundo, 414
East End Theatre District, 321
East Side Story, 50
Easy Rider, 151
Ebb, Fred, 165, 188, 207, 219
Ebersole, Christine, 291
Ebiary, Abo El Seoud El, 399
Ebinger, Blandine, 106
Ed Sullivan Show, 384
Eddy, Nelson, 162
Edge, Simon, 356
Edinburgh Fringe, 484, 520
Edinburgh Fringe Festival, 484
Edison, Thomas, 78
Edmonton, Dennis, 274
Edney, Kathryn, 173
Edwards, Alan, 345
Edwards, Gale, 346, 347, 348, 358, 361
Eenens, Paul, 243
Egnos, Bertha, 384, 557
Einstein, Albert, 102
Eisenstein, Sergei, 49
El amor de la estanciera, 406
El arroyo que murmura, 430
El barberillo de Lavapiés, 48
El Cóndor Pasa, 48, 417
El Diablo en el poder, 48
El Filibusterismo, 468
El gaucho de Buenos Aires, 407
El Gran Casino, 420
El Jorobado de Paris, 412, 413, 556
"El Manisero"
    Peanut Vendor, The. *See, See*
El otro yo de Marcela, 408
El quitrin, Flor de Yumuri, 430
El Rataplàn, 419
El Retrato de Dorian Gray, 424
El solar, 433
El Tango en París, 408
El último teatro del mundo, 425
Eleven Executioners, 104
Elgar, Edward, 17
Elgin Theatre, 294
Elisabeth, 63, 237, 443, 546

El-Leila El-Kebira, 402
Ellington, Duke, 150, 379, 431
Elliot, Cathy, 316
Elliot, Stephan, 355
Elliott, Benjamin, 312
Ellis, Sarah T., 193
Ellis, Vivian, 47, 88, 133, 141, 263, 271, 564
Elmer Gantry, 270
Embujo Theatre, 450
Emerald Hill Theatre, 339
Emerald Room, The, 349
Emigrants, The, 244
Emperor's New Clothes, 360, 448
Emperor's Waltz, The, 226
En Nu Naar Bed, 239, 556
    And Now to Bed. *See*
Enany, Sarah, 5, 397, 401
Eng, Thien Kwee, 493
Engel, Lehman, 7, 12, 27, 44, 80, 128-9, 133, 145, 154-6, 160, 168-9, 187, 192, 197-9, 205, 210, 213-4, 229, 279, 302, 312, 334, 445-6, 513, 523-4, 530, 540, 546, 564, 568
Enoch, Wesley, 354
Enrico 61, 246
Enright, Nick, 338, 340, 346, 555
Ensemble Theatre, 340
Entra na Faixa, 415
Epsenhart, Lauren, 418
Erdöd, Count Ferdinand Palffy von, 56
Es liegt in der Luft, 108
Esos invertidos amores, 425
Esplanade Centre, 488, 493, 498, 500, 503
Esse Mulato Val Sê Meu, 415
Esta noche me emborracho, 408
Establishment Club, 115
Eternal Road, The, 71
Etinger, Amos, 404
Eureka, 347
Eurobeat, 360
Eva, el gran musical argentino, 178, 411
Evangeline, 5, 314, 315
Everybody's Talking about Jamie, 513
Evie May, 364, 365
Evil Dead – The Musical, 297, 298, 556
Evita, 177, 219, 238, 406, 410, 413, 512, 557
Evita – Tango Popular Opera, 411, 557
Evita - Volveré y seré millones, 178, 411
Expresso Bongo, 154, 219, 266
Eyre, Sir Richard, 271
Eysler, Edmund, 60, 64
Fadel, Dalia Farid, 402
Faílde, Miguel, 429
Faisiang, Ingrid, 482
Faith, Percy, 277
Falabella, Miguel, 416

Falcone, Edoardo, 249
Fall, Leo, 60, 64, 96
"Falling in Love Again", 106
Falling Slowly, 252
Fallis, Terry, 312
Fame, 409, 486
Fancy Dress, 292
Fantasticks, The, 209, 404, 423, 450, 467
Farago, Peter, 236
Farnon, Robert, 277, 278
Farrar, Geraldine, 463
Fauré, Jean-Baptiste, 76
Faustus, 438
Favero, Alberto, 411
Fawzi, Mohamed, 400
Fayruz, 399
Fearless Vampire Killers (or, "Pardon Me But Your Teeth are in my Neck"), The, 238
Federico, Domingo, 411, 557
Feingold, Michael, 179
Fellner Jr., Ferdinand, 58
Fellowes, Julian, 139
Female Student, 477
Fenwick, John, 284
Feore, Donna, 251
Ferber, Edna, 126
Féria, Filipe La, 253
Fernandez, Doreen G., 461
Fernandez, Emilio, 420
Fernández, Joseito, 431
Ferré, Léo, 102
Ferrer, Horacio, 409
Festival of Asian Performing Arts, 490
Festival of Canadian Musical Theatre, 527
Feuersnot, 103
Feur, Cy, 167
Feydeau, Georges, 80
FFF, 323
Fiddler on the Roof, 29, 158, 159, 180, 207, 226, 391, 403, 409, 481
Fidelio, 56
Fielding, Harold, 447
Fields, Dorothy, 165
Fields, Joseph, 172
Filichia, Peter, 299
Finding Mr. Destiny, 472
Fings Ain't Wot They Used T'Be, 265, 529
Finian's Rainbow, 526
Finkle, David, 360
Firefly, 130
Fireweeds: Women of the Yukon, 316
Firqah Reda, 400
Fisher, Rodney, 343
Five Foot Broadway, 491, 557
Flash Jim Vaux, 339
Flatley, Michael, 250
Fledermaus (cabaret), 114

Fletcher, Jackie, 531
Fletcher, Mark, 351
Flor de nit, 246
Flores del Campo, Francisco, 414
Flory, Régine, 88
Flower Drum Song, 172, 174, 175, 436, 440
Flowered Port, 441
Floyd Collins, 362, 517
Fly, Robin, Fly, 237
Flynn, Patrick, 340
Foil, David, 42
Folies-Bergère, 22, 67, 78, 80, 81, 83, 85, 91, 92, 94, 548
Follies, 238, 467
Follies of the Day, 92
Fontaine, Robert, 165
Fonteyn, Margot, 329
Foote, Horton, 192, 447
Forbidden City, 436, 488, 493, 496, 498, 501, 557
Ford, Anne Kerry, 117
Ford, Lena Guilbert, 143
Ford, Nancy, 164
Foreign Hill, 448
Forever Plaid, 298
Forrest, David, 248
Forsyth, Julian, 109, 110
Forsyth, Marguerite, 110
Fortune Theatre, 384
Forty-Second Street, 485
Forty-second Street Moon, 6, 228
Fosse, Bob, 255, 539
Foster, Stephen, 142
Four Seasons Opera House, 310
Fox, Maxine, 195
Foxtrot, 240, 242
Francisquita, Doña, 48
François-les-Bas-Bleus, 81
Frankel, Scott, 543
Franklin, Benjamin, 170
Frattini, Manuel, 250
Frau Luna, 67, 74
Free Wind, The, 48
Freedman, Bill, 284, 285
Fregoli, 249
Fregoli, Leopoldo, 249
Freihaus-Theater auf der Wieden, 35
French Can-Can, 90, 99
"Fried Rice Paradise", 490
Friml, Rudolph, 130, 162, 163
Fringe of Toronto Festival, 287, 289
Frohman, Charles, 124, 309
"From a Prison Cell", 224
From A to Z, 332
From Russia With Love, 266
Frommermann, Harry, 110
Fronz, Oskar, 64
Frühling, 60
Fuentes, Fernando de, 420

573

Fugard, Athol, 384
Fulford, Robert, 275, 280, 283
Fulton Theatre, 87
Funny Girl, 329
Funny Thing Happened on the Way to the Forum, A, 80, 286
Furth, George, 362
Furtwängler, Wilhelm, 66
Fyshe, Anna, 169
Gabin, Jean, 91, 99
Gahely, Ezzat El, 399
Gaiety Theatre, 45
Galarraga, Gustavo Sanchez, 432
Galceran, Jordi, 246
Gamal, Samiya, 400
Gänzl, Kurt, 13, 52, 69, 85, 87, 93-4, 237, 267, 269, 378, 568
Garber, Victor, 313
Garbo, Greta, 245, 249
García, Cristina, 423
Garfunkel, Art, 48
Garinei, Pietro, 246, 249
Garland, Judy, 431
Garrick Gaieties, 130
Gasalla, Antonio, 410
Gate Theatre (Charing Cross, london), 332
Gates, Henry Louis Jr., 102
Gaudi, 246
Gay Hussars, The, 61
Gay, John, 22, 46, 72
Gay, Noel, 46
Gehry, Frank, 274, 310
Geistinger, Marie, 57, 58
Gélinas, Gratien, 267, 282
Genatt Haft, Simone, 485
Genée, Richard, 43, 58
George Ignatief Theatre, 289
George, Bruce, 338
Gerard, Frédéric "Frédé", 101
Gerard, Jeremy, 241
Gershwin, George, 11, 17, 27, 71, 88, 94, 109, 131, 133, 144, 146, 148, 150, 152, 227, 335, 362, 431, 445, 475, 514, 549, 552, 557
Gershwin, Ira, 11, 46, 133, 161
"Get Up and Boogie", 237
Gets, Malcolm, 299
Gevisser, Mark, 389
Gharam fi al-Karnak, 400
Ghazal al-banat, 399
Gielguid Theatre, 231
Gigi, 78
Gilbert, John, 249
Gilbert, Robert, 109
Gilbert, Sir William Schwenk, 7, 11, 23, 43, 45-6, 60, 109,122, 133, 141, 143, 252, 263, 541
Gill, André, 101
Gilliam, Terry, 415

Gilmore, David, 452, 453, 454
Gingold, Hermione, 332
Ginzler, Robert, 224
Giovannini, Sandro, 246
Gipsy Princess, The
  Die Csárdásfürstin, 61
Girl from Utah, The, 124
Girlfriends, 269
Giulietta e Romeo, 250
Give My Regards to Broadway, 144
Gladwell, Malcolm, 521
Glamorous Night, 139
Glasser, Mona, 370, 371
Glasser, Stanley, 370
Glasser, Susan, 254
Glee, 204, 543
Glickman, Will, 409
Global Search for New Musicals, 546
Glory of the Railwaymen, 50
Glow-Worm, 67
Gluckman, Arnald, 415
Gluckman, Leon, 372, 382
Godik, Giora, 403
Godspell, 197, 392, 451, 467
Godzilla, 443
Goebbels, Joseph, 66, 114
Goethe, Johann Wolfgang von, 438
Goetz, E. Ray, 83, 84
Goffin, Gerry, 147
Goh Boon Teck, 500
Goh Jung-min, 477
Goh, Robin, 490
Gokulsing, K. Moti, 456
Golan, Menahem, 404
Goldberg, Whoopi, 389
Golden Bat, The, 451
Golden Dawn, 62
Golden Valley, The, 48
Golderich, Arthur, 374
Goldman, Gabriel, 412
Goldoni, Carlo, 340, 395
Goldreich, Arthur, 371
Goldsmiths, University of London, 12, 374, 436, 518, 528, 564
Goldwyn, Samuel, 176
Gomeshi, Jian, 200, 544
Gomez, Jorge, 434
Gone with the Wind, 443, 447
Gontier, Robert, 303
Gonzáles, Inma, 245
Good Doctor, The, 477
Goodall, Howard, 18, 23, 148, 268, 271, 557
Goodbye for Now, 94
Goodbye to Berlin, 104
Goodeve, Piper, 164
Gooding, Neil, 5, 319, 349, 350, 358, 363, 365, 563
Goodloe, Kate, 164
Goodman, Benny, 109

Goodspeed Opera House, 165
Gordon, Maggie May, 347
Gorlero, Pablo, 407, 410
Gorney, Jay, 150
Gosford Park, 139
Goulet, Robert, 165, 313
Grady, Chris, 7, 9, 18, 159, 210, 212, 214, 514, 516, 519, 544, 563
Graham, Desmond Lyle, 342
Grainer, Ron, 337
Grammond, Peter, 39, 41
Grand Hotel, 440, 441
Grandage, Michael, 413
Granowsky, Andrew, 106
Grant, Bruce, 366
Grant, Mark N., 155
Grappelli, Stéphane, 102
Grattan, Harry, 88
Gray, John MacLachlan, 28, 186, 281, 285, 555
Grease, 194, 195, 423
Greco, Juliette, 218
Green, Adolph, 527
Greenbank, Percy, 124
Greene, Justin, 270, 559
Greenray Theatre Company, 459
Greenwell, Peter, 267
Greenwich Theatre, 518, 564
Greenwich, Ellie, 153
Greenwillow, 193
Greer, Germaine, 347
Grenet, Eliseo, 430, 432
Grey Gardens, 543
Grey, Clifford, 84, 333
Greyeyes, Michael, 316
Gribble, Harry Wagstaffe, 84
Griffi, Giuseppe Patroni, 249
Griffiths, Rudyard, 275
"Groovy Kind of Love", 153
Grosses Schauspielhaus, 68, 74
Grossmith, George, 60, 133
Grossmith, George Jr., 60
Grotowski, Jerzy, 391
Grudeff, Marian, 28, 281, 286, 287
Grünbaum, Fritz, 60
Grünbaum, Fritz, 114
Guang, Zhao, 481
Guerrero, Jacinto, 48
Guettel, Adam, 312, 362, 513, 519
Guevara, Nacha, 410, 411
Guild of Canadian Musical Theatre Writers, 27, 524, 525, 564
Guinovart, Albert, 246
Guiraud, Ernest, 42
Guitry, Sacha, 79, 86, 93
Gün, Aydın, 161
Gurr, Thomas Stuart, 330
Gussow, Mel, 452
Guthrie, Woody, 200
Guttman, Arthur H., 84

Guy Named Joe, A, 241
Guys and Dolls, 74, 157, 158, 193, 220, 226
Gypsy, 203, 224, 556
H.M. Tennent Ltd., 219
H.M.S. Pinafore, 45
Ha'penny Bridge, 250, 557
Habbema, Eddy, 241
Hackney Empire, 389
Hadfield, Chris, 280
Hafez, Abdel Halim, 400
Haggis, Paul, 278
Hague, Albert, 409
Hahn, Phil, 292
Hahn, Reynaldo, 79, 85, 86, 555
Hair, 154, 156, 340, 410, 532
Hairspray, 207, 294, 313, 485
Hales, Dr. Aaron, 488, 495, 496, 501
Hales, Jeff, 343
Halévy, Fromental, 38, 41
Halévy, Ludovic, 38, 40-2, 57
Haley, Bill, 146
Half a Sixpence, 266, 267
Hall, Henry, 219
Hall, Stephen, 343
Hamatateh, 403
Hamilton, 13, 417, 530, 540, 541, 542
Hamilton, Barbara, 284, 296
Hammerstein, Oscar (II), 25, 32, 42, 62, 70, 128, 133, 138, 151-2, 162, 168, 171, 172, 173, 174, 175, 197, 200, 208, 210, 213, 268, 341, 467, 485, 531, 537, 538, 539
Hampton, Christopher, 238
Hampton, Wilborn, 389
Han, A Reum, 476
Handel, George Frederic, 110
Hans Christian Andersen, 176
Hansard, Glen, 252
Hansel and Gretel, 71
Hansen, Helle, 519
Hansen, Max, 63
Hanslick, Eduard, 39
Happy End, 74, 190
Happy Time, The, 165
Harbach, Otto, 62, 162
Harburg, E.Y. "Yip", 130, 150
Harcourt, Peter, 326
Harkness Theatre, 386
Harmonists, The, 110
Harnick, Sheldon, 231, 241, 527, 542
Harriott, Chris, 349
Harrison, George, 263
Harrison, Rex, 168, 514
Harron, Don, 163, 282, 284, 296, 527, 555
Harron, Martha, 282
Harron, Mary, 282
Hart, Charles, 209
Hart, Lorenz, 62, 143, 153, 176, 205

Hart, Moss, 143
Harussi, Emmanuel, 403
Harvey, Michael Maurice, 347
Hasenclever, Walter, 106
Hata, Toyokichi, 438
Hatpin, The, 358, 359
Hatzidakis, Manos, 258
Hauptmann, Elisabeth, 72, 74
Have a Hearty Meal, 345
Hayes, Nancye, 329, 347
Hays, Matthew, 295
Heawood, John, 220
Hedley, Philip, 154, 352, 529, 530, 532, 533, 534
Hedwig and the Angry Inch, 483
Heerlijk duurt het Langst, 239
Hefer, Haim, 404-5
Hein, David, 5, 303, 304, 556, 563
Held, Anna, 92
Hellman, Lillian, 208
Hello, Dolly!, 57, 154, 158, 321, 409, 420, 422
Helmer, Hermann, 58
Helpmann, Sir Robert, 322
Helta, Jenő, 84
Hemmingway, Ernest, 67
Henderson, Bill, 317
Henderson, Dickie, 246
Heneker, David, 47, 219, 221, 229, 266, 557-8
Hennequin, Maurice, 257
Henry, Marc, 114
Her Majesty's Theatre, 166, 385
Her Majesty's Theatre (Brisbane), 336
Her Majesty's Theatre (Melbourne), 321, 322, 327
Her Majesty's Theatre (Sydney), 327, 346
Herbert, Alf, 368
Herbert, Sir Alan Patrick, 141
Herbert, Victor, 12, 129, 250
Herman, Jerry, 146, 513
Hermans, Toon, 115
Hero: The Musical, 476
Hervé, 37
Hesterberg, Trude, 107
Heuberger, Richard, 58
Hey, Sourpuss, 288
Higashi, Yutaka, 451
Higâzî, Shaykh Salama, 397
High School Musical, 456, 542
Higher than the Sky of Paris, 440
Highway, Thomson, 316
Highwayman, The, 333, 352
Hill, Alfred, 325
Hill, Brian, 298, 300, 307, 527
Hillman, Jessica, 180
Hindemith, Paul, 108
Hirasawa, Satoshi, 441
Hired Man, The, 268, 270

Hirobumi, Ito, 476
Hirsch, Foster, 72
Hirst, Sheba, 395
His Majesty's Theatre (London) Her Majesty's Theatre. *See*
Hitchcock, Alfred, 138
Hitchings, Henry, 272
Hitler, Adolph, 63, 66, 70, 75, 105, 108, 109, 114, 136, 194, 217
HMS Pinafore, 26, 122, 133
Hobson, Harold, 221
Hoile, Christopher, 282, 301
Holländer, Felix, 106
Holländer, Friedrich, 31, 67-8, 71, 75, 96, 105-9, 113, 115, 133, 188, 561
Holländer, Victor, 108
Holly, Buddy, 146
Hollywood - Ritratto Di Un Divo, 249
Holmes à Court, Janet, 352
Holmes, Eda, 300
Home and Beauty, 108
Honda, Hiroko, 455
Honda, Yoshihisa, 455
Honegger, Arthur, 83, 89, 100, 234
Hong Kong Rhapsody, 449
Honk!, 271, 498
Honolka, Kurt, 54, 56
Hood, Basil, 60
Hope, Bob, 184
Hope, Vida, 167
Hope-Wallace, Philip, 139
Hopper, Dennis, 151
Hornez, André, 90
Horwitt, Arnold B., 409
Hossein, Robert, 236
Hot Jazz Club of France, 102
Houdini, una ilusion musical, 413
House of Martin Guerre, The, 524
How Do, Princess, 139
How to Succeed in Business Without Really Trying, 507
Howes, Sally Ann, 332
"Hoy no me puedo levantar", 245
Hsu Po-yun, 458
Huairou Theatre, 485
Huddleston, Bishop Trevor, 367
Hui, Melissa, 316
Hùidae theatre, 470
Hull House Theatre, 194
Hummingbird Centre Sony Centre. *See*
Humperdinck, Engelbert, 71
Humphries, Barry, 334
Hunchback Of Notre Dame, The, 238
Hwang Gyudong, 482
Hwang, David Henry, 173, 174
Hydropathes, 98
Hylton, Jack, 377, 379
Hymne à l'Amour, 217
Hyslop, Jeff, 14

I Am a Camera, 104
I Can't Sing!, 270
"I Can't Touch You with Words", 301
"I Do I Do in the Sky", 289
"I Go to Rio", 346, 347
"I Love the Night Life", 355
I Love You, You're Perfect, Now Change, 364, 485
"I Remember Love", 290, 292
"I Will Wait for You", 230, 231
I'd Rather Be Right, 143
"I'll Never Smile Again", 277
I'm Alan Partridge, 270
"I'm Calm", 287
I'm Getting My Act Together and Taking it on the Road, 164
Ibarra, Benny, 423
Ibsen, Henrik, 323
Ichiro, Maki, 443
"If I Could Walk Freely", 478
"If I Ever Fall in Love Again", 267
Iglesias, Luis, 415
Ikeda, Riyoko, 442
Ikoku-No-Oka, 448
"Il a Raison", 220
Il Giorno Della Tartaruga, 248
Ilagan, Hermogenes, 462
Illya Darling, 258
Im weissen Rössl
    White Horse Inn, The. *See*
Impempe Yomlingo, 394
Imperial Theatre (St. John, NB), 280
Improbable Frequency, 252, 262
Imre, Zoltán, 62
In the Heights, 530
In the Mood for Sorrow, 481
In Tune Conference – Creating the Great Canadian Musical, 312
"Indian Love Call", 162
Indian Productions, 455
International New Aspect Educational and Cultural Foundation, 458
Into the Woods, 182, 539
Into The Woods, 238
Inverne, James, 457
Ipi-Tombi, 385
Irglová, Markéta, 252
Irma la Douce, 220, 222, 223, 227, 229, 235, 266, 557, 558
Irma La Douce, 78, 217, 219, 229
Is Australia Really Necessary?, 334
Isherwood, Charles, 252, 358
Isherwood, Christopher, 104
Isintu
    Kwa Zulu. *See*
Ismail, Ali, 400
Istana Budaya, 503
"It's a Grand Old Flag", 144
It's a Wonderful Life, 270

"It's an Over-rated World (With Seven Underwhelming Wonders)", 289
Itelman, Ana, 411
Ivaschenko, Aleksei, 254
Ives, Charles, 122
Ives, David, 238
"J'ai deux amours", 86
Jackman, Hugh, 329, 347
Jackson, Frederick, 88
Jackson, Jeffrey, 82, 98, 100
Jacobs, Jim, 194
Jacobsen, Amber, 308
Jacobson, Leopold, 61
Jahin, Salah, 402
James Adams Floating Palace Theatre, 127
James Hardie Industries, 343
James,Polly, 284
Jang Soyoung, 482
Janin, Jules, 38
Jardin de Paris, 92
Jarre, Maurice, 76
Je T'aime, 441
Jelavich, Peter, 103, 104
Jelly's Last Jam, 527
Jenbach, Béla, 61
Jeong Jiajin, 482
Jersey Boys, 319
Jessel, Raymond, 28, 89, 286
Jessop, Sonia Kolesnikov-, 500
Jesus Christ Superstar, 156, 235, 267, 313, 410, 423, 468, 512
Jewison, Norman, 181, 280, 318
Jiménez, José Alfredo, 420
Joaquim, Nick, 468
Joe, 241
Joe Starts Again, 351
Johann-Strauss-Theater, 61, 64
John Golden Theatre, 384
John, Alan, 340
Johnny Angel, 442
Johnson, Christine, 344
Johnson, Laurie, 265
Johnson, Lyndon, 474
Johnson, Melody, 301
Johnson, Reed, 414
Johnston, Dr. Peter Wyllie, 321, 323, 331, 334, 336, 338, 340, 341, 352, 353, 563
Jones, Arnold Wayne, 184
Jones, Chris, 195, 196
Jones, Deborah, 365
Jones, Laura, 386, 391
Jones, Sidney, 124
Jones, Tom, 152, 190, 192, 209, 450
Jonzi D, 533
Joplin, Scott, 154
Jorgensen, Peter, 312
Joseph and the Amazing Technicolor Dreamcoat, 158, 356

Joseph Papp Public Theater, 231
Joseph, Paul, 528
Jouy, Jules, 100
Joyner, Aaron, 5, 189, 350, 351, 356, 362, 363, 546, 563
Jubany, Miguel, 411, 557
Judía, 407
Jugar con fuego, 48
Julia, Raul, 112
Julissa, 423
Jung Sung San, 478
Jungr, Barb, 120
Junona i Avos, 254
Just a Kiss, 88
Just for Laughs, 298
Just So, 271
Justicia Criolla, 407
Kabarett der Komiker, 108
Kabuki, 178, 179, 436, 452, 454
Kálmán, Emmerich, 61, 64-5, 67-8
Kanagawa Arts Theatre, 449
Kander, John, 165, 188, 207, 223
Kanin, Garson, 58
Kanjanarat, Sangarun, 508
Kaouru, Irie, 442
Kaplan, Jonathan, 300
Kapur, Shekhar, 457
Karastamatis, John, 289
Karczag, Wilhelm, 58, 63
Karim, Mohammed, 398
Karloff, Boris, 169
Karmon, Jonaton, 405
Kärntnertortheater, 35
Kat and the Kings, 393, 558
Katharina Knie, 109
Katy, 468
Kauffman, Stanley, 384
Kaufman, George S., 127, 143
Kaverin, Veniamin, 254
Kaye, Danny, 176
Kazablan, 403
Kazantzakis, Nikos, 259
Keating, 120, 158, 354, 561
Keelan, Paul, 348, 559
"Keep the Home Fires Burning", 138, 143
Kelly, Conor, 252
Kelly, Dennis, 272
Kelly, Gene, 173, 232, 233, 400
Kelly, Laura Michelle, 205
Kelly, Veronica, 354
Kennedy, Chilina, 315
Kennedy, Jackie, 406
Kente, Gibson, 384
Kerby, Paul, 69
Kern, Jerome, 11, 27, 60-1, 123, 126, 129, 131-3, 144, 548
Kerr, Deborah, 230
Kerr, Walter, 224
Kesten, Hermann, 106

Khalek, Hisham Abdel, 181
Khan, Hazrat Inayat, 16
Khayri, Badie', 399
Kidman, Nicole, 394
Kikuta, Kazuo, 159, 441, 444
Kill or Kiss, 255
Killick, Dr. Andrew, 472
Kim Hee Gab, 475
Kim Jong-pil, 473
Kim Jun-myeon, 480
Kim Kyong Suk, 483
Kim Mi-hee, 477
Kim Wanwook, 482
Kim Young Su, 474
Kim, Patti, 474
"Kindred Spirits", 284
King and I, The, 59, 167-70, 172, 175-6, 187, 189, 210, 230, 403, 436
King Kong, 376, 377, 378, 379, 380, 384, 558
King, Carole, 147
King, David, 340
King, Francis, 236
King's Rhapsody, 141
King's Theatre (Melbourne), 324, 333
Kingston Mines Theatre, 194
Kingston, Claude, 324
Kipling, Rudyard, 271
Kiri no Mirano, 440
Kirk's Gallery, 340
Kishi, Nobusuke, 438
Kislan, Richard, 44, 73, 130-1, 512
Kiss Me Kate, 409
Kiss of the Spider Woman, 64, 238
Kissel, Howard, 225, 293
Kitchumnongpan, Peevara, 504, 510, 563
Kitt, Eartha, 384
Kleban, Ed, 198
Kleines Theater, 74
Klong, 505
"Klaikungwon" Musical on the Beach, 507
Knapp, Raymond, 122, 180, 190, 192
Kneebone, Tom, 119, 281
Knickerbocker Holiday, 132
Kobayashi, Ichizo, 437, 438, 439, 443
Koenig, Rhoda, 531
Kohl, Hannah, 426
Kojong, King, 470
Kolke, Shuichiro, 443
Kolle, Ray, 319, 563
Kollek, Teddy, 404
Kon, Stella, 190, 495, 563
Kong, Lily, 493
Koo Kam, 508
Kookaburra, 320, 322, 360, 361, 362, 363, 364
Kopit, Arthur, 21
Korda, Alexander, 109

Korie, Michael, 543
Korngold, Erich Wolfgang, 69
Kostelanetz, André, 129
Kracauer, Siegfred, 37, 38, 39, 40, 551
Kraft Durch Freude, 63
Kramer, David, 393, 558
Kramer, Gorni, 246
Krane, David, 182
Kretzmer, Herbert, 236, 244, 558
Kristina, 244
Krivoshei, David, 405
Kubelík, Jan, 130
Kuchwara, Michael, 293, 299
Kuhn, Jeffrey, 298
Kulabusaya, Rapeedech, 507
Kull daqqa fi qalbi, 400
Kullaha Yumayn, 397
Kunze, Dr. Michael, 63-4, 219, 237, 238, 443, 444, 556
Kuratomi, Shinichi, 440
Kwa Zulu, 386
Kwazulu
    Kwa Zulu. *See*
Kweyama, Mdu, 382
L'Amour Masqué, 79, 86
L'Attaché d'ambassade, 59
L'il Abner, 524
L'Impasse de la Fidélité, 225
La Basoche, 81
La Belle de Cadix, 93
La Belle Hélène, 39, 43, 68, 79
La Cage Aux Folles, 423, 507
La Calderona, 481
La canción de los barrios, 408
La cumparsita, Rascacielos, 408
La Femme du Boulanger, 87
La Fiaca, 412
La gatita blanca, 419
La Goualante du Pauvre Jean, 217
La Gran Via, 257
La Grande-Duchesse de Gérolstein, 39, 41, 79
La Grosse Valise, 229
La isla de cotorras, 430
La La Land, 233
La MaMa Experimental Theatre Club, 451
La muchachada del Centro, 407, 408
La Niña Rita, 432
La P'tite Lili, 217
La Pergola de las Flores, 414
La Périchole, 79
La Petite Functionnaire, 79
La Plume de ma Tante, 229
La Route Fleurie, 93
La Strada, 266
La Vie Parisienne, 39, 43
La Virgen Morena, 430
Labiche, Eugène Marin, 80
Lacámara, Carlos, 434

Lachiusa, Michael John, 513
Ladrão de Galinhas, 415
Lady in the Dark, 132
Lady Oscar, 443
Lafayette, Maximillien de, 97
Lagaan, 457
Lagrange, Frédéric, 397
Là-Haut, 88
Lahr, John, 155, 503
Lai, Francis, 76
Lakier, Gail, 385
Lamarque, Libertad, 420
LaMarsh, Judy, 278
Lamb, Andrew, 67, 74, 85, 93, 125
Lambert, Catherine, 307, 353
Lambert, Lisa, 286, 288, 291, 295, 297
Lamond, Stella, 328
Lamond, Toni, 329
Lamoureux, Robert, 217
Lan, David, 394
Landis, Barbara, 432
Landon, Margaret, 168
Landor Theatre, 119
Lang, Jennings, 512
lang, k. d., 276
Langdon, Harry, 328
Langrick, Maggie, 186
Lapin Agile, 99, 100, 101, 103
Lara, Agustín, 420
Larsen, Anika, 251
LaSalle College of the Arts, 497
Lascelles, Kendrew, 382
Last Empress, The, 436, 475
Latimer, Jeffrey, 298
Lauder, Sir Harry, 177
Laurence, Margaret, 281, 282
Laurents, Arthur, 203, 527
Lawrence, Gertrude, 168
Lay, Evelyn, 84
Layton, Joe, 445
Lazarus, Frank, 382
lbarra, Benny Sr, 423
Le Chef Grotesque, 287
Le Mariage aux lanternes, 57
Le Merliton, 99, 106
Le Passe Muraille
    Amour. *See*
Le Passe-Muraille, 234
Le Réveillon, 43, 57
Leander, Zarah, 63
Leander, Zarah, 74
"Learn Everything"
    "Open the Window". *See*
Leave it to Jane, 126
Leblebici Horhor Ağa, 261
Lecuona, Ernesto, 431, 558
Lee Haeje, 482
Lee Jangwoo, 6, 482, 563
Lee Jung Seop's 'Memory', 481
Lee Jung-Seop, 482

Lee Jung-Seop's Memory, 482
Lee Moon Roel, 475
Lee Myungil, 482
Lee Sunkyoung, 482
Lee, Baayork, 250
Lee, Chin Yang, 172
Lee, Dick, 449, 486, 492, 493, 494, 496, 497, 498, 499, 501, 502, 503, 557, 559, 560, 563
Lee, S.G., 280
Left Luggage, 242
Legaspi, Celeste, 468
Legrand, Michel, 31, 76, 218, 229-35, 555, 558, 562
Legrand, Raymond, 218
Lehár, Franz, 43, 59-60, 62, 64-5, 68
Lehrer, Tom, 148
Leibovitz, Liel, 108
Leila, 402
Leip, Hans, 114
Lemon, Jack, 226
Leningrad State Musical Comedy Theatre, 48
Lennon, John, 146, 263, 522
Lenya, Lotte, 73, 105, 152
Leon, Carlos, 421
Leon, Ruth, 236
Léon, Viktor, 43, 59
Leonowens, Anna, 169
LePage, Robert, 450
Lerner, Alan Jay, 13-4, 25, 41, 46, 61, 129-31, 149, 176-7, 202, 206, 208, 367, 514, 526, 531, 551-2, 568
Lerner, Sammy, 106
Les Aventures du Roi Pausole, 89
Les Belles et le gitan, 93
Les Brigandes, 79
Les Chasseurs d'images, 90
Les Demoiselles de Rochefort, 232, 235
Les Fridolinades, 282
Les Harengs Terribles, 218
Les Million, 90
Les Misérables, 10, 13, 25, 26, 37, 64, 76, 94, 156, 158, 164, 176, 234, 235, 241, 242, 251, 262, 279, 359, 360, 401, 412, 413, 443, 541
Les mômes de la clouche, 86
Les P'tites Michu, 81
Les Six, 99
Leschnikoff, Aspurach, 110
Lessing Theatre, 106
Letterman, David, 191
Levay, Sylvester, 63, 64, 237, 443, 556
Leveux, David, 180
Levinson, Mark L., 398
Li Ang, 459
Li Jinhui, 484
Li Tai-hsiang, 458, 459
Liang Wern Fook, 500
Lichtenberg, George, 227

Lift: The Slobodan Show, The, 255
Light in the Piazza, The, 312
Likes of Us, The, 267
Lilac Time, 331
Liliom, 168
Lillie, Beatrice, 130
Lim Chuang Yik, 501
Lim, Varian, 487
Lin Yu-lin, 485
Lincke, Paul, 67, 71, 74
Lincoln Center, 179, 226, 388, 391
Lincoln, Abraham, 129, 170
Lind, Jenny, 57
Linda, Solomon, 368
Linder, Cec, 322
Lindfors, Bernth, 379
Lingdai yu gaogenxie, 459
Lingenfelder, Charl-Johan, 6, 375, 382
Link, Peter, 18
Lion King, The, 79, 208, 238, 310, 392, 493
Lion of the East, 392
"Lion Sleeps Tonight, The", 369
Lion, Margo, 108, 109
Lipman, Daniel, 271
Lipovetsky, Anton, 312
Litchfield, Neil, 358
Little Johnny Jones, 145
Little Mercy's First Murder, 300
Little Night Music, A, 65, 450-1
"Little People", 236
Little Shop of Horrors, 238, 498, 524
Little Women, 362
Littlewood, Joan, 337, 529
Liu, Sissi, 484
Livermore, Reg, 340
Living Doll, 264
Llano Macedo, Luis de, 423
Llano Palmer, Luis de, 423
Lloyd Webber, Andrew, 138, 149, 151, 156, 166, 177, 178, 198, 205, 214, 238, 265, 266, 267, 268, 269, 308, 313, 362, 410, 413, 455, 457, 512, 517
Lloyd, Claudia, 395
Lock Up Your Daughters, 265
Loesser, Frank, 11, 25, 74, 107, 118, 131, 146, 176, 190, 193, 209, 211, 485, 513
Loewe, Edmund, 130
Loewe, Frederick, 12, 61, 130, 131, 176, 208, 514, 531
Löhner-Beda, Fritz, 59
Lola Montez, 335, 336, 558
London Pavilion, 83
London Road,, 273
London, Jack, 67
Longfellow, Henry Wadsworth, 314
Lonsdale, Freddie, 82
Look Back in Anger, 149

Lopez Ruiz, Oscar, 411
Lopez Tercero, Jose Antonio, 427
López Velarde, José Manuel, 425
Lopez, Daniel, 411
Lopez, Francis, 93, 217
López, Regino, 430
Lord of the Rings, The, 294, 310
Lorenzo's Oil, 340
Los amores con las crisis', 407
Los diamantes de la corona, 48
Lotherington, Dean, 351
Louÿ, Pierre, 89
Love Game, 508
"Love is Always Lovely in the End", 292
"Love is Blue", 222
Love Story, 269, 498
Love's Labours Lost, 528
Low, Ken, 490, 555
Lowe, Ruth, 277
Lozano, Jaime, 6, 417, 427
Lu'bat Râstûr wa Sheykh al-Balad wa al-Qawwâs, 395
Lubbock, Mark, 41, 128
Lucas, Craig, 312
Lucille Lortel Theatre, 164
Luhrmann, Baz, 90, 456
Lükûs Hayat, 262
Lully, Jean-Baptiste de, 39
Lulu, 90
Lumbera, Bienvenido, 467, 468
Lumière Brothers, 78
Luna de miel para tres, 408
Luna Park Arena, 412
Lunatic, 436, 477
Lund, Alan, 232, 283, 296
Lwanda, Man of Stone, 395
Lyen, Dr. Kenneth, 212, 491, 492, 494, 495, 496, 497, 498, 499, 500, 555, 558, 563
Lyric Stage, 184
Lyric Theatre, 222, 337
Lyric Theatre Hammersmith, 72
Lysistrata, 67
Lysistrata Jones, 507
M. Butterfly, 174
M. Theatre, 508
Mabaso, Corney, 382
Macbeth, 386
MacDonald, Jeanette, 162
Macdonoughy, Glen, 84
Macedo, Rita, 423
Machin, Antonio, 431
"Mack the Knife"
    "Ballad of Mack the Knife, The". *See*
Mack, Paul, 291
MacKellan, Greg, 6, 228
MacKenzie, David, 164

Mackintosh, Sir Cameron, 53, 76, 158, 166, 205, 235, 271, 483, 513
Maclaine, Shirley, 226
Mac-Nab, Maurice, 99
MacNeff, Stephen, 517
MacQueen-Pope, W. J., 140
Mad About the Boy", 47
Mad Dogs and Englishmen", 47
Madame Arthur, 241
Madame Butterfly, 489
Madame de Pompadour, 482
Madame et son filleul, 257
Madame Pompadour, 68
Madrid, Iker, 425
Mae Nak, 507, 508
Maen, Norman, 232
Magaña, Sergio, 421, 422
Maggie May, 266
Magic Flute, The, 23, 30, 34-6, 54, 55, 394-5, 547
Magic Paintbrush, The, 495
Magnificat, 436
Magnormos Productions, 350, 351
Magnormos Theatre, 189
Mahdiyya, Munira El-, 397
Mahidol University, 6, 506, 507
Mahler, Angel, 411, 413, 556, 558
Mahomed, Ismail, 393
Maid in the Mountains, 82
Maid of the Mountains, The, 330
Maipo Theatre, 411
"Mairzy Doats", 147
Makanplace, 486, 487
Make Me an Offer, 266
Makeba, Miriam, 371, 372, 389
Makeham, Paul, 352
Makhalipile, 368
Malefane, Pauline, 394
Malloy, Dave, 203
Maltby, Richard Jr., 166, 299, 508, 527, 537
Mama Mia!, 244, 313
Mame, 284
Mamma Mia!!, 238, 244, 308, 475, 539
Man of La Mancha, 78, 160, 198, 403, 422
Man Who Laughs, The, 481
Manana, the Jazz Prophet, 384
Mandela, Nelson, 367, 376, 389
Manet, Eduardo, 433
Manger, Itzik, 404
Mangkorn Slad Gled, 508
Manheim, Ralph, 112
Manitoba Theatre Centre, 311
Mankowitz, Wolf, 266, 370
Mann, Thomas, 300
Manning Clark's History of Australia – the Musical, 341
Mantovani, 337
Manufactured in Eretz-Israel, 403

Mar i cel, 246
Maraka, Lila, 257
Marche, Stephen, 275
Marconi, Saverio, 249
Marcos, Ferdinand, 465, 469
Margolis, Mac, 416
Marguerite, 230, 235
Maria de Buenos Aires, 409
María de la O, 432
Maria Severa, 300
Marie Antoinette, 238
Marigold, 332
Marischka, Hubert, 63
Marishka, Ernst, 69
Market Theatre of Johannsburg, 388
Marquis Theatre, 286, 293
Marshall, Rob, 207
Martell, Julie, 300, 301
Martí, José, 431
Martin Guerre, 498, 524
Martin, Bob, 286, 287, 288, 291, 294, 295, 296, 301, 556
Martin, Mary, 514
Martin, Steve, 102
Mary Bryant, 340
Mary Poppins, 271, 498
Mary Poppins Returns, 207-8
Masaaki, Hirao, 442
Masakela, Hugh, 371, 387
Masekela, Hugh, 368, 373, 388, 562
Masquerade, 241
Massary, Fritzi, 68
Massey Hall, 310
Masteroff, Joe, 188
Mastroianni, Marcello, 248
Masutti, Guillermo, 409
Matchmaker, Matchmaker, 207
Matchmaker, The, 57
Matilda, 120, 208, 272, 273, 513
Matshikiza, Esmé, 374-5
Matshikiza, Grace Ngqoyi, 369
Matshikiza, John, 370, 373
Matshikiza, Lindi, 381
Matshikiza, Samuel Bokwe, 369
Matshikiza, Todd, 368, 370, 558
Matsui, Rumi, 179
Maubon, Louis, 89
Maugham, Somerset, 108
Maurice Ravel, 18
Maurice, Ibrahim, 401, 402
Max Havelaar, 241
Max Reimer, 295
Max, Margarida, 414
Maxwell, Jackie, 300
May, Elaine, 116
Mayer, Louis B., 162
Mbube. *See* Lion Sleeps Tonight, The
MC Skolla, 531
McAnuff, Des, 313
McArthur, Colin, 177

McBroom, Amanda, 116
McBurney, Simon, 450
McCartney, Sir Paul, 146, 263
McClain, John, 224
McCollum, Kevin, 291
McCracken, Hugh, 153
McCutcheon, Martine, 205
McGuckian, Alastair, 250, 557
McGuickan, Garrett, 251
McHugh, Dominic, 171
McIntosh, Hugh, 324
McIntosh, Hugh D., 324
McKellar, Don, 286, 287, 288, 289, 291, 292, 295, 296, 556
McKelllar, John, 334
McLaughlin, Sarah, 118
McLuhan, Marshall, 13
McPherson, Jim, 348
Me and Juliet, 172
Meat Loaf, 238
Mecano, 245
Meehan, John Jr., 69
Meehan, Thomas, 297
Meged, Aharon, 404
Megileh, The, 404
Megilla of Itzak Manger, The. See Megilla, The
Meiga Arubamu, 439
Meilhac, Henri, 41, 57, 59
Meilhac, Henri, 39
Meilhac, Henri, 42
Meir, Golda, 404
Mekawy, Sayed, 402
Melba, Nellie, 330
Melbourne Repertory Theatre, 326
Melbourne Theatre Company, 339
Mellers, Wilfred, 34, 122
Melville, Alan, 332
Melville, Herman, 121
Memories of Matsuko, 453
Méndez, Memo, 424
Mendosa, Edmundo, 421
Menell, Clive, 371
Menell. Irene, 6, 303, 304, 305, 306, 371, 381, 556
Menopause – The Musical, 348
Mentiras, 425
Menuhin, Yehudi, 69, 368
Menzies, Robert, 338
Mercer, Johnny, 71
Mercure, 100
Mercury Musical Developments, 154, 513, 516, 518, 545
Mérimée, Prosper, 41
Mermaid Theatre, 265
Meropa
    Kwa Zulu. *See*
Merrick, David, 165, 223, 265
Merrily We Roll Along, 536
Merry Widow, 68

Merry Widow, The, 59, 62, , 130 *See*
"Message from a Nightingale", 290
Messager, André, 62, 79, 80, 81, 82, 85, 86, 560
Mestral, Marie-Claude, 227
Metropol Theater, 106
Metropolitan Opera, 42, 58, 129, 557
Metropolitan Theatre, 413
Mi querido capitán, 419
Mi Solar, 434
Michael, Kerry, 529, 531, 532, 533, 535, 563
Michell, Keith, 222-3, 322
Middleton, Jessie Edgar, 277
Midler, Bette, 357
Midsummer Nights' Dream, A, 68
Mikado, The, 46, 133
Milhaud, Darius, 100
Millar, James, 358, 557
Millar, Ronald, 337
Miller, Arthur, 62
Miller, Matthew, 108
Miller, Roy, 291
Miller, Scott, 155, 537
Million Dollar Quartet, 315
Milord, 217
Mimi, or A Poisoner's Comedy, 301
Minchin, Tim, 120, 272
Minelli, Liza, 24
Minervini, Rina, 387
Ming Wong, 490
Mini, Vuyusile, 390
Minim Bili, 383
Minim Export, 383
Minnie Moustache, 90
Minogue, Kylie, 319
Min-On Japan, 455
Minskoff Theatre, 238
Minsky's, 297
Miong, 465
Miori, Yumino, 441
Miracle, The, 68
Miralles, Esteve, 246
Miranda, Carmen, 92, 406, 416
Miranda, Lin-Manuel, 417, 530, 540
Mirande, Yves, 87
Mirisch, Walter, 226
Miroirs, 441, 561
Miroy, Jovi, 468
Mirvish Productions, 289, 290, 294, 308
Mishima, Yukio, 178
Misraki, Paul, 408
Miss Saigon, 78, 230, 279, 310, 436, 466, 468, 469, 475, 504, 510
Mistinguett, 83, 91
Mitchell, David, 343
Mitchell, Margaret, 444
Mitchell, Stephens, 444
Mitos Kamanalis, 418

Mitzi E. Newhouse Theatre, 388
Miyamoto, Amon, 159, 178, 179, 180, 295, 440, 441, 449, 563
Mkhumbane, 380, 559
Mo Faya, 395
Moberg, Vilhelm, 244
Moeketsi, Kippie, 374
Mofokeng, Jerry, 390
Mokdad, Linda, 398
Molière, 106, 395
Molina, Alfred, 181
Møller, Søren, 189, 518, 519, 534, 563
Molnár, Ferenc, 168
Mon Homme, 83, 90, 92
My Man. *See*
Mon Paris, 438
Moncrieff, Gladys, 330, 331
Mongkut, King, 168, 169, 172
Monk, Varney, 330, 331
Monnot, Marguerite, 31, 118, 217-8, 220, 224-7, 557-8
Monsieur Beaucaire, 82
Monsod, Ian, 465
Montalbán, Manuel Vázquez, 246
Montand and the French Lover, 481
Montaner, Rita, 431
Montes de Oca, J., 421
Montgomery, Lucy Maude, 164
Moody, Ron, 247, 264
Moon is East, The Sun is West, The, 452
Moore, Mavor, 27, 163, 267, 281, 282, 284, 296, 313, 555
Moore, Robin, 429
Moore, Tracey, 515
Moorish Maid, A, 327
Moosa, Matti, 396
Morales, Miguel Ángel, 422
Morán, José Luis, 245
Mordden, Ethan, 123, 299
More, Julian, 219, 220, 229, 266, 557, 558
Morehouse, Ward, 142
Morel, Steven, 289
Moretti, Bruno, 249
Morgan, Paul, 63
Moriones, Genera and Romualda, 419
Morley, Sheridan, 236
Morra, Guido, 249
Morris, Melissa, 298, 557
Morrison, Greg, 286, 288, 295, 556
Morriss, Elizabeth Rose, 527
Mortal Sins, 496
Mortifee, Ann, 7, 14, 28
Morugan Oyuki, 444
Mosman Town Hall, 330
Mossinzon, Yigal, 403
Motley theatre
Überbrettl. *See*
Motorcycle Diaries, The, 417
Motran, Khalil, 398

Motsieloa, Griffiths, 367
Mouezy-Eon, André, 89, 559
Mougy, Yehia El, 400
Moulin de la Chanson, 87
Moulin Rouge, 22, 78, 90, 91, 99, 438
Moulin Rouge (film), 456
Moulin, Jean-Pierre, 227
Mourad, Mounir, 399
Mouskouri, Nana, 259
Mozart (Kunze/Levay), 238
Mozart (musical play), 34, 35, 52, 55, 79, 86, 550
Mozart, Leopold, 53
Mozart, Leopold, 35, 36
Mozart, Wolfgang Amadeus, 23, 24, 35-6, 39, 41, 53, 69, 149, 269, 394-5, 547
Mr. Bean, 269
Mr. Cinders, 47
Mrs. Pretty and the Premier, 326
Msomi, Welcome, 386
Muangthai Ratchadalai Theatre, 504, 507
Mudugno, Domenico, 247
Munby, Jonathan, 382
Muraoka, Hanako, 285
Murdoch Mysteries, 186, 278, 280
Murphy, Colin, 251
Murphy, Frank, 339
Murphy, Gareth, 76
Murray Anderson's Almanac, 332
Musgrave Theatres, 325
Music Box Theatre, 234
Music Man, The, 190, 191, 192, 526
Musical Futures, 518, 564
Musical Theatre Educators Alliance, 545
Musical Theatre Limited, 212, 491, 495, 546, 555, 557
Musical Theatre Live, 518
Musical Theatre Matters, 514, 518
Musical Theatre Network, 518
Mussorgsky, Modeste, 48
Muthu, 455
Muthu, Dancing Maharaja, 455
My American Cousin, 186
My Beautiful Mother, 389
My Brilliant Career, 319
My Fair Lady, 14, 47, 61, 131, 158, 160, 176, 190, 240, 329, 403, 409, 423, 444, 514, 526
"My Man", 77, 83, 90, 92
"My Man's Gone Now", 525
"My Yiddishe Momma", 389
Myers, Peter, 247
"Nabasag ang Banga", 462
Nae maeumui punggeum, 477
Nahas, Edmond, 398
Nahas, Neguib, 398
Nakamura, Hideo, 451

Nakamura, Satoru, 441
Nallon, Steve, 176
Name of the Game, The, 426
Nanta, 475
Naqqash, Marun, 396
Narathippraphanphong, Prince, 508
Narkkong, Anant, 507
Nash, N. Richard, 165, 190, 192
Nasser, Gamal Abdel, 400
Nassour, Ellis, 238
Natasha, Pierre and the Great Comet of 1812, 203-4
Nathan, J. P., 500
National Alliance for Musical Theatre's Festival of New Musicals, 291
National Alliance of Musical Theatre Producers, 545
National Arts Centre, 295
National Arts Festival (Grahamstown), 393
National Institute of Dramatic Art, 329, 340
National Theatre, 178, 179, 271, 273
National Theatre (Buenos Aires), 408
National University of Singapore, 493
National Youth Music Theatre, 516
Natzler, Leopold, 60
Natzler, Sigmund, 60
Necessary Angel Theatre Company, 290
Ned Kelly, 340
Nederlander Worldwide Entertainment, 485
Neighbours, 319, 490
Neil Simon Theatre, 241, 313
Nelson, Rudloph, 105, 108
Nestroy, Johann, 56
Never on Sunday, 258
Never Say Goodbye, 443
Neville, John, 222
New London Theatre, 394
New Musicals Australia, 319, 350, 364, 365, 366, 546
New Theatre, 284
New Theatre (Melbourne), 338
New Tivoli Theatre, 331
New World Stage, 297
New York Musical Theatre Festival, 351, 360
New York Theatre Workshop, 252
Newman, Bill, 329
Newman, John, 329
Newman, Tommy, 418
Newton, Sir Isaac, 30
Next Stage Performing Arts Academy, 491
Next to Normal, 156
Ng Yi-Sheng, 486

Ngema, Mbongeni, 384, 386, 387, 388, 390, 391, 392, 562
Ni Fu, ni fa, 421, 422
Nice Work if You Can Get It, 507
Nicholaw, Casey, 291, 293, 297
Nicholls, Stewart, 139
Nichols, Mike, 116
Nicholson, Viv, 269
Nicholson, William, 382
Nicol, Eric, 281
Nieh Kuang-yen, 458
Nielsen, Carl, 189
Night and Day, 442
Night of the Hunter, 181
Night They Raided Minsky's, The, 297
Nightcap, 335
Nimrod Theatre, 339
Nine, 182, 413, 524
Nine Queens, 417
Nishimura, Kohji, 440
Nissay Masterpiece Theatre, 448
Nixon in China, 517
Nixon, Marni, 230
Nkosi Sikelel' iAfrika, 378
Nkosi, Lewis, 368, 376
No No, Nanette, 77, 79, 85, 328
No Ranch Fundo, 415
Noble, Peter, 140
Noh, 179, 454
Noli Me Tangere, 468
Nord-Ost, 254
Norman, Monty, 219, 229, 266, 557, 558
Norris, Rufus, 273
North by Northwest (Radio show), 544
Northwestern. University, 515
Norton, Frederic, 323
Not the Nine o'Clock News, 269
Nôtre Dame de Paris, 93
Nottingham Rep, 372
Novello Theatre, 294, 360
Novello, Ivor, 46, 47, 133, 138, 140-1, 263, 272, 552, 561
Novo, Salvador, 421
Nunn, Sir Trevor, 109, 235
Nyandeni, Thembi, 393, 394
O barbeiro de Niterói, 415
Ô mon bel inconnu, 86
O Vaftistikos, 257
O' Callaghan, Patricia, 251
O'Connor, Caroline, 329, 359
O'May, John, 321, 344
O'Neill, Eugene, 464
Oates, Jennifer, 177
Oberlin, Karen, 116
Octagon Theatre (Perth), 352
OCU Stripped, 516
Odós Oneirwn, 259
Oeda, Shinji, 442

Offenbach, Jacques, 22, 38-44, 57, 62, 68, 77-80, 93, 96, 99, 217, 233-4
Official Story, The, 417
Oh Boy!, 126
Oh Lady Lady!, 126
"Oh Lord, I'm On My Way", 525
Oh, Sang Joon, 476
Oh, What a Lovely War!, 529
Oklahoma!, 20, 41, 47, 55, 70, 141, 173, 187, 441, 464, 467, 516-7, 538
Okuni, Izumo-no-, 436
Old Vic, 372
Oles, Stephen, 209
Olivari, Carlos, 408
Oliver!, 31, 158, 209, 235, 264, 265, 266, 267, 268, 537
Oller, Joseph, 91
Omorphi Poli, 260
On a Clear Day You Can See Forever, 507
On connaît la chanson, 88
On the Street Where You Live, 176, 202, 526
Once, 252
Once in a Blue Moon (CD), 319
Ondeano, Felipe Fondesviela y, 428
One Fine Day, 460, 481
One Hundred Ten in the Shade, 190, 192
One Kiss, 87
Ong Teng Cheong, 492
Only Girl, The, 107
Onnasis, Aristotle, 386
Onshoudat el fou'âd, 398
Oon, Clarissa, 490
Open a New Window, 284, 552
Open the Window, 283, 284
Opera Ball, 59
Opéra Comique (London), 45
Opera do Malandro, 416
Opéra-Comique, 38, 41, 81, 87, 227
Oresteia, 68
Orfeo 9, 249
Orgambide, Pedro, 411
Orlando Rourke, 340
Orpheus in the Haymarket, 40
Orpheus in the Underworld, 22, 38, 41, 68, 78
Orr, William, 334
Osaka Samurai, 440
Osbourne, Charles, 132
Osbourne, John, 149, 151
Our Lady of the Camelias, 235
Our Language of Love, 220
Out of the Blue, 453, 454, 559
Ouzounian, Richard, 252, 290, 291, 294, 300, 301, 313, 317, 357
Over There, 142, 143, 145
Oyama, David, 178
Oz Showbiz Cares, 362
Özdemiroğlu, Attila, 262

Özgür, Sunay, 262
OzMade Musicals, 320, 350, 351, 546
Pabst, G.W., 73
Pacific 231, 89
Pacific Overtures, 178, 295, 436, 440, 449
Paget, Clive, 360
Pagnol, Marcel, 87
Paige, Elaine, 294
Pajama Game, The, 329
Pal Joey, 226
Pal, Graciela, 411
Palace Theatre, 333, 356
Palace Theatre (New York), 358
Palace Theatre (Sydney), 333
Palais des Sports, 235, 236
Palmer, John, 341, 343
Palmer, Robert, 387
Pam Ann, 120
Pan y toros, 48
Panasonic Theatre, 303, 310
Panella, Pasquale, 250
Pansera, Roberto, 411, 557
Panter, Howard, 28
Papadimitriou, Lydia, 5, 258
Paparelli, P.J., 196
Papp, Joseph, 112
Parade, 100
Parade Theatre, 340
Pardon Miss Westcott, 336
Parès, Phillipe, 90
Paris in the Rain, 95
Paris Olympia, 91
Paris Opéra, 41, 82, 85
Park Chung-hee, 480
Park Young Gu, 474
Park, Kolleen, 475
Park, Sam, 252
Parker, Dorothy, 126
Parker, Ross, 229
Parlor Match, A, 92
Parry, Nina, 6, 224
Pas sur la Bouche, 80, 87, 88, 561
Pasadena Playhouse, 372
Pascual, Armando, 421
Pasquel, Sylvia, 423
Passionnément, 80, 85
Patachou, 225
Patel, Dr. Aniruddh, 17
Paton, Alan, 380, 559
Patrick Street Productions, 312
Patterson, Vincent, 188
Paulsen, David, 405
Paulsen, Harald, 73, 108
Pavillion Theatre, 222
Paviot, Paul, 227
Pavlovsky, 'La', 410
Paz, Gaiza Guillermo, 409
Pedersen, Thomas Bay, 519
Pelagie, 200

Pélagie, 301
Pelay, Ivo, 407, 408
Pelléas et Mélisande, 82
Pen, *Polly*, 194
Penn State University, 515, 520
Peony Pavilion, The, 485
Perciavalle, Carlos, 410
Perfect Pitch, 518
Perfect Timing, 527
Perfect, Eddie, 354
Perkins, Rachel, 353
Perón, Eva, 177, 411
Perón, Juan, 178
Perryman, Jill, 321, 329, 346
Persephone Theatre, 311
Pet Sounds, 522
Peters, Bernadette, 166
Petersen, Taliep, 393, 558
Peterson, Eric, 285
Peterson, William, 493
Petito, Tony, 497, 498, 560
Phantom, 21
Phantom of the Opera, 10, 29, 158, 209, 212, 238, 267, 280, 309, 319, 422, 475, 504
Phillip Street Revues, 334, 340, 360
Phillip Street Theatre, 334
Phillips, Nicky, 303
Phi-Phi, 78, 82, 83, 84, 94, 220, 229, 559
Phoenix Players, 386
Phoenix Theatre, 231
Piaf, Edith, 77, 78, 86, 91, 102, 118, 217, 218, 260, 413, 548
Piattella, Tania, 249
Piazzolla, Astor, 217, 409
Pibulsonggram, Nitya, 168
Picadilly Theatre, 270
Picasso at the Lapin Agile, 102
Picasso, Pablo, 101, 102
Pickwick, 266, 267
Picnic at Hanging Rock, 319
Pimootewin (The Journey),, 316
Pinal, Silvia, 225, 423
Pinne, Peter, 5, 319, 339, 340, 345, 412, 413, 414, 424, 555
Pinochio, 250
Pinsent, Gordon, 185
Pinti, Enrique, 410
Pintó, David, 246
Pipe Dream, 172
Pippin, 197, 361, 423, 467
Pitre, Louise, 244, 308
Place To Stand, A, 165
Plain and Fancy, 408
Plamondon, Luc, 93
Planché, John Robinson, 40
Players Theatre, 167
Playhouse Theatre (Brisbane), 348
Playhouse Theatre (Canberra), 336
Plummer, Christopher, 280, 322

Plymouth Theater, 223
Plymouth Theatre, 332
Pokorny, Alois, 57
Pokorny, Franz, 57
Polanco, Fabian, 248, 419, 421, 422, 423, 424, 426
Polanski, Roman, 238
Polly, 22
Pondal, Sixto Rios, 408
Pooh, 250
Popp, André, 222
Popular, 173, 208, 411, 551, 553, 557
Porgy and Bess, 152, 160, 474
Porgy And Bess, 525
Porter, Cole, 11, 12, 46, 84, 94, 125, 146, 147, 150, 155, 168, 226, 239, 512
Portman, Jamie, 185
Pote tin Kyriaki. See Never on Sunday
Poulenc, Francis, 94, 100, 234
Poveri Ma Belli, 249
PraLor, 507
Prasartthong, Pradit, 508
Pratt Prize, 348, 351
Pratt, Jeanne, 348
Pratt, Richard, 348
Preston, Mary, 335
Previn, André, 17, 156, 226
Priestly, J.B., 149, 151
Primrose, 133
Prince Ananius, 129
Prince, Harold, 53, 178, 179, 208, 317, 513
Princes Theatre
    Shaftesbury Theatre. *See*
Princes Theatre (Manchester), 88
Princess of Wales Theatre, 251, 357
Princess Theatre, 126, 309, 330, 331, 341
Princess Theatre (Melbourne), 321, 327
Printemps, Yvonne, 77, 83, 86
Priscilla – Queen of the Dessert, 31, 308, 355, 357, 546
Prisoner Cell Block H, 339
Prissana, 508
Producers, The, 156, 255, 294
Prokofiev, Sergei, 17
Promises, Promises, 422, 507
Psy, 480
Puteri Gunung Ledang, 503
Pygmalion, 61, 109
Q, 544
Qabbani, Abu Khalil, 396
Quast, Philip, 329
Quatre Jours à Paris, 93
Qué Plantón!, 424
Que vachache, 408
Queens Theatre, 394
Quek, Jerome, 487
Querol, Beatriz, 421

Quinson, Gustave, 80, 87
Rachmaninoff, Sergei, 18
Radic, Leonard, 339
Raffenaud, François, 93
Ragtime, 515
Rahman, A. R., 457
Raimi, Sam, 298
Raimund Theater, 64
Raimund, Ferdinand, 64
Rainmaker, The, 165, 192
Rama-Hari, 467
Ramlie, Adlin Aman, 503
Ramos, Adrian, 423
Ramos, Santiago, 406
Randall, Carl, 333
Ranga, Dana, 50
Rangel, Martha, 422
Rapsodia Negra, 433
Rascel, Renato, 247, 248
Ratcliffe, Michael, 236
Rattigan, Terrence, 149, 263
Ravel, Maurice, 76, 94, 409, 431
Rayando el sol, 420
Really Useful Group, 362
Rebecca, 64, 238
Rebellato, Dan, 29
Red Dwarf, 269
Red, White and Boogie, 339
Reda, Aly, 400
Reda, Mahmoud, 400
Reddy, Helen, 329
Reds, 94
Reed, Rex, 383
Reedy River, 338
Reel to Real, the Movies Musical, 484
Reeves, David, 341
Reeves, Peter, 241
Regent Theatre (Melbourne), 321, 322
Reid, Bill, 317
Reid, Caroline, 120
Reinblatt, George, 297, 557
Reindhardt, Max, 75
Reinhardt, Django, 102
Reinhardt, Gottfried, 68, 69
Reinhardt, Max, 31, 53-4, 61, 68-70, 74, 104, 106, 108
Relâche, 100
Remarque, Erich Maria, 438
Renaldo in Campo, 247
Renard, Colette, 218, 222, 227
Renoir, Jean, 90, 91, 95, 99, 561
Rent, 26, 155, 156, 251, 279, 306, 309
Rentas congeladas, 422
Renzullo, Michele, 249
Resnais, Alain, 88, 561
Reviewing the Situation, 31, 537
Revill, Clive, 266
Revisor, 404
Revue '60, 334
Revue Nègre, La, 102

Rey, Cemel Reşit, 262
Rey, Ekrem Reşit, 262
Reyes, Jose Javier, 468
Reyes, Kresida, 506
Reyes, Napisi, 506, 563
Reynolds, Herbert, 124
Reynoso Compuesto, Antonio, 407
Rez Sisters, The, 316
Rhapsody in Blue, 71, 146, 431
Rhapsody in Blue', 146
Rhapsody on Songs of the People of the Soviet Union, 50
Riancho, Aurelio Gutiérrez, 430
Ricci, Nino, 318
Rice, Emma, 231
Rice, Sir Tim, 94, 151, 177, 219, 244, 267, 410, 411, 512, 518, 539
Rich, Frank, 388
Richard, Cliff, 264
Rickards, Harry, 324
Rihani, Naguib el-, 397, 399
Rimsky-Korsakov, Nikolai, 48
Ring of Fire, 313
Riordan, Arthur, 252
Rise and Fall of the City of Mahagonny, The, 70, 72
Rissi, Dino, 249
Ritchard, Cyril, 322, 332
Riveira, Chita, 157
Riverdance, 177, 250, 251
Riviera Girl, The
    Die Csárdásfürstin, 61
Rivoli, 288
Rizal, Dr. Jose, 468
Road to Qatar, The, 184
Robbins, Jerome, 414, 433
Robert and Elizabeth, 337
Roberts, Nick, 301
Robertson, Jennifer, 439
Robertson, Malcolm, 327
Robertson, Robbie, 276
Robertson, Tim, 341
Robitschek, Kurt, 108
Robledo, Alfredo, 421
Robles Godoy, Armando, 417
Robles, Daniel Alomía, 48
Robles, Daniel Alomía, 417
Rock Around the Clock, 146, 154
Rock Island, 191
Rockaybye Hamlet, 544
Rockin' with the Cave Men, 264
Rocking Rama, 507
Rocky Horror Show, The, 298
Rodgers, John, 354
Rodgers, Richard, 32, 39, 132-3, 147, 151, 168, 171, 187, 193, 203, 205, 208, 268, 341, 485, 519, 531, 553
Rodis, Girlie, 6, 468
Rodriguez, Agustin, 431
Roger, Elena, 413

Rogers, Ginger, 233, 284, 432
Rohter, Larry, 416
Roig, Gonzalo, 430
Roldán, Fred, 424
Rolls, Ernest C., 328
Romberg, Sigmund, 68, 131, 132
Rome, Florence, 445, 446, 447
Rome, Harold, 229, 444
Romeo and Juliet, 515
Romeril, John, 341
Ronchetti, Pierluigi, 250
Rongjun, Yu, 481
Ronnie Scott's, 115
Roodt, Daryl James, 389
Rooney, David, 299
Roosevelt, Franlin Delano, 170
Rosa, Noel, 415
Rosalinda, 69
Rose Marie, 88, 162, 163, 332
Rose Marie,, 162
Rose of Versailles, 190, 436, 442, 443, 561
Rosé, Bert, 408
Rose, Billy, 147
Rose-Marie, 77, 79, 130, 176, 331
Rosenbaum, Jonathan, 232
Rosenbaum, Thane, 181
Rosenberg, Deena, 527
Rosenkavalier, 110
Rosenthal, Jack, 166
Rosenwax, Nathalie, 330
Ross, Adrian, 60
Ross, Adrian, 124
Ross, Herbert, 247
Ross, Jerry, 513
Ross, Michael, 251
Ross, Peter, 363
Rossetto, Cecilia, 410
Rossini, Gioachino, 39, 415
Rostand, Edmond, 241
Rosti, Estafan, 398
Rota, Nino, 249
Rothenberg, David, 15
Roud, Richard, 227
Roundabout Theatre, 179
Roux, Michel, 219
Rowan and Martin's Laugh-in, 282, 335
Rowdyman, The, 185
Roy Thomson Hall, 310
Royal Alexandra Theatre, 162
Royal Canadian Air Farce, 120
Royal Opera House, 82
Royal Shakespeare Company, 236, 272, 273
Royal Winnipeg Ballet, 311
Rubens, Paul, 124
Rubinoff, Michael, 164, 302
Ruddell, Bruce, 317
Rudin, Scott, 540
Rudisill, Kristin, 456

Rufelle, Frances, 156
Rufen Sie Herrn Plim!
    Send for Mr. Plim. *See*
Rugantino, 247
Ruiz, Federico, 422
Runyon, Damon, 193, 220
Rush, Geoffrey, 295, 353
Russell, Jenna, 269
Rutherford, Peter, 358, 557
Rybnikov, Alexey, 254
Ryshpan, Arden, 543
Saedah Samat-Alkaff, 487
Sahl, Mort, 116
Saint-Saëns, Camille, 81
Sakellaridis, Theophrastos, 257
Sala, Xavier Bru de, 246
Salad Days, 287
Salinas, Carmen, 426
Salis, Rodolphe, 98
Salis, Rodolphe, 102
Saljjagi Obseoye, 474
Salonga, Lea, 436, 466, 469
Salten, Felix, 59
Salten, Felix, 114
Saludo, Ricardo, 466
Saludos Amigos, 415
Salys, Rimgaila, 49
Sams, Jeremy, 7, 95, 234, 244, 439, 441, 555
Samuels, Edmond, 332
Sancho Panza, 245
Sand, Paul, 453, 559
Sanders, Frank, 241
Sankoff, Irene, 303
Sanmao, 458
Santamaria, Iñigo, 6, 245
Santos, Freddie, 465
Sanu, Yaqub Rafail, 395
Sarafina!, 31, 379, 387, 388, 389, 390, 391, 392, 393, 562
Sarvil, René, 86
Satie, Eric, 94, 100
Saturday Girl, 336
Saturday Night Fever, 413
Savage, Lilly, 339
Savary, Jérôme, 227
Savoy Theatre, 332
Saward, Tim, 530, 532
Scaramouche, 246
Scaretto, 444
Scenario, 507
Schall und Rauch
    Sound and Smoke. *See*
Scheherazade, 397
Schepisi, Fred, 297
Schiffer, Marcellus, 108, 112
Schikaneder, Emanuel, 1, 35-6, 52, 53-6, 59, 547, 550
Schipa, Tito, 249

Schlesinger, Sarah, 7, 16, 210, 212, 213, 214, 527
Schmidt, Annie M. G., 116, 239, 242
Schmidt, Harvey, 152, 190, 192
Schönberg, Claude-Michel, 78, 230, 235, 236, 524, 554, 558
School for Scandal, 109
Schrödinger, Erwin, 252
Schultze, Norbert, 114
Schur, Danny, 311, 559
Schütz, Adolph, 63
Schwartz, Arthur, 131
Schwartz, Roberta Freund, 191
Schwartz, Stephen, 7, 56, 87, 197, 199, 219, 360, 467, 536, 542
Schweitzer, Marlis, 43
Scott, Allan, 357
Scott, Sir Walter, 177
Scotto, Vincent, 43, 83, 86-7, 93, 96, 118, 217, 559
Scottsboro Boys, The, 207
Scott-Stokes, Henry, 452
Script Lab, 155, 524, 527
Scrooge, 266
SCTV, 119
Se dice de mi, 407
Seal, Elizabeth, 6, 220, 221, 222
Second City, 119, 289, 296
Secrest, Meryle, 128
Seeger, Pete, 368
Selladoor Worldwide, 504
Seltzer, Dov, 5, 403, 404, 405
Selznick, David O., 444
Senczuk, John, 347
Send for Mr. Plim, 109, 112
Şendil, Sadık, 262
Sentimental Bloke, The, 32, 336, 337
Senza Luce, 307
Seo Sookjean, 482
Serban, Andrei, 231
Sergeant Pepper's Lonely Hearts Club Band, 522
Serra, Luis Maria, 411
Serrano, José, 48
Seung-hye, Kim, 472
Seven Little Australians, 341
Seventeen Seventy-six, 121, 184
Seventy-six Trombones', 192
Sevilla, Ninón, 420
Seward, Brian, 495, 558
Seymour Centre (Sydney), 322, , 342 358
Shaffer, Paul, 191
Shaftesbury Theatre (original), 88, 394
Shaiman, Marc, 207
Shakespeare, 112, 236, 272, 340, 455, 464, 528, 530
Shall We Dance?, 59
Shane Warne – The Musical, 354
Shanghai Blues, 500

Shanghai Conservatory of Music, 485
Shanghai Dramatic Arts Centre, 485
Sharman, Jim, 349
Shaw Festival, 300
Shaw, George Bernard, 61, 109, 250
Shaw, Loretta Leonard, 285
Shea, Tom, 230, 524
Sheldon, Tony, 328, 334, 336, 339, 346, 354, 355, 356, 358, 359, 563
Shemer, Naomi, 405
Shenton, Mark, 273, 362
Shepard, Richard, 404
Sheridan College, 302, 312, 518, 546
Sheridan Square Playhouse, 452
Sheridan, Richard Brinsley, 109, 395
Sherman, Hiram, 284
Sherman, Richard M., 271
Sherman, Robert B., 271
Shiba, Ryōtarō, 440
Shibata, Yukihoro, 440
Shiki Theatre Company, 285, 448
Shimoda, Itsuro, 451
Shinchi, Kuratomi, 442
Shippey, Dr. Theo, 387
Shire, David, 508
Shiro, 452
Short, Martin, 525
Show Boat, 20, 26, 128, 133, 332, 537
Show Off, 290
Showa Trilogy, 448
Shubert Organization, 84
Shulman, Milton, 247
Shuttleworth, Ian, 270
Si Eva se hubiese vestido, 408
Si Nos Dejan, 425
Sibande, Gert, 392
Sibi-Okumu, John, 395
Siburapha, 508
Sickinger, Robert, 194
Sideshow Alley, 348, 349, 362, 363, 559
Sidus FNH, 477
Signature Theatre, 165
Sikalo, 384
Sikov, Ed, 227
Silberg, Yoel, 403, 404
Silent Soprano, The, 466
Silk Stockings, 240
Silver Lake, The, 71
Simon, Jasmin Samat, 487
Simon, John, 405
Simon, Lucy, 25
Simon, Paul, 48, 149
Simons, Marlise, 241
Simons, Moisés, 83, 89, 431
Simplicissimus, 114
Simplicius, 59
Simpson, Professor Michael, 392
Sing Seng Kwang, 490
Sing to the Dawn, 498
Singapore Festival of the Arts, 491

Singapore Repertory Theatre, 493, 496, 498
Singh, Anant, 389
Singin' in the Rain, 230, 233, 464
Sirett, Paul, 528
Sitwell, Edith, 531
Skalenakis, George, 260
Sklar, Matthew, 297
Skywalk, 477
Slevogt, Esther, 70
Slings and Arrows, 296
Smash, 207, 543
Smith, Cecil Michener, 9
Smith, Harry B., 92
Smith, Janet, 312
Smith, Marlene, 279
Smith, Ron, 162
Smits, Sebastiaan, 243
Sneddon, Professor Elizabeth, 386
Snip en Snap, 115
Snow, Hank, 277, 553
Society of Cavaliers, 56
"Soldiers of the Lord", 345
Sollar, Fabien, 83, 559
Some Like It Hot, 153
"Someone is Waiting", 94
"Something in the Air", 527
Somewhere in the World, 298
Sommi, Leone de', 403
Son p'tit frère, 79, 87
Sondheim, Stephen, 18, 24, 43, 46, 65, 80, 88, 94, 149, 152, 155-7, 178, 191, 198-200, 203, 213-4, 219, 361-2, 450, 466, 485, 515, 524, 527, 530, 533, 536, 540
Song and Dance, 166
Song of the Dark, 481
Song of Yoon-A, 481
Song, Eric, 483
Songs for a New World, 360
Songs of a Sentimental Bloke, 337
Songs of the Megileh, 404
Sonneveld, Wim, 115, 239
Sons of France, 223
Sontonga, Enoch, 378
Sony Centre, 310
Sorcerer, The, 45
Soria, Ezequiel, 407
Sothart, Herbert, 162
Soto, Roberto, 419
Sound and Smoke, 68, 106, 107
Sound of Music, The, 193, 194, 295, 308, 341, 485
Sousa, John Phillip, 191, 192
South American Way, 416
South Pacific, 171, 173, 175, 187, 189, 436, 464, 467, 531, 568
Southern Cross, 448
Soy al rubio Pichinango, 407
Spamalot, 291

Sparks, John, 7, 21, 211-2, 524, 529, 534, 536
Spend, Spend, Spend, 270, 559
Spicer, David, 363
Spielberg, Steven, 186, 241, 271
Spitting Image, 270
Spoli Mills, 109
Spoliansky, Mischa, 31, 67-8, 71, 75, 96, 107, 109-13, 188, 559
Sportelli, Paul, 300, 560
Spring Awakening, 156
  original play, 104
Spring Thaw, 32, 119, 282, 286, 296, 334
St. Lawrence Centre, 310, 316
Stage Entertainment, 243
Stamp, Terrence, 356
Stand!, 312
Stange, Stan, 61
Stanley, Arthur, 62
Stanley, Edward, 377
Stanley, Ray, 342
Stannard, Peter, 335, 558
Star is Born, A, 431
Starr, Sir Ringo, 263
Stars, 497
State Theatre of South Australia, 340
Stavisky, 88
Stavrakopoulou, Anna, 256
Steam, 519
Steam-Family, 477
Steele, Tommy, 264
Stein, Joseph, 87, 159, 409
Stein, Leo, 43, 59, 61
Steiner, Maximilian, 57
Steinman, Jim, 64, 238
Stevens, Cat, 379
Stevens, Ray, 153
Stewart, Ian, 206
Stewart, Kris, 351, 365
Stewart, Sandy, 120
Steyn, Mark, 512, 531
Stickland, Dr. Leonie, 438, 440, 554
Stiles, George, 271, 272
Stoker, Bram, 411
Stoll Moss Theatres, 352
Stolz, Robert, 60, 68
Stone, Paddy, 116, 239, 441
Stone, Peter, 7, 10-13, 205, 549, 568
Stone, Peter, 568
Stone, Peter, 568
Stoneham, Reginald, 323
Stoppard, Sir Tom, 252
Story of My Life, The, 298, 299, 527, 544
Strampfer, Friedrich, 57
Stratford Festival, 251, 313
Straus, Oscar, 60-1, 68, 103-4, 114, 130
Strauss, Adele, 69
Strauss, Johann, 69
Strauss, Johann Jr., 43-4, 58-9, 61-2, 64, 67, 69, 141, 557, 561

Strauss, Richard, 67, 68, 103, 110
Stravinsky, Igor, 409
Strike!, 311, 559
Strindberg, August, 115
Strindberg, Frida, 115
Strouse, Charles, 11, 12, 146, 147, 217, 297, 524
Struble, John Warthen, 128
Stuart, Connie, 239
Stuart, Conny, 239
Styne, Jule, 166, 527
"Sugar, Sugar", 152, 154, 157
Sukee, Punnasak, 507
Sullivan Sir Arthur Seymour, 11, 23, , 43-6, 60, 67, 133, 141, 143, 252, 263, 541
Summer of '42, 233
Summer Rain, 340
Sunghuck, Bae, 6, 480, 483, 563
Sunrise, Sunset, 207
Sunset Boulevard, 238
Sunshine Club, The, 354
Suppé, 64
Suppé, Franz von, 57, 64
Surabaya Johnny, 74
Survival of St. Joan, The, 467
Suskin, Steven, 244
Suzman, Helen, 377
Sweeney Todd, 359, 450, 467
Sweet And Low, 332
Sweet Charity, 329
Sweeter And Lower, 332
Sweetest And Lowest, 332
Swillinger, Evi, 411
Syal, Meera, 457
Sydney Theatre Company, 340
Sydow, Max von, 244
Synge, J. M., 193
Ta Bouche, 80, 87
Ta Pediá tou Pireá, 258
Taber, Jane, 314
Tabor ukhodit v nebo, 255
Taillefere, Germaine, 100
Tait, E. J., 328
Tait, Frank, 328
Tait, John, 328
Tait, Nevin, 328
Taitte, Lawson, 184
Takarazuka Grand Theatre, 437
Takarazuka Revue, 189, 239, 437, 438, 439, 440, 441, 442, 443, 444, 448, 553, 554
Takio, Terada, 442
Tales of Hoffman, 42, 78
Tales of Hoffmann, 68
Talesnik, Ricardo, 412
Talking Stick, The, 316
Tallis, Sir George, 328
Tan, Selena, 490

Tango Argentino, 406
Tango por Dos, 413
Tangolandia, 408
Tanner, James T., 124
Taño, Tony, 434
Tapu, 325, 326
Tarkington, Booth, 82
Tarnow, Toby, 283
Tarragon Theatre, 300, 301
Tatárjárás, 61
Taubman, Howard, 224
Tautou, Audrey, 88
Tawil, Kamal El, 400
Taylor, Jeremy, 383
Taylor, Samuel A., 165
Taylor, Tiki, 329
Tchoukhajian, Tigran, 261
Teatro Argentino, 410
Teatro Astral, 408
Teatro de Ensayo, 414
Teatro de la Victoria, 407
Teatro Liceo, 413
Teatro Mazzi, 417
Teatro Municipal Sarmiento, 411
Teatro Olimpico, 407
Teatro Porteña, 407
Teatro Presidente Alvear, 408
Teatro Recreio, 414
Teatro Smart, 225
Tell Me on a Sunday, 166, 362
Teng Ky-gan, 492, 496, 501, 502, 503
Tennant, Neil, 23
Tenterfield Saddler, 346
Tetsuo, Miura, 448
Tevye and his Daughters, 481
Tezuka, Osamu, 442
Thalheim, Sabina, 173
Thammasat University, 508
"That Haircut Doesn't Suit You, Mr. Green", 287
"That's a Crime", 220
Thawiphop: The Musical, 507
"The Boys in the Back Room", 107
The Chocolate Soldier
  Der tapfere Soldat. *See*
The Merry Widow, 43
The Point (Dublin venue), 251
The Production Company, 348
"The Ragtime Pipes of Pan", 84
"The Song of the Young Sentry"
  Lili Marlene. *See*
"The Way We Were", 442
"The Words", 283, 284
Theater am Gärtnerplatz, 109
Theater am Schiffbauerdamm, 72
Theater an der Wien, 52, 55, 57, 58, 61, 63, 64, 114, 237
Theater and der Wien, 58
Theater auf der Wieden, 55
Theater der Stadt, 225

Theater zum lieben Augustin, 114
Théâtre Comte
  Theatre Bouffes-Parisiens. *See*
  Théâtre des Bouffes-Parisiens.
  See
Théâtre Daunou, 80, 87, 90
Théâtre de l'Athénée, 219
Théâtre de la Gaîté-Lyrique, 90
Théâtre de la Michodière, 80
Théâtre des Ambassadeurs, 225
Théâtre des Bouffes-Parisiens, 22, 38, 78, 80, 81, 82, 83, 88, 89, 234
Théâtre des Capicines, 79, 90
Théâtre des Nouveautés, 87
Théâtre des Variétés, 79
Théâtre du Châtelet, 90
Théâtre Edouard VII, 79
Théâtre Gramont, 217
Théâtre Marigny, 79
Théâtre Mogador, 79, 87, 162
Théâtre Montparnesse, 231
Théatre Nouveautés, 80
Theatre Passe Muraille, 289
Theatre Royal (Sydney), 225, 332, 361
Theatre Royal Drury Lane, 88, 162
Theatre Royal Stratford East, 154, 265, 352, 528, 531, 532, 535
Theatre Workshop, 337, 529
Theatreworks, 164, 487
Theodorakis, Mikis, 259
Theodorakis, Yannis, 260
Theory of Relativity, The, 307
"There is Only One Paris for That", 224
"There'll Always Be an England", 377
"There's a Bluebird on Your Windowsill", 277
Thespis, 45
"They Didn't Believe Me", 124
"They're in Love", 332
They're Playing Our Song, 422, 467
Thiessen, Vern, 312
"This Can't Be Love", 531
This Hour Has Seven Days, 119
Thlotothlamaje, Cocky, 386
Thomas Crown Affair, The, 233
Thommayanti, 507
Thompson, Fred, 84
Thompson, Peter, 347
Thomson, Lloyd, 336, 559
Thorburn, Sandy, 286
Thoroughly Modern Millie, 355
Thousand Islands Playhouse, 286
"Three Little Fishies (Boop Boop Diddum)", 147
Three Musketeers, 243
Threepenny Opera, 72, 73, 106, 108, 112, 113, 237, 416
Thring, F.W., 330, 331, 333
Tiatco, Anril P., 461

Tiffany, John, 252
Timlin, John, 341
Tinga-Tinga Tales, 395
Tingel-Tangel, 107, 115
Tinio, Rolando, 468
Tiongson, Nicanor, 470
Tisch School, 7, 12, 174, 210, 395, 417, 418, 436, 532
Tisch School of the Arts, 16, 518, 527, 529, 532
Tlatelolco, 417
To Kwok-Wai, Raymond, 500
To Live Another Summer, To Pass Another Winter, 405
Todorovic, Nenad, 255
Togni, Gianni, 249
Toho Company, 443
Toi c'est moi, 89
Tokugawa Iemitsu, 437
Tokura, Shun Ichi, 453, 559
Tokyo International Forum, 395
Tokyo Kid Brothers, 451
Toledo Surprise, 292
Toller, Ernst, 106
Tolstoy, Leo, 440
Tomá, matte, che, 406
Tommy, 512
Tongue, Cassie, 365
Touchstone Theatre, 312
Toulouse-Lautrec, Henri de, 91
Toy Factory, 500
Tracey, Andrew, 382
Tracey, Dr. Hugh, 382
Tracey, Paul, 382
Tranzac Club, 297
Trapp, Maria Augusta, 194
Traubner, Richard, 86, 96
Travers, P.L., 271
Treacher, Arthur, 84
Treemonisha, 154
Trenet, Charles, 77, 102
Trennet, Charles, 31
Très Très Snob, 223
Tretchikoff, Julie Jackson-, 325
Trevejo, Antonio Fernández, 428
Trial, 495
Trial By Jury, 45
Tricycle Theatre, 271
Tristan, 300, 560
Trois Gymnopédies, 94
Trotha, Gatti-, 60
Trovajoli, Armando, 247
Trudeau, Pierre, 163
Truscott, John, 343
Tsedu, Mpho, 393
Tsuneo, Kawasaki, 442
Tucholsky, Kurt, 105
Tucker, Percy, 372, 375, 377, 379, 383, 384, 385, 388
Tucker, Sophie, 389

Tudor, Daniel, 480
Tune, Tommy, 441
Tunisi, Bayram al-, 399
Tunku, 502
Turandot, 481, 482, 489
Turner, Ethel, 341
Turvey, 527
Turvey, Jay, 300, 560
Twain, Mark, 129, 319
Twala, Todd, 393
Twang!!, 266
Twilight of Springtime, The, 481
Twist of Fate, A, 498
Two Captains, The, 254
Two Gentlemen of Verona, 467
Two Hundred Pound Beauty, 477
Two Pianos, Four Hands, 314
Überbrettl, 103, 104
Uekrongtham, Ekachai, 490
Uhre, Mark, 301
Ullmann, Liv, 244
Ulvaeus, Björn, 244
Umabatha, 386
Umbrellas of Cherbourg, 233
Umbrellas of Cherbourg, The, 229, 231, 235
Umoja, 394
Un bolero en la noche, 430
Un día en el solar, 433
Unamuno, Miguel de, 536
Underhill, Jeff, 338
Une Femme par Jour, 90
Ungphakorn, Puey, 508
Union Theatre Repertory Company, 335
United Artistes Network, 491
Unity Theatre, 264, 337
Universal Amphiteatre, 118
Universexus, 411
University of Ballarat, 329
Uşaklıgil, Halid Ziya, 261
Uterus, 189, 302, 518, 519, 521, 546
Uxolo, 369
Valenzuela, Raimundo, 430
Valetti, Rosa, 106
Valse Millieu, 220, 223
Vámonos con Pancho Villa, 420
Van Cauwelaert, Didier, 234, 555
Van de Graaff, Janet, 288, 289
van den Ende, Joop, 241
Van den Ende, Joop, 243
van Dijk, Ad, 241
van Dijk, Bill, 241
van Dijk, Koen, 241
Van Loon, Nelles, 133, 205, 525, 526
Van Parys, Georges, 83, 90, 95, 99, 561
Vancouver Playhouse, 295
Vanderheyden, Tina, 279
Vanishing, The, 242
Vanloo, Albert, 81, 560

Variations, 166
Varney, Alphonse, 79
Vasilyev, Georgy, 254, 255
Vaughan Williams, Ralph, 18
Vaughan, Sarah, 408
Veber, Pierre, 257
Veber, Serge, 90
Venetian Twins, The, 340
Veronique, 78, 560
Véronique, 81
Very Good Eddie, 126
Victimas del Pecado, 420
Victor/Victoria, 239
Victoria, 108
Villanueva, Mario, 420
Villoch, Federico, 430
Vilsmaier, Joseph, 110
Vincy, Raymond, 93
Violettes impériales, 87
Virata ,Joy, 6, 465
Virata, Cesar, 465
Viravan, Takonkiet, 507
Vives, Amadeu, 48
Vives, Joan, 246
"Vluchten kan niet meer", 239
Volksoper, 64
Volpe, Mario, 398
Voltaire, 208
von Trapp, Baron Georg, 193, 194
Vosburgh, Dick, 202
Vournas, Tassos, 256
Voznesensky, Andrei, 254
Vrienten, Henny, 242, 556
Wada, Emi, 179
Wagdi, Anwar, 399
Wagner, Richard, 110
Wahab, Mohamed Abdel, 398, 399, 400
Wainaina, Eric, 395
Wainwright, Rufus, 90
Waissman, Ken, 195
Wait a Minim!, 382, 384
Waiting for Godot, 10
Wakao, Risa, 441
Walk a Little Faster, 130
Walker, Chet, 255
Walker, Joe, 381
Walker, Oliver, 376
Wallace, Shani, 222
Walley-Beckett, Moira, 278
Walsh, Enda, 252
Walsh, Michael, 263
Walsh, Mike, 342, 343
Walt Disney Company, 225, 271, 415, 442, 456, 536
Walton, William, 531
Waltz Dream, 68
War and Peace, 440
Wardle, Irving, 386
Waren, Dr. Stanley, 458

Waren, Florence, 458
Warrack, David, 525, 526, 559
Warren, Leslie Ann, 447
Warrior, The, 385
Washington, George, 170
Wat een planeet, 240
Waterfall, 508
Watermill Theatre, 270, 271
Watkins, Dennis, 338, 349
Watson, Don, 341
Watts, Matt, 288, 289
Watts, Richard Jr, 224
We Will Rock You, 308
"We'll Meet Again", 377
"We're Six Little Nieces of Our Uncle Sam", 514
"We're the Only Tulips on the Track Team", 287
Weaver, Harry, 223
Webb, Clifton, 84
Webb, Jimmy, 467
Webb, Marti, 166
Webber, Christopher, 48
Wedding Singer, The, 481
Wedekind, Frank, 104
Weidman, John, 178, 179
Weigl, Hans, 63
Weill, Kurt, 12, 23, 31, 67, 70-5, 106, 112-3, 117, 130, 132-3, 149, 152, 188, 190, 237, 269, 301, 338, 416, 550, 560
Weir, Peter, 319
Welch, Elisabeth, 267
Welles, Orson, 129
Wenn die beste Freundin, 108
West Side Story, 17, 203, 230, 235, 375, 379, 433, 467, 485, 535, 540
West Yorkshire Playhouse, 270
Western Australia Academy of Performing Arts, 340
Western Australian Academy of Performing Arts, 329
Whaley, Ben, 442
Wharton, Edith, 440
Wheeler, Hugh, 209
Whelan, Bill, 250
Whelan, Christie, 361
"When I Say My Say", 284
When in Rome, 246
Wherrett, Richard, 343
Whitcomb, Eleanor, 343
Whitcomb, Ian, 148
White Christmas, 432
White Horse Inn, The
  Im Weissen Rössl. *See*
White Horse Inn, The, 74
White Jacket, The, 121
White Rabbit Productions, 311
White, Onna, 223
Whiteman, Paul, 71

Whitfield, Sarah, 273
Whiting, Steven Moore, 100
Why Can't the English?, 176
Wicked, 197, 208, 238, 319, 419, 422, 448
Wie lernt man Liebe?, 109
Wiener Bürgertheater, 64
Wiener Frauen and *Der Rastelbinder*, 59
Wiener Stadttheater, 64
Wijnen, Maurice, 242, 556
Wilde Brühne, 107
Wilde, Oscar, 250
Wildeblood, Peter, 267
Wilder, Billy, 226
Wilder, Thornton, 57
Wildhorn, Frank, 443
Wilhelm, Kaiser, 67
Wilkinson, Alissa, 207
Willard, Kathy, 283
Willemetz, Albert, 83, 85, 87, 88, 89, 92, 93, 118, 559
Willett, John, 112
Williams, Albert, 195
Williams, Pat, 6, 16, 372, 375, 376, 379, 380, 381, 558
Williamson, J.C., 326, 327, 328, 329, 330, 331, 332, 333, 337, 554
Willner, A. M., 60
Willson, Meredith, 146, 190, 191, 513
Wilson, Angus, 378
Wilson, Brian, 146
Wilson, Clarence, 386
Wilson, Julie, 332
Wilson, Lambert, 88
Wilson, Monique, 469
Wilson, Sandra (film director), 186
Wilson, Sandy, 167, 186, 433
Windmills of Your Mind, The, 233
Wine, Toni, 153
Winter Garden Theatre, 290, 291, 294
Winter Sonata, 483
Wittman, Scott, 207
Witwatersrand University Great Hall, 376
WiwahPrasamut, 507
Wiz, The, 237, 243, 467
Wodehouse, P. G., 126
Wodehouse, P.G., 61, 124
Wolfe, George C., 527
Wolzogen, Ernst Von, 103, 104
Women xianzai de nianqingren, 484
Wong, Claire, 487
Wongsiri, Daraka, 508
Words, The, 284
Working in the Theatre, 288, 290, 291, 561
Wortman, Laura Farrell-, 177
Wright, Adrian, 141, 166, 267, 268

Wright, Katey, 312
Wrong Son, The, 301
Xanadu, 251
Xiaoquan, Zhou, 482
Ya ain, ya lail, 400
Ya Got Trouble, 191
Yabin, Wang, 481
Yajiro Shinagawa, 46
Yale University, 7, 372, 515, 548, 551
Yarnell, Bruce, 226
Ye, Jimmy, 500
Yedi Kokalı Hürmüz, 262
Yegrin Akdan, 473
Yeldham, Peter, 341, 344
Yellow Brick Road, The, 418
Yentl, 233
Yes, 79
Yeston, Maury, 14, 21, 23
Yishida, Yuko, 441
Yo Colón, 421
Yoduk Story, 478
Yoo-jeong, Jang, 472
Yoon Jeongin, 482
Yoshimatsu, Takashi, 452
You Are Beautiful, 174
You Could Drive a Person Crazy, 361
Youmanns, Vincent, 131
Young Vic, 394, 558
Young, Gary, 348, 559
Young, Josh, 313
Young, Neil, 286
Yūji, Koseki, 444
Yume Kara Samete Yume, 448
Yun Ho Jin, 475
Yuta to Fushigina Nakama-tachi, 448
Yuuko, Yoshida, 442
Yvain, Maurice, 79, 80, 83, 87, 88, 90, 92, 561
Zahim Al-Bakri, 503
Zakaria, Fareed, 21
Zaki, Mona, 402
Zequera, Manuel de, 428
Ziegfeld Follies, 464
Ziegfeld, Florenz, 53, 83, 92
Zimmermann, Tim, 520
Zitterbarth, Bartholomäus, 55
Zorba the Greek, 260
Zorro, 498
Zortman, Bruce, 75
Zuckmayer, Carl, 109
Zulu Dance Theatre, 386
Zulu, Lindewe, 390
Zuma, Dr. Nkosazana, 392
Zwar, Charles, 332, 334
Zwei Krawatten, 110

Endnotes

Acknowledgements

[1] Email to the author dated 9 June 2008.

Preface: A Search for Signs of Life

[1] Cecil Smith, *Musical Comedy in America: From The Black Crook to South Pacific*, Theatre Arts Books/Methuen, New York, 1987, p. 201
[2] Peter Stone, "The Musical Comedy Book" in *Dramatists' Guild Quarterly*, Vol. 25 No. 4, Winter 1989, p.13.
[3] Patsy Southgate, "Peter Stone: Musical Titan Writes the Book", *The East Hampton Star*, 29 May 1997.
[4] Stone, ibid.
[5] Stone, p. 23
[6] Lehman Engel, *Words With Music*, Schirmer Books, New York, 1981, p.6.
[7] Marshall McLuhan, *The Gutenberg Galaxy* Routledge & Kegan Paul, London, 1962, p.31
[8] Other names for it included "opéra-bouffe" or even "comédie-musicale", a term which pre-dates the American "musical comedy".
[9] Kurt Gänzl, *The Musical – A Concise History*, Northeastern University Press, Boston, 1997, p. xi.
[10] Alan Jay Lerner, *The Musical Theatre: A Celebration*, McGraw-Hill Book Company, New York, 1986, p. 236.
[11] Ginza is the theatre district of Tokyo.
[12] Scott Brown, "How Can Musical Theater be Saved?", Vulture.com, 24 May 2012, accessed 21 July 2012.
[13] "Mel Atkey has written lovely music": Quote from Laurel Graeber, "Family Fare" review of *A Little Princess*, *New York Times*, 7 November, 2003.
[14] A nickname for Vancouver derived from the intoxicated lotus-eaters in Homer's *The Odyssey*. It is a reference to the city's laid-back-to-the-point-of-falling-over attitudes.
[15] This name is attributed to producer David Y. H. Lui (1944-2011).
[16] I'm sure that many people can say this about their home towns, which is exactly my point.
[17] My history of musical theatre in Canada, *Braodway North: The Dream of a Canadian Musical Theatre* was published by Natural Heritage Books/Dundurn Press in 2006.

18 I had already seen a number of London shows during visits, beginning in 1969 with *Fiddler on the Roof* starring Alfie Bass.
19 David Rothenberg, "More than Words", *The Guardian and Observer Guides to Performing Part 2: Singing*, May 2009.
20 See Tom Phillips and Armand D'Angour (editors), *Music, Text, and Culture in Ancient Greece*, Oxford University Press, 2018.
21 H. I. Khan, *The Music of Life*, Omega Publications, Santa Fe, New Mexico, 1983, p. 335-6.
22 Pat Williams, *Our Knot of Time and Music*, Portobello Books, London, 2017, p. 210.
23 NYU Tisch School of the Arts Graduate Musical Theatre Writing Program course prospectus (no date indicated).
24 *New Scientist*, issue 2681, 11 November 2008, p. 17
25 Email to the author dated 15 April 2019.
26 Sofia Rizzi, "Why did Bernstein build West Side Story around 'The Devil's Interval'?", *Classic FM*, 27 March 2019, https://www.classicfm.com/composers/bernstein-l/bernstein-west-side-story-tritone/?fbclid=IwAR3VSvqY7yZ0f6aJj6_fOkpZ0Xn2Kv_I9OUNA4p3-ANgwBnOso0UnYVV7WQ, accessed 12 June 2019.
27 André Previn, *No Minor Chords*, Doubleday, New York, 1991, p. 101.
28 "Great Composers Scored on Language", *The Guardian*, London, 20 November 2004.
29 From a platform talk given at the National Theatre, London, 1 June 1993, interviewed by Jeremy Sams. *Platform Papers 5: Musicals… and Sondheim*, Royal National Theatre Publications department.
30 Goodall, *Big Bangs*, Chatto & Windus, London, 2000, p. 224.
31 David Manning, *Ralph Vaughan Williams on Music*, Oxford University Press, New York, 2008, p. 104
32 Email to the author dated 15 September 2018.
33 Fareed Zakaria, "The Rise of the Rest", *Newsweek*, 12 May 2008.
34 Email to author dated 13 July 2009.
35 Neil Tennant, "Out of Tune", *The Spectator*, 17 December 2011
36 Nick Curtis, "Why I'm Bringing Brando to the West End", *Evening Standard*, London, 10 August 2007.
37 Lehman Engel, *The American Musical Theater*, Collier Books, New York, 1975, pp. x-xi,
38 A reference to US President Richard Nixon's meeting with Mao Tse-tung in 1971. The assumption is that only a recognised political conservative could be trusted to open the US up to Communist China. "A Size-Up of President Nixon: Interview with

Mike Mansfield, Senate Democratic Leader", *U.S. News & World Report*, 6 December 1971, p. 61.

[39] For a more thorough discussion of this, please see my article "Do Musicals Need Hit Songs?" in my book *Breaking Into Song*, Friendlysong Books, Vancouver, 2017.

[40] *An Evening with Alan Jay Lerner*, recorded live at the Kaufmann Concert Hall of the 92nd Street Y, New York, as part of the Lyrics and Lyricist series, DRG Records, 1977.

[41] This was an email dated 18 February 2017, the author's name is withheld, although I do have it on file.

[42] Email to author from Katie Doyle dated 23 February 2017.

[43] Facebook message to author dated 24 June 2013.

[44] Email to author dated 17 December 2006.

[45] Email to author 17 June 2017.

[46] John Coulter, "The Canadian Theatre and the Irish Exemplar", *Theatre Arts Monthly*, July 1936, p. 505-506.

[47] Alistair Smith, "ATG to work with regional reps to find new British musicals", *The Stage*, 15 September 2011

[48] Rebellato, Dan, *Theatre and Globalization*, Palgrave MacMillan, Basingstoke, 2009, p. 60

[49] Rebellato, p. 41.

[50] The term "scientist" was coined in 1833 by English polymath William Whewell (1794-1866).

European Musical Comedy (Oops, I Mean Operetta)

[1] Wilfred Mellers, *Music in a New Found Land: Themes and Developments in the History of American Music*, Faber and Faber, London, 1987, p. 447.

[2] Officially the "Imperial and Royal Court Theatre of Vienna", although its mandate specified that it was to appeal to all classes.

[3] Letter of 30 January 1768 quoted in *The Letters of Mozart and his Family*, vol. 1 ed. And translated Emily Anderson, MacMillan and Co., London, 1938, p. 118.

[4] Played by Simon Callow in the film *Amadeus*.

[5] George Collerick, *From The Italian Girl to Cabaret*, Juventus, London, 1995, p.38.

[6] Exchange of letters dated 11 December 1780 and 16 December 1780 between Leopold Mozart and his song Wolfgang, cited in E.M. Batley, *A Preface to the Magic Flute*, Dennis Dobson, London, 1969, p.99.

[7] Eva Badura-Skoda, "The Viennese Singspiel, Haydn and Mozart", from Michael Cherlin, Halina Filipowicz, Richard L. Rudolph, *The*

Great Tradition and Its Legacy, Berghahn Books, New York, 2003, p.177

[8] Siegfried Kracauer, *Offenbach and the Paris of His Time*, Constable, London, 1937, p. 129

[9] Kracauer, pp 33-34.

[10] Cited in Richard Traubner, *Operetta: A Theatrical History*, Routledge, 2003.

[11] Kracauer, p. 266, citing Eduard Hanslick, *Aus Meinem Leben*, 2 volumes, Berlin, 1911.

[12] Kracauer, p. 129.

[13] Peter Gammond, *Offenbach*, Omnibus Press, London, 1980, p. 42.

[14] Gammond, ibid, p.8.

[15] Kracauer, p. 174.

[16] Kracauer, pp 273-5.

[17] *The Tomahawk*, 24 August 1867, p. 174-175.

[18] Leslie Baily, *Gilbert & Sullivan and Their World*, Thames and Hudson, London, 1973, p. 30

[19] In fact, Offenbach's first show in New York was *Les Deux Aveugles* in 1857.

[20] Gammond, ibid, pp 140-41.

[21] Mark Lubbock, "The Music of 'Musicals'", *The Musical Times*, Vol. 98, No. 1375 (Sep., 1957), pp. 483-485.

[22] Lerner, p. 19.

[23] David Foil, *Carmen*, Black Dog & Leventhal Publishers, New York, 1996, p.24.

[24] Joan Peyser, Bernstein – A Biography, Billboard Books, New York, 1998, p.334.

[25] Marlis Schewitzer, "'Darn that Merry Widow Hat' : The on-and offstage life of a theatrical commodity circa 1907-1908", *Theatre Survey*, 2009, p. 190

[26] *Oxford Concise Dictionary of Music*, Fifth Edition, Michael Kennedy and Joyce Bourne Kennedy, eds., Oxford University Press, Oxford, 2007

[27] George Colerick, *Romanticism and Melody*, Juventus, London, 1995, p. 63.

[28] Loud, boisterous.

[29] Stephen Sondheim, *Finishing the Hat – Collected lyrics (1954-1981), with attendant Comments, Principles, Heresies, Grudges, Whines and Annecdotes*, Virgin Books, London, 2010, p. 332.

[30] Engel, *The American Musical Theater*, p. 137.

[31] Richard Kislan, *The Musical*, Prentice-Hall Inc., Englewood Cliffs, NJ, 1980, p. 94.

[32] Baily, p. 33.

[33] Baily, p. 36.
[34] William Schwenck Gilbert, "William Schwenck Gilbert: an Autobiography", *The Theatre: A Monthly Review of the Drama, Music, and the Fine Arts*, vol. 1, 2 April 1883, pp. 217–24, reprinted in *Gilbert and Sullivan: Interviews and Recollections*, ed. Harold Orel, University of Iowa Press, Iowa City, 1994, p. 8.
[35] Gerald Bordman, *American Operetta*, Oxford University Press, New York, 1981, p. 16
[36] I once suggested to Japanese director Amon Miyamoto that he should stage *The Mikado* in Japan using Japanese actors made up to look English. Shocked, he said "You can't do that!"
[37] Stephen Sondheim, *Finishing the Hat*, Virgin Books, London, 2010, p. 212.
[38] House of Commons Culture, Media and Sport Committee, Fifth Report of Session 2004-05, The Stationery Office, London, 2005, Ev85.
[39] Geoffrey Macnab, "Homme fatal", *The Guardian*, London, 10 January 2004.
[40] According to Iñigo Santamaria, author of *Guía Ilustrada del Teatro Musical en España*, "'zarzuela' is not really related in meaning with bushes (zarzas), more with a kind of mixture, usually refering to a culinary specialty that mixes different types of fish and s[h]elfish in the same plate (as does 'zarzuela' with music and text, as opposed to opera).
[41] Christopher Webber, *The Zarzuela Companion*, Scarecrow Press, Metuchen, New Jersey, 2002.
[42] http://www.zarzuela.net/com/vives.htm, accessed 22 April 2010.
[43] Rimgaila Salys, *Laughing Matters – The Musical Comedy Films of Grigorii Alexsandrov*, Intellect, Bristol, 2009, p.7
[44] Graham Greene, "Jazz Comedy/Two for Tonight", *The Spectator*, 27 September 1935.
[45] Richard Taylor and Ian Christie, eds. "Party Cinema Conference Resolution: The Results of Cinema Construction in the USSR and the Tasks of Soviet Cinema", *The Film Factory, Russian and Soviet Cinema in Documents 1896-1939*, Routledge, London, 1994, pp. 211-12.
[46] Dana Ranga, *East Side Story*, Anda Films, Berlin, 1997.

Musicals for the Masses: Emanuel Schikaneder and the Theater an der Wien

[1] Email to author dated 9 July 2010.

² Michael Cherlin, "Conflict and Crossroads in Viennese Music", *The Great Tradition and Its Legacy*, Berghahn Books, New York, 2003, pp. 141-142..

³ Colerick, *Romanticismm and Melody*, p.63.

⁴ Kurt Honolka, *Papageno – Emanuel Schikaneder Man of the Theater in Mozart's Time*, Translated by Jane Mary Wilde, Amadeus Press, Portland, Oregon, 1990, pp 7-8.

⁵ Honolka, p.95.

⁶ Adolf Bäuerle, *Memoiren*, Wien, 1858, Vol. 1, p. 112, cited in Kurt Homolka, p. 187.

⁷ Honolka, p. 207.

⁸ Email to author dated 23 November 2015.

⁹ Several of the great Broadway lyricists were also composers, or were at least musically trained, including Sheldon Harnick and Alan Jay Lerner; Frank Loesser and Stephen Sondheim began their careers as lyricists, and like Genée, graduated to writing the score as well.

¹⁰ While *The Magic Flute* and *The Merry Widow* are popularly known in the English-speaking world by their translated names, people seem happy to refer to *Die Fledermaus* by its German title, perhaps because producers knew that if they called it *The Winged Rodent*, box office queues would evaporate like a puddle in a heat wave. Similarly, Cameron Mackintosh resisted any temptation to call *Les Misérables* "The Wretched".

¹¹ Simon Broughton, "Return to Dreamland: Has the musical killed off operetta? " *Independent*, 17 October 1992.

¹² Peter Herz, "Der Fall Franz Lehár. Eine authentische Darlegung von Peter Herz", *Die Gemeinde* 24 April 1968.

¹³ Now the site of the Vue Cinema.

¹⁴ *New York Times*, 7 July 1909.

¹⁵ Lerner, p.42.

¹⁶ Ellwood Annaheim, "Shaw's Folly – Straus' Fortune", Opening Remarks, February 2002 *Musical Theater Research Project* performance, archived on 20 June, 2005. https://web.archive.org/web/20050620092840/www.geocities.com/musictheater/chocolate/chocolate.html

¹⁷ Richard Traubner, *Operetta: a Theatrical History*, Routledge, New York, 2003, p.266.

¹⁸ Zoltán Imre, "Operetta beyond borders: The different versions of *Die Csárdásfürstin* in Europe and the United States (1915-1921) ", *Studies in Musical Theatre*, 7:2, p. 198-9.

¹⁹ Not to be confused with Austria's national theatre, the Burgtheater ("Imperial Court Theatre"), built in 1741.

Give My Regards to Friedrichstrasse

[1] In fact, recent DNA evidence has suggested that Hitler's family had North African and even Jewish ancestry. See Heidi Blake, "Hitler 'had Jewish and African roots', DNA tests show", *the Telegraph*, 24 August, 2010.
[2] Furtwangler was the subject of the Ron Harwood play *Taking Sides*.
[3] *Deutschen Allgemeine Zeitung*, 11 April 1933.
[4] Cited by Wolf Lepenies in "Die Nationalsozialisten und die Kultur", *Berliner Morgenpost*, 18 May 2008.
[5] Andrew Lamb, *150 Years of Popular Musical Theatre*, Yale University Press, New Haven, CT, 2000, p.226.
[6] Radio interview conducted by William H. Marshall, Assistant District Director of Immigration and Naturalization at Ellis Island on the NBC Blue Network, 9 March 1941. Weill-Lenya Research Center, Ser.122/3
[7] Email to author dated 18 November 2009.
[8] A denomination of old German coinage.
[9] Gottfried Reinhardt, *The Genius – A Memoir of Max Reinhardt*, Alfred A. Knopf, New York, 1979, pp. 68-69.
[10] Email to author dated 14 July 2010.
[11] Yehudi Menuhin, *Unfinished Journey*, MacDonald & Jane's, London, 1977, cited in Reinhardt, *Genius*.
[12] "Light-Opera Boom", *Time*, 9 November 1942.
[13] Reinhardt, p. 74.
[14] Gusti Adler, *Max Reinhardt*, Festungsverlag, Salzburg, 1964, p. 43, cited in Michael Patterson, "Populism versus Elitism, *The Great Tradition and Its Legacy*, Berghahn Books, New York, 2003, p. 73.
[15] Esther Slevogt, "A hard-nosed Utopian", *signandsight.com*, 25 January 2006, originally published in German in *Die Tageszeitung*, 28 December 2005.
[16] John Willett and Ralph Manheim, "Introduction", *Collected Plays One by Bertolt Brecht*, Methuen, London, 1970, p.vii-xvii
[17] Colerick, *From The Italian Girl to Cabaret*, p.70.
[18] Foster Hirsch, *Kurt Weill on Stage*, Limelight Editions, New York, 2002, p. 18.
[19] John Willett, translator, *Brecht on Brecht*, Methuen, London, 1964, p.131-2, cited in Michael Bawtree, *The New Singing Theatre*, Oxford University Press, New York, 1991, p.60.
[20] Richard Kislan, *The Musical – A Look at the American Musical Theater*, Pretice-Hall, Englewood Cliffs, NJ, 1980, p.192

[21] Lamb, ibid.
[22] Bruce Zortman, *Hitler's Theater: Ideological Drama in Nazi Germany*, Firestein Books, El Paso, Texas, 1984, p. 7.

Paris: Where Musicals Were Born, and Where they Go to Die

[1] Margaret Vermette, *The Musical World of Boublil and Schönberg*, Applause Theatre and Cinema Books, New York, 2006, p.20.
[2] Sheridan Morley and Ruth Leon, *Hey Mr. Producer*, Back Stage Books, New York, 1998, p.102.
[3] Gareth Murphy, "Parisian Radar"!, *The Journal of Music*, Galway, Vol. 1 No. 1, April 2009, p. 36.
[4] "New Plays in Manhattan", *Time*, New York, 18 March 1929.
[5] Email to the author dated 25 June 2008.
[6] Engel, *Words With Music*, p.143.
[7] Stephen Sondheim, *Finishing the Hat*, p.80.
[8] Jules Bertaut, *Paris: 1870-1935*, translated by R. Millar, Eyre and Spottiswoode, London, 1936, p. 256.
[9] Jeffrrey H. Jaclson, *Making Jazz French*, Duke University Press, Durham, NC, 2003, p.2.
[10] Société des Auteurs, Compositeurs et Éditeurs de Musique
[11] Confédération Internationale des Société d'Auteurs et Compositeurs
[12] "Five New Productions Next Week", *The Times*, London, 28 August 1919, p. 8.
[13] "E. Ray Goetz Returns", *New York Times*, 3 May 1920.
[14] *The Daily Mirror*, London, 2 June 1922, p. 7.
[15] *The Daily Mirror*, London, 5 June 1922, p. 7.
[16] Edward Behr, *Thank Heaven for Little Girs – The True Story of Maurice Chevalier's Life and Times*, Hutchinson, London, 1993, p.96.
[17] Gänzl, *The Musical*, p. 163.
[18] Richard Traubner, *Operetta: A Theatrical History*, Routledge, 2003, p. 313.
[19] Cited in Jacques Damase, *Les Folies du Music-Hall*, Anthony Blond, London, 1962, p. 63.
[20] Kurt Gänzl, *Encyclopedia of the Musical Theatre*, Blackwell, Oxford, 1994, p.1292.
[21] Maurice Yvain, *Ma Belle Operette*, Editions de la Table Ronde, Paris, 1962, cited in www.cinemagia.ro accessed on 5 June 2008.
[22] Yvain, loc. Cit.
[23] *The Times*, London, 9 September 1926, p. 10.
[24] Peter Bogdanovich, introduction to the Criterion Collection DVD of *French Cancan*, 2004.

[25] Cited in Pierre Mariel, *Paris Revue*, translated by Peter Munk, Neville Spearman, london, 1962, p. 21.
[26] *Musical Stages*, Issue 45, Spring 2005, p.10.
[27] Kim Willsher, "An American (musical) in Paris. Once seen as lowbrow, Broadway shows now ride high in France", *Los Angeles Times*, 15 December 2017.
[28] Gänzl, *Encyclopedia*, p. 890.
[29] Andrew Lamb, *150 Years of Popular Musical Theatre*, Yale University Press, New Haven, p.236
[30] Kurt Gänzl, *Musicals*, Carlton Books, London, 2001, p. 236.
[31] *Encyclopedia of popular music (online ed.)*, Oxford University Press. 2006.
[32] The Schola opened in 1896 as an alternative to the more operatic Paris Conservatoire.
[33] See Steve Swayne, *How Sondheim Found His Sound*, University of Michigan Press, Ann Arbor, 2005, p.22

Declaration of Independence

Cabaret: From "le Chat Noir" to the Algonquin Room

[1] Richard Traubner, *Operetta: A Theatrical History*, Routledge, 2003, p.10.
[2] Maximillien de Lafayette, *Entertainment Divas, Cabaret, Jazz Then and Now*, iUniverse, Lincoln, NE, 2006, p.47.
[3] The modern sense of the word "camera" comes from "camera obscura", a darkened room in which a reflected image of the world outside is projected. This came to be used for an optically similar device for recording pictures on emulsion.
[4] This is a point where even "facts" become subjective. The Hydropathes existed from at least 1878, and the Lapin Agile – in its previous incarnation as "Cabaret des Assassins" – had been in business since 1860.
[5] Alfred Fierro, *Histoire et Dictionnaire de Paris*, Robert Laffont, 1996, pg. 738
[6] Jeffrey H. Jackson, *Making Jazz French*, Duke University Press, Durham, 2003, p. 35.
[7] Lisa Appignanesi, *The Cabaret*, Yale University Press, New Haven, CT, 2004, p. 1-2.
[8] Jackson, ibid, p. 118.

[9] Philip Dennis Cate and Mary Shaw, editors, *The Spirit of Montmartre*, Rutgers, new Brunswick, NJ, 1996, p. 190.
[10] Henry Louis Gates Jr. and Karen C. C. Dalton, *Josephine Baker and La Revue Nègre*, Harry N. Abrams, Inc., New York, 1998, p.7.
[11] Ute Lemper *Blue Angels and Pirate Jennys* BBC Radio 4, 25 February 2006
[12] Cited in Colerick, *From the Italian Girl to Cabaret*, p.67.
[13] Possibly an ironic play on Nietsche's word Übermensch ("superman")
[14] Peter Jelavich, *Berlin Cabaret*, Harvard University Press, Cambridge, MA, 1993, p.61
[15] Christopehr Isherwood, *Goodbye to Berlin*, Hogarth Press, London, 1939, p.38.
[16] Cited in Jelavich, p.96.
[17] Appignanesi, p.187.
[18] Cited by Jon Stewart, *Rolling Stone*, 29 September 2011
[19] The fact that Berlin was also home to the Ufa film studios no doubt helped to create a large talent pool.
[20] Davies, Cecil William, *The Plays of Ernst Toller: A revaluation*, Routledge, New York, 1996, p. 355.
[21] Liel Leibovitz and Matthew Miller, *Lili Marlene – The Soldier's Song of World War II*, W. W. Norton & Co., New York, 2009, p.45.
[22] Michael Billington, "Life and soul of the cabaret", *The Guardian*, London, 31 August 1999.
[23] Liner notes to the 1976 New York Shakespeare Festival cast recording of *Threepenny Opera*, CBS Records PS 34326.
[24] Roger Boyes, "Life is a cabaret in Kohl twilight zone", *The Times*, London, 29 August 1998.
[25] Email to the author dated 5 May 2008.
[26] Email to the author dated 4 May 2008.
[27] Email to the author dated 4 May 2008.
[28] Email to the author dated 4 May 2008.
[29] Email to the author dated 29 June 2008.
[30] www.videocab.com
[31] Sandy Stewart, *Here's Looking at Us*, CBC Enterprises, Toronto, 1986, p. 160.
[32] Barb Jungr, "Thriving Cabaret Scene Down Under", *The Stage*, London, 4 October 2007.
[1] Actually, the pronunciation "zee" comes from an English minority dialect dating back to the 1670s. It died out in the mother country but lived on in the colony.

[2] Herman Melville (1819–1891), U.S. author. *White-Jacket* (1850), ch. 36, *The Writings of Herman Melville*, vol. 5, eds. Harrison Hayford, Hershel Parker, and G. Thomas Tanselle (1969).
[3] Wilfred Mellers, *Music in a New Found Land: Themes and Developments in the History of American Music*, Faber and Faber, London, 1987, p.3.
[4] Raymond Knapp, *The American Musical and the Formation of National Identity*, Princeton University Press, Princeton, NJ, 2005, pp 32-33.
[5] Mellers, ibid., p.39.
[6] Ethan Mordden, *Broadway Babies: The People Who Made the American Musical*, Oxford University Press, New York, 1983, p. 27.
[7] "New Maker of Melodies Talks About His Trade", *World*, New York, 14 September 1913.
[8] Alec Wilder, *American Popular Song: The Great Innovators, 1900–1950*, Oxford University Press, New York, 1972, pp 34-35.
[9] Lamb, p.152
[10] David Lehman, *A Fine Romance – Jewish Songwriters, American Songs*, Schocken Books, New York, 2009, p. 45 See also Robert Kimbell, *The Complete Lyrics of Cole Porter*, Knopf, New York, 1983.
[11] Benny Green, *P. G. Wodehouse – A Literary Biography*, Pavilion Books, London, 1981, p 110.
[12] Edna Ferber, *A Peculiar Treasure*. Doubleday. New York, 1960, pp. 297–304.
[13] Mark Lubbock, *The Complete Book of Light Opera*, Appleton-Century-Crofts, New York, 1962, pp. 753–56
[14] Jason Green (moderator) "The Greatest Musical: "I Can't Live With 'West Side Story' Not Being Among the Finalists", *New Yorker*, 9 January 2011.
[15] Engel, *The American Musical Theater*, p.8
[16] Meryle Secrest, *Leonard Bernstein – a Life*, Bloomsbury, London, 1995, p.52
[17] John Warthen Struble, *History of American Classical Music*, Checkmark Books / Facts on File, New York, 1995, p.188
[18] Lerner, p.44.
[19] Engel, Ibid.,p.7.
[20] Lerner, ibid., p.117.
[21] Kislan, p. 102.
[22] Biographer Gene Lees disputes this.
[23] Gene Lees, *The Musical Worlds of Lerner and Loewe*, Robson Books, London, 1990, p. 11.
[24] Lerner, ibid., p.71.
[25] Kislan, ibid, p. 99-100.

[26] Charles Osbourne, *The Dictionary of Composers*, The Bodley Head, London, 1977, p.376.
[27] Foster Hirsch, *Kurt Weill on Stage*, Limelight Editions, New York, 2003, p. 352.
[28] Max Wilk, *They're Playing Our Song*, Atheueum, New York, 1973, pp 12-13.
[29] Wilk, ibid, p.88.
[30] Email to the author dated 3 July 2003.

Between the Wars

[1] Webb, Paul. "Novello, Ivor", *Grove Music Online*, Oxford Music Online, accessed 17 March 2011.
[2] Stewart Nicholls, "West End Royalty: Ivor Novello", *The Oxford Hanbook of the British Musical*, Oxford University Press, 2016, p. 218.
[3] Julian Fellows discusses Ivor Novello with Thos Ribbits, *Musical Talk* podcast dated 8 September 2013.
[4] Peter Noble, *Ivor Novello – Man of the Theatre*, The Falcon Press, London, 1951, p. 267
[5] *The Critics*, BBC, 15 January 1950.
[6] Noble, p. 228
[7] Noble, p. 249.
[8] Ivor Novello interviewed by Charles Hamblett in *Illustrated*, 17 September 1949. Cited by Wright, *Tanner's*, p. 38.
[9] Noble, p. 281.
[10] Noble, p. 227.
[11] Adrian Wright, *A Tanner's Worth of Tune – Rediscovering the Post-War British Musical*, The Boydell Press, Woodbridge, 2010, p. 15.
[12] Gerald Bordman, *Jerome Kern – His Life and Music*, Oxford University Press, New York, 1980, p. 47.
[13] Ward Morehouse, *George M. Cohan – Prince of the American Theatre*, J. B. Lippincott Company, New York, 1943, p. 15.
[14] Cited by Morehouse, ibid, p. 174.
[15] Laurence Bergreen, *As Thousands Cheer – The Life of Irving Berlin*, Da Capo Press, New York, 1996, p. 72.
[16] Morehouse, ibid, p. 196.
[17] Morehouse, ibid, pp 200-201.
[18] In 1904, when "Give My Regards to Broadway" was written, Broadway was not yet established as a world theatre capital. Originally known in Dutch as "Breede Weg", the theatre district had only recently begun to establish itself in the area of Times Square. Previously, it had been based around an area south of there known as the Rialto.

[19] Bergreen, loc cit.
[20] Lehman Engel, *Words With Music*, p. 248

The New World(s)

The Rock 'n' Roll Syndrome

[1] http://news.bbc.co.uk/go/pr/fr/-/1/hi/entertainment/8297635.stm, accessed on 9 October 2009

[2] Clive Barnes, "Hair is a shaggy happening set to rock music that grooves along with pot, peaceniks and a startling tableau of nudes", *Saturday Evening Post*, 10 August, 1968.

[3] 1956 hearings of the Anti-Trust Subcommittee of the House Judiciary Committee, cited in Ian Whitcomb, *After the Ball*, Limelight Editions, New York, 1972/1989, p. 209.

[4] "Richard Rogers Expresses Views on Rock and Roll", Footage Film, YouTube, cited in Lurence Maslon, *Broadway to Main Street*, Oxford University Press, 2018, p. 158.

[5] Originally written by Bulee Gaillard (1916-91) and Leroy Stewart (1914-87) as "flat foot floozie", referring to a promiscuous woman. "Floy floy" was a reference to venereal disease. The publishers made them change the first reference, but left the second one alone.

[6] Howard Goodall, *Big Bangs*, p.206.

[7] Tom Lehrer, *An Evening Wasted with Tom Lehrer*, Reprise Records, 1959.

[8] Whitcomb, ibid, pp 211-212.

[9] Paul Simon, "George on my mind", *The Observer*, 6 September 1998, © New York Times Syndication.

[10] Not that this approach was always successful – following a performance of *Othello* at London's Old Vic in the early nineteenth century, the great actor Edmund Keane snarled at the audience: "I have played in every civilised country where English is the language of the people, but in all my life I never acted to such a set of ignorant, unmitigated brutes as I now see before me." – (from "Where the Old Vic belongs", *Tribune Magazine*, 1 October 1948.)

[11] Alan Jay Lerner, preface to *Camelot*, Random House, New York, 1961.

[12] Lyrics by E. Y. Harburg, Music by Jay Gorney, "Brother Can You Spare a Dime?", Warner/Chappell Music, Inc., Shapiro Bernstein & Co. Inc., Next Decade Entertainment,Inc.

[13] Mel Atkey, "An Epiphany", *Musical Stages*, Issue 25, October 2000, p. 14.

[14] Email from Ron Dante to author dated 26 August, 2000

[15] Marilyn Stasio, "…And Still Champion", *Cue*, 30 September 1974, p. 10.
[16] Engel, *Words With Music*, p 127
[17] Understood by only a few.
[18] Mel Gussow, "Sondheim Scores With 'Company'", *New York Times*, 28 April 1970.
[19] Engel, ibid, pp. 129-30.
[20] Mark N. Grant, *The Rise and Fall of the Broadway Musical*, Northeastern University Press, Boston, 2004, p. 161.
[21] John Lahr, *Automatic Vaudeville*, Alfred A. Knopf, New York, 1984, p. 101-102
[22] Email to author dated 2 July 2003.
[23] Scott Miller, "But That Was Once Upon a Time", *The Bad Boy of Musical Theatre – Random Musings from a Bad-ass Cultural Warrior*, 13 July 2011.
[24] Previn, p. 63.

Universality Part 1: "Do They Understand This Show in America? It's So Japanese!"

[1] Cameron Mackintosh in letter to the author dated 18 July 2003, cited in Mel Atkey, *Broadway North: The Dream of a Canadian Musical Theatre*, Natural Heritage Books, Toronto, p.138.
[2] Cited in Peter Stone, Jerry Bock, Sheldon Harnick and Joseph Stein, "Landmark Symposium: Fiddler on the Roof", *Dramatists Guild Quarterly*, New York, 1983, Vol.20, No.1, p. 27
[3] Wayne Hoffman, "A 'Fiddler' in Tokyo", *Tablet*, 8 January 2018 www.tabletmag.com
[4] Barbara Isenberg, *Tradition! The Highly Improbable, Ultimately Triumphant Broadway-to-Hollywood Story of Fiddler on the Roof, the World's Most Beloved Musical*, St. Martin's Griffin, New York, 2014, p. 173.
[5] Engel, *Words With Music*, p.4-5.
[6] Lyrics by Dubose Heyward and Ira Gershwin, *Porgy and Bess*, © 1935 Warner/Chappell Music Inc.
[7] Max Wilk, *They're Playing Our Song*, Atheneum, New York, 1973, pp 91-92.
[8] Lehman Engel, *Porgy in Ankara*, an unpublished manuscript in the archives of Yale University Music Library.
[9] Letter from Ira Gershwin to Lehman Engel dated 15 July 1969, courtesy of Ira and Leonore Gershwin Trusts
[10] Ron Smith, "Rose Marie: I Don't LoveYou", Thompson Rivers University, 2006.

[11] Pierre Berton, *Hollywood's Canada – The Americanization of Our National Identity*, McLelland and Stewart, Toronto, 1975, p. 234.
[12] However, they were not too embarrassed to hand over control of their image to the Walt Disney Company for a brief period in the 1990s.
[13] Ibid, p. 139.
[14] Don Harron, *Anne of Green Gables The Musical – 101 Things You Didn't Know*, White Knight Books, Toronto, 2008, p. 133.
[15] Ibid, p. 72.
[16] Under US copyright law, anything published before 1923 is automatically up for grabs, whereas in most other countries, the copyright would last until 70 years after the author's death.
[17] "The Other Anne", Kate Goodloe, *Ottawa Citizen*, 5 May 2007.
[18] "Warning Sent to New York's Anne", CBC News, 10 May, 2007, http://www.cbc.ca/arts/theatre/story/2007/05/10/newyork-anne.html
[19] Faye Hammill, "'A new and exceedingly brilliant star': L. M. Montgomery, "Anne of Green Gables," and Mary Miles Minter". *The Modern Language Review*, July 2006. 101 (3) pp. 652–670.
[20] James Inverne, *Wrestling With Elephants*, Sanctuary, London, 2003, p.121.
[21] Adrian Wright, *Must Close Saturday – The Decline and Fall of the British Musical Flop*, The Boydell Press, Woodbridge, 2017, p. 159.
[22] Inverne, p. 143.
[23] Michael Coveney, *The Andrew Lloyd Webber Story*, Arrow Books, London, 2000
[24] Vida Hope, "*The Boy Friend* on Broadway", *Plays and Players*, Christmas 1954, p. 12.
[25] Letter to Christopher Cox, *Boston Herald*, September 19, 1997.
[26] Cited in Meryle Secrest, *Somewhere for Me: A Biography of Richard Rodgers*, Bloomsbury, London, 2001, p. 287.
[27] Alfred Habegger, *Masked: The Life of Anna Leonowens, Schoolmistress at the Court of Siam*, University of Wisconsin Press, 2014, p. 354.
[28] Engel, *The American Musical Theater*, p. 49.
[29] Given the fate of the National Film Board of Canada's 1982 Oscar winning documentary of Dr. Helen Coldicott's anti-nuclear lecture *If You Love This Planet* – which was branded "foreign government propaganda" by the Reagan adminsitration – (meaning that anybody viewing the film must give their names to the U.S. Justice Department) – you never know.

30 "Broadway's lost chords and Hollywood's cut tracks uncovered by University of Sheffield's researchers", University of Sheffield Press Release, 11 February 2019.
31 Facebook message dated 12 February 2019.
32 *New York Herald-Tribune*, 25 March 1951
33 Richard Rodgers, *Musical Stages: an Autobiography*, Random House, New York, 1975, p. 273.
34 In an email dated 12 August 2010, Peter Pinne told me, "Last year when I was in Thailand as a guest of the Thai Tourist Agency I actually asked about *The King and I* and they said that the movie had been screened there, the songs were sung there, and that nobody these days worried about the depiction of Thailand in it.
35 Kathryn Edney, "Integration through the wide open back door: African Americans respond to *Flower Drum Song* (1958)", *Studies in Musical Theatre*, Vol. 4 No. 3, 2010, p. 263.
36 Sabina M. Thalheim, *A Hundred Million Messages: Reflections on Representation in Rodgers and Hammerstein's Flower Drum Song*, MA Thesis from Ohio State University, 2013, p. 58
37 "A New Musical by Rodgers and Hwang", *New York Times*, 13 October 2002.
38 Facebook message to the author dated 3 September 2019.
39 *The Globe and Mail*, Toronto, 6 May 2003.
40 Jared Brown, *Moss Hart – A Prince of the Theatre*, Back Stage Books, New York, 2006., p.295
41 Steve Nallon, "The Britishness of the British Musical", published in *Musical Stages*, London, 2000 (no date or volume given)
42 Jennifer Oates , "Brigadoon: Lerner and Loewe's Scotland", Studies in Musical Theatre, Vol. 3 No. 1, 2009, p. 91
43 Colin McArthur, Braveheart, Brigadoon and the Scots: Distortions of Scotland in Hollywood Cinema, I.B. Taurus, London, 2003, pp 2-3.
44 Laure Farrell-Wortman, "The Riverdance phenomenon and the development of Irish identity in the global era", *Studies in Musical Theatre*, Vol 4 No 3, pp. 317-318.
45 Jean Graham-Jones, "'The truth is... My Soul is With You': Documenting a Tale of Two Evitas", Theatre Survey, May 2005, p. 76.
46 Cited in Philip Freund, *Oriental Theatre*, Peter Owen, London, p. 745.
47 Ben Brantley, "Genuinely Ugly Americans, as Viewed by the Japanese", *New York Times*, 11 July 2002
48 *Village Voice*, New York, 16 July, 2002

[49] William Andrews, "From Broadway to Yokohama as Japanese theater gets a new home", CNN Asia, 8 February 2011, http://www.cnngo.com/tokyo/visit/broadway-yokohama-873802

[50] *Village Voice*, 30 November, 2004

[51] Lisa Lambert, Greg Morrison, "Message from a Nightingale", from *The Drowsy Chaperone*. © SOCAN

[52] Raymond Knapp, The American Musical and the Formation of National Identity, Princeton University Press, Princeton, NJ, 2005, p. 279-80

[53] Jessica Hillman, "Goyim on the Roof: embodying authenticity in Leveaux's Fiddler on the Roof", Studies in Musical Theatre, Portsmouth, Vol. 1 No. 1, p. 25

[54] "A Legacy Cut Loose", Thane Rosenbaum, *Los Angeles Times*, 15 February, 2004.

[55] Email to author dated 21 February 2005.

[56] Stephen Cole, "The Road to the Road to Qatar", *Dramatists Guild Quarterly*, November/December 2008

[57] Email to author 24 November 2008.

[58] Kathryn Boughton, "The Quiet Composer", *Litchfield County Times*, 12 June 2009.

[59] Lawson Taitte, "Autobiographical Road to Qatar proves a bubbly tour of creating a musical", *Dallas Morning News*, 11 October 2009

[60] *Dallas Voice*, 16 October 2009.

[61] Mel Atkey, *Broadway North: The Dream of a Canadian Musical Theatre*, Natural Heritage Books, Toronto, 2006, p17-18

Universality Part 2: A Sense of Time and Place

[1] Gordon Pinsent, *By the Way*, Stoddart, Toronto, 1992, p. 232

[2] *Montreal Gazette*, 22 July 1976.

[3] Gordon Pinsent (with George Anthony), *Next*, McClelland and Stewart, Toronto, 2012, p. 156.

[4] Atkey, *Broadway North*, p. 14.

[5] Engel, *Words with Music*, p. 131.

[6] *Blue Angels and Pirate Jennys*, BBC Radio 4, 25 February 2006.

[7] Engel, ibid, p.263.

[8] When I was in high school, my drama teacher even told me that *The Music Man* was based on *The Rainmaker*, the source of *110 in the Shade*. However, Meredith Willson began writing *The Music Man* in 1951, and *The Rainmaker* wasn't produced until 1954.

[9] Raymond Knapp, *The American Musical and the Formation of National Identity*, Princeton University Press, 2005, p. 144.

10 Roberta Freund Schwartz, "Iowa Stubborn: Meredith Willson's musical characterization of his fellow Iowans", *Studies in Musical Theatre*, Volume Three, Number One, Intellect Ltd., Bristol, 2009, p. 31.
11 Stephen Sondheim, *Look, I Made a Hat – Collected Lyrics (1981-2011)*, Virgin Nooks, London, 2011, p.309
12 Meredith Willson, *But He Doesn't Know the Territory*, University of Minnesota Press, 2009, p. 48.
13 Ibid, p. 37.
14 Engel, *Words with Music*, p. 247.
15 Tom Jones, "The Making of 110 in the Shade", *Theatre Week*, 20 July 1992.
16 Tom Jones, *Making Musicals*, Limelight Editions, New York, 1998, p. 112.
17 John S. Wilson, "'110 in the Shade' 1963 musical, revived", *New York Times*, 8 June 1982.
18 "Never Will I Marry", from *Greenwillow*, music and lyrics by Frank Loesser, © Frank Music Corp.
19 *New York Times*, 20 March 1960.
20 *Time*, 21 March 1960.
21 Sarah T. Ellis, "Establishing (and re-establishing) a sense of place: musical orientation in *The Sound of Music*", *Studies in Musical Theatre*, Vol. 3 No. 3, Intellect Ltd., 2009.
22 At the time a part of the Austro-Hungarian Empire that was later lost to Italy and is now in Croatia.
23 Albert Williams, "The Jim and Warren Show", *The Bleader*, 9 January 2009.
24 Rick Kogan, "The original 'Grease' was born in Chicago, wild, funny and new in 1971", *Chicago Tribune*, 29 January 2016
25 Chris Jones, "Bring back our own, original R-rated 'Grease'", *Chicago Tribune*, 8 January 2009.
26 Robert Simonson, "Grease returns to its raunchy roots", *Playbill*, 31 March 2011.
27 Kevin McKeough, "NOT TEEN ANGELS: The original version of the sanitized 1978 film opens at American Theater Company", *Chicago Magazine*, 3 May 2011
28 Chris Jones, "Young, tough and heartfelt, it's the real 'Grease'", *Chicago Tribune*, 4 May 2011.

Craft

1 Letter to the author dated 17 February 1982.
2 Letter from the Guild of Canadian Musical Theatre Writers to the author dated 26 July 1984.
3 Atkey, *Broadway North*, p.136.

[4] "The Sounds of Silence", © 1964 Paul Simon
[5] "Leonard Cohen on Hallelujah", telegraph.co.uk, 19 December 2008, accessed on 11 June 2009.
[6] "Bob Dylan: The Paul Zollo Interview", *American Songwriter*, 9 January 2012.
[7] Email to author dated 16 March 2012.
[8] Stephen Sondheim, *Finishing the Hat*, p. xxv-xxvi.
[9] "My Cup Runneth Over", from *I Do! I Do!*, lyrics by Tom Jones, music by Harvey Schmidt © 1966 Chappell & Co. Inc.
[10] Sondheim, p. xxvii
[11] Ibid.
[12] Lyrics by Alan Jay Lerner, Music by Frederick Loewe, Chappell-Harms, 1956. From *My Fair Lady*.
[13] Pop music boasts its own ideas of craft, but that is outside of our remit.
[14] http://howlround.com/a-slushy-in-the-face-musical-theater-music-and-the-uncool accessed 24 June 2014.
[15] Email from Nelles Van Loon dated 3 July 2003.
[16] William Grimes, "'Titanic' Adds Another Feather to His Cap", *New York Times*, 18 May 1997, p. 34.
[17] *An Evening with Alan Jay Lerner*.
[18] Ian Stewart, "Where have all the melodies gone?", tokafi.com/news/where-have-all-the-melodies-gone 2009 Accessed 6 January 2019.
[19] Alissa Wilkinson, "Mary Poppins Returns – with a sadder story and forgettable songs", *Vox*, 18 December 2018.
[20] Steven McIntosh, "Mary Poppins Returns cast defend 'forgettable' songs", BBC Entertainment & Arts, 19 December 2018.
[21] Rupert Christiansen, "Where are the great new musicals?", *Telegraph*, 14 March 2015.
[22] Joan Peyser, *Bernstein: A Biography*, Beech Tree Books, New York, 1987, p. 248.
[23] Mel Atkey, *Breaking Into Song: Essays, Articles and Interviews on Musical Theatre*, Friendlysong Books, Vancouver, 2017, p. 83.
[24] Tom Jones, *Making Musicals*, p. 89
[25] Based on a play by Sidney Howard (1901-1939).
[26] Some sources give Franklin Lacey (1917-88) as a co-author of the story, although Willson is the sole credited author of the actual book. Judging by Willson's memoir, Lacey may have been more a dramaturg than a co-author.
[27] Almost; I and a few others will continue to fight for them.
[28] Deborah Brevoort and Fred Carl traveled to Nairobi, Kenya in 2018, which grew out of their relationship with Kenyan musician

Eric Wainaina (1973-), whom they had met at the Sundance Institute's theatre lab. He is the author and composer of *Lwanda, Man of Stone*, based on Kenyan folklore. (More on him in the chapter "Africa: Freedom is Coming".)

[29] *Be More Chill* music and lyrics by Joe Iconis and book by Joe Tracz based on a novel by Ned Vizzini. Produced at Pershing Square Signature Center in 2018, intended to transfer to Lyceum Theatre in February 2019. It officially opened on 10 March of the same year, and closed on 11 August 2019.

[30] Email dated 4 December 2018.

[31] Email dated 5 December 2018.

[32] Could this have been done if the show had been written by multiple authors? You tell me.

[33] We attended Goldsmiths together in 2014-15.

[34] Facebook message dated 4 December 2018.

[35] See Aristotle's *Poetics*.

[36] Email from Susan Cluff dated 1 July 2003.

[37] Email to the author, dated 22 August 2003.

Europe after Hitler

[38] In France, this was not the first time this had happened; after the fall of the Second Empire, Offenbach and all that he stood for largely fell out of favour.

[39] Cited in the liner notes for the 1967 Paris revival cast CD, VEGA 826-2

[40] Email to author dated 21 September 2009.

[41] This has been a common practice. A quarter of a century later, the French working classes in *Les Misérables* spoke with a cockney, and in the Dutch version of *My Fair Lady*, Eliza Doolittle speaks with a Jordanees dialect (from the working class De Jordaan area of Amsterdam).

[42] Cited in Tom Vallance, David Heneker obituary, *The Independent*, London, 8 March 2001., and in Didier C. Deutsch's liner notes for the 1961 Original Broadway Cast CD of *Irma la Douce*, Sony Broadway SK 48018

[43] Ira Henry Freeman, "Comprenez-vous Irma?", *New York Times*, 25 September 1960.

[44] Peter Brook, *The Shifting Point*, Harper & Row, New York, 1987, p.37.

[45] Email from Elizabeth Seal to the author dated 12 May 2019.

[46] Harold Hobson, "Irma Translated", *Sunday Times*, 20 July 1958.

[47] *Punch*, 23 July 1958.

[48] *The Times*, 18 July 1958, p.3.

[49] Philip Hope-Wallace, *Manchester Guardian*, 18 July 1958.
[50] *Obsevrer*, London, 20 July 1958.
[51] Harry Weaver, "What's Irma Got?", *Daily Herald*, 18 July 1958.
[52] Anthony Cookman, "Good, clean fun in the Place Pigalle", *The Tatler & Bystander*, 30 July 1958.
[53] During the number "There is Only One Paris for That"
[54] Email to the author dated 28 May 2019.
[55] Howard Taubman, "Place Pigalle Genially Satirized; 'Irma la Douce' Has Debut at Plymouth Gallic Musical Turns Vice Into Innocence", *New York Times*, 30 September 1960.
[56] *Time*, 10 October 1960.
[57] *Daily News*, New York, 30 September 1960.
[58] *Journal American*, New York, 30 September 1960.
[59] *New York Post*, 30 September 1960.
[60] *Herald-Tribune*, New York, 30 September 1960.
[61] Howard Kissel, *David Merrick – The Abominable Showman*, Applause Book,s New York, 1993, p. 193.
[62] Ed Sikov, *On Sunset Boulevard – The Life and Times of Billy Wilder*, Hyperion, New York, 1998, p. 470.
[63] Walter Mirisch, *I Thought We Were Making Movies, Not History*, University of Wisconsin Press, 2008, p. 156
[64] Ibid, p.471.
[65] *The Guardian*, 14 February 1964.
[66] Katherine Knorr, "'Irma': Bravos for a Good Laugh", *New York Times*, 4 August 2009
[67] *La Dennière Heure*, 25 February, 1971, cited in the liner notes for the 1967 Paris revival cast CD, VEGA 826-2.
[68] Email to the author dated 27 December 2010.
[69] *La Dennière Heure*, ibid.
[70] "New Revue in Manhattan", *Time*, 24 November 1958
[71] Tom Shea, *Broadway's Most Wanted*, Brassey's Inc., Washington, D.C., 2004, p.157.
[72] Agnès Varda, *L'Univers de Jacques Demy*, Ciné Tamaris, 1995 (Distributed by Optimum Releasing with the DVD *The Umbrellas of Cherbourg*).
[73] Varda, ibid.
[74] *The Guardian*, London, 22 March 2011.
[75] *Variety*, 22 March 2011.
[76] Document supplied by Grover Dale to the author, dated 9 May 2019.
[77] Jonathan Rosenbaum, "Not the same old song and dance", *Chicago Reader*, 17 March 2000.

[78] Bill Higgins, "Before 'La La Land,' 'Umbrellas of Cherbourg' Had Tinseltown Singing", *Hollywood Reporter*, 9 January 2017.
[79] Alan Riding, "The Real Paradox: Musical Comedy Made in France", *New York Times*, New York, October 20, 2002
[80] Ben Brantley, "A French Milquetoast's Talent Lights the Fuse of Mischief", *New York Times*, 21 October 2002.
[81] Email to the author dated 10 October 2009.
[82] Behr, Edward. *"The Complete Book of Les Misérables"*. Arcade Publishing, London, 1989, p.50
[83] Sheridan Morley and Ruth Leon, *Hey Mr. Producer!*, Back Stage Books, New York, 1998, p.91.
[84] Email to the author dated 25 January 2019.
[85] Vermette, p.24
[86] Kurt Gänzl, *Musicals*, Carlton Books, London, 2001, p. 247.
[87] Nancy Rosati, "What's New on the Rialto? Interview with Michael Kunze of Dance of the Vampires", *Talkin' Broadway*, 27 October 2002.
[88] Email to the author dated 9 June 2009.
[89] Ellis Nassour, "Michael Kunze: The Sondheim and Lloyd Webber of Europe", *Broadway Stars*, 5 December 2002.
[90] Rialto was the name of New York's previous theatre district (from the 1870s until the turn of the century), located on Broadway between 14th and 23rd streets, in the area of Union Square. This in turn was named after the commercial area of Venice. "Rialto gossip" is a New York expression for the showbiz grapevine. It may have originated with "News and Gossip of the Rialto", a column in the *New York Times*.
[91] Email to the author dated 18 May 2009.
[92] Patrick Van Den Hanenberg, "DE MUSICALS VAN ANNIE M.G. SCHMIDT In nieuwe versie van 'Heerlijk' wordt de titel wel verklaard", ("The Musicals Of Annie M.G. Schmidt In new version of 'Heerlijk' ('Delicious'), the title does get explained"), *De Volkskrant*, 9 October 1998, re-edited on 16 January 2009 (translated from Dutch for the author by René Driessen).
[93] Ibid
[94] Ibid
[95] Ibid
[96] Marliese Simons, "THEATER: A Musical 'Cyrano': Can a Dutch hit sell on Broadway?", *New York Times*, 21 November 1993.
[97] Ben Brantley, "Cyrano's Flights Have Touched Down on West 52nd Street", *New York Times*, 22 November 1993.
[98] *Variety*, 22 November 1993.
[99] *Musical Stages*, Issue 60, Winter 2008/9, p. 21.

[100] Email to author dated 9 July 2009.
[101] Email to author dated 7 April 2010
[102] *Variety*, 24 Sept 2009
[103] 15 March 2010 https://www.abbaontv.com/2010/description-hall-of-fame.html (accessed 22 July 2018)
[104] Email to the author dated 29 June 2018.
[105] John Francis Lane, "Pietro Garinei, obituary", *The Guardian*, London, 5 June 2006
[106] Ron Moody, *A Still Untitled (Not Quite) Autobiography*, JR Books, London, 2010, p. 74.
[107] Milton Shuman, *Evening News*, London, 4 July 1963.
[108] Email to author dated 25 June 2018.
[109] "Theater: 'Rugantino' Is Transplanted From Rome; An Italian Musical With English Titles Opens", *New York Times*, 7 February 1964.
[110] *Guardian*, ibid.
[111] Fabian de la Cruz Polanco, *Magia pura y total – (Historia del Teatro Musical en la Ciudad de México 1952-2011)*, Segunda edición, Mexico City, 2012, p. 6.
[112] "L'amico In Più", www.aggiungiunpostoatavola.info/piattella.htm (accessed and translated 22 June 2018)
[113] Michael Ross, "A Ha'penny for his thoughts", *The Sunday Times*, London, 12 June 2005.
[114] Patricia O' Callaghan, RTE. 15 June 2005.
[115] Colin Murphy, "Colin Murphy ventures upriver to check out the Ha'penny Bridge", *The Village*, Dublin, 1 July 2005.
[116] Richard Ouzounian, "Ha'penny Bridge Topples in Toronto", *Variety*, 20 February 2008.
[117] Richard Ouzounian, "Producer cancels North American premiere of Ha'penny Bridge", *Star*, Toronto, 21 February 2008.
[118] Email to author dated 22 May 2009.
[119] Charles Isherwood, "It's That Old Story: Spies, Physics and Gaelic", *New York Times*, 5 December 2008.
[120] Ben Brantley, "A Love Affair With Music, Maybe With Each Other", *The New York Times*, 6 December 2011.
[121] Peter Baker and Susan Glasser, *Kremlin Rising: Vladimir Putin's Russia and the End of Revolution*, Simon and Schuster, New York, 2005, p.156
[122] Annalisa Quinn, "A Musical About Slobodan Milosevic Stirs Memories in Kosovo", *New York Times*, 7 March 2018.
[123] See Dr. Michael Scott's BBC documentary series *Ancient Greece: The Greatest Show on Earth* first broadcast 27 August 2013 on BBC Four.

[124] David L. Ulin, "In David Prudhomme's graphic novel 'Rebetiko,' a music revolution", *Los Angeles Times*, 1 October 2013.
[125] Gail Holst, *Road to Rembetika: Music Of A Greek Sub-Culture, Songs Of Love, Sorrow And Hashish*, Anglo-Hellenic Publishing, 1975
[126] Lydia Papadimitriou,"More Than a Pale Immitation: Narrative, Music and Dance in Two Greek Film Musicals of the 1960s", *Musicals: Hollywood and Beyond*, edited by Bill Marshall and Robynn Jeananne Stilwell, Intellect, 2000, p. 121/
[127] "Greek farce: 'Mother' play satirizes corruption", *Washington Times*, 4 January 2010. https://pulitzercenter.org/reporting/greek-farce-mother-play-satirizes-corruption Accessed 11 April 2018.
[128] Thodōros Chatzēpantazēs and Lila Maraka, *Athinaiki epitheorisi*, Ekdotikē Hermēs, 1977, p. 22, cited (and translated) in Hans van Maanen, S.E. Wilmer, *Theatre Worlds in Motion: Structures, Politics and Developments in the Countries of Western Europe*, Brill | Rodopi, Leiden, Netherlands, 1998, p. 269.
[129] Aliki Bacopoulou-Halls, "Theatre Systems of Greece", *Theatre worlds in motion : structures, politics and developments in the countries of Western Europe* edited by Hans van Maanen and S E Wilmer, Rodopi, Amsterdam, 1998.
[130] *Embros*, 9 August 1915.
[131] Lydia Papadimitriou, *The Greek Film Musical – A Critical and Cultural History*, McFarland & Company, Jefferson, North Carolina, 2006, p. 25
[132] John Chapman, "Melina Dazzles Broadway", *Daily News*, New York, 13 April, 1967.
[133] Gaver, Jack, " 'Illya Darling' Depends Largely on Greek Star", *St. Petersburg Times'*, April 13, 1967
[134] CD liner notes for *Street of Dreams* Music by Manos Hadjidakis, Lyrics by Manos Hadjidakis, Alexis Solomos, Iakovos Kambanelis, Nikos Gatsos and Minos Argyrakis. EMI 50999 516433 2 4
[135] Nana Mouskouri, "Chante la Grèce", Fontana 6325303
[136] Papadimitriou, p. 45.
[137] Giannis Soldatos, *Istoria tou Ellinikou kinematographou*, [History of the Greek Cinema] Volume 2, Egokeros, Athens, 1989, p. 246 (translation by Lydia Papadimitriou)
[138] Eleftheria Pantziou, " Anthony Burk: 'You don't choose to become an actor, it's a need!', *Embassy News*, 13 April 2016. embassynews.net/2016/04/13/anthony-burk-you-dont-choose-to-become-an-actor-its-a-need-interview/
[139] Leon Kontente, *Smyrene et l'Occident, de Antiquité au XXIe siècle*, Montigny, 2005, pp. 570, 581, cited in Philip Mansell, *Levant – Spleandour and Catastrophe on the Mediterranean*, Yale University Press, New Haven, 2010, p. 165.

"Who Will Buy?" Lionel Bart and the Post-war British Musical

[1] Michael Walsh (with Mary Cronin), "Magician of the Musical", *Time*, New York, 18 January 1988.
[2] *The Stage*, London, 1 April 2010, p.5
[3] Ron Moody, *A Still Untitled (Not Quite) Autobiography*, p.158.
[4] Ibid, p. 159.
[5] Michael Coveney, "Oliver!: The real story of Britain's greatest musical", *The Independent*, 9 January 2009.
[6] David Roper, *Bart!*, Pavillion Books, London, 1994, pp. 59-60.
[7] Liner notes from the original cast recording of *Passion Flower Hotel*, 1965. CBS BPG62598
[8] Italian for "realism", referring to an Italian movement in both opera and literature towards naturalism.
[9] Wright, *Tanner's*, p. 139.
[10] Wright, *Tanner's* p. 168.
[11] Gänzl, *The Musical*, p.341.
[12] Lerner, *The Musical Theatre*, p.225, 234.
[13] Michael Coveney, *Financial Times*, 2 November 1984.
[14] Kurt Gänzl, *The British Musical Theatre Vol. II*, Macmillan, London, 1986, p. 1127.
[15] Ian Bradley, *You've Got to Have a Dream – The Message of the Musical*, SCM Press, London, 2004, p. 190.
[16] Piers Ford, "Big Spender: Barbara Dickson", *Show Music*, Vol. 16, No.1, Spring 2000.
[17] *Evening Standard*, London, 14 April 2011
[18] *The Guardian*, 14 April 2011.
[19] George Stiles, "Don't Sing the Blues", *The Stage*, 8 October 2011.
[20] *The Times* 10th December 2010

[21] *The Independent*, 14 December 2010

[22] Henry Hitchings, *Evening Standard*, 10 Dec 2010
[23] "RSC already set to recoup on Matilda the Musical", *The Stage*, 12 January 2012.
[24] Sarah Whitfield, "Two different roads to new musicals in 2011 London: *London Road* and *Road Show*", *Studies in Musical Theatre*, Vol. 5 No. 3, pp309-310.
[25] *The Stage*, London, 21 April 2011.

Canada – "Still Deciding What it Will Be"

[1] Robert Fulford, "Mary Pickford, Glenn Gould, Anne of Green Gables, and Captain Kirk: Canadians in the world's imagination" Lecture at The Hebrew University, Jerusalem, June 5, 1997
[2] Rudyard Griffiths, *Who We Are – A Citizen's Manifesto*, Douglas & McIntyre, Vancouver, 2009, pp. 148-49.
[3] Sara Miller Llana, "Northern Composure", *The Christian Science Monitor Weekly*, 25 February 2019, p. 28
[4] Interview by Richard Williams in *Melody Maker*, London, 29 May, 1971.
[5] *The Times Magazine*, London, 27 November 2004, p. 13.
[6] Jason Schneider, *Whispering Pines: The Northern Roots of American Music from Hank Snow to the Band*, ECW Press, Toronto, 2009, p. 7.
[7] J.E, Middleton, "The Theatre in Canada", *Canada and Its Provinces Vol. 12*, Publishers Association of Canada Ltd., Toronto, 1913, p. 661.
[8] Bernard K. Sandwell, "The Annexation of Our Stage", *Canadian Magazine*, Vol. 38. No. 1, November 1911, p. 23.
[9] Murray Ginsberg, *They Loved to Play – Memories of the Golden Age of Canadian Music*, East End Books, Toronto, 1998. p.116
[10] Pierre Berton, *The Last Good Year*, Doubleday, Toronto, 1997.
[11] Tom Hawthorn, *The Year Canadians Lost Their Minds and Found Their Country*, Douglas & McIntyre, Vancouver, 2017, p. 7.
[12] You could go back even further; *Due South* built on the foundations of *Seeing Things*, Louis del Grande's 1980s comedy series about a newspaper reporter who receives psychic visions.
[13] *Time Out Toronto*, Time Out Guides, London, 2007, p. 218.
[14] S.G. Lee, "Size Matters: A Consideration of the Canadian Musical", *Brock Review*, Vol. 12, No. 2, Brock University, 2012.
[15] Letter to the author dated 28 April 1986.
[16] Tom Kneebone passed on only two weeks after I interviewed him. In fact, the first thing I did when I heard the news was check the tape to make sure it had recorded…
[17] Eric Nicol and Peter Whalley, *Canada Cancelled Because of Lack of Interest*, Hurtig Publishers, Edmonton, p.130.
[18] "In the Air", *Winnipeg Citizen*, July 14 1948, cited in Christian Riegel, *Challenging Territory: The Writing of Margaret Laurence*, University of Alberta Press, Edmonton, 1997, pp 204-205.
[19] Christopher Hoile, "Les Fridolinades", *Eye Weekly*, Toronto, 1 November, 2010
[20] Atkey, *Broadway North*, p.54.
[21] Mary Harron grew up to direct the films *American Psycho* and *The Notorious Betty Page*
[22] Harron, p. 16.

[23] Fulford, ibid.
[24] Atkey, p. 110.
[25] ibid, p. 112.
[26] ibid, p. 113.
[27] Sandy Thorburn, "Who is the Drowsy Chaperone's Muse?", *Thousand Islands Theatre Programme*, 2009 (courtesy of Lisa Lambert and Sandy Thorburn)
[28] Ibid.
[29] "The Drowsy Chaperone", *Working in the Theatre*, American Theater Wing/City University Television, April 2006
[30] Email to the author dated 2 August 2009.
[31] Susan Dominus, "In The Drowsy Chaperone, Bob Martin's Birthday [sic] present Became His Broadway Debut", *New York Times*, 30 April 2006.
[32] Gordon Bowness, "Musically fanatical", *Xtra!*, Toronto, 28 June 2001.
[33] *NOW*, 25 November 1999.
[34] Phil Hahn, "From the fringes to Broadway: The Drowsy Chaperone", *CTV.ca*, 7 June 2006 http://edmonton.ctv.ca/servlet/an/local/CTVNews/20060607/drowsy_chaperone_060607 accesed 30 July 2009
[35] Email to CASTRECL dated 10 July 2006, used by permission.
[36] *Associated Press*: 1 May 2006
[37] "'Drowsy Chaperone' a sleeping beauty", *New York Daily News*, May 1 2006
[38] "Nostalgic 'Drowsy Chaperone' Opens on Broadway", *New York Times*, May 1 2006
[39] *Star*, Toronto, 24 September 2007.
[40] Matthew Hays, "Can't Stop the Music", *Equity Quarterly*, Canadian Actors' Equity Association, Winter 2010, p.13.
[41] *Working in the Theatre*, ibid.
[42] Email to the author dated 2 August 2009.
[43] "Quaint musical demands we care", Robert Cushman *National Post*, Saturday, November 11, 2006
[44] Ben Brantley, "Male Bonding – It's a Wonderful Friendship", *New York Times*, February 20, 2009.
[45] *Variety*, February 20, 2009
[46] Michael Kuchwara, "Frienship Flowers in 'The Story of My Life'", *Associated Press*, February 20, 2009.
[47] Peter Filichia, "The Story on 'The Story of My Life'", Theatremania.com, February 23, 2009.

[48] Peter Filichia, email dated 24 February 2009, citing Ethan Mordden's *The Happiest Corpse I've Ever Seen : The Last 25 Years of the Broadway Musical* , Palgrave MacMillan, New York, 2004.
[49] Email to the author dated 6 August 2009.
[50] Gary Smith, "The good and the gobblers of 2007", *Hamilton Spectator*, Hamilton, Ontario, December 29, 2007
[51] http://www.niagarafallsreview.ca/ArticleDisplayGenContent.aspx?e=3410, retrieved 22 November 2008.
[52] Richard Ouzounian, "Shaw's Tristan – Too Little, Too Late", *The Star*, Toronto, July 30, 2007.
[53] Jon Kaplan, "Ranney's Double Act", *Now*, Toronto, August 30, 2007.
[54] *Variety*, 9 August 2011.
[55] *The Star*, Toronto, 6 August 2011.
[56] *National Post*, 9 August 2011.
[57] Richard Ouzounian, "Mimi is wickedly, deadly delicious", *The Star*, Toronto, 24 September 2009.
[58] Robert Cushman, "The emancipation of Mimi is a success", *National Post*, 24 September 2009.
[59] *Eye Weekly*, Toronto, 29 September, 2009.
[60] *Downstage Center*, American Theater Wing/XM Satelite Radio, 2 June 2006.
[61] Sheridan College press release dated 4 April 2012.
[62] Facebook message from Michael Rubinoff dated 18 February 2019.
[63] Ben Brantley, "Review: 'Come From Away,' a Canadian Embrace on a Grim Day" *The New York Times*, March 12, 2017
[64] Henry Hitchings, "Touching tale of kindness in face of terror sees human spirit soar", *Evening Standard*, 19 February 2019.
[65] Catherine Lambert, "Come From Away is a hit and a masterpiece", *Sunday Herald Sun*, Melbourne, 20 July 2019.
[66] "West End Comes West", Kamal Al-Solaylee, *Globe and Mail*, Toronto, 14 December, 2006.
[67] Email from Darcie Kennedy dated 20 April 2012.
[68] Robert Enright CBC Manitoba 990 Radio review, May 27, 2005
[69] Morley Walker, *Winnipeg Free Press*, 28 May 2005.
[70] See email to author dated 16 November 2006.
[71] Janet Smith, "Theatre takes centre stage", *The Georgia Straight*, Vancouver, 21-28 June 2012.
[72] "Jesus Christ still a superstar 40 years on", *Evening Standard*, London, 23 March 2012.

[73] Richjard Ouzounian, "Jesus Christ superstar: Five reasons it flopped on Broadway", *Star*, Toronto, 20 June 2012.
[74] Press Release: "Investing in Cultural Spaces That Inspire Performance Excellence: The Governments of Canada and Prince Edward Island Support a Retrofit to the Confederation Centre of the Arts", Office of the Minister of Canadian Heritage and Official Languages, 13 February 2009.

[75] Richard Ouzounian, "Adam Brazier new artistic director at Confederation Centre of the Arts in Charlottetown", *The Star*, 4 November, 2013.
[76] Email dated 1 March 2018.
[77] Jane Taber, "How Ted Dykstra's Evangeline finally made it to the stage", *The Globe and Mail*, 8 July 2013.
[78] David Cooper, "Ted Dykstra's Evangeline doesn't feel fresh, but it tells an important story", *The Globe and Mail*, 6 November 2015, updated 22 March 2018.
[79] Richard Ouzounian, "Evangeline: A triumph from a Canadian tragedy", *The Star*, 7 July 2013.
[80] www.cbc.ca.arts/theatre/story/2009/04/03/cree-opera.html accessed 20 May 2009.
[81] Peter Birnie, "Beyond Eden builds a beautiful bridge", *Vancouver Sun*, 25 January 2010.
[82] "CBC cancels shows, slashes 88 news jobs", http://www.cbc.ca/news/canada/story/2012/04/10/cbc-budget-programs.html, accessed 11 April 2012.
[83] Norman Jewison, *This Terrible Business Has Been Good to Me*, Key Porter Books, Toronto, 2004, p.44.
[84] Quoted in Edward Keenan, "Making a Scene: A Bunch of Youngish Indie Rockers, Political Activists and Small Press Literati are Creating the Cultural History of Toronto", *UTOpia – Towards a New Toronto*, Edited by Jason McBride and Alana Wilcox, Coach House Books, Toronto, 2005, p.24.

Larrikins and Sentimental Blokes: Musicals Down Under

[1] Mark Twain, *Following the Equator*, American Publishing Company, New York, 1897, cited in Tim Flannery, *The Birth of Sydney*, William Heinemann, London, 2003, p. 321.
[2] *Broadway at Bedtime*, JOY-FM, Melbourne, 16 April, 2006.
[3] Agricultural trainee.

4 Except for the *Virgin Encyclopedia of Stage & Film Musicals*, which incorrectly declares he was "Austrian" – only one of many errors in that tome.
5 Claude Kingston, *It Don't Seem a Day Too Much*, Rigby, Adelaide, 1971, p.73
6 *The Advertiser*, Adelaide, 6 September 1920.
7 C.J. De Garis, *The Victories of Failure*, Modern Printing Company, Melbourne, 1925, p. 377.
8 *Sunday Times*, Sydney, 10 October 1920.
9 *The Herald*, Melbourne, 11 October 1920, cited in Frank Van Straten, "The Riddle of *FFF*, a forgotten Australian musical comedy", *Australasian Music Research*, No. 6, 2001, p. 116.
10 Julie Jackson-Trechikoff, "Amateur operatics in Auckland: musical theatre's last frontier", *Studies in Musical Theatre*, Vol. 2 No. 2, Intellect, Bristol, 2008, p.196.
11 Ibid, p.197.
12 *New Zealand Times*, 17 February 1903.
13 Peter Harcourt, *Fantasy and Folly*, Steele Roberts, Wellington, 2002.
14 Cited in Viola Tait, *A Family of Brothers*, Heinemann, Melbourne, 1971, p.215.
15 Malcolm Robertson, "The Australian Theatre: The Situation in the Seventies", *Biala*, Prahran College of Advanced Education, Vol. 1, 1977, No. 13.
16 Cited in "It's Australian—and it's good! The Australian musical Collits' Inn", *National Library of Australia News*, December 2003 Volume XIV Number 3
17 Edmond Samuels, *If the Cap Fits*, Modern Literature Co., Sydney, 1972, p. 74
18 According to English theatre historian Philip L. Scowcroft, author of *British Light Music Composers*, some additional songs were contributed to the London production by musical director Percival Mackey.
19 Ibid, p.90.
20 Really Useful Theatres archives
21 Letter from Peter Stannard, dated 11 May 2012.
22 Letter to the author dated 9 November 2012.
23 The word has a number of possible origins, all English: it could be a corruption of "larking"; a Cornish word "larrikin" meaning "hooligan", or a Black Country name for "togue", i.e. an outspoken person.
24 In *A Family of Brothers*, Viola Tait says it was in 1957.

[25] Viola Tait says it tried out at Sydney's Empire Theatre in front of an audience of fifty.
[26] Interview with Nancy Brown by Beryl Davis, 15 March 1989, Transcript, p. 39, National Library of Australia Oral History Collection, ORAL TRC 2426, cited in Margaret Marshall and Simon Platt, *Making a Song and Dance*, a booklet to accompany the exhibition of the same name at the Victorian Arts Centre, Melbourne, 2004.
[27] Robyn Archer, "The Politics of the Musical", *Australasian Drama Studies*, Vol. 1 No. 2, April 1983.
[28] *The Age*, Melbourne, 22 December 1958.
[29] Cited by Peter Pinne, *ON STAGE*, Spring 2003 Vo.04 No.04
[30] Document from Peter Pinne dated 29 December 2008.
[31] Leonard Radic, "Local Novel Set to Music", *Age*, 16 May 1966.
[32] Jean Battersby, "Bright Musical from Australian Novel", *Canberra Times*, 7 June 1966.
[33] Clark Forbes, *Sun News–Pictorial*, January 1988
[34] D. L. G., "The Drama Report", *The Armidalian – The Magazine of The Armidale School, N.S.W.*, December 1978, Volume 80
[35] Ray Stanley, "Whispers, Rumours and Facts", *Theatre Australia*, September, 1979.
[36] Norman Kessell, "Whispers, Rumours and Facts", *Theatre Australia*, February, 1980.
[37] LinkedIn message to author dated 16 July 2018.
[38] A Melbourne TV variety show that ran between 1957-1970.
[39] Leonard Radic, "The winning ways of little Australians", *The Age*, Melbourne, 24 June 1988, Retrieved 1 March 2016.
[40] Debbie Kruger, "Seven Little Australians Review", *Variety*, July 6, 1988.
[41] Peter Pinne interviewed by Rob Morrison, *Musical Theatre Melodies*, InnerFM, Melbourne, 26 June, 2018.
[42] Letter to author dated 12 March 2009.
[43] Ben Brantley, "Theater Review: Flash Of 70's Sequins", *The New York Times* , 17October 2003, accessed 13 November, 2017
[44] Robin Usher, "How to Stage an Epic", *The Age*, 13 September 2004.
[45] *Broadway at Bedtime*, ibid.
[46] *Talking Heads with Peter Thompson*, 13 August 2007, http://www.abc.net.au/talkingheads/txt/s2001093.htm
[47] "Musical a sure hit", *Courier-Mail*, Brisbane, January 12, 2007.
[48] Gary Young, "Creating an Australian musical freak show", *Arts Hub*, 2 february 2007,

http://www.artshub.com.au/au/news.asp?sType=view&catId=1069&sc=&sId=152277 accessed 16 January 2008

[49] Bryce Hallett, "Knockout Aussie tale puts life back into musicals", *Herald-Sun*, Melbourne, February 5, 2007.

[50] Rosemary Duffy, *State of the Arts*, February 8, 2007

[51] Email to the author dated 28 June 2018.

[52] Makeham, Paul B, "Singing the landscape: 'Bran Nue Dae'". *Australasian Drama Studies*(28) (1996):pp. 117-132.

[53] J, Eccles, "Bran Nue Dae", *The West Australian*, 5 March 1991.

[54] Catherine Lambert, "Top Talent Tripped by Production", *Sunday Herald Sun*, 11 July 1993.

[55] Robyn Archer, "The music of survival, pride and indominability", http://www.australiacouncil.gov.au/__data/assets/pdf_file/0018/32382/04_aia_music.pdf accessed 28 April 2012.

[56] Veronica Kelly, "Shadows After the Sunshine", *The Australian*, December 1999.

[57] "Priscilla hits the West End", *Australian Times*, London, 17 March 2009, p.7.

[58] Ben Wardle, "Donovan a king among queens", *London News*, 24 March 2009, p.3.

[59] Martha de Lacey, "Carry on camping, Jase", *London Lite*, 24 March 2009, p.27.

[60] *Daily Express*, London, 24 March 2009.

[61] "Wild ride for Priscilla Queen of the Desert", *Evening Standard*, London, 24 March 2009.

[62] Michael Billington, "Priscilla: queen of the desert but not the Palace theatre", *The Guardian*, 24 March 2009, p. 9.

[63] *Independent*, London, 24 March 2009.

[64] *Spectator*, London, 28 March 2009, p. 9.

[65] *Variety*, 27 October 2010.

[66] Patrick Healy, "A Broadway Makeover for 'Priscilla' Queens", *New York Times*, 10 March 2011.

[67] Healy, ibid.

[68] *New York Times*, 21 March 2011.

[69] *Broadway at Bedtime*, ibid.

[70] *Stage Whispers Performing Arts Magazine*, May-June 2008, Volume 17, Number 3.

[71] *Theatremania*, 21 September 2008.

[72] *Sydney Morning Herald*, 21 July 1007.

[73] *The Observer*, London, 22 July 2007.

[74] *The Stage*, London, 24 July 2007.

⁷⁵ Rosemary Neill, "Nobody can stop the music", *The Australian*, November 10, 2007.

⁷⁶ Diana Simmonds, "This Kookaburra Is Mort", http://www.stagenoise.com/newsdisplay.php?id=219, January 4th 2009
⁷⁷ http://theatrenotes.blogspot.com/2007/07/sondheim-not-happy.html (accessed 7 July 2018)
⁷⁸ David Spicer, "What Cooked Kookaburra?", *Stage Whispers*, March-April 2009 Vol. 18 No. 2, p. 52.
⁷⁹ Peter Cousens, "My biggest regret is not being able to carry on", *Sydney Morning Herald*, 2 June 2009.
⁸⁰ Bryce Hallett and Louise Schwartzkoff, "Troubled Kookaburra retreats into silence", *Sydney Morning Herald*, 5 March 2009.
⁸¹ Deborah Jones, *The Australian*, Sydney, 17 October 2018.
⁸² Cassie Tongue, "This new musical takes an intriguing slice of Australian theatrical history", *Time Out Sydney*, 18 October 2018.
⁸³ *The Age*, Melbourne, 15 February 1958, p. 19

South Africa: "Freedom is Coming"

¹ Lerner, *The Musical Theatre*, p. 9.
² P.J. Powers, *Here I Am*, Penguin, London, 2014
³ Anthony Sampson, *Drum: The Making of a Magazine*, Jonathan Ball Publishers, Johannesburg, 2005, p. 197.
⁴ Lewis Nkosi, *Home and Exile*, Longmans, 1965, p. 19.
⁵ From the foreward by Harry Bloom to *King Kong – The Superb African Jazz Opera*, Fontana Books, London, 1961, p. 9-10
⁶ Incidentally, one of the co-adapters of "The Lion Sleeps Tonight", George David Weiss was also partly responsible for "I Can't Help Falling in Love", which was based on "Plaisir d'amour", written in 1784 by Jean-Paul-Égide Martini (1741-1816). Weiss was also a collaborator on three Broadway musicals: *Mr. Wonderful* (1956), *First Impressions* (1959) and *Maggie Flynn* (1968).
⁷ By this, he presumably means British Actors Equity and the Musicians Union, two separate organisations.
⁸ Bloom, p. 10.
⁹ "King Kong and Toxic Nostalgia", *sigwenjazz*, 12 January 2017, https://sisgwenjazz.wordpress.com/2017/01/12/king-kong-and-toxic-nostalgia/
¹⁰ Mona Glasser, *King Kong – A Venture in the Theatre*, Norman Howell, Cape Town, 1960, p. 3
¹¹ Glasser, p. 13.

[12] Todd Matshikiza and John Matshikiza, *With the Lid Off – South African Insights from Home and Abroad 1959-2000*, M&G Books, Milpark, 2000, p. 99.
[13] Bloom, *King Kong*, p. 14.
[14] Glasser, p. 11.
[15] Goldreich turned out to be a communist agitator who would later stage a rather sensational jail-break.
[16] Glasser, p. 37.
[17] Pat Williams, *King Kong – Our Knot of Time and Music*, Portobello Books, London, 2017, p. 73
[18] Matshikiza & Matshikiza, *With the Lid Off*, p. 100
[19] , p. 68.
[20] Ibid., p.127.
[21] Glasser, p. 13.
[22] Bloom, *King Kong*, p. 11-12.
[23] Glasser, p. 33.
[24] Matshikiza & Matshikiza, *With the Lid Off*, p. 95.
[25] David Coplan, *In Township Tonight! South Africa's Black City Music and Theatre*, Jacana Media, Auckland Park, 2007, p. 214
[26] Hugh Masakela (with D. Michael Cheers), *Still Grazing – the Musical Journey of Hugh Masakela*, Three Rivers Press, New York, 2004, p. 98.
[27] My alma mater.
[28] Andrew Walter Oliphant and Ivan Vladislav, editors, *Ten Years Of Staffrider 1978-1988*, Ravan Press, Johannesburg, 1988
[29] Todd Matshikiza, *Chocolates for My Wife*, Hodder & Stoughton, London, 1961, 122-3
[30] Email to the author, 18 November 2017.
[31] Matshikiza, *Chocolates*, p.122-3, 125
[32] Email to the author, 13 November 2017.
[33] Email to the author, 18 November 2017.
[34] Williams, p.80.
[35] Email to author dated 31 July 2018.
[36] Tucker, p. 129.
[37] Matshikiza & Matshikiza, *With the Lid Off*, p. 14.
[38] Williams, p. 149.
[39] Lewis Nkosi, *Home and Exile*, pp 23-4.
[40] Tucker, p. 132.
[41] *The Star*, Johannesburg, 7 August 1959.
[42] Matshikiza & Matshikiza, *With the Lid Off*, p. 96.
[43] There is controversy as to whether Sontonga wrote both music and lyrics, orwhether he used a melody by Welsh composer Joseph

Parry (1841-1903). Xhosa poet Samuel Edward Krune Mqhayi (1875-1945) later added seven more verses.
[44] Email to the author dated 21 October 2008.
[45] Matshikiza & Matshikiza, *With the Lid Off*, p. 100
[46] Angus Wilson, "South Africa – A Visit to My Mother's Land", *Reflections in a Writer's Eye*, Viking Penguin, New York, 1986, p. 72.
[47] *Times*, London, Feb 24, 1961.
[48] Bernth Lindfors, "Charles Dickens and the Zulus", *Africans on Stage: Studies in Ethnological Show Business*, Inadiana University Press, Bloomington, 1999, p. 78.
[49] Williams, p. 203.
[50] Tucker, p.133.
[51] "Cape Town Charge Against Author",*Times*, London, Feb 24 1961.
[52] David Coplan, *In Township Tonight! South Africa's Black City Music and Theatre Second Edition*, Jacana Media (Pty) Ltd, 2007
[53] Tucker, p. 131.
[54] Williams, p. 207
[55] Tucker, p.134.
[52] Williams, p. 243.
[57] Bob Hitchcock, "'King Kong' went all wrong", *Rand Daily Mail*, Johannesburg, May 3, 1979.
[58] Email to the author, 8 November 2017.
[59] A "minim" is a half note in British English.
[60] Tucker, p. 161.
[61] https://www.youtube.com/watch?v=0Hr75pqA8bo accessed 29 November 2017
[62] Words & Music - Jeremy Taylor © 1961 MPA
[63] Rex Reed, "Fun From South Africa", *New York Times*, March 20, 1966.
[64] *Times*, April 10, 1964.
[65] *New York Times*, March 8, 1966.
[66] Tucker, p. 158.
[67] Tucker, p.45.
[68] Tucker, p. 297.
[69] *Times*, London, 20 November 1975, p. 10.
[70] *Sunday Times*, 23 November 1975. P.35.
[71] *Time*, 24 January 1975, p. 35.
[72] Jones, ibid., p.68.
[73] *Times*, 4 April 1972, p. 6.
[74] Irving Wardle, "Unfaked Happiness", *The Times*, 25 July 1975, p.7.
[75] SOuth WEstern TOwnships

76 Robert Palmer, "A Musical Born of South African Prtoest", *New York Times*, October 25, 1987.
77 Rina Minervini, "Life with Big Daddy Ngema", Time Out, *Sunday Star*, Johannesburg, June 14, 1987.
78 Percy Tucker, *Just the Ticket!*, Jonathan Ball Publishers, Johannesburg, 1997, p.458.
79 *Sunday Times*, Johannesburg, June 21, 1987.
80 *New York Times*, October 26, 1987.
81 *Christian Science Monitor*, Boston, October 28, 1987.
82 Masakela and Cheers, Ibid, p. 348.
83 Wilborn Hampton . "Cast of 'Sarafina!' Evokes Their Lives In South Africa", *New York Times*, March 13, 1988

84 Mark Gevisser, "I should be paid a million rands", *Weekly Mail & Guardian*, March 8, 1996.
85 Jerry Mofokeng, "Theatre and Change in South Africa", edited by Geoffrey W. Davis and Anne Fuchs, page 85, Harwood Academic Publishers, 1996
86 Nigel Noble, *Voices of Sarafina!*, New Yorker Video, 1988
87 Lee Hirsch, *Amandla! A revolution in Four Part Harmony*, Artisan Entertainment, 2003.
88 Ibid.
89 Laura Jones, *Nothing Except Ourselves –The Harsh Times and Bold Theater of South Africa's Mbongeni Ngema*, Viking, New York, 1994, p. 9.
90 Jones, ibid, p. 128.
91 John Donnelly, "On South African stage, learning song, dance, and history", *Boston Globe*, May 28, 2004
92 Email to author dated 26 September 2008.
93 *Mail & Guardian Online*, 19 August 2008. http://mg.co.za/article/2008-08-19-sarafina-iii-a-hot-potato accessed 13/04/2011.
94 Ibid.
95 *New York Times*, August 20, 1999
96 Terri-Liza Fortein, "Umoja cast gumbooted out of Canada", *Saturday Argus*, March 15, 2008.
97 Michael Church, "Mozart magic meets African brilliance", *The Independent*, London, 4 February 2008
98 Matti Moosa, *The Origins Of Modern Arabic Fiction*, Three Continents Press, 1997, p. 43.
99 Moosa, *Origins*, p. 40.
100 Note all of these "fathers" from the same time period, showing that Egyptian musical drama really is quite new.

[101] An ensemble that consists of *oud*, the *qanun*, the *kamanjah*, the *ney*, the *riq*, and the *darabukkah*.
[102] Frédéric Lagrange, October 1994, From: *Shaykh Sayed Darwish [1892-1923] Artistes Arabes Associés AAA 096 Les Archives de la Musique Arabe - Shaykh Sayed Darwish*, Contributed by Lars Fredriksson, http://almashriq.hiof.no/egypt/700/780/sayed-darweesh/ accessed 19 September 2018.
[103] "Darwish remembered", *Al-Ahram Weekly*, 25 Sept. - 1 Oct. 2003, Issue No. 657
[104] Mark L. Levinson, *The Levant*, 9 July 1995. http://almashriq.hiof.no/egypt/700/780/abdel-wahab/abdel-wahab-bitton.html accessed 15 September 2018.
[105] Linda Y. Mokdad, "Egypt", Linda Y. Mokdad and Corey K. Creekmur (Editors), *The International Film Musical*, Ediburgh University Press, 2013, p. 214.
[106] While the Ottoman Empire had been defeated by the British, Napoleon Bonaparte occupied Egypt from 1798-1801, and France still maintained a strong economic presence.
[107] Nour El-Bastawisy, American University of Cairo audio course entry, Spring 2018, https://soundcloud.com/nourelbastaweesy/egyptian-musical-theater-from-the-past-till-the-present-day
[108] Ati Metwaly, "Fabrica troupe: from Les Miserables to a creative commotion", *Al Ahram Weekly*, Sunday 23 Mar 2014.
[109] **Mary Aravani,** "Fabrica Brings Puppetry To Life In El Leila El Kebira", *Caravan*, 16 November, 2014.
[110] Samia Farid Shihata, "Leila: An Egyptian Musical", *Enigma*, 2 July 2017.
[111] Richard F. Shepard, "Theater: Manger Megilla", *New York Times*, 10 October 1968.
[112] Dan Almagor, "Musical Plays on the Hebrew Stage", *The Israel Review of Arts and Letters*, 16 July 1998, #103
[113] Email to the author dated 29 September 2018.
[114] Clive Barnes, "Theater: Pleasant Revue", *New York Times*, 22 October 1971.
[115] John Simon, "Up From Various Ghettos", *New Yorker*, 8 November 1971.

"Down South American Way" – Musical Theatre in Latin America

[1] Milonga was a precursor to the tango. It originated in the Rio de la Plata in the 1870s and is generally in 2/4 time.

[2] Email to author dated 20 June 2009.
[3] Email to the author from Guillermo Masutti dated 8 March 2010
[4] Astor Piazzolla, *A Memoir*, Natalio Gorin, Amadaeus, pp. 70-1.
[5] Email from Pablo Gorlero to the author dated 20 June 2009.
[6] *Clarin.com*, 19 May 2005
edant.clarin.com/diario/2005/05/19/espectaculos/c-1101.htm accessed and translated 26 June 2010.
[7] Read Johnson, "Brazil goes Broadway yet keeps its own beat", *Los Angeles Times*, 31 July 2005.
[8] Larry Rohter, "The Real Carmen Miranda Under the Crown of Fruit", *New York Times*, 13 December 2001.
[9] Mac Margolis, "Way, Way Off-Broadway; Brazilian producers are mastering the art of the musical", *Newsweek International*, 30 August 2004.
[10] Apuntes. *Historia de Huanuco, Revista antológica* N° 4, ago. 2000, pp. 15-23 "Daniel Alomía Robles en primera persona".
[11] *La República* Peru, Tuesday, April 13, 2004
[12] "Lin-Manuel Miranda Talks IN THE HEIGHTS, HAMILTON MIXTAPE, SMASH, Superpowers and More in Reddit AMA", *Broadway World*, 5 March 2014.
https://www.broadwayworld.com/article/Lin-Manuel-Miranda-Talks-IN-THE-HEIGHTS-HAMILTON-MIXTAPE-SMASH-Superpowers-and-More-in-Reddit-AMA-20140305 accessed 1 September 2018.
[13] Mariza Bafile, "Jaime Lozano: la música entró en su vida con la fuerza de los amores imprevistos", *Vice Versa Magazine*, 31 January 2016.
[14] Bafile, ibid.
[15] Bafile, ibid.
[16] Email to author dated 2 September 2018.
[17] Marlena Fitzpatrick, "CHILDREN OF SALT: Broadway's Mexican Infusion", *Latino Rebels*, 20 June 2016
www.latinorebels.com/2016/06/20/children-of-salt-broadways-mexican-infusion/ accessed 1 September 2018
[18] Email to the author from Fabian Polanco dated 15 October 2018.
[19] Mario Villanueva, loc. cit.
[20] "Canción ranchera" refers to the genre of Mexican folk music that emerged following their revolution.
[21] https://www.senatehouselibrary.ac.uk/blog/capturing-monster-mexico-city-literature accessed 17 September 2019. See also Salvador Novo, *Nueva grandeza mexicana / por Salvador Novo. Ensayo sobre la ciudad de México y sus alrededores en 1946.* Editorial Hermes, México, 1946

[22] Fabian Polanco, *Magia pura y total*, Samsara Editorial, Mexico City, 2012, p. 12.
[23] Polanco, p. 12.
[24] Mario Villanueva, "Teatro Chico, Carpas Y Políticos", *Opera Mundi*, 18 February, 2010 http://www.operamundi-magazine.com/2010/02/teatro-chico-carpas-y-politicos.html
[25] Polanco, p. 12.
[26] Polanco, p. 15.
[27] Polanco, p. 133.
[28] Polanco, p. 14.
[29] Polanco, p. 14.
[30] Named for a mathematical game.
[31] Polanco, p. 12.
[32] Document submitted by Peter Pinne to author 5 September 2018.
[33] Liliana Hernández, "José Manuel López Velarde: Hay muchas ganas de hacer teatro, pero no audiencia", *Crónica*, 17 July 2018, www.cronica.com.mx/notas/2018/1086996.html, accessed and translated 4 September 2018.
[34] Brisa Granados, "José Manuel López Velarde, no todo son 'Mentiras'", *Revista Central*, 18 Noviember, 2015
[35] Hernández, ibid.
[36] Polanco, p. 16.
[37] Bafile, ibid.
[38] "Bringing Musical Theatre Training To Mexico City", American Musical and Dramatic Academy, 24 April 2015 https://www.amda.edu/news/bringing-musical-theatre-training-to-mexico-city
[39] Polanco, p. 19-20.
[40] Polanco, p. 7.
[41] Others argue that the inventor may have been Manuel Saumell (1818-70).
[42] Robin Moore, "The *Teatro Bufo*: Cuban Blackface Theatre in the Nineteenth Century", *Soundscapes from the Americas*, Ashgate Publishing, Farnham 2014, p. 40-41.
[43] Some sources date it to either 1900 or 1880.
[44] *San Bernardino County Sun/Associated Press*, 18 February 1935.
[45] John von Rhein, "A girl named Maria sings to an Afro-Cuban beat", *Chicago Tribune*, 2 June 2010.
[46] Letter from Héctor Quintero to Lionel Enriquez dated 15 September 1970, cited in Elizabeth Schwall, "Sweeping gestures: Alberto Alonso and the revolutionary musical in Cuba", *Studies in Musical Theatre*, Volume 13 Issue 1, p. 41.

[47] Humberto Arenal, "Por que *Los Novios*", Teatro Musical de la Habana performance programme, 7 May 1964, Biblioteca Juan Marinello, Archivo Central del Ministerio de Cultura, Fondo Consejo Nacional de Cultura, Cajuela 202, cited in Elizabeth Schwall, "Sweeping gestures: Alberto Alonso and the revolutionary musical in Cuba", *Studies in Musical Theatre*, Volume 13 Issue 1, p. 42.

"The Theatre Is Alive" – Musical Theatre in Asia

[1] Named for Emperor Meiji (1852-1912)
[2] Leonie Stickland, *Gender Gymnastics: Performers, Fans and Gender Issues in the Takarazuka Revue of Contemporary Japan,* Doctoral thesis at Murdoch University, 2004, p.72.
[3] Email to author dated 4 October 2010.
[4] Jennifer Robertson, *Takarazuka – Sexual Politics and Popular Culture in Modern Japan,* University of California Press, Berkeley, 1998, p.156
[5] Leonie Stickland, *Gender Gymnastics: Performing and Consuming Japan'' Takarazuka Revue,* Trans Pacific Press, Melbourne, 2008.
[6] Ichizō Kobayashi, *Takarazuka Manpitsu* ("Takarazuka Jottings"), Hankyu Dentetsu, 1980, p. 38
[7] Kerry Short, "Legendary Song and Dance Man, Tommy Tune, Taps His Way to the Maltz Jupiter Theatre", *Haute Living*, 16 November 2017.
[8] Email from Jeremy Sams dated 5 October 2010.
[9] Ben Whaley, bwhaleyjapan.blogspot.com, accessed 31 May 2009.
[10] Email from Dr. Michael Kunze dated 15 June 2009.
[11] David Jortner, Keiko McDonald, Kevin J. Wetmore, Modern Japanese Theatre and Performance, Lexington Books, 2007, p.238
[12] Freund, p. 730
[13] In fact they had done several, but never – at this point – involving Broadway personnel.
[14] Florence Rome, *The Scarlett Letters*, Random House, New York, p. 42.
[15] Rome, p. 43.
[16] Email from Ed Weissman dated 24 May 2019.
[17] Lehman Engel, *One Bright Day*, MacMillan Publishers, New York, 1974, p. 335-6.
[18] Rome, p. 64.
[19] Rome, p. 205.
[20] Atkey, *Broadway North*, p. 113.

[21] Nobuko Tanaka, "Amon Miyamoto: Globe-trotting dramatist seeks new horizons", *Japan Times*, 5 June 2011.
[22] Tanaka, *Japan Times*, ibid.
[23] *Chopsticks New York*, 1 April 2010, www.chopsticksny.com/people/2010/04/01 Accessed 19 June 2010.
[24] Founded in 1961 by African-American Ellen Stewart (1919-2011) whose followers called her "Mama".
[25] Cited in Freund, pp. 733-4.
[26] Mel Gussow, "Stage: 'Japanesque' Samurai Musical", *New York Times*, 15 November 1981.
[27] https://blog.fromtheboxoffice.com/2016/08/01/the-20-worst-musicals-in-history/ accessed 5 August 2018.
[28] *Stage Door podcast* December 2014 https://itunes.apple.com/gb/podcast/stage-door-podcast/id950184785?mt=2
[29] A form of Japanese musical drama dating to the fourteenth century, it is the oldest remaining of Japan's theatrical forms.
[30] Ibid.
[31] Paul Taylor, "The sins of the fathers : THEATRE", *The Independent*, 4 February 1995
[32] *Musical Stages*, Issue 31, Christmas 2001, p.7.
[33] Mihir Bose, *Bollywood – A History*, Tempus, Stroud, 2006, p. 226.
[34] Bose, ibid, p. 234.
[35] K. Moti Gokulsing, K. Gokulsing and Wimal Dissanayake, *Indian Popular Cinema: A Narrative of Popular Change*, Trentham Books, 2004, pp 98-99.
[36] "Baz Lurhman Talks Awards and *Moulin Rouge*", http://movies.about.com/library/weekly/aa030902a.htm.
[37] Rudisill, K. "'My School Rocks!' Dancing Disney's *High School Musical* in India", *Studies in Musical Theatre* Volume 3 Number 3, Intellect Ltd., pp. 253-271, 2009.
[38] James Inverne, *Wrestling with Elephants*, Sanctuary, London, 2003, p.191.
[39] I have my own personal experiences of Hsu Po-yun and New Aspect, but that's another book: see *Running Away with the Circus – or – "Now is the Winter of our Missing Tent*.
[40] "A Novel Idea", *Taiwan Today (Free China Review)*, 1 December 1987. https://taiwantoday.tw/news.php?unit=12,20,29,33,35,45&post=22566 (Accessed 25 August 2018.)
[41] *Taiwan Today*, loc. cit.
[42] *Taiwan Today*, loc. cit.

43 Pepe Diokno, "Who Killed Philippine Cinema?", Independently organised TED event, https://youtu.be/plNNkf90jUU accessed 14 March 2018.

44 Sometimes called Filipino, Tagalog shares one great advantage with Italian and Spanish: lots of open vowel sounds, making it very attractive to composers.

45 "Poverty in the Philippines", Asian Development Bank, https://www.adb.org/countries/philippines/poverty Accessed 27 March 2018.

46 Sir Anril Pineda Tiatco , "Performing Like a Concert King or a Queen: Producing Original Filipino Musicals", *The Palgrave Handbook of Musical Theatre Producers*, edited by Laura MacDonald, William A. Everett, Palgrave Macmillan, New York 2017

47 Asia-Pacific Cultural Centre for Unesco, Asia-Pacific Database on Intangible Cultural Heritage https://www.accu.or.jp/ich/en/arts/A_PHL1.html, accessed 16 March 2018.

48 Or sometimes "sarsuwela".

49 Doreen G. Fernandez, "Zarzuela to Sarswela: Indigenization and Transformation", *Philippine Studies* Vol. 41, No. 3 (Third Quarter 1993), Ateneo de Manila University, Manila, 1993, p 328.

50 Email to the author dated 27 May 2018.

51 Nick Deocampo, *Film: American Influences on Philippine Cinema*, Anvil Publishing, Manila, 2017

52 Tiatco, loc. cit.

53 A passion play, from the Spanish *cenaculo*, "upper room".

54 Doreen Fernandez, *The American Colonial and Contemporary Traditions in Philippine Theater*, Sentrong Pangkultura ng Pilipinas, Manila, 1994.

55 Just as they didn't really want Hawaii, they just needed Pearl Harbour as a refueling base.

56 A debate in verse.

57 "Pabása ng Pasyón", Reading of the Passion

58 Neighbourhoods.

59 Email to author from Joy Virata dated 19 March 2018.

60 Email to author from Ryan Cayabyab dated 19 March 2018

61 An ancient instrumental music form using a row of small gongs, accompanied by larger gongs and drums.

62 "Filipino Film 'Ang Larawan' Sets the Bar High for Movie Musicals", KQED Inc., https://www.kqed.org/arts/13818736/filipino-film-ang-larawan-sets-the-bar-high-for-movie-musicals accessed 25 March 2018.

63 Oliver Oliveros, "ANG LARAWAN is Lavish, Absorbing Family Drama", BroadwayWorld.com, 19 December 2017.

[64] Antonio D. Sison, "In musical "The Portrait", beauty and truth resist materialism", *National Catholic Review*, 22 January 2018.
[65] Walter Ang, "Hey, Madam Producers!", *Philippine Daily Inquirer*, 22 March 2014, lifestyle.inquirer.net/154687/hey-madame-producers/ Accessed 28 March 2018.
[66] I.e. "culture", "entertain".
[67] Nicanor Tiongson, "The Winds of Change: 1986-1994", *Genesis*, December 2009, Cultural Center of the Philippines.
[68] There may have been indoor theatres built for the foreign diaspora, but not accessible to ordinary Koreans.
[69] Herbert Henry Austin, Angus Hamilton, Masatake Terauchi, *Korea, its History, Its People, and Its Commerce*, J. B. Millet Co, Boston, 1910, p. 196-7
[70] Kim Seung-hye, "Theater shifts gears, draws new patrons", *Joongang Daily*, 16 July 2013.
[71] Email to author dated 23 July 2009
[72] Email to author dated 3 August 2009.
[73] See Ji Hyon Yuh, "Korean Musical Theatre's Past: Yegrin and the Politics of 1960s Musical Theatre", *The Palgrave Handbook of Musical Theatre Producers*, Edited by Laura MacDonald and William A. Everett, Palgrave MacMillan, New York, 2017, p. 255.
[74] Chun Young-Gi and Kang Jin-Kyu, "Music's role in the revolution", *Korea JoongAng Daily*, 9 July 2015.
[75] Some cite *Gyeonwoo Jingnyeo* a love story between an earth-bound man and a heavenly fairy filmed in 1960.
[76] The National Ch'anggŭk Company of Korea has performed a version of *Baebijangjeon*, the same story that inspired the first Korean musical, *Saljjagi Obseoye*.
[77] Yaisana Huidrom, "'Sweet, Come to Me Stealthily' returns", 14 December 2012, http://mystickorea.blogspot.com/2012/12/sweet-come-to-me-stealthily-returns.html accessed 29 August 2018
[78] Don Kirk, "'Last Empress,' Musical Echo of Korea's History", *New York Times*, 27 March, 1998.
[79] Ibid.
[80] Rachel Saltz, "Politics, History and All That Jazz: Good vs. Evil in 34 Songs", *New York Times*, 29 August 2011.
[81] See Sun Hyo-rim and Kim Jong-eun, "Korean Musical Industry: Splendors and Woes", *Korea Focus*, The Korea Foundation, 23 July 2014, http://www.koreafocus.or.kr/design2/layout/content_print.asp?group_id=105523, accessed 29 August 2018.
[82] Han Sunhee, "Korean film industry tunes up stage musicals", *Variety*, 22 July 2008

[83] "S. Korean musicals market to nearly triple in 2-3 years.", *Asia Pulse*, 7 March 2006
[84] Han Aran, "Comedian-turned-musical director sets bar high", *Korea.net*, 10 July 2008
http://www.korea.net/news/News/NewsView.asp?serial_no=20080709001&part=113&SearchDay= accessed 30 December 2008.
[85] Barbara Demick, "Les Miserables' of North Korea", *Los Angeles Times*, 22 February 2006.
[86] www.korea.net/Events/Performances/view?articleId=3811 accessed 25 April 2018.
[87] Park Jae-sang (1977-)
[88] Daniel Tudor, *A Geek in Korea – Discovering Asia's New Kingdom of Cool*, Tuttle Publishing, Tokyo, 2014, p. 14.
[89] Daegu International Musical Festival Program Book, 2019, p. 13.
[90] Zhang Qian, "A nostalgic, feel-good musical taking us back to the 1990s", *Shine (Shanghai Daily)*, 24 November, 2017
https://www.shine.cn/feature/entertainment/1711246893/
[91] Emily Macel Theys, "Meet Yabin Wang, The Coolest Chinese Choreographer You've Never Heard Of", *Dance*, 2 November 2018, https://www.dancemagazine.com/meet-yabin-wang-the-coolest-chinese-choreographer-youve-never-heard-of-2617450860.html
[92] "Original Chinese Musical Lights Up The Stage", *Shanghai Eye*, 11 December 2018
https://www.shanghaieye.com.cn/musical/ Accessed 24 July 2019
[93] "New Stage Theater gained rights to the first Korean musical Turandot – when will it be introduced?", 8 July 2018.
https://tech2.org/slovakia/video-new-stage-theater-gained-rights-to-the-first-korean-musical-turandot-when-will-it-be-introduced-life-in-the-city/
[94] The "Flower Drum" is a type of double-skinned Chinese hand drum.
[95] Siyuan Liu, editor, *Routledge Handbook of Asian Theatre*, Routledge, London, p. 534.
[96] Alistair Smith, "Multimillion pound Chinese musical is Ed Fringe first", *The Stage*, London, 15 July 2010.
[97] Email from Simone Genatt dated 28 September 2010.
[98] Ng Yi-Sheng, "Five things that make a Singaporean musical", www.esplanade.com accessed 10 November 2018.
[99] "The world's her stage", *The Star*, Kuala Lumpur, 1 September 2003.
[100] 100 Dr.Aaron Hales, *The State on Stage: A Socio-Political Critique of Singaporean Musical Theatre*, Doctoral Thesis, University of Western

Australia School of Music and School of Social and Cultural Studies, September 2009, p. 79-80.
[101] Dr. Aaron Hales, p. 119
[102] Clarissa Oon, "Who am I? Musicals and Identity", www.esplanade.com/tributesg/performing-arts/dick-lee Accessed 10 November 2018.
[103] Lok Meng Chue, "Who am I? Musicals and Identity", www.esplanade.com/tributesg/performing-arts/dick-lee
[104] S Y Chua, "A triumph for Asia", *Malaysian Business*, Kuala Lumpur, Mar 16, 2002
[105] Ong Teng Cheong, *Report of the Advisory Council on Culture and the Arts*, Government of Singapore, 1989, p.12.
[106] William Peterson, *Theatre and the Politics of Culture in Contemporary Singapore*, Wesleyan University Press, Middletown, CT, 2001, pp. 195-6.
[107] Katharine Ee, "Tip of the peninsula", *The Stage*, London, 3 November 2011.
[108] Lily Kong, "Cultural Policy In Singapore: Negotiating Economic And Socio-Cultural Agenda", Geoforum, For Special Issue on "Culture, Economy, Policy" 2000
[109] Dr. Hales, p. 70.
[110] Dr. Hales, p. 61.
[111] Dr. Hales, p. p. 147.
[112] *Front* Season 3, Episode 6, Arts Central TV, Singapore, broadcast 21 December 2007
[113] A dialect native to the Minnan region of Fujian Province, China.
[114] Chue
[115] Sonia Kolesnikov-Jessop, "In Singapore, Musical Theater That Prefers Its Own Local Flavor", *New York Times*, 24 May 2010.
[116] "Xīn" is an abbreviation for Singapore; "Yáo" means "song".
[117] Ibid.
[118] Dr. Hales, p. 230.
[119] Dr. Hales, pp. 253-4.
[120] Email to the author dated 24 November 2014.
[121] John Lahr, *Automatic Vaudeville*, Alfred A. Knopf, New York, 1984, p.5
[122] Siyuan Liu, editor, *Routledge Handbook of Asian Theatre*, p. 356.
[123] Amritha Amrinand, "Dragon's Heart Returns", *Bangkok Post*, 26 August 2016.
[124] This is also a problem in other cities, including Toronto and Melbourne.

New Musicals: "You Have to Kiss a Lot of Frogs"

[1] Richard Kisland, *The Musical: A Look at the American Musical Theater*, Prentice Hall Inc., Englewood Cliffs, NJ, p.255

[2] Mark Steyn, *Broadway Babies Say Goodnight*, Faber and Faber, London, p. 163

[3] Mattthew Hemley, "Don Black Defends Lloyd Webber's TV Talent Shows", *The Stage*, London, 1 May 2008.

[4] Roger Foss, "Join the Parade", *What's On Stage*, London, September 2007

[5] Robert Viagas, "Where in the World is Cameron Mackintosh?", *Show Music*, Vol. 15 No. 1, Spring 1999.

[6] "Kiss of the Spider Woman", *Working in the Theatre*, American Theatre Wing/ City University of New York, September 1993

[7] Lees, p. 101.

[8] See Brown, *Moss Hart*, p. 338.

[9] Max Wilk, *They're Playing our Song*, Atheneum, New York, 1973, p. 237

[10] Tracey Moore, "The Out-of-Town tryout Goes Back to School", *Studies in Musical Theatre*, Vol. 3 No. 3, Intellect Ltd., 2010, p.304.

[11] House of Commons Culture, Media and Sport Committee, Theatre, Fifth Report of Session 2004-05 Volume III Oral and written evidence Ordered by The House of Commons to be printed 15 March 2005, HC 254-111 [Incorporating HC 1153-i, Session 2002-03] Published on 30 March 2005 by authority of the House of Commons London: The Stationery Office Limited

[12] Mel Atkey, *Breaking Into Song*, Friendlysong Books, Vancouver, 2017, p. 45

[13] Email to author dated 22 August 2003.

[14] Letter to author from Billie Bridgman, Guelph Spring Festival, dated 11 September 1987.

[15] Email to author dated 11 March 2018.

[16] Malcolm Gladwell, *Outliers – The Story of Success*, Allen Lane, London, 2008, p. 137

[17] John Cleese, "The Importance of Mistakes", speech made to the British-American Chamber of Commerce in 1988, http://my.ilstu.edu/~eostewa/ART309/Mistakes.htm

[18] Tom Shea, *Broadway's Most Wanted*, Brassey's, Washington, D.C., 2004, p.66.

[19] 19 Scott Brown, "How Can Musical Theater be Saved?", Vulture.com, 24 May 2012, accessed 21 July 2012

[20] "Lehman's Terms", BMI Lehman Engel Musical Theatre Workshop Newsletter Vol 3, No. 7 June/July, 2000

[21] Letter from the Guild of Canadian Musical Theatre Writers dated 9 August 1982.
[22] Email to the author dated 4 July 2003.
[23] Email to the author dated 2 July 2003.
[24] Email to the author dated 3 July 2003.
[25] Email to the author dated 4 July 2003.
[26] Email to the author dated 1 July 2003.
[27] George Jean Nathan (1882-1958) believed that Lerner had based *Brigadoon* on a story by Friedrich Gerstäcker (1816-72) about the disappearing village of Germelshausen in Germany, but Lerner maintained that he hadn't heard of this story until after he had written *Brigadoon*'s first draft. (See "Drama Mailbag", *The New York Times*, 30 March, 1947, p. X3.) Some claim that the title comes from the Brig o' Doon, a medieval bridge in Ayrshire.
[28] Although Meredith Willson's 1957 musical *The Music Man* has a similar plot to the 1954 play *The Rainmaker*, Willson's musical had been in development for a number of years when the other opened.
[29] see Engel, *Words With Music*, p.116.
[30] Email from Nelles Van Loon to the author dated 3 July 2003.
[31] Lee Davis, "Two Days in Musical Theatre Paradise", *Show Music*, Vol. 15 No. 2, Summer 1999
[32] *The Indepnedent*, London, 29 April 2004
[33] Philip Headley, "The Theatre Royal Stratford East's Musical Theatre Journey", *The Big Life* (published script), Oberon Books, London, 2004, p. 4.
[34] Email to the author dated 27 December 2008.
[35] Episode 26, *Musical Talk*, 4 March 2008. (podcast)
[36] Sondheim, *Look, I Made a Hat*, p.xxi.
[37] Steyn, ibid., p. 226.
[38] http://www.britishtheatreguide.info/reviews/daboyz-rev.htm, accessed 1 April 2009
[39] *The Independent*, London, 9 May 2003.
[40] Charlotte Cripps, "Hip hop don't stop", *www.breakinconvention.com*, 27 April 2004 (accessed 1 April 2009)
[41] Email to author sent 27 December 2008.
[1] Miguel de Unamuno, *Vida de D. Quijote y Sancho: Según Miguel de Cervantes Saavedra: Explicada y Comentada por Miguel de Unamuno*, Libreria de Fernando Fe, Madrid, 1905, p. 175-6.
[2] "Sondheim decries modern Broadway", *The Times*, London, 6 March 2012.
[3] Email from Richard Maltby Jr. to the author, dated 15 August 2004.

[4] *Time*, 29 December 1961, cited in *The Complete Works of W. H. Auden*, Princeton University Press, 1988, p. 465
[5] Scott Miller, "But That Was Once Upon a Time".
[6] Sarah Green, "The Wicked Stage: Can Musical Theatre Ever Be Naturalistic?", *a Younger Theatre*, 18 December 2011.
[7] David Benedict, "Win When You're Singing", *The Guardian*, 16 June 2002, https://www.theguardian.com/film/2002/jun/16/features.review2 accessed 16 July 2019.
[8] Platform talk given at the Royal National Theatre's Lyttelton Theatre, 24 May 1990, chaired by Mark Steyn. *Platform Papers 5. Musicals… and Sondheim*, RNT Publications Dept.,
[9] Scott Brown, "How Can Musical Theater be Saved?", Op. cit.
[10] In fact, his wedding was even set to the music of "To Life" from *Fiddler on the Roof*.
[11] Jody Rosen, "The American Revolutionary", *New York Times*, 8 July 2015.
[12] Rebecca Mitzoff, "Lin-Manuel Miranda on Jay Z, *The West Wing*, and 18 More Things That Influenced *Hamilton*", Vulture, New York, 29 July 2015
[13] See Clive Barnes' review of *Henry, Sweet Henry*, *New York Times*, 22 December 1967. See also Clive Barnes, "Hair is a shaggy happening set to rock music that grooves along with pot, peaceniks and a startling tableau of nudes", *Saturday Evening Post*, 10 August, 1968.
[14] *Equity Quarterly*, Canadian Actors' Equity Association, Winter 2010.
[15] Jessie Thompson, "Let it go – and surrender to magical musicals", *Evening Standard*, London, 5 August 2019, pp 22-23.
[16] Bradley, p. 198.
[17] Email to the author dated 9 April 2012.
[18] This isn't new. The CBC cancelled *Don Messer's Jubilee* in the 1960s because, although it still attracted a reasonably large audience, it didn't appeal to the all-important "baby boomers".
[19] Full disclosure: a colleague of mine, Shel Piercy, had a special in development for that program based on my book *Broadway North: The Dream of a Canadian Musical Theatre*. Needless to say, it was aborted.
[20] Simon Tait, "The Writing's on the Wall", *The Stage*, London, February 26, 2009.

Other Books by Mel Atkey:

An anthology of thirty years of interviews, articles and essays on musical theatre, including a 1980 interview with Stephen Schwartz and a 1982 interview with the late Reid Shelton, *Annie*'s original Daddy Warbucks.

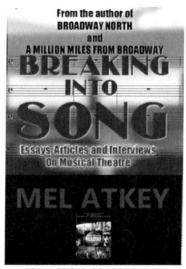

ISBN 978-0-9916957-3-7
Order from Lulu.com or Amazon

Running Away with the Circus (or, "Now is the Winter of our Missing Tent"

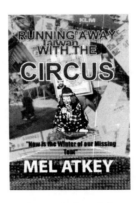

"If some clairvoyant had told me that I'd be spending my nights in a shipping container in Taiwan, guarding seven tigers, six Chihuahuas, five bears, four sea lions, three geese, two horses and a 'killer dog' named Ludwig, I'd have said 'You're supposed to read the tea leaves, not smoke them.'" –
Mel Atkey

ISBN 9780991695713
Order from Lulu.com or Amazon

***Something Magic*** A Collection of songs from musicals written by Mel Atkey. Mr. Atkey has been writing musicals ever since he was in high school in his native Vancouver. He was a finalist for the Musical of the Year competition in Aarhus, Denmark, and his work has been short-listed for the Vivian Ellis Prize, the Quest for New Musicals, the Ken Hill Prize and Musical Stairs. His two-character musical *Perfect Timing* was a finalist in the 1996 Musical of the Year competition in Aarhus, Denmark, and was showcased at Greenwich Theatre, London, in 2005. He made his New York debut in 2001 with *O Pioneers*, and followed it in 2003 with *A Little Princess*, both with book by Robert Sickinger.

ISBN 978-0-9916957-2-0
Order from Lulu.com or Amazon

"This is a story as long and rich as it is entertaining, which Mel Atkey expertly points out in this beautifully produced book, replete with countless photographs. But you don't have to be an theatre expert to enjoy it... Atkey's well-researched and delightful account, makes it easy to see why Hollywood has been permanently packed with stage-struck Canadians since the days of Quebec-born Mack Sennett." – *Canada Post*, London (UK)

"Atkey's book (long in the making) is an important service in the cause of the Canadian musical." – Keith Garebian, *Stage and Page*

"Mel Atkey's book is so full of interesting detail and entertaining anecdotes, by the time I had reached the last page I found myself caring about all the projects and personalities I had read about. To my delight, the book also confirms once and for all the extreme arrogance of Broadway and the West End. The idea that a musical is not a musical until it has been recognised by either of those giant arbiters of taste is, of course, idiotic; but that opinion certainly exists in New York and is voiced by some in London... Thank you, Mel Atkey, for an informative and affirming book." – Ken Caswell, *Musical Stages*, London

"If you're a Canadian and a show-tune buff, you'll probably be interested in this book... it's full of information and pictures about our musical theatre that no one has ever collected before." – Richard Ouzounian, Toronto *Star*

"A most intriguing new book... The stories of the creation of *Anne of Green Gables* and *Billy Bishop Goes to War* are well told." – Brad Hathaway, *Potomac Stages* (Washington, D.C.)

"*Broadway North* should be required reading for all Canadian students and practitioners of musical theatre. And for members of the general public with an interest in the arts in general, Atkey will forever dispel the notion that "Canadian musical theatre" is the ultimate oxymoron." – Danny Schur, *Winnipeg Free Press*

Did you know that the idea behind the Radio City Music Hall Rockettes was first tried out in Toronto? That Canada produced the world's longest-running annual revue? Few people realize the Canadian influences that are at the heart of American and British culture.

Author **Mel Atkey**'s research for ***Broadway North*** included interviews with Norman and Elaine Campbell and Don Harron, creators of *Anne of Green Gables-The Musical*; Mavor Moore, founder of the Charlottetown Festival and of *Spring Thaw*; John Gray, author of *Billy Bishop Goes to War*; Ray Jessel and Marian Grudeff, *Spring Thaw* writers who had success on Broadway with *Baker Street*; Dolores Claman, composer of the *Hockey Night In Canada* theme, who also wrote the musicals *Mr. Scrooge* and *Timber!!!*; and Galt MacDermott, the composer of *Hair* who started out writing songs for the McGill University revue *My Fur Lady*. Atkey also draws on his own experience as a writer and composer of musicals, and tells the story of why a show that should have starred James Doohan (*Star Trek*'s Scotty) *didn't* happen.

Composer, lyricist and author, **Mel Atkey** is currently based in the U.K. Proud of his Canadian cultural roots, he has long been fascinated with the notion of a distinctive Canadian musical theatre.

Broadway North: The Dream of a Canadian Musical Theatre
By: Mel Atkey
Number of pages: 336
ISBN: 1897045085
Published by Natural Heritage/Dundurn

We encourage individuals to buy books from their local bookstore as much as possible. Most bookstores offer a "special order" service, where they will obtain the books you want and let you know when they have arrived at the store.

Alternatively, our books can be ordered online. Most Natural Heritage titles are carried by Indigo/Chapters, Amazon Canada, Amazon US and Amazon UK.